edition **seventh**

MANAGEMENT INFORMATION SYSTEMS

Kenneth J. Sousa
Bryant University

Effy Oz
The Pennsylvania State University,
Great Valley

CENGAGE
Learning·

Australia • Brazil • Mexico • Singapore • United Kingdom • United States

Management Information Systems, Seventh Edition

Kenneth J. Sousa and Effy Oz

Product Director: Joe Sabatino

Product Manager: Clara Goosman

Senior Content Developer: Kate Mason

Development Editor: Deborah Kaufmann

Product Assistant: Brad Sullender

Market Development Manager: Heather Mooney

Marketing Coordinator: Eileen Corcoran

Design and Production Service: PreMediaGlobal

Manufacturing Planner: Ron Montgomery

Senior Rights Acquisition Specialist: Christine Myaskovsky

Cover Image(s): © Nikada/Getty Images

For product information and technology assistance, contact us at
Cengage Learning Customer & Sales Support, 1-800-354-9706

For permission to use material from this text or product,
submit all requests online at **www.cengage.com/permissions**
Further permissions questions can be e-mailed to
permissionrequest@cengage.com

Library of Congress Control Number: 2013950990

ISBN-13: 978-1-285-18613-9

ISBN-10: 1-285-18613-3

Cengage Learning
200 First Stamford Place, 4th Floor
Stamford, CT 06902
USA

Cengage Learning is a leading provider of customized learning solutions with office locations around the globe, including Singapore, the United Kingdom, Australia, Mexico, Brazil, and Japan. Locate your local office at: **www.cengage.com/global.**

Cengage Learning products are represented in Canada by Nelson Education, Ltd.

For your course and learning solutions, visit **www.cengage.com.**

Purchase any of our products at your local college store or at our preferred online store **www.cengagebrain.com.**

Instructors: Please visit **login.cengage.com** and log in to access instructor-specific resources.

Notice to the Reader

Publisher does not warrant or guarantee any of the products described herein or perform any independent analysis in connection with any of the product information contained herein. Publisher does not assume, and expressly disclaims, any obligation to obtain and include information other than that provided to it by the manufacturer. The reader is expressly warned to consider and adopt all safety precautions that might be indicated by the activities described herein and to avoid all potential hazards. By following the instructions contained herein, the reader willingly assumes all risks in connection with such instructions. The publisher makes no representations or warranties of any kind, including but not limited to, the warranties of fitness for particular purpose or merchantability, nor are any such representations implied with respect to the material set forth herein, and the publisher takes no responsibility with respect to such material. The publisher shall not be liable for any special, consequential, or exemplary damages resulting, in whole or part, from the readers' use of, or reliance upon, this material.

Printed in the United States of America
1 2 3 4 5 6 7 17 16 15 14

To my father, Henry, and in memory of my mother, Virginia, and my sister, Karen.
—Kenneth J. Sousa

In Memoriam: Dr. Effy Oz

Dr. Oz was a passionate and beloved teacher at The Pennsylvania State University, Great Valley. He wrote several books, including six previous editions of this popular textbook on management information systems. He touched the lives of many students at Boston University, Boston College, Wayne State University, and Penn State. With this revision, we honor his legacy and careful thought about MIS education.

brief CONTENTS

detailed CONTENTS

preface

The goal of *Management Information Systems, Seventh Edition* is to provide a real-world understanding of information systems (ISs) for business and computer science students. Like its predecessor, this Seventh Edition provides students with a firm foundation in business-related information technology (IT) on which they can build successful careers regardless of the particular fields they choose. They may find themselves formulating strategic plans in executive suites, optimizing operations in businesses or on factory floors, fine-tuning plans for their own entrepreneurial ventures, designing ISs to optimize their organization's operations, working as consultants, augmenting business activities on the web, or creating valuable new information products in any number of industries. Ultimately, the integration of technology into the strategy and operations of a business is an important factor in its success.

This Seventh Edition is organized in 14 chapters that contain the most important topics for business students. The fundamental principle guiding this book is that ISs are everywhere in business. Information systems are pervasive because information is the single most powerful resource in every business function in every industry. Knowledge of IT is not always explicitly stated as a job requirement. However, a solid understanding has become an essential element of success in virtually any position. Not everyone in business needs to have all the technical skills of an IT professional, but everyone needs a working knowledge and exposure of the subject to know how to use IT in his or her profession. These skills are imperative in the increasingly digital and networked business world.

Management Information Systems provides students with the proper balance of technical information and real-world applications. No matter what field they undertake, students will enter the business world knowing how to get information to work for them. They will know enough about IT to work productively with IT specialists, and they will know enough about business applications to get information systems to support their work in the best way possible.

Approach

Ongoing Business Case Shows IS Principles in Action

In this edition, one business example is used as the foundation to integrate business case material for each Part and each Chapter. Part One introduces the textbook case, Kimball's Restaurant. The restaurant case provides a practical, "real world" example of a business scenario. In the succeeding chapters, material is added to the case to communicate a scenario tailored to each chapter's content. Each chapter case provides a narrative similar to the challenges and opportunities a business professional or entrepreneur would encounter in a company. Ultimately, the case scenario gives students the opportunity to integrate business IT principles, view IS issues in action, and to solve business problems related to IT just as they arise in the real world. The running case approach shows students how the full range of business functions operate while gaining an in-depth knowledge of a specific business. The textbook case is integrated into the text in several ways:

- **The Case:** Each chapter begins with a case based on the textbook running case, Kimball's Restaurant. The case is structured to be sequential in nature, beginning as a small restaurant then expanding to a new location at the Lakeside. In each chapter, a new "episode" of the restaurant's expansion is framed with new strategic and operational issues. Students are encouraged to "embed" themselves as a consultant to the business by (1) identifying the problems and opportunities, (2) applying general business and information technology concepts, (3) analyzing the alternatives to resolve the issues, and (4) recommending a suitable solution to focus on the success of the business.

- **The Business Challenge:** At the beginning of each Part in the textbook, a series of statements introduces the restaurant's challenges, which are outlined in more detail in each chapter case.
- **Kimball's Revisited:** At the end of each chapter, the textbook revisits issues framed in the chapter opening case and sets the environment for students to analyze the specific challenges facing Kimball's in two sections. Students can assume the role of consultants, providing advice to the restaurant's owners.
- **What Is Your Advice?:** This section communicates the various strategic and operational problems and issues confronting the restaurant. Students should carefully read the discussion points, analyze the issues, and integrate the technology concepts to provide specific advice.
- **New Perspectives:** In this section, students have an opportunity to answer questions that introduce a wide variety of "what ifs," reaching beyond the original scope of the case and asking students to think creatively and assume various different roles to meet business challenges.

Emphasis on the Real World

Management Information Systems is not afraid to warn about the limitations and challenges of ISs. The text also explains the great potential of many information technologies, which many organizations have not yet unleashed. Of course, this book includes chapters and features that provide a thorough, concise—and refreshingly clear—focusing on the technology of information systems, because all professionals in successful organizations are actively involved in making decisions about hardware, software, and telecommunications. But, through current, detail-rich, real-world case studies throughout the book, and a dedication to qualifying each presentation with the real-world factors that may affect business, this book provides issues and topics that are directly related to the business workplace in its presentation. It is important to understand the basic issues and concepts associated with information systems. However, business organizations continue to require its professionals to reinvent, integrate, and create a competitive advantage using information systems.

Attention to New Business Practices and Trends

Large parts of the text are devoted to discussing innovative uses of information technology and its benefits and risks. Contemporary concepts such as supply chain management systems, Big Data and data warehousing, business intelligence systems, knowledge management, social media, web-based electronic data interchange, and software as a service are explained in plain, easy-to-understand language.

Illustration of the Importance of Each Subject to One's Career

Business students often do not understand why they have to learn about information technology. The reason many students are frustrated with introductory MIS courses is that they do not fully understand how information technology works or why it is important for them to understand it. One of the primary goals of this book is for its entire presentation to make the answers to these questions apparent. First, all subjects are explained clearly that even the least technically oriented student can understand them. Technology is never explained for technology's sake, but to immediately demonstrate how it supports successful business strategies and operations. For instance, networking, database management, and web technologies (Chapters 6 through 8), which are often confusing topics, are presented with clear, concise, and vivid descriptions to paint a picture of technology at work. In addition, each chapter includes a feature titled **Why You Should**, which explains to students how being well-versed in that chapter's aspect of IT is important to their careers.

Emphasis on Ethical Thinking

The book puts a great emphasis on some of the questionable and controversial uses of information technology, with special treatment provided in the **Ethical & Societal Issues** boxes. The students are required to weigh the positive and negative impacts of technology and to convincingly argue their own positions on important issues such as privacy, free speech, and professional conduct. Successful businesses focus not only on profit and revenue, but also on ethical and transparent interaction with their stakeholders.

Emphasis on Critical Thinking

Critical thinking is used throughout the text as well as in the book's many features. For instance, the students are put in the midst of a business dilemma relating to the running case of each chapter and required to answer **What Is Your Advice?** questions. The questions motivate students to evaluate many aspects of each situation and to repeatedly consider how quickly IT evolves. Similarly, many of the **Discussion Questions** at the end of chapters call for their evaluation and judgment.

Additional Emphases in the Seventh Edition

Building on the success of the Sixth Edition, *Management Information Systems, Seventh Edition* includes a uniquely effective combination of features.

Updated Textbook Running Case Study

This Seventh Edition introduces a modified and dynamic pedagogical tool: one running case focusing on a business entity that incorporates a wide array of real-world events and challenges that dramatize how information technology is integrated into everyday business. The integration of one business example, rather than several different cases across chapters, focuses the attention of students on gaining an intimate and up-close perspective on one business. As students progress through the textbook, their analysis and insights will expand as they leverage the previous knowledge and information on Kimball's Restaurant. Additionally, the one case example helps students develop a distinct perspective on the maturation and development of one business as it wades through a variety of obstacles and challenges.

Strong Foundation in Strategic ISs in Business Functions

In addition to a complete chapter on strategic uses of ISs (Chapter 2), strategic thinking is an underlying theme throughout the book. Current examples are used to illustrate how information systems can help give businesses build and sustain a strategic competitive advantage.

Up-to-date Coverage of Web-Enabled and Mobile Commerce

Reflecting the use of web technologies in so many business activities, the book integrates the topic seamlessly throughout the text, just as it has become integrated into business in general. But the text goes beyond the well-worn discussions of the topic (and the handful of sites everyone knows about) to tell the students what works about e-commerce and what doesn't work. In addition, the rapid adoption of mobile technology through the use of tablets and smartphone technology is integrated throughout the textbook.

Current Real-world Examples Reflect a Wide Variety of Businesses

The textbook incorporates more applications, cases, and projects in the full range of business functions and industries throughout the book. The cases at the end of the chapter, in the **From Ideas to Application: Real Cases** sections, have been carefully selected to include critical thinking questions to guide students to apply what they have learned. Most of these cases are new to this edition and others have been updated and reflect current technology and trends. In addition, for strong pedagogical reinforcement, examples are embedded throughout the book.

Coverage of Global Issues

Globalization has become an important issue both economically and technologically. An entire chapter, Chapter 9, is devoted to discussing challenges to global information systems, from legal discrepancies through cultural issues to time zone issues. The chapter also discusses how the challenges can be met successfully. This topic receives little coverage in similar textbooks. The breadth and depth of coverage of challenges to global uses of IT in this book has been enthusiastically received by adopters.

New Aspects of Ethical and Societal Issues

The coverage of **Ethical & Societal Issues** in *Management Information Systems* builds on the strong foundation started in the first six editions. However, new issues have emerged, such as data security, Big Data and privacy, and offshoring, which are discussed in this edition.

New Student Assignments for Reinforcement of Material

This Seventh Edition continues to provide an updated selection of assignments at the ends of chapters, mainly assignments that require the use of relevant software and the web. Many of these assignments, including **Applying Concepts**, **Hands-On Activities**, and **Team Activities**, have been updated for this Edition. Responding to instructors' recommendations, more assignments require research involving the web. In addition to the hands-on exercises in each chapter, students and instructors will find a host of additional new hands-on work available at the student companion website, which is discussed later in this Preface.

More Points of Interest

Responding to instructors' enthusiastic reception of **Points of Interest**, a wealth of updated sidebar statistics, anecdotes, and short stories were added to this edition which add an interesting and entertaining aspect to the main chapter text. Except for a few entries believed to have remained accurate, all points of interest are updated in this edition.

Instructor's Package

Management Information Systems, Seventh Edition, includes teaching tools to support instructors in the classroom. The ancillaries that accompany the textbook include an Instructor's Manual, Solutions, Test Banks and Test Engine, PowerPoint presentations, and Figure Files. This textbook is one of the few accompanied by an Instructor's Manual written by the text author, ensuring compatibility with the textbook in content, pedagogy, and philosophy. All teaching tools available with this book are available on Cengage.com.

The Instructor's Manual

The text author has created this manual to provide materials to help instructors make their classes informative and interesting. The manual offers several approaches to teaching the material, with sample syllabi and comments on different components. It also suggests alternative course outlines and ideas for term projects. For each chapter, the manual includes teaching tips, useful websites, and answers to the Review Questions, Discussion Questions, and Thinking about the Case questions. Having an Instructor's Manual created by the text author is particularly valuable, as the author is most familiar with the topical and pedagogical approach of the text.

Solutions

We provide instructors with solutions to Review Questions and Discussion Questions as well as for quantitative hands-on work in each chapter. If appropriate, we will also provide solution files for various activities.

Cengage Learning Testing Powered by Cognero

A flexible, online system that allows you to:

- author, edit, and manage test bank content from multiple Cengage Learning solutions
- create multiple test versions in an instant
- deliver tests from your LMS, your classroom, or wherever you want

PowerPoint Presentations

Microsoft PowerPoint slides are included for each chapter. Instructors might use the slides in a variety of ways, including as teaching aids during classroom presentations or as printed handouts for classroom distribution. Instructors can add their own slides for additional topics introduced to the class.

Figure Files

Figure files allow instructors to create their own presentations using figures taken directly from the text.

Organization

Management Information Systems, Seventh Edition is organized into five parts, followed by a glossary and an index. It includes the following major elements.

Part One: The Information Age

Part One of the book includes three chapters. Chapter 1, "Business Information Systems: An Overview," provides an overview of information technology (IT) and information systems (ISs) and a framework for discussions in subsequent chapters. Chapter 2, "Strategic Uses of Information Systems," discusses organizational strategy and ways in which ISs can be used to meet strategic goals. Chapter 3, "Business Functions and Supply Chains," provides a detailed discussion of business functions, supply chains, and the systems that support management of supply chains in various industries. Together, these three chapters address the essence of all overarching ideas that are discussed at greater depth in subsequent chapters.

Part Two: Information Technology

To understand how ISs enhance managerial practices, one must be well versed in the technical principles of information technology, which are covered in Part Two. Chapters 4, "Business Hardware," 5, "Business Software," and 6, "Business Networks and Telecommunications," provide a concise treatment of state-of-the-art hardware, software, and networking technologies in business. Chapter 7, "Databases and Data Warehouses," covers database management systems and data warehousing, which provide the technical foundation leading to an expanded discussion of business intelligence and knowledge management in Chapter 11.

Part Three: Web-Enabled Commerce

Part Three is devoted to networked businesses and their use of the Internet. Chapter 8, "The Web-enabled Enterprise," is fully devoted to a thorough discussion of relevant web technologies for business operations. All chapters were updated to include mobile computing, tablets, and social media. Chapter 9, "Challenges of Global Information Systems," highlights cultural and other challenges organizations face in planning and using the web and international information systems.

Part Four: Decision Support and Business Intelligence

Part Four provides a view of state-of-the-art decision support and expert systems in Chapter 10 and business intelligence in Chapter 11. Electronic decision aids have been integrated into other systems in recent years, but understanding of their fundamentals is important. Business intelligence applications, such as data mining, Big Data, and online analytical processing, are essential tools in a growing number of businesses. Ample examples have been provided to demonstrate their power and benefits for businesses.

Part Five: Planning, Acquisition, and Controls

Part Five is devoted to planning, acquisition, and controls of information systems to ensure their successful and timely development and implementation, as well as their security. Chapter 12, "Systems Planning and Development," discusses how professionals plan information systems. It details traditional and agile methods of software development. Chapter 13, "Choices in Systems Acquisition," presents alternative acquisition methods to in-house development: outsourcing, purchased applications, end-user systems development, and software as a service. Additional material and recent trends in outsourcing and offshoring have been integrated as alternatives in systems acquisition. Chapter 14, "Risks, Security, and Disaster Recovery," discusses the risks that information systems face and ways to minimize them, as well as approaches to recovering from disasters.

New Features of this Edition

We listened carefully to our adopters, potential adopters, and reviewers in planning and writing this Seventh Edition of *Management Information Systems*. We kept the number and organization of chapters the same as in the previous edition to suit optimal coverage, pedagogy, and allow for flexibile term management. The major changes and improvements in this edition are:

- Complete update to integrate a running case into all 14 chapters
- Updated and extended coverage of the latest technologies and trends in MIS, including information security, mobile computing, social media, cloud computing, and Software as a Service
- New Point of Interest boxes throughout each chapter
- All end-of-chapter case studies were updated with recent examples
- New or revised end-of-chapter exercises

Some instructors would like students to consider careers in IT. Therefore, the discussion of IT careers was moved to Chapter 1, "Business Information Systems: An Overview." This allows the students to learn what IT professionals do early on.

Supply chain management (SCM) systems and customer relationship management (CRM) systems have become important staples in businesses. Therefore, they are now introduced early in Chapter 1, thoroughly explained in Chapter 3, "Business Functions and Supply Chains," and discussed widely throughout the text in various contexts. While we still discuss information systems by business function in Chapter 3, a large part of the chapter is devoted to enterprise applications such as SCM, CRM, and ERP systems.

Chapter 4, "Business Hardware," now includes shorter discussions of the innards of computers and extensive discussions on external memory devices and networked storage technologies such as SAN, NAS, and cloud storage.

In Chapter 5, "Business Software," the discussion of programming language generations was significantly cut to make room for more important discussions of software that all students will encounter in most organizations. The growing trend of using open source software is extensively discussed and students are exposed to a plethora of open source applications.

Chapter 6, "Business Networks and Telecommunications," focuses on the use of various networking technologies in business. A new section covers the latest wireless technologies, as this is the future of networking in communities, businesses, and homes. A detailed discussion of RFID technologies is included to provide the technical foundation for further discussion of current and future application of this technology in business.

The major web technologies are discussed and demonstrated in Chapter 8, "The Web-Enabled Enterprise." The chapter reflects the latest technologies. The section on alternatives in establishing commercial websites reflects the latest array of hosting options. Chapter 9, "Challenges of Global Information Systems," is devoted to illuminating the challenges and efficiencies of managing business information systems on a global scale.

Many current examples of decision support systems and artificial intelligence are provided in Chapter 10, "Decision Support and Expert Systems." Chapter 11, "Business Intelligence and Knowledge Management," combines discussions that were included in different chapters in earlier editions. The concept of employee knowledge networks is explained and demonstrated in examples.

Chapter 12, "Systems Planning and Development," discusses the traditional "waterfall" approaches such as the systems development life cycle, but also devotes a thorough discussion to agile methods, which have become so popular among software developers.

Chapter 13, "Choices in Systems Acquisition," discusses alternatives to in-house software development, such as Software as a Service.

Security and disaster recovery are discussed in Chapter 14, "Risks, Security, and Disaster Recovery," with more attention to increasingly severe risks, such as phishing. The discussion of threats to privacy were updated to address new technologies such as RFID tags and location-based services.

Except for very few entries, all the *Point of Interest* box features are new. All *Ethical & Societal Issues* discussions have been updated.

Nearly all of the end-of-chapter Real Cases are new. As in previous editions, all are real-world examples reported in a wide range of major business and technology journals.

Acknowledgments

I am honored to have been selected to revise the successful textbook that Effy Oz created. Dr. Oz was an exceptional educator and author, and my first and primary acknowledgment is to him. It is my hope that my efforts will continue his legacy and his great work.

Revising a textbook is a challenging process that requires commitment and unwavering discipline. However, as in any long, challenging initiative, a project such as this could not be successful without the contribution of many people. I would first like to thank my colleagues in the business, consulting, IT, and academic organizations whose ideas, efforts, and opinions over all these years have helped me understand the educational needs of our students and the marketplace. Without them, it would be impossible to have attained the experience and knowledge required to compile this textbook. I also must recognize the indirect but important contribution of the many students I have taught. Their comments (and criticism) helped me refine and sharpen my teaching. Over 20 years of teaching, they have helped me to comprehend the points that needed extra emphasis, a different presentation, or an experiential assignment to make topics that may be overwhelming clearer and more interesting. I have learned that teaching only prepares students for today, but educating builds skilled and mature professionals for life.

Many thanks go to Kate Mason for being so enthusiastic about this project. She was always there for me with advice, encouragement, and patience as a new author. Kate demonstrated and exerted unbounded energy while leading this project. Her active guidance and constant involvement made an immense contribution to this edition. Kate also handled the smooth coordination of the instructor's package, web materials, and more. Arul Joseph Raj, the Content Product Manager, guided the textbook through its production while managing the process in a very orderly and timely manner. The design and art managers at PreMediaGlobal ensured the textbook and photos were visually appealing, and the team of artists skillfully rendered our ideas. I extend both my personal and professional gratitude to these talented professionals.

Deb Kaufmann, the developmental editor, has demonstrated again her excellent skills and high integrity. I was very fortunate to have Deb on the team because of her involvement with Dr. Oz for the sixth edition. It was wonderful to work with an editor who excels not only in improving style and organization but who is also so knowledgeable in the subject matter. She is a consummate professional who helped me tremendously through her broad perspective while always attending to the details that were essential ingredients supporting my work.

Reviewers are the most important aides to any writer, especially when preparing a college textbook. I would like to thank the reviewers who carefully reviewed each chapter for this edition:

Merlin Amirtharaj, *Stanley Community College*
Don Danner, *San Francisco State University*
John Delalla, *University of Arizona South*
Lewis Todd, *Belhaven University*
Patricia Wallace, *The College of New Jersey*

A special thanks goes to Charles McCormick, who retired from Cengage in 2012, for supporting me to author this textbook.

This textbook would not be possible without the contribution of my research assistant. Jerry Theiler, a senior accounting student, assisted with the research and compilation of updates for this edition. Jerry is a diligent, intelligent, and mature young man who provided me with quality work throughout this revision.

Lastly, I would like to thank my mother Virginia, who recently passed away, and my father Henry. They have provided me with the work ethic, integrity, and loyalty that that has been the bedrock of my achievements. This textbook and other accomplishments in my life could not have been gained without their exceptional influence and support. Additionally, I would like to acknowledge my many friends and former students as well as my colleagues at Bryant University for their constant encouragement and support. As Kingman Brewster said, "*There is no greater challenge than to have someone relying upon you, no greater satisfaction than to vindicate their expectations.*" It is my hope that I have fulfilled your expectations.

I welcome suggestions and comments from our adopters and their students to continue developing a quality textbook as well as to continue Dr. Oz's legacy and contributing to the education of students that this textbook will provide.

Kenneth J. Sousa
author@sousamis.com

THE INFORMATION AGE

Textbook Case: KIMBALL'S RESTAURANT

Liz and Michael Kimball dreamed about opening their own restaurant. They believed that they could use their talents and experience to operate a successful restaurant. Liz was a great cook and had accumulated many family recipes for appetizers, entrees, and bakery desserts. Michael had a degree in business and several years of experience in business management. They believed that it was the right time to think about new careers and realize their dream.

Michael began his career in the human resources department of a local manufacturing business. Over the course of his 20 years in human resources, he was responsible for recruiting, compensation evaluation, and employee orientation. He also managed employees' performance evaluations for the production departments. While he has some accounting and budgeting experience, it was specific only to human resources, not for an entire business organization.

Liz started work as a customer service rep for a financial services company right after high school. Her 15 years of customer service experience has given her some ability to manage people. She does not have a formal culinary education, but she has an excellent sense of food preparation, ingredient selection, and meal planning. These skills should provide a foundation for the menu development and food preparation that a restaurant will require. However, her lack of a formal culinary education and experience in commercial kitchen operations might require some additional training.

The Kimballs live in Lakeside Heights, a suburb of a metropolitan city. Their community and the adjacent towns consist of primarily middle-income households. Many of the adults in the community are college-educated and have professional jobs in business and manufacturing. The population of the town and surrounding communities is approximately 40,000 people. The city, about 12 miles from Lakeside Heights, has a population of 110,000.

Michael and Liz believe that a restaurant serving Liz's specialties of "home style" American, Italian, and seafood dishes would be a good choice for their location. They are excited about the possibility of providing quality food at a reasonable cost. The same family and friends that enjoy Liz's cooking would match their expected customers. They want to offer a quiet, relaxed dining environment offering mid-priced meals.

■ Researching the Business

As they talked about the details, their dream gathered momentum. However, they both knew that they couldn't build their business on dreams alone. They would need additional business advice and perspective to ensure that their business concept was realistic. First, they checked out the numbers.

Liz and Michael, along with their advisors and friends, assessed the capital required for starting a restaurant. They agreed that Liz and Michael had sufficient funds to use as start-up capital for the new venture.

Tom, a family friend employed as a marketing consultant, felt that their business model would be well suited for their location. They had their eye on a strip mall location that was vacant and could be suitable for a small family restaurant. They contacted the local real estate agent, Anne Marie Simmons, to ask about its rental cost, availability, and size. Liz and Michael visited the location with Anne Marie. The agent said that the store housed a diner for three years before it closed. She speculated that the diner might not have been able to compete against the fast-food franchises in the area. The agent also believed that the owners did not have the proper financial and marketing plan to be successful.

Liz studied the store's floor plan and dimensions. The store had floor space to accommodate about 50 diners as well as a full kitchen operation and storage areas. The strip mall location had plenty of parking as well as access on a major road. The gas, plumbing, and electrical infrastructure were in good working order. The décor and kitchen appliances need to be purchased as well as all restaurant fixtures (pans, dishes, flatware, etc.) if they signed a lease to occupy the restaurant.

In order to be efficient and leverage their individual skills, Liz and Michael segregated the various research tasks necessary to compile business projections and forecasts. Michael focused his attention on the front-house operations, sales, and marketing plan while Liz analyzed the kitchen operations, inventory, and menu planning. Each of them compiled forecasts for the startup and operational costs in their areas of specialty. These costs included the labor, materials, food, utilities, rent, and other necessary costs. These forecasts would be the foundation of their business, financial, and operations plan.

■ Creating the Business Plan

Michael continued to work with Tom on the marketing and promotion of the restaurant. Their first thought was to gather sales, customer, and meal data from the previous owner. To protect the anonymity of the new owners, Michael asked Anne Marie to contact the previous owner. She provided three years of weekly data on the number of meals and tables served. Unfortunately, the previous owner could not or did not want to provide any sales data. Michael entered 164 weeks of data into a simple Excel spreadsheet to review. The spreadsheet contained three data points: week ending date (Sunday), total checks, and total meals served. Michael and Tom reviewed the spreadsheet to attempt to find some relevant information for their marketing and forecasting projections.

The diner had been open seven days a week. However, the data Michael received was not broken down by the day of the week. Therefore, the data could not be used to analyze daily traffic and sales, but only to analyze weekly trends without information on daily traffic and sales.

Tom coached Michael on how to analyze the data through a "rough" first glance. He separated the data into three spreadsheet tabs by year, where the first row of weekly data was the first week in the calendar year. He added a column that calculated the average meals per check. Then, to gain an understanding of the restaurant's customer load, he ranked both the number of meals and checks within the year. These values provided a basic sense of the high and low weeks for the previous restaurant. He then sorted each of the three calendar years by the meal count (descending with the highest ranking first).

The lack of daily data limited the depth of analysis that could be completed. Tom looked at the hardcopy of three years of data side by side. After reviewing the three years of data, Tom pointed out that their weekly data showed only one clear trend: Some weeks showed lower sales than the other periods. Upon further analysis, it appeared that they were holiday periods (Thanksgiving and Christmas weeks) as well as some summer weeks. Without the daily data, it was impossible to determine the distribution or trending of customer sales.

Liz completed another tour of the restaurant location. The kitchen was equipped with an operational walk-in refrigerator, exhaust fan, several tables, and shelving units. She assembled a tentative new floor plan for the kitchen and food preparation area. From the floor plan, she compiled a cost estimate listing the appliances and fixtures still needed for the kitchen.

In addition to seating about 50 people comfortably with 15 tables, Michael believes that a bar can be built to seat an additional 10 patrons. He created estimates for dining room and bar equipment, furniture and fixtures, including all labor installation costs.

Tom helped them create a spreadsheet using various factors to estimate the weekly sales. They used some of the previous owner's data to calculate the seasonal and weekly trends. With the menu that

Liz compiled, they estimated the weekly sales for the restaurant for the first year. The entire spreadsheet calculated the variable costs (labor, food) based on the number of meals served. The list of fixed overhead costs (like utilities, taxes, and rent) then helped to generate the monthly cash flow and profit estimates. The spreadsheet calculated three scenarios: aggressive, reasonable, and conservative. The most conservative estimate resulted in a small loss for most months. They felt comfortable with the range of projections they had compiled. Tom believed that Liz and Michael could present these forecasts and a business plan to a bank for a loan for the startup costs.

■ Launching the Dream

Kimball's Restaurant opened in the strip mall location. As with any new business, the restaurant started out slowly with sales closer to the conservative estimates. However, as their reputation for quality, reasonably priced meals developed, Liz and Michael knew their dream had become a reality.

Three years later, Kimball's was operating successfully and profitably. Their dining room was often at capacity with both new and returning customers. They often had a small waiting line on weekend nights. Liz and Michael were very satisfied with their dream. What would be next?

BUSINESS CHALLENGES

In the next three chapters, you will learn what Michael and Liz need to get started in harnessing the power of information systems to help build and grow their restaurant. They will need to understand how information systems can help with a restaurant's short-term (operational) needs as well as plan for long-term initiatives (strategic) to expand the business.

- In Chapter 1, "Business Information Systems: An Overview," you learn the various types of information systems businesses use and why familiarity with information technology is important for your career. You also are introduced to some of the major ethical and societal concerns about acquiring, storing, and reporting potentially sensitive information.

- In Chapter 2, "Strategic Uses of Information Systems," you learn how to use information strategically, and how to harness information technology for competitive advantage.

- In Chapter 3, "Business Functions and Supply Chains," you learn how you might best use information technology to help manage a business, whether you need to order inventory and track sales, generate financial statements, or automate payroll systems. You also learn how supply chain management systems serve whole enterprises.

BUSINESS INFORMATION SYSTEMS
An Overview

Learning Objectives

It is likely that you are carrying or using an information system. This is so if you have a smartphone, a tablet, or a laptop computer. Information systems pervade almost every aspect of our lives. Whether you are withdrawing money from a bank's automatic teller machine, surfing the web, or making a hotel reservation on your cell phone, hardly a day goes by without our feeding data into, or using information generated by, an information system. In business especially, digital information systems generate most of the information we use. Information systems receive and process data from various sources. These systems have become essential to successful business operations.

When you finish this chapter, you will be able to:

- Explain why information technology matters.

- Define digital information and explain why digital systems are so powerful and useful.

- Explain why information systems are essential to business.

- Describe how computers process data into useful information for problem solving and decision making.

- Identify the functions of different types of information systems in business.

- Describe careers in information technology.

- Identify major ethical and societal concerns created by widespread use of information technology.

The restaurant has been operating successfully for three years. Although they experienced challenges, Liz and Michael believe that they developed a great dining establishment. Sales forecasts have steadily increased over the last three years. Thankfully, the growth was not so fast as to cause any "growing pains" or problems with their business. Michael found that during most weeks, they had reservations for 50 to 100 percent of their dining capacity.

Processing Orders and Payments

Michael believed his analysis was fairly accurate, but it took a lot of effort to compile his information. The servers wrote the customer orders on multipart paper checks. One copy of these checks went to the kitchen for preparation. The server tabulated totals on the original copy and gave it to the customer when the meal was complete. At that point, the customer paid the cashier directly with cash or a credit card and the hardcopy of the check was saved. Several times a week, Michael used the paper checks to enter the sales and table information in an Excel spreadsheet for analysis. Because he was so busy with other operational priorities, the spreadsheet data entry and subsequent analysis was often delayed.

The restaurant processed its payroll through a local service. Employees maintained their timecards manually. Each week, the timecard data was validated by Michael and sent to the payroll service for processing and check printing. Michael was not comfortable with the manual entry of employee time punches, but he did not have a simple, cost effective alternative.

Michael used a small business accounting package to track the restaurant's expenses, process payable checks to suppliers, and record deposits. The software was easy to use and provided the balance sheet and income statement needed for the business. It also generated the required tax information for his accountant to file the appropriate tax forms. However, it did not track a level of information needed for analyzing the business operations and forecasting sales. From his experience in human resources, Michael understood the need for quality data and business information. At his former employer, the information technology department provided that expertise and assistance. Unfortunately, those skills were not available at the restaurant.

Michael knew that his time was limited and that he needed to focus more on the operations rather than data entry, but he also wanted to collect and analyze data about his business to manage it and plan effectively.

Their son, Tyler, finished his education to complete a business degree, specializing in marketing and

management. He had worked in the restaurant during the summers and semester breaks as a busboy and server so he had some familiarity with the business. He was also anxious to gain more experience to try out some of the skills he had learned in business school. Liz and Michael decided it was a good time for Tyler to join the business.

Defining the Problems

Michael told Tyler that he would like to streamline the front- and back-house operations and gather more information for analysis without relying on manual data entry. Tyler understood the challenges because some of the problems in these areas were directly related to issues that Tyler encountered while he was a server at the restaurant. The issues could be categorized into two areas: completeness and accuracy of guest check information, and check payment.

Because the guests' orders were handwritten, sometimes parts of the orders were not legible. In addition, especially with new servers, some of the information needed to complete a meal was either inaccurate or incomplete for that meal choice (cooking preferences, toppings, special preparation). This issue added time for the server and cooking staff as well as reduced customer satisfaction. Check payment was another problem. Often, it was not clear to the customers whether they should pay the server or the cashier. Michael wanted to control the cash and credit-card processing at a central location, but was willing to review this policy.

Tyler talked to the servers and kitchen personnel to gain perspective on the guest check and payment problems. The staff was pleased to be asked for input. They confirmed that guest check accuracy and payment were issues, but additional issues were uncovered. As in many restaurants, at Kimball's the servers were responsible for any checks not paid by the customer. However, it was impossible for the server to know if the customer paid the cashier or left without paying. The servers would prefer that customers settle their payment directly with the server so that they could know if a customer has paid. Servers also conveyed that even when they wrote out the order legibly and completely, meals sometimes were not prepared properly. The kitchen staff said that changes to guest orders are often "rushed" and disrupted the completion of other meals in progress. On many occasions, servers submitted changes after the order was ready to deliver to the table. Kitchen staff said a new process was needed to communicate order changes before the table's meals were cooked. Unfortunately, it was impossible to tell from the current checks which orders required changes. Therefore, no data was available to objectively assess the magnitude of the problem.

Collecting Data to Address Problems and Make Decisions

Tyler then focused his attention on the data analysis. He asked his parents to define two lists of questions: (1) What do you know from the information you currently maintain? and (2) What answers would you like to know that would help you operate the business more efficiently and profitably? They responded that they knew how many tables were seated by day as well as the total check amounts. The checks separated the liquor and food totals for tax purposes, but the daily totals for these categories did not provide any details about the individual customers' orders. Michael would also like to know more details, such as ... What meals did they order? Did they order appetizers? How many patrons were at the table (adults and children)? Did the customer take advantage of any of the specials? Liz wanted to know, how much food do I need to order based on past sales?

Tyler said that these questions were a great start. He categorized their questions into two areas: marketing/promotion and operational. He knew that additional marketing information was needed to determine menu planning, promotions, and customer satisfaction. He wondered how many people were returning or new customers. How did they learn about the restaurant? For operational issues, was there any monitoring of the operations as issues occurred?

Does Information Technology Matter?

The Denver-based hamburger chain Smashburger developed more than a secret recipe for its hamburgers. It used social media giants, Facebook and Twitter, by inviting bloggers to promote the opening of new locations in their area. Instead of relying solely on paid media promotion, Smashburger engaged their consumers directly through the use of social media.

A survey compiled by Boston-based Aite Group of 1,000 consumers demonstrated their adoption of mobile devices to complete banking transactions. Approximately one-third of the consumers conveyed that they have increased their use of mobile banking applications to check their account balances; an increase of 10 times within one year (Cerny, 2011).

These examples, as well as many other observations, show that IT can no longer be the sole domain of IT professionals. Business professionals can no longer count solely on IT specialists to make decisions on development, purchasing, and deployment of information systems. Social media and mobile computing clearly rely on a well-developed strategy across all functions of business organizations. Today's business professionals are expected to know how to develop and use IT significantly more than just a few years ago. Regardless of their major field of expertise, those who have the proper IT knowledge and skills stand a better chance of receiving more lucrative job offers and faster promotions.

The Power of Digital Systems

We are accustomed to using 10 digits to represent quantities. We call it the decimal counting system. However, we could also use a system consisting of only two digits, zero and one, to represent quantities. This is the binary counting system. Because computers and related devices use the binary system—a system that uses two *digits*—they are referred to as **digital systems**. However, digital systems are not used only to represent information that contains numbers, or quantities. They can also represent any information as combinations of zeroes and ones, or, more accurately, the two states that represent zeroes and ones.

Digital information consists of zeroes and ones representing two states. When you have a mechanism that can represent two states, such as electrically charged and uncharged elements, magnetized and non-magnetized areas, light and no light, you have a way to represent the zeroes and ones. Based on such signals, information can be represented, stored, communicated, and processed *digitally*.

Unlike analog systems (systems based on a continuous signal that varies in strength or quantity), digital systems are capable of delivering data and information—quantities, text, sound, pictures, video, and any other type of information—so that the original information can be re-created with complete accuracy. That is, a digital copy is an exact copy of the original. For example, an analog copy machine reproduces images by reflection or a similar technique. The copy may be good, but it is never as good as the original. And as you make a copy from the copy, the quality deteriorates. When you make a copy of a digital file, such as an image file or a musical file, the system you use first captures the combinations of signals (the digits, zeroes and ones) that make up the file. When processed by the proper hardware and software, the digits are transformed back into the image, or music, or whatever other information you copied. As long as your computer or other digital device can capture all the digits that make up the information, the original information can be re-created fully.

Digital information is stored and communicated by way of electromagnetic signals—electricity, magnetism, and light. These processes involve few or no moving parts. Therefore, storage, retrieval, processing, and communication of digital information are extremely fast. These capabilities—accuracy and speed—make digital systems powerful and therefore useful and important in so many fields: business, education, entertainment, and many others.

The Purpose of Information Systems

People require information for many reasons and in varied ways. For instance, you probably seek information for entertainment and enlightenment by viewing television, watching movies, browsing the Internet, listening to the radio, and reading newspapers, magazines, and books. In business, however, people and organizations seek and use information mainly to make sound decisions and to solve problems—two closely related practices that form the foundation of every successful company.

What is a problem? A *problem* is the root cause of an undesirable situation. When you are stuck in the middle of nowhere with a flat tire, you have a problem. If you know that some customers do not pay their debts on time, but you don't know who or how much they owe, you have a problem. You can solve both problems with the aid of information. In the first case, you can call a towing company, which might use a computerized tracking system to send the tow truck closest to your location; in the second case, simple accounting software can help.

An organization or individual that identifies more than one way to solve a problem or a dilemma must make a *decision*. The problem "2+2=?" does not require decision making because it has only one solution. However, as a manager, you might face a dilemma such as "Which is the best way to promote the company's new car?" There are many potential ways to promote the new car—television advertising, radio advertising, newspaper advertising, web advertising, auto shows, direct mail, social media, or any combination of these methods. This dilemma calls for decision making.

Both problem solving and decision making require information. Gathering the right information efficiently, storing it so that it can be used and manipulated as necessary, and using it to help an organization achieve its business goals—all topics covered in this book—are the keys to success in business today. The purpose of information systems is to support these activities. In addition to solving problems and making decisions, businesses use information systems to support daily operations, such as electronic commerce, making airline reservations, and many other activities. As a professional, you need to understand and apply information fundamentals to succeed.

WHY YOU SHOULD   Be Well-Versed in Information Systems

You might be surprised at how much information technology (IT) knowledge your prospective employer will expect of you when you interview for your next job, even if the position you seek is not in the IT area. Today's corporations look for IT-savvy professionals, and with good reason. Information is the lifeblood of any organization, commercial or nonprofit; it is essential to sound problem solving and decision making, upon which business success is built. In fact, the main factor limiting the services and information that computers can provide within an organization is the budget.

Because of rapid changes in technology, information systems, unlike many other business components, are quickly changing in form and content. A computer considered fast and powerful today will be an outdated machine in 18–24 months. In 12–24 months, a better application or technology model will surpass one that is considered innovative right now. The dynamic nature of information technology is like a moving target. Your new idea or product concept using information technology will be replaced by someone else's new idea or product concept.

A professional who does not stay informed is of diminishing value to an organization. All knowledge workers—professionals, scientists, managers, and others who create new information and knowledge in their work—must be familiar with IT. Moreover, they must know which IT is relevant for their work and what information they can obtain with a certain technology or networked resource.

Professionals must at all times maintain a clear picture of their organizations and the outside business environment. They must know what resources are available to them and to their competitors. Information technology provides excellent tools for collecting, storing, and presenting facts. But to be truly effective, those facts must be manipulated into useful information that indicates the best allocation of various resources, including personnel, time, money, equipment, and other assets. Regardless of the operations being managed, information systems (ISs) are important tools. Successful professionals must know which ISs are available to their organizations and what systems might be developed in the future.

Data, Information, and Information Systems

We use the words "data," "information," and "system" almost daily. Understanding what these terms mean, both generally and in the business context, is necessary if you are to use information effectively in your career.

Data vs. Information

The terms "data" and "information" do not mean the same thing. The word **data** is derived from the Latin *datum*, literally a given or fact, which might take the form of a number, a statement, or a picture. Data is the raw material in the production of information. **Information**, on the other hand, is facts or conclusions that have meaning within a context. Raw data is rarely meaningful or useful as information. To become information, data is manipulated through tabulation, statistical analysis, or any other operation that leads to greater understanding of a situation.

Data Manipulation

Here's a simple example that demonstrates the difference between data and information. Assume that you work for a car manufacturer. Last year, the company introduced a new vehicle to the market. Because management realizes that keeping a loyal customer base requires continuously improving products and services, it periodically surveys large samples of buyers. It sends out questionnaires that include 30 questions in several categories, including demographic data (such as gender, age, and annual income); complaints about different performance areas (such as ease of handling, braking, and the quality of the sound system); features that satisfy buyers most; and courtesy of the dealer's personnel.

Reading through all this data would be extremely time consuming and not very helpful. However, if the data is manipulated, it might provide highly useful information. For example, by categorizing complaints by topic and totaling the number of complaints for each type of dissatisfaction and each car model, the company might be able to pinpoint a car's weaknesses. The marketing analysts then can pass the resulting information along to the appropriate engineering or manufacturing unit.

Also, the company might already have sufficient data on dealers who sold cars to the customers surveyed, the car models they sold, and the financing method for each purchase. But with the survey results, the company can generate new information to improve its marketing. For instance, by calculating the average age and income of current buyers and categorizing them by the car they purchased, marketing executives can better target advertising to groups most likely to purchase each car. If the majority of buyers of a particular type of car do not ask for financing, the company might wish to drop this service option for that car and divert more loan money to finance purchases of other cars. In this way, the company generates useful information from data.

Generating Information

In the examples just cited, calculating totals and averages of different complaints or purchasers' ages may reveal trends in buying habits. These calculations are processes. A **process** is any manipulation of data, usually with the goal of producing information. Hence, while data is essentially raw materials, information is output. Just as raw materials are processed in manufacturing to create useful end products, so raw data is processed in information systems to create useful information (see Figure 1.1). Some processes, however, produce yet another set of data.

FIGURE **1.1**

Input-process-output

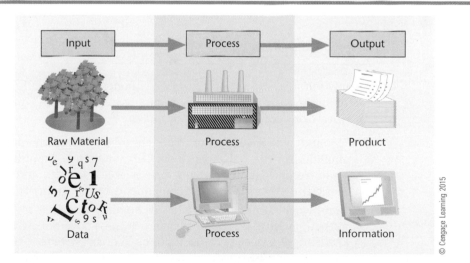

Sometimes, data in one context is considered information in another context. For example, if an organization needs to know the age of every person attending a basketball game, then a list of that data is actually information. But if that same organization wants to know the average price of tickets each age group purchases, the list of ages is only data, which the organization must process to generate information.

Information in Context

Information is an extremely important resource for both individuals and organizations, but not all information is useful. Consider the following story. Two people touring in a hot-air balloon encountered unexpected wind that soon blew them off course. When they managed to lower their balloon, they shouted to a farmer on the ground, "Where are we?" The farmer answered, "You are right above a cornfield!" The balloonists looked at each other, and one groaned, "Some information! Highly accurate and totally useless!" To be useful, information must be relevant, complete, accurate, and current. And in business, information must also be obtained economically, that is, cost effectively. Figure 1.2 lists characteristics of useful information.

FIGURE 1.2

Characteristics of useful information

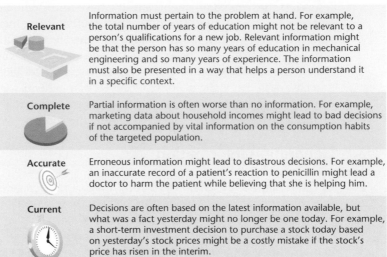

Relevant	Information must pertain to the problem at hand. For example, the total number of years of education might not be relevant to a person's qualifications for a new job. Relevant information might be that the person has so many years of education in mechanical engineering and so many years of experience. The information must also be presented in a way that helps a person understand it in a specific context.
Complete	Partial information is often worse than no information. For example, marketing data about household incomes might lead to bad decisions if not accompanied by vital information on the consumption habits of the targeted population.
Accurate	Erroneous information might lead to disastrous decisions. For example, an inaccurate record of a patient's reaction to penicillin might lead a doctor to harm the patient while believing that she is helping him.
Current	Decisions are often based on the latest information available, but what was a fact yesterday might no longer be one today. For example, a short-term investment decision to purchase a stock today based on yesterday's stock prices might be a costly mistake if the stock's price has risen in the interim.
Economical	In a business setting, the cost of obtaining information must be considered as one cost element involved in any decision. For example, demand for a new product must be researched to reduce risk of marketing failure, but if market research is too expensive, the cost of obtaining the information might diminish profit from sales.

© Cengage Learning 2015

What Is a System?

Simply put, a **system** is an array of components that work together to achieve a common goal, or multiple goals, by accepting input, processing it, and producing output in an organized manner. Consider the following examples:

- A sound system consists of many electronic and mechanical parts, such as a laser head, an amplifier, an equalizer, and so on. This system uses input in the form of electrical power and sound recorded on a medium such as a CD or DVD, and processes the input to reproduce music and other sounds. The components work together to achieve this goal.

- Consider the times you have heard the phrase "to beat the system." Here, the term "system" refers to an organization of human beings—a government agency, a commercial company, or any other bureaucracy. Organizations, too, are systems; they consist of components—people organized into departments and divisions—that work together to achieve common goals.

Systems and Subsystems

Not every system has a single goal. Often, a system consists of several **subsystems**—components of a larger system—with subgoals, all contributing to meeting the main goal. Subsystems can receive input from, and transfer output to, other systems or subsystems.

Consider the different departments of a manufacturing business. The marketing department promotes sales of the organization's products; the engineering department designs new products and improves existing ones; the finance department plans a budget and arranges for every unused penny to earn interest by the end of the day. Each department is a subsystem with its own goal, which is a subgoal of a larger system (the company), whose goal is to maximize profit.

Now consider the goals of a manufacturing organization's information system, which stores and processes operational data and produces information about all aspects of company operations. The purpose of its inventory control subsystem is to let managers know what quantities of which items are on hand and which may soon have to be reordered. The purpose of the production control subsystem is to track the status of manufactured parts. The assembly control subsystem presents the bill of material (a list of all parts that make up a product) and the status of assembled products. The entire system's goal is to help deliver finished goods at the lowest possible cost within the shortest possible time.

Figure 1.3 shows an example of a system found in every business: an accounting system. An accounting system consists of several subsystems: accounts payable, records information about money that the organization owes to suppliers and service providers; accounts receivable, records sums owed to the organization and by whom; a general ledger, records current transactions; and a reporting mechanism, generates reports reflecting the company's financial status. Each subsystem has a well-defined goal. Together, the subsystems make up the organization's accounting system.

FIGURE **1.3**

Several subsystems make up this corporate accounting system

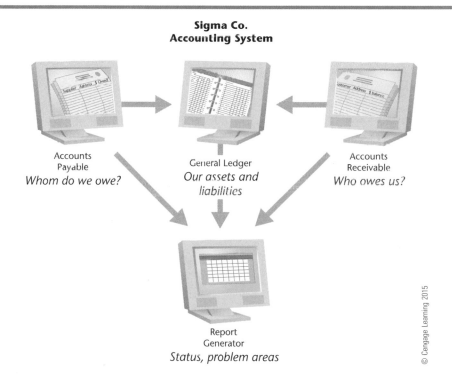

**Sigma Co.
Accounting System**

Accounts Payable
Whom do we owe?

General Ledger
Our assets and liabilities

Accounts Receivable
Who owes us?

Report Generator
Status, problem areas

© Cengage Learning 2015

All professionals must understand systems, both organizational and physical. They need to understand their position in an organization so they can interact well with coworkers, employees of business partners, and customers. They need to understand information systems so that they can utilize them to support their work and interactions with other people.

Closed vs. Open Systems

Systems are closed or open, depending on the nature of the information flow in the system. A **closed system** stands alone, with no connection to another system: nothing flows in from another system; nothing flows out to another system. For example, a small check-producing system that prints and cuts checks when an employee enters data through a keyboard is a closed system. The system might be isolated for security purposes. An **open system** interfaces and interacts with other systems. For example, an accounting system that records accounts receivable, accounts payable, and cash flow is open if it receives its payroll figures from the payroll system. Subsystems, by definition, are always open, because as components of a bigger system, they must receive information from, and give information to, other subsystems.

Increasingly, companies are implementing open—interfaced—information systems. Each system may then be referred to as a module of a larger system, and the modules are interconnected and exchange data and information. For better cooperation, many organizations have interconnected their information systems to those of their business partners, mainly suppliers and clients.

Information Systems

With an understanding of the terms "information" and "system," the definition of an information system is almost intuitive: an **information system (IS)** consists of all the components that work together to process data and produce information. Almost all business information systems consist of many subsystems with subgoals, all contributing to the organization's main goal.

Information and Managers

Thinking of an organization in terms of its suborganizations or subsystems—called systems thinking—is a powerful management approach because it creates a framework for excellent problem solving and decision making. To solve problems, managers need to identify them, which they do by recognizing the subsystems in which the problems occur and solving the problems within those subsystems' constraints and strengths.

Systems thinking can also help keep managers focused on the overall goals and operations of a business. It encourages them to consider the entire system, not only their specific subsystem, when solving problems and making decisions. A satisfactory solution for one subsystem might be inadequate for the business as a whole. For example, when the sales department creates a web site to take online customer orders, it automates a formerly labor-intensive activity of the sales subsystem. This saves cost. However, increased orders may cause understocking of finished goods. With systems thinking, improving the sales process could also improve other company processes. Without systems thinking, managers from other departments aren't involved in the decision, so they don't benefit. In the case of the sales department, if other managers are involved in planning for automated online ordering, they could suggest that sales data recorded on a shared **database**—a large collection of electronic records—connected to the web also be accessible to other departments such as shipping and manufacturing. The shipping department could use the records to expedite packaging and shipping, thanks to the information that appears on a computer monitor rather than a sheet of paper. The manufacturing units could use the order records for planning resources such as laborers and inventory. Figuratively, by applying systems thinking, effective managers view their areas of responsibility as puzzle pieces. Each piece is important and should fit well with adjacent pieces, but the entire picture should always be kept in view.

One of an information system's most important contributions to the sound workings of an organization is the automation of information exchange among systems. Redbox offers DVD and video game rentals through kiosks but there are other ways to rent. Customers can also reserve a DVD or video game on a mobile phone or through the web and pick it up at a selected Redbox kiosk. Redbox uses an inventory and reservation database to synchronize all three channels of reservation processing (Chipchase, 2011).

Innovation in sales systems can be the competitive advantage a company needs to survive in a harsh economic environment. For example, Redbox uses vending machines to distribute and collect DVDs that they rent for only $1 per night. Redbox strategically places kiosks in high-footfall areas and does not have the labor expenses that traditional retail video stores experience, thus creating financial advantage. Their location placement strategy has created rapid sales growth; 31.2 percent revenue growth in the first quarter of 2011 (Anonymous, 2011; Pruitt, 2007). A May 2011 research report indicated that consumers spent 8 percent more on movies rented at kiosks, mail or streaming while renting or purchasing a DVD at a retail store decreased 8 percent. (Gruenwedel, 2011).

The **information map** of a modern business—that is, the description of data and information flow within an organization—shows a network of information subsystems that exchange information with each other and with the world outside the system. In an ideal organization, no human would need to retrieve information from one IS and transfer it to another. The organization would capture only new raw data, usually from its operations or from outside the organization. Then, data captured at any point in the system would automatically become available to any other subsystem that needs it. Thus, systems thinking is served well by **information technology (IT)**, a term that refers to all technologies that collectively facilitate construction and maintenance of information systems. Systems thinking is the basic reasoning behind equipping organizations with enterprise software applications. Enterprise software applications are systems that serve many parts of the organization by minimizing the need for human data entry and ensuring timely, useful information for the organization's entire supply chain, including taking customer orders, receiving raw materials, manufacturing and shipping, and billing and collection. In the service sector, companies often use document management systems, enabling workers from many departments to add information and signatures to a document from request to approval, or from draft to a final document. You will learn about these systems throughout this book.

Information Systems in Organizations

In an organization, an information system consists of data, hardware, software, telecommunications, people, and procedures, as summarized in Figure 1.4. An information system has become synonymous with a computer-based information system, a system with one or more computers at its center, and which is how the term is used in this book. In a computer-based information system, computers collect, store, and process data into information according to instructions people provide via computer programs.

FIGURE 1.4

Components of an
information system

Data	Input that the system takes to produce information
Hardware	A computer and its peripheral equipment: input, output, and storage devices; hardware also includes data communication equipment
Software	Sets of instructions that tell the computer how to take data in, how to process it, how to display information, and how to store data and information
Telecommunications	Hardware and software that facilitate fast transmission and reception of text, pictures, sound, and animation in the form of electronic data
People	Information systems professionals and users who analyze organizational information needs, design and construct information systems, write computer programs, operate the hardware, and maintain software
Procedures	Rules for achieving optimal and secure operations in data processing; procedures include priorities in dispensing software applications and security measures

Several trends have made the use of information systems (ISs) very important in business:

- The capacity of data storage devices has grown while their prices have decreased.
- The variety and ingenuity of software applications have increased.
- A "bring your technology with you" environment has become mainstream with the adoption of mobile computing, tablets, and **cloud computing**.
- Quick and reliable communication lines and access to the Internet and the web have created affordable software applications using **Software as a Service (SaaS)** implementation methodologies.
- The fast growth of the Internet has opened opportunities and encouraged competition in global markets.
- The convergence of technology innovations such as smart phones, mobile applications, organizational systems, and cloud storage systems have expanded both technology adoption and functionality.
- An increasing proportion of the global workforce is computer literate.

In this environment, organizations quickly lag behind if they do not use information systems and skills to meet their goals. Moreover, they must continuously upgrade the features of their information systems and the skills of their employees to stay competitive.

The Four Stages of Processing

All information systems operate in the same basic fashion whether they include a computer or not. However, the computer provides a convenient means to execute the four main operations of an information system:

- Entering data into the IS (**input**).
- Changing and manipulating the data in the IS (**data processing**).
- Getting information out of the IS (**output**).
- Storing data and information (**storage**).

A computer-based IS also uses a logical process to decide which data to capture and how to process it. This process will be discussed later.

Input

The first step in producing information is collecting and introducing data, known as input, into the IS. Most data an organization uses as input to its ISs are generated and collected within the organization. These data elements result from transactions undertaken in the course of doing business. A **transaction** is a business event: a sale, a purchase, a payment, the hiring of a new employee, and the like. These transactions can be recorded on paper and later entered into a computer system; directly recorded through a **transaction processing systems (TPS)**, such as a point-of-sale (POS) machine, scanner, or camera; or captured online when someone transacts through the web. A TPS is any system that records transactions. Often, the same system also processes the transactions, summarizing and routing information to other systems; therefore, these systems are transaction *processing* systems, not just transaction *recording* systems.

Input devices (devices used to transfer data into an IS) include the keyboard, handheld devices that read and sense graphic codes, voice recognition systems, and touch screens. Chapter 4, "Business Hardware," describes these and other means to input data. The trend has been to decrease the time and effort of input by using devices that allow scanning or auditory data entry.

Processing

The computer's greatest contribution to ISs is efficient data processing. The computer's speed and accuracy enable organizations to process millions of pieces of data in seconds. For example, managers of a national retail chain can receive up-to-date information on inventory levels of every item the chain carries and then order accordingly; in the past, obtaining such information would take days. The huge gains in the speed and affordability of computing have made information the essential ingredient for an organization's success.

Output

Output is the information an IS produces and displays in the format most useful to an organization. The most widely used output device is the video display, or video monitor, which displays output visually. Another common output device is the printer, used to print hard copies of information on paper. However, computers can communicate output through speakers in the form of music or speech and also can transmit it to another computer or electronic device in computer-coded form, for later interpretation.

Storage

One of the greatest benefits of using IT is the ability to store vast amounts of data and information. Technically, storing a library of millions of volumes on magnetic or optical storage media is feasible. Publishers, libraries, and governments have done that. For example, YouTube estimates that 72 hours of video are uploaded to its site every minute. Based on this statistic, YouTube's total storage would increase by approximately 21.6 billion bytes of storage per minute. As of 2011, Amazon stored 762 billion objects within its Simple Storage Service (S3). These statistics clearly illustrate our world's growing appetite for data storage (Anonymous, 2012b).

Computer Equipment for Information Systems

To support the four data processing functions, different types of technologies are used. Figure 1.5 illustrates the five basic components of the computer system within an IS:

- Input devices introduce data into the IS.
- The computer processes data through the IS.
- Output devices display information.
- Storage devices store data and information.
- Networking devices and communications lines transfer data and information over various distances.

FIGURE **1.5**

Input, process, output, storage and networking devices

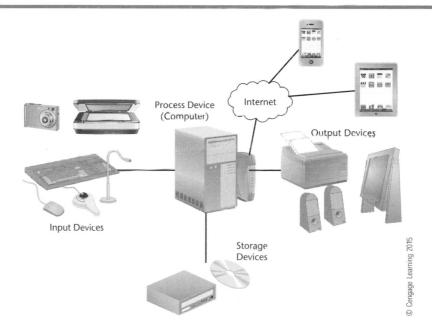

In addition to communication that takes place between computer components, communication occurs between computers over distances (called **telecommunications**). The distance to communicate can be as small as a few feet for a Bluetooth mouse or Wi-Fi handheld scanning device, a few hundred yards for computers connected through a local area network (LAN) within the same building, or thousands of miles for global network systems between continents. Communications technology lets users access data and other electronic resources of many computers, all connected in a network. This way, the capabilities of a single computer might be augmented with the power of an entire network.

From Recording Transactions to Providing Expertise: Types of Information Systems

Different types of information systems serve different functions—for particular types of organizations, functions within organizations, business needs, and management levels of an organization. Business enterprises differ in their objectives, structure, interests, and approaches. However, ISs can be generally categorized based on the level of a system's complexity and the type of functions it serves. ISs in business range from the basic transaction processing system that records events such as sales to sophisticated expert systems, which provide advice and reduce the need for the expensive services of a human expert. In recent years, the capabilities of many applications have been combined and merged. It is less likely that you will find any of the following applications as stand-alone systems with a single capability. Managers and other professionals plan, control, and make decisions. As long as a system supports one or more of these activities, it may be referred to as a **management information system (MIS)**.

Transaction Processing Systems

Point-of-sale (POS) machines are a universal type of transaction processing system

©iStockphoto.com/LuminaStock

Transaction processing systems (TPSs) are the most widely used information systems. The predominant function of TPSs is to record data collected at the boundaries of organizations, in other words, at the point where the organization transacts business with other parties. They also record many of the transactions that take place inside an organization. For example, they record the movement of parts from one phase of manufacturing to another, from raw materials to finished products. TPSs include POS machines, which record sales; automatic teller machines, which record cash withdrawals, deposits, and transfers; and purchase order systems, which record purchases. A typical example would be the purchase of gasoline at a pump, using a credit card. The purchase is recorded by the gasoline company and later at the credit-card-processing bank. After these data elements are collected, the IS can automatically process the data immediately and store it for later access on demand. Transaction processing systems provide most of the data in organizations for further processing by other ISs.

Supply Chain Management Systems

The term "supply chain" refers to the sequence of activities involved in producing and selling a product or service. In industries that produce goods, the activities include marketing, purchasing raw materials, manufacturing and assembly, packing and shipping, billing, collection, and after-the-sale services. In service industries, the sequence might include marketing, document management, and monitoring customer portfolios. Information systems that support these activities and are linked to become one large IS providing information on any stage of a business process are called **supply chain management (SCM) systems**.

Often, such systems are called **enterprise resource planning (ERP) systems**, because the information they provide supports the planning of shipping resources such as personnel, funds, raw materials, and vehicles. However, ERP is a misnomer for the systems, because they mainly serve managers in monitoring and modifying business processes as they occur, and not only for planning. The term "supply chain," too, is somewhat misleading. Business processes do not always take the form of a sequence; some processes take place in parallel. This is true in manufacturing, where two or three teams work on different parts of a product, and in services, where two or three different people peruse a document online and add their input to it within a certain period of time rather than sequentially. In the production of goods and services, some modules of SCM systems provide support to the major processes. These components include human resources (HR) information systems and cost accounting systems.

SCM systems are the result of systems thinking and support systems thinking. They eliminate the need to reenter data that has already been captured somewhere else in the organization. An SCM is an **enterprise application** because the systems that support each business process are connected to each other to form one large IS. Technically, anyone with access to the system can know the status of every part of an order received by the business: whether the raw materials have been purchased, which subassemblies are ready, how many units of the finished product have been shipped, and how much money has been billed or collected for the order. HR managers can tell which workers are involved in any of the processes of the order. Accountants can use their module of the system to know how much money has been spent on the order and what the breakdown of the cost is in labor, materials, and overhead expenditures. The figure shown below combines several performance metrics into one screen called a dashboard. This dashboard from iNetSoft shows the various sales, inventory, and quota metrics to monitor organizational performance based on data processed by various transaction processing systems.

With enterprise applications, many units of the organization can access the same data and share information for their own management tasks or further processing

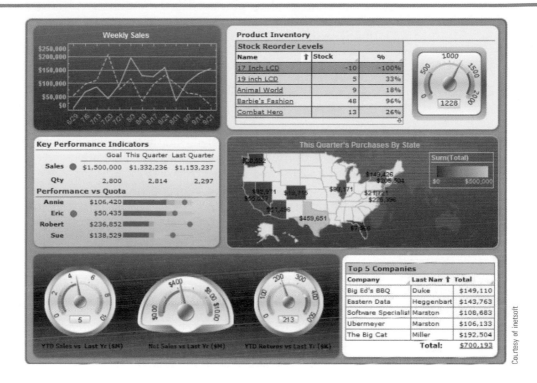

Courtesy of inetsoft

Customer Relationship Management Systems

Customer relationship management (CRM) systems help manage an organization's relationships with its customers. The term refers to a large variety of information systems, from simple ones that help maintain customer records to sophisticated systems that dynamically analyze and detect buying patterns and predict when a specific customer is about to switch to a competitor. Many CRM systems are used by service representatives in combination with a telephone. When a customer telephones, the representative can view the entire history of the customer's relationship with the company: anything that the customer has purchased, deliveries made, unfulfilled orders, and other information that can help resolve a problem or help the customer find the desired product or service. The convergence of various technologies has provided innovative methods of

Customer relationship management systems help support customers and glean business intelligence

© wavebreakmedia/Shutterstock.com

providing customer service with online chat and callback services. Some companies offer a "call back" feature where customers place their requests in a queue, which allows customers to do other tasks while awaiting a phone call. Businesses have adopted online chat customer service through their websites to reduce telephony costs and increase customer service personnel productivity. The main goals of CRM systems are to increase the quality of customer service, reduce the amount of labor involved in serving customers, and learn as much as possible about the buying habits and service preferences of individual customers.

CRM systems are often linked to web applications that track online shopping and process online transactions. Using sophisticated applications, a company can learn what makes a customer balk just before submitting an online order, or what a customer prefers to see displayed on webpages. Online retailers such as Amazon.com, Buy.com, and Target.com use applications that construct different webpages for different customers, even when they search on the same keywords. The pages are constructed to optimally suit the individual customer's interests as inferred from previous visits and purchases. CRM systems provide important data that can be accumulated in large databases and processed into business intelligence.

Effective CRM systems are accessible to both sales and service people. They enable continuous and smooth interaction with everyone from prospective customers to buyers who need after-the-sale service. Both salespeople and service crews can view the entire record of a customer and the product purchased and fit the service according to the product service schedule. Because retaining loyal customers is significantly less expensive than acquiring new ones, CRM systems may increase an organization's profitability.

Business Intelligence Systems

ISs whose purpose is to glean from raw data relationships and trends that might help organizations compete better are called **business intelligence (BI)** systems. Usually, these applications consist of sophisticated statistical models, sometimes general and sometimes tailored for an industry or an organization. The applications access large pools of data, usually transactional records stored in large databases called **data warehouses**. With proper analysis models, BI systems might discover particular buying patterns of consumers, such as combinations of products purchased by a certain demographic group or on certain days; products that are sold at faster cycles than others; reasons for customers' churns, that is, customers leaving a service provider for a competitor; and other valuable business intelligence that helps managers quickly decide on changing a strategy.

Decision Support and Expert Systems

Professionals often need to select one course of action from many alternatives. Because they have neither the time nor the resources to study and absorb long, detailed reports of data and information, organizations often build information systems specifically designed to help make decisions. These systems are called **decision support systems (DSSs)**. While DSSs rely on models and formulas to produce concise tables or a single number that determines a decision, **expert systems (ESs)** rely on artificial intelligence techniques to support knowledge-intensive decision-making processes.

Decision support systems help find the optimal course of action and answer "What if?" questions. "What if we purchase raw materials overseas? What if we merge our warehouses? How many first-time buyers were gained from our social media sites?" These questions seek answers like, "This is how this action will impact our revenue, or our market share, or our costs." DSSs are programmed to process raw data, make comparisons, and generate information to help professionals glean the best alternatives for financial investment, marketing strategy, credit approval, and the like. However, it is important to understand that a DSS is only a decision aid, not an absolute alternative to human decision making.

Many environments are not sufficiently structured to let an IS use data to provide the one best answer. For instance, stock portfolio management takes place in a highly uncertain environment. No single method exists to determine which securities portfolio is best, that is, which one will yield the highest return. Medical care is another unstructured environment. There might be many methods of diagnosing a patient on the basis of his or her symptoms. Indeed, a patient with a particular set of symptoms might receive as many different diagnoses as the number of doctors he or she visits.

Using ESs preserves the knowledge of retiring experts and saves a company the high cost of employing human experts. After gathering expertise from experts and building a program, the program can be distributed and used repeatedly. The expertise resides in the program in the form of a knowledge base consisting of facts and relationships among the facts. You will learn about DSS and ES in detail in Chapter 10, "Decision Support and Expert Systems."

Geographic Information Systems

In some cases, the information decision makers need is related to a map or floor plan. In such cases, special ISs called **geographic information systems (GISs)** can be used to tie data to physical locations. A GIS application accesses a database that contains data about a building, neighborhood, city, county, state, country, or even the entire world. By representing data on a map in different graphical forms, a user is able to understand promptly a situation taking place in that part of the world and act upon it. Examples of such information include flood-prone regions, population levels, the number of police officers deployed, probabilities of finding minerals, transportation routes, and vehicle allocation for transportation or distribution systems. Thus, when a supermarket chain considers locations for expansion, executives look at a map that reflects not only geographic attributes but also demographic information such as population growth by age and income groups. GISs are often used to manage daily operations as well as for planning and decision making. They also have been used to provide service via the web, such as helping residents find locations of different services on a city map or plan travel routes. Many GISs that support operations use information from global positioning system (GPS) satellites, especially to show the current location of a vehicle or person on a map or to provide directions or information on traffic congestion, alternate routes, or various services along a route. This mobile type of GIS has become popular, preinstalled in vehicles, sold as a portable device, or integrated into a smartphone.

Geographic information systems, such as Google Maps, help associate information with locations and regions. This map identifies ATM locations

Courtesy of Google, Inc.

Commonly used GISs on the web are Google Earth and Mapquest. They combine maps with street addresses, points of interest, directions, distances, and travel time calculations. Other web-based GISs provide real estate information. One such popular system is Zillow (www.zillow.com), which provides maps and information about homes for sale, recent sales, and price estimates. Many businesses, such as hotels, integrate external GIS systems within their web-based systems to provide more information to consumers. The figure shows an example of Google Maps that identifies automated teller machines in a geographic area.

Information Systems in Business Functions

ISs serve various purposes throughout an organization in what are known as functional business areas—in-house services that support an organization's main business. Functional business areas include, but are not limited to, accounting, finance, marketing, and human resources. As previously mentioned, in a growing number of organizations these systems are modules of a larger enterprise system, an SCM, or ERP system. Chapter 3, "Business Functions and Supply Chains," discusses business functions and their systems in detail.

Accounting

In accounting, information systems help record business transactions, produce periodic financial statements, and create reports required by law, such as balance sheets and profit-and-loss statements. In the United States, the Sarbanes-Oxley Act of 2002 has forced companies to modify their ISs or install new systems to comply with more demanding accounting rules. ISs also help create reports that might not be required by law, but that help managers understand changes in an organization's finances. Accounting ISs contain controls to ascertain adherence to standards, such as a double entry accounting method.

Finance

While accounting systems focus on recording and reporting financial changes and states, the purpose of financial systems is to facilitate financial planning and business transactions. In finance, information systems help organize budgets, manage cash flow, analyze investments, and make decisions that could reduce interest payments and increase revenues from financial transactions.

Marketing

Marketing's purpose is to pinpoint the people and organizations most likely to purchase what the organization sells and to promote the appropriate products and services to them. For instance, marketing information systems help analyze demand for various products in different regions and population groups in order to more accurately market the right product to the right consumers. Marketing ISs provide information that helps management decide how many sales representatives to assign to specific products in specific geographical areas. The systems identify trends in the demand for the company's products and services. They also help answer such questions as, "How can an advertising campaign affect our profit?" The web has created excellent opportunities both to collect marketing data and to promote products and services by displaying information about them. That is why organizations conduct so much of their marketing efforts through ISs linked to the web.

POINT OF INTEREST   Texting to Help Social Causes

New information systems have allowed mobile phone users to donate more quickly and easily than ever. During the aftermath of the earthquakes in Haiti in 2010, the Red Cross utilized this ability to quickly raise over $30 million, just through text message donations. By sending "GIVE" to a number, mobile phone users automatically donated $10 which was added to their next phone bill.

For example, in Africa, mobile phone users can remind patients to take their medicines and warn farmers when elephants are coming so they can ward them off rather than kill them. These examples demonstrate how mobile communications hasten the efficient transmission of money and information in a fast moving world.

Source: Alter, L. (2012). Texting Becomes Key Tool for Philanthropy. http://tlc.howstuffworks.com/home/texting-changing-philanthropy.htm

Human Resources

Human resource (HR) management systems help mainly in record-keeping, employee evaluation, and employee benefits. Every organization must maintain accurate employee records. Human resource management systems maintain such records, including employees' pictures, marital status, tax information, and other data that other systems, such as payroll, might use. For example, the sample screen from Mipis Software shown here gives the experience captured from an employee's resume and stored in the database.

Human resource management systems, like Mipis Software, help users hire and promote employees

Courtesy of Mipsis

Performance evaluation systems provide essential checklists that managers can use to assess their subordinates. These systems also offer a scoring utility to quantify workers' strengths and weaknesses.

HR management systems have evolved to serve many purposes: recruiting, selection, placement, benefits analysis, requirement projections (how many employees with certain skills will be required in so many months?), and other services. Many companies enable employees to use online systems to compare and select benefit packages such as health insurance and pension plans.

Web-Empowered Enterprises

The most exciting intersection of IT and business in recent years has been networked commerce—buying and selling goods and services via a telecommunications network—or as it is popularly called, **e-commerce**. The development of the web and the opening of the Internet to commercial activities spawned a huge surge in business-to-business and business-to-consumer electronic trade. Now, every individual and small business can afford to use a network for business: the Internet.

The Internet is a vast network of computers connected across the globe that can share both information and processing. The web is capable of displaying text, graphics, sounds, and moving images. It has enticed thousands of businesses to become involved in commercial, social, and educational initiatives. Social networking through sites such as Twitter, Pinterest, Foursquare, and Facebook provide a virtual meeting place for people and an opportunity to advertise and promote business organizations to mass audiences with minimal effort. Thus, the web is not only a place to conduct e-commerce, but also an emerging advertising medium, gradually replacing other media such as television and newspapers. Almost every brick-and-mortar business has extended its operations to the web. Chapter 8, "The Web-Enabled Enterprise," discusses web technologies and how they are used in business activities. Because of its great influence on the use of information technology, the web's impact on the use of information systems is discussed throughout the book.

It does not require much effort to consider the positive impact of technology in our daily lives. However, it often also has undesirable or unintended effects. This was true of the labor-saving machines that prompted the industrial revolution (introducing 16-hour workdays and child labor under harsh conditions), and it is also true about information technology. Think of the effect of IT: it makes our work more productive because a few keystrokes on a computer keyboard prompt the computer to calculate and print what would otherwise take many human hours. It educates us via technologies such as multimedia classes delivered online. It opens new economic opportunities such as trading with overseas consumers via the Internet. It makes the world smaller by letting people work and socialize together over great distances via networks such as the web. It creates communities and establishes closer, more interactive relationships with customers through social media sites. And it puts at our fingertips information on practically every imaginable subject. So, what's the downside? There are quite a few downsides, which we will discuss in the following chapters. Here is a sample of the main issues and the questions they raise.

- **Consumer Privacy.** The ability to inexpensively and quickly collect, maintain, manipulate, and transfer data enables every individual and organization to collect millions of personal records. When visiting a commercial website, chances are the site installs a little file, a "cookie," on your computer's hard disk. This file helps track every click you make on that site, so companies specializing in consumer profiling can learn your shopping and buying habits. When you use a mobile phone to search for a restaurant, it records your exact location. Using an electronic toll payment device on your car stores the location, day, and time each time you pass through a highway or bridge toll booth. Every time you pay with a credit card, the purchase is recorded to a personally identifiable record. All this data is channeled into large databases for commercial exploitation. Your control of such data is minimal. While consumers, patients, and employees might consent to the collection of information on one aspect of their lives by one party and on another aspect by another party, the combination of such information might reveal more than they would like. For example, using the data gathered from a retailer's "frequent shopper card," a firm can easily and inexpensively purchase your data from several consumer goods companies, combine the data into larger records, and prepare a dossier about you: your name, age, and gender; your shopping habits; the drugs you take (and through this information, the diseases you might have); the political party to which you contributed; and so on.

  Civil rights advocates argue that IT has created a Big Brother society where anyone can be observed, monitored, and tracked. Lawmakers have passed legislation to regulate the collection and dissemination of private data. Are you willing to give up some of your privacy to help companies better market to you products and services you might be interested in? Do you accept the manipulation and selling of your personal data? Do you know how each of the businesses that you visit on the web utilizes and shares your personal data?

- **Employee Privacy.** IT helps employers monitor their employees, not only via the ubiquitous video camera, but also through the personal computers they use. Employers feel it is their right to monitor keystrokes, email traffic, the websites employees visit, and the whereabouts of people whose wages they pay while on the job. So, while IT increases productivity, it might violate privacy and create stress. Which is more important: your employer's right to electronically monitor you, or your privacy and mental well-being?

- **Freedom of Speech.** On the web anyone can become a publisher without censorship. The use of social media, blogging, and other technologies encourage netizens (Internet users) to opine about anything from products to their employers' misdeeds. Some of the material published may be violent or embarrass people. If someone posts slurs about your ethnic group at a website, do you want the government to step in and ban or penalize such postings? To what extent should web server operators be responsible for what others publish through their sites? Is unsolicited commercial email (spam) a form of free speech?

- **Online Annoyances.** Everyone has been a target of spam email. It is often a nuisance, but how do you accept this? And if you own a new small business and want to advertise via email to reduce your promotion costs, wouldn't you want the freedom to do so? While surfing the web, you encounter many pop-up windows. Or your computer contracts spyware. Sometimes special software hijacks your browser and automatically takes you to a commercial site that you do not care for. Are these annoyances acceptable, or should they be stopped by legislation?

- **Phishing and Identity Theft.** Millions of people have fallen prey to phishing, the practice of enticing netizens to provide personal information to imposters. Email recipients are directed to copycat sites that purport to be legitimate sites of banks and other businesses where they are requested to "update" or "correct" their Social Security numbers, credit-card account numbers, passwords, and other information. This information is used by the phishers to make fraudulent purchases and obtain loans. Businesses and consumers become victims and sometimes lose money. In many cases when phishers steal an identity, the victims experience a long ordeal with authorities and businesses to deal with the damage from fraudulent activities.

- **IT Professionalism.** IT specialists play an increasing role in the lives of individuals and the operations of organizations. The information systems they develop and maintain affect our physical and financial well-being tremendously. If IT specialists are considered professionals, why don't they comply with a mandatory code of ethics as other professionals, such as physicians and lawyers, do?

We will discuss these and other ethical and social issues throughout this book. As you will see, these issues are not easy to resolve. The purpose of these discussions is to make you aware of issues and provoke your thoughts. Remember that the purpose of education is not only to develop skilled professionals but also to remind professionals of the impact of their work on the welfare of other people, and to encourage professionals to be socially responsible.

POINT OF **INTEREST** — **Malware Attacks Target Social Media and Mobile Devices**

Over the last several years, the adoption of portable technology has increased significantly with the increasing use of smartphones, laptops, and tablets. At the same time, consumers have increased their use of social media sites. A recent Internet Security Threat report published by Symantec shows that the combination of social media sites and mobile devices has provided a wealth of new targets for malware attacks. The report identified more than 3.1 billion attacks by 286 million unique variants of malware in 2010. The attacks used a variety of methods, including shortened URLs, SMS (text) messages, and destructive applications. In addition, the report states that these attacks depended on users failing to be attentive to the permissions being accepted.

Source: Anonymous. (2011, April 11, 2011). Mobile Devices and Social Networks Key Malware Targets, Wall Street Journal (Online), p. n/a.

Careers in Information Systems

Regardless of the career you choose, you are almost certain to interact with IT professionals. The IT trade is made up of people engaged in a wide variety of activities. According to a forecast by the U.S. Bureau of Labor Statistics, demand for IT professionals in the United States will continue to grow. The Bureau estimates an increase of 22 percent in demand for computer and information technology specialists for the decade 2010–2020. These positions consist of information security analysts, web developers, and computer network architects with a median salary of $75,000 (Anonymous, 2012a).

The following sections review the responsibilities of IT professionals in typical areas of specialization and show excerpts of posted online help wanted ads from employers seeking IT professionals. These IT positions were selected due to their significant job growth projections. In addition, these positions, specifically the "chief" job titles, describe the management potential for IT professionals.

Systems Analyst

Many IT professionals start their careers as programmers, or **programmer/analysts**, and then are promoted to **systems analysts**, positions that require a broad range of skills. A programmer/analyst is partly involved in the analysis of business needs and ISs, but the greater part of the job involves setting up business applications. A systems analyst is responsible for researching, planning, and recommending software and systems choices to meet an organization's business requirements. Systems analysts are normally responsible for developing cost analyses, design considerations, implementation timelines, and feasibility studies of a computer system before making recommendations to senior management. A big part of this job includes developing alternative system plans based on (1) analyzing system requirements provided by user input, (2) documenting development efforts and system features, and (3) providing adequate specifications for programmers.

To succeed, systems analysts must possess excellent communication skills to translate users' descriptions of business processes into system concepts. They must understand a wide range of business processes and ways in which IT can be applied to support them.

Most importantly, systems analysts must always keep in mind that they are agents of change, and that most people resist change. Unlike many other occupations, theirs often involves the creation of new systems or the modification of existing ones. Because new or modified systems often affect human activities and organizational cultures, systems analysts must be able to convince both line workers and managers that change will benefit them. Thus, these IS professionals must possess good persuasive and presentation skills.

Senior systems analysts often advance to become project leaders. In this capacity, they are put in charge of several analysts and programmers. They seek and allocate resources, such as funds, personnel, hardware, and software, that are used in the development process, and they use project management methods to plan activities, determine milestones, and control the use of resources.

POINT OF INTEREST — Technology Jobs and Women

According to a 2012 study by the National Center for Women & Information Technology, 57 percent of 2010 undergraduate degree recipients were women. However, only 18 percent of 2010 Computer and Information Sciences undergraduate degree recipients were women. From 2000 to 2011, there has been a 79 percent decrease in the number of first-year undergraduate women interested in majoring in Computer Science. While 57 percent of professional occupations in the 2011 U.S. workforce were held by women, they only accounted for 25 percent of professional computing occupations. Considering the US Labor Department's increased projections for information technology positions, there are substantial opportunities for women to secure quality, successful positions.

Source: National Center for Women & Information Technology. (March 3, 2012). Women in IT: By the Numbers. http://www.ncwit.org/sites/default/files/legacy/pdf/BytheNumbers09.pdf

---

Database Administrator

The **database administrator (DBA)** is responsible for the databases and data warehouses of an organization—a very sensitive and powerful position. Since access to information often connotes power, this person must be astute not only technologically but politically as well. He or she must evaluate requests for access to data from managers to determine who has a real "need to know." The DBA is responsible for developing or acquiring database applications and must carefully consider how data will be used. In addition, the DBA must adhere to federal, state, and corporate regulations to protect the privacy of customers and employees.

A growing number of organizations link their databases to the web for use by employees, business partners, and consumers. Attacks on corporate databases by hackers and computer viruses have made the DBA's job more difficult. In addition to optimizing databases and developing data management applications, this person must oversee the planning and implementation of sophisticated security measures to block unauthorized access but at the same time to allow easy and timely access to authorized users. The DBA is also highly involved in the implementation of SCM systems, because they access corporate databases.

Network Administrator

Among the many IT areas, the one that has seen the most exciting developments in recent years is networks and telecommunications. Not surprisingly, this area has also seen the greatest increase in corporate allocation of IT resources in many organizations. The emergence of new technologies, such as Voice over Internet Protocol and Wi-Fi, which are discussed in Chapter 6, "Business Networks and Communications," is expected to sustain this trend for some years, allowing network professionals to be in great demand and to command high salaries.

The **network administrator** is responsible for acquiring, implementing, managing, maintaining, and troubleshooting local area networks throughout the organization and their interfaces with the wide area networks such as the Internet. He or she is also often involved in selecting and implementing network security measures such as firewalls and access codes.

System Administrator

A **system administrator**—often referred to as "sys admin"—is responsible for managing an organization's computer operating systems. System administrators often manage and maintain several operating systems, such as UNIX and Microsoft Windows and ensure that the operating systems work together, support end users' business requirements, and function properly. System administrators are also responsible for the day-to-day maintenance of an organization's operating systems, including backup and recovery, adding and deleting user accounts, and performing software upgrades.

Mobile phone application development is a rapidly growing information technology career

J. Emilio Flores/Corbis

Mobile Applications Developer

The explosive use of smartphones and other mobile devices has created a new position for information technology professionals: **mobile applications developer**. These positions require technical expertise relating to the various software development tools for mobile devices and programming languages such as Java, ASP, and SQL. Mobile applications developers are often required to have experience with designing and gathering information about the specific needs of an application. Communication and system design skills are important for this type of professional. Because mobile applications are used directly by consumers, it is also important to understand their product preferences and needs.

Webmaster

The rapid spread of the web, intranets, and extranets has increased the responsibility and stature of the organizational webmaster. A **webmaster** is responsible for creating and maintaining the organization's website as well as its intranet and extranet. Webmasters are increasingly involved in creatively deciding how to represent the organization on the web. These decisions involve elements of marketing and graphic design. Since many organizations use the web for commerce, webmasters must also be well-versed in web transaction software, payment-processing software, and security software. In small organizations, the website may be the responsibility of a single person. In large organizations, the webmaster often manages a crew of programmers who specialize in developing and updating code specifically for webpages and their links with other organizational ISs.

Chief Security Officer

Because of the growing threat to information security, many organizations have created the position of **chief security officer (CSO)**, or chief information security officer (CISO). In most organizations, the person in this position reports to the chief information officer (CIO) (see next section), but in some cases the two executives report to the same person, usually the chief executive officer (CEO). The rationale is that security should be a business issue, not an IT issue. A major challenge for CSOs is the misperception of other executives that IT security is an inhibitor rather than an enabler to operations.

Chief Information Officer and Chief Technology Officer

The fact that a corporation has a position titled **chief information officer (CIO)** reflects the importance that the company places on ISs as a strategic resource. The CIO, who is responsible for all aspects of an organization's ISs, is often, but not always, a corporate vice president. Some companies prefer to call this position **chief technology officer (CTO)**. However, you might find organizations where there are both a CIO and a CTO and one reports to the other. There is no universal agreement on what the responsibility of each should be. Yet, in most cases when you encounter both positions in one organization, the CTO reports to the CIO.

A person who holds the position of CIO must have both technical understanding of current and developing information technologies and business knowledge. As Figure 1.6 shows, the CIO plays an important role in integrating the IS strategic plan into the organization's overall strategic plan. He or she must not only keep abreast of technical developments but also have a keen understanding of how different technologies can improve business processes or aid in the creation of new products and services.

FIGURE 1.6

Traits of a successful CIO

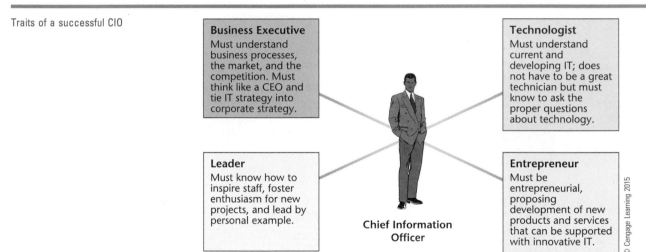

Business Executive
Must understand business processes, the market, and the competition. Must think like a CEO and tie IT strategy into corporate strategy.

Technologist
Must understand current and developing IT; does not have to be a great technician but must know to ask the proper questions about technology.

Leader
Must know how to inspire staff, foster enthusiasm for new projects, and lead by personal example.

Entrepreneur
Must be entrepreneurial, proposing development of new products and services that can be supported with innovative IT.

Chief Information Officer

© Cengage Learning 2015

Summary

- Today's business professionals are expected to know how to develop and use IT significantly more than just a few years ago, regardless of their major field of expertise.

- Digital systems quickly and accurately store, process, and communicate information of any type.

- Computer-based information systems pervade almost every aspect of our lives. Their ability to help solve problems and guide decisions makes them indispensable in business and management. Computer-based information systems take data as raw material, process the data, and produce information as output. Although data sometimes can be useful as is, it usually must be manipulated to produce information that is useful for reporting and decision making.

- A system is a set of components that work together to achieve a common goal. An information system (IS) consists of several components: hardware, software, data, people, and procedures. The components' common goal is to produce the best information from available data.

- Often, a system performs a limited task that produces an end result, which must be combined with other products from other systems to reach an ultimate goal. Such a system is called a subsystem. Several subsystems might make up a system. Sometimes, systems are also classified as closed or open. A stand-alone system that is not interfaced with other systems is called a closed system. A system that interfaces with other systems is an open system.

- Data processing has four basic stages. In the input stage, data elements are collected and entered into the computer. The computer then performs the next stage, data processing, which is the manipulation of data into information using mathematical, statistical, and other tools. The subsequent stage, output, displays or presents the information. We often also want to maintain data and information for later use. This activity is called storage.

- Any information system that helps in management may be referred to as a management information system (MIS). MISs use recorded transactions and other data to produce information for problem solving and decision making.

- There are several types of information systems. They include transaction processing systems (TPSs), supply chain management (SCM) systems, customer relationship management (CRM) systems, business intelligence (BI) systems, decision support systems (DSSs), expert systems (ESs), and geographic information systems (GISs). Often, some or all of these systems are linked to each other or to other information systems.

- Enterprise application systems, such as SCM or ERP systems, are information systems that tie together the different functional areas of a business, such as order entry, inventory management, accounting and finance, and manufacturing. Such systems allow businesses to operate more efficiently by avoiding reentry and duplication of information. The systems can provide an up-to-the-minute picture of inventory, work-in-progress, and the status of an order to be fulfilled. Businesses that link each of their information systems have an infrastructure to utilize data for effective operational and strategic decisions.

- ISs are used in many business functions, most commonly accounting, finance, marketing, and human resources. These systems aid in the daily operations of organizations by maintaining proper accounting information and producing reports, assisting in managing cash and investments, helping marketing professionals find the most likely buyers for their products and services, and keeping accurate employee records and assisting with their performance evaluations.

- The job prospects for IT professionals are bright. Among the typical careers in this field are systems analyst, database administrator, network administrator, system administrator, webmaster, chief security officer, chief information officer, and chief technology officer.

- IT has many advantages, but it also has created societal concerns. Issues such as privacy, phishing and identity theft, free speech on the web, spam, and web annoyances are viewed by many people as serious ethical issues. And while IT professionals increasingly affect our lives through the systems they develop and maintain, they are not required to adhere to any code of ethics as other professionals are. These and related issues are discussed throughout the book.

KIMBALL'S REVISITED

Now that Chapter 1 has helped you understand how businesses use data, information, and information systems, let's reexamine the *Kimball's Restaurant* case. Michael is spending significant time entering the restaurant's sales data. He does not have the time to manage the business during its operating hours as well as maintain the financial records. He is responsible for rent payments, sales tax reports, and paying suppliers for operating expenses and materials. He needs a better system to maintain the guest check and meal information for forecasting.

What Is Your Advice?

1. What would you suggest to Tyler to improve the restaurant's operational efficiency? Examine the business's inputs, processing, and outputs. Formulate recommendations to streamline the business transactions. What type of reports do Liz and Michael need? How would you alter the back-office work to better suit their needs?

2. Based on Tyler's request, his parents provided some questions. Michael knows that some meals are selling better than others, but he can only guess which ones. What sales and operational data do they need to maximize revenues and profits while minimizing costs? What data will help them to make decisions on how to operate

and manage their business? What information technology system(s) would you recommend for gathering and reporting the necessary information?

New Perspectives

1. The restaurant industry is not static; new competitors and challenges always arise. Consider the following challenges:

   - *Economic trends.* When economic downturns occur and disposable income decreases, consumers tend to dine out less. Dining establishments need to be creative in order to counteract the possible loss of sales revenue.

   - *Operational efficiency.* Like any business, *Kimball's* has both fixed and variable costs. Fixed expenses can be budgeted and planned. However, the variable expenses, if not managed properly, can reduce profit and cash flow rather quickly.

   - *Marketing and promotional data.* The former owners did not gather and report any data on their operations for analyzing marketing trends. What can be done differently?

2. Explain how information technology and systems can help *Kimball's* to comply with gathering this data.

Key Terms

Review Questions

1. What does the word "processing" in data processing mean?

2. Give three examples in which raw data also serves as useful information.

3. Give three business examples (not mentioned in the text) of data that must be processed to provide useful information.

4. Give three examples of subsystems not operating in the context of IT. Why are these considered subsystems and not systems?

5. How do TPSs and DSSs differ?

6. What is a problem? Give an example of a business problem and discuss how a computer-based information system could solve it.

7. "An information system consists of hardware and software." Why is this statement inadequate?

8. In which situations does one need to make a decision? Give three examples not mentioned in the chapter.

9. How can a DSS help make decisions?

10. Note the word "support" in decision support systems. Why are these applications not called decision-*making* systems?

11. Who is considered a knowledge worker? Will you have a career as a knowledge worker? Explain.

12. When would a business use mobile computing or web-based information systems in their operations? Discuss an example of a business function that could be implemented on each platform, and explain why that platform would be preferred over the other platform.

13. TPSs are usually used at the boundaries of the organization. What are boundaries in this context? Give three examples of boundaries.

Discussion Questions

14. No longer the domain of technical personnel, information systems are the business of every professional. Why?

15. For information systems projects and initiatives, what would you expect your involvement to be as a business professional?

16. Assume that computers can recognize voices easily and detect their users' exact meaning when talking. Will the necessity for written language be reduced to zero? Why or why not?

17. Information systems cannot solve some business problems. Give three examples and explain why technology cannot help.

18. Practically all knowledge workers must know how to use information systems. Why?

19. Think of two examples of fully web-based businesses. What made the web so attractive for these entrepreneurs?

20. We will soon stop talking of e-commerce and simply speak of commerce. Why?

21. Help wanted advertisements do not use the term "computer specialists"; rather, they use the term "information system professionals" or "information technology professionals." Why?

22. How do traditional commerce and web-based commerce differ? What aspects of traditional shopping do you prefer over online shopping? How has mobile computing altered web-based commerce?

23. Information technology might bring people together, but it also isolates them. Explain the latter claim and give an example. How does social media help or harm inter-relationships between business professionals? Business organizations?

24. Give two examples of phenomena that are a social concern because of information technology. Explain.

25. What irritates you about the web? What would you do to minimize this irritation?

26. Do you foresee an IT-related societal or ethical concern that is not a current concern? Explain.

27. Identity theft existed before the advent of the Internet. However, increased identity theft is one of the unintended, undesirable results of using the Internet. What is the role of educating the public in containing this crime?

Applying Concepts

28. Recall what you did yesterday from the moment you got up until the moment you went to bed. How many times did you use a computer or receive data or information from someone who used a computer? (Do not forget ATMs, POS machines, automated kiosks, personal devices, etc.) Write a two-page essay on your daily experience with IT and on society's dependency on computers.

29. Contact a business organization and ask permission to observe a business process. Pinpoint the segments in the process that a computer-based information system could aid. Write a report detailing your observations and suggestions.

30. Observe activities in a supermarket: shoppers looking down aisles for specific products; lines forming at the POS machines; workers putting new prices on items. Prepare a list of shoppers' and workers' activities that could be carried out with less use of human time and more accuracy if they were aided by IT. Explain how you would change those activities.

Hands-On Activities

31. Consider the Weather Channel Facebook app example shown in a Point of Interest box earlier in this chapter. List some initiatives that could develop a new product or service by integrating social media for business organizations.

32. Use a résumé template in your word-processing program to type your résumé. If you don't have a lot of direct work experience, remember to include all types of work, whether it's babysitting, camp counseling, mowing the lawn, or volunteer work. Now turn your résumé into one that can be displayed well as a webpage.

33. Prepare a list: what information that you currently receive through other means could you receive through your computer? The list should include text, images, audio, and animated information. Would you prefer to receive this information on the computer or as you do now?

Team Activities

34. Form a team with two other students. Each team member should play the role of a vice president in charge of a business function: human resources, accounting, marketing, finance, and so on. Each vice president should enumerate information he or she needs to perform his or her function. Now list information that two or more of the functions must share and data produced by one function that another function uses.

35. Team up with another two students. Brainstorm and try to think of a new business opportunity that you would like to pursue in which you will not need IT. You should be able to convince your professor that IT cannot improve the operations of this business.

From Ideas to Application: Real Cases

The Personal and Portable Touch

FedEx is an organization that never sleeps. The foundation of its business is "fast," and every minute counts. Each business day, the company's more than 300,000 team members handle an average of 9 million packages, using over 663 aircraft and 90,000 motorized vehicles. During the holiday season, its operations experience significantly increased package volumes and high customer expectations. The company, which generated $37 billion in revenue in 2012, serves more than 220 countries and territories. Customers use FedEx because they want reliable delivery in a compressed timeframe. When anything disrupts the timely and safe delivery of those packages, FedEx's customer service reps are likely to receive a call from a customer.

Prompt, efficient customer service is extremely important for staying in this highly competitive global shipping industry, let alone doing so with a satisfactory profit. Incoming telephone calls at the FedEx customer service centers are answered by FedEx reps. Sitting in front of computer monitors in a cluster of cubicles with headsets on, these agents barely have time to stretch their limbs.

A caller complains that her package hasn't arrived, which is a common complaint. Another asks if he can change his pickup time. A third caller is confused about signature: is he supposed to sign for the delivery or will the package just be dropped at his doorstep? The reps are confident and friendly. They welcome any question or complaint even if they have heard it a thousand times before. The words "I am sorry" are uttered often. They are careful not to give the customers a feeling of being rushed, but try to resolve complaints quickly. Time is money.

Several years ago FedEx installed software that reps at the call centers can use to provide faster service. Many of the callers are already registered in the company's database. One of the most frequent requests is to send a FedEx worker to pick up a package. Using the software, a rep can handle such a request in 20 seconds. All she needs to do is enter a name, which leads to a zip code, which in turn leads to a tracking number. That number uniquely identifies the package. Some complaints are more complex. For example, a FedEx driver misunderstood a note a caller had left for him and therefore misdelivered a package. A complaint like that takes no more than 10 minutes to resolve.

An experienced and efficient rep can handle about 10 callers in 45 minutes. Ideally, though, nobody would call. If FedEx had its way, at least six of the ten callers would use their computers to go to

FedEx's website and solve their problem by themselves—because about 60 percent of FedEx's clients have a computer connected to the Internet. Like other companies, FedEx tries to save labor by directing callers to its website. Yet, many people prefer to use the phone and talk to a human helper.

Every time a customer decides to use the company's website instead of telephoning, the company saves up to $1.87. Efforts to divert callers to the site have been fruitful. In 2005, FedEx call centers received 470,000 calls per day, 83,000 fewer than in 2000. This difference in calls translates into a saving of $57.56 million per year. The company's website handles an average of 60 million requests to track packages per month. Operating the website does cost money. Each of these requests costs FedEx 3 cents, amounting to $21.6 million per year. However, if all these requests were made by phone, the cost would exceed $1.36 billion per year. As it is impossible to divert all callers to the website, the company must maintain call centers. The annual cost of these call centers is $326 million. This cost might decrease over the years, as more and more customers use the website, but there will probably always be call centers, because FedEx does not want to lose frustrated customers.

In 2000, management purchased customer relationship management software called Clarify. A new policy was established: systems and customer service experts are equally responsible for the call centers. Using PCs, reps can pull up historical data on customers whenever customers call. Customer records that are immediately available to reps include shipping histories, preferences, and images of the paper bills. Customers are happier now than they were just a few years ago. So are the reps. Turnover of service reps has decreased 20 percent.

Interestingly, customers are not interested in friendliness, but in quick and accurate information. FedEx constantly follows customer reactions to different help styles. Managers discovered that when reps' time is not limited, they tend to speak with customers beyond the time required to solve the problem. Customers perceive them as too talkative, and they get a bad impression about FedEx. Thus, reps are encouraged to get off the phone as soon as the problem is resolved rather than try to be "nice."

The web has clearly transformed customer service. However, mobile computing now allows the customer to "carry the company" with them. While FedEx has a website version for smartphones, a fully optimized mobile version was released in late 2010.

Mobile-based websites generate a fraction of the traffic realized by the traditional website. However, FedEx experienced steady growth on the mobile-based product. The increasing adoption of the new technology forced an examination of the new product. They believed that a more robust product was needed to support FedEx's operations.

Ultimately, FedEx developed a product that offered a broader functionality using smartphone technology on popular devices such as Apple iPhones and Android phones. FedEx plans to track the use of the apps and the mobile site against any cost savings realized through reduced calls placed to their call centers.

The availability of quality, fast customer service continues to be realized by integrating information technology with the latest mobile technologies. FedEx, like many business organizations, continues to improve through innovative technology initiatives.

Sources: FedEx. (2012). About FedEx. Retrieved 13 September, 2012, from http://about.van.fedex.com/; Gage, D. (2005). Personal Touch; Fedex already saves big bucks by steering inquiries to its web site. So how can it justify spending $326 million a year on call-center reps? Baseline, 1(39), 54-54; Gordon, R. (2010). FedEx mobile strategy aims for customer loyalty. www.dmnews.com/fedex-mobile-strategy-aims-for-customer-loyalty/article/181706/

Thinking About the Case

1. What is CRM in general? Give examples of *different* CRM applications.

2. Enumerate and explain the various ways in which the CRM applications discussed here save costs or help in other ways.

3. Which metrics would you use to measure *before* and *after* performance regarding the information technologies implemented in this case? Consider cost, service quality, cycle time, and any other performance factor and provide a specific metric (i.e., ratio, product, or absolute value).

4. What are the challenges of implementing mobile technology? Are the savings similar to web-based systems?

5. As an executive for FedEx or a similar company, what else would you implement using mobile computing and the Internet?

Blooming with Technology

The use of information technology is needed by every industry size and type of business. Small businesses can realize the positive effects through adopting technology. However, small businesses often do not have the resources and expertise of large corporations to implement information technology strategies. However, the benefits of technology for small and medium-sized enterprises (SMEs) are just as crucial to business operations and strategy.

Consider Four Seasons Greenhouse and Nursery, located in Colorado. This small nursery was like many other small businesses and garden centers. They used manual registers to track and maintain its inventory as well as determine which products were realizing the most profit. The profits from the nursery were either "negligible" or a loss. They did not have access to useful operational data to effectively manage their business. For example, they did not track or review the margins of individual products. However, they believed that they needed to do something different for their $1M business operation.

Enter a new point-of-sale system (POS) in 2008. The system allowed the owners to track useful business data from the sales transactions immediately at the time of the sale; eliminating the need for tracking sales manually. The system processes and stores data from the sale while updating the inventory as well as compiling a sales history. This eliminates reliance on manual entry of sales transactions and reduction of inventory units for the items sold. POS systems provide much more than a cash register. These systems provide more robust functionality in inputting, tracking, and distributing data to provide useful information to operate and manage the business.

Accurate inventory data maintained by the POS helped with decision making. Decisions on how many units of a product to order were no longer based on speculation about current inventory units. Now, accurate inventory counts eliminate the guesswork on how much to order, helping the business to operate on leaner inventory units. The system's reporting can provide the detail transactions for an inventory item, such as how many were purchased, discarded, and sold.

The implementation of a POS system also confirmed that the owners did not know as much about their business as they thought they did. As they reviewed reports from the new system, they saw that some products were less profitable than they thought. The more detailed cost reporting by item helped them to understand which products contributed the most profit to the operation. Their new perspective of the "real costs" provided the opportunity to shift production to the higher-profit items, thereby gaining more profit. Prior to implementing the POS system, they simply did not have the time to approach this level of decision making.

Knowledge of their detailed product costs helps them to price products more profitably. Price changes can be implemented temporarily (for a promotion) or permanently and still remain within acceptable product margins. The accurate and timely reporting of this information assists them to be more effective managers of their business operations. The ability of the system to process sales, inventory, and purchasing transactions immediately reduces the need for data entry of paper information. The time savings can be used for managing the business rather than mundane clerical functions.

The new system has expanded Four Seasons's management control over employee schedules to review and allocate labor expenses to specific departments and functions. An additional benefit allows the owners to delegate more responsibility to the staff and establish accountability. Instead of the owners establishing goals, they provide the system's data and ask staff to submit their sales goals for the next reporting period. Ultimately, the information technology system creates a solid infrastructure to process and report the businesses operations for the entire enterprise.

The garden center is an excellent example of how technology can realize benefits for a business. The ability for organizations to remain competitive and agile is crucial. These systems allow organizations large and small to leverage business data to gain a competitive advantage and operational efficiency.

Source: Jones, R. (2011, May). Garden Center 2.0. Today's Garden Center, 8, 14-16.

Thinking About the Case

1. Why do point-of-sale systems process business activities more effectively? Can the information be tracked manually in an effective manner? Why or why not? What types of questions could be answered effectively? How could the information be used to better manage the business?

2. Why do small business owners avoid the use of information technology?

3. Consider the types of information systems discussed in the chapter. What other systems could interact with the POS system as it processed a sale?

References

Anonymous. (2011). Coinstar Reports 2011 1st Quarter Results. *Entertainment Close-Up*.

Anonymous. (2012a). Information Security Analysts, Web Developers, and Computer Network Architects. www.bls.gov/ooh/computer-and-information-technology/print/information-security-analysts-web-developers-and-computer-network-architects.htm

Anonymous. (2012b). Youtube Statistics. Retrieved September 8, 2012, from www.youtube.com/t/press_statistics

Cerny, J. (2011). Making the MOVE to MOBILE. *Mortgage Banking, 71*(11), 68-70, 72-73.

Chipchase, J. (2011). "Innovation lessons from a vending machine." Retrieved 10 September 2012, from http://globalpublicsquare.blogs.cnn.com/2011/06/13/innovative-vending-machines/

Gruenwedel, E. (2011). Analyst: Consumers Prefer Lower-cost Movie Rentals. *Home Media Magazine, 33*(22), 6.

Pruitt, A. (2007). Tiny Redbox's DVD Kiosks Grow, *Wall Street Journal*, p. B.5D.

CHAPTER two

STRATEGIC USES OF INFORMATION SYSTEMS

Learning Objectives

Executives know that information technology is not merely a resource to support day-to-day operations. Clever use of IT can significantly change an organization's long-term strategic position. Often, innovative use of information systems radically changes the way a firm conducts its business. Some information systems even change a firm's product or service, such as when innovative software is integrated into a physical product or when a service is readily available on the web. Therefore, information systems are now an integral part of strategic planning for nearly all organizations.

When you finish this chapter, you will be able to:

- Explain what business strategy and strategic moves are.

- Illustrate how information systems can give businesses a competitive advantage.

- Identify basic initiatives for gaining a competitive advantage.

- Explain what makes an information system a *strategic* information system.

- Identify fundamental requirements for developing strategic information systems.

- Explain circumstances and initiatives that make one IT strategy succeed and another fail.

KIMBALL'S RESTAURANT: Using Information Strategically

Kimball's business has steadily grown over its first three years. With all their hard work and long hours, Liz and Michael were pleased to see their dining room full of customers on many nights. The bar developed a strong, local clientele for weekday sporting events and "after work" gatherings. Several nights a week, there was standing room only in the bar area. The implementation of a point-of-sale system helped the dining and kitchen operations and provided several benefits over their antiquated hardcopy guest check process. The new system tracked and stored each meal and customer check information. This additional detail provided data for analysis without the need to enter data from the paper guest check method.

Restaurant sales continued to grow. As they grew, Mike and Liz wondered if they should consider expansion. Michael's analysis of customer checks and sales showed that their current location's capacity was an issue. However, they did not want to expand just for the sake of expanding.

An Opportunity

Liz and Michael were approached by Shaun Reilly, whose family owned a lakeside campground property about five miles from the restaurant. The campground business closed after his parents retired. With changing consumer behavior and lifestyles, Shaun did not think the property could continue successfully as a campground. Therefore, he was looking to sell or lease the property for an alternative use.

The campground's picturesque view of Lake Zephyr was an excellent location for a restaurant. The main building had housed a medium-sized restaurant for the campground. Several areas could be easily converted to expand the current dining room area. In addition, the building included a spacious covered patio area that was used as a lounge area for campers. The patio area could be used for additional lakeview dining during the warmer months.

Intrigued by Shaun's proposal, Liz and Michael visited the campground. Although the building was over 30 years old, Shaun's family had maintained the property meticulously. The kitchen area was ample to cook, prepare, and store food. The additional three rooms in the building could be redesigned easily to serve as two dining areas and a lounge/bar area. One of the dining rooms could also be used as a small function room for business meetings or family events. The views of the lake provided a remarkable atmosphere for a unique dining experience.

Michael estimated that the dining area would increase their dining capacity to 110 seats and the lounge area to 25. Liz thought "Could this location support a successful restaurant?" Would Liz and Michael damage a successful restaurant to seek out a larger establishment? They expressed some concern about whether it would be a viable business opportunity. Or were they leaning toward the safe, no-risk approach? Or should they remain with the current location and business model they currently have?

Looking Before They Cook

Michael and Liz spoke to their son, Tyler, about the opportunity. They all agreed that it would be better to revisit their original business plan. Because Tom's marketing expertise was so valuable when they first planned the business, they hired him to update the plan in terms of the proposed new location. Michael provided the detailed menu item and daily sales summary data that he had collected since Kimball's point-of sale-system was installed. At a first glance, it was clear to Tom that the restaurant was doing well. With the new point-of-sale system, Michael captured more data than the previous owner had from the manual guest check system.

Tom analyzed the time customers spent at each table, known as table turnaround. The higher the value of this metric, the more efficiently the tables were being used, meaning less time spent by customers at tables. Michael had never tracked this data, or understood the range of information that was available from the new system.

Tom worked with the data to develop several factors that he could use to forecast sales and expenses for the proposed new location. He extracted the average for the total check amount, dining time, and number of people per table. Tom analyzed this data by day of the week, specific timeframe (holidays, etc.), and months. These different summaries of the data provided a wide view of the factors to compile a more accurate sales forecast. Michael had never reviewed the data from the POS system using this approach. He was a bit surprised by what the data could report.

Michael and Liz then had a meeting with Terri Jordan, the restaurant's accountant. She prepared all of the restaurant's financial statements, state sales tax reports, and income tax filings. Over the last two years, Terri reported that while the restaurant was doing well, their total expenses also increased. The financial statements showed that the cost of goods sold as well as labor expenses increased disproportionately compared to total sales. Although sales increased, the net profit margin decreased slightly each month. Liz asked Terri to tell them what they were doing wrong and how they could fix it.

Terri saw two possible factors in the declining profits: excess inventory and labor costs. She had analyzed the restaurant's financial data, operations, and invoices. The information system did not maintain data for direct inventory costs for meals or spoilage. Terri was frustrated that she could not directly compare the meal sales to inventory in order to calculate the amount of spoilage (if any). However, using summary data, she felt that Liz might be purchasing more food than necessary based on forecasted sales. Without the ability to forecast food purchases based on past meal sales, it is difficult to maintain accurate inventory and to reduce spoilage costs.

Terri also looked at the labor costs for servers and kitchen staff. She reviewed and compared the weekly personnel schedules. The comparison clearly indicated that the hours scheduled did not match the anticipated number of diners. Terri noticed that the staff schedules did not change from day to day, even though some days' sales were consistently lower. This could potentially explain the increased labor costs.

Liz and Michael thought about the information from Tom and Terri. Both advisors discussed that the increased sales and customers probably distracted the owners from managing the business from a strategic perspective. The owners admitted that as the business became popular, they felt that they did not need to manage costs and operations as strictly. Tom said this was a common mistake that a lot of small business owners make, and Terri had commented that the restaurant still had strong, stable sales and remained popular with customers. Therefore, they just needed to focus on a few things to increase profitability. The easy solution would be to raise prices, but either Michael or Liz wanted to do that. Michael decided that their first task would be to implement some strategies to strengthen their existing business before expanding.

Moving Forward

Liz, Michael, and Tyler met again with Shaun. Liz and Michael loved the location and were excited by its possibilities, but after their discussions with Tom and Terri, they realized that they weren't ready to take on the expansion.

Tyler agreed that the business was doing fine, but they needed to focus their attention to building some strategies in operations and information technology to strengthen their business in the current location. He said that this focus could provide the results to leverage in a new location. Expanding the restaurant with a "critical eye" toward a lean operation would create a perfect transition to the new location when the time was right.

A solid action plan was in place!

Strategy and Strategic Moves

A survey of 2,335 CIOs by Gartner Research highlighted the ever-changing role of IT as an integral player in corporations. The Gartner *2012 CIO Agenda Report* noted that 61 percent of the CIOs conveyed that their organization's mobility strategy will be a top priority (Anonymous, 2012b). The majority of the respondents set a goal of being a "market leader" in their industry specific to their use of mobile computing. The Gartner study also reported that CIOs business priorities will focus on enterprise growth and attracting and retaining customers. One-third also believed that IT innovation could enhance the customer experience. Clearly, IT is expected to contribute to business strategy.

The word "strategy" originates from the Greek word *strategos*, meaning "general." In war, a strategy is a framework, or an approach, to obtaining an advantageous position. Other disciplines, especially business, have borrowed the term. As you know from media coverage, corporate executives often discuss actions in ways that make business competition sound like war. Businesspeople must devise decisive courses of action to win—just as generals do. In business, a strategy is an approach designed to help an organization outperform its competitors. Unlike battle plans, however, business strategy often takes the form of creating new opportunities rather than beating rivals.

Although many information systems are built to solve problems, many others are built to seize opportunities. And, as anyone in business can tell you, identifying a problem is easier than creating an opportunity. Why? Because a problem already exists; it is an obstacle to a desired mode of operation and, as such, calls attention to itself. An opportunity, on the other hand, is less tangible. It takes a certain amount of imagination, creativity, and vision to identify an opportunity, or to create one and act on it. Information systems that help seize opportunities are often called **strategic information systems (SISs)**. They can be developed from scratch, or they can evolve from an organization's existing ISs. They are not defined by their technical features per se, but by how they are used, that is, for strategic advantage.

In a free-market economy, it is difficult for a business to do well without some strategic planning. Although strategies vary, they tend to fall into some basic categories, such as developing a new product, identifying an unmet consumer need, changing a service to entice more customers or retain existing clients, or taking any other action that increases the organization's value through improved performance.

POINT OF INTEREST — IT as a Strategic Tool

E-business is one of the fastest growing industries in the United States as electronic commerce sales totaled $61.2 billion in first quarter 2013, a 2.7 percent increase from the previous quarter. According to eMarketing Inc., sales from electronic commerce sources are projected to grow to $434 billion by 2017. Small- to medium-size firms feel pressured to develop an e-business strategy by using the Internet to effectively fulfill customer orders and communicate with members of their supply chain. By doing so, they can create new markets for their products and services thus, create competitive advantages. In addition, effective integration of e-business information technology can also create operational efficiencies and lower the cost of processing a sale.

Sources: Anonymous. (2013). U.S. Census Bureau News. Washington, D.C.; Enright, A. (2013). U.S. e-commerce sales could top $434 billion in 2017. Internet Retailer. www.internetretailer.com/2013/04/25/us-e-commerce-sales could-top-434-billion-2017; Gupta, M. (2010). The enabling role of E-business technologies in strategic operations management. *Journal of International Technology and Information Management*, 19(2), 109–IV.

Many strategies do not, and cannot, involve information systems. But increasingly, corporations are able to implement certain strategies—such as maximizing sales and lowering costs—thanks to the innovative use of information systems. A company achieves **strategic advantage** by using strategy to maximize its strengths, resulting in a **competitive advantage**. When a business uses a strategy with the intent to *create* a market for new products or services, it does not aim to compete with other organizations that make the same product, because that market does not yet exist. Therefore, a strategic move is not always a competitive move in terms of competing with similar products or services. However, in a free-enterprise society, a market rarely remains the domain of one organization for long; thus, competition ensues almost immediately. So, we often use the terms "competitive advantage" and "strategic advantage" interchangeably.

The most innovative companies are battling on the front lines to create the next "got-to-have-it" technology. In 2012, the battle revolved around mobile payment technology. Paying on-the-go with a smartphone allows you to make purchases quicker and easier than ever. Starbucks agreed to a partnership with Pay with Square, a mobile payment company, to process credit card transactions via the Pay with Square smartphone app at 7,000 locations in the United States To use the app, users activate a tab in the app that notifies the Starbucks of their arrival and then the customer can pay simply by saying their name at the register. Mobile payment technology is taking retail consumerism to the next level. Practically any mobile-based system that gives a company competitive advantage is a strategic information system.

Consider competitive advantage in terms of a for-profit company, whose major goal is to maximize profits by lowering costs and increasing revenue. A for-profit company achieves competitive advantage when its profits increase significantly, most commonly through increased market share. Figure 2.1 lists eight basic initiatives that can be used to gain competitive advantage, including offering a product or service that competitors cannot provide or providing the same product or service more attractively to customers. It is important to understand that the eight listed are the most common, but not the only, types of business strategy an organization can pursue. It is also important to understand that strategic moves often consist of a combination of two or more of these initiatives and other steps, and that sometimes accomplishing one type of advantage creates another. The essence of strategy is innovation, so competitive advantage is often gained when an organization tries a strategy that no one has tried before.

FIGURE **2.1**

Eight basic ways to gain competitive advantage

Initiative	Benefit
Reduce costs	A company can gain advantage if it can sell more units at a lower price while providing quality and maintaining or increasing its profit margin.
Raise barriers to market entrants	A company can gain advantage if it deters potential entrants into the market, enjoying less competition and more market potential.
Establish high switching costs	A company can gain advantage if it creates high switching costs, making it economically infeasible for customers to buy from competitors.
Create new products or services	A company can gain advantage if it offers a unique product or service.
Differentiate products or services	A company can gain advantage if it can attract customers by convincing them its product differs from the competition's.
Enhance products or services	A company can gain advantage if its product or service is better than anyone else's.
Establish alliances	Companies from different industries can help each other gain advantage by offering combined packages of goods or services at special prices.
Lock in suppliers or buyers	A company can gain advantage if it can lock in either suppliers or buyers, making it economically impractical for suppliers or buyers to deal with competitors.

© Cengage Learning 2015

For example, Amazon gained a competitive advantage when it created a new subscription service, Amazon Prime. For $79 a year, subscribers enjoy free two-day shipping on everything plus access to over 25,000 movies and TV shows that can be streamed instantly. Prime members also are allowed to borrow books for their Kindle e-readers from the Kindle Owners Lending Library for no additional fee. Figure 2.2 shows that a company can use many strategies together to gain a competitive advantage, as Amazon did.

FIGURE 2.2

Many strategic moves can work together to achieve a competitive advantage

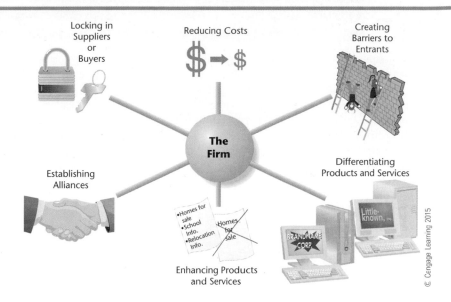

Initiative #1: Reduce Costs

Customers like to pay as little as possible while still receiving the quality of service or product they need. One way to increase market share is to lower prices, and the best way to lower prices is to **reduce costs**. For instance, if carried out successfully, massive automation of any business process gives an organization competitive advantage. The reason is simple: automation makes an organization more productive, and any cost savings can be transferred to customers through lower prices. We saw this happen in the auto industry. In the 1970s, Japanese automakers brought robots to their production and assembly lines and reduced costs—and subsequently prices—quickly and dramatically. The robots weld, paint, and assemble parts at a far lower cost than manual labor. Until their competitors began to employ robots, the Japanese had a clear competitive advantage because they were able to sell high-quality cars for less than their competitors. A similar approach gave Intel, the computer microprocessor maker, a strategic advantage that it maintains to this day: much of the labor involved in making and testing microprocessors has been automated by information technology and robots. This enabled the company to substantially reduce the prices of its products.

In the service sector, the web has created an opportunity to automate what until recently was considered an activity that only humans could perform: customer service. An enormous trend toward automating online customer service began with companies such as FedEx, which initially gave customers an opportunity to track their parcels' status by logging on to a dedicated, private network and database. The same approach is now implemented through the web. Many sites today include answers to FAQs (frequently asked questions). Others have special programs that can respond to customer questions. Online service gives businesses two major benefits: it changes service from being labor intensive to technology intensive, which is much less expensive, and it provides customers easy access to a service 7 days a week, 24 hours a day. Any executives of companies that operate call centers will tell you that they work hard to shift callers off the phone and to their websites to receive the help they need. It not only cuts the costs of expensive human labor but also of telephone and mailing charges. Companies that are first to adopt advanced systems that reduce labor enjoy competitive advantage for as long as their competitors lag behind.

Although devising strategic moves is mainly the responsibility of senior management, let us remember Napoleon's words: "Every soldier carries a marshal's baton in his knapsack." To paraphrase: every junior worker is a potential senior executive. Thus, it is incumbent on every professional to try to think strategically for his or her organization. In fact, employees at the lowest levels have proposed some of the most brilliant strategic ideas. In today's highly competitive market, strategy might determine an organization's rise or fall.

An increasing number of strategic moves are possible only with the aid of ISs or by having ISs at the center of their strategy—that is, technology provides the product, service, or method that gains the organization strategic advantage. The potential for new business models on the web is still great. Thus, professionals must understand how to use technology in strategic moves. Understanding how strategic information systems are conceived and implemented might help you suggest good ideas for such systems in your organization and facilitate your promotion up the organizational ladder.

Initiative #2: Raise Barriers to Market Entrants

The smaller the number of companies competing within an industry, the better off each company is. Therefore, an organization might gain competitive advantage by making it difficult, or impossible, for other organizations to produce the product or service it provides. Using expertise or technology that is unavailable to competitors or prohibitively expensive is one way to bar new entrants.

Companies **raise barriers to entrants** in a number of ways. Obtaining legal protection of intellectual property, such as an invention or artistic work, bars competitors from freely using it. Microsoft, IBM, and other software powerhouses have gained tremendous strategic advantages by copyrighting and patenting software. Numerous examples of such protection can be found on the web. Priceline.com holds a patent for online reverse ("name your own price") auctioning, which has prevented competitors from entering its business space. Amazon.com secured a patent for one-click online purchasing, which enables customers to enter shipping and credit card information once and to place subsequent orders while skipping a verification webpage. Although the software is quite simple, Amazon obtained a patent for it in 1999 that will not expire until 2017. Amazon successfully sued Barnes & Noble (B&N) when BN.com implemented a one-click technology. Now B&N, along with Apple, pays Amazon to use the technology. In October 2010, Amazon patented the one-click order process in Canada. However, by November of the following year, the patent was being appealed in Canada's Federal Court of Appeals. The one-click process also faced difficulties in Europe where it was denied a patent in 2011 because the process was deemed not genuinely inventive enough. As a result, European companies can use the one-click process without a fee while American companies must pay Amazon to use it. Although technology can create a barrier to entry for other businesses, it can also come with legal issues in a global market.

Another barrier to potential new market entrants is the high expense of entering the particular market. Industries such as airlines have a significant barrier to entry due to the investment of information technology for central reservation and other operational systems. However, while technology can create an impediment for new market entrants, it can also have the reverse effect. For example, manufacturing businesses rely heavily on technology to manage their product lifecycle processes (from design, manufacture, service and disposal). Traditionally, due to the cost and complexity of implementing product lifecycle management (PLM) technology systems were reserved only for large manufacturing businesses; ultimately creating a barrier to entry for smaller companies. However, as new low-cost alternatives for PLM systems have become available, many smaller manufacturing businesses have adopted this technology, decreasing the barrier maintained by large manufacturers (Waurzyniak, 2012).

Initiative #3: Establish High Switching Costs

Switching costs are expenses incurred when a customer stops buying a product or service from one business and starts buying it from another. Switching costs can be explicit (such as charges the seller levies on a customer for withdrawal from a contract) or implicit (such as the indirect costs in time and money spent adjusting to a new product that competes with the old).

Often, explicit switching costs are fixed, nonrecurring costs, such as a penalty a buyer must pay for terminating a deal early. In the mobile phone service industry, you can usually get an attractive deal, but if you cancel the service before the one- or two-year contract ends, you have to pay a hefty penalty. So although another company's service might be more attractive, you might decide to wait out the full contract period because the penalty outweighs the benefits of the new company's service. When you do decide to switch, you might discover that your phone is not suitable for service with any other mobile service provider. The cost of the phone itself, then, is another disincentive to switch.

A perfect example of indirect switching expenses is the time and money required to learn new software. Once a company trains its personnel to use one word-processing or spreadsheet program, a competing software company must offer a very enticing deal to make switching worthwhile. The same principle holds for many other applications, such as database management systems, webpage editors, and graphical software. Consider Microsoft's popular Office productivity suite. Google Docs and OpenOffice.org offer products that can be used or downloaded at no cost and are compatible with Office applications. This cost savings and inter-product compatibility could significantly lower the switching costs for an office productivity product. Yet, few organizations or consumers who are accustomed to MS Office are willing to completely switch to Google Docs or OpenOffice.org.

Manufacturers of laser and ink-jet printers sell their printers at cost or below cost. However, once you purchase a printer, you must replace a depleted ink or toner cartridge with a costly cartridge that the printer manufacturer sells, or take a risk with other cartridges whose quality is often low. You face high costs if you consider switching to another printer brand. Thus, establishing high switching costs often locks in customers. Locking in customers by any means is a way to accomplish a strategic advantage, and is discussed later in this chapter.

High switching costs are often more prominent when a company uses proprietary software, especially when the software is expensive, such as an ERP or human resource management system. In addition to the initial price of the system, the client incurs other costs, some tangible and some not. Tangible costs include modification to suit the special needs of the client's unique business processes. Intangible costs include employees' learning the new system and the establishment of smooth working relations with the service unit of the software vendor.

Initiative #4: Create New Products or Services

Clearly, the ability to **create a new and unique product or service** that many organizations and individuals need gives an organization a great competitive advantage. Unfortunately, the advantage lasts only until other organizations in the industry start offering an identical or similar product or service for a comparable or lower price.

Examples of this scenario abound in the software industry. For instance, Lotus Development Corporation became the major player early on in the electronic spreadsheet market after it introduced its Lotus 1-2-3 program. When two competitors tried to market similar products, Lotus sued for copyright infringement and won the court case, sustaining its market dominance for several years. However, with time, Microsoft established its Excel spreadsheet application as the world leader, not only by aggressive marketing but also by including better features in its application.

Another example of a company creating a new service is eBay, the firm that dominates online auctions. The organization was the first to offer this service, which became very popular within only a few months. While other firms now offer a similar service (e.g., Amazon.com and Yahoo! Auctions), the fact that eBay was the first to offer it gave the company a huge advantage. It quickly acquired a large number of sellers and bidders, a network that is so critical to creating a "mass" of clients, which in turn is the main draw for additional clients. It also gave eBay an advantage in experience and allowed it to open a gap that was difficult for competitors to close, even for giants such as Amazon.com. eBay is an example of an entire business that would be impossible without the web and the information technologies that support the firm's service.

eBay's success demonstrates the strategic advantage of the **first mover**, an organization that is the first to offer a new product or service. By the time other organizations start offering the same product or service, the first mover has usually created some assets that cannot be held by the competitors: a superior brand name, a better technology or method for delivery, or a **critical mass**. A critical mass is a body of clients that is large enough to attract many other clients. In many cases, first movers simply enjoy longer experience, which in itself is an advantage over competitors.

eBay gained a first mover advantage by marketing products to a mass audience

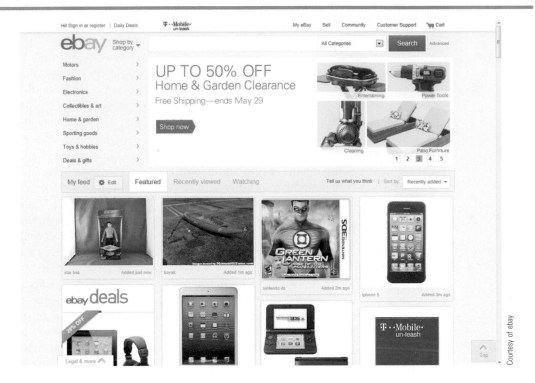

Courtesy of ebay

XM and Sirius satellite-based radio services have changed radio broadcasting. The two pioneers in this market have reaped the rewards of being first movers since 2001. Satellite broadcasts release radio services from the constraints of territorial boundaries and from national content regulation. Because of this, many radio personalities and radio stations offer programs on satellite radio, hoping to participate in its strategic advantage. In 2008, Sirius Satellite Radio's $5 billion buyout of XM Radio was approved but the U.S. Department of Justice, despite strong disapproval from consumer groups and lobbying from the land-based radio industry. The Department of Justice said the merger was unlikely to hurt competitors or consumers, citing the development of mobile broadband Internet devices as the upcoming replacement for satellite radio. Sirius/XM had close to 23 million subscribers in 2012. In this case, both companies were first movers and competition did not allow them to profit, so they agreed to merge.

A good example of a new product is Apple's iPhone. Handheld devices that combine telephony and computers had been around for many years. When the iPhone was introduced in 2007, it developed a new concept: no physical keys. All the functions are activated by using touchscreen keys, and therefore can be more intuitively operated and offer more options. While the original iPhone created a market advantage for a new product, the touchscreen concept was quickly adopted by many competitors. This example clearly identifies that the advantage of a new product or service, especially for technology, can rapidly fade.

The iPhone continues to be the most popular smartphone device

©iStockphoto.com/franckreporter

Since the release of the original iPhone, Apple has continued to make improvements with every model. The iPhone 5 boasted a larger screen, reduced weight and width, and other enhancements. Even though it had record setting pre-order sales (2 million in 24 hours), its competitor Samsung immediately seized on its shortcomings and promoted features in their own mobile phone such as instant video sharing that the iPhone lacked. This is another illustration of how being a first mover with cutting-edge technology can be a difficult position to maintain.

Some websites were the first to offer certain services that soon attracted millions of visitors per day. The high traffic they have created gives them a significant strategic asset in the form of advertising potential. Two successful social media outlets, Facebook and Twitter, are using their massive user base to bring in advertising revenues; 1.1 billion and 554 million users respectively (Anonymous, 2013c, 2013d). Both social media sites contain advertisements on their websites. With the exponential growth of mobile computing, these social media giants are attempting to please investors by expanding revenue by streaming news feed ads to users' mobile devices. However, this type of advertising can be irritating to some users, because the ads are often placed in the middle of the screen. What may have been passive ignorance of these screen areas may irritate users (Winkler, 2012). Facebook and Twitter are taking cautious approaches to mobile advertising in order to not lose users.

YouTube is another social media giant that has benefited from first mover advantage. YouTube enables individuals and corporations to upload video clips for viewing by its visitors. By January 2012, the site was streaming more than 4 billion videos per day. Its popularity has increased significantly since it was acquired for $1.65 billion by Google. Many businesses have created YouTube accounts to advertise their products and services. YouTube's marketing reach, search engine capabilities, and no-cost model provide an effective environment for corporate promotions and outreach. Broadcast networks and movie studios have uploaded video content as another venue for their products. As shown in the figure, broadcast networks and media organizations have leveraged YouTube as an additional method to distribute and promote their content.

YouTube continues to be used to promote television shows and other media content

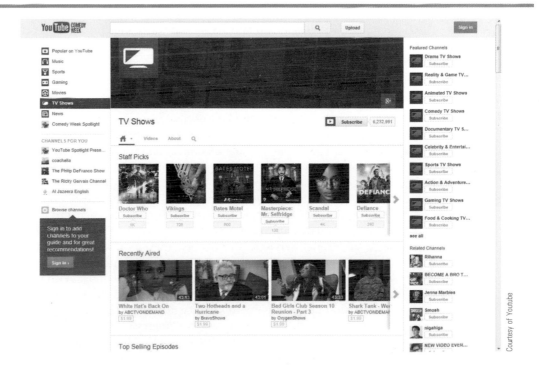

Courtesy of Youtube

Being a first mover is not always a guarantee of long-term success, however. One example of how a first-mover strategic advantage can be lost within just a few months is in the web browser arena. Netscape Corporation (now part of AOL) dominated the web browser market, which was new in 1994. By allowing individual users to download its browser for free, it cornered up to 95 percent of the market. The wide use of the browser by individuals moved commercial organizations to purchase the product and other software compatible with the browser. Netscape's dominance quickly diminished when Microsoft aggressively marketed its own browser, which many perceived as at least as good as Netscape's. Microsoft provided Internet Explorer free of charge to anyone and then bundled it into the Microsoft Windows operating system software distributed with almost all PCs. Even after the court-ordered unbundling, its browser still dominated.

Other first movers have lost market share because they neglected to improve the service they pioneered. Few web surfers may remember Infoseek, the first commercial search engine. Google, which entered the search engine arena in 1998, improved the quality and speed of web searches, offering a clutter-free home page. The strategy of its two young entrepreneurs was simple: provide the best search engine, and refrain from commercializing it for a while. Over a period of about three years Google established itself as the best search engine. In time, it started to capitalize on this prominence by selling sponsored links (the right side of the results of a user's search, and later the top shaded results). Most importantly, the organization never stopped improving its search algorithms and periodically has offered new services. The strategy has succeeded so much that "google it" has become synonymous with "search for it on the web."

Initiative #5: Differentiate Products or Services

A company can achieve a competitive advantage by persuading consumers that its product or service is better than its competitors'. Called product **differentiation**, this advantage is usually achieved through advertising and customer experience. Consider Skype. Although the software was not the first to offer free phone calls over the Internet, its quality was higher than similar applications. People noticed the difference, and hundreds of millions now use the application. When the user base was large, the company (which was acquired by Microsoft) added many features, including video chat. It makes money by selling features for videoconferencing, long distance voice services, and mobile devices.

Brand-name success is a perfect example of product differentiation. Think of Levi's jeans, Chanel and Lucky perfumes, and Gap clothes. The customer buys the brand-name product, perceiving it to be superior to similar products. In fact, some products *are* the same, but units sold under a prestigious brand name sell for higher prices. You often see this phenomenon in the food, clothing, drug, and cosmetics markets.

Initiative #6: Enhance Products or Services

Instead of differentiating a product or service, an organization might actually **enhance existing products or services**, that is, add to the product or service to increase its value to the consumer. For example, car manufacturers might entice customers by offering a longer warranty period for their cars, and real-estate agents might attract more business by providing useful financing information to potential buyers.

Since the Internet opened its portals to commercial enterprises in the early 1990s, an increasing number of companies have supplemented their products and services. Their websites provide up-to-date information that helps customers utilize their purchased products better or receive additional services. Companies that pioneered such Internet use reaped substantial rewards. For example, Charles Schwab gained a competitive advantage over other, older brokerage companies by opening a site for online stock transactions. Within months, half its revenue came from this site. All brokerage houses followed suit and allow customers to trade through a website.

Other companies use the Internet to maintain their competitive edge by continually adding to and enhancing their online services. The Progressive Casualty Insurance Company, ranked 169 on the Fortune 500 list, is an excellent example. The company enables insured drivers to place a claim and follow its progress at the company's site. The company has connected its information systems with those of car dealerships and financing institutions. When a car is totaled (i.e., fixing it would cost more than purchasing a new car), the owner can receive a check to purchase a new car. However, since the company knows that purchasing a new car can be a hassle, the insured owner can use, free of charge, the company's Total Loss Concierge service. The company developed special software that retrieves details about the totaled vehicle. The details are shared with a network of dealerships, and the concierge selects the best alternatives in terms of compatibility with the client's needs and the price. The agent accompanies the client in the contacts with the dealerships. If the client still owes money to a lender, the Progressive agent uses the system to retrieve the financing information and sends it to a network of financing firms. The agents send the client the best alternatives. In the auto insurance industry, the Total Loss Concierge service is an enhancement offered only by Progressive. Recently, Progressive integrated technology innovation into their business operations, offering mobile apps to access their site and the Snapshot® device to track good driving habits. Each of these initiatives fulfills the strategies of Gartner's CIO report discussed earlier; attracting new customers and adding mobile applications.

Initiative #7: Establish Alliances

Companies can gain competitive advantage by combining services to make them more attractive (and usually less expensive) than purchasing services separately. An alliance may also be created to enable customers to use the same technology for purchases from different companies. These **alliances** provide two draws for customers: combined service is cheaper, and one-stop shopping or using the same technology is more convenient. The travel industry is very aggressive in this area. For example, airlines collaborate with hotel chains and car-rental firms to offer travel and lodging packages. Credit-card companies offer frequent flier miles for every dollar spent, discounts on ticket purchases from particular airlines, or discounts on products of an allied manufacturer. In all these cases, alliances create competitive advantages.

As Figure 2.3 indicates, by creating an alliance, organizations enjoy synergy: the combined profit for the allies from the sale of a package of goods or services exceeds the profits earned when each acts individually. Sometimes, the alliances are formed by more than two organizations. Consider the benefits you receive when you agree to accept a major credit card: discounts from several hotel chains, restaurant chains, flower delivery chains, and other stores; free insurance when renting a car; and frequent flier miles, to name a few. Similarly, travel websites such as Kayak and Orbitz offer you the opportunity to reserve lodging and car rental at discounts while you make your airline reservations. These companies have established alliances with hotel chains and car-rental companies.

FIGURE **2.3**

Strategic alliances combine services to create synergies

Before Strategic Alliance

Airline   Floral Shop

After Strategic Alliance

Vacation Package

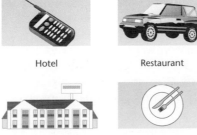

Telephone Carrier   Car Rental

Hotel   Restaurant

© Cengage Learning 2015

What is the common denominator among these companies? They each have an information system that tracks all these transactions and discounts. A package of attractive propositions entices clients who need these services (and most businesses do). Would this offer be feasible without an IS to track transactions and discounts? Probably not.

The growth in e-commerce and reduction of logistics costs has created new alliances. Consider United Parcel Services (UPS), well known for its delivery services, and Medtronic, a Minneapolis-based medical device company. UPS now fills pharmacy orders at their Louisville, KY facility. UPS pharmacists log into Medtronic's system to fill orders for medical devices ordered by their patients. These medical devices are also stored at the UPS facility for immediate shipment. Medtronic has closed its own warehouse facility and significantly reduced the costs of processing its orders. Again, a clever IT initiative and corporate alliance enable an operational efficiency strategy that will have positive benefits for business organizations.

On the web, an obvious example of alliances is an **affiliate program**. Anyone can place links to commercial sites on his or her personal website. When a visitor clicks through to a commercial site and makes a purchase, the first site's owner is paid a fee. Some online retailers have thousands of affiliates (sometimes referred to as associates). The early adopters of these programs, such as Amazon.com, Buy.com, Priceline.com, and other large e-retailers, enjoyed a competitive advantage in gaining new customers. It is easy for any website holder to become an associate of Amazon.com.

Business affiliating with Amazon can earn revenue by adding a link to a specific product

The web has generated strategic alliances that would probably never be created offline. Can you imagine Wal-Mart inviting Sears to sell Sears' merchandise from Wal-Mart stores? This is exactly what Amazon does. Its site has links to products of other companies. When you search for an item on Amazon, you might find links not only to its own products but also to those of competitors, such as Ace Hardware, the consumer hardware store. If this sounds strange, consider the rationale: Amazon wants customers to compare its price and its competitors' price for the same item and see that Amazon's is lower, mainly because Amazon manages its warehouses more efficiently than any other retailer. Even if customers decide to purchase from the competitor through the Amazon site, Amazon receives a commission from the seller.

A growing number of companies use software to help analyze the vast amounts of data they collect. Some share the data and business intelligence with business partners because if their partners do better, so will they. For example, Marriott, the large hotel chain, provides online and traditional travel agencies with analyses about pricing, joint promotions, and inventory. The analytical results help the agencies optimize their operations, which results in more customers for Marriott.

Initiative #8: Lock in Suppliers or Buyers

Organizations can achieve competitive advantage if they are powerful enough to **lock in** suppliers to their mode of operation or buyers to their product. Possessing bargaining power—the leverage to influence buyers and suppliers—is the key to this approach. As such, companies so large that suppliers and buyers must listen to their demands use this tactic nearly exclusively.

A firm gains bargaining power with a supplier either when the firm has few competitors or when the firm is a major competitor in its industry. In the former case, the fewer the companies that make up a supplier's customer base, the more important each company is to the supplier. In the latter case, the more important a specific company is to a supplier's success, the greater bargaining power that company has over that supplier.

The most common leverage in bargaining is purchase volume. Companies that spend billions of dollars purchasing parts and services have the power to force their suppliers to conform to their methods of operation, and even to shift some costs onto suppliers as part of the business arrangement. Consider Wal-Mart, one of the world's largest retailers. Not only does the company use its substantial bargaining power to pressure suppliers to lower prices, but it also requires them to use information systems that are compatible with its own automated processes. The suppliers must use ISs that tell them when to ship products to Wal-Mart so that the giant retailer is never left understocked or overstocked. In recent years this power allowed the company to require its suppliers to use radio frequency identification (RFID) devices in packaging to allow more accurate tracking of ordered, shelved, and sold items. This bargaining power and tight control of inventory enables Wal-Mart to enjoy considerable cost savings, which it passes on to customers, which keep growing in numbers thanks to the competitive prices. Many suppliers are locked in with Wal-Mart because of the sheer volume of business they have with the company: some sell a third to one-half of everything they produce to this single retailer, and some, such as the giant consumer products maker Procter & Gamble, have a "Vice President, Wal-Mart" as a member of the senior management.

One way to lock in *buyers* in a free market is to enjoy a situation in which customers fear high switching costs. In the software arena, enterprise applications are a good example. This type of software helps organizations manage a wide array of operations: purchasing, manufacturing, human resources, finance, and so forth. The software is expensive, costing millions of dollars. After a company purchases the software from a firm, it is locked in to that firm's services: training, implementation, updates, and so forth. Thus, companies that sell enterprise software, such as SAP, Oracle, and BMC Software, make great efforts to improve both their software and support services to maintain leadership in this market.

Another way to lock in clients is to **create a standard**. The software industry has pursued this strategy vigorously, especially in the Internet arena. For example, Microsoft's decision to give away its web browser by letting both individuals and organizations download it free from its site was not altruistic. Microsoft executives knew that the greater the number of Internet Explorer (IE) users, the greater the user base. The greater the user base, the more likely organizations were to purchase Microsoft's proprietary software to help manage their websites. Also, once individual users committed to IE as their main browser, they were likely to purchase Microsoft software that enhanced the browser's capabilities.

Similarly, Adobe gives away its Acrobat Reader software, an application that lets web surfers open and read documents created using different computers running different operating systems, such as various versions of Windows, the Mac operating system, and UNIX. When the Reader user base became large enough, organizations and individuals found it economically justifiable to purchase and use the full Acrobat application (the application used to create the documents) and related applications. Using this strategy put Adobe's PDF (portable data format) standard in an unrivaled position.

Adobe uses a similar strategy for its Flash software used to create webpage animations. It offers the Flash player for download free of charge but sells the development tool. Like PDF, Flash created a symbiotic situation to augment a market: the more individuals download the player, the more businesses are willing to purchase the development tool. The more companies engage Flash modules in their webpages, the more individuals download the player, without which they cannot enjoy those animations.

The simplest way to lock in buyers is to create a physical or software limitation on using technology. This can be in the form of a company designing a socket for add-on plugs that takes only a specific size or form, or designing files so that they run only on its software. Apple Computer's iTunes is a classic example of the latter. The online music store is a popular site for purchasing music files. However, the files contain FairPlay DRM (digital rights management) software, which ensures the files run only on Apple devices. Digital music players made by competitors are locked out. Apple's decision had a significantly positive impact on its profits.

Creating and Maintaining Strategic Information Systems

IT might offer many opportunities to accomplish a competitive edge, especially in industries that are using older software, such as the insurance industry. Insurance companies were among the early adopters of IT and have not changed much of their software. This is why some observers say the entire industry is inefficient. Once an insurance company adopts innovative software applications, like the Progressive insurance mobile app described in the section on Enhancing Existing Products or Services, it probably will gain competitive advantage. Customers can submit a claim through the mobile app and use the phone's camera to upload pictures of the accident scene. Airlines are another example of an industry that still uses antiquated hardware and software. As you'll learn later in the chapter, when JetBlue was established, it adopted the latest technologies, and this was a major reason for its great competitive advantage.

Companies can implement some of the strategic initiatives described in the previous section by using information systems. As we mentioned at the beginning of the chapter, a strategic information system (SIS) is any information system that can help an organization achieve a long-term competitive advantage. An SIS can be created from scratch, developed by modifying an existing system, or "discovered" by realizing that a system already in place can be used to strategic advantage. While companies continue to explore new ways of devising SISs, some successful SISs are the result of less lofty endeavors: the intention to improve mundane operations using IT has occasionally yielded a system with strategic qualities.

Strategic information systems combine ideas for making potentially winning business decisions and ideas for harnessing information technology to implement the decisions. For an information system to be an SIS, two conditions must exist. First, the information system must serve an organizational goal rather than simply provide information; and second, the organization's IS unit must work with managers of other functional units (including marketing, finance, purchasing, human resources, and so on) to pursue the organizational goal.

Creating an SIS

To create an SIS, top management must be involved from initial consideration through development and implementation. In other words, the SIS must be part of the overall organizational strategic plan. The danger always exists that a new SIS might be considered the IS unit's exclusive property. However, to succeed, the project must be a corporate effort, involving all managers who use the system.

Figure 2.4 presents questions that management should ask to determine whether to develop a new SIS. Executives meet to try to identify areas in which information can support a strategic goal. Only after completing the activities outlined in Figure 2.4 will management be able to conceptualize an SIS that seizes an opportunity.

FIGURE 2.4

Questions to answer in a strategic information system idea-generating meeting

1. What would be the most effective way to gain an advantage?

2. Would more accessible or timely information to our employees, customers, or suppliers help establish a significant advantage? If so, how?

3. Can an information system be developed that provides more accessible and timely information?

4. Will the development effort be economically justified?

   ◆ Can existing competitors afford to fund the development of a similar system?
   ◆ How long will it take the competitors to build their own, similar system?
   ◆ Can we make our system a moving target to the competition by constantly enhancing it, so that it always retains its superiority?

5. What is the risk of not developing such a system?

6. Are alternative means of achieving the same goals available, and if so, how do they compare with the advantages and disadvantages of a new SIS?

7. Will technology add value to the customer's experience? If so, how?

© Cengage Learning 2015

A word of caution regarding Question 4 in Figure 2.4, the issue of economic justification of an SIS: an increasing number of researchers and practitioners conclude that estimating the financial benefits of information systems is extremely difficult. This difficulty is especially true of SISs. The purpose of these systems is not simply to reduce costs or increase output per employee; many create an entirely new service or product. Some completely transform the way an organization, or an industry, does business. Because so many fundamental business changes are involved, measuring the financial impact is difficult, if not impossible, even after implementation, let alone before. For example, if a bank is considering offering a full range of financial services via the web, how can management know whether the move justifies the cost of the necessary software? It is difficult to estimate the success of such a bold approach in terms of how many new customers the bank would gain.

Recently, many business organizations have been focusing on providing value as well as enhancing the customer's experience, and technology has been pivotal to their strategies. Retailers can provide product videos on the retail floor to promote their products. Supermarkets can offer scanning devices to reduce checkout time as well as offer specials and promotions to their customers. E-tailers can offer suggestions of new products and specials based on past searches and purchases. Hotels can offer room upgrades at a special price or destination information for an upcoming stay at their property. Each of these examples leverages information technology strategies to add value to the customer experience, thereby creating additional revenue, retention of customers, and increasing organizational brand value.

Yet, a great number of SISs are the unintended consequence of exploiting information technology to support activities that are not strategic. For example, in the 1990s, Owens & Minor, a distributor of hospital supplies, built a data warehouse from which to glean business intelligence. However, both its customers (mainly hospitals) and its suppliers (drug and medical instrument makers) agreed to pay for mining the data warehouse to improve their decision making. In this case, the company did not plan to create an SIS, but the data warehouse and the tools that help mine it may become one, increasing Owens & Minor's profit in a business that has little to do with its original business.

Reengineering and Organizational Change

To implement an SIS and achieve competitive advantage, organizations sometimes must rethink the entire way they operate. While brainstorming about strategic plans, management should ask: "If we reestablished this business process from scratch, how would we do it?" The answer often leads to the decision to eliminate one set of operations and build others from the ground up. Changes such as these are called **reengineering**. Reengineering often involves adoption of new machinery and elimination of management layers. Frequently, information technology plays an important role in this process.

Reengineering's goal is not to gain small incremental cost savings, but to achieve great efficiency leaps—of 100 percent and even 1000 percent. With that degree of improvement, a company often gains competitive advantage. Interestingly, a company that undertakes reengineering along with implementing a new SIS cannot always tell whether the SIS was successful. The reengineering process makes it impossible to determine how much each change contributed to the organization's improved position.

Implementation of an SIS requires a business to revamp processes—to undergo organizational change—to gain an advantage. For example, consumer electronics and appliance manufacturer LG decided that it needed to apply its product innovation tactics to its supply chain management system. In 2007, management found inconsistent practices for 115 factories and subsidiaries within LG. Senior management believed that they need to reengineer its supply chain to better manage its relationship with suppliers. Originally, they allowed each division to negotiate its own agreements with suppliers. Therefore, the procurement personnel managing a chip supplier for cell phones might not be aware of their colleague's purchase of the same chips from the same supplier for televisions at another LG manufacturing plant.

LG reengineered its procurement process to require that purchase orders be processed by a centralized function. The analysis of their operations created a streamlined process, and they compiled a single procurement manual. Ultimately, the new process replaced its fragmented and uncoordinated purchasing procedures with consolidated procedures, saving the company $2 billion; a savings of 6.7 percent. Coincidentally, these savings helped LG to be better prepared for the forthcoming global downturn. This example reinforces the lesson that business organizations should not ignore opportunities during successful times and rush to identify opportunities only during challenging times. Being prepared for downturns is an important strategy. For its reengineering efforts and results, LG was named as an innovator by *Business Week* in 2010.

Interestingly, most reengineering of the 1990s and early 2000s failed and simply resulted in massive layoffs. Executives found it impossible to actually change many business processes. Business processes eventually did change in companies that adopted enterprise systems, commonly called ERP systems. The reason: the new systems forced managers and employees to change their way of work.

Competitive Advantage as a Moving Target

As you might have guessed, competitive advantage is often short-lived. In time, competitors imitate the leader, and the advantage diminishes. So, the quest for innovative strategies must be dynamic. Corporations must continuously contemplate new ways to use information technology to their advantage. In a way, companies' jockeying for the latest competitive advantage is a lot like an arms race. Side A develops an advanced weapon, and then side B develops a similar weapon that terminates the advantage of side A, and so on.

In an environment where most information technology is available to all, SISs that are originally developed to create a strategic advantage quickly become an expected standard business practice. A prime example is the banking industry, where surveys indicate that increased IS expenditures did not yield long-range strategic advantages. The first banks to provide ATMs and online banking reaped some rewards in terms of labor savings and new customers, but the advantage disappeared because most banks now offer these services.

A system can only help a company sustain competitive advantage if the company continuously modifies and enhances the system, creating a moving target for competitors. American Airlines' Sabre—the online reservation system for travel agents—is a classic example. The system, which was designed in the 1950s, was redesigned in the late 1970s to sell travel agencies a new service, online airline reservations. But over the years, the company spun off an office automation package for travel agencies called Agency Data Systems. The reservation system now encompasses hotel reservations, car rentals, train schedules, theater tickets, and limousine rentals. When the Internet became accessible to businesses and consumers, the system was redesigned to let travelers use Sabre from their own computers. The system has been so successful that in some years American earned more from the technology than from its airline operations. The organizational unit that developed and operated the software became a separate IT powerhouse at AMR Corp., the parent company of American Airlines, and now operates as Sabre Holding Corporation, an independent company. It is the leading provider of technology for the travel industry. Travelocity, Inc., the popular web-based travel site, is a subsidiary of Sabre, and, naturally, uses Sabre's software. Chances are you are using Sabre technology when you make airline reservations through other websites, as well.

We return to Amazon as an example of how ISs help companies maintain competitive advantage. Management believes that it must add new features to its website to attract buyers over and over again. The company continuously improves its webpages' look and the online services it provides. Amazon has moved from merely selling books through the web to providing best-seller lists, readers' reviews, and authors' interviews; selling almost any consumer product imaginable; streaming audio and video; and posting consumer wish lists, product reviews by customers, and other "cool stuff." The constant improvements help the company maintain its dominant position in online retailing.

However, all of these features have been imitated by competitors. Amazon now also offers web hosting services and space for rent in its warehouses worldwide. Amazon has extended its products and services to sell what it already does well; warehousing, fulfillment, and web-based sales processing. If you are a small business, you can contract with Amazon to create the "look and feel" of a major supplier and gain the order and fulfillment efficiencies of a larger business organization. Ultimately, the small business can focus on its core competencies of manufacturing its product without the "back house" order fulfillment issues. Amazon has also opened much of its software for developers to use.

Similarly, Google has offered access to some of its software. For example, it enables webmasters and other website owners to use software that finds out why Google's crawler—software that searches the web and indexes new pages for search—has difficulties in indexing pages. The result: the site owners get their new pages indexed so the public can access them, and Google receives free labor in fixing problems its crawler faces. Organizations can integrate Google mapping software into their own intranets to map customer locations, track shipments, manage facilities, and perform other activities that are map-related. Amazon and Google have augmented the portfolio of services they provide to increase the circle of organizations and individuals who depend on them, thereby strengthening their strategic positions.

We usually expect entrepreneurs to enter a new and profitable industry, not an old, money-losing one. However, with the proper technology and management methods, it seems that some energetic people can gain strategic advantage where others have been hurting. The U.S. airline industry has seen mainly bad times since the industry's deregulation in the 1970s. The situation deteriorated as the 1990s drew to a close, and grew even worse after the terrible events of September 11, 2001. In 2001, the industry lost $7.7 billion, but JetBlue had a profit of $38.5 million on revenue of $320.4 million. It continued to be profitable in 2002, 2003, and 2004 along with only one other carrier, Southwest Airlines, while all other U.S. carriers had losses. JetBlue's revenues grew from $998.4 million in 2003 to $1.27 billion in 2004. The organization continues to be profitable, posting net income of $86M and $128M in 2011 and 2012 respectively (Anonymous, 2013b).

For jetBlue, information technology is at least as important as fuel

© iStockphoto.com/Boarding1Now

JetBlue was established in February 2000 by David Neeleman, who served as its CEO. Two decades earlier, in 1984, Neeleman cofounded Morris Air, a small airline in Salt Lake City, Utah, which was the first airline to offer ticketless travel, a program that was developed inside the company. Working with a college student he developed Open Skies, a computer program that integrates electronic ticketing, Internet reservations, and revenue management. Revenue management tools help an airline plan the most profitable routes and ticket pricing. Morris Air was sold to Southwest Airlines, which enthusiastically adopted the e-ticket idea. Neeleman became an executive at Southwest but left in frustration, because he believed that an airline could achieve much more efficiency with information technology. JetBlue gained a significant strategic advantage over larger and older airlines. The company's success was the result of understanding customers' priorities and gaining marked efficiencies through automating whatever IT can automate. Management also learned to break away from practices that inhibit efficiency and agility.

In a highly competitive industry that traditionally has had a narrow profit margin, JetBlue managed to gain strategic advantage by *reducing cost*, therefore reducing the price to the customer, and *improving a service*, especially in terms of on-time departures and arrivals.

Massive Automation

We usually think of manufacturing organizations when mentioning automation, but benefits can also be gained by automating services. JetBlue uses Open Skies, the software that Neeleman developed. It is a combination reservation system and accounting system, and supports customer service and sales tracking. Using JetBlue's system directly to purchase a ticket, the company avoids the cost of commission by booking a ticket through a travel agent. In addition, JetBlue saves office space rent and electricity by using reservation agents who work from home (telecommuting is discussed in Chapter 6, "Business Networks and Telecommunications") and use VoIP (Voice over Internet Protocol, also discussed in Chapter 6) for telephoning. This reduces its handling cost per ticket to $4.50.

Because all tickets are electronic, there is no paper handling or related expense. JetBlue encourages customers to purchase their tickets online, and most of them do so, saving the company much labor. The cost of handling a ticket ordered via the web is reduced to only 50 cents, as opposed to $4.50 paid to a reservation agent, and a far cry from the commission when booking through a travel agent.

JetBlue automates other aspects of running an airline as well. Its maintenance workers use a maintenance information system from Dash Group to log all airplane parts and their time cycles, that is, when the parts must be replaced and where they can be found. The system reduces manual tracking costs.

Flight planning to maximize yield—the number of seats occupied on a flight—is executed on a flight-planning application from Bornemann Associates. It reduces planning costs and makes operations more efficient. JetBlue also uses an application that its team of IT professionals developed in-house, called Blue Performance. It tracks operational data that is updated flight by flight. The company's intranet enables its employees to access the performance data. Managers have up-to-the-minute metrics, so critical in airline operations, which enable them to respond immediately to problems.

When on the ground, employees use wireless devices to report and respond to any irregular event, from weather delays to passenger injuries. The response is quick, and the events are recorded in a database for later analysis.

When training pilots and other employees, no paper records are kept. An aviation training management system provides a database to track each employee's training record. It is easy to update and efficient for record retrieval.

Away from Tradition

JetBlue decided not to use the hub-and-spokes method of routing its airplanes, a practice used by all major airlines. Instead of having its airplanes land in one or two hubs and undergo maintenance there before taking off for the next leg of a route, it simply uses the most profitable routes between any two cities. All flights are point to point—no hubs, no spokes.

JetBlue was the first airline to establish paperless cockpits. The Federal Aviation Authority (FAA) mandates that pilots and other aircrew members have access to flight manuals. The manuals are the documents showing information about each flight, including route, weight, how the weight is spread on board, fuel quantity, and even details such as how many pets are on board. JetBlue was one of the first airlines to maintain electronic flight manuals, and the pilots and first officers access and update the manuals on laptop computers that they carry into the cockpit. As soon as the data have been entered, employees have access to the information. The advantage once realized by the paperless cockpit has been adopted by several airlines. Recently, tablet technology has been implemented to provide pilots with paperless access to operational data (Anonymous, 2012c, 2013a). Data can be updated directly from the cockpit to cloud data servers or PDFs sent directly back to operations centers.

The laptops enable the pilots and first officers to calculate the weight and balance of their plane with a few keystrokes instead of relying on dispatchers at headquarters to do the calculations for them. JetBlue saves paper and time by having employees enter flight data. The company subscribes to SharePoint, a web-based portal that enables electronic updates to flight manuals. This cuts 15 to 20 minutes from preflight preparations for every flight. The result is a savings of about 4,800 hours per year and planes that take off and land on time.

JetBlue continues to harness IT to maintain the strategic gap between the company and its competitors. Management planned a paperless frequent flier program, cockpit-monitoring cameras transmitting through satellites so that ground crews can monitor activity, and biometric applications in airport terminals. Biometrics use physical characteristics of people, such as fingerprints and retina scans, for authentication and access to physical places and online information systems. Biometrics are more secure than access codes.

Enhanced Service

Much of the technology that helps JetBlue employees provide better service is invisible to the customers, but it also has some more obvious winning features. JetBlue offers leather seats and individual real-time television on all its airplanes. When they began offering these services, other airlines did not offer such seats on economy class, and offered only recorded television programs, now others have followed. United Airlines has equipped 200 of its fleet with television entertainment with over 100 channels free for first-class passengers and for a fee for coach (Anonymous, 2013f).

Its use of IT technologies also placed the airline at the top of the list for on-schedule departures and arrivals, a service that is very important, especially to business travelers. Perhaps even better, JetBlue ranks at the top as having the fewest mishandled bags. Thanks to constant updates to the Open Skies system, the company has managed to maintain check-in time at less than one minute. When passengers arrive at JetBlue's terminal at JFK airport, they are directed by a large LCD display with a computer-generated voice telling them which window is available to serve them. Usually, checking baggage takes 45 seconds. When passengers arrive at their destination, they do not have to wait for their suitcases. Their electronically tagged suitcases wait for them at the baggage claim area.

The most important metric in the airline industry is cost per available seat-mile (CASM), which is how much it costs to fly a passenger one mile of the journey. JetBlue was able to maintain the lowest or next to lowest CASM in its first three years of operations. A February 2012 Airline Economic Analysis Report compiled by Oliver Wyman reported JetBlue's CASM at 11 cents for 2011. Only two carriers posted lower costs, Spirit and Virgin America (Hazel, Stalnaker, & Taylor, 2012).

Late Mover Advantage

Some observers cite the fact that JetBlue is a late competitor as an important factor in its success. The company is not burdened with antiquated information systems, or as IT professionals like to call them, legacy systems. This allowed them to implement the latest available technologies: fast databases, VoIP, a slick website, laptop computers with the latest algorithms for fast calculation of routes and loads in the cockpit, and other technologies. This situation illustrates the strategic advantage of the **late mover**.

JetBlue executives quip that while other airlines run on fuel, theirs runs on information technology. Its CIO said that up to 40 percent of the software the company was using was beta or new software. Beta software is software that the developer gives to potential adopters for trial use. Talk about being on the cutting—and possibly bleeding—edge! Yet, competitors took notice. Many of them began to mimic JetBlue's innovations, including live TV.

When ice storms wreaked havoc with airlines in February 2007, one of JetBlue's major problems was that crews who were supposed to be in a certain city were stranded in another, and therefore staffing of flights was affected. While the crisis was on, the IT team developed a special database and application to let crews call in their location and to replace it with the location still stored in the system. The development process took a mere 24 hours. The IT team also devised ways to communicate better with customers through broadcasting automated flight alerts via email and mobile devices.

POINT OF INTEREST   Costly Battles

In 2007, Microsoft was sued by i4i Inc., a Toronto-based software firm, for patent infringement of a small piece of software code that was used in Microsoft Word. Four years later, the small Canadian technology company had spent over $10 million in legal fees. Microsoft had appealed the case to the U.S. Supreme Court. Two lower courts had ruled against Microsoft with one jury awarding i4i $290 million. By summer of 2011, the U.S. Supreme Court had upheld the position of the lower courts and Microsoft was charged $290 million. Because of the enormous value of patents in the tech industry, patent lawsuits are very frequent, costly, and require significant corporate resources.

Source: Greene, Jay. (June 9, 2011). Supreme Court rules against Microsoft in i4i patent case. http://news.cnet.com/8301-10805_3-20070308-75/supreme-court-rules-against-microsoft-in-i4i-patent-case/

At what point do the public and the courts start to consider a successful strategy as a predatory, unfair business practice that makes competition from other businesses impossible, even if their products are better? For instance, should a firm that takes bold entrepreneurial steps to become a business leader be curbed when it succeeds in becoming powerful? Several court cases against software industry leader Microsoft have focused on these questions. However, the questions are not simply legal issues. They are also important because they impact the economy and, as a result, society.

- **Historical Background.** In the 1970s, Microsoft was a small software company headed by its young president, Bill Gates, who established the company at age 19. The company was fortunate to find and buy an operating system from a small company in Seattle, Washington, for $50,000. An operating system (OS) is the software program that "mediates" between any computer program and the computer. Every application is developed with a particular operating system, or several operating systems, in mind. To a great extent, the operating system determines which applications a computer can run. Therefore, it is an extremely important program. We discuss operating systems and other types of software in Chapter 5, "Business Software."

People who purchased a computer had to consider the OS to determine which applications they could run. After Microsoft bought the operating system, it entered into a contract with IBM, the most powerful computer manufacturer at that time. IBM needed an operating system for its new creation, the IBM PC, and they chose Microsoft's DOS (Disk Operating System). While Microsoft did not make much money on the IBM deal, its executives realized the strategic potential of contracting with "the big guy."

Indeed, the strategy paid off. Soon, Compaq (later part of Hewlett-Packard) and many other manufacturers started to market IBM PC clones, cheaper computers that performed as well as IBM PCs and that could run the same operating system and applications. Because Microsoft's contract with IBM allowed it to sell DOS to other parties, it made a fortune selling DOS to Compaq and others. Later, Microsoft developed Windows, an improved operating system, and the success story repeated itself. To this day, the majority of buyers of personal computers also buy a copy of some version of Windows.

One major key to gaining a decent share of the new Internet market was the widespread use of web browsers. In the mid-1990s, more than 80 percent of web surfers used Netscape's browsers. Netscape was a young, entrepreneurial company selling innovative products. Microsoft decided to increase its own browser's market share of about 15 percent to a leading position. If a great number of people used its browser, Microsoft could expect hefty

sales of related software, such as server management applications.

No one would deny that Microsoft's attempt to compete in the browser market was legitimate. While Netscape gave its browsers away to individuals and educational institutions but charged for-profit organizations, Microsoft gave its browser to everyone free of charge. Also, the company took advantage of Windows dominance; it started bundling its browser with Windows, practically forcing any PC maker who wanted to sell the machines with the operating system installed to also install Internet Explorer (IE). The great majority of new PC owners used IE without even trying any other browser.

Within two years, a majority of web surfers were using IE. But Netscape, the U.S. Department of Justice, and many individuals considered Microsoft's tactics unfair. Microsoft used its muscle in the operating system market to compel sellers of personal computers to include a copy of Internet Explorer with Windows. Furthermore, the browser was inseparable from newer Windows versions. Since sellers had to include Windows on every machine, and because it was practically the only operating system most buyers would accept, sellers had no choice but to succumb to the pressure. The U.S. Department of Justice and the Attorneys General of several states filed lawsuits claiming Microsoft violated fair trade practices. Subsequently, legal authorities in other countries, such as the European Union (EU) and Taiwan, also either probed the company or sued it. In 2004, the EU's antitrust office fined Microsoft 497 million euros ($665 million) for abusively wielding Windows' monopoly and for locking competitors out of the software market.

- **Controversial Practices.** In 2009, Microsoft settled with the European Union for $2.2 billion for monopolizing the world's Internet searches. Their controversial practices led to $400 billion in sales and domination of Internet browsing. The fine is only one-half of one percent of sales over the 10-year period in which Microsoft was fighting the European Commission and selling Windows outfitted to run only their own browser, Internet Explorer. As part of the settlement, Microsoft has been forced to alter its "bundled" packages of software, which has allowed rival browsers to run on Windows including Safari, Chrome, and Firefox. The move benefits consumers who can choose their Internet browser and encourages web innovation from entrepreneurs.

The U.S. government opted not to extend the antitrust oversight of Microsoft in 2011. The twice-extended oversight forced Microsoft to release key software to assist competitors and cooperate with a three-person committee that ensured Microsoft did not engage in any predatory practices. However, since the settlement in 2002, Microsoft has seen its share of the browser market decrease (check http://en.wikipedia.org/wiki/Usage_share_of_web_browsers to see the current share statistics). The U.S. antitrust oversight against Microsoft was completed in May 2011 (Goldberg, 2011). Microsoft was fined in March 2013 in relation to its non-compliance with stricter anti-trust regulations imposed by the European Union (Foo, 2013).

Contrary to public perception, the United States, the European Union, and many other countries do not outlaw monopolies. They only forbid unfair use of monopolistic power. Because anyone may compete in any market, it would be unfair to punish an entrepreneur for marketing unique products and mustering market power of any magnitude. Of concern in the eyes of U.S. law, for example, are two issues: (1) have any unfair practices helped the company gain monopolistic power, and (2) does the monopolistic situation serve customers well, or does it hurt them?

- **Up Side, Down Side.** Microsoft argues that although it could charge higher prices for Windows, it has not, because it wants to make Windows affordable to all. Microsoft also argues that, unlike typical monopolists, it invests huge amounts of money in research and development,

which eventually benefits society in the form of better and less-expensive products. Microsoft's rivals in the software industry claim that Microsoft's practices stifle true competition. Both claims are difficult to measure. Some observers argue that allowing the same company to develop operating systems and many applications is good for consumers: the applications are compatible with each other; all use the same interface of menus and icons. Others suggest that Microsoft should be broken into two organizations, one that develops operating systems and another that develops only applications and competes fairly in that market. And some organizations and individuals simply fear the great power that a single person can have. Recent changes in two large organizations, Microsoft and Apple, clearly highlight the impact of visionary leaders on technology companies. Apple's Steve Jobs and Microsoft's Bill Gates both influenced the product development and innovation within their businesses as well as our economy and society.

What is your opinion? What would you do about this issue? Has the transition of their leadership impacted Apple and Microsoft? Technology innovation?

Ford on the Web: A Failure Story

Sometimes what seems to be a great, forward-looking strategic move ends up as a colossal failure. It might be because of lack of attention to details or simply because the innovator could not predict the response of customers or business partners, or had an idea too far ahead of its time. Such was the great initiative of Jacques Nasser, the former CEO of Ford Motor Company, the second largest U.S. automaker. In some cases, an early failure in a technology adoption can later lead to a success through a change in industry practices and operations. The timing of initiatives often is a key factor of success in business and some advances in technology are "before their time" and may have a future and successful impact.

The Ideas

When Nasser was appointed CEO of Ford in 1999, he regarded himself as an agent of change. He was eager to push the company into the web, which was then at the height of the "dot-com bubble." "We are now measuring speed in gigahertz, not horsepower," he said at the 2000 North American International Auto Show in Detroit. The concept cars sported, among other innovations, mobile Internet access. Ford Motor Co., he said, would put the Internet on wheels.

Ford launched Wingcast telematics, devices that would be installed in the company's vehicles and enable drivers and passengers to access the web. To this end the company formed an alliance with Qualcomm, Inc., a telecommunications company, and Yahoo!

Ford created a joint venture with General Motors Corp. and DaimlerChrysler to establish Covisint, a website that served as an electronic market for parts suppliers who could bid online on requests for proposals posted by the automakers. Although not announced this way, the automakers' hope was that suppliers would fiercely compete in an open bidding process and cut their prices dramatically, so the auto companies could enjoy cost cuts. This was the business-to-business (B2B) part of Nassers's grand plan.

The business-to-consumer (B2C) idea was bolder: Ford wanted to push vehicle sales to the web. Nasser wanted to bypass dealerships and retail the vehicles online directly to consumers. Consumers would go to the website, take a virtual test-drive, see images of a vehicle in all its available colors, order a vehicle, pay for it online, and then have it driven to their door. Ford would not only provide a great service but also save the dealer fees. The company called the site FordDirect.com. A special organizational unit, ConsumerConnect, was established to build the website and handle the direct sales. Today, many manufacturers such as Toyota, Chevrolet, and Honda have integrated the functionality of building a vehicle on their websites. What once was viewed as a failure changed the approach to selling vehicles on automakers' websites.

Hitting the Wall

Apparently, buyers were not as enthusiastic about having web access in their vehicles as Nasser predicted. In June 2001, Ford eliminated the Wingcast project. The B2B effort, Covisint, worked for a while, but not as expected. It was later sold to Compuware, a software development company. The B2C initiative failed.

The failure was not the result of faulty technology. There were web technologies that would support retail through the web. There is no reason why a car cannot be selected, paid for, and delivered (with the help of companies that specialize in such delivery from the manufacturer to the buyer) via the web (and in fact this model became popular several years later, with some changes). The company failed because it did not carefully consider state laws and its relationships with dealers.

Many state laws do not permit cutting an agent out of the sale. State franchising laws did not allow Ford to bypass its dealers. Also, since Ford would still rely on dealers to sell cars to people who do not have access to the Internet or who like to sit in a physical car and test-drive it, it could not cut the relationship all at once. Ford still needed the collaboration of the dealers, if it could overcome the legal hurdles, in order for direct sales to take off.

The Retreat

The circumstances convinced Ford to abandon its plan to sell directly to consumers. The ConsumerConnect unit was disbanded. FordDirect.com morphed into a site that allows consumers to build and price their own cars, compare vehicles, and search inventory—but working with Ford dealers rather than trying to bypass them. Like any car dealer, the site also offers used cars for sale, which is not what Ford originally wanted to do. The price tag of this failed experiment was reported to be a hefty portion of the $1 billion Ford spent on its Internet initiative under Nasser's leadership. While other automakers were making modest profits in the period from 2000 to 2001, Ford posted losses. Nasser was forced to leave the company.

Ford's management can find some solace in the continued operation of FordDirect.com. Although Nasser's grand plan did not materialize, the site is the origin point of tens of thousands of sales transactions per month. The site saves dealers marketing cost. A FordDirect sale costs dealers only $160 (Anonymous, 2011). Ford also says the site helps it predict sales. FordDirect continues to add new features to its system, such as DealerConnection for dealers (Anonymous, 2012a).

The Bleeding Edge

As you might often hear, huge rewards go to whomever first implements a new idea. Innovators might enjoy a strategic advantage until competitors discover the benefits of a new business idea or a new technology. However, taking such steps before competitors have tested a system involves great risk. In some cases, failure results from rushing implementation without adequately testing a market. But even with careful planning, pioneers sometimes get burned.

For example, several supermarket chains tried self-checkout stations in the mid-1990s. Consumers were expected to ring up their own purchases. By and large, investment in such devices failed at that time not because the technology was bad, but because many consumers either preferred the human touch, or because they did not want to learn how to correct mistakes when the devices did not pick up the price of an item or picked it up twice. Recently, barcode scanners at both the checkout and handheld scanners that allow shoppers to enter their purchases as they shop have been installed by several chains. Consumers are finding these more user friendly and less error prone, and their popularity is growing, as the technology has matured.

While it is tempting to take the lead on new technology, the risk of business failure is quite high. Several organizations have experienced disasters with new business ideas, which are only magnified when implementing new technology. When failure occurs because an organization tries to be on the technological leading edge, observers call it the **bleeding edge**. The pioneering organization "bleeds" cash on a technology that increases costs instead of profits. Adopting a new technology involves great risk: there is no experience from which to learn, no guarantees that the technology will work well, and no certainty that customers, employees, or business partners will welcome it.

Being on the bleeding edge often means that implementation costs are significantly higher than anticipated, that the new technology does not work as well as expected, or that the parties who were supposed to benefit—employees, customers, or suppliers—do not like using it. Thus, instead of leading, the organization ends up bleeding, that is, suffering from high cost and lost market share. For this reason, some organizations decide to let competitors test new technology before they adopt it. They risk losing the initial rewards they might reap, but if a competitor succeeds, they can quickly adopt the technology and even try to use it better than the pioneering organization.

Microsoft generally takes this approach. It seizes an existing idea, improves it, and promotes the result with its great marketing power. For instance, the company did not invent word processing, but Word is the most popular word-processing application today. The company did not invent the electronic spreadsheet, but Excel is the most popular spreadsheet application. And Microsoft was not the first to introduce a PC database management application, but it sells the highly popular Access. The company joined the Internet rush late, but it developed and gave away Internet Explorer, the market leader in web browsers. You might call this approach competing by emulating and improving, rather than competing by being on the leading edge.

Sometimes, companies wait quite a long time to ensure that a technology has matured before they start using it, even at the risk of diminishing their strategic position. Although data warehousing—the organization and summarization of huge amounts of transactional records for later analysis—has been around since the mid-1990s, The Home Depot, Inc., decided only in 2002 to build a data warehouse. Home Depot is the world's largest home improvement retailer. It started the project years after its main rival in the United States, Lowe's, had implemented a well-functioning data warehouse, which it used effectively for strategic decision making.

Summary

- Some ISs have become strategic tools as a result of strategic planning; others have evolved into strategic tools. To compete better, executives need to define strategic goals and determine how new or improved ISs can support these goals. Rather than waiting complacently until a problem occurs, businesses actively look for opportunities to improve their position with information systems.

- An IS that helps gain strategic advantage is called a strategic information system (SIS). To assure optimal utilization of IT for competitive advantage, executives must participate in generating ideas and champion new, innovative uses of information systems. In recent years, many of these ideas involved using the Internet.

- A company achieves strategic advantage by using strategy to maximize its strengths, resulting in a competitive advantage.

- Strategic advantage is often achieved by one or a combination of the following initiatives. Cost reduction enables a business to sell more units of its products or services while maintaining or increasing its profit margin. Raising barriers to potential entrants to the industry lets an organization maintain a sizable market share by developing systems that are prohibitively expensive for competitors to emulate. By establishing high switching costs, a business can make buying from competitors unattractive to clients. Developing totally new products and services can create an entirely new market for an organization, which can also enjoy the advantage of being a first mover for that product and market. And if the organization cannot create new products or services, it can still enjoy competitive advantage by differentiating its products so that customers view them as better than a competitor's products. Organizations also attain advantage by enhancing existing products or services. Many new services are the fruits of alliances between companies: each contributes its own expertise to package services that entice customers with an overall value greater than that offered by the separate services individually. Locking in clients or suppliers, that is, creating conditions that make dealing with competitors infeasible, is a powerful strategy to gain advantage.

- In the software industry, creating standards often creates strategic advantage. A standard is an application used by a significant share of the users. To this end, many companies go as far as giving software away. When the standard has been established, the company enjoys a large sales volume of compatible and add-on software.

- Reengineering is the process of redesigning a business process from scratch to save hundreds of percentage points in costs. Almost always, reengineering involves implementing new ISs.

- Strategic advantages from information systems are often short-lived, because competitors quickly emulate the systems for their own benefit. Therefore, looking for new opportunities must be an ongoing process. Companies can maintain the strategic advantage gained through an IS by continuously augmenting the services they provide.

- To maintain a strategic advantage, organizations must develop new features to keep the system on the leading edge. But they must be mindful of the bleeding edge, the undesirable results (such as huge ongoing costs and loss of customers) of being the first to use new technology with the hope of establishing a competitive advantage. Early adopters find themselves on the bleeding edge when the new technology is not yet fully reliable or when customers are uncomfortable with it.

KIMBALL'S REVISITED

Tyler's perspective was crucial in helping his parents become aware of the strategic and operational challenges of their business. He knows if he could design and implement efficient changes to operations as well as some information technology, the business would be even more successful. Additionally, these changes would build a solid business foundation to objectively analyze the expansion decision.

What Is Your Advice?

1. Kimball's has several challenges to resolve in its operations to improve its current business and prepare for a potential expansion. What changes has Kimball's implemented to positively impact their business? Can you identify the strategic initiatives that Kimball's can implement? What could Tyler recommend to move the business forward? Be sure to consider the following ways of gaining a competitive advantage:

   - Reduce costs
   - Raise barriers to entrants
   - Establish high switching costs
   - Create new products and services
   - Differentiate products and services

   - Enhance products or services
   - Establish alliances
   - Lock in suppliers or buyers

2. Review the advice of the professional advisors, Tom and Terri. Do you believe they have some merit? What would you recommend to move forward to resolve their perspective of the problem(s)? What type of information technology could be implemented?

New Perspectives

1. Considering the POS system, what information do the owners need to manage and lead the restaurant? What data can help Liz and Michael monitor their operations to ensure positive results or take corrective action?

2. Michael and Liz operated the business without the use of data from their operations. The oversight and management of their operations associated with inventory and labor appear to have been overlooked. How do these categories of expenses affect the profitability of the restaurant? How can an information system assist with the management of these functional areas?

Key Terms

affiliate program, 46

alliance, 45

bleeding edge, 58

competitive advantage, 37

create a new and unique product or service, 41

create a standard, 47

critical mass, 42

differentiation, 44

enhance existing products or services, 44

first mover, 42

late mover, 54

lock in clients or suppliers, 47

raise barriers to entrants, 40

reduce costs, 39

reengineering, 50

strategic advantage, 37

strategic information system (SIS), 37

switching costs, 41

1. In what respect does business strategy resemble military strategy?

2. Refer to Chapter 1's discussion of different types of information systems. Which types of ISs can gain strategic advantage and which cannot? Why?

3. What should an information system achieve for an organization in order to be considered a strategic information system? How do strategic information systems compare with operational information systems?

4. What strategic goal can an IS attain that does not involve wresting market share from competitors? Provide some business examples.

5. What conditions must exist in an organization planning an SIS?

6. Sometimes it is difficult to convince top management to commit funds to develop and implement an SIS. Why?

7. An SIS often offers a corporation short-lived advantages. How so?

8. What is reengineering? Why is reengineering often mentioned along with IT?

9. Why have most reengineering projects failed? What has eventually affected reengineering in some companies?

10. Software developers have made great efforts to "create a standard." What does creating a standard mean in the software industry, and why are companies doing it?

11. What should an organization do to sustain the strategic benefits of an IS?

12. Adobe encourages PC users to download its Acrobat Reader and Flash Player free of charge. How does this eventually help Adobe strategically? If they give the application away, how does their generosity help them make money?

13. Referring to the list of strategic moves (see Figure 2.2), classify the initiatives of JetBlue.

14. What were the reasons for the failure of the original purpose of FordDirect.com? Who eventually gained from the system and what were the gains?

15. The executives of well-established airlines are not less smart than those at JetBlue, and yet, their larger airlines have not done what JetBlue has done. Why?

16. What does the term "first mover" mean?

17. Can a *late mover* have any strategic advantage with IT? What is the risk that a late mover takes?

18. What does the term "bleeding edge" mean?

19. Can an off-the-shelf computer program be used as an SIS? Why or why not?

20. The organizations that eventually use the systems, not consulting firms that try to help organizations, develop more successful SISs. What might be the reasons for this?

21. You head a small company. You have an idea for software that can give your company an advantage over competitors. Since you do not have a staff that can develop and implement the software, you decide to approach a software company. Other than the company's technical offerings, what additional company aspects are desirable?

22. Some argue that an SIS gives a company an unfair advantage and might even cause the demise of smaller, weaker companies that cannot afford to build similar systems. Is this good or bad for customers? Explain your opinion.

23. Why is the web the arena of so much competition today?

24. Information systems play a major role in almost every reengineering project. Why?

25. Accounting and payroll ISs have never become SISs. Why? What other types of ISs are unlikely to ever provide strategic advantage for their owners?

26. Give two examples of products or services whose delivery time could be cut from days to minutes with the aid of IT.

27. What is the role of ISs in alliances such as airlines and credit-card issuers? Why would such alliances be practically infeasible without IT?

28. JetBlue used new software that had not been tested by other companies. If you were a CIO, would you use software that is still in beta (untested with live data) in your organization?

29. You are an executive for a large organization that provides services to state and federal agencies. A software development firm approached you with an offer to implement new software that might give your organization a strategic advantage by reducing the service delivery cycle by several days. What would you do to avoid putting your organization on the "bleeding edge" while still considering the new software?

30. When a software developer creates a *de facto* standard (i.e., not the official standard, but something so widely used that it becomes a standard), it has monopolistic power. Should governments intervene to prevent this practice? Explain your opinion.

31. Suppose you are a venture capitalist considering a proposal to invest millions of dollars in a new online business. What questions would you ask the enthusiastic young people who have approached you for funds?

32. What are the potential risks of a single organization controlling much of the market for essential software?

33. Can you think of any other first movers/technologies that might replace satellite radio?

Applying Concepts

34. Although Apple Computer Inc. introduced a personal computer and software that was superior to those produced by IBM and other companies, it failed to capture the lion's share of the PC market. However, it did capture a large share of several markets: the digital music player, cell phone, and tablet. Complete some research. What was the difference in the company's approach to the two types of products? What is your conclusion regarding the proper approach when developing a new digital product?

35. Prepare a brief essay that includes an example of each of the following strategic moves: raising barriers to entrants (*Hint*: intellectual property), establishing high switching costs, creating a new product or service (*Hint*: the web), and establishing alliances. The examples do not necessarily have to involve IT. Do not use examples already presented in the text. You may use examples from actual events or your own suggestions, but the examples must be practical.

36. A publishing company wants to publish electronic books that can be downloaded and read on both tablets and electronic readers. At least two firms have developed e-book technologies that the publisher can adopt. The publisher hires you as a strategic consultant. Write a report explaining the strategic moves you suggest. What would you advise the company to do: try to develop its own e-book reader or purchase a license for existing technology? Who should be the initial target audience for the product? What should be the company's major goal in the first two or three years: profit, market share, user base, technological improvement, or perhaps having the largest sales force in this industry? Should the company give anything away? Prepare a detailed report enumerating and explaining your suggestions.

37. You are a software-marketing expert. A new software development firm has hired you to advise it on pricing and marketing strategies of its new application. After some research, you conclude that the firm can be successful either by selling at a high unit price (in which case, probably only businesses would purchase licenses to use the application), or at a very low price, which would be attractive to many individuals and companies. You estimate that by the end of the sixth year of the marketing effort competing software will be offered, which will bring the number of units sold to zero. For alternative A, the price would be $350 per license, and you expect 600 adopters in the first year and an annual growth of adopters of 50 percent. For alternative B, the price would be $25, and you expect 25,000 adopters in the first year and an annual growth of adopters of 5 percent. Use a spreadsheet application to calculate revenue, and tell the firm which strategy is expected to bring in greater revenue. Enter the prices and number of first-year adopters for each alternative only once, each in a single cell, and use absolute referencing to those cells.

Hands-On Activities

38. Use PowerPoint or other presentation software to present the ideas you generated in Question 34 or 35 of "Applying Concepts." Use the program's features to make a convincing and visually pleasing presentation.

39. Research business journals and magazines such as the *Wall Street Journal, BusinessWeek, Forbes,* or *Fortune.* Find a story on a business's strategic use of data, information, or information systems. Be aware that the writer may not have specifically identified the system as strategic in nature. Gain an understanding of the new system's goals and determine whether it is strategic. Prepare a report explaining the opportunity seized. Did the organization create a new product or service, improve one, or manage to capture a

significantly greater market share of an existing product or service? How did the data, information, or information system play a major role in the strategic move?

40. Consider the information provided in the "Ethical & Societal Issues" box of this chapter. Prepare extensive lists of pros and cons. The pros should aim to convince an audience why Microsoft, or a similar company, should be left alone to practice its business maneuvers. The cons should aim to convince an audience why governments should intervene in how corporations such as Microsoft behave and explain what such interventions are meant to accomplish. How has the global market for software changed the legal issues?

Team Activities

41. Brainstorm with your team to answer the question: "Which information technology over the past two years has epitomized a unique product or service that was 'ahead of the curve' for a significant amount of time?" This might be a physical product using IT or an online service that was, or still is, unique. List the reasons each of the team members liked this product or service.

42. Some information technologies had a certain original purpose but were creatively used to serve additional purposes. For example, companies have used caller ID to retrieve customer records as soon as a customer telephones. This saves labor and increases service quality. You and your teammates are consultants who work with many businesses. Offering your clients original ideas will increase your success. Select an information technology or an IT feature that can be leveraged in ways not originally conceived. How can your

clients (in manufacturing, service, or any other business sector) use this feature to gain strategic advantage? Prepare a rationale.

43. Sirius and XM Radio had the first mover advantage in the satellite radio industry. They had radio stations dedicated to celebrities, music stars, and most major sports including the NFL, NHL, and MLB. By 2006, they had close to 14 million users. They merged in 2008 to cut operating costs. The barriers to entry in the Internet radio industry are relatively low because it is simple for a webcaster to pay royalties for a song and broadcast it. iPods, cell phones, and Internet radio are all competing for time in the customers' ear. Do you think the Sirius-XM merger was a business move to eliminate competition between each other and defend against other upcoming forms of radio? What are some other reasons to explain their merger? Provide an analysis and rationale for your position.

Finish Line Finishes First

Finish Line is a clothes and shoe retailer with over 640 locations in malls across the United States. In late 2012, Finish Line was about to unleash its new in-store POS technology to engage more shoppers. Although Finish Line was initially criticized for the timing of the roll-out, director of store applications and delivery, Rob Baugh, knew from the start it was going to be a home-run. From previous research conducted by the National Retail Federation, Finish Line knew an astounding 95 percent of retail purchases were still occurring in physical stores. Thus, an opportunity awaited retailers that could engage more customers to make more in-store purchases. Baugh knew the goal of the POS system was to provide service to the customer, when the customer needed it.

Before Finish Line could make any technological improvements, it required network upgrades and additional wireless access points. Mobile receipt printers were placed throughout stores to aid sales associates performing mobile POS transactions. To leverage the opportunity at hand, Finish Line implemented a mobile POS system to aid and engage shoppers through their entire in-store shopping experience. To enable mobile payments, it upgraded its POS system to a platform from MICROS Systems and implemented a customer engagement solution from VeriFone. Their new electronic payment options included magnetic stripe and PIN-based debit/credit cards, chip-enabled smartcards, and mobile payments. The multimedia processors were high-speed, color, and supported full-motion video for additional shopper appeal. iPod Touch devices used Micros' MyStore application and VerFone's PAYware Mobile Enterprise software, which supported all device transaction functionality.

High confidence in the success of the new system led to a 36-store, 3-month pilot program from May to August. Each store featured five mobile devices that could process a variety of business activities. Customers appreciated using the mobile POS units to interact with sales associates. The overall results of the pilot were very positive and one month later, the positive results led to a companywide roll-out, right before the crucial holiday season. Finish Line issued five devices per store and added barcode scanners to allow users to conduct price checking and inventory management processes. Transactions completed on the mobile units are sent through the retailer's centralized system to consolidate its sales and inventory data.

Finish Line's new POS system and mobile payments acceptance has changed its in-store shopping experience. Finish Line did its research and pursued an opportunity to change in-store consumers' shopping experience and put the customer first.

Source: Amato-McCoy, D. M. (2012). Perfect Timing. Chain Store Age, 88(7), 28–28.

Thinking About the Case

1. Why do retailers want to provide customers with more product/service information when they come into a retail store?
2. How does Finish Line put the customer first?
3. Why is it important to monitor the results of newly implemented technology, even when it is previously deemed successful?
4. Would you be more inclined to shop at Finish Line or one of their competitors, and why?

Realizing the Goal Helps Reach Results

Businesses aiming to expand, gain a larger market share, or compete with competitors can accomplish these goals through reducing costs, raising barriers to market entrants, or creating new products or services. Additionally, each of these goals can be accomplished through the use of innovative technologies. When companies explore uses for innovative technologies with a specified goal in mind, they can experience tremendous results in their attempts in shaping consumer behavior, changing their shopping experience, or even altering the backhouse operations. Other times, when technology reaches maturity, it has other unforeseen uses. In both of the following short case examples, the exhibited company uses technological innovations to either differentiate itself in the market place, attract new customers, lock in customers, offer a new product or service, or some combination of the previous.

Peapod is an online grocery ordering service provider whose goal was to use branding as a way to promote an innovative product-service combination. Peapod placed virtual walls in commuter rail stations and other public locations that looked like products on a grocer's shelves. These virtual walls offered branding and advertising which attracted customers and served as a reminder of Peapod's innovative service which is online grocery ordering and delivery. Shoppers can use the Peapod app on their smartphone to order groceries and have them delivered the next day. Although their technology is changing the way consumers approach grocery shopping, the added conveniences soothe the transition. The goal is to allow customers to see the branding, use the app, and have groceries delivered the next day; all while waiting for a train home. The ultra-modern shopping experience is just another way retailers are altering consumers' expectations of how shopping should be conducted.

This idea has been expanded further by other companies such as Sears Holdings Corp. Sears and Kmart used QR code-driven "toy walls" to produce a wall-driven shopping experience. Toy walls were featured in high-traffic locations such as malls, airports, and movie theatre lobbies. This shopping approach is cost efficient because the virtual walls do not require any floor space. Shoppers then could simply scan the wall's QR code to order toys while on the run.

One of Amazon's keys to financial success is not the sales revenue collected by their e-reader, the Kindle, but the sales that the Kindle provokes subsequently. Digital sales of books, movies, and TV shows are where Amazon expands its revenue sources. To encourage more Kindle sales to hesitant buyers, Amazon opened a physical store location in Seattle, Washington so potential customers could come in and tryout a Kindle before purchasing one. The idea of opening a brick-and-mortar location will increase Kindle sales which would then create more demand for digital content and additional sales for Amazon. After a customer has purchased the Kindle, the digital sales expand and the customer is locked in for future sales.

The innovative technologies aforementioned had incredible results, primarily because they were implemented with a specified goal in mind. Peapod is utilizing game-changing virtual walls to turn passersby into shoppers and Amazon is locking in future customers by easing their initial purchase; the most important one. There are a number of different ways to attract new customers, lock in customers, and produce differentiation with a new product/service combination when utilizing innovative technologies. In doing so, the most important key to success is to realize a destination early, plan the course of action, and adjust for adversities.

Source: Anonymous. (2012). What is Game-Changing Innovation? Chain Store Age, 88(5), 2–4A, 5A.

Thinking About the Case

1. What benefits are provided to the shopper by Peapod's services? How does their innovative product/service combination provide additional benefits beyond the average grocery store with delivery service?

2. "Toy walls" could be found in malls, airports, and movie theater lobbies during the 2011 holiday season. Why were they featured in these locations and what additional locations would be ideal? Explain why.

References

Anonymous. (2011). FordDirect Dealer News. Retrieved May 22, 2013, from http://forddirect.xpsitehosting.com/FD1106/

Anonymous. (2012a, 2012-02-09). FordDirect Launches DealerConnection Elite Service for Dealers. *Travel & Leisure Close-Up*.

Anonymous. (2012b). The 2012 Gartner CIO Agenda Report (pp. 10). Stamford, CT.

Anonymous. (2012c). Why Operations Take the Tablets. *Flight Evening News* (3), 3–3.

Anonymous. (2013a). App will aid advance towards the paperless cockpit. *Flight International*, 183, 22–22.

Anonymous. (2013b). JetBlue Announces 2012 Annual Profit.

Anonymous. (2013c). Number of active users at Facebook over the years. Retrieved May 22, 2013, from http://news.yahoo.com/number-active-users-facebook-over-230449748.html

Anonymous. (2013d). Twitter Statistics. Retrieved May 22, 2013, from www.statisticbrain.com/twitter-statistics/

Anonymous. (2013f, 2013-05-15). United Airlines; United Airlines Introduces 200th Aircraft With Live Television. *Entertainment Newsweekly*, 112.

Foo, Y. C. (2013, Mar 07). EU slaps $731 million penalty on Microsoft, *Chicago Tribune*, p. 1.

Goldberg, A. (2011). US to end antitrust oversight of Microsoft, *McClatchy-Tribune Business News*.

Hazel, B., Stalnaker, T., & Taylor, A. (2012). Airline Economic Analysis (p. 41). New York, NY.

Waurzyniak, P. (2012). PLM Systems Further Extend Reach to the Shop Floor. *Manufacturing Engineering*, 149(5), 67–70, 72–75.

Winkler, R. (2012). Facebook, Twitter: Space Invaders, *Wall Street Journal*, p. B.16.

three

BUSINESS FUNCTIONS AND SUPPLY CHAINS

Learning Objectives

In an economy that produces and consumes so much information, professionals must know how to use information systems in virtually every business activity. Managers must have an overall understanding of all elements of a system, so that they know what options are available to control quality, costs, and resources. Modern information systems encompass entire business cycles, often called supply chains.

When you finish this chapter, you will be able to:

- Identify various business functions and the role of ISs in these functions.

- Explain how ISs in the basic business functions relate to each other.

- Articulate what supply chains are and how information technology supports management of supply chains.

- Enumerate the purposes of customer relationship management systems.

- Explain enterprise resource planning systems.

KIMBALL'S RESTAURANT: The New Location

Liz and Michael carefully reviewed the marketing, financial, and operational forecasts for expanding their business to the new lakeside location and closing the current location. They felt that their forecasts were reasonable. In January, they agreed to leasing terms with Shaun to move the restaurant into the former campground location. They planned to take several months to complete the design and renovations and prepare for opening "Kimball's by the Lakeside" in late May.

Tyler had convinced his parents to take their advisors' advice and focus on operating their business more profitably before the move. This focus would also benefit them in their expansion, because they would need additional management to create efficiency in operations and build a more effective strategy for the restaurant. The increased number of customers at the new location would also require more employees, food purchases, and coordination with suppliers. If the backhouse operations were not managed and controlled properly, the expansion could create more problems than it solved. If they can't operate more efficiently in the new location, their profits could evaporate, even with the additional clientele.

Currently, Kimball's marketing activities were limited to small advertisements in a local newspaper. Although they had a solid clientele at the current location, it would be important to extend their reach to the nearest metropolitan city, about 12 miles away. Tyler hoped to use the four months before opening the new location to develop new marketing and promotions to build their customer base.

Planning the Transition: Operations and Marketing

Liz, Michael, and Tyler met to discuss the transition plan. Tyler had several thoughts about the operational changes that needed to be implemented. The company that sold Kimball's the point-of-sale software used by the servers had additional software available, although additional research needed to be completed. He wondered, "If reliable software was available, when would be the right time to install and use the new system?"

Since the expansion decision was behind them, he wondered if additional software to help the business could be installed before the move. Using this approach, the employees and management could use the system in the current location and gain more experience with it. Liz asked, "If we installed the software now, wouldn't that be twice as much work to then reinstall it in the new location?" Tyler responded that the current hardware and software would need to be shut down, packed, transported, and installed in the new location anyway. The purchase of any new software would be "carried over" to the new location without any additional expense.

Michael and Liz thought about the alternatives that Tyler presented. Liz recalled the planning process for their current location, and how issues arose at the start of the business, even with their careful planning. Experience told her that similar issues could come up at the new location. Michael said, "Maybe it's not a bad idea to install the new software now. We can train people in a familiar and established operation for a month or two." Liz believed that the new location might need more hardware based on the larger dining and kitchen area. They all agreed that if a suitable system to help with the backhouse operations could be installed in their current location, it should be purchased and implemented.

Michael and Tyler then focused their attention on marketing. They agreed that they needed to expand their clientele to include people in the nearby metropolitan area. They also wanted to keep and increase their local clientele and to continue hosting "after work" customers from local businesses. The additional seating at the new location could be promoted for breakfast, lunch, and dinner meetings for businesses as well. Michael, Liz, and Tyler agreed that it was important for them to retain Kimball's "local" feel while promoting the new location to a wider audience.

Effectiveness and Efficiency

In customer service departments, the ringing tone from telephones was a common occurrence. Major business organizations would receive millions of calls from customers to ask a variety of questions on their accounts. Telephones at the offices of Capital One Financial Corp., a leading credit-card issuer and a Fortune 500 company, probably do not ring as often as they did two or three decades ago. Cardholders who once called to ask about their balance or to ensure that the company received their recent payment now have other alternatives such as smartphones, websites, or directly entering their account information into an automated phone service.

If you do connect with a customer service agent, technology is still involved in your call. Information technology uses the caller's telephone number to search the company's huge databases. Inferring from previous calls and numerous recorded credit-card transactions of the caller, the computers may predict the reason for calling. Based on the assumed reason, the computers channel the call to an employee who can best handle the situation. Important information about the caller is brought up on the employee's computer monitor without having to ask or enter the caller's account number. Although callers usually do not contact the company to make purchases, the computer also brings up information about what the caller might want to purchase. As soon as the customer service representative provides the caller with satisfactory answers, he or she also offers the cardholder special sales. Many callers do indeed purchase the offered merchandise. All of these steps—accepting the call, reviewing and analyzing the data, routing the call, and recommending merchandise—take the computers a mere tenth of a second. Because of Capital One's effective operations and efficient response, they were recognized by J.D. Power and Associates for their outstanding customer service in 2012.

It is often said that the use of information technology makes our work more effective, more efficient, or both. What do these terms mean? **Effectiveness** defines the degree to which a goal is achieved. Thus, a system is more or less effective depending on (1) how much of a particular goal it achieves, and (2) the degree to which it achieves better outcomes than other systems do.

Efficiency is determined by the relationship between resources expended and the benefits gained in achieving a goal. Expressed mathematically,

$$\text{Efficiency} = \frac{\text{Benefits}}{\text{Costs}}$$

One system is more efficient than another if its operating costs are lower for the same or better quality product, or if the product's quality is greater for the same or lower costs. The term "productivity" is commonly used as a synonym for efficiency. However, **productivity** specifically refers to the efficiency of *human* resources. Productivity improves when fewer workers are required to produce the same amount of output, or, alternatively, when the same number of workers produces a greater amount of output. This is why IT professionals often speak of "productivity tools," which are software applications that help workers produce more in less time. The closer the result of an effort is to the ultimate goal, the more effective the effort. The fewer resources spent on achieving a goal, the more efficient the effort.

Suppose your goal is to design a new car with fuel economy of 60 miles per gallon. If you manage to build it, then you produce the product effectively. If the car does not meet the requirement, your effort is ineffective. If your competitor makes a car with the same features and performance, but uses fewer people and resources, then your competitor is not only as effective as you but also more efficient. ISs contribute to both the effectiveness and efficiency of businesses, especially when serving specific business functions, such as accounting, finance, and engineering, and when used to help companies achieve their goals more quickly by facilitating collaborative work.

One way to look at business functions and their supporting systems is to follow typical business cycles, which often begin with marketing and sales activities (see Figure 3.1). Serving customers better and faster, as well as learning more about their experiences and preferences, is facilitated by **customer relationship management (CRM)** systems. When customers place orders, the orders are executed in the supply chain. Often, information about the customer is collected as orders are taken. This information may be useful down the road. Customer relationship management continues after delivery of the ordered goods in the forms of customer service and more marketing. When an organization enjoys the support of CRM and supply chain management (SCM) systems, it can plan its resources well. Combined, these systems are often referred to as enterprise resource planning (ERP) systems.

FIGURE 3.1

Business activities consist of customer relationship management, supply chain management, and supporting functions

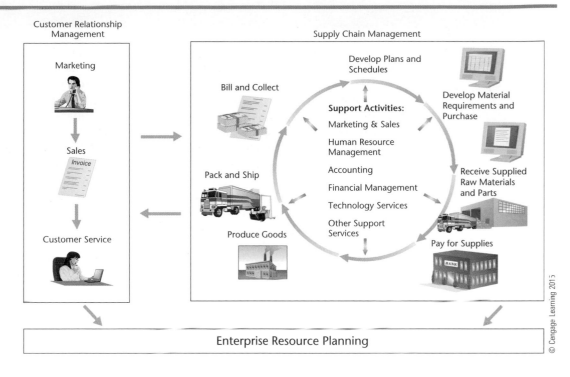

Enterprise Resource Planning

© Cengage Learning 2015

Figure 3.2 shows some of the most common business activities and their interdependence. For example, cost accounting systems are linked to payroll, benefits, and purchasing systems to accumulate the cost of products manufactured by a company; and information from purchasing systems flows to both cost accounting and financial reporting systems. The following discussion addresses the role of information systems, one business function at a time.

FIGURE 3.2

Information systems in different business functions are interdependent

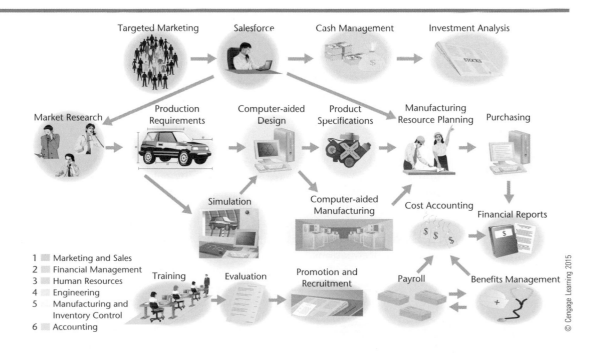

1 ▢ Marketing and Sales
2 ▢ Financial Management
3 ▢ Human Resources
4 ▢ Engineering
5 ▢ Manufacturing and Inventory Control
6 ▢ Accounting

© Cengage Learning 2015

The purpose of accounting is to track every financial transaction within a company—from a few cents expenditure to a multimillion-dollar purchase, from salaries and benefits to the sale of every item. Without tracking the costs of labor, materials, and purchased services using a cost-accounting system, a company might discover too late that it sells products below what it costs to make them. Without a system of accounts receivable, managers might not know who owes the company how much money and when it is due. Without an accounts payable system, they cannot know how much money the company owes suppliers and when payments are due. Without a system that records and helps plan cash flow, managers cannot keep enough cash in the bank to make payments on schedule. At the year's end, the company cannot present a picture of its financial situation—called a balance sheet—and a profit-and-loss report, unless it maintains a general ledger to record every transaction with a financial impact. Accounting systems are required by law and for proper management. General ledger, accounts receivable, accounts payable, and cash-flow books conveniently lend themselves to computerization and can easily generate balance sheets and profit-and-loss statements from records (see Figure 3.3). The word "books" in this reference is now a relic of former times. Accounting ISs are, of course, fully electronic.

FIGURE 3.3

Accounting information systems include features that reflect up-to-date performance of the organization in financial terms

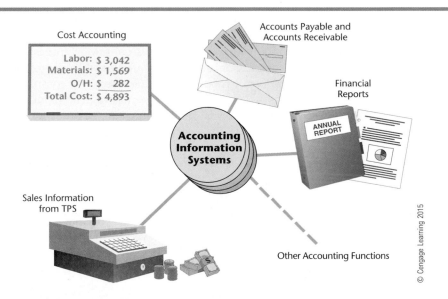

Typically, accounting ISs receive records of routine business transactions—such as the purchase of raw materials or services, or the sale of manufactured goods—from transaction processing systems (TPSs), which include point-of-sale (POS) machines. Such a system automatically routes every purchase of raw materials or services to the accounts payable system, which uses it to produce checks or transfer funds to a vendor's bank account. Whenever a sale is recorded, the transaction is routed to the accounts receivable system (which generates invoices) and other destinations. Totals of accounts receivable and accounts payable can be automatically transferred to a balance sheet. Data from the general ledger can be automatically compiled to generate a cash-flow report or a profit-and-loss report for the past month, quarter, or year. Accounting ISs can generate any of these reports on demand, as well as at scheduled times.

Today's professionals are expected to be knowledgeable not only in their specific line of work but also in other areas. And since practically every business process involves information technology, new hires are expected to know, or quickly learn, how to use the proper ISs in their respective positions. Many employers look for generalists rather than specialists and focus on the techno-manager, a manager well-versed in information technology as it relates to the entire supply chain.

Because many ISs serve multiple functions and interface with other systems, it is extremely important for a professional to be familiar with the way ISs facilitate work in areas outside his or her expertise. If you work for a commercial organization, you are bound to be part of a supply chain or work for a unit that supports a supply chain. Knowledge of systems in different business areas helps you cooperate with your peers and coordinate efforts that cross departmental boundaries. Because professionals often have opportunities to be promoted to positions in other disciplines, the more you know, the better your chances of being "cross-promoted."

When a company develops and manufactures a new product that has never been available on the market, how can it determine a price that covers costs and generates a decent profit? It must maintain a system that tracks the costs of labor, materials, consulting fees, and every other expense related to the product's development and manufacture. Cost-accounting systems, used to accumulate data about costs involved in producing specific products, make excellent use of IT to compile pricing data. ISs also help allocate costs to specific work orders. A **work order** is an authorization to perform work for a specific purpose, such as constructing a part of an airplane. When interfaced with payroll and purchasing ISs, a cost-accounting system automatically captures records of every penny spent (and originally recorded in the payroll and purchasing systems) and routes expenses to the appropriate work order. Because work orders are associated with specific products and services, the company now knows how much each product or service costs, or how much making a part of a final product costs. This can help the company in future pricing of products or services.

Accounting ISs are also used extensively for managerial purposes, assisting in organizing quarterly and annual budgets for departments, divisions, and entire corporations. The same systems help managers control their budgets by tracking income and expense in real time and comparing them with the amounts predicted in the budget. Budget applications are designed with proper controls, so that the system does not allow spending funds for a specific purpose beyond the amount that was budgeted.

Finance

A firm's health is often measured by its finances, and ISs can significantly improve financial management (see Figure 3.4). The goal of financial managers, including controllers and treasurers, is to manage an organization's money as efficiently as possible. They achieve this goal by (1) collecting payables as soon as possible, (2) making payments at the latest time allowed by contract or law, (3) ensuring that sufficient funds are available for day-to-day operations, and (4) taking advantage of opportunities to accrue the highest yield on funds not used for current activities. These goals can be best met by careful cash management and investment analysis.

FIGURE 3.4

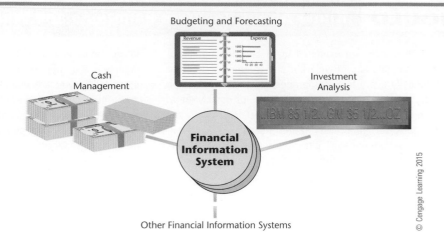

Cash Management

Financial information systems help managers track a company's finances. These systems record every payment and cash receipt to reflect cash movement, employ budgeting software to track plans for company finances, and include capital investment systems to manage investments, thus balancing the need to accrue interest on idle money against the need to have cash available. The information on expected cash receipts comes from sales contracts, and the information on cash outlays comes from purchasing contracts as well as payroll and benefits schedules. Systems that deal specifically with cash are often called **cash management systems (CMSs)**. One common use for a CMS is to execute cash transactions in which financial institutions transfer huge amounts of money using **electronic funds transfer (EFT)**. EFT is the electronic transfer of cash from an account in one bank to an account in another bank. More than 80 percent of all payments of the U.S. government are made using EFT systems.

Investment Analysis and Service

Every investor's goal is to buy an asset and later sell it for more than it cost. When investing in securities, such as stocks and bonds, it is important to know the prices of securities in real time, that is, *right now*. The ability of financial ISs to record millions of securities prices and their changes over long time periods, coupled with the ability to manipulate numbers using software, puts powerful analysis tools in investment managers' hands. Within seconds, an investment analyst can use a financial IS to chart prices of a specific stock or bond over a given period, and then build or use preprogrammed models to estimate what might happen to securities prices in the future.

Even the smallest investment firm can provide clients with an inexpensive online service for buying and selling securities, providing on-demand statements listing the stocks they own (called a portfolio), periodic yield, and the portfolio's current value. Clients serve themselves through the websites of brokerage firms to place, buy, and sell orders. Execution of orders takes only a few seconds.

Nearly instantaneously, ISs provide subscriber brokers and their clients with financial news, stock prices, commodity prices, and currency exchange rates from multiple locations across the world. Consider what happens when a foreign currency's exchange rate fluctuates a fraction of a percent. A brokerage house can make a profit of several thousand dollars within two minutes of buying and selling several million dollars' worth of the foreign currency.

Financial managers need to consider many factors before they invest in a security. Some of the most important factors to consider are (1) risk, measured as the variability (degree of change) of the security's past yield; (2) expected return; and (3) liquidity, a measure of how fast an investment can be turned into cash. Special programs help calculate these factors and present the results either in tables or graphs to allow timely decision making.

Engineering

The time between generating an idea for a product and completing a prototype that can be mass-manufactured is known as engineering lead time, or **time to market**. As discussed in Chapter 2, business organizations offering a new product or service can create a first-mover advantage. This competitive advantage requires a rapid, efficient product design and development strategy. Collaterally, it is imperative to ensure products are more "leading edge" than "bleeding edge" by integrating quality in a rapid development environment.

Engineering includes **brainstorming** (the process of a group of colleagues meeting and working collaboratively to generate creative solutions and new ideas), developing a concept, creating mock-ups, building prototypes, testing, and other activities that require investments of time, labor, and money. Minimizing lead time is key to maintaining a competitive edge: it leaves competitors insufficient time to introduce their own products first. ISs can contribute significantly to this effort. Over the past two decades, automakers have used engineering and other ISs to reduce the time from product concept to market from 7 years to 18 months.

IT's greatest contribution to engineering is in the area of **computer-aided design (CAD)** and **rapid prototyping** (creating one-of-a-kind products to test design in three dimensions). Engineers can use computers to modify designs quickly and store drawings electronically. With collaborative software, they perform much of this process over the Internet: engineers can conduct remote conferences while viewing and developing plans and drawings together. The electronic drawings are then available to make rapid prototypes.

Rapid prototyping allows a model of a product to be produced within hours, rather than days or weeks. The model required is often a mock-up to show only the physical look and dimensions of a product, without the electronics or other components that are part of the full product. First, an image of the object is created on a computer. The computer is connected to a special machine that creates a physical, three-dimensional model by laying down hundreds or thousands of thin layers of liquid plastic or special resin. The model can be examined by engineers and marketing managers in the organization, or shown to clients.

When the prototypes are satisfactory, the electronic drawings and material specifications can be transferred from the CAD systems to **computer-aided manufacturing (CAM)** systems. CAM systems process the data to instruct machines, including robots, how to manufacture the parts and assemble the product (see Figure 3.5).

FIGURE 3.5

Engineering information systems assist engineers in designing new products and simulating how they operate

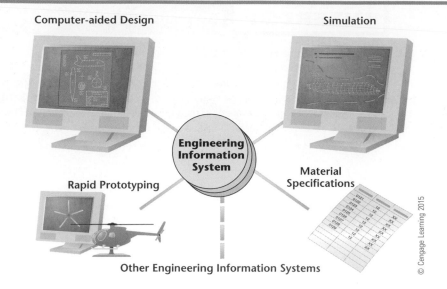

Computer-aided Design

Simulation

Engineering Information System

Rapid Prototyping

Material Specifications

Other Engineering Information Systems

© Cengage Learning 2015

As we mentioned, automakers needed years to turn a concept into actual vehicles rolling out for sale. Now, thanks to CAD, CAM, rapid prototyping, and collaborative engineering software, the lead time has been reduced to months. The digital design of vehicles saves not only time but also the cost of cars crashed in tests; many of the tests can be performed with sophisticated software rather than with real cars. Similar benefits have been accomplished in aerospace and many other engineering and manufacturing industries. The illustration below shows the use of SolidWorks CAD software to design a blender.

Computer-aided design systems significantly shorten the time necessary to produce drawings and complete the design for new products

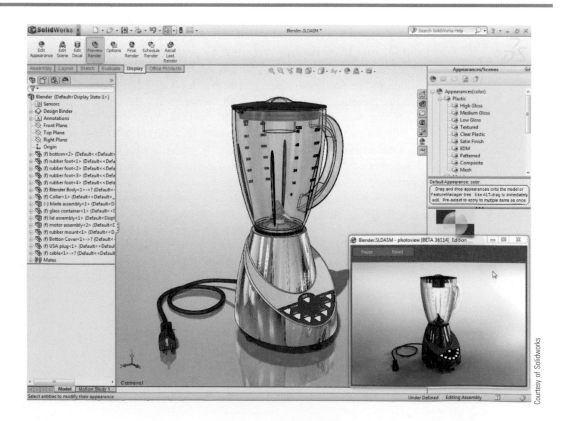

Courtesy of Solidworks

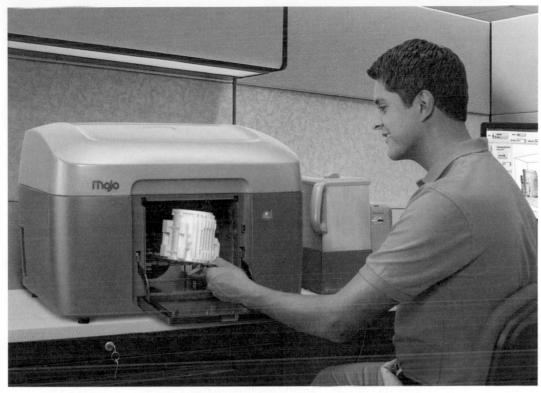

Rapid prototyping shortens time to market; with 3-D printers like this one, engineers can quickly create plastic models of parts

Supply Chain Management

In its fundamental form, a **supply chain** consists of three major phases: procuring raw materials, processing the materials into intermediate and finished goods, and delivering the goods to customers. Processing raw materials into goods is manufacturing. **Supply chain management (SCM)** consists of monitoring, controlling, and facilitating supply chains, as depicted in the right side of Figure 3.1. Supply chain management (SCM) systems are information technologies that support SCM. SCM systems have been instrumental in reducing manufacturing costs, including the costs of managing resources and controlling inventory (see Figure 3.6). In retail, the manufacturing phase does not exist, so the term "supply chain" refers only to the purchasing of finished goods and the delivery to customers of those goods. In the service industries the term "manufacturing" is practically meaningless, because no raw materials are purchased and processed.

FIGURE **3.6**

Manufacturing and inventory control information systems help reduce cycle times and the cost of maintaining inventory

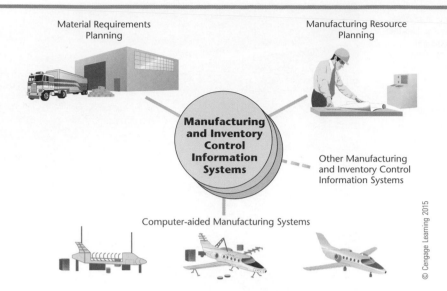

Material Requirements Planning

Manufacturing Resource Planning

Manufacturing and Inventory Control Information Systems

Other Manufacturing and Inventory Control Information Systems

Computer-aided Manufacturing Systems

© Cengage Learning 2015

As is clear from the previous discussion, much of the data required for manufacturing processes can flow directly from CAD systems to CAM systems as well as to inventory control systems and other systems that support planning and execution of manufacturing. While CAM systems participate in physical activities such as cutting and welding, other information systems help to plan and monitor manufacturing.

Information technology helps in the following manufacturing activities:

- Scheduling plant activities while optimizing the combined use of all resources—machines, personnel, tooling, and raw and interim materials.
- Planning material requirements based on current and forecasted demand.
- Reallocating materials rapidly from one order to another to satisfy due dates.
- Letting users manage inventories in real time, taking into consideration demand and the responsiveness of all work centers.
- Grouping work orders by characteristics of items ordered, such as color and width of products.
- Considering the qualifications of each resource (such as qualified labor, set-up crews, and specialized tools) to accomplish its task. For instance, people and raw materials can be moved from one assembly line to another to respond to machine breakdown or customer emergency, and design changes can be implemented quickly to respond to changes in customer wishes.

Material Requirements Planning and Purchasing

MRP systems help reduce inventory costs while ensuring availability of product to fulfill customer demand

© Vasily Smirnov/Shutterstock.com

One area of manufacturing that has experienced the greatest improvement from IS is inventory control, or **material requirements planning (MRP)**. Traditional inventory-control techniques operated according to the basic principle that future inventory needs are based on past use: once used up, inventory was replaced. By contrast, replenishment in MRP is based on *future* need, calculated by MRP software from demand forecasts. MRP programs take customer demand as their initial input. The main input to MRP programs is the number of product units needed and the time at which they are needed; the programs then work back to calculate the amounts of resources required to produce subparts and assemblies. The programs use long-range forecasts to put long-lead material on order.

Other important input to MRP applications includes a list of all raw materials and subcomponent demands (called the **bill of materials**, or **BOM**)

Computer-aided manufacturing systems control costs

REUTERS/Rebecca Cook/Landov

and the economic order quantity of different raw materials. The **economic order quantity (EOQ)** of a specific raw material is the optimal quantity that allows a business to minimize overstocking and save cost, without risking understocking and missing production deadlines. A special program calculates EOQ for each item. It considers several factors: the item's cost, the discount schedule for large quantities, the cost of warehousing ordered parts, the cost of alternative uses of the money (such as the interest the money could earn had it not been spent on inventory), and other factors affecting the cost of ordering the item. Some MRP applications are tied to a purchasing IS, to produce purchase orders automatically when the quantity on hand reaches a reorder level. The purchase order includes the economic order quantity.

Manufacturing Resource Planning

Manufacturing resource planning (MRP II) combines material requirements planning (MRP) with other manufacturing-related activities to plan the entire manufacturing process, not just inventory. (The "II" in MRP II is simply to distinguish this term from material requirements planning, another term with the same acronym.) MRP II systems can quickly modify schedules to accommodate orders, track production in real time, and fix quality slippage. The most important input of MRP II systems is the **master production schedule (MPS)**, which specifies how production capacity is to be used to meet customer demands and maintain inventories. Virtually every report generated by an MRP II package starts with, or is based on, the MPS. Purchases of materials and internal control of manufacturing work flow, for example, start with the MPS, so the MPS directly affects operational costs and asset use.

MRP II systems help balance production economies, customer demands, manufacturing capacity, and inventory levels over a planning horizon of several months. Successful MRP II systems have made a significant contribution to **just-in-time (JIT)** manufacturing, where suppliers ship parts directly to assembly lines, saving the cost of warehousing raw materials, parts, and subassemblies.

MRP and MRP II systems gave ERP systems their name. MRP II modules are now integrated into ERP systems. While MRP and MRP II were, indeed, used mainly for planning, the "P" in ERP is somewhat misleading, because ERP systems are used mainly for daily operations, in addition to planning.

Ideally, the ISs of manufacturing organizations and their suppliers would be linked in a way that makes them subsystems of one large system. The MRP II application of an organization that manufactures a final product would plan and determine the items required, their quantities, and the exact times they are needed at the assembly lines. Suppliers would ship items directly to assembly lines just before they are incorporated into the final product (hence the term *just-in-time manufacturing*). Manufacturing organizations have not yet reached the point where JIT is accomplished with every product, but they have made great progress toward this ideal.

The Internet facilitates such system linking. Companies that were quick to link their systems to their suppliers' systems attained strategic advantages. One such company is Cisco Systems, a world leader in design and manufacturing of telecommunications devices. The company used to maintain many manufacturing plants. In 2001, it had sold all but two. The company's ISs are linked through the Internet to the ISs of its suppliers, some of whom purchased the very plants that Cisco sold. Managers can track orders using these systems. They can tell Cisco clients the exact status of their orders and the time of delivery. Cisco managers keep track of the products they order and know at what phase of manufacturing and delivery each item is—as if *they* were running the manufacturing plants. More than 80 percent of what Cisco orders never passes through the company's facilities; the manufacturers ship the products directly to Cisco's clients.

Monitoring and Control

Information systems have been designed to control manufacturing processes, not just monitor them. Controlling processes is important to ensure quality. For example, Ford Motor Company implemented software that it calls Project Execution, which combines bar-coding and wireless technology to ensure quality. Since each vehicle is assembled on a chassis, each chassis is tagged with a unique bar code. A bar-code sensor is installed in each stop of the assembly line. The sensor transmits wireless signals to computers and electronically controlled gates. The "gates" are not physical ones, but points where the vehicle is checked. The purpose of the system is to ensure that no assembly steps are skipped, and that each vehicle passes a series of performance and quality tests along the way. If a step is missed, the gate does not let the vehicle leave the plant. Mazda North America also implemented information technology to assist with monitoring its manufacturing process. In 2009, Mazda North America implemented a system that manages its vehicle logistics network in the United States and Canada. This system maintains and tracks various performance measures and estimated delivery dates for all of their supply partners.

Shipping

When the process of manufacturing products is complete, the next link in the supply chain is shipping. Shipping is performed either by the manufacturer or by a hired shipping company. The variables that affect the cost and speed of shipping are numerous: length of routes, sequence of loading and unloading, type of shipped materials (e.g., perishable, hazardous, or fragile), fuel prices, road tolls, terrain and restricted roads, and many more. Therefore, the use of sophisticated software to optimize shipping time and the cost of labor, equipment use, and maintenance helps companies stay competitive.

Today's trucks are equipped with computers, global positioning systems (GPS), and satellite communication devices. You might have seen small antennas on trucks. The antenna receives real-time orders from a central shipping office, especially when routing changes are necessary, and transmits information about the truck, such as current location, the previous point of loading or unloading, and the next point of loading or unloading. Truckers rarely visit shipping offices. These systems allow them to be on the road doing productive work all the time, thanks to constant communication with the office.

The GeoBase mapping system (Figure 3.7) was released in 2009 by Telogis, a global platform for location-based services for the enterprise. The system allows organizations to use traffic and commercial vehicle turn restrictions to design dispatching and navigation solutions, as well as custom routes. Real-time updates can be accessed by laptops and mobile operating systems. The flexibility of the new system allows drivers to edit maps and routes in the field, which can be incorporated into the back-end database of the enterprise. Software like this allows workers to quickly adjust to accidents and closed roads and best utilize time and resources.

FIGURE 3.7

GeoBase optimizes
transportation routing,
navigation, and mapping
along with real-time traffic
data

Supply chain management software in transportation helps load trucks, ships, and airplanes in an optimal manner both in terms of space utilization and sequence of unloading. Figure 3.8 provides a visual description of an optimal loading of boxes on a truck before its dispatch using CargoWiz software from Softtruck. Figure 3.9 illustrates how information is communicated between a truck and a shipper's office.

FIGURE 3.8

CargoWiz is truck and
container loading
software that optimizes
shipping space to
transport cargo

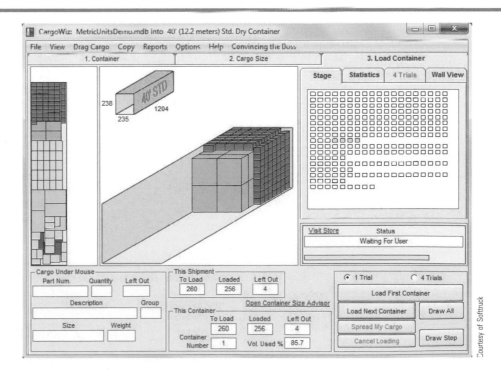

FIGURE 3.9

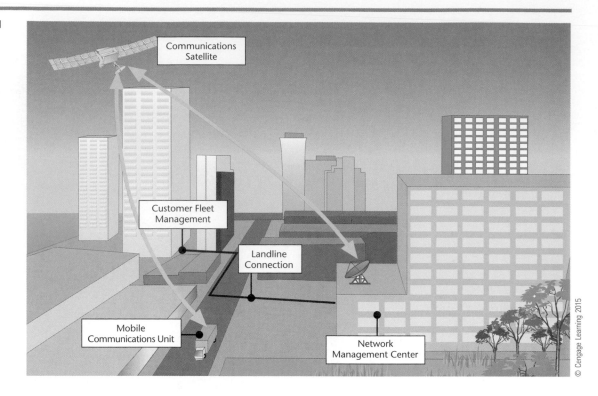

RFID in SCM

The most important development in hardware to support SCM has been a technology called **radio frequency identification (RFID)**. We discuss the technology itself in Chapter 6, "Business Networks and Telecommunications." RFID tags contain circuitry that allows recording of information about a product. When attached to a product, it contains an **electronic product code (EPC)**, which provides much more information than the universal product code (UPC). The tag can include the date of manufacturing, the plant in which the product was made, lot number, expiration date, destination, and many other details that help track its movement and sale. The information can be read and also revised by special RFID transceivers (transmitter-receiver devices). Figure 3.10 shows an example of an RFID product and its small size. Figure 3.11 shows an example of how RFID is used in a supply chain. Items with rewritable tags can contain maintenance history of products, which helps optimize maintenance of the items.

FIGURE 3.10

An example of an RFID
device in relation to the
size of a grain of rice

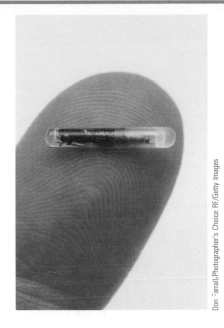

Don Farrall,Photographer's Choice RF/Getty Images

FIGURE 3.11

An example of how RFID
technology is integrated
into a supply chain

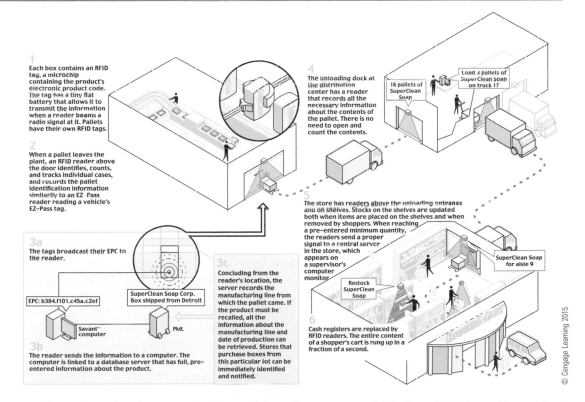

1
Each box contains an RFID tag, a microchip containing the product's electronic product code. The tag has a tiny flat battery that allows it to transmit the information when a reader beams a radio signal at it. Pallets have their own RFID tags.

2
When a pallet leaves the plant, an RFID reader above the door identifies, counts, and tracks individual cases, and records the pallet identification information similarly to an EZ–Pass reader reading a vehicle's EZ–Pass tag.

3a
The tags broadcast their EPC to the reader.

EPC: b384.f101.c45a.c2ef

Savant™ computer

SuperClean Soap Corp. Box shipped from Detroit

PML

3b
The reader sends the information to a computer. The computer is linked to a database server that has full, pre–entered information about the product.

3c
Concluding from the reader's location, the server records the manufacturing line from which the pallet came. If the product must be recalled, all the information about the manufacturing line and date of production can be retrieved. Stores that purchase boxes from this particular lot can be immediately identified and notified.

4
The unloading dock at the distribution center has a reader that records all the necessary information about the contents of the pallet. There is no need to open and count the contents.

16 pallets of SuperClean Soap

Load 3 pallets of SuperClean Soap on truck 17

5
The store has readers above the unloading entrance and on shelves. Stocks on the shelves are updated both when items are placed on the shelves and when removed by shoppers. When reaching a pre–entered minimum quantity, the readers send a proper signal to a central server in the store, which appears on a supervisor's computer monitor.

Restock SuperClean Soap

SuperClean Soap for aisle 9

6
Cash registers are replaced by RFID readers. The entire content of a shopper's cart is rung up in a fraction of a second.

© Cengage Learning 2015

The same technology can also be used for other purposes, including detection of items that should be recalled because of hazardous components and accurate condemnation of expired items, such as drugs and auto parts. When a pattern of defects is discovered in a product, RFID helps pinpoint the plant at which it was produced and the particular lot from which it came. Only products from that lot are recalled and replaced or fixed. It does not take too long to determine the particular manufacturing phase in which the defect was caused. When the expiration date of an item arrives, a transceiver detects the fact and alerts personnel to remove the item from a shelf. Packaging of drugs and other items contain RFID tags with unique identifiers. Transceivers can detect whether the products are genuine.

No commercial organization can survive without selling its products or services. Thus, businesses seek to provide products and services that consumers want—and to entice them to buy what the business produces. Businesses exert marketing efforts to pinpoint demographic groups that are most likely to buy products, to determine features that consumers desire most, and to provide the most efficient and effective ways to execute a sale when a consumer shows interest in the product or service. Because these efforts depend mainly on the analysis of huge amounts of data, ISs have become key tools to conceiving and executing marketing strategies. When marketing succeeds, ISs support the sales effort; to entice customers to continue to purchase, ISs support customer service (see Figure 3.12).

FIGURE **3.12**

Customer relationship management systems help marketing, sales, and customer service departments target interested and profitable customers

Customer relationship management (CRM) systems are designed to support any and all relationships with customers. Mostly, they support three areas: marketing, sales, and customer service. Modern CRM systems can help capture the entire customer experience with an organization, from response to an online advertisement to automatic replenishment of products to proactive service. With growing competition and so many options available to consumers, keeping customers satisfied is extremely important. Many executives will tell you that their companies do not make money (and might even lose money) on a first sale to a new customer because of the substantial investment in marketing. Thus, they constantly strive to improve customer service and periodically contact anyone who has ever purchased something from them to ensure repeat sales and to encourage customer loyalty. Any information technology that supports these efforts is considered a CRM system, but in recent years the effort has been to combine applications that support all three areas—marketing, sales, and customer service—to better understand what customers want, to be able to collect payment sooner, and to ensure timely shipping.

POINT OF INTEREST | Too Much, Too Little, or Just Right

Bars and clubs are inherently known for having high shrinkage costs due to spilled drinks, overpouring, not charging, and theft. However, the use of RFID can limit those costs significantly. LiquorInventory.Net's Liquor Inventory System is a replacement pour spout in the end of a liquor bottle that is equipped with an RFID transmitter. Every time the bartender pours a drink the RFID registers it in real time and tracks it over the Internet. This allows managers and bar owners to increase customer satisfaction by more closely monitoring their inventory levels and accurately charging patrons the correct amount.

Source: Kaplan, A. (2011). Tag! you're it! Beverage World, 130 (1818), 49.

CRM systems also provide an organization with an important element: all employees of the company who directly or indirectly serve a customer are "on the same page." Through their individual computers, everyone has immediate access to the status of an order for an item, a resolution of a buyer's complaint, or any other information that has to do with the customer. All who serve the customer are well-informed and receive the information from the same source. This is especially important in a long, complex sales cycle, because it minimizes response time and improves the quality of service for customers.

Market Research

Few organizations can sell their products and services without promotion; fewer still can promote successfully without market research. Market research systems help to find the populations and regions that are most likely to purchase a new product or service. They also help analyze how a new product fares in its first several months on the market.

Through interviews with consumers and retailers, market researchers collect information on what consumers like and dislike about products. When the researchers collect sufficient data, the marketing department uses statistical models to predict sales volumes of different products and of different designs of the same product. This critical information aids in planning manufacturing capacities and production lines. It is also extremely important for budgeting purposes. When questionnaires are involved, many companies offer web-based forms instead of paper questionnaires. In some cases, respondents use telephones to answer questions after a purchase, usually for a chance to win money prizes. The entered data is channeled into computer databases for future analysis. Dunkin' Donuts utilizes the data gained from its guest satisfaction survey to continually monitor the performance of its stores and the quality of its products. The chain gathers customer feedback by promoting the completion of a web-based survey at the bottom of a receipt.

A portion of a sales receipt showing Dunkin' Donuts invitation for a customer to participate in market research at its website

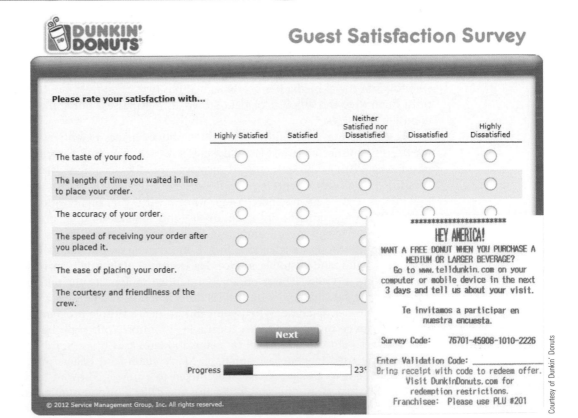

Targeted Marketing

To save resources, businesses use IT to promote to people most likely to purchase their products. This activity is often referred to as **targeted marketing**. Great advances in database technology enable even the smallest low-budget business to use targeted marketing. The principle of targeted marketing is to define the prospective customer as accurately as possible, and then to direct promotional dollars to those people most likely to purchase your product. Perhaps the best evidence of how much companies use ISs for targeted marketing is the use of the Internet for mass communication of unsolicited commercial email, a practice called spamming. Many people loathe spamming, but it is certainly the least expensive method of advertising. Another controversial, but apparently effective, method is pop-up advertising, in which a small window pops up either in front of or behind a web browser's window.

To define their target markets, businesses collect data everywhere they can: from sales transactions and warranty cards, or by purchasing databases with information about organizations and individuals. Using database management systems (DBMSs)—special programs to build and manipulate data pools—a company can sort and categorize consumers by age, gender, income, previous purchase of a related product, or any combination of these facts and other demographic information. The company then selects consumers whose characteristics match the company's customer profile and spends its promotional dollars to try to sell to those select customers.

The massive amount of personal information that corporations collect and purchase lets them prepare electronic dossiers on the interests, tastes, and buying habits of individuals. The information they possess lets them target "a market of one," namely, an individual rather than a group. Online purchase transactions and online product registrations by consumers provide a wealth of information to corporations. Vendors sort the information to send promotional material via ground mail or email only to those customers whose profiles indicate potential interest.

Aetna faced the challenge of targeting small business owners interested in health insurance. They wanted to identify the sole proprietorships that did not have coverage while ensuring that the target list did not include small business owners who had coverage through employers or other sources. Aetna targeted a direct mail campaign, which integrated search keyword buys (purchased from search engines) and display ads from various networks. Their efforts resulted in more than $1M annually while reducing their cost per acquisition by 10 to 25 percent.

For decades, organizations have integrated the use of data to implement marketing initiatives. However, recently, the flood of marketing data from websites, affinity cards, smart phones, and social media has overwhelmed business organizations. The new term "big data" not only quantifies the amount of data stored by businesses, but the challenges of mining large, complex databases.

Telemarketing (marketing over the telephone) makes extensive use of IT. The telemarketer uses a PC connected to a large database, which contains records of potential or existing customers. With a retrieved record displayed on the screen, a marketer dials the number by pressing a single key or clicking the mouse. The telemarketer speaks to the potential buyer while looking at that person's purchasing record with the organization or other organizations. Universities and charitable organizations use the same method to solicit donations.

Computer telephony integration (CTI) is a technique enabling a computer to use the digital signal coming through a telephone line as input in a computer system. It has been used often in marketing, sales, and customer service. For example, mail-order firms use caller ID to better serve their customers. Caller ID was originally intended to identify the telephone number from which a person calls, but mail-order businesses quickly found a new use for the gadget. They connect it to their customer database. When you call to order, a simple program searches for your number, retrieves your record, and displays it on a PC monitor. You might be surprised when the person who receives your call greets you by name and later asks if you want to use the same credit-card number you used in your last purchase. Many credit-card issuers utilize CTI to activate a new credit card sent to a customer. A label affixed to a new credit card asks the customer to call an 800-number to activate the card. CTI gains the caller's phone number to validate that the call is originating to the customer's phone number in their account. The use of this technology not only reduces the customer's time to activate the card, but also increases the security of the transaction.

Techniques such as data mining take advantage of large data warehouses to find trends and shopping habits of various demographic groups. For example, the software discovers clusters of products that people tend to purchase together, and then the marketing experts promote the products as a combination, and might suggest displaying them together on store shelves. You will learn more about data mining in Chapter 11, "Business Intelligence and Knowledge Management."

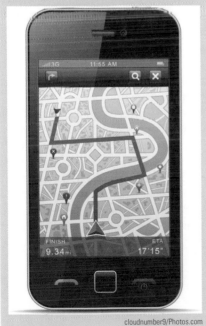

Location based services using a smart phone allow customers to find businesses based on their current location

cloudnumber9/Photos.com

With the proliferation of set-top boxes (devices that allow for personal programming and recording for digital televisions), several software companies have developed applications that may allow television networks to transition from the wasteful and expensive 30-second commercial to more personal advertising. Relying on information provided by households through these interactive boxes, they can select and transmit to each subscriber commercials only for products in which the subscriber is interested. For example, you will not receive commercials about pet food if you do not have pets, but you will receive commercials for gardening products and services if this is your hobby.

Use of information technology for targeted marketing has taken sophisticated forms on the web. More than just targeting a certain demographic group, web technologies enable retailers to *personalize* marketing when shopping and buying are conducted online. Special software used by online retailers tracks every visit consumers make and captures their "click streams" (the sequence of selections they make) and the amount of time they spend viewing each page. The retailer's software combines this information with data from online purchases to personalize the pages whenever consumers revisit the site. The reconstructed page introduces information about the products that the individual visitor is most likely to purchase. For example, two people with different purchasing records at Amazon.com who revisit the company's home page will find that they are looking at slightly different versions of the page. Amazon's software custom-composes the elements for each person according to his or her inferred interests in products. The ones that the software concludes might be of the highest interest are displayed or linked on the page.

Location-Based Services

Marketing personnel continue to design new methods of targeting customers by gathering more effective information about them. **Location-based services** offer the ability to accurately and efficiently gather various dimensions of consumer information, such as when and where they shop and what they buy, in a real-time environment. With location-based services, location and time data can be recorded when an action is performed. Smart phones with GPS (global positioning service) technology, combined with mobile apps and social media, can offer a significant new element for marketing strategy. About half of the people equipped with a GPS-enabled device have enabled location-based services.

Pepsico has tested a new initiative by rewarding consumers for purchasing their products in grocery and convenience stores. Location-based social networks such as Foursquare and CheckPoints provide incentives for users and their friends to purchase products from nearby vendors, then gather real-time data on the purchases. Ultimately, the location-based services on smartphones are "leading" prospective customers to their businesses thereby increasing sales and promoting their location.

Customer Service

Companies have saved millions of dollars per year by shifting customer service from employees to their website. Web-based customer service provides automated customer support 24 hours per day, 365 days per year. At the same time, it saves companies the cost of labor required when humans provide the same service. For example, letting customers pay their bills electronically not only provides convenience but also saves (both customers and companies) the cost of postage and paper and saves the company the time required for dealing with paper documents. Online billing costs only a small fraction of paper billing. The business research firm Gartner estimates the average invoice-to-payment cycle at 41 days, while online invoice and payment shortens the period by at least six days. Customers appreciate the discounts that many companies offer for accepting statements and paying bills online.

A 2009 Forrester Research study states that the top business drivers are those that improve customers' website experiences and reduce the cost of web operations (63 percent). Business drivers are focused initiatives or activities that provide direct, substantial influences on the business. Many businesses are focusing their technology and organizational strategy on expanding and improving the customer experience while driving down costs. United Illuminating's new online system increases customer engagement as well as reduces their energy costs. The use of UI's portal increased by over 400 percent during the first four years of operation.

Some companies are using online chat to help customers. Snapfish, currently owned by HP, is one of the world's largest online photo retailers with over 90 million members in 20 countries. The company provides unlimited online storage for photos, and provides tools to make photos into gifts and novelties. Customers sometimes need help while designing a photo book or other item. Snapfish had integrated software developed by LivePerson (see figure) to provide real-time customer interaction for customer service and to answer technical questions. Snapfish expanded its use of the live-chat technology to deepen the engagement with customers, assisting them with more complex products and design tasks. Using LivePerson Enterprise technology, Snapfish was able to target and connect with customers during their shopping cart and check out process and to provide quick responses for customers. The strategic use of this technology significantly increased the average order value by 33 percent while increasing customer satisfaction scores to 87 percent. Ultimately, Snapfish achieved the grand prize by simultaneously increasing revenue, delivering quality customer service, and increasing agent productivity by 14 percent (Anonymous, 2009).

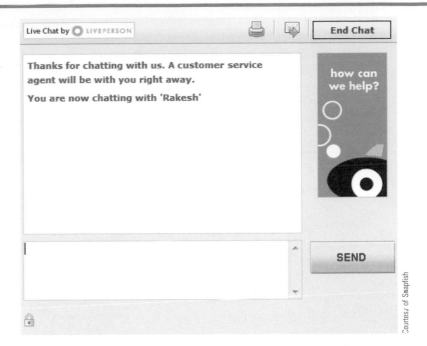

Online chat software integrated into a company's webpage can provide a convenient and cost-effective approach to customer service

Online customer service applications have become increasingly sophisticated. They help track past purchases and payments, update online answers to frequently asked questions (FAQs) about products and services, and analyze customers' contacts with the company to maintain and update an electronic customer profile. The FAQ pages of many companies have been replaced with options for open-ended questions; instead of looking up a question that is similar to what you would ask, you can simply type in your question. Employing artificial intelligence software, the site will "understand" your question and provide a short list of links where you can find an answer.

Salesforce Automation

Salesforce automation equips traveling salespeople with information technology to facilitate their productivity. Typically, salespeople are equipped with laptop or tablet computers that store promotional information for prospective customers, software for manipulating this information, and computerized forms. Many salespeople carry laptop computers or smartphones that contain all the information they need, and which allow them to connect to their organizational information systems through the Internet. Salesforce automation can increase sales productivity significantly, making sales presentations more efficient and letting field representatives close deals on the spot, using preformatted contracts and forms.

Salesforce automation increases the sales and productivity of sales personnel

byryo/Photos.com

Information technology lets salespeople present different options for products and services on the computer, rather than asking prospective customers to wait until the main office faxes or mails the information. At the end of the day or the week, salespeople can upload sales information to a computer at the main office, where it is raw input to the order-processing department, the manufacturing unit, or the shipping and invoicing departments.

Using smartphones, laptops, or tablets that can establish a wireless or cellular connection to the Internet enables salespeople to check prices, confirm availability of the items in which a customer is interested, and place an order away from the office. The salespeople can then spend more time on the road, increasing direct contact with prospective customers.

Human Resource Management

Human resource management (HRM) has become more complex due to the fast growth in specialized occupations, the need to train and promote highly skilled employees, and the growing variety of benefits programs. Human resource management can be classified into five main activities: (1) employee record management, (2) promotion and recruitment, (3) training, (4) evaluation, and (5) compensation and benefits management (see Figure 3.13).

FIGURE **3.13**

Human resource management information systems help managers optimize promotion and recruitment, training, evaluation, and compensation activities

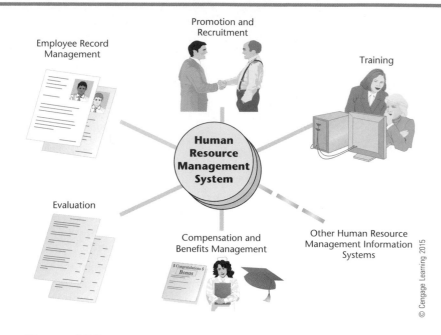

© Cengage Learning 2015

Employee Record Management

ISs facilitate employee record management. Human resource departments must keep personnel records to satisfy both external regulations (such as federal and state laws) and internal regulations, as well as for payroll and tax calculation and deposit, promotion consideration, and periodic reporting. Many HR ISs are now completely digitized (including employees' pictures), which dramatically reduces the space needed to store records, the time needed to retrieve them, and the costs of both.

POINT OF **INTEREST** | Job Fishing? Start with Proper Baits

A growing number of companies require an electronic copy of your résumé when you apply for a position. The résumé is added to a database. Human resource managers search the database by keywords. The search yields a list of résumés containing words that match the keywords. Therefore, you can enhance your chances of obtaining the position you want by including as many relevant keywords in your résumé as you can. One effective way to find these keywords is to examine online and print ads for the position you are seeking. Include these keywords—sometimes called "buzzwords"—and increase the chances of your résumé coming up in the recruiters' search. However, there are negative "buzzwords" as well. LinkedIn, a professional networking site, released a list of the top 10 most overused words job seekers use in résumés and job applications. The list includes creative, organizational, and motivated, to name a few. Using these words can make your résumé or application blend in with the many others that use the same words. In order for your resume to stand out, it is important to use "buzzwords" so your resume is recognized by the database, as well as unique words so it stands out and makes an impression on the potential employer.

Source: Olson, Lindsay. (December 13, 2011). 10 Buzzwords to Avoid on Your Resume. http://money. usnews.com/money/blogs/outside-voices-careers/2011/12/13/10-buzzwords-to-avoid-on-your-resume

Promotion and Recruitment

To select the best-qualified person for a position, a human resource manager can search a database of applicants and existing employees' records for set criteria, such as type and length of education, particular experience, specific talents, and required licenses or certifications. Automating the selection process significantly minimizes time and money spent on recruitment, but it does require that a current database be maintained.

Intranets (intraorganizational networks that support web applications) help HR managers post position vacancy announcements for employees to peruse and consider from their own PCs. This system is especially efficient in large organizations that employ thousands of workers, and even more so at multisite organizations.

With the growing number of job applicants, many companies refuse to receive paper applications and résumés. In 2011, Starbucks received 7.6 million job applications, while Proctor & Gamble received almost a million. McDonald's and its franchises received over one million applications and hired 62,000 people on its national hiring day, April 19, 2011. Therefore, it is no wonder that some companies may accept such documents via email, but that others accept only forms that are filled out and submitted online. Using keywords, recruiting officers can then use special software to scour a database for the most-qualified candidates. HR consultants say that this process reduces the time spent on a typical search from several hours to several minutes. Some software companies sell automated recruiting and selection software to support such activities. For example, PeopleAdmin, Inc. offers software by the same name. HR managers save the cost of publishing help wanted ads and can start reviewing résumés as soon as applicants respond online instead of waiting the typical 6–8 days from traditional advertising.

Some companies use the entire web as a database for their search. Across industries, companies using traditional recruiting systems experience a cost per hire of $5,000–$12,000, depending on the set of skills required and the level of the position. Wonderlic, Inc. develops web-based recruiting, assessment, and retention solutions. Early in 2010, they introduced their Automated Staff Acquisition Platform (ASAP) designed to help home healthcare organizations more efficiently hire talented employees (Anonymous, 2010b, 2010c). ASAP for Home Healthcare is a web-based solution that automatically gathers candidates' skills and information and displays the findings in an easy-to-read style. This allows organizations to quickly compare all findings and select the top candidates to interview. ASAP for Home Healthcare reduces the time managers spend interviewing candidates by 75 percent and produces noticeably better results than interviews alone. ASAP for Home Healthcare streamlines the process by eliminating candidates who do not meet minimum requirements, which allows managers to quickly determine which candidates are most likely to succeed. Wonderlic offers the ASAP tailored to other industries as well. One company using ASAP for property management gained a 20 percent reduction in turnover for onsite positions. By 2010, 46 percent of U.S. firms were outsourcing all or part of their human resource function. Large firms are more likely to outsource HR. The average cost-per-hire in the United States for firms using modern recruitment systems based on outsourcing and multichannel sourcing is between $2,500 and $3,500 with smaller firms bearing the larger recruiting costs (Anonymous, 2010a). This cost-per-hire figure has decreased significantly in recent years due to innovations in the recruiting process, such as ASAP software.

Training

One important function of human resource departments is improving employee skills. In both the manufacturing and service sectors, multimedia software training is rapidly replacing training programs involving classrooms and teachers. Such applications include interactive, three-dimensional simulated environments. Some applications contain sophisticated virtual reality components. For example, one such application trains workers to handle wrought iron that must be hammered manually. The worker wears special goggles and holds a hammer in one hand and a piece of metal in the other, over an anvil. The worker "sees" the metal piece through the goggles, "hears" the hitting sound through earphones, and receives a programmed, realistic jolt every time he "hits" the metal. This safely prepares the worker for the dangerous work instead of putting him at risk for injury before he has enough experience to do the actual work. Although the initial investment in multimedia training systems might be high, human resource managers find the systems very effective. Surgeons train using similar systems to operate on virtual patients rather than risk injuries to human patients.

Training software emulates situations in which an employee must act and includes tests and modules to evaluate a trainee's performance. In addition to the savings in trainers' time, there are other benefits. The trainee is more comfortable because he or she controls the speed at which the sessions run. The software lets the trainee go back to a certain point in the session if a concept is missed. Also, the software can emulate hazardous situations, thereby testing employee performance in a safe environment. And if training in a real environment involves destruction of equipment or consumption of materials, virtual reality training applications accomplish the same results in skill enhancement without destruction or waste.

Developments in IT enable organizations to reduce training costs dramatically. Aspect is an internationally recognized software provider that focuses on unified communications for the contact center. Their PerformanceEdge eLearning with integration to the Aspect© Unified IP© platform allows for real-time monitoring of service levels and recognizes when agents need new eLearning sessions. Managers can schedule eLearning sessions for agents without compromising the overall quality of service. PerformanceEdge eLearning software improves training and coaching by providing agents and supervisors with the appropriate content at the appropriate time. For companies with limited hiring resources, especially smaller companies where the cost-per-hire can be very high, eLearning sessions can help improve the skill sets of current agents rather than recruiting new ones. By using the software, recruitment centers experience reduced hiring costs and improved agent retention. This leads to improved customer service because the best agents are hired.

Evaluation

Supervisors must periodically evaluate the technical ability, communication skills, professional conduct, and general behavior of employees. While objective factors are involved in evaluation—such as attendance rates and punctuality—employee evaluation is often very subjective. Assessing performance and effort levels, and their relative weights of importance, varies significantly, depending on who is evaluating. A supervisor might forget to include some factors altogether or might inappropriately weigh a particular aspect of performance. Subjectivity is particularly problematic when several employees are being considered for a promotion and their evaluations are compared to determine the strongest candidate. By helping to standardize the evaluation process across employees and departments, evaluation software adds a certain measure of objectivity and consistency.

In an evaluation, a supervisor provides feedback to an employee, records the evaluation for official records and future comparison, and accepts input from the employee. Software helps managers standardize their employee evaluations by providing step-by-step guides to writing performance reviews, a checklist of performance areas to include in the evaluation (with the option to add or remove topics), scales to indicate how strong the employee is in each area, and the ability to select the relative importance each factor should hold in the overall evaluation. Performance areas include written and oral communication, job knowledge, and management skills, with each topic broken down into basic elements to assist the supervisor in creating an accurate evaluation. A typical application guides the supervisor through all necessary factors and includes a help guide. When the evaluator finishes entering data, the application automatically computes a subtotal for each category and a weighted grade, which can then be electronically stored as part of the employee's record.

Compensation and Benefits Management

ISs help HR officers manage compensation (salaries, hourly pay, commissions, and bonuses) efficiently and effectively. Programs can easily calculate weekly, monthly, and hourly pay according to annual salaries and can include federal, state, and local tax tables to assist in complying with compensation regulations. This same system can also automatically generate paychecks or direct deposits, which are the electronic transfer of funds from the firm's bank account to the employee's.

Special software helps the HR department manage benefits such as health insurance, life insurance, retirement plans, and sick and leave days, which are determined by seniority; amounts individuals pay into plans; and other factors. To optimize benefits, some companies use special software, incorporating expert systems (ISs that emulate human expertise) that determine the optimal health and retirement plans for each employee based on factors such as marital status, age, occupation, and other data.

Using intranets, many organizations allow their employees to access the benefits database directly and make changes to their preferences, such as selecting another health-care insurance program, or adding a family member as a beneficiary in a life insurance plan. When the company engages a third party for managing pension funds or other benefits, employees can go directly to the website of that company, not involving their own company resources at all.

St. Vincent's Hospital in Alabama implemented a self-service system for employees to access their compensation information and manage their benefits. The system expands their access to information to 24/7 from a traditional 9-to-5 when human resource personnel are available. Employees choose their benefits through this system during the open enrollment period, eliminating manual entry of benefit elections. The system has reduced costs by $1 million through eliminating printing and mailing checks as well as reduced paper and printing costs. By making the changes directly from their PCs, employees reduce the amount of work of the HR staff and decrease the company's overhead costs. Ultimate Software is one company that produces customized human resource software that allows employees to manage their own benefits (see figure).

Human resource software can provide employees with self-service access to manage their benefits

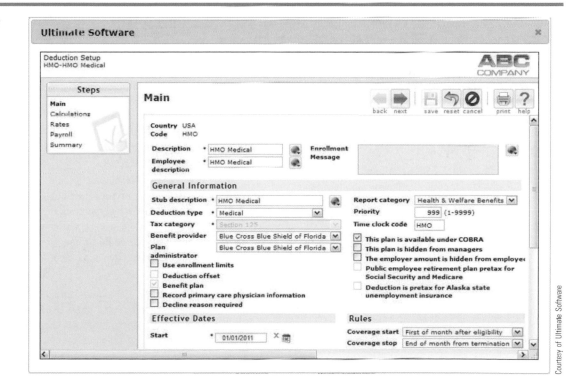

CRM systems, and IT in general, help businesses serve us better at lower costs. But in the process, we may lose some privacy. Consider the following scenario: you agree to give some financial information about yourself to a car dealership to finance the car you have just purchased. At a later date, you provide medical information when you purchase a prescription drug. Your credit-card company has enough information from your purchasing activity to know your culinary and fashion tastes better than you do. Whenever you interact with an organization online, information is recorded; and if you provide personally identifiable information—which is always the case when you make an online purchase—the information is added to your record held by this organization. It may also be recorded by a third party that contracts with the vendor. Finally, without your knowledge or consent, yet another organization gathers all this information and puts it in one big record that is practically a detailed personal dossier.

Organizations collect huge amounts of personal information. Every time you pay with your credit card you leave a personal record; the few details of your purchase are often used to update an already hefty dossier about your buying habits. Every time you provide personal information at a website, you either help open a new dossier with an organization or help other organizations update their dossier about you. When you pass through a highway toll booth, the electronic pass device in your car tracks the date, time, and location of your travels. GPS and location-based services monitor your movement in a similar manner. In their zeal to market more effectively, businesses often violate consumer privacy.

- **What Is Privacy?** In the context of information, privacy is your right to control information about yourself. For example, you maintain your privacy if you keep to yourself your college grades, medical history, or the name of the organization with which you interviewed for a position. Someone who receives such information without your permission is violating your privacy.

- **Business Arguments.** Business leaders argue that they must collect and use personal data. Without personal data, they would have to waste time and money to target likely buyers. They need to know the repayment histories of individuals to help make prudent decisions on extending loans and credit. This ability to purchase and manipulate large amounts of consumer information makes the business world more democratic than it used to be. Small companies now have the same chances of targeting prospective buyers with good credit as big companies, creating more opportunities and more competition, which eventually benefit consumers.

- **Consumer Arguments.** Consumers usually accept that they must divulge some private information to receive services, but many do not accept the mass violation of privacy. They resent unsolicited mail and email sent by companies who know much about them although they have never provided personal details to these companies. They hate telephone calls from salespeople who obtained their records from companies that were supposed to keep their records confidential. And their greatest concern might be the "dossier phenomenon."

- **Losing Control.** In many cases, you volunteer information in return for some benefits, such as consumer loyalty points or participation in a sweepstakes. In others, you simply cannot receive the service or product unless you agree to provide certain personal details. In such cases, you give implicit or explicit informed consent to obtain information about yourself. However, once you provide information, you have little control over it. With some newer technology, such as RFID, you might not even be aware of who and when information is collected about you. You have just stepped out of a department store with your new clothing purchases. All are RFID-tagged. The store's systems recorded your visit and detailed what you purchased. Can you be sure that nobody else has the proper device to read and record what you purchased? Unless you removed the tag, the serial number embedded in the EPC of the sweater you purchased may uniquely identify you to a stalker whenever you wear it.

- **The Eight Commandments of Personal Data Collection and Maintenance.** In a free, market-oriented society, not allowing organizations to collect personal data is inconceivable. What can businesses do to help protect privacy? They can adhere to these rules to avoid misuse:

Purpose. Companies should inform people who provide information of the specific, exclusive purpose for which the company maintains its data, and only use the data for another purpose with the subjects' consent. For example, this practice could protect people with a genetic proclivity for certain diseases from higher health insurance premiums.

Relevance. Companies should record and use only data necessary to fulfill their own purposes. For example, an applicant's credit record should not contain membership in political or religious organizations because that information is irrelevant in credit considerations.

Accuracy. Companies should ensure that the personal records they maintain are accurate. For example, many loan applicants have had terrible experiences because some of the data maintained by credit companies is erroneous. Careful data entry and periodic verification can enhance accuracy.

Currency. Companies should make sure that all data about an individual is current. If currency cannot be guaranteed, then data should be discarded periodically. Outdated information can create seriously negative repercussions. For example, a person who might have been unemployable due to past illness might not be able to get a job, even though he or she might be healthy now.

Security. Companies should limit access to data to only those who need to know. In addition to passwords, audit trails (which identify every employee who accesses a personal record and for what purpose) are also very effective tools for ensuring security. Extra caution must be practiced when personal data is accessible online by business partners.

Time Limitation. Companies should retain data only for the time period necessary. For example, there is no reason for a landlord to maintain your credit record after you move out.

Scrutiny. Companies should establish procedures to let individuals review their records and correct inaccuracies.

Sole Recording. When using a recording technology, a company should ensure that no other party can take advantage of the technology to record the same information. For example, if a store records an individual's purchases using RFID technology, it must ensure that the RFID tags embedded in the packaging or items are disabled as soon as the customer leaves the store.

Of course, many consumers will still feel that their privacy is invaded even if every business adopts these "commandments." How can you protect your privacy? Do not furnish your name, Social Security (or any other identifying) number, address, or any other private information if you do not know how it will be used. If you do provide detailed information, indicate that you do not wish the data to be shared with any other organization or individual. You can usually check a box to this effect on paper or web forms. To avoid junk mail or junk email, again check the proper box on web forms. Do not fill out any online or paper forms with detailed data unless an opt-out option is available. Of course, many services we receive depend on our willingness to provide personal data, so at least some organizations must have personal information, but you can be selective. Always carefully weigh what you gain against the privacy you might lose. And finally, always read and understand the terms of service and privacy policies associated with social media venues. Learn the various settings to protect yourself and your information.

Supply Chain Management Systems

U.S. Department of Commerce statistics show two important patterns over the past two decades: the fluctuations in inventory as a percentage of gross domestic product (GDP) and the absolute ratio of inventory to GDP have steadily decreased. In 2011, the ratio of changes of private inventory to GDP was .243 percent. This means that the U.S. GDP is growing while less and less money is tied to inventory. The smaller the inventory, the more money can be spent on other resources. Much of this trend can be attributed to the use of ISs, especially SCM systems.

The organizational importance of supply chain management has clearly increased. According to a survey by Tompkins Supply Chain Consortium, over half of several industries claimed they employ a supply chain leader at the executive level: manufacturing (51 percent), apparel and automotive (100 percent), and food and beverage (57 percent).

According to IBM, companies that implemented SCM systems have reduced inventory levels by 10–50 percent, improved the rate of accurate deliveries by 95–99 percent, reduced unscheduled work stoppages to 0–5 percent, reduced cycle time (from order to collection) by 10–20 percent, and reduced transportation costs by 10–15 percent. For example, while a significant dialogue continues to focus on healthcare costs, two healthcare facilities have addressed the issue by implementing supply chain management systems. Methodist Health System in Dallas has automated the supply chain using a web-based system. Their system improved workflow and increased service levels, cutting its staff by approximately one-half. Management estimates that this system has saved $5.5 million; much of that saving was realized by renegotiating lower product costs with its vendors with the new supply chain data. St. Joseph's Hospital Health Center in Syracuse, NY implemented a just-in-time supply chain initiative with a distributor. The new materials management system reduced inventory size and storage space.

Several enterprise applications, such as ERP systems, also serve as SCM systems. As Figure 3.14 illustrates, many such systems enable managers not only to monitor what goes on at their own units or organization but also to follow what goes on at the facilities of their suppliers and contractors. For example, at any given point in time managers can know the status of the following: an order now being handled by a contractor, by order number; the phase of manufacturing the produced units have reached; and the date of delivery, including any delays and their length. When purchasing parts, managers use the systems for issuing electronic purchase orders, and they can follow the fulfillment process at the supplier's facilities, such as when the parts were packed, when they were loaded on trucks, and when they are estimated to arrive at the managers' floor or the floor of another business partner who needed the parts. You, as a consumer, can get a sense of what SCM systems provide when you purchase a product on the web and track its shipment status and delivery.

FIGURE 3.14

A shared supply chain management system monitors the movement of raw and finished goods

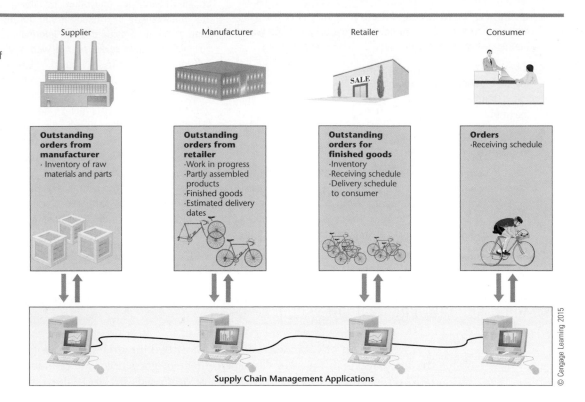

SCM applications streamline operations throughout the chain, from suppliers to customers, lowering inventories, decreasing production costs, and improving responsiveness to suppliers and clients. Harnessing the global network, managers can supervise an entire supply chain regardless of the location of the activity—at their own facilities or another organization's, at the same location or thousands of miles away. Older SCM systems connected two organizations. New ones connect several. For example, a distributor can reorder products from Organization A and simultaneously alert Organization B, the supplier of Organization A. The systems let all parties—suppliers, manufacturers, distributors, and customers—see the same information. A change made by any organization that affects an order can affect a corresponding change in scheduling and operations in the other organizations' activities.

Companies that have adopted SCM systems have seen improvement in three major areas: reduction in inventory, reduction in cycle time (the time it takes to complete a business process), and, as a result, reduction in production cost. Companies can reduce their inventory by communicating to their suppliers through a shared SCM system the exact number of units of each item they need and the exact time they need them. In ideal situations, they do not need to stockpile any inventory, saving warehouse costs. The management consulting firm Aberdeen Group estimates that companies using SCM systems through the Internet reduce purchase order processing cycles by 70–80 percent and pay 5–10 percent less for the items they purchase.

The Importance of Trust

SCM systems accomplish the greatest efficiencies when all businesses in the chain link their systems and share all the information that is pertinent to planning, production, and shipment. For example, BP PLC, Royal Dutch Shell PLC, Chevron Corp.'s Texaco, and other large oil companies are requiring their franchises to update their convenience store checkout systems to become more efficient. The proposed technological advances include a small, touch-screen PC like those seen at restaurants or bars. The most sophisticated versions of the machines would be able to track inventory and place orders when supplies run low on items in the store. The increased efficiency will save gas stations money by monitoring sales and inventory in one system.

However, not all organizations are willing to collaborate with their business partners. One reason is the fear that when Organization A purchases from Organization B and has access to Organization B's demand figures, it might disclose the information to competitors in an attempt to stir more competition and enjoy favorable prices. Another fear is that if Organization B realizes that at a certain point in time Organization A is in dire need of its raw materials, Organization B might take advantage of the situation and negotiate higher prices.

The first type of fear can be found in initial reluctance of suppliers to share information with large buyers such as Wal-Mart. Only the bargaining power of Wal-Mart and its insistence on sharing such information convinced suppliers to link their systems with those of Wal-Mart. The second type of fear still exists between trading partners such as General Motors and its main tire supplier. For example, Goodyear could enjoy lower inventories if it had GM's demand schedule for tires. It could then calibrate its own order for raw materials and its manufacturing capacity to suit those of GM, save money, and pass at least some of the savings to its client in the form of cheaper products. It could always replenish its client's inventory of tires before GM ran out of them. Better yet, it could deliver the tires directly to the assembly lines just when they are needed, saving both GM and itself warehousing costs. Yet, GM is guarding its production schedule as confidential.

Thus, effective supply chain management between companies is not only a matter of appropriate technology but also a matter of trust and culture change. So far, most of the successful collaborations have been between a large company and its business partners, whereby the company uses its power to dictate collaboration. However, some large companies have tied their SCM systems out of mutual understanding that this would benefit both companies, even if the shared information reveals some unpleasant facts. For example, Procter & Gamble, Inc., the giant supplier of household products, has had its systems connected to those of Wal-Mart since 1987, when the term "supply chain management" was not even in use. By providing its retail information to P&G, Wal-Mart ensures that it never runs out of P&G products. A culture of sharing—you show me some of your information and I show you some of mine—is essential for the success of both companies and creates a sense of mutual dependence and true partnership.

SCM systems can be taken a step beyond the sale. The systems can be used for after-the-sale services. For example, Beckman Coulter, Inc., in Fullerton, California, makes blood analyzers and other medical devices. After it sells a machine, the company uses the Internet to link the machine from the client's facility to a computer in its Fullerton factory. Software on the computer runs 7 days per week, 24 hours per day to monitor the sold machine. When a problem occurs, the computer alerts a Beckman technician, who can repair the machine before it stops working. Beckman estimates that the system provides savings of $1 million annually, because malfunctions are captured at an early stage, which avoids the higher cost of fixing a more damaged machine. The added benefit is increased customer satisfaction. As business partners see the benefits of sharing data, trust has grown, and the fear of linking IS to those of other organizations is waning.

Continuous Attention to Inventory

Recall the wonderful trend cited in the beginning of this section: the dollar value of inventory for U.S. businesses was growing at about 60 percent of the growth of GDP. However, much of the trend took place in the 1981–1991 period. In the 1992–2004 period, inventory as a percentage of GDP stayed fairly static at about 3.5 percent. Recently, in 2012, inventories reduced real GDP by .39 percent and .46 percent in the first and second quarters respectively. Apparently, while large corporations have the resources to install and run SCM systems to cut their own inventory, the ratio of inventory to revenue in small enterprises is growing because they do not use such systems. And sometimes, the companies that suffer the inventory ripple effect are not small. They might be powerful, and they even might manage their own SCM system, but their system might not be linked to their buyers' systems, so they cannot plan their production to reduce inventory.

For an example, let us return to the relationship between General Motors and Goodyear. The world's largest auto manufacturer improved "inventory turns" 55.2 percent between 1996 and 2001. Inventory turns is the number of times a business sells (or "turns over") its inventory per year. It is calculated by dividing the sales revenue by the average value of inventory. The greater the inventory turns number, the better. During the same period, Goodyear, GM's tire supplier, experienced a 21 percent decrease in inventory turns. The likely conclusion is that GM avoided purchasing tires from Goodyear until it needed them at the assembly line, but Goodyear did not have enough information on when, exactly, those tires would be required, and therefore kept overstocks. Had the SCM systems of the companies been linked, Goodyear could reduce inventory and see its inventory turns rise rather than fall. It is also reasonable to assume that, due to the cost savings, Goodyear would be able to sell tires to GM at a lower price. GM and other companies have created a situation where each company tries to "sit" with a lean inventory while, inadvertently, leaving another "standing" with an overstock. In order for all involved in a supply chain to enjoy efficiencies, the musical chairs, or "hot potato" situation, must stop.

Collaborative Logistics

The web enables organizations from totally different industries to streamline operations through collaboration. In recent years an increasing number of businesses found a new way to cut shipping costs: they combine freight with other businesses, sharing their own trucks or the vehicles of trucking companies. The collaboration reduces partially empty trucks, or empty trucks between stops. To this end, the companies connect their SCM systems to the site of a company that specializes in optimization of logistics, such as Nistevo Corporation, now owned by IBM. The company manages the site and uses sophisticated software to calculate the shortest routes between departure and arrival points and the best combination of loads from two or more companies to share trucks and routes. The SCM systems of subscribing companies provide daily data into the shared system. The IS takes into consideration the type of freight to ensure safety and adherence to regulations. For example, the software is designed not to combine chemicals with food. Therefore, typical allies of food manufacturers have been paper manufacturers, for instance. The cost savings have been impressive.

The spice maker McCormick & Co., Inc. has reduced freight costs by 5–15 percent, while General Mills has realized savings of up to 7 percent of its overall logistics costs. Manufacturers of household paper products such as Georgia-Pacific and International Paper Co. share about 80 long-distance routes with General Mills on a regular basis, cutting freight costs for those shipments 5–20 percent. Because the success of collaborative shipping is so impressive, some experts expect competitors to share trucks, leaving competition to some other areas of their operations, such as development and manufacturing processes. A 2009 study by Transport Intelligence found that 94 percent of businesses responding expressed a desire to engage in supply chain collaboration with another company.

Another area where some companies have explored collaboration is warehousing. The principle here is the same: try to maximize the use of warehouse space, and if you cannot use all of it, allow other businesses to use the extra space. The way to accomplish this, again, is through the web; a third party specializing in warehousing optimization combines warehousing needs and availability from member companies to offer optimal solutions.

Some companies are also extending their collaboration with retailers. Coca-Cola initiated a new collaborative store order program with Wegmans Food Markets. Coke optimized sales and inventory by compiling a "perfect order" by using store sales data. The use of store-level POS information provided value to production planning, forecasting, and inventory management as well as order fulfillment and delivery.

Enterprise Resource Planning

A growing number of organizations elect to replace old, disparate ISs with enterprise applications that support all or most of the business activities we have described. As mentioned before, these systems are often referred to as **enterprise resource planning (ERP)** systems, although they are used not only for planning but also for managing daily operations. Designers of ERP systems take a systems approach to an enterprise. For example, the Manufacturing Resource Planning component of the system uses the information recorded on a sale to retrieve product specifications; the data is used to generate purchasing information such as items, quantities, and the timetable for suppliers to deliver for the purchasing department. As products are manufactured, the system tracks the stages of the work in progress. When items are ready to be shipped, the shipping department can retrieve information on the items for its operations. The system keeps shipping information such as content and destination, along with billing information, to help produce shipping and billing documentation. The system also records financial transactions involved in these activities, such as payment made from a bank account. The accounting component records the transactions. In addition, ERP systems also provide human resource modules for payroll, employee benefits management, and employee evaluation software. CRM components are also available and are tied to other components through orders, applications, and sales records. In terms of 2012 revenue, the ERP market was divided among four vendors. SAP (25 percent), Oracle (13 percent), Sage (6 percent), and Infor (6 percent) (Columbus, 2013). SAP and Oracle have been the leaders in this field for several years. Oracle's market share has increased mainly through acquisitions of other ERP developers, such as J.D. Edwards and Siebel Systems.

Challenges and Disadvantages of ERP Systems

With successful ERP implementation, organizations can reap substantial rewards. However, ERP systems pose many challenges. The software packages are quite complex. Because they are not tailored to the needs of specific clients, they often require adjustment and fine-tuning for specific organizations. Therefore, their installation and testing involve experts who are usually employees of the software vendor or professionals who are certified for such work by the vendor.

Even with adjustments—often called "tweaking"—potential adopters must remember that the system was designed for an entire industry, not for the way an individual organization does business. If the organization has a competitive advantage thanks to a unique set of business processes, this advantage may diminish or disappear when the system is installed, because to a large degree the system dictates how business processes should be conducted. The system requirements are quite rigid, and therefore customization of ERP systems is limited.

ERP applications are expensive; modules cost millions of dollars. Buyers usually must allocate several more million dollars to pay for installation and modifications. Installation often takes many months to complete, and budget and time overruns are common.

The greatest advantage of ERP systems, the integration of many business processes, may become a challenge for the adopter. Because the operational lines between business units become blurred, there may be arguments over responsibility and accountability when something goes wrong. For example, the sales department may argue that the responsibility for an erroneous invoice is the accounting department's or even of a manufacturing unit that entered incorrect costs for the order. Also, a process that becomes a weak link in the supply chain may negatively affect other processes.

Implementation of ERP systems can fail because of formidable challenges: the gap between system capabilities and business needs, lack of expertise on the consultant's part, and mismanagement of the implementation project. The business research firm Standish Group found that only 10 percent of ERP implementation projects are completed as planned, on time, and within budget. Fifty-five percent are completed late or over budget (which usually means loss of business and revenue), and the other 35 percent of such projects are canceled because of difficulties. At Hewlett-Packard, one of the world's largest computer and IT equipment makers, a $400 million loss in the third quarter of 2004 was blamed on poorly managed migration to a new ERP system. Previous cases of difficult implementations of ERP systems are Hershey Foods and Nike. In both cases, the adopters blamed losses of hundreds of millions of dollars on late completions of ERP system installations. In one case, an industry leader was bankrupt as a result of unsuccessful implementation of an ERP system.

In 2006, Shane, a jewelry company with $200 million in sales, spent $36 million on an ERP project that was cancelled after three years. It is believed that the project was oversized and too large for the company. Research calculates that the average business spends 9 percent of its annual revenue on an ERP project; Shane spent twice as much. The failures associated with ERP projects focus on hiring inexperienced consultants/integrators, ineffective project management, and changing requirements.

Providing the Missing Reengineering

In our discussion of reengineering of business processes in the previous chapter, we noted that in the 1990s, most reengineering projects failed. Interestingly, in the late 1990s and early 2000s, ERP systems helped realize many of those reengineering ideas because the systems forced changes in processes. At the least, ERP systems integrated information from various organizational units, resulting in less labor, greater accuracy, and shorter cycles.

ERP systems also help organizations move away from the traditional silos of functional units to business processes, an approach that helps many of them operate better. Suppliers and customers do not care whose responsibility it is to take care of their orders and payments. Therefore, organizations are better off planning and managing processes rather than organizational units. Despite the risks and the high costs involved, a growing number of companies adopt ERP systems.

Summary

- Effectiveness is the degree to which a task is accomplished. The better a person performs a job, the more effective he or she is. Efficiency is measured as the ratio of output to input—the greater the ratio, the more efficient the process. ISs can help companies attain more effective and efficient business processes. Productivity is the measure of people's efficiency. When people use ISs, their productivity increases.

- ISs have been integrated into almost every functional business area. In accounting and payroll, because of the routine and structured nature of accounting tasks, the systems automatically post transactions in the books and automate the generation of reports for management and for legal requirements.

- Financial ISs help managers track cash available for transactions, while ensuring that available money is invested in short- or long-term programs to yield the highest interest possible. Investment analysis ISs help build portfolios based on historical performance and other characteristics of securities.

- Computer-aided design (CAD) systems help engineers design new products and save and modify drawings electronically. Computer-aided manufacturing (CAM) systems direct machines in manufacturing parts and assembling products.

- Supply chain management systems optimize workload, speed, and cost in the supply chains for procurement of raw materials, manufacturing, and shipping of goods. ISs, especially MRP and MRP II systems, facilitate production scheduling and material requirements planning, and shorten lead time between idea and product. Shipping ISs help speed up delivery and cut costs. RFID technology helps promote and operate supply chain management (SCM) systems. Radio frequency identification (RFID) tags carry product information that can be tracked and updated.

- Customer relationship management (CRM) includes the entire cycle of relationships with customers, from marketing through sales to customer service. CRM ISs collect information about shoppers and customers and help target the most likely buyers of a product or service. Online customer service systems help customers help themselves via the web 24 hours per day, 7 days per week, and save the company labor and telephone expenses. Salesforce automation allows salespeople to spend more time with customers and less time in the office.

- Human resource management systems expedite staff selection and record keeping. An increasing amount of recruiting is done via the web. Managers often use evaluation software to help assess their subordinates' performance. Employees can use expert systems to choose health care and other benefits programs that best suit their situation.

- Companies can link their SCM systems to monitor the status of orders at their own facilities but also at those of their business partners, usually their suppliers. Such cooperation can create further efficiencies, but it requires a high degree of trust between organizations.

- Rather than use disparate ISs for business functions, many organizations opt to install a single system that encompasses all their business processes, or at least the major ones. They employ enterprise resource planning (ERP) systems to support their supply chain management and customer relationship management. Installation of ERP systems is expensive and challenging, and often involves budget and time overruns.

KIMBALL'S REVISITED

Michael understands that the expansion of the business is dependent on two issues: (1) gaining efficiencies in backhouse operations and (2) defining marketing and promotional strategies to gain additional customers. Help Michael and Tyler assess their current systems and plan to address those issues.

What Is Your Advice?

1. Using the classifications in this chapter, identify the business functions within Kimball's. What business functions could assist Kimball's to gain efficiencies in the backhouse operations? List those functions and their benefit to the business.

2. What software applications should Tyler research? What questions could he ask his current software vendor? What types of metrics and ratios could be used to help monitor the business operations?

3. How would you develop a target market plan to increase clientele for the restaurant? What types of marketing data would you need for this effort? Could social media be used as a component of the target marketing plan? What information systems could be utilized to assist with this marketing and promotion effort? What data is necessary to gather in order to track and monitor those efforts?

New Perspectives

1. Should Kimball's develop any initiatives to gain feedback from customers directly? Could social media provide that feedback?

2. What information technology systems could help Kimball's to gather and store the important data elements for the marketing?

Key Terms

bill of materials (BOM), 76
brainstorming, 73
cash management system (CMS), 72
computer-aided design (CAD), 73
computer-aided manufacturing (CAM), 73
customer relationship management (CRM), 68
economic order quantity (EOQ), 77
effectiveness, 68

efficiency, 68
electronic funds transfer (EFT), 72
electronic product code (EPC), 80
enterprise resource planning (ERP), 97
just-in-time (JIT), 77
location-based services, 85
manufacturing resource planning (MRP II), 77
master production schedule (MPS), 77

material requirements planning (MRP), 76
productivity, 68
radio frequency identification (RFID), 80
rapid prototyping, 73
supply chain, 75
supply chain management (SCM), 75
targeted marketing, 84
time to market, 73
work order, 71

Review Questions

1. What is a supply chain? What is the purpose of supply chain management systems?

2. What is the purpose of cost accounting ISs?

3. What is the relationship between CAD and CAM systems?

4. What are the concerns in cash management, and how do cash management ISs help financial managers?

5. What is time to market? How have ISs affected time to market?

6. In brief, what is the purpose of customer relationship management systems?

7. What are the typical components of ERP systems?

8. Although technologically the full linking of the SCM systems of suppliers and buyers is feasible, many buyers are reluctant to do so. Why?

9. Why do the ERP installation and testing of systems require that experts be involved? Why does the implementation of so many ERP systems face severe challenges or totally fail?

10. What is EOQ? Which two problems do ISs that calculate EOQ help minimize?

11. What is JIT? How do MRP and MRP II systems help achieve JIT?

12. For the human resource managers of some organizations the entire web is a database of job candidates. How so?

13. What information technologies play a crucial role in marketing?

14. Many sales reps have no offices, yet they have access to huge resources, and their productivity is great. Explain how that is possible.

15. What is RFID, and what role does it play in SCM?

16. In the supply chain, shipping software helps mainly in two ways. What are they?

Discussion Questions

17. You established a small shop that manufactures a single product that you sell by mail. You purchase raw materials from several vendors and employ five full-time employees. For which business functions would you certainly use software?

18. Which of the ISs you listed for Question 17 would you link to each other, and for what purpose?

19. Why is it so important to have a quick response of online investment ISs? Give two examples of how such systems are critical.

20. Some experts say that ISs have great potential in manufacturing. Explain why. (*Hint:* Consider business process reengineering.)

21. Over the past decade, banks and investment firms have offered many services that would be impossible without ISs. Describe three such services and explain how IT makes them possible.

22. ISs in both the manufacturing and service sectors often help to *optimize*. Give two examples of what they optimize.

23. The web has significantly cut the cost of collecting data about shoppers and buyers. Explain how.

24. Sellers of consumer products argue that targeted marketing serves not only them but also their consumers. How so?

25. If you had to evaluate your own subordinates, would you prefer to evaluate them in written, open-ended form, or would you prefer to use employee evaluation software? Why?

26. As an employee, would you prefer that your supervisor evaluate you with the aid of employee evaluation software or without it? Why?

27. Try to remember the last time you gave someone your personal data, such as an ID number, email address, or a physical address. What was the reason for asking for the data? Do you know how the data will be used by the receiver?

28. Some consumer advocates argue that organizations should pay every individual whenever they sell data about him or her to another organization. (They suggest 5 or 10 cents per sale.) Do you agree? Why?

29. Examine the list of precautions suggested in "Ethical & Societal Issues" for ensuring minimum invasion of privacy when businesses use personal data. Which steps can be taken without, or with minimal, added cost? Which steps would impose financial burdens on businesses? Why?

30. RFID tags are increasingly embedded in almost every type of good, from soda six-packs to clothing items. Consumer advocates fear that the technology might cause massive violation of privacy. Describe at least two ways in which this can happen. What controls or limitations would you impose on RFID tags and use to minimize the fears of invasion of privacy?

Applying Concepts

31. You are the CEO of a company that runs 2 plants, manufactures 12 different products, and sells them in 15 world regions. List all the items of information (totals, metrics, etc.) that you would like to know at least on a quarterly basis. State which information can or cannot be obtained through company operated ISs and why.

32. Choose three distinct but related business functions (e.g., inventory control, purchasing, payroll, accounting, etc.). Write a short paper describing how interfacing the information systems of these three functions can improve an organization's performance.

33. Select a business process (possibly at a local firm) not mentioned in this chapter. Write an essay explaining how IS technology could make the process (1) more efficient and (2) more effective.

34. Write a three-page essay titled "Factory of the Future." Your factory will not require anybody in the manufacturing organization to enter any data into information systems. All the necessary information will come from customers at one end and suppliers at the other end. There will also be no need to type in any data for payments and collections. Explain how all this will work.

Hands-On Activity

35. Many companies use email to advertise their products. Your company is trying to sell a new product and is advised to use email. All the email addresses are of people who have agreed to receive promotional email about products such as the one you try to sell. The profit on each unit sold is $200. Developing the attractive email message, use of 2,750,000 email addresses, and sending the message would cost $25,000. Experience shows that 5 percent of the initial recipients forward such messages to friends and family. Experience also shows that 2 percent of all recipients actually click the web address included in the message and visit the commercial site. Of these visitors, 0.5 percent end up purchasing the advertised item.

Using Microsoft Excel or another spreadsheet, answer the following questions: (1) Would you generate a profit if you used this advertising opportunity? (2) Would you profit if you could email only 1,000,000 people?

Develop a rationale for integrating social media into the email initiative. How can the integration of social media be used along with a direct email campaign? Research the strategy of various businesses as a model for your recommendations.

36. Form a team and design an IS for a small business that sells manufactured parts to other businesses. The system must handle customer order processing, sales, salesperson commissions, billing, and accounts receivable. Prepare a report describing the system's different components and their points of interface. What files are necessary? How will the business use data in each file? If you have command of Microsoft Access, create the tables for the above objects, and populate each one with three to five records.

37. Assume that you and your teammates are about to start a web-based business for sporting goods. You wish to email information to potential customers. Determine the demographic characteristics of your target audience. Search the web for companies that sell consumer data that can serve you. Prepare a report about three such companies: their names, services, and prices (if available).

From Ideas to Application: Real Cases

Winning the Bet

International Game Technology (IGT) is a leading manufacturer of slot machines and lottery machines for casinos and government lotteries. Headquartered in Reno, Nevada, with sales headquarters in Las Vegas, the company also maintains sales, manufacturing, and service sites in Africa, Australia, Europe, and South America. Its Reno site alone produces 140,000 machines annually. It has been profitable for many years. In 2005, it had a profit of $437 million on revenue of $2.4 billion, apparently a situation that would lull executives of other companies to think "If it ain't broke, don't fix it." Not IGT managers.

Until 2002, each business function had its own information system. IGT had different systems for handling sales, customer orders, manufacturing, and accounting. When managers wanted to receive information about a specific customer order, they had to go to each functional unit to receive a different piece of the information: customer details from the sales department, status of the machines being manufactured from the manufacturing units, and payment status from accounting. The accounting department itself had several software applications that handled different books, such as accounts receivable, accounts payable, and the general ledger.

As business was growing, managers complained that they could not get comprehensive information on orders. The IT department developed interface software to connect the systems, but there were still complaints that information was not coherent. The IT specialists admitted that they were maintaining a mishmash of software. The loudest complaints came from the accountants. Every year it took them two weeks "to close the books."

The accounting department pressured management to purchase a new system that would make their work more efficient. The CIO understood their plea but was afraid that satisfying this department's request would trigger similar requests from other units, such as engineering and manufacturing. The result might be a better information system for each department, but disparate systems that still were not connected to each other. On the CIO's advice, IGT management decided to implement an ERP system.

A steering committee and project team were assembled. Their members focused on business functionality rather than the technology. After the first selection, systems from three companies were considered: SAP, Oracle, and J.D. Edwards (which was later acquired by Oracle). After further consideration, SAP won the contract, and IGT embarked on a two-year effort. In 2003, the company switched to using the R/3 ERP system. IGT did not disclose the cost of the project, but analysts estimate it was well over $10 million.

When the system was ready, three functions were incorporated into one enterprise system: product development, manufacturing, and finance. Like other ERP systems, R/3 is highly structured even when modified for a particular customer. As often happened, the new system forced IGT to change some of its business processes. However, the company chose SAP's system because it found it less rigid than other ERP systems. This was important to IGT, because it builds machines to order.

The system afforded the company several benefits. Price proposals are made based on more accurate information and estimates. Managers on the manufacturing floor can view or print out manufacturing process sheets at their own PCs. Employees can no longer ignore specifications or "cut corners." The system does not allow a process to continue when an attempt such as this is made. The products are made more efficiently and with fewer errors. The system connects all of the company's sites around the globe. One of the system's modules is project management, which enables managers to monitor design changes and costs involved in new product development.

The new system replaced the old MRP (material requirements planning) system, but the company still uses its internally developed factory control system, which has been successfully integrated into the SAP system. The factory control system enables managers to know which machines are built at which plant.

IGT reduced the average period of order to shipping from 9–10 weeks to 7–8 weeks. When a rush order is entered, IGT can now fulfill it in four weeks instead of seven weeks. Between 2002 and 2005 the error rates in orders for raw materials decreased from 10 percent to almost 0. Inventory turn increased from 6.3 to 8.4 percent per year.

IGT's CIO admits that the implementation was challenging. The company makes a variety of machines, which meant that many bills of materials had to be entered into the system (and new ones will have to be entered for new products). Adapting some features to the way IGT operates was not easy. However, the implementation was successful. The CIO credits the success to strong support from senior management, the establishment of a steering committee with members from all affected units, a capable project management team, a training program to help employees understand how to use the new system, and the rigorous testing the system underwent before it was used.

Source: Bartholomew, D., "ERP: Gaming Company Hits Jackpot," Baseline, October 2, 2006; (www.igt.com), 2007.

Thinking About the Case

1. What problems did IGT face before the implementation of the ERP system?

2. How does the new system help control processes?

3. Compared to the situation in 2002, what are the benefits of the ERP system?

4. IGT decided to continue operating its older factory control system. Why do you think it did so?

Resting on Electronic Mail for Effective CRM

For service industries, providing the customer with a great experience is key to success. Very often, very small details are what surprise customers and create a lasting positive impression. The foundation of CRM methodologies focuses not only on maintaining relationships with customers, but with profitable customers.

When email adoption increased significantly in the 1990s, many businesses shifted their marketing and communication focus from direct mail to electronic mail. This new technology was viewed as a low-cost, efficient method to communicate with customers. However, the benefits of communicating by email quickly became a "double edged sword" to consumers. Overusing email could quickly create overcommunication with their customers that would result in customers becoming turned off.

The combination of government regulation and the popularity of social media have reduced the reliance on electronic mail. A 2010 report by Nielsen confirmed that the share of time relating to email has declined to 28 percent, while time spent with social media increased to 43 percent. Ironically, while social media may be popular, consumers remain loyal (42 percent) to email as the source to obtain information about specials and advertisements. An eConsultancy study found that only 3 percent use social-networking sites and 1 percent use Twitter. Forrester Research's 2011 report found that consumers delete fewer emails without reading them.

The hotel industry continues to provide properties with amenities that are desired by customers. With over 7,000 hotels, Wyndham Hotel Group has more than 8 million members in its loyalty program. Wyndham wanted to use email campaigns to increase revenue and occupancy at their properties as well as promote their brand. However, it would be important to balance their campaigns so they did not overcommunicate with members. The competitive nature of the hotel industry creates a fickle customer. The promotions offered by a hotel can often complicate the issue of coordinating email campaigns. However, an effective email campaign requires the same approach as for any other business: discipline.

Although Wyndham implemented many email promotions, they were not receiving the results that they planned. Coupled with the effort needed to implement these campaigns, they knew that a new approach was needed. Working with a marketing firm, Acxiom, a more targeted approach was developed. With the outside consultants, they applied best practices to determine the timing and sequences of messages. They created webpages and various email versions along with custom Subject text. These emails would be sent to a subset of their rewards members in the United States.

It was important to tailor future emails to customers based on their past actions. Wyndham developed an automated email engine that operated based on such data. For example, a confirmation email was sent based on the completion of a registration. A variety of emails would be sent to rewards members based on a specific purpose, ranging from free nights to vacation specials to reward point specials. With the focus on email distribution, Wyndham continued to offer members the ability to opt out of receiving emails.

Their strategy and use of email technology was successful compared with their previous email campaigns. Wyndham's total revenue linked directly from email solicitations increased by 187 percent. Various other metrics showed positive gains as well. The rate of emails that were opened by users increased by 8.2 percent while registration rates for a summer promotion increased by 43 percent over a previous campaign.

Sources: Aquino, J. (2012). Don't count out email yet. Customer Relationship Management, 16-19. Aquino, J. (2012). Wyndham hotels' targeted emails break records. Customer Relationship Management, 16, 37. Rubel, S. (2010). Hot or not: Email marketing vs. social-media marketing. Advertising Age, 81(29), 16.

Thinking About the Case

1. Why was it important for Wyndham to re-examine their email campaign approach rather than just abandon it?

2. What do you believe was the turning point for this effort?

3. Why have marketing professionals approached email campaigns differently than other promotional methods?

4. Consider the emails that you receive from businesses. Contrast and compare the approach of these businesses versus Wyndham's approach.

References

Anonymous. (2009). Success Story — SnapFish. www.liveperson.com/sites/default/files/pdfs/Snapfish_CaseStudy.pdf

Anonymous. (2010a). Recruiting Still the HR Function Most Likely to Be Outsourced. *Staffing Management, 6*, 9–9.

Anonymous. (2010b). Wonderlic Launches ASAP for Home Healthcare(TM) A Web-Based Solution That Helps Home Healthcare Firms to Quickly Hire Capable, Service-Oriented Staff, *Business Wire.*

Anonymous. (2010c). Wonderlic Rolls Out ASAP for Property Management Hiring. *Professional Services Close-Up.*

Columbus, L. (2013). 2013 ERP Market Share Update: SAP Solidifies Market Leadership. *Forbes.com.* www.forbes.com/sites/louiscolumbus/2013/05/12/2013-erp-market-share-update-sap-solidifies-market-leadership/

INFORMATION TECHNOLOGY

BUSINESS CHALLENGES

Liz and Michael understand the strategic and functional uses of information technology for their restaurant business. Now they need to analyze and assemble the hardware, software, and networking requirements that will support their strategic and operational decisions. In addition, Liz and Michael will need to determine what information is needed to support their business operations.

- In Chapter 4,"Business Hardware," you learn how to evaluate hardware needs and determine what hardware will support the daily operations of a business entity.

- In Chapter 5, "Business Software," you learn how to determine the types of software needed to provide the functions for an organization's staff and management.

- In Chapter 6, "Business Networks and Telecommunications," you learn about the network and telecommunications strategies that various businesses use to support the technology and business functions.

- In Chapter 7, "Databases and Data Warehouses," you learn the importance of an organization's significant asset—databases—and understand how database technology can be leveraged for both strategic advantage and operational efficiency.

CHAPTER four

BUSINESS HARDWARE

Learning Objectives

At the core of any modern information system stands at least one computer. Few machines have changed human life as radically as the computer, and few such complex machines have become so affordable to so many businesses and individuals in such a short time. Because computers and other hardware devices are central to information systems and to business, to successfully implement ISs, you need to understand them. Businesses have many hardware choices, ranging from computers and mobile devices to input and output devices. Understanding the capabilities of hardware and the options available can save companies millions of dollars. This chapter provides you with the knowledge to make intelligent decisions about computer hardware in your professional career.

When you finish this chapter, you will be able to:

- List major hardware components of computers and explain their functions.

- Classify computers into major categories, and identify their strengths and weaknesses.

- Identify and evaluate key criteria for deciding what computers or related devices to purchase.

- Discuss the possible health hazards of computer use.

KIMBALL'S RESTAURANT: Hardware for the Appetite

Tyler and Michael have worked on the marketing plan for the new location. They believe that it will be successful in expanding their marketing reach to gain new customers for Kimball's lakeside location. Now it was time to turn their attention to improving the operational aspect of their business. At the top of their list was determining what restaurant software would best fit their needs for the new location, and if their current computer hardware could handle it.

Talking Technical

Tyler and his parents agreed that upgrading their information system would help create a more efficient operation at the existing restaurant, and provide a solid base for launching their new location. They also were excited about having access to additional data and reporting capabilities to help them evaluate and plan more efficiently and effectively. What they didn't know was what hardware and software they needed to achieve their goals.

Tyler contacted Clark Howard at PosiDining Systems (PDS), the software company that installed their current POS system. They selected PDS's entry-level version several years ago as a low-cost option to automate the operations.

Since the installation of the PDS system, some of the issues have been reduced (see previous chapter cases for additional explanation). However, he is concerned that the version of the system they are using may not be enough for the new location. He was concerned that the servers manually entered orders into the system based on notes taken at the table. There could be mistakes in either the writing or entry of the customer orders.

Tyler explained the estimated volume that was anticipated at the new restaurant as well as some of the management issues that were anticipated at the new location. Clark and Tyler reviewed the number of workstations needed by the wait and kitchen staff as well as the dining and bar area seating chart. Clark told Tyler that the more robust version of PDS's product would be able to operate the new location effectively, provide more data for management, and avoid some of the problems they're currently experiencing with the POS system.

Although Tyler wanted an information system that could help his family operate and manage the restaurant effectively, he was also concerned about the cost and the learning curve associated with a new system for both staff and management. Clark understood his concerns. Tyler asked if it would be possible to install the upgraded system at the current location for 2-3 months while the lakeside location was being prepared. Although there might be some additional cost to install and reinstall the hardware and software, they could train people at the current location so the transition to the new location would be less stressful.

Clark said he would prepare a proposal for this phased-in approach that would detail the associated costs for the restaurant.

Computer Hardware Components

eBay, the world's largest auction business, sold $4.0 billion of electronics in the first quarter 2013 and serves more than 116 million active users worldwide. The influence of mobile computing has been significant, 33 percent of all eBay transactions are mobile-based. These activities require a huge amount of hardware. The company uses 50,000 servers. (eBay, 2012, 2013; Sverdlik, 2013). The company's computers are spread all over the world, and are connected through the Internet.

Hardware, in computer terms, refers to the physical components of computers and related digital devices such as tablets, scanners, and smartphones. (Software, covered in the next chapter, refers to the sets of instructions that direct the hardware to perform particular tasks.) In corporate decision making, managers should consider software first, not hardware. Businesses need to first identify the tasks they want to support and the decisions they want to make, and therefore the information they need to produce. This information will help them determine the appropriate software, and they can then purchase the best hardware to run the software. A new organization can often make software-related decisions first. However, in a great majority of cases, established organizations already have a significant investment in hardware and, therefore, must often consider adopting new software within the constraints of their existing hardware. Regardless of size, age, function, or capability, most computers have the same basic components (see Figure 4.1) and operate according to the same basic principles. A computer must handle four operations: (1) accept data, (2) store data and instructions, (3) process data, and (4) output data and/or information. In recent years, data communication over a network has become an essential aspect of input and output for almost every computer, whether stationary or portable.

FIGURE 4.1

Most computer systems
have the same basic
components

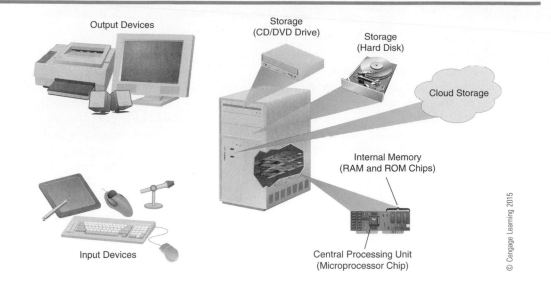

© Cengage Learning 2015

In general, every computer has these components:

- **Input devices** receive signals from outside the computer and transfer them into the computer. Common input devices are computer keyboards, mice, and touch screens, but some input devices accept voice, image, or other signals.

- The **central processing unit**, or **CPU**, is the most important part of any computer. The CPU accepts instructions and data, decodes and executes instructions, and stores results (output) in memory for later display. In technical terms, a CPU is a chip made of silicon, transistors, and numerous tiny soldered wires that form complex circuitry. The circuitry is built and programmed so that it can interpret electrical signals to run computers. Some computers have several CPUs. The increase in the power of computers and decrease in their prices have in large part been the result of engineers' ability to increase the number of transistors on these chips without increasing the chips' size.

- **Internal memory**, also called primary memory, is located near the CPU and stores data and instructions just before and immediately after the CPU processes them. This includes programs currently running on a machine, intermediate results of arithmetic operations, intermediate versions of documents being word processed, and data elements that represent the pictures displayed on a computer screen and the sounds played by the speakers. Most of a computer's internal memory is **RAM (random access memory)**, and a smaller amount is **ROM (read-only memory)**. RAM holds data and program instructions, and is volatile by design, that is, its contents are cleared when the computer is turned off or when a computer program is allowed to replace the data in it. ROM is nonvolatile. It contains data and instructions that do not change, mostly instructions the computer uses to load programs when it is powered on. The amount of RAM—often simply called memory—and the speed at which it operates are two of the properties that determine the power of a computer. The CPU and primary memory are usually plugged into a circuit board in the computer case called the **motherboard** or system board.

- **Storage** is different types of media—such as magnetic disks, magnetic tapes, optical discs, DVDs, and flash memory—that store data and information; however, unlike RAM, external memory allows for permanent storage. Thus, many external storage media are portable and can be moved from one computer to another. Online or cloud storage (storing data on remote storage devices over the Internet or a private network) is an increasingly popular form of storage.

- **Output devices**, most commonly computer monitors and printers, deliver information from the computer to a person. Additional output devices include speakers and digital audio players for audio output and specialized output devices such as digital scoreboards.

Recall the explanation of digital information in Chapter 1, "Business Information Systems: An Overview." Computers and other digital devices use two states to represent zeroes and ones. Representing only two states is easier than representing many states, and two states can be more accurately detected—that is, received—than many states.

The amount of data that computers process and store is measured in bits and bytes. A **bit** is a binary digit, a 0 or 1. A **byte** is a combination of eight bits. All data stored and processed by a computer, including text, images, video, and audio, is represented by bits and bytes. Computer memory and storage capacity are measured in megabytes (MB, millions of bytes), gigabytes (GB, billions of bytes), and terabytes (TB, trillions of bytes) and beyond, as shown in Figure 4.2.

FIGURE 4.2

Measuring amounts of digital data

1 KB (kilobyte) = 1,000 bytes
1 MB (megabyte) = 1,000,000 bytes
1 GB (gigabyte) = 1,000,000,000 bytes
1 TB (terabyte) = 1,000,000,000,000 bytes
1 PB (petabyte) = 1,000,000,000,000,000 bytes
1 EB (exabyte) = 1,000,000,000,000,000,000 bytes
1 ZB (zettabyte) = 1,000,000,000,000,000,000,000 bytes
1 YB (yottabyte) = 1,000,000,000,000,000,000,000,000 bytes

© Cengage Learning 2015

Classification of Computers

Computers come in a wide variety of classes, from supercomputers to handheld smartphones. Computers are classified by their power, which is determined mainly by processing speed and memory size. However, the lines between the classes have become blurred, and the class names have changed over the years. In general, the more powerful the computer, the higher its price.

Supercomputers

Supercomputers are the most powerful computers at any given time, but are built especially for assignments that require arithmetic speed. They would be overly expensive and impractical for most business situations. Usually, supercomputers are also the largest in physical size and the

Supercomputers are used predominantly by research institutions and government agencies for complex calculations

Eimantas Buzas/Photos.com

most expensive. Universities, research institutions, government agencies, and large corporations engaged in research and development are most likely to use them. Supercomputer manufacturers include IBM, Cray, Fujitsu, Hitachi, and NEC. Supercomputers' RAMs consist of billions of bytes, and their processing speed is trillions of instructions per second. They usually cost at least in the millions of dollars. The Titan supercomputer, discussed later in a point of interest, cost $100 million (Munger, 2012).

Supercomputers contain multiple processors that let them perform **parallel processing** and run at great speeds. For example, NASA uses a supercomputer system for its scientific research and space exploration. Its Pleiades supercomputer system, made by SGI, has 182 racks, 11,776 nodes, 23,552 processors and 233 TB of memory (Anonymous, 2012e). However, even this machine is slow in comparison to the Blue Gene used at the U.S. Department of Energy's Lawrence Livermore National Laboratory. This IBM computer has 1.6 M processors capable of processing 16 thousand trillion calculations per second with 1.6 PB of memory (Brodkin, 2012). The size of its processing power is small compared to the 3,000 square feet required to house this computer system.

In parallel processing (sometimes called **multiprocessing**), several CPUs process different data at the same time. Uses of supercomputers include calculation of satellite orbits, weather forecasting, genetic decoding, optimization of oil exploration, and simulated testing of products that cannot otherwise be tested because of price or physical difficulty.

POINT OF INTEREST — The World's Most Powerful Computer

Oak Ridge National Laboratory turned on their newest supercomputer, Titan, for the first time in October 2012. The supercomputer is projected to be the fastest in the world and will be used to research and develop biofuels, combustion engine efficiency, magnetics, astrophysics, climate studies, nuclear science, and atomic-level materials science. Titan has 10 times the processing power of its predecessor, Jaguar, and occupies the same amount of space. The speed of the Titan is equal to every one of earth's 7 billion people executing 3 million calculations per second.

Source: Hoover, J. N. (2012). Energy Dept.'s Titan Supercomputer: Record Breaker? Informationweek - Online. http://www.informationweek.com/government/enterprise-applications/energy-depts-titan-super computer-record/240012478

In lieu of one large supercomputer, some organizations link a "cluster" of smaller computers via networks to create and enjoy similar computing power. Instead of a single machine with multiple processors, **clustering** uses the CPU power of multiple computers, with the same effect. A computer cluster is comprised of a group of connected computers which complete computing requests together to improve processing performance. This can be done with special software that links the CPUs of servers via a private or public network such as the Internet, all or part of the time.

Mainframe Computers

Mainframe computers are less powerful in computational speed and significantly less expensive than supercomputers. They cost several thousand to several hundred thousand dollars. Businesses that must handle business transactions and store large amounts of data in a central computer often use mainframes, which some IT professionals fondly call "big iron." These businesses include banks, insurance companies, large retail chains, and universities. Well-known mainframe manufacturers include IBM, Fujitsu, and Unisys. While the processing speed of mainframes is usually not higher than that of the fastest PCs, they often have multiple processors and their memories are significantly larger, measured in terabytes. By some estimates, a significant amount of the world's business data resides on mainframes. Like supercomputers, these computers are largely invisible to the public, although we access them often via the Internet.

POINT OF INTEREST — Supercomputing for All

Accessibility of supercomputers has been a problem because of their enormous size and cost. They can cost over $20 million to build and suck up millions more each year in power and cooling costs. However, Jason Stowe, the CEO of Cycle Computing, has solved this problem for small businesses and researchers desiring large-scale computations without the large price. Cycle Computing's software communicates to Amazon.com's cloud-computing service and organizes over 50,000 of its computers to work on one problem. Cycle Computing divides up computing problems into small pieces that can be spread out over all the machines and then puts the results back together. The low price, $1,000 per hour, makes the service affordable even to someone with a modest research grant and challenging questions.

Source: Vance, Ashley. (2012). Supercomputers for Rent. BloombergBusinessweek. Retrieved from, http://www.businessweek.com/articles/2012-07-26/supercomputers-for-rent

---

Servers

A midrange category of computers, often referred to as **servers**, are smaller than mainframes and less powerful. They are usually used as a shared resource, connecting hundreds of users to a variety of computers from desktops, laptops, and other servers. Therefore, these computers are used to communicate to other computers and "serve" applications and data, both through the Internet and locally within organizations. Like mainframe computers, servers sometimes use multiple processors.

Personal Computers

Personal computers (PCs) is the collective name for several types of computers: notebook computers, desktops, netbooks, and handheld computers. More powerful personal computers are sometimes called **workstations**. Workstations are typically used for computer-aided design (CAD), computer-aided manufacturing (CAM), complex simulation, graphical rendering, and scientific applications. As the performance of PCs steadily improves, computers that in the past were classified as midrange computers are now marketed as PCs, and the lines between computer categories continue to blur.

The power of PCs in terms of speed and memory capacity doubles about every two years. Most PCs now sold to individuals and businesses cost less than $900. However, a growing number of personal computers are not desktop PCs, but laptops and tablet computers.

Computers on the Go: Notebooks, Tablets, and Smartphones

Computers are increasingly used outside the home, office, or school. Notebook or handheld computers are used to record and retrieve data for people on the go. The **notebook computer** (also called a laptop) is a compact, light, personal computer that can be powered by a rechargeable battery. These computers can operate for up to eight hours without recharging their batteries. All recent notebook computers have internal circuitry that enables them to connect wirelessly to networks and the Internet. (Wireless technology is covered in Chapter 6, "Business Networks and Telecommunications.") Notebooks have matched the power of desktop PCs in terms of speed, memory, and hard disk capacity.

One highly popular class of computing machinery is the handheld computer. Handheld computers called **personal digital assistants (PDAs)** appeared on the market in the early 1990s but became popular only toward the end of the decade. These devices were small enough to fit in the palm of your hand, and typically a **stylus** (a pen-like pointing and drawing device) was used to enter data through a touch screen, although some had a small keyboard or could plug into a folding portable keyboard. By the mid-2000s, almost all new PDAs also served as mobile phones, and were increasingly called by the new term, **smartphone**.

POINT OF INTEREST — Is it a Phone, a Tablet, or Both?

The Samsung Galaxy Note II, released in 2012, eliminates the need to carry around a mobile phone, camera, and tablet; it is all of those things and more. Its 5.3-inch screen sizes it in between traditional smartphones and tablets. It can execute the tasks of the traditional mobile phone such as making calls and text messages, as well as taking high quality pictures that can be instantly uploaded to social media sites. The "S pen" can be used for notetaking and drawing. Sloppy handwriting? No worries. Your handwriting can be automatically converted to text. The Galaxy Note II has great call quality and fast upload/download speeds. Samsung has created a demand for their product by making one device that has the capabilities of many devices.

Source: Mies, G. (2012). Samsung Galaxy Note: Impressive, but Not for All. PC World, 30, 54.

Another mobile computing device is the **tablet computer**, often called tablet for short. Instead of a mouse, you use your fingers or a stylus on a touch screen to execute commands. Tablets can be laptop PCs with touch screens that can operate either in "traditional" monitor mode with a keyboard, or swivel to operate in "slate" mode using the touch screen. Other tablets are smaller in size without a built-in keyboard, such as the Apple iPad, Microsoft Surface, and many others. Most tablets have high-definition displays and excellent audio and video capabilities, as well as Wi-Fi and/or cellular network connectivity.

The applications for tablets have exponentially expanded in recent years. Users can surf the web, read books, shop, video chat, watch movies, listen to music, play games, and much more. Access to online "app" stores gives users instant access to songs, books, movies, and games. Tablets are popular among people of all ages because of their wide range of applications. In addition to their use for entertainment, one of the most beneficial uses for tablets is in schools, where students use them to download electronic texts, take notes on lectures, and communicate with teachers about assignments. The cost of supplying each student with a tablet can be less than constantly replacing outdated textbooks.

Medical professionals can leverage the portability of a tablet device to access and update patient information

Hongqi Zhang/Photo.com

Some tablets evolved from e-readers. For example, the original Kindle e-reader offered by Amazon.com performed the basic task of displaying the pages of a book. However, many e-readers have evolved to perform as many tasks as tablets. The Kindle Fire HD has a tablet-size screen and can use high-speed cellular networks. Users can download movies, songs, and books, as well as check email and surf the web. It is becoming increasingly difficult to distinguish what is a tablet and what is an e-reader because they are evolving to perform the same tasks.

The popularity of the Apple iPad, Kindle Fire, and other tablet computers has created an alternative to traditional desktop and laptop computers. The combination of a high definition display, network capabilities, and the proliferation of application software provides a solid product. Tablet technology offers business professionals the computing capability they need to perform their jobs more efficiently on the go.

Converging Technologies

As you've seen in the previous section, in recent years, we have experienced an increasing trend of **technology convergence**, building several technologies into a single piece of hardware. Smartphones are a prime example. In the early 1990s, PDAs became popular devices, placing computing power in a handheld-sized unit. Cell phones were becoming popular at the same time. The rapid adoption of both cell phones and PDAs converged to create a new product, the smartphone, which combined the computing power of a PDA with the calling functionality of cell phones. In addition, smartphones integrated media technologies such as MP3 players, video recording, and digital cameras. Smartphones also can connect to personal computers or networks to synchronize data (calendars, contacts), connect to printers, and access cloud storage systems. The convergence of several technologies—cellular telephone, data and networking, media, and cloud storage—in the smartphone has significantly extended the ability of individuals to "take their computers on the go."

POINT OF INTEREST   Today the Mobile Way

In 2012, the number of Chinese who accessed the Internet via mobile phone outnumbered desktop Internet users for the first time. The 388 million Chinese who used their mobile phone to surf the web was 22 percent more than in 2011. That leaves 380 million still accessing the Internet through a desktop computer. About 50 percent of all new Chinese Internet users are from rural areas, and 60 percent of them access the Internet from mobile phones. Tech companies are reacting by offering expanded services to mobile phone users and by targeting the rural population.

Source: Tsuruoka, D. (2012). Mobile Phones Now Top Way To Access Internet In China, Investor's Business Daily.

A Peek Inside the Computer

Smartphones provide extensive computing, networking, and phone capabilities in one small unit

Oleksiy Mark/Photos.com

It is not necessary to look under a car's hood to drive it, but it is important to know enough about how a car is built to know which car to buy. Similarly, professionals must know enough about the major components of a computer to understand what computing power and capabilities they buy or recommend for buying. The following discussion introduces the computer's most common parts and peripheral equipment and describes in some detail how these devices work.

The Central Processing Unit

The CPU is the computer's brain, where all processing takes place. The CPU consists of two units: the **control unit** and the **arithmetic logic unit (ALU)**. These units store and process data. The CPU is a silicon chip with multiple circuits. It carries signals that execute all processing within a computer. Because the chip is so small, it is often called a **microprocessor**, or simply a processor. Most modern computers use processors that combine two or more CPUs or "cores" on a single chip, called **multicore processors**. Multicore processors are capable of performing more than one task at a time. For example, they can carry out a calculation in a spreadsheet and process a graphical design simultaneously. Processing more than one program, or processing several parts of a program, at the same time is often called **multithreading**, whereby each process is a thread.

Microprocessors

Microprocessors are made of silicon embedded with transistors. A transistor is a semiconductor, a component that can serve as either a conductor or an insulator, depending on the voltage of electricity that tries to flow through it. This property is excellent for computer communications, because it provides a means to represent binary code's two states: a 1 (voltage conducted) or a 0 (voltage not conducted). Thus, transistors can sense binary signals that are actually encoded instructions telling the computer to conduct different operations.

The greater the number of transistors that can be embedded in the chip—which means the greater the number of circuits—the more powerful the microprocessor. Current processors can contain several hundred million circuits. Current technology enables chip makers to print circuits on silicon that is 0.1 micron thick, one thousand times thinner than a human hair. New processor-making technologies let engineers increase the processing speed of computers while enabling them to use less energy and give off less heat.

The Machine Cycle

When a program starts running in a computer, the CPU performs a routine sequence, illustrated in Figure 4.3 for a simple arithmetic function. First, the control unit, one of the two parts of the CPU, fetches an instruction from a program in primary memory and decodes it, that is, interprets what should be done. The control unit transmits this code to the other part of the CPU, the arithmetic logic unit (ALU), which executes the instruction. Usually, the operation's result is needed for further operations. Therefore, the control unit takes the result and stores it in primary memory, or it leaves it in a memory location called register for a following instruction to use. The control unit then fetches the next instruction, decodes it, and "puts" it in the ALU, which executes the instruction. The control unit stores the result in primary memory, and so on, until the entire program is executed, or something happens that stops the cycle. Anything that stops the cycle is called an interrupt. It might be an instruction in the program itself, a power failure, or any other event that stops the CPU.

FIGURE 4.3

What happens inside the CPU in one machine cycle

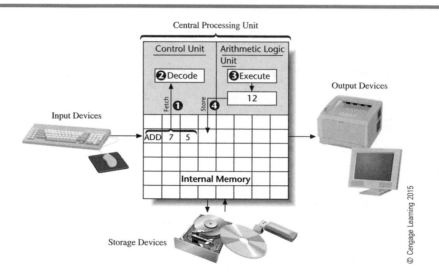

© Cengage Learning 2015

As you can see, the CPU performs four functions in every cycle: fetch, decode, execute, and store. Each cycle is called a **machine cycle**. CPUs can perform billions of machine cycles per second. The sequence of CPU operations must be paced so that different tasks do not collide. To this end, the control unit uses special circuitry called a **CPU clock**, which synchronizes all tasks. The clock is programmed to run operations at the maximum rate allowable. The number of pulses per second is called frequency, or **clock rate**. A machine cycle takes several clock pulses. CPU frequencies are measured in megahertz (MHz, millions of hertz) or gigahertz (GHz, billions of hertz). During the time it takes your eye to blink (about 0.2 second), a computer can execute hundreds of millions of instructions. Therefore, timing of computer operations is measured in very small fractions of a second (see Figure 4.4).

FIGURE 4.4

The timing of computer processing operations

1 millisecond = 1/1,000 (0.001) second

1 microsecond = 1/1,000,000 (0.000001) second

1 nanosecond = 1/1,000,000,000 (0.000000001) second

1 picosecond = 1/1,000,000,000,000 (0.000000000001) second

© Cengage Learning 2015

Interestingly, many computers now have a lower clock rate than computers of several years ago. This does not mean that such computers work more slowly. They have multicore processors, which are more efficient. They execute more instructions per machine cycle than the older single-core processors, and therefore are faster despite the lower clock rate. Therefore, both the cycles per second and instructions per cycle (IPC) should be considered when comparing speeds of processors.

The Word

The **data word** (or "word" for short) is the maximum number of bits that the control unit can fetch from primary memory in one machine cycle. The word's size is determined by the size of the CPU circuitry that holds information for processing. Obviously, the larger the word, the more instructions or data can be retrieved per second. Therefore, all other things being equal, the larger the word, the faster the computer. Current microcomputers have words of 32 and 64 bits.

The Arithmetic Logic Unit Operations

The ALU is the part of the CPU where all arithmetic and logic operations take place. Arithmetic operations include addition, subtraction, multiplication, division, exponentiation, logarithmic calculations, trigonometric computations, and other complex mathematical tasks. Logic operations compare numbers and strings of characters. For example, comparisons such as greater than, less than, and equal to are logic operations. The ALU also compares character strings that are not quantitative. For example, when you try to find a word in the text of a word-processing document, the ALU compares all words in the text to that specific word until it finds an identical word.

Computer Power

What makes one computer more powerful than another? The two major factors to consider are processing speed and memory capacity. A computer's speed is determined, among other factors, by the CPU clock rate (measured in MHz or GHz), and the amount of information the CPU can process per cycle (determined by the size of the data word and the capacity of internal data communication). However, the architecture of the various computer components also plays a significant role in determining processing speed. To mention one, consider the discussion of multicore CPUs. When two computers are built with the same components except the number of cores, the computer with the greater number of cores is faster.

All other things being equal, the greater the clock rate, the faster the machine. This is due to the fact that it can fetch, decode, execute, and store more instructions per second. Similarly, the larger the data word, the faster the computer. A larger word means that in each trip to the primary memory, the control unit can retrieve more bits to process. Therefore, the CPU can execute a program faster.

You might have seen advertisements promoting a "64-bit computer." This means the data word's capacity is 64 bits. You must be cautious with regard to word size. A larger word does not always mean a faster computer, because the speed at which the bits move between the CPU and other components depends on the capacity of internal communication lines. The system bus—also called simply the **bus**—which is the electronic lines or traces used for communication inside the computer, might have a width of only 32 bits, while the word might contain 64 bits. The number of bits is also referred to as the width of the bus.

Buses have their own clock rate. The bus that computer makers usually mention in ads is the front side bus, which is the bus connecting the CPU to the memory. A typical front side bus clock rate is 1600 MHz. The combination of bus width and clock rate determines throughput. **Throughput** is the number of bits per second that the bus can accommodate. Considering both factors, CPU clock rate (so many GHz) and bus throughput, enables you to compare properly the speeds of different computers.

Computer speed is also measured in **MIPS** (millions of instructions per second), which is not an accurate measure, because instructions have various levels of complexity. However, computer speed expressed in MIPS is often used to indicate overall processing speed because all factors that determine speed are considered: clock rate, data word size, and bus throughput, as well as other speed factors that we do not discuss here. Computer speeds expressed in MIPS have been used to indicate the dramatic reduction in the cost of computing; observers often divide the MIPS by the cost of a computer and marvel how the cost of computer power has decreased dramatically, from MIPS per dollar to MIPS per cent. In recent years, computer makers have also used the term "transactions per minute" (TPM), referring mainly to database transactions, but this ratio, too, is not an absolute measurement.

Input Devices

Computers must receive input to produce desired output. Input devices include all machines and other apparatuses used to enter instructions and data into the computer. Popular input devices include the keyboard, mouse, trackball, touch screen, microphone, and various types of scanners. The most common input device is the keyboard.

Keyboard

The keyboard contains keys that users press to enter data into primary memory and instructions for programs to run. All keyboards include the basic letters of the alphabet, numbers, and punctuation marks—plus several function keys numbered F1, F2, and so on, that can be activated to execute preprogrammed functions, such as copying a highlighted sentence in a text file created with a word processor. With the growing use of the web and use of computers to play music and video clips, keyboard manufacturers have added keys that facilitate web browser commands such as Back and Forward, and music keys such as Volume and Play/Pause. On some keyboards you can bring up your email application by pressing the Mail key or the calculator by pressing the Calculator key.

QWERTY and Dvorak Keyboards

The standard keyboard layout is called QWERTY, an acronym based on the top row of letter keys from left to right. Interestingly, the QWERTY keyboard was originally designed to slow down typing, because early mechanical typewriters jammed when users typed too fast. Today's electrical devices make this layout counterproductive. Other keyboard designs facilitate faster typing. On the Dvorak keyboard, the most frequently used keys are in the home, or central, row. Using this keyboard can increase typing speed by 95 percent. Some operating systems, such as Windows, let users map QWERTY keys into a Dvorak layout. Most computer users are reluctant to retrain themselves for the Dvorak map. In France and some other European countries, the A and Q keys are swapped, and the Z and W keys are swapped. These keyboards are known as AZERTY keyboards.

Ergonomic Keyboards

Many people prefer to use ergonomic keyboards for additional comfort while typing

Hemera Technologies/Photos.com

One of the most prevalent computer-related work injuries is carpal tunnel syndrome, the pain or numbness caused by holding the forearms in an unnatural position for long periods. The repetitive motion of typing exacerbates this problem, causing repetitive-stress injuries (RSIs). In response, ergonomic keyboards are gaining popularity. **Ergonomics** is the study of the comfort and safety of human beings in their working environment. Ergonomic keyboards are split in the middle, and the two parts are twisted outward to better fit the natural position of the forearms.

Mouse, Trackball, and Trackpad

A **mouse** is an input device that controls an on-screen pointer to facilitate the point-and-click approach to executing different operations. It is most commonly used with a keyboard, although some programs use it exclusively. Mice have one

Szymon Mazurek/Photos.com

to five buttons that let the user place the pointer anywhere on the screen, highlight portions of the screen, and select items from a menu.

When the user moves the mouse on the surface of a desk or a pad, the computer detects the movements, translates them into digital coordinates on the screen, and moves the pointer to imitate the mouse's movement. The buttons are used for clicking, locking, and dragging displayed information. A **trackball** is similar to a mouse, but the ball moves within the device, rather than over a surface. With a **trackpad**, a user controls the cursor by moving his or her finger along a touch-sensitive pad. Many notebook computers have built-in trackpads. Many mice and trackballs have a built-in wheel that scrolls pages displayed on the monitor.

Mice, trackballs, and keyboards are also available as wireless units that use infrared or radio technology. These units give users more flexibility, especially in software-based presentations, in which the presenter may move around holding the mouse.

Touch Screen

Sometimes a single device, such as a **touch screen**, may serve both as an input and output device. A touch screen lets the computer user choose operations by touching the options on the computer screen. Some common public applications use touch screens to provide advice to tourists, select lottery numbers, and ring in grocery items at self-serve supermarket checkouts. On handheld computers, the screen serves as both a display (output) and input device. The user enters commands and data either by touching a stylus on icons and menu items, or by touching the screen with the fingers.

More and more, computers and other information devices are operated through touch screens. Microsoft Windows 8 was designed specifically to utilize touch screen technology. Global positioning systems (GPSs) have offered this convenience for some time. Smartphones and tablets have touch screens. Touch screen technology is available in larger varieties such as walls, tablets, transparent touch screens, and interactive systems. The *Hawaii Five-0* and *CSI* television shows use DoubleTake Technologies or FlickIt technology to transfer graphics or other content from a table-top monitor to other displays on the walls surrounding the actors (Anonymous, 2012c).

Integrating computer software with touch screen hardware

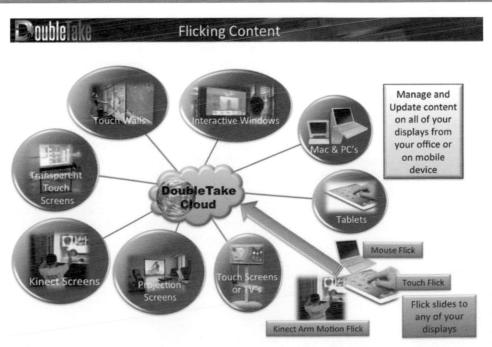

Courtesy of WordPress

Source Data Input Devices

In some businesses, the speed of data entry is a top priority. These businesses use machine reading devices, such as bar-code scanners, known as **source data input devices**. They copy data directly from the source, such as a bar code or magnetic-ink characters, without human intervention. They can also record data directly from other sources, including checks and credit cards. Source data input technologies are widely used in banking, retail, credit-card processing, and shipping.

Source Data Technology

Mark-recognition devices are essential to successful source data entry. Special devices use *optical mark recognition* to detect the positions of marks on source documents, such as standardized test response forms. *Optical bar recognition* senses data encoded in the series of thick and thin black bars in bar codes.

A less accurate technology used for source data entry is *optical character recognition (OCR)*. Unlike optical mark recognition, OCR technology is often used to try to interpret handwritten and printed texts not originally designed for source data entry. A special scanner scans the page and translates each character into a digitized representation. Software then tries to correlate the images with characters and stores interpreted text for further processing. Postal services around the world have experimented with OCR to replace human eyes and hands in the tedious job of mail sorting.

Note that OCR is not optical mark sensing. In optical mark sensing, the scanner senses a mark's *position*, not what the mark actually is. The mark's position determines the input. Because the mark's position rather than its shape determines the input data, mark sensing is far more accurate than OCR.

A new optical mark format that uses a two-dimensional bar code (matrix) has become popular, especially for marketing and consumer advertising. These Quick Response Codes, or QR codes, were originally developed in Japan and used by automobile manufacturers due to their increased storage capacity as compared to traditional UPC barcodes. The QR code matrix consists of black- and white-squares. The convergence of smartphone, digital camera, and mobile technologies and applications has facilitated the use of QR codes. Prospective customers can use their smartphones to scan QR codes on a billboard or in a magazine to access additional information about a product. Home shopping channels show a QR code as a product is being introduced. The customer can simply scan the code to see more information and link to purchase options.

The fastest growing source data technology is **radio-frequency identification (RFID)**. It uses a device known as an RFID tag along with an RFID reader, an efficient and cost-effective data entry method. RFID transfers data without physically touching the hardware device. In fact, unlike bar code technology, RFID tags can be embedded in an object, and does not require a direct line of sight. It transmits data in the kilohertz, megahertz, and gigahertz frequency ranges. The tags gain their power either from batteries or from the radio frequency waves emitted from the reader.

RFID technology differs from standard barcode technology. When you are in a grocery store, each product has a bar code, called a **Universal Product Code (UPC)**, which is scanned by the cashier to identify the product and its price. However, this value identifies only the product, but not a specific unit of the product. In contrast, an RFID tag contains an Electronic Product Code (EPC) that uniquely identifies each unit. For example, an RFID tag could be attached to each carton of vaccine to identify its specific manufacturing date and origin. This level of information could help the pharmaceutical company track the distribution of specific products as they are transported to their final destinations.

A QR code can be used to easily access a web site by scanning through a smartphone app

© Cengage Learning 2015

OCR has recently been integrated into mobile devices. For example, Samsung sells a cellular phone that can help save time entering information into the phone's address book. When you use the phone's digital camera to photograph a business card, the built-in character recognition software captures the information from the picture and enters it into the address book.

Banking

Sometimes the development of new technology removes the reliance on older technology. In the past, commercial banks and the Federal Reserve Bank processed millions of checks daily. Entering check data manually would make the process extremely expensive and slow. The bank identification number, account number, and check number are printed in special magnetic ink at the bottom of each check, as shown in Figure 4.5. A device called a magnetic-ink reader uses **magnetic-ink character recognition** (**MICR**, pronounced MIKE-er) to detect these numbers. A person at the bank enters the amount of the check, also in magnetic ink. The bank then records its check deposits by placing a large number of checks in a MICR device, which records check amounts and accounts from which the money is drawn.

Because of the convergence of scanning technology with existing ATM devices, banking customers at some ATMs are able to insert a check directly into an ATM, which reads the pertinent information (check amount, account, and bank information) and immediately processes the check without any additional processing by the bank (see POI below).

However, the greater trend is toward eliminating or reducing the use of paper checks in favor of a process that is mostly or entirely electronic. Increasing numbers of people are paying their bills through electronic banking using a bank's website, significantly reducing labor and increasing operational efficiency.

FIGURE 4.5

Banks use magnetic-ink character recognition (MICR) to automate part of the check clearing process

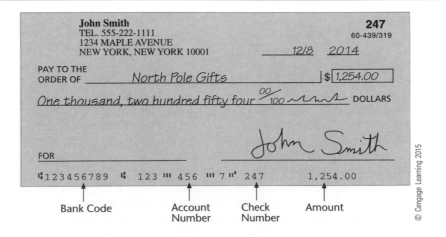

© Cengage Learning 2015

Credit and Debit Cards

Credit and debit cards, too, facilitate source data entry. Card number and holder information are coded on the magnetic strip on the card's back. When you charge a purchase with your credit card, the card is passed through the reader at the point of sale (POS) to record the account number and your name and address. The total amount charged is either keyed manually or recorded automatically from the cash register (often from a bar code on the item purchased).

The Square card reader hardware can process sales on a mobile phone

Courtesy of Squareup.com

One of the newest input devices available to consumers and merchants is the Square card reader. In late 2008, a frustrated glass artist lost out on a $2000 sale because he could not accept credit cards, and the idea of Square was born. Square is a small, square device that plugs into the audio jack of a smartphone with a slit to slide credit cards through. The device reads the card information and converts it to an audio signal. Software on the phone decodes the information before sending it over the cell phone network to be authorized by Square's servers. Customers can sign by drawing their signature on the smartphone screen, and credit card information is deleted from the phone after the purchase goes through. Square was introduced for iPhones, and has expanded to offer software for the iPad and Android phones. This revolutionary point-of-sale input device allows even the smallest of merchants to easily accept credit and debit cards and keep track of customer purchases. As the popularity of cashless payments continues to rise, the ability for small merchants to accept debit and credit cards will lead to increased sales.

Shipping and Inventory Control

You might have noticed that every package you receive through shipping companies such as UPS and FedEx has a bar code on it. Bar codes use the optical bar recognition techniques described earlier to represent information for both inventory control and shipment tracking. A package is scanned before it leaves the shipping facility, and the information is channeled into a computer that stores information such as the recipient's name and address. Whenever the item reaches a station, the bar code is scanned again. This information is combined with the identification information of the station. So, anyone with access to the shipping company's database can see exactly where the item has been and when, right up to the point of delivery. You can track an item by logging on to the shipping company's website and entering the item's tracking number. Since quick delivery is essential, source data input is extremely important in the shipping industry, because it is highly accurate and saves much labor and time. As discussed in Chapter 3, "Business Functions and Supply Chains," bar codes are being replaced with RFID tags for both shipping and inventory control.

Imaging

A growing number of organizations are **imaging**, or image processing, their documents. Doing so allows not only the storage of enormous amounts of data in less space than paper, but also much more efficient retrieval and filing. By scanning and indexing images, many companies have already reduced millions of paper documents to digitized pictures. They use the technology to store invoices, shipping documents, insurance policies and claims, personnel files, checks, and many other document types. The images are indexed and linked to relevant records in large databases, from which they can be retrieved and displayed on computer monitors. This technology is particularly useful when documents include signatures and graphics.

Once scanned, the original document can be destroyed because an exact copy can be generated on demand. Since it is in electronic form, it can be indexed. Indexing enables you to search a document by keywords and numbers. This reduces the average time of searching a document from several hours to about five seconds. In the United States, checking account holders receive one or two sheets of imaged canceled checks from their banks instead of a stack of their original checks. Customers who do their banking online can retrieve these images at any time. This system saves banks millions of dollars in paper, space, and handling costs. The images are often stored on DVDs. Because imaging reduces the amount of paper in organizations, some of the most enthusiastic adopters of imaging are companies in paper-intensive fields such as law, retail, insurance, banking, health care, and shipping.

Imaging technologies continue to progress. A global financial services company saved $56–$80 million in paper costs. Another financial services firm claims a 100 percent return on investment in eight months and saved $3.6 million in paper and copying costs over a one year period. A property insurance company focused on long cycle times for processes based on hardcopy documents. The insurer implemented technology to capture, archive, and retrieve documents and reduced the cost of issuing new policies by 33 percent with a savings of over $6 million per year (Anonymous, 2012a; Medina & Andrews, 2009). These examples prove that substantial cost savings are realized through document imaging technology. The efficiency of several business processes, such as invoicing, customer service, collections, and purchasing, can be affected positively with the use of this technology.

POINT OF INTEREST — Deposit Your Check in a Flash

The banking world has found another solution to make standing in line for the next available teller a thing of the past. Banking customers can download an app on their iPhone, Android, or Windows smartphones, sign in, and snap a picture of the front and back of the check to deposit it. Wells Fargo, Bank of America, Chase, and Citibank have already implemented ways for customers to deposit checks using their smartphones. The innovation saves customers time because they do not have to visit a bank branch. The financial institution saves money because the check is immediately scanned into the system, eliminating the need for bank personnel to process the check as well as reducing transactions processed by a teller.

Source: Avalos, G. (2012). Checks Go Cellular, Providence Journal.

Speech Recognition

The way we communicate with computers is changing. We already mentioned touch screens. However, in some work environments, using manual input devices is either impossible or inconvenient. In other situations, such as customer service, using a computer to respond automatically to spoken customer queries can save labor costs. Instructing machines by speech can help in these instances. **Speech recognition**—also called voice recognition—is the process of translating human speech into computer-readable data and instructions. Although speech recognition systems vary in sophistication, all receive voice input from a microphone or telephone and process it with software.

Since help-desk labor is an area of great potential for reducing costs, several companies have developed speech recognition software. Nuance Communications, Inc. offers Dragon Naturally Speaking for dictating text in word processors and email. Microsoft's Tellme software provides voice services for automated 411 (telephone directory) services and enterprise customer service. The convergence of smartphone and voice recognition technologies has made possible applications to assist with dialing contacts, text and email messaging, as well as initiating a search.

Navigation systems have become a standard feature in many vehicles. Toyota installs VoiceBox software in the navigation systems of its new cars as well as car voice innovations; IBM's Embedded ViaVoice is used in General Motor's OnStar and other dashboard command systems. So far a GPS system is capable only of providing voice directions; with the new system, you will be able to verbally ask the GPS system for directions, and it will speak them back. Apple's Siri is used on iPhones and iPads to receive voice commands as input to GPS.

Currently, the customer service departments of many companies use interactive voice recognition (IVR) to understand simple commands from telephone callers, who can utter answers to questions and receive recorded responses. IVRs can provide the most efficient method for customers to get assistance. Some companies can direct up to 90 percent of their incoming calls to IVR systems (Fluss, 2012). However, customer complaints prod companies to employ more sophisticated voice recognition systems. A recent study of consumers indicates that most still prefer speaking to a live agent rather than using an IVR system (Gray, 2012). However, updating the organization's IVR application will realize a cost-effective investment to increase its performance (Fluss, 2012).

A Commanding Voice

Emerging as the most common scene for voice recognition systems is mobile phones. Many mobile phones offer some type of speech recognition system that allows users to issue basic voice commands. Android-powered smartphones are taking it a step further. Users of newer Android smartphones can download an app that allows Google to recognize the pattern of their speech. The service gradually becomes accustomed to the user's voice and over time will more accurately understand voice commands. Accurate speech recognition in mobile phones is extremely convenient for people without a free hand or who are driving.

Source: San Jose Mercury, N. (2010). Google launches next phase of speech-recognition service, The Salt Lake Tribune.

Output Devices

Output devices include all electronic and electromechanical devices that deliver results of computer processing. We receive most information in visual form, either on screen or on paper. Therefore, this discussion focuses on the most popular output devices: monitors and printers. Output also includes audio signals, received through speakers and earphones, or downloaded to digital audio players. Soon we might also be able to enjoy smell output using digital technology.

Monitors

The most common output device is the computer monitor, which looks like and uses technology similar to a television screen. The two major types of monitors are cathode-ray tube (CRT) and flat-panel display. CRT is an older technology, and most monitors today are flat-panel. Images on a monitor are made up of small dots called **pixels** (*pi*cture *el*ements, with the addition of an *x* for easier pronunciation).

In a **CRT (cathode-ray tube)** monitor, the inner side of the screen has a layer of tiny phosphoric dots, which make up the pixels. These dots respond to electronic beams by displaying different colored light. An electron gun receives instructions from the computer and sweeps the rows of pixels, spraying a ray of electrons. When electrons hit a pixel, the pixel emits light for a limited time. The electronic gun bombards some pixels and skips others, creating a picture on the screen. This type of monitor has rapidly vanished as a means of displaying data.

Flat-panel monitors have gained popularity for personal computers and handheld computers, after years of use in notebook computers. The advantages of flat-panel monitors are their slim profile, sharper images, and lower power consumption. The most common type of flat-panel monitor is the **liquid crystal display (LCD)**. The price of LCD monitors has decreased sharply over the past several years, making them the most popular type of monitor. In addition, the lower cost of flat-panel monitors has made it possible and popular to use two monitors on one personal computer, increasing the number of active applications at any one time. In LCD, a conductive, film-covered screen is filled with a liquid crystal, whose molecules can align in different planes when charged with a certain electrical voltage. The proper voltage applied to segments of the screen disrupts the crystal's regular structure in those areas, causing it to block light. Light continues to pass through the rest of the liquid. This combination of light and dark areas produces images of characters and pictures.

Oleksiy Mark/Photos.com

Any type of high definition television (HDTV) set can be connected to a computer (if it has the proper socket) and serve as a computer monitor.

The price of a monitor depends primarily on its size, measured as the diagonal length of the screen. Other price factors include brightness (the brighter the better), contrast ratio (the higher the better), and pixel pitch (how close the pixels are to each other; the closer the better).

The greater the number of pixels per unit area on the screen, the sharper the picture. Picture sharpness is called **resolution**. It is expressed as the number of pixels that fit the width and height of a complete screen image. Monitors come in various resolutions. If you multiply these numbers, you get the total number of pixels on the screen. Common resolutions are 1024 × 768, 1280 × 1024, 1366 × 768, 1600 × 1200, 1920 × 1080, and 2560 × 1600.

Good color monitors can display more than 16 million colors and hues. The number of colors and the overall quality of pictures also depends on the quality of the video card used inside the computer. The video card contains memory and circuitry to manipulate and display two- and three-dimensional images.

Printers

Printers can be classified into two basic types—nonimpact and impact—based on the technology they use to create images on paper.

Nonimpact Printers

The printer most commonly used today in businesses is the laser printer, which is a **nonimpact printer** because it creates images on a page without mechanically impacting the paper. Nonimpact printers include laser, ink-jet, electrostatic, and electro-thermal printers. Laser printers are also page printers, because they print one whole page at a time. Laser and ink-jet printers produce very high-quality output, including color. Laser printing technology can create typeset quality equal to what you see in magazines and textbooks. Ink-jet printers can be used for photo-quality output, and therefore are often used to print pictures captured by digital cameras. All nonimpact printers have fewer moving parts than impact printers and are, therefore, significantly quieter. They are also much faster. The excellent quality of their output makes laser printers the choice of many individual and corporate users for desktop publishing.

Two qualities to check when purchasing a laser or ink-jet printer are speed, measured in pages per minute (PPM), and density, measured in dots per inch (DPI). The higher the density, the sharper the output. Desktop printers produce output at 300, 600, and 1200 DPI or more. Ink-jet printers are capable of producing output at much higher density, such as 4800 × 1200 DPI. The speed of desktop laser printers is 17 to 60 PPM. Color laser printing is somewhat slower due to the time it takes the printer to compose the image. Larger, commercial laser printers reach speeds of more than 400 PPM.

The low prices of laser and ink-jet printers might be misleading. Over the life of the printer, the buyer will spend much more money for the cartridges than for the printer. For example, a color laser printer that costs $200 typically requires four cartridges, each costing about $40. Just a single set of new cartridges costs almost as much as a new printer. If a new printer is to be used for high-volume printing, the initial larger expenditure on a laser printer makes business sense because the per-page cost of laser cartridges is lower than the per-page cost of ink-jet cartridges. However, ink-jet printers are more suitable for photo-quality prints because of their higher resolution, that is, a greater DPI density.

Impact Printers

Printers are considered **impact printers** if they reproduce an image on a page using mechanical impact. Of this type, the only printers you might still encounter are dot-matrix printers. The printhead of **dot-matrix printers** consists of a matrix of little pins. When certain pins strike the ribbon against the paper, they mark the shape of a character or another form on the paper. Thus, each character or other image is made up of tiny dots. Dot-matrix printers produce low-quality output but are still in use in many businesses, because they can print multi-copy forms.

Storage

To maintain programs, data, and information for later use, data must be stored on a nonvolatile medium, that is, a medium that retains data even when not connected to electric power. Often, we also want to move stored data to a computer that is not part of a network, and we need to back up important programs and data as well. For these purposes, we use storage media. Although media are the materials on which information is stored, and the storage device is the media and the mechanism that stores and retrieves the information, the terms "storage media" and "storage devices" are often used interchangeably.

Storage devices come in different forms and use different materials, each with strengths and weaknesses. Cost, capacity, access speed, and access mode should all be considered when evaluating storage devices. Capacity is the amount of data the medium can hold, access speed is the amount of data that can be stored or retrieved per time unit, and access mode refers to the organization of data on the medium, either random or sequential.

Storage devices differ in the technology they use to maintain data (such as magnetic or optical) and in their physical structure (disks, tapes, or other forms). Physical structure might limit ways in which data can be organized on the medium. While disks allow any type of organization, tapes allow only sequential organization. This section discusses modes of access, looks at specific media and technologies, and considers the trade-offs that managers must consider when evaluating what type of storage solution is best for a particular business.

Modes of Access

The two basic types of access modes for data storage are sequential and direct (random) access (see Figure 4.6). In **sequential storage**, data is organized one record after another. With sequential storage (the only option for magnetic tapes), to read data from anywhere on the tape, you have to read through all the data before that point on the tape. Retrieving files from sequential devices is slower and less convenient than on devices that utilize direct access. In **direct access**, records are not organized sequentially, but by the physical address on the device, and can be accessed directly without going through other records. Devices that allow direct access storage are often called DASD (DAZ-dee), short for direct access storage device. They include magnetic and optical disks as well as **flash drives**, small storage devices that connect to a computer via a **universal serial bus (USB)** receptacle.

FIGURE 4.6

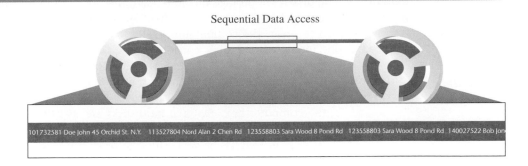

Sequential Data Access

Direct Data Access

© Cengage Learning 2015

Magnetic Tapes

Tape cartridges are an inexpensive method to back up data

Ray Johnson/Photos.com

Magnetic tapes similar to those used in tape recorders are also used to store computer data. While some tape drives still use open reel tapes, most use tape cartridges. Many of these cartridges look, in general, like the tapes used in audio tape players. One of the most popular types of tape cartridges is the Linear Tape-Open (LTO). In 2012, Quantum, a storage media manufacturer, offered tape cartridges with a capacity of 3 TB (terabytes) that access data at a rate of 280 MB per second (Anonymous, 2013). The cost of storage is measured in how much money is spent on each byte of storage capacity. Tapes provide the lowest cost in terms of cents per GB. The Quantum 3 TB LTO-5 tape (retailing at $35 each) costs 1.1 cents per GB.

Backing up all or a designated part of data from its original storage medium needs to be done regularly. The entire hard disk of a PC can be backed up, or, in organizations, large amounts of data are backed up in case a hard disk crashes or an incident occurs that makes the original data irretrievable. Backing up can be done manually or automatically with the help of software. When the backup is done for an organization, often the organization makes use of a storage area network, a dedicated area where disk (and possibly tape) storage devices are connected through communication lines to organizational ISs for the sole purpose of data backup. Such networks are discussed later in this chapter. Backup and recovery procedures are discussed in Chapter 14, "Risks, Security, and Disaster Recovery."

Tapes are inexpensive but they have two major flaws. It takes a long time to copy from a tape. This is a serious concern when terabytes of data must be recopied to a disk from a tape. Tapes are also unreliable after about five years. To extend this period, a magnetic tape must be reeled back and forth every few months to maintain an even tension. Uneven tension, which always develops over time, may render some of the stored data unreadable.

Magnetic Disks

The most widely used storage medium is the **magnetic disk**. Magnetic disks include hard disks and floppy disks, though floppy disks are rarely found today. As with information on magnetic tape, information on magnetic disks is coded in magnetized spots on the disk's surface.

PCs usually come with at least one hard disk built in. Hard disks are often mistakenly called hard drives. The disk is the storage medium itself; the drive is the mechanism that stores data to it and retrieves data from it. (However "hard disk," "hard drive," and "hard disk drive" are commonly used to mean the combination of the two, because the drive and disk are sold and installed as one unit.) A **hard disk** consists of one or more rigid platters installed in the same box that holds the CPU and other computer components, or attached externally to the computer, usually through a USB port. An external hard disk is portable; it easily can be connected to or disconnected from the computer without opening the computer box. External hard disks are usually more expensive than internal disks with the same capacity. Hard disks for desktop computers are capable of storing up to 3 TB of data. The cost of storing 1 GB has decreased to less than 5 cents.

Magnetic disks are available in several forms, such as the internal disk shown here, or external USB or Firewire-connected disks

franz pfluegl/Photos.com

The storage and use of corporate data has become a major IT initiative. In recent years, the most important impetus for the acquisition of hard disks has been the construction of data warehouses, large databases that maintain mainly consumer purchase records. A 2011 study by McKinsey & Company projects that the growth of global data will increase by 40 percent per year. The amount of data stored by 15 out of the 17 sectors in the United States is greater than the contents of the Library of Congress (235 TB in April 2011) (Manyika et al., 2011).

POINT OF INTEREST Tera Firma

An external hard drive with storage capacity of 3 terabytes can be purchased for less than $140. How much information can a hard disk with a capacity of 1 terabyte hold? It would store about 300 hours of good quality video. Ten terabytes could store the printed collection of the Library of Congress, approximately 155 million items.

Source: Anonymous. Fascinating Facts. Retrieved June 4, 2013, from http://www.loc.gov/about/facts.html; Anonymous. (2013). Megabytes, Gigabytes, Terabytes ... What Are They? Retrieved June 4, 2013, from http://www.whatsabyte.com/

The quickly decreasing cost of magnetic disks enables storage and streaming of thousands of video clips on the web. McKinsey & Company estimates that a $600 disk drive could store all of the world's music. In just two years of operations, YouTube (now part of Google) amassed a collection of video clips that required 45 terabytes of storage space. The company says it receives and stores about 72 hours of videos every minute. Using the factor of 1 GB per hour of video content, YouTube would require 172 TB per day to accommodate new uploaded videos by their users (Anonymous, 2012f; Manyika et al., 2011).

Optical Discs

Optical discs are recorded by treating the disc surface so it reflects or does not reflect light. A special detecting device detects the reflections or nonreflections, which represent ones and zeroes of digital coding. The two basic categories of optical discs are **compact discs (CDs)** and **digital video discs (DVDs),** also known as digital versatile discs. CDs come in several types: CD-ROM (Compact Disc, Read Only Memory), CD-R (recordable), and CD-RW (rewritable). Recordable DVDs come in a variety of recording options. The main advantage of optical discs is their storage capacity and portability. CDs and DVDs are also less expensive than hard disks in terms of bytes per dollar, although the cost gap is closing. Standard DVDs can store 4.7 GB per side for a total of 9.4 GB. More advanced DVDs, using techniques called blue laser and double storage, can reach capacities of 50 GB; a dual layer disc which is the industry standard for full-length video discs. However, the disadvantage of all optical discs is that the speed of storage and retrieval is currently slower than that of hard disks.

karam miri/Photos.com

Solid-State Storage

Solid-state storage, also known as **flash memory**, is becoming popular for both primary memory (memory inside the computer) and external storage. **Solid-state storage** can be rewritten and hold its content without electric power. It consumes very little power and does not need a constant power supply to retain data when disconnected. It offers fast access times and is relatively immune to shock or vibration. These qualities make solid-state storage an excellent choice for portable devices such as MP3 players, digital cameras, and mobile phones, or as independent portable storage. Unlike other types of memory, erasing data can only be done in blocks of bytes, not individual bytes, and hence the name: a whole block of bytes is erased in a flash.

As an independent memory device, flash memory takes two main forms: as a memory card (often used in digital cameras and other portable devices), and as a **USB drive**, sometimes called a thumb drive or USB flash drive. Many computers and some monitors and printers include multiple built-in card readers that accommodate the most popular flash memory cards, such as SD (Secure Digital) and CF (Compact Flash). USB drives are about the size of an adult's thumb, and act as portable storage. (The name "drive" is a misnomer; there are no moving parts or disks in flash memory.) They plug into the computer through a USB port. As USB ports become standard in most computers, it is easy to use a thumb drive to save data or transfer data between computers. There is usually no need to set up any software once the USB drive is plugged in. The device is recognized as an additional external storage device. USB drives come in storage capacities of up to tens of gigabytes, and their cost is decreasing rapidly.

Flash memory cards are ideal for portable devices such as digital cameras and portable voice recorders

Courtesy of Sandisk

Solid state memory accesses information without any moving parts

In addition to its use in USB flash drives and memory cards, flash memory is used in solid-state disks. A **solid-state disk (SSD)** is an alternative to magnetic disks. Again, the word "disk" is a misnomer, because this type of storage involves no disk and no moving parts. SSDs are attached to computers in a similar way to magnetic disks. The fact that there is no need to wait for a disk to rotate in order to locate data—a period of time called latency—makes SSDs up to 250 times faster than magnetic disks, especially if the SSD comes with its own CPU. The function of such CPUs is specifically to speed up data processing. SSDs are used by organizations to store frequently used software to prevent data processing "bottlenecks." SSDs are also becoming popular on high-end PCs.

Chesky_W/Photos.com

DAS, NAS, and SAN

Organizations increasingly rely on storage systems that allow multiple users to share the same storage media over a network. In **direct-attached storage (DAS),** the disk or array of disks is directly connected to a server. The storage devices might also be tapes, especially if the storage is for backup. Other computers on the network must access the server to use the disks or tapes. DAS is relatively easy to deploy and manage, and involves relatively low cost. However, speed of access to data might be compromised because the server also processes other software, such as email and databases. Also, if the server is down, the other computers cannot access the storage devices. DAS might be suitable for localized file sharing, which is typical in small businesses. It is not easily scalable, because each additional server and its storage devices must be managed separately. **Scalability** is the ability to add more hardware or software to accommodate changing business needs.

Two other arrangements place the storage devices on the organization's network so that they can be accessed directly by all other computers. These approaches are known as network-attached storage (NAS) and storage area network (SAN).

Network-attached storage (NAS) is a device or "appliance" especially designed for networked storage. It comprises both the storage media, such as hard disks, and management software, which is fully dedicated to serving (accessing) files over the network. NAS relieves the server of handling storage, so the server can process other applications, such as email and databases. Disks can store many terabytes of data in a small, centralized space, and managing such large storage in one place saves money. NAS is highly scalable. While in DAS each server runs its own operating system, NAS can communicate with servers running various operating systems, and therefore allow much flexibility when adding computers and other devices to the network.

Storage area network (SAN) is a network fully devoted to storage and transfer of data between servers and storage devices. The storage devices are part of this dedicated network, which is managed separately from the organization's local area network. (Networks are covered in Chapter 6, "Business Networks and Telecommunications.") A SAN may combine DAS and NAS devices. The communication lines in this network are high-speed optical fibers. The data transfer standards used in a SAN are different from those used by a NAS, and generally support higher speeds. NAS identifies data by files, or, as professionals say, at the file level. SAN identifies much larger quantities of data, called data blocks, and therefore can transfer and back up much larger amounts of data at a time. This is important when high speed of data transfer is important, such as in online business transactions that involve a large number of records in a stored database. A large number of users can simultaneously access data without delays. SANs are highly scalable. For these reasons, SANs are used by organizations that conduct business on the web and require high-volume transaction processing. However, SANs are relatively expensive and their management is complex. In recent years, the technical differences between NAS and SAN have blurred.

DAS, NAS, and SAN often include **RAID** (redundant array of independent disks), whereby data is replicated on different disks to enhance processing speed and fault-tolerance. **Fault tolerance** is the ability of the system to sustain failure of a disk, because the same data also appears on another disk.

Several companies specialize in NAS and SAN systems and the software that manages them, including Hewlett-Packard, Hitachi, and IBM.

Cloud Storage

The significant increase in the data storage needs of consumers and organizations, coupled with the exponential increase in Internet and other network use, has created a new technology product, cloud storage. Simply defined, **cloud storage** is the availability of network-accessible storage from an off-site computer or technology device. Based on the 1970s model of application service providers (ASPs), these systems are usually maintained by a third-party organization through a subscription charge based on several factors and service models.

With cloud storage, consumers can store their personal files "in the cloud" and access them with several devices. For example, a customer can purchase and upload MP3 files to their cloud storage area. The music files can then be accessed and played through their smartphone, personal computer, or tablet without the need to store the music on each device. The storage location associated with the cloud provides an efficient single point of storage and access to various files.

Business professionals can use cloud storage to centralize their file storage and access while traveling and telecommuting. As an alternative to storing data on multiple devices or transporting data on USB flash drives, cloud storage maintains one version of a data file, which can be accessed from various devices for editing and printing. In addition, the cloud offers a more secure location for storing sensitive data than on flash drives and portable devices that can be stolen.

Business organizations can also use cloud storage to reduce the cost of storing and managing data. Although data storage costs are decreasing, the increased use of corporate data remains a significant cost of information technology overhead. Cloud storage vendors, sometimes called **storage-as-a-service**, offer corporations an alternative to on-site data storage by outsourcing data storage services. Cloud storage can also provide an efficient alternative to store corporate data for compliance and archiving purposes, leveraging additional internal storage infrastructure for live and production data needed for operational business activities.

However, cloud storage has its disadvantages. The off-site storage of data increases the reliance on networks, and has associated network costs. Even with all the assurances of cloud storage vendors, that security of corporate data stored in the cloud remains a significant issue. Off-site storage creates an additional point of failure that could risk the security of sensitive corporate data. Therefore, the tradeoffs of on-site vs. off-site storage must be considered and analyzed.

IBM and Iron Mountain Digital are two major players in the corporate SaaS market. However, companies such as Amazon and Apple are capitalizing on the consumer demand for cloud storage. Amazon provides 5 GB of cloud storage at no cost for its customers to store videos, photos, music, documents and other digital files. The cloud storage is accessible through its desktop application for the personal computer as well as its Kindle Fire tablets. Amazon's strategy is to offer Kindle Fire owners access to their cloud storage as an additional benefit. Apple iCloud stores iOS and Mac device users' content. Microsoft Office 2013 product offers more cloud access features than previous versions; its Office 365 product is advertised as "Office in the cloud" to access Office tools from any location.

As of 2010, according to the U.S. Census Bureau, about 77 million Americans use computers at work, at school, and at home (Anonymous, 2012b). An increasing number of studies show that working with computers threatens workers with a variety of hazards. These risks include repetitive-stress injuries (RSIs) due to long periods of repeated motions. According to the U.S. Occupational Safety and Health Administration (OSHA), RSIs cost American businesses an estimated $20 billion annually in workers' compensation claims (Anonymous, 2012d). The U.S. Department of Labor reported that injuries and illnesses attributed to repetitive motion tasks accounted for three percent of all injury and illnesses in 2011. However, these cases required a median of 23 days of work absences, nearly three times as much as all types of injuries and illnesses (Anonymous, 2012d). As computer-aided work has grown, RSIs have grown, too, to the extent that some scientists call these injuries an epidemic.

The most common computer-related type of RSI is carpal tunnel syndrome. It is the result of repetitive use of a keyboard. The injury causes pain in the forearms due to swelling and pressure on the median nerve passing through the wrist. Carpal tunnel syndrome may cause permanent disability. In rare cases workers lost their ability to return to work due to this injury.

Our eyes, too, are strained from computer work. Studies found that a programmer's eyes make as many as 30,000 movements in a workday. These are movements up, down, and to the sides, which strain the eye muscles. However, other studies found that while staring at a computer monitor people blink at one-sixth of the frequency that they blink normally. Blinking is important for moisturizing the eyeball, which helps kill harmful germs and eases eye strain. A study by The National Institute for Occupational Safety and Health (NIOSH) found that short breaks from work with computers that involve keyboards and video displays reduce eye soreness, visual blurring, and upper-body discomfort, while quantity and quality of work were not compromised. The agency estimates that more than half of computer users who stare at computer displays for long hours develop a health problem called computer vision syndrome (CVS), which is any combination of headaches, loss of focus, burning eyes, double vision, or blurred vision.

The argument has been made that it is an employer's moral obligation to educate employees about such risks and to provide an environment that minimizes them. Both factors, the economic and ethical, have moved many employers to try to reduce the increasing "injuries of the Information Age." They do so by purchasing and installing ergonomic equipment, training employees how to use computers in a way that minimizes injuries, and enforcing periodic breaks from repetitive activities such as typing. The breaks help prevent both RSIs and eye strain. OSHA maintains a website, *www.osha.gov/SLTC/ computerworkstation*, that provides useful tips on safe computer work. As a professional, it is likely you will spend much of your workday sitting in front of a computer. Read the tips and apply them to maintain your good health.

To minimize these risks, you can download and install on your computer one of several free programs such as Workrave that prompt the user to take brief breaks and less frequent but longer rest breaks. It also limits the daily total time a worker can use a computer. When the computer is networked to other computers in the office, it does not allow the worker to use any of the others that are part of the network when a break or daily time limit is enforced. Working times of all workers whose computers are connected are recorded and tabulated on a server for review and analysis. The application also provides an animated exercise guide for the shoulders, arms, and eyes.

Business Considerations in Evaluating Storage Media

Before spending money on storage devices, professionals must consider several factors: the purpose of data storage, the amount of data to be stored, the required speed of data storage and retrieval, how portable the device needs to be, and, as always, cost.

Use of Stored Data

The first consideration before adopting storage media is how the data will be used, mainly, whether it will be used for current operations or as backup. If it is to be used for backup only, and not processing, magnetic tape, flash drives, external drives, CDs, or DVDs would be a proper choice. Magnetic tape is less costly and holds more data per reel or cassette than a single CD; this should be a consideration, too. If the users need to access individual records quickly, then magnetic hard disks are the best choice. Thus, a business that allows customers to retrieve their records online should use fast magnetic disks. If the information is archival, such as encyclopedias or maps used by library patrons, the library should place the information on CDs or DVDs, because the user needs fast, direct retrieval of specific information (records), and might not tolerate sequential search on a tape. However, with the speed and low cost of external disk drives, it is easy to justify the use of these storage devices (usually on servers) for instant information access. Archival information that should not be changed should be stored on write-once media.

The use of cloud storage to access and store data should also be considered. The low cost and availability of online servers eliminate the businesses oversight and management of data storage functions. For example, as a business begins to approach its capacity of on-site storage, new disk drives (or servers) must be purchased and installed. But when additional storage is needed in a cloud storage environment, it simply is accessed without any active effort on the part of the business.

Amount of Data Stored

When storage volume is the most important factor, professionals must first consider price per megabit or megabyte, that is, the ratio of dollars spent to storage capacity. If the medium is to be used solely for backup, their low cost makes magnetic tapes and DVDs an ideal choice. If the medium is to be used for fast retrieval, magnetic disks would be the best choice.

For some purposes, the capacity of the device is important. When a set of very large software applications and/or data must be stored on a single device, a device with a large capacity must be selected. For example, if a sales rep must be able to demonstrate applications totaling 4 GB, it might be more economical to store the data on five CDs, but this would be impractical because the rep would either have to first copy the content of all the CDs onto every PC where she makes a demonstration (which for security reasons might be prohibited by the hosting party), or she would have to swap the CDs throughout the demonstration. A small portable hard disk or USB flash drive of at least 4 GB would be a more practical option, albeit significantly more expensive.

Speed

The speed of magnetic disks (also called spindle speed) is often measured in rotations per minute (RPM). Current disks come with speeds of 5,400 to 15,000 RPM. For disks of the same size, a higher RPM means shorter data transfer time and usually better performance overall. While the great capacity and low cost of CDs and DVDs are appealing, the transfer rate of magnetic hard disks is still significantly better. If very high speed is required, SSD is currently the best choice, although its price is significantly higher than that of magnetic disks.

Accessing data in the cloud is heavily dependent on the network bandwidth (speed and volume of data that can be transferred). With internal storage, businesses control the access to servers containing storage devices. The speed of accessing data is faster because the connection is local. The speed of accessing data in a cloud environment will be based on the network (Internet) service and bandwidth purchased.

POINT OF INTEREST — Don't Place This Laptop on Your Lap

Defects in Sony batteries caused one of the largest recalls in computer history. The batteries in several models of laptop computers overheated. Some exploded, and others burst into flames. Dell replaced the batteries in 4 million computers, Apple in 1.8 million, and Lenovo in 0.5 million. In 2006, The Federal Consumer Safety Products Commission (CPSC) issued this helpful advice: "Do not use your computer on your lap." The CPSC has offered several tips on notebook use including the placement of laptops on soft surfaces as well as using appropriate batteries and chargers.

Source: Horowitz, A., Jacobson, D., McNichol, T., Thomas, O., "101 Dumbest Moments in Business," *Business 2.0*, January/February 2007, p. 100; CPSC Releases Tips on Notebook Computer Use, September 2006, http://www.cpsc.gov/CPSCPUB/PREREL/prhtml06/06271.html

Unit Space and Portability

Sometimes the cost of a gigabyte stored is not the most important consideration, but the physical size of the storage medium is. A portable hard disk drive might be economical and fast, but it might be more practical for a traveling salesperson to carry a CD rather than an external hard disk. And even though a CD is significantly less expensive than a USB flash drive, the salesperson might find it more convenient to carry a USB drive. CDs do not fit in shirt pockets, while a USB flash drive can be attached to a key chain or clipped to a shirt pocket. Even if storage cost is not as attractive as that of CDs, portability and the fact that USB ports are ubiquitous in PCs might push one toward selecting a USB flash drive. Many business professionals today who travel and need network connectivity and limited local disk storage are opting to use tablet computers or even smartphones to access their applications and data.

Cost

Once professionals agree on the best type of data storage device for a particular business use, they need to consider cost. The approach is simple: obtain the greatest storage capacity for the smallest amount of money. In other words, for each proposed device, consider the ratio of cents per gigabyte of capacity. The lower the ratio, the more favorable the product. It is easy to find the ratio. If a 1 TB hard disk costs $80, the ratio is $80/1 TB, or 8 cents per gigabyte. The cost per gigabyte of a 3 TB drive that costs $135 would be 4.5 cents. If a 32 GB thumb drive costs $20, the cost per gigabyte is $20/32 GB, or 62 cents per gigabyte. Thus, if the convenience and portability of a thumb drive is important to you, you will pay significantly more per GB of storage capacity.

Use of cloud storage changes the cost curve of additional capacity as the business operations warrant. As the internal capacity is approached, additional storage devices must be purchased and installed. If the capacity of the server housing the storage reaches its capacity, the server must also be upgraded. Therefore, the incremental cost is higher as each new capacity level is added. With cloud storage, the additional cost of additional capacity is incrementally smaller as more capacity is needed.

Reliability and Life Expectancy

Although this is usually not the highest priority, businesses must also consider the storage medium's reliability and life expectancy. For instance, optical discs are more reliable and durable than magnetic disks. Magnetically stored data remains reliable for about 10 years, whereas CDs and DVDs are expected to store data reliably for 50 to 100 years (although they have not been around long enough to prove that).

While the management and oversight of managing off-site data storage through the cloud eliminates costs for businesses, it also creates a potential issue. The reliability and availability of the cloud data to business personnel and management is only as good as the vendor's management and operations. Therefore, it is crucial to research and analyze the various cloud vendors for cost, reliability, and uptime statistics.

Trade-Offs

As you can see, several factors must be considered when purchasing storage media, and often you must trade one quality of the device for another. For example, while USB drives are convenient and fast, they are also expensive and unacceptable for storing large amounts of transactional data, or even backing up large amounts of data, because of their relatively small capacity. Figure 4.7 summarizes characteristics of the most popular storage media. Obviously, terms such as "moderate cost" and "high capacity" are relative. Storage capacities and speeds of almost all storage media have increased over the years, and costs have decreased. Thus, the specific capacities, retrieval speeds, and costs change all the time. The table is presented for general comparison and reference, whereby "high" and "low" for each medium are relative to the other media.

FIGURE 4.7

Characteristics of digital storage media for business purposes

Medium	Capacity per Device Size	Recording and Retrieval Speed	Cost ($/GB)	Ideal for...	Capacity per Device	Limitations
Magnetic Hard Disk	High	Very Fast	High	Immediate Transactions	Very High	Bulky, Heavy
Magnetic Tape	High	Slow	Very Low	Backup	Very High	Not Suitable for Immediate Processing
Optical Tape	Very High	Fast	Low	Backup	Very High	Limited Market
Recordable CD	Very High	Medium	Very Low	Backup, Distribution of software	Low	Low Capacity per Device
Recordable DVD	Very High	Fast	Very Low	Backup	Medium	Low Capacity per Device
Flash Memory	High	Fast	High	Backup, Portability	Medium	Expensive

© Cengage Learning 2015

Considerations in Purchasing Hardware

Decisions about purchasing computers are usually made by an organization's IT professionals or with the help of a consulting firm. But surveys show an increasing trend of involving other employees in the decision-making process. More and more companies realize that effective use of computers depends on whether their employees are satisfied with the computers and other equipment installed in their workplace.

Before deciding what to purchase, consider the following variables:

- *The equipment's power:* Its speed, its memory size, and the capacity of its storage devices, such as the hard disk installed in the computer. Increased internal memory (RAM) should always be considered to increase processing and calculation time.

- *Expansion slots:* Computers should have enough slots to add circuitry cards for additional purposes, such as adding more powerful graphic cards and wireless cards on the motherboard (the board on which the CPU and other circuitry are installed). Additional memory cards increase the speed of processing by allowing more concurrent programs and data to run.

- *The number and type of external ports:* **Ports** are sockets used to connect a computer to external devices such as printers, hard disks, scanners, remote keyboards and pointers, and communication devices. More ports give more flexibility. Because so many external devices—hard disks, printers, scanners, thumb drives, digital cameras, presentation "clickers," and many others—connect to the computer through a USB port, the greater the number of USB ports, the more external devices can be added at the same time. Although USB hubs (devices that connect to a single port and provide several) can be used, this may cause inconvenience and increased costs. Built-in multiple card readers for flash memory make it convenient to read data from the cards instead of connecting the device that houses them, such as digital cameras.

- *The monitor type and resolution:* Higher resolution is more pleasing and less straining to the eyes. Larger monitors allow viewing the windows of many software applications simultaneously and require less scrolling. Multiple monitors should be considered when applications requiring large screens can increase the productivity of the computer user. Touch screens are important where keyboard data entry is impractical and inefficient.

- *Ergonomics:* Ergonomic equipment does not strain the back, arms, and eyes. For example, working with the keyboard must be comfortable. Traditional keyboards cause muscle pain when used for long sessions. Consider purchasing an ergonomic keyboard. Consider a trackball instead of a mouse; it requires only moving fingers rather than the forearm or the entire hand.

- *Compatibility:* IT managers must ensure that new devices will integrate with existing hardware, software, and networks. A new computer might have a different operating system or internal architecture. If it is to be used to host an important application, care must be taken to ensure that the application will run on the new machine. For example, commercial software vendors guarantee that their applications will run on a list of processors and operating systems. Professionals must consider **backward compatibility**, in which newer hardware is compatible with older hardware. (The same term applies to software.) For example, USB 2.0 devices are backward-compatible with USB 1.1 ports (although the communication speed then deteriorates to the speed of the older port). Compatibility between hardware and networks is also important. Newer handheld devices such as bar-code scanners might use an updated communication standard and no longer communicate with an existing warehouse network, because the new devices are not backward-compatible with the older standard transceivers.

- *The hardware footprint:* If space is scarce, you might want to consider the size of the computer and its peripheral equipment. The footprint is the area that a computer occupies. A smaller footprint leaves more desk space for other devices. All-in-one personal computer units have become popular with computer users with minimal desk space.

- *The reliability of the vendor, the warranty policy, and the support given after the warranty expires:* Ask if the vendor provides a website and 24-hour help via telephone. Try to assess how soon the equipment will be obsolete, a difficult task given the reality of fast development in computer equipment.

- *Power consumption and noise:* Computers that consume less power help save money on electricity and usually also give off less heat. Computers use fans to cool down the circuitry. Quiet fans will make the work environment more pleasant.

- *Cost:* All of the preceding factors must be weighed against cost. Careful study might yield hardware with excellent performance for an affordable price. Perusing print and web-based trade journals is helpful. Many periodicals provide tables evaluating comparable hardware, based on laboratory tests by impartial technicians. You do not have to be an IT professional to understand their evaluations.

Figure 4.8 summarizes the factors discussed in this chapter that you should consider when purchasing hardware. When comparing computers from different vendors, it is useful to establish a 10-point scale and score each category to indicate how well each computer addresses each important item. Your organization's, or even your department's internal needs, may require you to add some factors. The equipment receiving the highest score is the best in the evaluator's opinion.

FIGURE **4.8**

Example of an evaluation form to assist with the purchase of hardware

Factor	What to look for	Score
Power		
Speed	Greater frequency and word size	———
RAM capacity	Larger	———
Expandability	Greater number of board slots for additional devices and memory	———
Ports	Greater number of ports for printer, external hard disk, communication devices, and other peripherals	———
Ergonomics	Greater comfort and safety	———
Compatibility		
with hardware	Compatibility with many other computers and peripheral devices from the same and other manufacturers	———
with software	Compatibility with many software packages currently used and potentially to be used	———
with network	Compatibility with network infrastructure	———
Footprint	Smaller area	———
Support	Availability of telephone and online support for troubleshooting	———
	Supply of information on new upgrades	———
Warranty	Longer warranty period	———
Cost	Lower cost	———

Scalability and Updating Hardware

IT managers try to extend the productive life of hardware by ensuring that any equipment they buy is scalable. The principle of scalability implies that resources—in this case, hardware—can accommodate a growing amount of work either with or without upgrading. A scalable system can provide increased power as demands increase. For instance, many servers are designed to use multiple processors—4, 8, or 16 is not uncommon. If the server is initially installed with only a small number of processors, say two, then processors can be added over time to increase computing power. This way the machine will not have to be discarded too soon, and this helps protect the organization's initial investment. The same can be done for memory, storage, and other components.

However, some hardware is not scalable. Businesses tend to update their software, especially operating systems (such as Windows), when a new version is available, but many still maintain old hardware. While they avoid the cost of purchasing new hardware, this might actually cost the companies in lost productivity: newer software cannot run as fast or as reliably on the old machines. Often, excellent features of newer software are not available if it runs on older machines. For example, although Windows Vista offered greater security, faster file management, and superior visual effects over earlier Windows versions, most PCs at the time of its introduction were not powerful enough to run the new operating system.

Hardware should be disposed of and new hardware should be installed to avoid performance gaps between software and hardware. One rough formula to help determine when to replace hardware is the ratio of the average age of hardware pieces to the average age of the operating systems running on the machines. If the ratio is less than one, it might be time to replace some or all of the hardware.

If you are concerned that the equipment's useful life might be short because more powerful computers might be available within months, you can lease your system instead of buying it. Many vendors offer leasing programs. However, note that vendors are also aware of how quickly hardware becomes obsolete and price the leases accordingly; thus, you might find that the lease payment often covers the purchase price within a mere 18–24 months. Yet, many firms prefer leasing their PCs and notebook computers to purchasing them.

As you will see throughout this book, hardware components are combined in many different configurations to help businesses streamline operations and attain strategic goals. But hardware is rarely the first consideration in acquiring a new IS. When planning a new IS, managers should first determine their business needs and then consider which software can support those needs. Only then should they select the hardware that supports the software. The next chapter focuses on software.

Summary

- More professionals outside the IT field find themselves in the decision-making role regarding the purchase and use of computer hardware. Therefore, understanding hardware is important.

- For ease of reference, computers are classified into several categories according to their power. The most powerful are supercomputers, used mainly by research institutions for complex scientific calculations. Somewhat less powerful, but more suitable for business operations, are mainframe computers; many organizations still use them to process large databases and perform other tasks that require speed and large primary memory. Midrange computers are less powerful than mainframe computers and are often used as servers. Microcomputers include PCs and smaller computers, such as notebook, handheld, and tablet computers.

- Regardless of their size and power, all computers must have several components to function. The "brain" of every computer is its central processing unit (CPU), which consists of circuitry on a piece of silicon wafer and controls four basic operations: (1) it fetches instructions from memory, (2) it decodes them, (3) it executes them, and (4) it stores the results in memory.

- The rate at which the CPU does all this is the computer's clock rate.

- A computer's data word is the number of bits that can move through its CPU in one machine cycle.

- Speed, memory size, and the number of processor cores are among the determinants of a computer's power.

- The larger part of a computer's memory, RAM (random access memory), is volatile; that is, it keeps data only as long as electrical power is supplied. ROM (read-only memory) is nonvolatile. Unlike data in RAM, data stored in ROM stays in ROM when you turn the computer off. Similarly, all secondary storage media, such as magnetic disks, optical discs, and flash cards, are nonvolatile.

- Imaging devices help process large amounts of text and graphic data and have made the work of banks and other industries more productive.

- When evaluating storage media, factors to consider are capacity, transfer rate, portability, and the form of data organization that it allows. The latter determines the mode of access (sequential or direct).

- Data stored on tapes can only be organized and retrieved sequentially, therefore tapes are good for backup but not for transactions. Direct access storage devices, such as RAM, magnetic disks, optical discs, and solid-state disks, allow random organization and retrieval. Direct organization provides faster storage and retrieval of records that must be accessed individually and quickly, such as records in airline reservation systems. Only direct-access devices are suitable for processing databases.

- When purchasing computers, professionals should consider computer power and other factors in addition to cost. Professionals should consider expandability of RAM, the availability of sockets (ports) for connecting peripheral equipment, and compatibility with existing hardware and software.

- Like many new technologies, information technology may pose health risks to users. The most common problems computer users experience are carpal tunnel syndrome and repetitive-stress injuries caused by the repetitive use of the keyboard over long time periods. Today, manufacturers of computer equipment pay more attention to health hazards and try to design devices ergonomically.

KIMBALL'S REVISITED

While Liz and Michael are focused on the marketing, renovation, and grand opening projects for the new location, it is difficult for them to focus on information technology. They will need to rely on Tyler's knowledge from his college courses and the business. Tyler needs some guidance to understand the issues to make an informed decision.

What Is Your Advice?

1. Tyler wants to brand the new location with the service-oriented environment, providing timely and quality service for its customers. He believes that the use of technology would not only create that environment, but also show customers a well-managed business using technology. What alternatives could fulfill this branding for a restaurant? Should they use handheld devices to process customer orders at the tables? Would this be an efficient method of entering orders? What types of devices could be used?

2. The reliance on the new system will require some type of backup of the production data. What advice would you offer Tyler for this important function?

3. Consider the entire operation of a restaurant. Identify and discuss the various hardware devices that Tyler should expect to install.

New Perspectives

1. Would it be appropriate for Kimball's to solely rely on the handheld devices for customer orders? Analyze and discuss this point.

2. Review the marketing, promotional and social media discussion from the previous chapter. What type of hardware should Tyler recommend to assist with these initiatives?

Key Terms

arithmetic logic unit (ALU), 115
backward compatibility, 136
bit, 111
bus, 117
byte, 111
central processing unit (CPU), 110
clock rate, 116
cloud storage, 131
clustering, 112
compact disc (CD), 128
control unit, 115
CPU clock, 116
CRT (cathode-ray tube), 124
data word, 117
digital video disc (DVD), 128
direct access, 126
direct-attached storage (DAS), 130
dot-matrix printer, 126
ergonomics, 118
fault tolerance, 130
flash drive, 126
flash memory, 129
flat-panel monitor, 124
hard disk, 128
hardware, 109
imaging, 122
impact printer, 126
input device, 110

internal memory, 110
liquid crystal display (LCD), 124
machine cycle, 116
magnetic disk, 127
magnetic-ink character recognition (MICR), 121
magnetic tape, 127
mainframe computer, 112
microprocessor, 115
MIPS, 117
motherboard, 110
mouse, 118
multicore processor, 115
multiprocessing, 112
multithreading, 115
network-attached storage (NAS), 130
nonimpact printer, 125
notebook computer, 113
optical disc, 128
output device, 110
parallel processing, 112
personal computer, 113
personal digital assistant (PDA), 113
pixel, 124
port, 135
radio-frequency identification (RFID), 120

RAID, 130
RAM (random access memory), 110
resolution, 125
ROM (read-only memory), 110
scalability, 130
sequential storage, 126
server, 113
smartphone, 114
solid state disk (SSD), 129
solid state storage, 129
source data input device, 120
speech recognition, 123
storage, 110
storage area network (SAN), 130
storage-as-a-service, 131
stylus, 113
supercomputer, 111
tablet computer, 114
technology convergence, 114
throughput, 117
touch screen, 119
trackball, 119
trackpad, 119
universal serial bus (USB), 126
USB drive, 129
workstation, 113

Review Questions

1. You have decided to buy parts and build your own personal computer. At the minimum, what are the components that you would need for this device to be considered a computer?

2. Modern CPUs contain cores. What is a core?

3. Multicore CPUs facilitate multithreading. What is multithreading?

4. Most people never get to see a supercomputer, let alone use one. Why? What are the most frequent uses of this type of computer?

5. News about the death of mainframe computers has been greatly exaggerated. Explain.

6. IT professionals often speak of the merging of technologies. Think of handheld computers and cell phones. Give an example of such merging.

7. When a computer is offered for sale, one of its advertised characteristics is something such as "2.9 GHz." What does this mean, and what does it measure?

8. Why are computers said to be processing data digitally?

9. What is the difference between volatile and non-volatile memory? Give one example of volatile memory and one example of nonvolatile memory.

10. What are the main qualities to look for in an LCD monitor?

11. Among the external storage devices discussed in this chapter, all but one store data on the surface of some material, and one in circuitry. Which one stores data in circuitry?

12. What is DVD technology? How does it differ from CD technology?

13. What does footprint mean in hardware? When is a footprint important in the office?

14. What are the most important features to consider before purchasing a PC?

15. On a continental tour, a traveling salesperson makes software-based presentations at every place he stops. He has ensured that there is a PC and projecting equipment at every site he visits. Occasionally, he needs to change the content of his presentation. He wants to carry as small a storage device as possible. What data storage device would you recommend he carry?

Discussion Questions

16. Computers fail significantly less frequently than copy machines and printers. Why?

17. Comment on this statement: large computers, such as mainframes and supercomputers, have no future.

18. Because information technology advances so rapidly, business professionals find it difficult to make informed decisions regarding computer and peripheral equipment purchases. What factors cause this difficulty? What advice would you provide to help with the decision?

19. End users' role in making hardware purchasing decisions is growing. Analyze the technological and operational reasons for this trend.

20. Would you replace a PC with a tablet computer for your studies or work? Why or why not?

21. Which storage medium would you use in each of the following situations: (1) airline reservations system, (2) information on employee benefits and professional conduct, and (3) online answers to customers' frequently asked questions (FAQs)? Explain your choices.

22. The miniaturization and merging of technologies into highly portable devices has caused some annoyances. Give some examples.

23. Comment on the following statement: the useful life of a PC is about two years, therefore, it is not important whether the vendor is still in business in two or three years.

24. Thanks to DVD and other advanced technologies, a PC can combine the functions of a computer, telephone, fax machine, and television set. Would you give up your home telephone and television set if you could use your PC to make calls and watch television? Why or why not?

25. Sometimes useful information might be lost, not because the medium on which it was stored deteriorated or was damaged, but because no device was available to retrieve the information. How could that happen? Can you give examples?

26. You might have heard of the e-reader, a handheld device that allows readers to read a book from internal memory or cloud storage. What are the advantages and disadvantages of such devices when compared with traditional books? Think in terms of portability, text clarity, searching for specific words or pages, and so on. What would you prefer: an electronic book or a paper book? Why?

27. Observers say that personal computers have become a commodity. What does the term "commodity" mean? How could this development impact businesses and homes?

28. Try to count how many hours per week you use a personal computer: at your home, in the PC lab, in the library, or elsewhere. Do you consider yourself "computer addicted"?

29. What do you expect will be the most popular storage devices for personal use in five years? What will be the most popular non-portable storage devices for corporate use in five years? Why?

30. Almost daily a new electronic device, often one that combines several technologies, is offered for sale. People sometimes refer to these devices as "gadgets," which hints that they might be nice to have but not really necessary or even useful. How do *you* delineate the difference between a gadget and a helpful device?

Applying Concepts

31. Analyze each of the business scenarios outlined below. Recommend a hardware configuration for each of the scenarios listed using the table. Develop a rationale of your configuration selections. Assume that the cost of the hardware configurations will be approved based on your rationale.

Features	Computer Configuration			
	A	B	C	D
Processor				
Speed (clock rate)				
Internal Storage, RAM (GB)				
Internal storage, hard disk				
Monitor (size, resolution)				
Video Graphics (memory, resolution)				
Printer (type, PPM, DPI)				

a. An artist creates complex graphics. The software required to develop these graphics require large and complex programs. While the quantity of their graphic printouts is not substantial, they must be high quality.

b. The administrative personnel use a computer for editing and printing documents and small reports using word-processing software. These employees will maintain the document files on their computer system. These documents will require professional and quality appearance.

c. The data analysts require access to corporate databases to complete complex statistical analysis. These queries and data analysis can require significant time to complete the mathematical calculations. The analysts will print reports consisting of the results of their data analysis in reasonable quality and speed.

d. The corporation's accountants need a computer system that will be able to develop reports as well as substantial spreadsheets. They will need to access their software-as-a-service accounting software through a browser as well as download financial data. Their reports need to be professional and or reasonable quality.

32. Assume you can choose among magnetic tapes, magnetic hard disks, recordable optical discs (CD-R: write once, read many), and flash memory USB drives. Consider each scenario independently of the others. For each of the following purposes, explain which one of the media you would choose and why. Start by saying which medium you have chosen. Then explain why.

a. You need to store thousands of employee records for several years. This is only a backup procedure. The information will never be processed from the backup medium.

b. The storage medium is used as part of an airline reservation system.

c. Your business sells machines that must be maintained well by your clients. You wish to provide them with a digital version of the maintenance manual. The manual includes an index (like the one at the end of a book) with links to the proper pages.

d. You are a sales manager who travels often. You must store a large PowerPoint presentation that you show to prospective customers in their office. You do not carry a laptop computer, but there is a PC wherever you go. You do not want to carry CDs, because you found that the graphic-rich presentation moves too slowly from CDs.

e. You have a business on the web. You maintain your own server and site. You provide much textual and graphical information from the site.

Customers can search products and make purchases.

f. You want to store all the paintings of impressionist painters for use by your local library patrons. Patrons can search by artist name, artist nationality, or the painting's topic. The library would like multiple copies of what you store, and to be able to loan them to patrons for viewing at home.

g. You use the medium for a large database that your employees manipulate frequently.

h. You work for the IRS, and you need to archive the tax records of millions of taxpayers for several years. The archiving is done after all processing of tax filings are complete and after all refunds and payments have been made. IRS employees must occasionally go back and retrieve specific records from these files, and when they need a record, they want to access it directly.

Hands-On Activities

33. Your company is about to open a new branch. You were selected to equip the office with 20 personal computers, 10 laptop computers, and 5 laser printers. Management has asked that you purchase all the equipment from a single online vendor. Each PC must be purchased complete with a 20-inch LCD monitor. After interviewing employees about their typical computing needs, you developed the following scale:

PCs: Every 1 MHz of clock rate receives 1 point; every 1 GB of RAM receives 10 points; every 1 GB of hard disk storage receives 1 point. For CD-RW, each 1X of reading speed receives 1 point (writing and rewriting speeds are not essential, but the capabilities are required).

LCD monitors: Every 1:100 of contrast ratio gets 10 points. Other features are not essential.

Laptops: The same scoring as for PCs.

Printers: Every 1 PPM receives 100 points; every 1 DPI receives 1 point.

Research three online vendor sites for this equipment. Prepare a spreadsheet table with three columns, one for each vendor, and enter the information you found about each piece of equipment for each vendor. Enter a formula to add up the total number of points at the bottom of each column. Do not consider any factor that is

not mentioned here. Find the vendor whose total points per dollar is the highest.

34. Use a spreadsheet application to prepare a table that clearly shows (both in text and numbers) how to calculate the following. A music CD contains 750 million bytes. How long does it take to play all the music on it, assuming the disc plays at 1X? If the CD contains data, how long would it take to retrieve all the data from it into a computer's RAM, if you used a 60X CD drive?

35. Imagine you are the head of the sales department for a regional paper company. As part of your responsibility, you must select new hardware for your department, which consists of two administrative personnel, ten inside salespeople, six outside salespeople, and four inside sales executives. While selecting the new hardware, it is important to remember the types of employees that make up the office:

- Administrative personnel who create office memos and take care of paper work

- Inside salespeople who use a software as a service (SaaS) for sales and marketing software for customer contacts

- Outside salespeople that need access to customer contact information on the road (through the SaaS application) and send memos, emails, etc.

- Inside sales executives who are mostly internal but sometimes travel

Headquarters has allowed you to choose from the following new hardware: laptop computers, desktop computers, and tablets. Administrative personnel and inside salespeople will receive one new piece of hardware and outside salespeople and inside sales executives will receive two new pieces of hardware. In a formal purchase order proposal, determine which employees should receive what types of hardware and why. Make sure you specify why the selected hardware will fit the responsibilities of the employee you choose it for. Include the following items which would be presented to your purchasing manager. Conduct online research to determine the competing laptops, desktops, and tablets and create three tables, one for each of the three types of hardware being purchased, that shows the features and costs of the hardware. Record the cost per unit and total costs of the new hardware purchases. Include in the proposal features of the hardware that will make it beneficial for the tasks it needs to perform. Do not forget installation or transition costs if they are applicable.

Team Activities

36. Your team has received $1,000 to purchase a computer system. Assume you have no equipment; everything needs to be purchased. Use the evaluation form in Figure 4.8. Visit the websites of three computer hardware vendors, and write down specifications of three sets of equipment. Include in each set a computer, a keyboard and mouse (or trackball), a compatible 22- or 24-inch LCD monitor, and a color laser printer. Your team should evaluate the features of each configuration, on a scale of 1 to 10 (1 = worst; 10 = best), and total the points. Which configuration (and, therefore, vendor) would you recommend to your fellow students? If you cannot spend your entire $1,000, any surplus should be considered a benefit. Be ready to explain your recommendation.

37. As in Activity 36, assume you have $1,000 available. You are to purchase your ideal PC, monitor, and printer, while utilizing all or almost all of your budget. Shop the web for these devices, list them (item name, vendor, and capabilities) and their prices, and rationalize why this is the ideal system for your needs and desires.

Better Storage for Our Best Friends

"At Petco animals always come first," says the website of Petco Animal Supplies, Inc. Established in 1965, the company is a leading retailer of pet supplies, from cat collars to aquariums to pet food. It operates more than 1150 stores nationwide. To accommodate customers, it also operates an online store.

Because Petco maintains thousands of products in its warehouses, and because receiving and shipping takes place often, it must track in real time the location of each item. In its three main warehouses, workers use handheld devices equipped with both barcode and RFID capabilities. They are used to scan product barcodes, record inventory receipts, and track shipping instructions and execution. Because of the large number of stores and the huge variety of items, Petco is highly sensitive to disruptions and downtime of its information systems. Downtime may cause significant financial damage due to lost sales.

All this data must be recorded and backed up. Petco used magnetic tapes to back up data every few hours, but the approach was far from ideal. Tape backup is reliable, but the latency of a few hours posed a risk. If electric power was lost, so was several hours of data that could not be recorded. Also, recording on tape is labor-intensive, because tapes must be manually mounted and dismounted. Rewinding tapes is time-consuming, and therefore delays availability of new tapes for recording.

Another issue with data storage was that the company used the DAS (direct-attached storage) approach: each computer backed up to its own magnetic disk. The data could not be shared by all computers. This created two problems. Many of the disks were underutilized; much space—up to 50 percent—was never used. As the company grows, the total underutilized disk space grows as well. In addition, sharing the stored data was challenging.

To overcome these problems, Petco IT staff tried mirroring. In disk mirroring, the entire disk is automatically copied to a backup disk. While this reduces labor and makes data available immediately from the mirror disk, it also presents a problem. If the original disk is corrupt, such as infected with a virus, so is the mirror disk.

The IT staff examined SAN (storage area network) and NAS (network-attached storage) solutions. It found that SAN would require much maintenance, while NAS required much equipment to handle data communications. Petco opted for a system called iSCSI provided by Network Appliance, Inc., better known as NetApp. The system of backing up to DAS was replaced with backing up the Petco computers to

NetApp servers over the Internet. iSCSI (pronounced "eye scuzzy") utilizes the existing Internet standards and network, and provides very fast data transfers. The adopter does not need to incur the typical expense of optical fiber networks associated with SAN. The magnetic disks and the software that manages them were implemented in the three main warehouses.

Compared to the DAS approach, using such a system reduces the total amount of required storage capacity, because much of the capacity of directly attached disks is never used. The new arrangement does not require as much storage planning as was required with DAS. The company can add storage capacity whenever data management needs require it. This eliminates wasted money spent on excess capacity. Thus, the storage system is scalable. It is easy and inexpensive to add more disks at any of the three warehouses.

Another benefit of using this technology was that the system could be installed without interruption to warehouse operations. In fact, warehouse workers did not notice the change. They left work on Friday, and when they returned on Monday morning everything looked the same to them.

Source: Pettis, A., "Petco's New Storage Gear is the Cat's Meow," eWeek, March 13, 2000, (www.petco.com), March 2007.

Thinking About the Case

1. What were the data backup problems when Petco used tapes?

2. What were the data backup problems when Petco used mirroring?

3. What are the disadvantages of using DAS, and how are these disadvantages compounded when a company grows?

4. What benefits did Petco acquire when adopting the current technology for backing up warehouse data?

Food in Transit

As you sit to eat a meal, you may wonder how many processes and activities must be completed before the product gets to your table. Consumers want quality, fresh food products at a reasonable price. Each of those characteristics requires food manufacturers to operate efficiently to remain in business and stay competitive.

Consider Texas-based Mission Foods, one of the largest manufacturers of Mexican food products in the U.S. Their operations consist of 16 plants and 50 distribution centers. Mission's distribution model uses a network of independent distributors to deliver their products over 2,300 routes. The distributors deliver directly to supermarkets and retail locations. Mission used an antiquated paper-based, batch methodology to manage its route delivery operations. Some of their distributors communicated invoicing and receipt acknowledgement information to Mission via modems. The remainder of the invoices was processed through the original hard copies, which required scanning for processing. On any given day, Mission could process about 30,000 documents nationwide. These processes were inefficient and labor intensive, extending the time to process invoices accurately by the company's information systems.

A 2010 survey completed by ARC Advisory Group determined that the top four mobile technologies used for supply chain management are smartphones, handheld computers, cellular networks, and mobile bar code scanners. Mission's management believed that the technology advancements in networking and mobile computers could help end the inefficient picking and packing processes. Their analysis determined that a device was needed that would be able to enter and store information and be able to transmit information using a variety of methods:

- Wide area wireless connection in the field
- Wireless 802.11b standard within Mission's facilities
- Bluetooth capabilities at a customer site

Mission was able to procure one hardware unit that was capable of the three communication methods. The distributor can gain a customer's signature on the handheld device in real time when the product is accepted. At this point, the invoicing data is immediately transmitted and processed by Mission's information systems over AT&T's cellular network. As always, network connections can be disrupted. However, if the network is unavailable at the time of delivery, the system will store the information on the handheld and attempt to resend the data. Any transactions that have not been sent during the day will be transmitted when the distributor returns to Mission's distribution center through their wireless LAN.

Several years later, the success of this initiative led Mission to look inside its warehouses to gain additional efficiency using handheld devices. Their warehouse activities still used paper order picking lists to gather full cartons of a product and place them onto a delivery pallet. Their current system created two problems: incorrectly picked products and improper selection of recently manufactured products before older products.

With the first problem, the incorrect product is shipped. With the second, employees selected boxes that did not have the oldest expiration date, which caused the company to scrap expired products.

Misson's solution consisted of implementing special handheld devices capable of scanning barcodes directly from the product cartons. The devices included special terminal emulation software that mimicked the data entry terminals used by Mission's information system. As an employee scanned the pick location and the product in the warehouse, the system would ensure that the accurate product and quantity was being selected. Any discrepancies would be immediately communicated to the warehouse employee.

Source: Napolitano, M. (2011). Mission foods' wireless evolution. Logistics Management (2002), 50(4), 46–48, 50.

Thinking About the Case

1. Is there any benefit for Mission to deploy this technology for its independent distributors? For the consumer?

2. What types of handheld devices could be used today for a system like this? Compile some research on the hardware solutions for a similar product.

3. Why would it be important for Mission to know that a customer acknowledged the receipt of products delivered from the independent distributors?

4. These information technology initiatives required capital investments by Mission for the hardware, software, and networking costs. What would you expect the benefits to be gained by Mission? What cost savings and other benefits would be needed to justify the investment?

References

Anonymous. (2012a). 10 Ways Imaging Systems Deliver Strong ROI to AR. *IOMA's Report on Managing Credit, Receivables & Collections, 12*(3), 12-13.

Anonymous. (2012b). Adult Computer and Adult Internet Users by Selected Characteristics: 2000 to 2011 (pp. U.S. Census Bureau). Washington, D.C.

Anonymous. (2012c). DoubleTake's new FlickIT Technology makes Hawaii Five-O and CSI TV fake touch screen photo flicking a reality! Retrieved May 30, 2013, 2013, from http://doubletaketech.com/2012/03/07/doubletakes-new-flickit-technology-makes-hawaii-five-o-and-csi-tv-fake-photo-flicking-a-reality/

Anonymous. (2012d). Nonfatal Occupational Injuries and Illnesses Requiring Days Away From Work, 2011.

Anonymous. (2012e). Pleiades Supercomputer. Retrieved May 30, 2013, 2013, from http://www.nas.nasa.gov/hecc/resources/pleiades.html

Anonymous. (2012f). Youtube Statistics. Retrieved September 8, 2012, 2012, from http://www.youtube.com/t/press_statistics

Anonymous. (2013). Quantum LTO-6 Drives. Retrieved June 4, 2012, 2013, from http://www.quantum.com/products/tapedrives/ltoultrium/lto-5/index.aspx

Brodkin, J. (2012). With 16 petaflops and 1.6M cores, DOE supercomputer is world's fastest. *Information Technology*. http://arstechnica.com/information-technology/2012/06/with-16-petaflops-and-1-6m-cores-doe-supercomputer-is-worlds-fastest/

eBay. (2012). Who We Are Overview. from http://www.ebayinc.com/who

eBay. (2013). 1eBay Marketplaces Fast Facts At-A-Glance (Q4 2013).

Fluss, D. (2012). IVRs Get a Bad Rap. *Customer Relationship Management, 16*, 8-8.

Gray, P. (2012). Just Getting the Job Done is Not Enough. *Customer Inter@ction Solutions, 30*(9), 24-24, 26.

Manyika, J., Chui, M., Brown, B., Bughin, J., Dobbs, R., Roxburgh, C., & Hung Byers, A. (2011). Big data: The next frontier for innovation, competition, and productivity.

Medina, R., & Andrews, L. (2009). New Impetus for Going Paperless. *Infonomics, 23*(3), 40-42.

Munger, F. (2012). The cost of Titan. Retrieved from http://blogs.knoxnews.com/munger/2012/11/the-cost-of-titan.html

Sverdlik, Y. (2013). An eBay server's worth. *Datacenter Dynamics*. http://www.datacenterdynamics.com/focus/archive/2013/03/ebay-servers-worth

BUSINESS SOFTWARE

Learning Objectives

Hardware, as powerful as it might be, is useless without software. Software consists of instructions that tell the computer and its peripheral devices what to do and how to do it. These instructions are called programs or applications. Many IT professionals refer to computer programs as "systems" because they are composed of components working to achieve a common goal. As a professional, you must be able to make educated decisions regarding software selection. To do so, you need to understand the factors involved in developing, selecting, and using software.

When you finish this chapter, you will be able to:

- Explain the difference between application software and system software.

- Enumerate the different generations of programming languages and explain how they differ.

- Cite the latest major developments in application and system software.

- Identify and explain the roles of web programming languages.

- Explain the types and uses of website design tools.

- Clarify the differences between proprietary software and open source software.

- List characteristics that are important in evaluating packaged software applications for business use.

- Understand the problem of software piracy and how it affects businesses and consumers.

KIMBALL'S RESTAURANT: Software Added to the Bill

Michael knew that the "front house" operations were important for customer service and efficient functioning of the restaurant. However, he knew that the restaurant could not survive on the efficiency of its front-house operations alone. He remembered their accountant's emphasis on the need to pay more attention to the purchase of food. The profits of a restaurant depend significantly on ordering and forecasting, reducing spoilage by not ordering more product than they need. Michael has learned that there is a careful balance between ordering too much and running out of food. He wondered also if he could manage his suppliers better with more accurate data on the restaurant's needs. Could he reduce his deliveries from a supplier to ask for a larger discount? Negotiate better prices by consolidating orders to specific suppliers?

Accounting for Success

As he thought about these questions, he wondered how he could collect and access better data. The new point-of-sale system recorded the sales of each menu selection and type, from appetizers, entrees, and desserts to side orders. The management information from the new system surely could help him to project the number of patrons on any given night and the sales of individual menu items. How could he use that information? Would he need input from Liz and the kitchen operations?

He decided to discuss it with both Tyler and his wife. Michael asked Liz to provide some details on her ordering process. She said that she gives a standard order to the suppliers for the main components of the menu items. She then used those order quantities as a basis for her next order. "Sometimes I may order more or less based on what I see in the food storage areas, freezers and refrigerators," she said. "It's just a guess, but I think it is working pretty well." She also said that she is meticulous about marking the delivery dates of perishable items so that she does not use spoiled materials.

Tyler then asked, "How do we know what is thrown out because of spoilage? Or when we run out of a product?" Michael also explained that he wants to make sure they are ordering efficiently based on accurate forecasts rather than just by guess. Food costs are a significant

percentage of their total operating costs. He did not want to ask, but he believed that Liz did not ask or negotiate prices with the suppliers. He asked Tyler to complete an inventory of the food for a week to gain more understanding of the situation. Tyler wondered if he could design a simple spreadsheet to develop an order list for the various suppliers in order to simplify the process.

As Michael considered basing their food purchases on a forecast, he also wondered if scheduling their serving, kitchen, and busing personnel could be done in a similar manner. Also, they are currently using a payroll service to pay employees and generate all the necessary regulatory reporting; maybe there is a better way to manage the labor costs to gain efficiency and reduce costs.

Putting Software to Work

Most of the menu and promotional materials for the restaurant have been created using a local graphic artist and print shop. This service added costs to their operation as well as increased turnaround time to complete the materials. Tyler wondered if they might be able to purchase some software for their new computer system that would allow them to create and print some of the promotional, marketing, and menu materials on their own color laser printer. For the grand opening, they will need additional materials for the marketing, promotion, menus and other administrative functions.

As another important part of the promotional process, moving to the new location could be a perfect opportunity to upgrade their website. Currently, the website consists of a few simple pages containing a few pictures of the restaurant, their location and directions, and a sample menu; the website had not been changed in the last two years. They want to give it a new "look" and presentation to match the new location, and add some dynamic content for specials and updates to create more interaction with customers. Tyler knows a little about building a website from his college courses, but he has no graphical or web design skills. He wonders if there are any software tools out there that could help him "kick up" their website in order to prepare for the new location and draw new customers.

Software: Instructions to the Hardware

If you have ever walked to the back of a restaurant, you might have seen a touch screen computer station where servers bring your check. The computer runs software that collects front-house information and sends it to back-house operations. The specialized computers can calculate check totals, keep track of inventory, and save historical records of purchases. This data allows managers to monitor customer trends or patterns and keep track of supplies.

You use software all the time, not just when you use your computer. You use software when you drive a car, upload a video from your smartphone, and when you use the self-checkout station at a store. The purpose of much of the software used by organizations is to increase productivity.

When executives talk about productivity tools, they really mean computer programs, commonly known as software **applications**. Word processors, electronic spreadsheets, web browsers, project management tools, collaborative work programs, and many other types of productivity tools are software that runs on computers and enables workers to produce more products and services in a given amount of time. This chapter discusses the differences between system software and application software, programming languages that are used to write software, and the types of business software tools currently available.

Software is a series of instructions to a computer or other digital device to execute any and all processes, such as displaying text, mathematically manipulating numbers, or copying or deleting documents. Digital devices only understand instructions made up of electrical signals alternating between two states, which eventually close or open tiny electrical circuits. Different sequences of signals represent different instructions to the computer. In the early days of computers, programming a computer meant actually changing the computer's wiring by opening and closing switches or moving plugs from one circuit to another. Because programs today consist of instructions that require no hardware reconfiguration, the skill of composing software programs is independent of building or directly manipulating hardware. Software is executed not only on computers, but in every device that uses microprocessors, such as motor vehicles, digital cameras, and mobile phones. However, in this chapter we will focus mainly on computer software that serves organizations.

The two major categories of software are application software and system software. **Application software** enables users to complete a particular application or task, such as word processing, investment analysis, data manipulation, or project management. **System software** enables application software to run on a computer, and manages the interaction between the CPU, memory, storage, input/output devices, and other computer components. Both types of software are discussed later in the chapter.

Programming Languages and Software Development Tools

Programs are needed for absolutely every operation a computer conducts. An operation can be as simple as adding 1 + 2, typing a word, or emitting a beep—or as involved as calculating the trajectory of a spacecraft bound for Mars. The process of writing programs is **programming**, also known as "writing code" and "software engineering."

Remember, the *only* language that computer hardware understands is a series of electrical signals that represent bits and bytes, which together provide computer hardware with instructions to carry out operations. But writing programs in this language—called **machine language**—requires a programmer to literally create long strings of ones and zeroes to represent different characters and symbols, work that is no longer required thanks to programming languages and other software development tools. **Assembly languages** made programming somewhat easier because they aggregated common commands into "words," although many of the "words" are not English-like. Higher-level **programming languages** enable the use of English-like statements to accomplish a goal, and these statements are translated by special software into the machine language.

Software development kits (SDKs) are even easier to use because they require practically no knowledge of programming languages to develop software. An SDK typically offers a set of software development tools for a particular hardware system (like a video game console or the Apple iPhone), operating system, or programming language. SDKs provide several software tools that integrate together to increase the productivity of software development professionals and reduce software costs. Adobe's Creative Suite includes a portfolio of software including Photoshop, Illustrator, and InDesign to assist with print design and digital publishing.

Programmers have at their disposal literally thousands of different programming languages, such as Visual Basic, Java, and C++. Programmers and nonprogrammers alike can use webpage development tools such as Adobe Dreamweaver or Avanquest WebEasy Professional, which provide menus, templates, and palettes that the developer can select or click to create intricate webpages, forms, animation, and links to organizational information systems. To develop the software development tools themselves, and to develop highly specialized software, programmers still have to write code in programming languages.

Figure 5.1 shows how programming languages have evolved dramatically over the years. The different stages of development are known as generations. First-generation (machine language) and second-generation (assembly) languages were quite inefficient tools for code writing. They required lengthy written code for even the simplest procedures. In third- and fourth-generation languages, shorter, more human-friendly commands replaced lengthy code. Ultimately, it would be nice to be able to program using the daily grammar of your native language—English, Spanish, Hebrew, or any other language. But even then, the so-called natural language would have to be translated by another program into machine language.

FIGURE 5.1

The evolution of programming languages

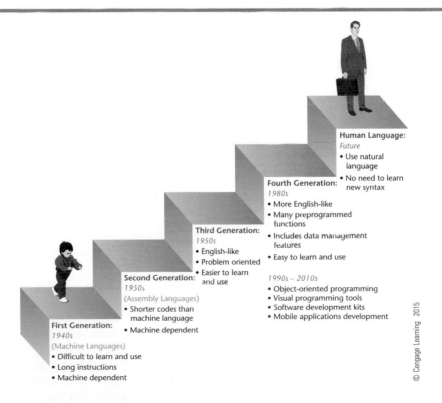

First Generation:
1940s
(Machine Languages)
• Difficult to learn and use
• Long instructions
• Machine dependent

Second Generation:
1950s
(Assembly Languages)
• Shorter codes than machine language
• Machine dependent

Third Generation:
1950s
• English-like
• Problem oriented
• Easier to learn and use

Fourth Generation:
1980s
• More English-like
• Many preprogrammed functions
• Includes data management features
• Easy to learn and use

1990s – 2010s
• Object-oriented programming
• Visual programming tools
• Software development kits
• Mobile applications development

Human Language:
Future
• Use natural language
• No need to learn new syntax

© Cengage Learning 2015

Third-generation languages (3GLs) are considered "procedural" because the programmer has to detail a logical procedure that solves the problem at hand. Third-generation languages reduced the programmer's time spent producing code. One 3GL statement is equivalent to 5–10 assembly language statements. Some common procedural languages include FORTRAN, COBOL, BASIC, RPG, Pascal, and C. Some of them, such as RPG and COBOL, are no longer in use or in limited use.

Fourth-generation languages (4GLs) make application development even easier. They are built around database management systems that allow the programmer to create database structures, populate them with data, and manipulate the data. Many routine procedures are preprogrammed and can be recalled by including a single word in the code. A single 4GL statement is equivalent to several 3GL statements, and therefore to dozens of assembly statements.

4GL commands are more English-like than commands in 3GL procedural languages. In fact, 4GLs are significantly less procedural than 3GLs. With 4GL commands, the programmer often only needs to type what is to be done, but doesn't need to specify how the procedure accomplishes the task. For example, if one column in a database is AGE, the programmer can simply use the preprogrammed command LIST AVERAGE(AGE) to display on the screen the average age, which is calculated from the age values in all the records. Similarly, preprogrammed functions are provided for total, standard deviation, count, median, and many more tasks. The list of preprogrammed functions in electronic spreadsheets such as Microsoft Excel has become so comprehensive that some people refer to them as 4GLs.

Structured Query Language (SQL) is a 4GL used by many database management software packages. SQL is a nonprocedural language that consists of simple commands and keywords to manipulate, extract, and update data in a relational database. For example, the following SELECT statement in SQL will list six fields (customer number, name, street, city, state, and balance due) from a database table (tblCustomer) for all customers whose balance due is greater than $1000.

```
SELECT CustNumber, CustName, CustStreet, CustCity, CustState,
    BalanceDue
FROM tblCustomer
WHERE BalanceDue > 1000;
```

WHY YOU SHOULD   Be Software Savvy

As a professional, you should regard software as a tool to further your productivity and education. Software can automate many processes that professionals must accomplish. Even the simplest of software applications, such as electronic spreadsheets, can be used to build decision support applications. Electronic spreadsheets are extremely useful for organizing and comparing data, and database software allows users to efficiently sort through large amounts of client information. Software vendors offer a huge variety of programs with various functions and features. While it is challenging for individuals to be knowledgeable about all available software, an understanding of the types of software and some particular applications lets you make informed comparisons and suggestions for improving your organization's software portfolio and your own library of personal software. In addition, the various categories and uses of software tend to follow the trends in hardware innovations. For example, the integration of mobile computing applications has created a market for mobile development software. The more knowledge you have about software trends, the more valuable you will be to your organization.

4GLs speed up the programming process. They are relatively easy to use by people who are not professional programmers, and therefore enable non-IT employees in many companies to produce applications on their own. The produced code is usually easy to change, which reduces the cost of software maintenance. Because 4GLs are very English-like, **debugging**—locating and fixing programming errors—is relatively easy.

Higher-level programming languages have their advantages, but also some disadvantages (see Figure 5.2). Therefore, programming languages are chosen based not only on programming productivity but also on the amount of control over the resulting software that is desired.

FIGURE 5.2

Advantages and
disadvantages of using
higher-level programming
languages

Advantages of Higher-Level Programming

◆ Ease of learning the language

◆ Ease of programming

◆ Significantly shorter code

◆ Ease of debugging

◆ Ease of maintenance (for example, modification of a procedure)

Disadvantages of Higher-Level Programming

◆ Less control over hardware

◆ Less efficient memory use

◆ Program runs more slowly

© Cengage Learning 2015

Visual Programming

To accelerate their work, programmers can use one of several **visual programming languages**, such as Microsoft Visual Basic, Embarcadero Delphi, Micro Focus COBOL, ASNA Visual RPG, and Visual C++. These languages let programmers create field windows, scroll-down menus, click buttons, and other objects by simply choosing the proper icon from a palette. They can then use a flexible tool to shape and color these objects. (Note that here the term "object" is used loosely, not with its special meaning in the context of object-oriented languages, as discussed in the next section.) Seeing exactly and immediately how boxes and menus look on screen reduces the chance of bugs and helps programmers finish their jobs faster than if they had to write code. The appropriate code is written automatically for them when they click on elements. However, the programmer can always go back to the code and add or change statements for operations that cannot easily be accomplished by using the visual aids. Thus, knowledge of the programming language is still required. Visual Basic software from Microsoft is used to develop forms that can allow users to enter data and click on a button to process the data.

Using Visual Basic, programmers develop a form that includes a clickable button to execute a command such as Print

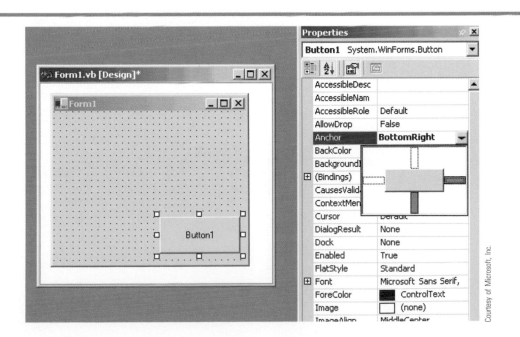

Courtesy of Microsoft, Inc.

Object-Oriented Programming

An increasing amount of software is developed using **object-oriented programming (OOP) languages**. These languages use a modular approach, which offers two great advantages: ease of maintenance and efficiency in applications development (see Figure 5.3). In traditional programming, programmers receive specifications of how a program should process data and how it should interact with users, and then they write code. If business changes and the program must be modified, the programmer must change the code. In traditional programming, data and the operations to manipulate the data are kept separate from each other. In object-oriented programming, on the other hand, operations are linked to the data. For example, if the operation is to calculate an employee's gross pay, taxes, and net pay, selecting and clicking the record triggers the calculation. Routine, frequent operations are kept with the data to be processed. Thus, OOP's primary emphasis is not on the procedure for performing a task, but on the objects involved in the task.

FIGURE 5.3

Advantages of object-oriented programming (OOP) over procedural languages

OOP Advantages

- Requires less code than other languages
- Requires less time than programming in other languages
- Enhances program modularity and reusability
- Makes code maintenance easier
- Enhances ability to create user-friendly interface
- Appropriate for graphic- and sound-enhanced applications

© Cengage Learning 2015

What Is an Object in OOP?

Figure 5.4 illustrates how an object in OOP encapsulates a data set with the code used to operate on it. Data elements in the object are called data members. They might be records, whole files, or another type of data structure. Data members have *attributes* that define the nature of the data, such as Social Security number, last name, and hourly rate. The code elements of the object are called *methods*. These procedures operate on the data, such as calculating an employee's gross pay for the week. In object-oriented software, there is no direct access to data members of an object; they can be accessed only through the methods, which are part of the object. In our example, the object includes four methods: Hourly Rate, Weekly Pay, Overtime Pay, and Age. Weekly Pay calculates each employee's gross and net pay, Overtime Pay calculates each employee's overtime gross pay, and Age computes all employees' average age.

FIGURE 5.4

A representation of the
object EMPLOYEE

Employee Maintenance

Attributes   Employee ID

Last Name

First Name

Address

Date of Birth

Methods   Hourly Rate

Weekly Pay

Overtime Pay   Close

Age

© Cengage Learning 2015

Ease of Maintenance and Development

Typically, about 80 percent of all work associated with software is spent on maintaining it. Maintenance primarily involves modifying programs to meet new business needs, but also debugging errors that were not detected when testing the developed code. In object-oriented programming, software developers treat objects as parts, or standardized modules that work together and can be used and reused. Instead of creating large, complex, tightly intertwined programs, programmers create objects. Objects are developed in standard ways and have standard behaviors and interfaces. These modules enable software to be assembled rapidly rather than written laboriously.

OOP also makes creating programs easier for nonprogrammers. The inexperienced developer does not need to know *how* an object does what it does, only *what* it does. Thus, the developer can select and combine appropriate objects from an object library, which is a repository of developed objects, to build a desired application.

Object-Oriented Programming Languages

The most popular OOP languages are Java, C++/C#, and Visual Basic. Smalltalk, developed by Xerox, was an early object-oriented programming language. C++ has become the major commercial OOP language because it combines traditional C programming with object-oriented capabilities. Java, developed by Sun Microsystems, is a popular object-oriented language designed to be platform independent, that is, to run on any computer regardless of the CPU or operating system. Another popular language, Visual Basic, enables the programmer to use graphical objects, but does not fulfill all the requirements of a true OOP language. For example, moving an icon to another application does not move the code associated with it. Some OOP languages are designed specifically for use in developing **graphical user interfaces** (GUIs). Elements of GUIs include windows, icons, scroll boxes, and other graphical images that help the user interact with the program with minimal effort.

Languages for the Web

Because an increasing amount of software is developed for websites and to link applications via the Internet, special software languages and tools have been developed for these tasks. Such programming languages include Java, JavaScript, and PHP. The main advantage of Java and JavaScript is that the code produced—often called **applets**—can be executed well regardless of the operating system that the computer uses. Therefore, the same applet will be executed the same way on a computer running Windows or one running Mac OS X. This is a significant benefit, especially when the applets are developed to be posted at a website.

The use of web-based applications can reduce costs for an organization. Consider a municipality that maintains a fleet of vehicles for public services and safety. The total cost of ownership of the fleet (purchase and operational costs) has a direct impact on municipal budgets and taxes paid by property owners. Using fleet management software, management can monitor the maintenance of vehicles. Management Reporting Suite, developed by Chevin, provides a web-based fleet management system necessary for organizations to gather and aggregate real-time data to improve key business areas such as total cost of ownership, fuel cost, mobility, and carbon dioxide reduction (Geoghegan, 2013).

In recent years an increasing number of applications have been developed in Microsoft's .NET "environment." .NET is software that supports building and linking applications that can "talk to each other" on the Internet and enable web browsers to invoke information resources, such as databases. Applications developed using .NET tools run on Microsoft operating systems, such as Windows. IBM's WebSphere is another application software portfolio designed to integrate enterprise-wide web applications across various technology platforms. As technology offerings have become decentralized consisting of different operating systems and hardware, WebSphere provides the development environment to develop applications for various business processes in an agile technology infrastructure (Anonymous, 2013a, 2013c). We discuss operating systems later in this chapter.

Development for Mobile Applications

In the late-1990s, the proliferation of web-based applications exploded with the integration of e-commerce technology. The rapid technological evolution of cell phones into smartphones has created a huge demand for mobile applications. The same consumers who adopted the use of web-based applications for purchasing, business transactions, and information gathering were the perfect audience for mobile applications. Consequently, the market for mobile software development kits increased based on the demand for these new software applications.

The specific platform that will be used to implement the mobile application needs to be considered. The most popular mobile platforms are Android, Apple, Windows, and Blackberry. Each of these mobile technology platforms uses specific variations to develop its applications. For instance, Apple's Developer provides a software development environment to create mobile applications for its iPhone product. For Android-based products, there are several alternatives.

Language Translation: Compilers and Interpreters

Recall that computers understand only machine language. Just as assembly languages need assemblers, procedural languages need special programs to translate **source code**, which is the program as originally written, into **object code**, which is the same program in machine language. (Unfortunately, the word "object" is used for several different contexts. In the context of this section it has nothing to do with object-oriented languages.) The two types of programming language translators are compilers and interpreters. **Compilers** translate the higher-level code into an equivalent machine language code, but do not execute the code; the translated code must be run to check for programming errors. **Interpreters** translate each program statement and execute it.

A compiler (see Figure 5.5) scans the entire source code, looking for errors in the form (syntax) of the code. If it finds an error, it does not create the object code; instead, it generates an error message or a list of error messages. If the compiler finds no syntactic errors, it translates source code into object code, which the computer can execute. At this point, the programmer can save the object code. From now on, the user can simply run only the object code. This saves translation time.

FIGURE 5.5

A compiler converts higher-level language code (source code) into machine language (object code), which the computer can execute

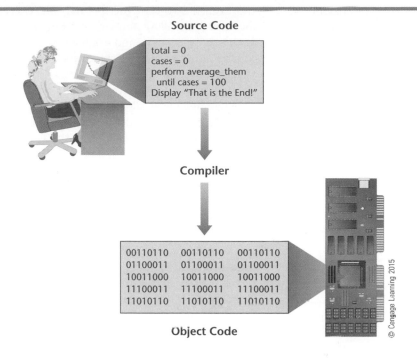

Source Code

```
total = 0
cases = 0
perform average_them
    until cases = 100
Display "That is the End!"
```

Compiler

Object Code

```
00110110   00110110   00110110
01100011   01100011   01100011
10011000   10011000   10011000
11100011   11100011   11100011
11010110   11010110   11010110
```

© Cengage Learning 2015

An interpreter checks one statement at a time. If the first statement is free of syntactic errors, it interprets the statement into object code and makes the computer execute it. If the statement is erroneous, the interpreter issues an error message. In some environments, the programmer can immediately correct the statement. The computer then executes the corrected statement, and the interpreter moves on to check the next statement. Error-free statements are executed immediately.

Code written in interpreted programming languages can run only on machines whose disks store the interpreter. In contrast, compiled code is ready to run because it is in machine language and does not need to be translated. Most Visual Basic and Java translators are interpreters. Translators of FORTRAN, COBOL, C, C++, and most other 3GLs are compilers.

When you purchase an application, whether a computer game or a business program, you purchase a compiled version of the code, that is, the object code. There are three reasons for this. First, the application is executed immediately because there is no need to compile the code. Second, most users do not have the compiler for the source code. Third, the vendor does not wish buyers to modify the code. If the program is sufficiently modified, the modified copies may be sold without violating intellectual property laws such as patents and copyrights. Source code can be modified by anyone who knows the programming language in which it was written; modifying object code is very difficult.

While testing code, programmers can use programming language translators to find syntactic errors. When they execute the program, they can find execution errors—also called runtime errors—such as division by zero or an excessive use of memory (memory leak). However, only the programmer can detect and prevent logical errors, because the logic relies, and should rely, solely on the way the programmer translated a way to produce a result into code.

Application Software

As noted earlier, an application is a program developed to address a specific need. An application can also be software that lets nonprogrammers develop such programs. Most programs that professionals use are application programs, such as word-processing programs, spreadsheet programs, payroll programs, investment analysis programs, and work-scheduling and project management programs.

Programs designed to perform specific jobs, such as calculating and executing a company's payroll, are collectively called **application-specific software**. Programs that serve varied purposes, such as developing decision-making tools or creating documents, are called **general-purpose application software**. Spreadsheets and word processors are general-purpose applications.

General-purpose applications are available as **packaged software**; that is, they come ready to install from an external storage medium such as a CD or a file downloaded from a vendor's website. Application-specific software is not always so readily available. Managers must decide whether an off-the-shelf software package meets all of their needs. If it does, the company can simply purchase it. But if off-the-shelf or other ready-made software cannot address an organization's specified needs, managers must have a program developed, either within the organization or by another organization specializing in that type of software. Therefore, it is important to clearly define the business's functional and information requirements before acquiring software. We discuss alternative ways to acquire ready-made software in Chapter 13, "Choices in Systems Acquisition."

Office Productivity Applications

The purpose of business software is to make the work of people more productive and businesses more efficient in the processing of their daily operations. However, applications that help employees in their routine office work often are called simply "productivity tools." They include word processors, spreadsheets, presentation tools, file and database management software, graphics programs, personal information managers, desktop publishing tools, and project management applications, as well as many others for more specialized purposes. Web browsers are also included in this group, because they help so many employees to find and communicate information in their daily work. These tools were developed to support home and office users on their personal computers.

While *word processors* are used mainly to type letters, articles, and other text documents, they also automate otherwise laborious tasks such as creating tables of contents and indexes. Some enable users to plan the binding and look of books up to the point of handing files to a high-quality printer for the production of the physical book. Examples of word processors include Microsoft Word or Corel WordPerfect.

Spreadsheets such as Microsoft Excel no longer limit users to entering numbers and performing basic arithmetic calculations. They include a long list of complex mathematical, statistical, financial, and other functions that users can integrate into analysis models. These functions are so powerful that statisticians often use them. Executives can build their own decision-support models with this robust tool. Spreadsheets also provide a large array of preformatted charts from which the user can select for presentation purposes.

Presentation tools such as Microsoft PowerPoint enable professionals and salespeople to quickly develop impressive presentations. One does not need to be a graphics expert, because the tools provide wide selections of font types and sizes and allow users to embed almost any art that they find (with permission!) or have created in graphics programs. Animations, sound, and video clips can be integrated into presentations and slide shows that can be posted to run on the web as videocasts.

POINT OF INTEREST   10/20/30 Rule

Guy Kawasaki was the chief evangelist of Apple and is the author of ten books including *Enchantment* and *How to Drive Your Competition Crazy*. In another one of his books, *The Art of the Start*, he teaches readers how to become a successful entrepreneur through his experiences. One of the most important and easily remembered lessons from his book is the "10/20/30" rule for PowerPoint presentations in a business setting: 10 slides, 20 minutes, 30 point font. His reasoning is that the presenter should do most of the talking by using the slides as reference points and 30 point font provides sufficient white space to keep the audience's attention. He gets his point across through his humorous tone; "I don't care if you're selling dog food, permanent life, nano particles, optical components, or the cure to cancer: Ten slides and twenty minutes is all you get."

Source: Kawasaki, Guy. (n.d.). "Official" Bio. http://www.guykawasaki.com/about/; Kawasaki, Guy. (2004). The Art of the Start: The Time-Tested, Battle-Hardened Guide for Anyone Starting Anything. New York, New York: Penguin Group (USA) Incorporated.

File management and data management tools enable the creation and manipulation of local or shared databases. Popular database management systems such as Microsoft Access are relatively easy to learn and create simple databases. They often include features that professional developers can use to create more complex databases.

Graphics programs make it easy to create intricate images and manipulate digital photographs. They are often used to create graphics to be placed on webpages. The large selection of these tools includes Adobe's Illustrator and Photoshop, Corel Paint Shop Pro, and Xara Designer Pro, as well as the free IrfanView and Gimp.

Desktop publishing tools, such as Microsoft Publisher, Adobe InDesign, and Serif PagePlus, enable both expert and novice to easily create professional looking pamphlets, newsletters, cards, calendars, and many other items for publication on paper or as webpages. More professional tools, such as Quark, by a company of the same name, have significantly increased the productivity of the publishing industry.

Project management tools, such as Microsoft Project, Basecamp, or free software alternatives such as Open Workbench and OpenProj, help managers of any type of project—such as building construction, product development, and software development—to plan projects and track their progress. Project managers enter information such as tasks and their expected completion dates, milestones, and resources required for each task: labor hours, materials, and services. The software alerts planners when they enter illogical information, such as scheduling a worker to work 120 hours in one week, and when tasks violate interdependencies. The latter happens when, for instance, planners schedule the start of Phase D before the completion of Phase C, though they had previously indicated that Phase D depends on the completion of Phase C.

Project management software facilitates the planning, execution and monitoring of projects

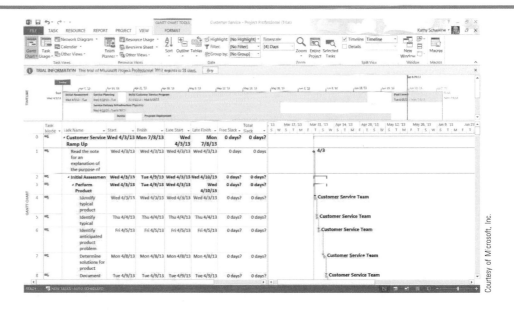

Courtesy of Microsoft, Inc.

Software developers often create **suites** of productivity tools. For example, most versions of Microsoft Office suite include a word processor (Word), spreadsheet (Excel), presentation application (PowerPoint), and an email application (Outlook). Microsoft added OneNote into its Office suite. OneNote allows users to consolidate various links, videos, webpages, and other files into their notes. Other examples of suites are IBM Lotus SmartSuite, and the free Apache OpenOffice.org. When productivity tools are integrated into a software suite, the documents created can be interdependent using technologies such as object linking and embedding (OLE). You can create tables in a spreadsheet, copy them into a word-processed document or a presentation, and ensure that when you modify the tables in the spreadsheet they also change in the document or presentation. A Microsoft Word document can link various objects with additional information, spreadsheets, and charts, embedded within the text to present a report more effectively.

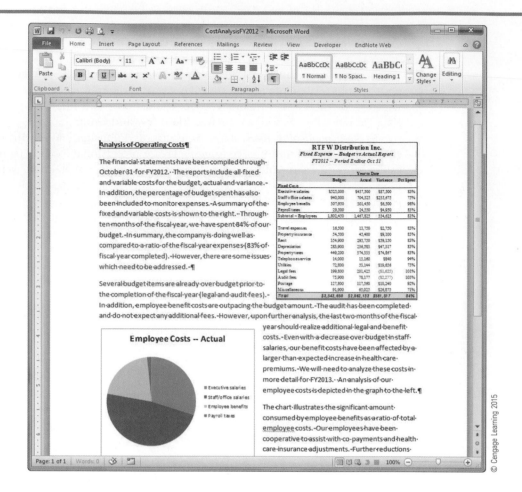

© Cengage Learning 2015

You can also embed links to websites in your documents. Linking among documents involves hypermedia technologies, and embedding information such as sound and video clips in documents uses multimedia technologies. These technologies are discussed in the next section. A growing number of web-based office applications are offered free of charge; all one needs is a web browser. Typically, all the documents the user creates are saved at the application's server. This way, both the applications and documents can be accessed from anyplace with an Internet link. For example, ThinkFree, offered by the company of the same name, is an online suite that includes a word processor, spreadsheet, graphical application, and a presentation application in a cloud office environment. It is promoted as a free online alternative to Microsoft Office implemented within a collaborative, multi-device environment (desktop, laptop, tablet, and smartphones). Google offers Google Drive (formerly known as Google Docs) an environment similar to ThinkFree. Microsoft Office itself now offers WebApps. The new environment of office productivity tools offers cloud storage and access to data files, along with applications such as calendaring and contact managers across all hardware platforms and devices. The world of application software has broadened by offering quality alternatives to off-the-shelf software.

Hypermedia and Multimedia

Hypermedia is a feature that enables a user to access additional information by clicking on selected text or graphics. Hypermedia is the web's most essential ingredient. When first conceived, the concept was limited to text and was called hypertext. Now, hypermedia is very common, used widely in various types of software, and essential to web-based documents as well as documents, charts, and presentations created using productivity tools. Any text or icon that can be clicked to jump to another place in a document or open a new document is called a link, whether on the web or not. Often, we say that a word or icon is "clickable." Hypermedia enables linking text, pictures, sounds, animations, and video.

Hypermedia features are enabled by **webpage authoring tools**. They are also part of other applications, such as some word processors and presentation tools. You can easily create a PowerPoint presentation with marked text or an icon that calls up a picture, a sound, or an animation, or one that takes you to another slide. Programs that can handle many different types of data are called **multimedia software**. Multimedia is a powerful means of communicating, because it does not limit the method of communication. A natural extension of the computer's capabilities, it provides flexibility that lets people work the way they think, integrating all types and forms of information. Multimedia is tightly associated with hypermedia, because it often uses embedded links. These links are the essence of hypermedia and are used to communicate pictures, sounds, and video as part of the same message in a way that is similar to an educational lecture or a product manual. A few examples of the uses of multimedia are described in the following sections.

Multimedia in Education and Research

One of the most common uses of multimedia is in education. A student taking a multimedia-based lesson can view a scenario in one window and view text in another while listening to a recording or webcast of his or her professor. The student might then be asked to answer questions interactively, providing responses in another window on the screen. The same program might be designed to provide the student with feedback on her performance. With voice recognition software, multimedia programs used in language training can ask a student to pronounce certain words and evaluate the student's performance.

Another common use of multimedia is in compiling and integrating data from research. For instance, a researcher might use multimedia programs to view written articles and television news footage and to listen to radio clips.

Multimedia in Training

In many industries, multimedia is commonly used to simulate real-world situations for training exercises. For example, multimedia products that use video and voice and allow users to respond to questions about various situations have been used to teach workers for an electric utility company how to solve high-voltage wire problems. If they attempted to solve the same cases in the field, their lives would be jeopardized. Flight simulators use extensive multimedia software to simulate takeoff, landing, and other flight situations when training pilots before they fly real planes.

Multimedia in Business

Multimedia can be very useful in business situations as well. Consider this example: one manager writes a document that includes digitized photographs or video clips and possibly a "live" spreadsheet, which lets the user enter numbers and execute calculations. The manager sends the document to a colleague for review; the colleague tacks on a video and voice clip requesting clarification of a certain point. The compound document can be filed electronically, retrieved, altered, and communicated as appropriate, without ever being transformed into a paper document. In fact, multimedia by its very nature cannot be transferred to a paper document. Many websites include multimedia because of its interactive nature.

Mashups

Many companies, including Amazon.com, eBay, Flickr, Google, and Yahoo!, have opened their applications so that the applications, or some of their features, can be integrated with other software to create new useful applications. These integrated applications are called mashup applications, or simply **mashups**. For example, an amateur programmer can combine a mapping application from one website—such as Mapquest, Apple Maps, or Google Maps—with a local database of charity associations to show the locations and details of the associations on a map. The mapping application continues to provide its regular features, such as directions to and from the organizations' locations.

The programmer uses software elements from different applications and combines them, or some of their features, into a hybrid application. Since these software elements are constantly available on the web, users of the mashup can enjoy it whenever their computers are connected to the Internet.

One of the most educationally useful mashups on the web is Khan Academy. Khan Academy is a not-for-profit online institution designed by a graduate of Harvard and MIT, which offers lessons on a broad range of subjects from arithmetic to calculus to molecular science to the French Revolution. The website has delivered over 200 million lessons by embedding YouTube videos into their webpages. In the YouTube videos, the instructor talks students through lessons and problems using the mouse pointer arrow and uses different colors on a black background to help students visualize what's going on. After watching the video, students can post comments and questions, similar to other YouTube videos. Khan Academy's strategy of combining a traditional website with embedded YouTube videos has created an effective mashup that is more valuable than the sum of its parts. The YouTube videos allows students to work at their own pace and the comments section lets them get help from other students, just as if they were sitting in class. It's not just a lecture; it's an interactive, social learning experience.

Website Design Tools

As a growing number of organizations established websites, and many needed to change the content of the webpages daily or even hourly, the need for web design tools grew. Popular webpage development packages include Microsoft SharePoint Designer and Expression Web, Avanquest WebEasy Professional, and Adobe CS2/Dreamweaver. Many Internet service providers (ISPs) and website hosting companies also provide online tools and templates to design and implement personal and commercial websites.

Webpage development packages expedite development of webpages. Like other visual tools, they provide menus, icons, and other features from which the developer can select. Therefore, developers have to write code only when a feature is not readily available. When using ready-made options, such as fill-in forms and animation effects, the code is automatically added. Since much of the code is in nonproprietary languages such as HTML and XML (which we discuss in Chapter 8, "The Web-Enabled Enterprise"), a programmer can start work with one development tool, such as WebEasy Professional, and continue the work with another, such as Dreamweaver. Developers alternate if they find one tool is easier to use for quick development of icons, for example, whereas another offers a more appealing way to develop animations.

Recently, a new method of developing websites has become popular. Small businesses and individuals have implemented websites using a blog environment, such as Wordpress. The blog environment can then be tailored using an automated web design program such as Artisteer. Products such as Artisteer give users who have limited web design experience the ability to customize a blog to operate as a website. The example shown here illustrates a website design for a cake and coffee shop that could be developed through Artisteer.

Groupware

Multimedia technologies are any applications that allow sharing of ideas and information resources among group members. Most of these applications are integrated with web technologies. **Groupware** applications are programs that enable workers to collaborate in real time over the web. They not only eliminate the need to travel and sit in the same physical room but also facilitate expression of ideas by demonstrating them through the combination of text, images, drawings, sound, animation, and video. Collaboration software includes various productivity tools used for team-based environments and projects where human interaction (either synchronous or asynchronous) is necessary. The specific functions vary by software application but can include project/task management, shared calendars, video/audio/text chatting, email, voice messages, and file sharing. Wiggio is an example of collaboration software. With over 1.1 million users, the software provides an environment to connect a group of people working on a project or initiative. A project representative (group leader) begins the process by creating a group and then adding members. Members can be assigned or prohibited from various functions within the group environment. The revision of this textbook was completed using Wiggio between the author and research assistant.

Google Drive, formerly called Google Docs, is a cloud-based feature that allows users to work with others on a document, presentation, spreadsheet, form, or drawing and save it online. You can upload an existing file or create a new one using Google's software. While working on a file, the user can see who else is working on that file and what changes they are making. Files are saved to the cloud so they can be opened by those granted access. Using Google Drive saves businesses time and transportation costs while providing an accessible medium for team collaboration.

3-D Geographic Software

An increasing number of applications are being developed to create 3-D models of geographic areas and whole cities, down to every hydrant and shrub. The raw materials are land and aerial photographs that cover the targeted area. The digital photographs are "sewn" together to allow a continuous "walk" or "travel" on a city street or university campus. This helps with navigation, whereby one can recognize buildings and landmarks by their similarity to the software images. This type of information can be delivered through the web. When tied with a global positioning system (GPS), the software helps people who have never been to a place to navigate easily. In the near future, 3-D software such as this will help property rental companies manage their assets. For example, a manager will be able to click on an apartment on the 12th floor of a building and check information about the unit and let a potential renter have a view from the windows or balcony. Maintenance staffs will be able to virtually go into the walls and check pipes and electrical wiring, and fire companies will be able to navigate quickly and locate hydrants on their way to put out fires.

Trimble SketchUp is a type of 3-D geographic software that is also used to create virtual cities and areas, though it is effective on a smaller scale as well. Inventive business owners use the software to create their own machines or products rather than creating virtualizations of already existing buildings or places. The potential for SketchUp is endless. Users can start by creating a small component such as a two-by-four piece of wood and eventually design an entire house and the rest of the block it's on. For those less inventive, the SketchUp library allows users to download components created by other users. Examples of these components include anything from pallets and framed walls to train stations and skyscrapers. SketchUp even connects to Google Maps, which allows the option for users to place a house where it is in real life. 3-D geographic software is important in the business world because of its capacity to virtualize existing tangible items and create new ones.

Model of the Old Salem Town Hall developed using SketchUp, a 3-D modeling tool

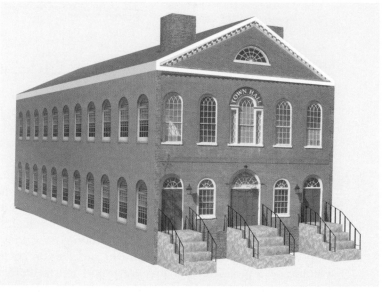

Beryl Reid

System Software

System software includes programs that are designed to carry out general routine operations, such as the interface between user and computer, loading a file, copying a file, or deleting a file, as well as managing memory resources and operating peripheral equipment such as monitors and printers. The purpose of system software is to manage computer resources and perform routine tasks that are not specific to any application. On one hand, system software is developed to work in partnership with as many applications as possible; on the other, applications can work with system software only if they are developed to be compatible with that software. The following discussion covers major types of system programs. Note that compilers and interpreters, which were discussed earlier, are also classified as system software.

Operating Systems

The **operating system (OS)** is the single most important program that runs on a computer and the most important type of system software. As Figure 5.6 illustrates, operating systems perform basic tasks, such as recognizing input from the keyboard and mouse, sending output to the computer display, keeping track of files and directories (groups of files) on disks, sending documents to the printer, and interfacing with network devices. Without an operating system, no application can run on a computer. An operating system is developed for a certain microprocessor or multiple microprocessors. Programmers know which operations each microprocessor can perform and how it performs them. The OS must address technical details such as CPU circuitry and memory addresses. Therefore, OSs are usually developed with the aid of low-level programming languages, such as assembly languages, or with a language that can access low-level machine functions, such as C.

FIGURE 5.6

The operating system mediates the computer system's resources and application software as well as controls peripheral and network devices

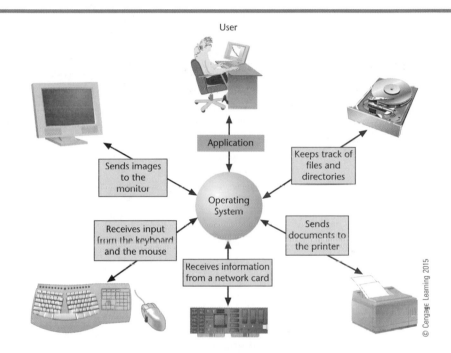

The OS is sometimes called the "traffic cop" or the "boss" of computer resources. Indeed, it is charged with control functions such as optimally allocating memory locations for an application program, copying the application from an external storage medium into memory, passing control to the CPU for execution of program instructions, and sending processing results to output devices. Operating systems are also often referred to as "platforms," because they are the platform on which all other applications "ride" when interacting with the hardware.

When application developers write code, they use the **application program interfaces (APIs)** for the operating system on which the application will run. APIs are software included in the operating system. A good API makes it easy to develop an application. Applications using the same API have similar interfaces.

From User to OS to CPU

Figure 5.7 shows the OS's position in the logical operation of a computer. The user interacts with the user interface using menus, icons, and commands provided by the application. The application converts some of the user's input into commands the OS understands, and the OS commands the CPU to carry out the operation. (Some commands are not delivered to the OS but directly from the application to the hardware.) The OS ensures that applications can use the

CPU, memory, input and output devices, and the file system. The file system is software that stores, organizes, and retrieves files.

FIGURE 5.7

Computer systems operate on a number of layers, beginning with the user interface and moving into the computer's hardware

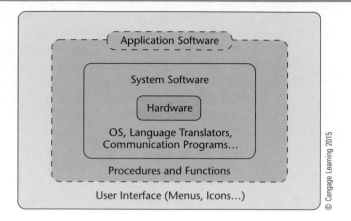

For example, assume that you are using a word processor. You select a paragraph you wish to copy and paste. You select Copy from the menu. The word processor converts your choice into an appropriate command for the OS, which then instructs the CPU to copy the paragraph. A similar action takes place when you select Paste from the menu. Assume that you like a picture on a webpage and have permission to copy it. You right-click the picture and choose to copy it. The web browser's menu might not look the same as the word processor's menu. However, when you select Copy Image, the operating system receives a command from the application that is identical to the one it received when you used the word processor. And when you paste, the Paste command that the OS receives from the browser is the same one it received from the word processor. Thus, developers of these two applications did not need to program the copy and paste operations; they only needed to know how their programs must call up these operations from the OS.

In addition to performing input and output services and controlling the CPU, many OSs perform accounting and statistical jobs, including recording times when a user logs on and logs off, the number of seconds the operator used the CPU in every session, and the number of pages a user printed. Some OSs also perform **utilities** such as hardware diagnostics, file comparison, file sorting, and the like. However, not all OSs provide all the utilities that might be necessary, in which case special utility programs must be used. Operating systems also include a number of security functions, such as the ability to set user passwords and restrict access to files and computer resources.

Operating System Functions

Operating systems provide several services, the most important of which is system management. System management refers to the efficient allocation of hardware resources to applications and includes tasks such as prompting the user for certain actions, allocating RAM locations for software and data, instructing the CPU to run or stop, allocating CPU time to different programs running at the same time, and instructing co-processors and peripheral equipment.

User Interface   An important part of the OS is the user interface. A graphical user interface (GUI) makes the use of the computer intuitive and easier to learn. The interface takes the form of easy-to-understand frames, icons, and menus. Users find it helpful to have most of the interface features identical regardless of the application they use, unless the application requires an interface element for a unique feature.

Memory Allocation   One of the most important functions of an operating system is memory management, especially for RAM—the memory where data and program code must reside before being executed. Ideally, an entire application and all the data it processes reside in RAM until processing ends. However, when many applications are open concurrently, or when applications and data pools exceed the computer's RAM capacity, the operating system may use virtual memory. **Virtual memory** lets the user proceed as if significantly more RAM were available than really exists. Virtual memory uses the hard disk as an extension of RAM. A special module of the OS continually detects which parts of the application program are used frequently. The OS keeps these parts in RAM while leaving on the disk the least frequently used parts. Professionals call this activity "page swapping"—"pages" are program parts of equal size that the OS swaps between RAM and the disk, and the space on disk used as memory is called "swap space." Because hard disks are slower than RAM, opening many applications at the same time may reduce the speed at which programs are running. However, virtual memory enables concurrent use of many and large programs without need to purchase more RAM, which is significantly more expensive than disk memory.

Plug and Play   A good operating system should also facilitate fairly simple changes to hardware configuration. When a new device, such as an external hard disk, DVD burner, external communication device, or joystick, is attached to a computer, the operating system's job is to recognize the new attachment and its function. If the OS can do so (without your intervention) immediately after you attach the device, it is a **plug-and-play (PnP)** OS, and the device, too, is referred to as a plug-and-play device. To do so, the operating system must have access to the attached device's driver. A **driver** is the software that enables the OS to control a device, either one installed inside the computer (such as a second video card) or an external device such as a flash memory drive. Thus, a true PnP OS, such as Windows 8 or Mac OS X, includes the drivers for many devices, or at least is fully compatible with a driver that is installed either from a disc or after it is downloaded from the web. In recent years, almost all external devices have been built to attach to a computer through a USB port. (USB ports were discussed in Chapter 4, "Business Hardware.")

Increasing Services from OSs   The trend in OS development is to incorporate more and more services that used to be provided by separate software. These services include database management, networking, and security. For instance, users now expect an OS to perform such security measures as tracking account numbers and passwords, controlling access to files and programs, and protecting the computer against viruses. OSs also check for access codes to ensure that only authorized users can access the computer. Modern operating systems provide networking functions previously handled by separate programs.

Current Operating Systems   As mentioned earlier, operating systems are designed to work with a particular microprocessor; consequently, different computers and types of microprocessors use different OSs. While specific operating systems exist for supercomputers, mainframe computers, midrange computers, and handheld computers, most people use a personal computer (PC) operating system. Popular operating systems for PCs include Windows, Linux, and Mac OS. Smartphones and tablets have their own operating systems geared toward the mobile environment, such as Apple iOS, Google Android, and Microsoft Windows RT. Figure 5.8 provides a list of popular operating systems. Some may come bundled with other applications. For example, i5/OS (formerly, OS/400) comes with powerful DB2 database management systems.

FIGURE 5.8

Popular operating
systems for various
hardware platforms

Typically run on...	Name	OS Developer
Mainframe	z/OS (zSeries) Clearpath OS2200	IBM Unisys
Midrange	i5/OS Solaris	IBM Sun Microsystems
Personal Computers	Windows Linux (Fedora, Red Hat, Smallfoot) OS X BSD	Microsoft Various Apple FreeBSD
Servers	Microsoft Server 2012 HP-UX 11i Unix	Microsoft HP Bell Labs (original developer) with various Unix-like OSs derived by others
Smartphones	Blackberry OS iOS Windows Phone Jelly Bean, Ice Cream Sandwich	Blackberry Apple Microsoft Android, Inc (original developer, now Google), licensed under Apache license
Tablets	iOS (iPad) Microsoft RT (Surface) Android (various)	Apple Microsoft Google

© Cengage Learning 2015

One OS that has grown in popularity is Linux, which can be obtained free of charge. Linux is based on UNIX, an operating system developed by AT&T Bell Labs in 1969 to run on midrange computers, and for 10 years was distributed free of charge. Different companies and individuals modified UNIX, developing variations of the OS such as Linux (developed by Linus Torvalds and others) and Solaris (developed by Sun Microsystems). Linux and other "open source" software is discussed in the next section.

One of the most important qualities of an OS is its *stability*. A stable OS does not cause the computer to freeze or produce error messages. It is expected to continue to function even if the user makes a mistake, in which case it should gracefully notify the user what happened and give an opportunity to resolve the problem, rather than stop functioning. Early versions of Windows were notoriously unstable. Although mishaps do occur with later versions of Windows, they are significantly more stable. OSs based on UNIX are known to be highly stable, and their stability is the main reason for their popularity, especially for running servers. Mac OS X versions are based on UNIX. Linux, too, is considered to be very stable.

Although Mac OS is installed on fewer than 10 percent of the world's computers, its share is growing (Anonymous, 2013b). From the start, Mac operating systems have been more intuitive and user-friendly than Windows operating systems. In many respects they set the standards that Windows OSs later followed. Many current popular applications, such as Excel, were first designed for the Mac OS, and only later adapted for Windows, when the latter provided user interfaces similar to those of the Mac OS. Mobile operating systems are also steadily increasing their share of the OS marketplace.

Other System Software

While operating systems are the most prevalent type of system software, other types of system programs include compilers and interpreters (discussed previously), communications software, and utilities. Some people also include in this class database management systems, which are discussed in Chapter 7, "Databases and Data Warehouses."

Communications software supports transmission and reception of data across computer networks. We discuss networking and telecommunications in Chapter 6, "Business Networks and Telecommunications." Utilities include programs that enhance the performance of computers, such as Symantec's Norton 360, which checks PCs for inefficiencies and fixes them. It also includes online backup facilities. Utilities also include antivirus programs, firewalls, and other programs that detect and remove unwanted files and applications, such as cookies and spyware, or block data from being transmitted into or out of a networked computer. We discuss these topics in Chapter 8, "The Web-Enabled Enterprise," and Chapter 14, "Risks, Security, and Disaster Recovery."

Open Source Software

The great majority of business and individual software is proprietary, that is, software that is developed and sold for profit. The developers of **proprietary software** do not make the source code of their software public. The developer retains the rights to the software. In most cases you do not actually own the copies of applications that you purchase; you only purchase licenses to use those applications. In contrast to proprietary software, some programmers freely contribute to the development of a growing number of computer programs not for profit. The developers of **open source software** can obtain the source code free of charge, usually on the web. Anyone who can contribute features or fix bugs is invited to do so. Anyone who wishes to download the latest version can do so free of charge. An open source program can be developed by a random group of programmers, rather than by a single company. Programmers share an application's basic code, find its weaknesses, debug it, and contribute new pieces. This process might yield better results than the traditional "closed" process of proprietary software, because so many talented programmers continuously try to show their prowess in improving the program. Some historians find the beginning of the open source "movement" in people such as Richard Stallman and his allies in the Free Software Foundation, who believe that software should be as free as the air we breathe and never sold for money.

The advantages of open source software over proprietary software are clear: the software has fewer bugs because thousands of independent programmers review the code, and it can offer more innovative features by incorporating ideas from a diverse set of experts from different countries and cultures who collaborate. The motive for developing and improving open source software is not monetary, but rather the satisfaction of solving programming problems and the recognition of one's contribution. Programmers who improve such software do it for fame and recognition by their peers the world over. They collaborate mainly via the Internet. They post patches of code that improve current code, or add extensions and plug-ins to enhance functionality of an application. These extensions are free for all to download and use. The major disadvantage is that development and support depend on the continued effort of an army of volunteers.

A recent study conducted by BearingPoint reveals that the critical drivers for adopting open-source software focus on competitive differentiation, reduced deployment cost, increased customization agility, and avoiding software vendor lock-in (Anonymous, 2012). The pressure to reduce costs in a competitive environment has forced banks and financial services businesses to take a second look at open source software, driving IT costs downward (Yeaton, 2013).

The need for agile software development with the transition to consumer-focused platforms such as the web and mobile, only heighten the popularity of open source software. The expanding focus on customer engagement by businesses requires a development agility that can be provided by open source software. Acquia believes that implementing social publishing using open source technology provides that agility. Customer engagement functions such as blogs, wikis, forums, and other user-generated content can be implemented more cost effectively using open source software. A cost savings of 75-85 percent over proprietary software alternatives can be realized (Anonymous, 2011).

For all of the advantages of implementing open source software, there are several issues to consider before adoption. The advantages of reduced costs and increased return on investment (ROI) are losing relevance. A *Computerworld* study found that 42 percent of organizations using open source software did not calculate ROI and total costs (Collett, 2011). A 2010 study by Accenture found that quality, reliability, and security were rationales for selecting open source software. Organizations are focusing on the value that can be achieved by adopting an open source environment. Institutional issues such as training and help desk costs are also important factors. Open source software includes hundreds of useful applications, such as the popular web browser Mozilla Firefox, the content-management system Drupal, the relational database management system MySQL, and the powerful programming language PERL (Practical Extraction and Report Language). The OpenOffice.org suite, which can be freely downloaded at www.openoffice.org, provides an alternative to Microsoft's Office suite of productivity applications. With the OpenOffice.org suite, users can create 3-D graphical designs, multimedia presentations, documents, spreadsheets, and databases.

OpenOffice.org provides free application software to complete various productivity tasks

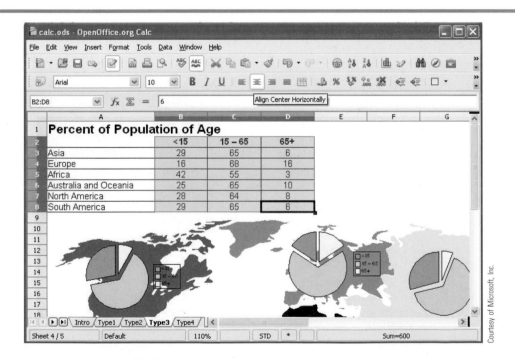

Courtesy of Microsoft, Inc.

Linux is the best known open source operating system. A Finnish graduate student named Linus Torvalds developed it for his own use, but he has never claimed rights to the software. Hundreds of programmers have contributed code to Linux. Over time, Linux evolved into many different variants, some of which are free, such as Ubuntu, Red Hat Fedora, and Smallfoot, while others such as Red Hat Enterprise Edition and SUSE charge for additional interface features and support services. Linux has become the OS of choice of many Internet service providers to run their Internet servers. The major disadvantage of using Linux is the limited number of applications that can run on it, compared with the Windows platform.

Reputable software and hardware companies including IBM, Intel, Hewlett-Packard (HP), and Dell have committed to supporting Linux by developing applications that run on it. A growing number of corporations have adopted it, including Burlington Coat Factory, Tommy Hilfiger, and Toyota Motor Sales U.S.A. Many major brokerage houses on Wall Street use Linux, including the New York Stock Exchange. Linux is popular not only because it is stable, but because it is versatile: it can run on mainframe computers, PCs, handhelds, and electronic devices. The oil company Amerada Hess uses Linux on a supercomputer to help find oil and gas deposits. Pixar Animation Studios has used Linux machines to render digital animated characters. TiVo, the television recording device, runs on Linux. So do many game consoles and television sets that are connected to the Internet. A version of Linux, Linux Mobile, operates on some handheld computers and mobile phones.

While many versions of Linux can be downloaded free of charge from the web, most firms prefer to purchase a packaged version. Companies such as Novell, Red Hat, and VA Software sell the software and promise technical support. Usually, contracts also include software updates. Companies such as IBM and HP have made millions of dollars by bundling Linux with other system software and business applications, such as database management systems.

Software Licensing

The next time you "purchase" software, read carefully the "purchase" contract. You might be surprised to learn that you do not own the software you have just obtained. As noted earlier, most of the software that organizations and individuals obtain is not purchased; it is licensed. The client receives a software license, limited permission to use the software, either indefinitely or for a set time. When the use is time-limited, the client pays annual license fees. The only exceptions to this rule occur when an adopter uses its own employees to develop the software, when it hires the work of a software development firm, or when the adopter uses software developed by people who explicitly allow the user to change the software and sell the product.

Software Licensing Models

Software licensing comes in several models. The *permissive* model allows anyone to use, modify, and make the software into a product that can be sold or licensed for profit. The Berkeley Software Distribution (BSD) UNIX operating system is an example of software under this model. Another is the *General Public License* (GPL), which permits anyone to use, modify, and make applications with the code, but not to use it in proprietary products for sale or licensing. This is the approach taken by the Free Software Foundation. Much of the software we use is *proprietary*, which means the code is owned by someone who has the right to sell or license it to us.

POINT OF INTEREST   The eBay & Skype Licensing Battle

When Internet auctioneer giant eBay, Inc. bought Skype in 2005, some of the core software to run its Internet-calling service remained with the Skype founders so the founders could keep leverage. So in 2009 when eBay began designing new software to run the service to avoid a licensing dispute with the founders, the founders used their leverage and threatened to withdraw all the underlying technology. eBay sued the founders to prevent them from pulling the technology. To complicate the matter, eBay put Skype up for sale in the middle of this litigation. The final result gave 14 percent of Skype back to the founders and spun Skype off into its own company, which owned the key technology that started the whole litigation in the first place. In 2011, Microsoft bought Skype for $8.5 billion.

Source: Hartley, M. (2009). EBay builds its own software for Skype; Licensing dispute, National Post; Stone, B. (2009, Nov 07). Founders Win a Piece Of Skype From eBay, New York Times, p. B.3.

Microsoft, SAP, Oracle, and all other for-profit organizations that develop software own their software and license it. Such licensing takes several forms, such as a fee per user per year, or a site license for a limited or unlimited use regardless of how many users use the software. The latter type of agreement is sometimes signed between a software vendor and a higher-education institution.

Software as a Service

One alternative to software licensing is for organizations to develop their own software, either in-house or outsourced to technical professionals. Such software would be owned by the company free from licensing. However, as the strategic and operational needs of the organization change, the application software used to process its activities also needs to be modified. Therefore, the maintenance and support of the organization's application software must be provided by information technology professionals at a significant cost to the organization.

Recently, another variation of software licensing has become very popular with businesses from small to large. The **software as a service (SaaS)** model provides application software developed and maintained by a third-party provider and offered to organizations for a recurring fee. In a manner similar to leasing a car, the third-party, sometimes called an application service provider (ASP), develops and maintains the software on their hardware. All software maintenance, support, and hardware operations are provided by the ASP and included in the monthly fee.

Businesses access SaaS through network connections between their locations and the SaaS software provider. Instead of processing and storing the organization's transactions on their local computers, data processing and software execution is processed in a cloud environment through a thin client using a standard web browser. The thin client is a low-level personal computer system designed only to initiate the connection to the SaaS provider and operate the software remotely.

This contemporary software delivery method reduces the organization's application software development cost by amortization in the monthly leasing fees. Therefore, the initial cost is significantly reduced, and the software is operational immediately with SaaS. In addition, maintenance and support of any software modifications are handled by the SaaS provider, not by the business. One of the disadvantages of SaaS is that businesses are not able to customize the software to their specific needs. Using the SaaS software delivery model requires the use of the mainstream product. While SaaS can offer some customization, the inherent operation and "mechanics" of the software have been developed to appeal to a mass market.

POINT OF INTEREST   Wall Street's Adoption of SaaS

The financial sector is the second largest industry user of software as a service or SaaS, only following the technology sector. However, while many smaller firms have fully embraced SaaS, many larger firms are hesitant to adopt. Morgan Stanley, Merrill Lynch, and Citibank use hosted customer relationship management (CRM). They are reluctant to rely on hosted software for more complex and time-sensitive applications because of the enormity of their databases and their security concerns. Larger firms do not experience the same ease of adoption level as smaller firms because smaller firms have a much easier time with the integration of data from different applications. Despite the fact SaaS offerings can integrate data with other programs, they run more efficiently when data is stored by the SaaS provider's data center.

Source: Crosman, P. (2008, 2010-06-07). SaaS Gains Street Traction—Providers are pitching Software-as-a-Service as a universal answer to application needs. But will Wall Street firms adopt SaaS beyond CRM?, Wall Street & Technology, p. 37.

The Los Angeles County Sheriff's Department purchased a license to install software offered by DataWall, Inc. The license allowed the department to install 3,700 copies of the software, but it installed 6,000 copies. The department claimed that the number of employees using the software concurrently could not exceed 3,700. The sheriff's department was sued. An appellate court did not accept the department's argument. The defendant ended up paying over $750,000 in fines and attorney fees.

Software piracy, the illegal copying of software, is probably one of the most pervasive crimes. Software piracy has several forms: making copies from a single paid copy of the software; using the Internet to download software from a website without paying for it, or copying software through use of peer-to-peer applications; using one licensed copy to install an application on multiple computers; taking advantage of upgrade offers without having paid for a legal copy of the updated version; using for commercial purposes copies that were acquired with discounts for home or educational use; and using at home a copy that was purchased by an employer under a license to use only on the employer's premises. The software industry established two organizations to protect software developers from piracy: Business Software Alliance (BSA) and the Software & Information Industry Association (SIIA). The two organizations were established by major software companies and are supported by the majority of the world's software development firms. Both organizations have websites that encourage everyone to report pirated software. Occasionally, the organizations sponsor studies that estimate the proportion and financial damage that piracy causes in various world regions.

As the amount of software sold on the market grows, so do the estimated losses that the software industry suffers from piracy. In the 1980s and 1990s, the global financial damage was estimated at $10–$12 billion annually. A study completed by the Business Software Alliance estimates the cost of unlicensed software at $63 billion in 2011, up 8 percent from 2010. Bootleg software increased by 12 percent in the Asia Pacific region to a record of $21 billion. The study reported that there is a significant difference relating to the average piracy rates between emerging and mature markets; 68 percent to 42 percent respectively. A spokesperson for BSA explained that piracy deprives local governments of tax revenue, costs jobs in the technology supply chain (developers, distributors, retailers), and cripples local software companies.

While some people believe that software piracy saves money, it can increase costs beyond litigation and fines. Pirated software can be infested with malware or viruses. In a study completed by IDC and commissioned by Microsoft, infected software was found in 30 percent of businesses. The global study studied 270 websites and networks and interviewed over 250 information technology managers. The study estimates that consumers could spend 1.5 billion hours and $22 billion while the cost to businesses globally is $114 billion.

The cost of software piracy extends beyond the cost of virus-embedded software. In May 2013, a U.S. company agreed to pay a $115 thousand fine to settle a case of unlicensed software copies from four software companies. Unlicensed software can subject businesses to costs associated with litigation, fines, and settlements, not to mention any adverse publicity that can arise from the offense.

Critics question the methods used to reach these estimates. Furthermore, they say that even if the estimates of pirated software are correct, the conclusions are exaggerated, because not all who pirated software would necessarily acquire it if they had to pay for it. Thus, if everybody was forced to pay for the software, the software companies would not collect the entire worth of installed software, but much less. Still, it is reasonable to assume that many pirates actually needed the software, and would pay for it had piracy not existed.

Laws in most countries treat software the same way as they do books, DVD movies, and other types of intellectual property: copies (except for one copy of the software for archival purposes) may not be made without permission of the copyright or patent holder. Yet, the crime is pervasive because it is easy to commit and rarely is punished.

Sources: Anonymous. (2012, 2012-07-24). Software piracy tab surpasses $63 billion. Network World, 29, p. 10; Anonymous. (2013, 2013-03-13). Microsoft Corporation: Software Piracy Costs Billions in Time, Money for Consumers and Businesses, Computer Weekly News, p. 3933.

Considerations for Packaged Software

When an application is developed especially for an organization, specific program goals and custom requirements are considered during the development process. Such requirements include business needs, organizational culture needs, the need to interface with other systems, and performance issues, such as response time. However, organizations find ways to satisfy many needs with ready-made software as well. Figure 5.9 summarizes important factors and outlines what you should look for when purchasing software.

FIGURE **5.9**

Factor	What to Look For	Score
Fitness for purpose	◆ Try to maximize the number of needs satisfied.	_____
Ease of learning to use	◆ The shorter the learning time, the better.	_____
Ease of use	◆ The easier a program is to use, the better. ◆ Try to minimize the number of commands that need to be memorized. ◆ The more intuitive the icons, the better.	_____
Compatibility with other software	◆ Try to maximize compatibility with related software and with other operating systems. ◆ Try to maximize portability of data and output to other programs.	_____
Reputation of vendor	◆ Use professional contacts and references to gather background information on the vendor. ◆ Be sure the vendor can deliver what it promises. ◆ Be sure the vendor stands by its pricing.	_____
Availability and quality of telephone and online support	◆ Ask references about their experience. ◆ Look for knowledgeable staff on Web and phone support.	_____
Networking	◆ Try to maximize ability of many computers to share the software.	_____
Cost	◆ Seek detailed pricing information. ◆ Seek the best price, while maintaining quality and performance. ◆ Consider the total cost of ownership: annual license fees, support cost, necessary hardware upgrades, and other costs associated with use of the software.	_____

© Cengage Learning 2015

While Figure 5.9 provides a general framework for evaluating ready-made software, each item might be augmented with further inquiry, depending on the program's main purpose. For example, potential buyers often test a word-processing program for features such as availability of different fonts, dictionary size, response time to search operations, ability to create tables of contents and indexes, and other features. Electronic spreadsheet programs are tested for speed of recalculation of formulas, charting, and other features typical of this type of software. Webpage development applications are tested for ease of creating various layouts and graphical designs, as well as the ability to maintain desired template appearance and integrity of links among related pages and associated media. Many trade journals and websites, such as CNET, *PC World*, and *PC Magazine*, maintain labs in which they test competing applications. Experts test different applications on the same computer and report the results.

When considering the selection of packaged software, it is important for businesses to differentiate their needs versus "nice to haves." This process does not suggest that important business functions should be disregarded for the sake of purchasing a particular software package. However, in the fast-paced competitive environment of evolving business models, reducing the time to implement information technology can have a positive effect on businesses and give them a competitive edge. Just as the "time to market" is important in a new product release, so is the implementation timeframe associated with new information technology initiatives.

The factors to be considered when purchasing large software packages such as ERP software are significantly more complex. The purchasing organization must consider not only the cost of the software, which is usually millions of dollars, but also the amount of time it will take to implement the software, the cost of interrupting ongoing operations, the difficulty and cost of modifying the software for the organization's specific needs, and many other issues.

Summary

- "Software" is the collective term for computer programs, which are sets of instructions to computer hardware.

- Software is classified into two general categories. System software manages computer resources, such as CPU time and memory allocation, and carries out routine operations, such as translation and data communication. Application software is developed specifically to satisfy some business need, such as payroll or market analysis. Application software can include programs that carry out narrowly focused tasks, or general-purpose applications, such as spreadsheets and word processors.

- To develop software, programmers use programming languages and software development tools. Third-generation languages (3GLs) are more English-like than machine language and assembly languages, and allow more productive programming, meaning that they require less time to develop the same code. Fourth-generation languages (4GLs) are even more English-like and provide many preprogrammed functions. Object-oriented programming (OOP) languages facilitate creation of reusable objects, which are data encapsulated along with the procedures that manipulate them. Visual programming languages help programmers develop code by using icons and other graphics while code is developed automatically by manipulating the graphics.

- As an increasing amount of software is linked to the Internet, many software tools have been created especially for development of webpages and the software that links webpages with organizational information resources, such as databases. They include programming languages such as Java, JavaScript, and PHP, and webpage development packages. Java and other languages for the web produce code that runs on various computers and therefore is very useful for the web.

- All code written in a programming language other than machine language must be translated into machine language code by special programs, either compilers or interpreters. The translation creates object code from the source code. Software offered for sale is usually object code.

- Some application programs are custom-designed, but many are packaged. The majority of packaged applications are purchased off the shelf, although "off the shelf" might actually mean downloading the application through the Internet.

- Office productivity tools help workers accomplish more in less time. The most pervasive of these tools include word processors, spreadsheets, presentation tools, file and database management software, graphics programs, desktop publishing tools, and project management tools. Some of them are offered as suites.

- Hypermedia and multimedia technologies are useful tools for training, education, research, and business.

- Groupware combines hypermedia and multimedia with web technologies to help people in separate locations collaborate in their work.

- Three-dimensional geographic software helps model city blocks and campuses. Combined with other information, it is useful in city service planning and real estate management.

- A growing number of applications are developed using web programming languages and software tools such as those included in Microsoft .NET. The applications support web services and access to information resources from web browsers.

- The most important type of system software is operating systems, also referred to as "platforms." Operating systems carry out an ever-growing number of functions, and include networking and security features. System software also includes utility programs.

- Open source software is being adopted by a growing number of businesses and governments. The source code and its documentation are open to all to review and improve. Open source applications and system software can be downloaded from the web. Programmers continually improve the code, not for monetary remuneration, but to prove their programming prowess and gain the appreciation of the users. This practice yielded the powerful operating system Linux as well as hundreds of useful applications.

- Almost all software is licensed. The user purchases or agrees that they have the right to use the software for a limited time or indefinitely, but does not own the software. Software as a Service (SaaS) is an alternative to traditional software licensing in which application software is developed and maintained by a third-party provider and offered to organizations for a recurring fee.

- Businesses should follow a systematic evaluation to determine the suitability of ready-made software to their needs. Consideration of software includes many factors, among which are fitness for purpose, ease of learning to use, ease of use, reputation of the vendor, and expected quality of support from the vendor.

- While software prices have decreased over the years, software piracy is still a problem. The latest estimate of the cost of software piracy is $114 billion.

Michael, Liz, and Tyler have been focused on the renovations and the move to the new location. Currently, the computer systems are used to interact with the restaurant point-of-sale system for management reporting and system administration functions. With their new computer system, Tyler believes that they can do more, especially in the area of operations. He knows that the operations of the restaurant should focus on more than simply the system that places the orders from customers, sends the orders to the kitchen, and prints the guest checks. The point-of-sale system must store important data that could be used by other functions to operate the business.

What Is Your Advice?

1. What types of software are needed by Kimball's to assist them with their operations? What application software do you believe would complement their point-of-sale system?

2. Research various restaurant point-of-sale systems. Can Kimball's use any packaged productivity software or integrate with this software to help manage the restaurant?

3. Tyler has heard a great deal about the differences between Windows and Mac-based software for graphics and artistic work. Now that you have two new Windows-based personal computers for the restaurant, should you consider additional hardware components or software to work on their graphs needs?

New Perspectives

1. Liz is very cautious about using past information for ordering food from suppliers. She never has done that and the restaurant seems to be doing well. Discuss your rationale with her relating to a better approach to this activity.

2. What advice would you give to Tyler to help him with the development of the initial website for the new location? What would you suggest to help with the marketing and promotion of the new location (from previous chapters)?

3. Can you use the initial website design to help the restaurant? Or do you think you need to scale up to a larger website solution to gain effectiveness?

Key Terms

applet, 155
application, 150
application program interface (API), 165
application software, 150
application-specific software, 158
assembly language, 151
compiler, 156
debugging, 152
driver, 167
general-purpose application software, 158
graphical user interface (GUI), 155

groupware, 163
hypermedia, 160
interpreter, 156
machine language, 151
mashup, 161
multimedia software, 161
object code, 156
object-oriented programming (OOP) language, 154
open source software, 169
operating system (OS), 165
packaged software, 158
plug-and-play (PnP), 167
programming, 150

programming language, 151
proprietary software, 169
software, 150
software as a service (SaaS), 172
source code, 156
suite, 159
system software, 150
utilities, 166
virtual memory, 167
visual programming language, 153
webpage authoring tools, 161

Review Questions

1. What are the most popular operating systems for mainframe computers? Personal computers?

2. If you were going to develop a new mobile application for the Android, what are the various software development kits that you would consider?

3. The use of 4GLs is said to contribute to programmer productivity. How so?

4. What is multimedia? Give five examples of how this technology can be used in training, customer service, and education.

5. With so many ready-made software packages available, why do some companies commission software development projects?

6. Office applications are often called productivity tools. Why?

7. Electronic spreadsheets are great tools for modeling. Give an example of a model that shows gradual growth of a phenomenon and describe how you would implement it in a spreadsheet.

8. What are the different media in multimedia?

9. What is the importance of 3-D geographic software? For which types of organizations is it useful?

10. What is the difference between system software and application software?

11. What are the advantages of developing a website using a tool such as Artisteer or Joomla? Are there any disadvantages?

12. Linux is a free and stable operating system, which is a great advantage. What are the disadvantages of adopting it?

13. What is the difference between an interpreter and a compiler?

14. To a compiler or interpreter any logic is legitimate, even if it results in a bad program. Why can't compilers and interpreters detect logic errors in a program?

15. What are the main elements to consider when purchasing ready-made software for an organization?

16. What is open source software? To what does the word "source" refer?

17. Give three reasons why Linux has become a popular server operating system.

Discussion Questions

18. Why has the trend been to purchase software rather than have it tailor-made for organizations?

19. Think of a standard application such as a payroll system. What might drive an organization to develop its own payroll application rather than purchase a ready-made application?

20. Practically all operating systems that run on PCs have graphical user interfaces. What additional (or different) elements would you like to see in operating systems and applications to make them more intuitive?

21. A decision to adopt Linux or another open source operating system is not an easy one for IS managers. What are their concerns? (*Hint*: Think of the relationships between OSs and applications.)

22. Some companies sell open source software, such as Linux. Companies and many individuals buy the software rather than download it free of charge. Why? Would you buy such software or simply download it from the web?

23. Widespread free application software, such as OpenOffice.org, that runs on a variety of OSs, as well as web-based applications such as Google Drive, threatens to eat into Microsoft's potential revenue. Why?

24. The more an application takes advantage of a GUI, the more suitable it is for international use. How so?

25. Increasingly accurate voice recognition software and sophisticated software that can interpret commands in natural language are bringing us closer to the days of operating a computer by speaking to it. Would you rather speak to a computer than use a keyboard, mouse, or some other input device? Why or why not?

26. Why is software piracy so pervasive? What are your innovative ideas to reduce this problem?

27. Most pressure to legislate and enforce copyright laws for software has come from North America and Western Europe and not from other parts of the world. Why?

28. Do you think open source software will proliferate or disappear?

29. If you were so proficient in programming languages that you could improve open source code (such as the Linux operating system, the Firefox browser, or any of hundreds of applications), would you do it for no monetary compensation? Why or why not?

30. In what ways can young people who seek IT careers benefit by participating in improving open source software?

31. Some observers compare open source software to water. Both the software and water are free, but some companies manage to generate revenue from selling them. How?

Applying Concepts

32. HeadHunter, Inc., is a new personnel recruiting and placement company. The well-established and cash-rich management consulting company that founded HeadHunter is intent on providing adequate financial resources for the new firm to acquire information systems. HeadHunter has opened offices in eight major U.S. cities and two European cities.

   Recruiting specialists exchange written correspondence with prospective clients, both managers looking for new positions and companies that might hire them. Records of both recruits and client companies must be kept and updated. All 10 branches should be able to exchange information in real time to maximize the potential markets on both continents. HeadHunter professionals will often travel to make presentations before human resource managers and other executives.

   The majority of HeadHunter's own personnel are college graduates who lack programming skills. HeadHunter management would like to adopt software that is easy to learn and use.
   a. List the types of software the firm needs, both system software and applications.
   b. Research trade journals and online sources. Suggest specific software packages for the firm.
   c. Develop an evaluation matrix (as shown in Figure 5.9) for each software package alternative.

Hands-On Activities

33. Honest Abe and Cars R Us are two fiercely competitive car dealerships. Recently, both started to sell Sniper Hybrid, a new model from Green Motors. Dealers' cost of the car is $19,600. Green Motors pays a dealership $300 for each car sold, and the dealership also keeps whatever markup it adds to the cost. Both dealers start selling the car at the price of $20,600.

   Immediately after the two dealerships started to offer the car, each decided to lower the price until the other dealership stopped selling the car. However, their price reduction policies differed. Honest Abe's policy is as follows: at the end of each day, the company sets the price for the next day at the competitor's price minus $50. Cars R Us's policy is the following: at the end of each day, the company sets the price for the next day at the competitor's price minus one percent.

   Each dealership decided to stop selling the car as soon as it sells a car at a loss instead of a profit.

   Using a spreadsheet application, enter the initial numbers and build a model that will help you answer the following questions:
   a. Which dealer will stop selling the car first?
   b. How many days after it starts to sell the car will this dealer stop selling it?
   c. How much money will this dealer lose per car on the first day it loses money on this car?
   d. If the Honest Abe changes his price reduction to $25, how will this change the results?

34. Team up with other students from the class. Each student must select a personal desktop computer, tablet, or a laptop to analyze. Create a group on Wiggio.com with yourself and your teammates. Create a folder for each of the devices. Within each folder create one spreadsheet and one document. In the spreadsheet, create a table that shows the price, specifications, brand, and features. In the document, write a short rationale of the device you chose (2-3 paragraphs) based on the information from the spreadsheet.

Use Wiggio's team environment to edit and review your teammates' work. Select a competing device researched by one of your teammates.

a. Download and edit their spreadsheet. Create additional columns to the right to provide your evaluation of their device using the same evaluation criteria. Upload your new version of the spreadsheet to their folder.

b. Download and edit their document. Compile a short narrative that compares your device to their selection. Update your new version of the document to their folder.

c. Add your professor to the group so he/she can see the previous versions of the documents and spreadsheets and grade your work.

At the end of the assignment, jointly write a 1-2-page response to the Team Assignment answering the following questions:

a. How did Wiggio help your group during this activity?

b. What features of Wiggio were most useful? Least useful?

c. What did you think of groupware? How did using groupware affect the completion of this assignment?

Less May Be More

Sometimes, the best is the worst enemy of the good. In software, too much sophistication may alienate customers instead of improve service. Managers at one successful business learned this the hard way.

Citizens National Bank of Texas has a long history. It was established in Waxahachie, Texas, in 1868, and is still privately held. The bank has 16 offices. It does not try to compete with big banks, but rather caters to small communities of 500–25,000, and emphasizes friendly customer service. The extra care has paid off: the bank enjoys two to two and a half cross-sales per customer, a ratio considered high in banking. This means that, on average, each customer has purchased more than two products, such as a checking account, savings account, or home loan. Banks' profitability is highly related to the number of services the same customer purchases. Citizens' best customers use six or seven products.

For many years the bank tracked customer contacts manually. Relationship bankers—as the bank's salespeople are called—wrote down on paper the details of contacts. Every Monday, management received a sales report covering the previous week and the calls each banker was going to make that week. With 50,000 customers and many prospective ones, this information soon became reams of paper. The documents contained good information, but the information was difficult to glean and manage.

In 2001, management decided to install a customer relationship management (CRM) system. The product chosen was a CRM package from Siebel Systems (which was later acquired by Oracle). Citizens National hoped to enable the CEO and the 16 relationship bankers to improve tracking of prospective customers and increase the number of contacts the bankers made.

The bank hired a local consulting firm that specializes in installing software for small businesses. The cost of the new software was $150,000. Installing it and adapting it to the bankers' needs cost another $350,000. Siebel's CRM software is recognized as very good, but it was overkill for the bankers, who were typically old-fashioned sales-people not keen on using technology. The system has many features that the bankers did not need, and lacked simple features that they did need. It was too sophisticated for Citizens' simple handling of customers. Much of the adaptation time was spent turning off unused features.

Large companies often use CRM systems to set up customer support cases, which are files with details of complaints and how they were resolved, from beginning to end. The bank did not need this function. When customers call to complain, the call center handles the complaint immediately, or channels it to the appropriate officer for immediate resolution. If a customer needs a new checkbook, the call center sends an email message to the proper bank worker who handles checkbook orders. The request for the activity is scheduled, and the bank worker handles such requests in the order in which they come in. The new system did not support this simple way of operation.

The bankers found navigating the new system challenging. Moving from a window to another relevant window was not intuitive, and the bankers wasted much time. They expected to see the typical opportunities to sell more services to a customer listed in the record of the customer. For example, they expected to see an opportunity to offer the customer a business loan listed. However, such opportunities must be entered by the system's users when the customer record is set up.

Different relationships with the same customer might be on different screens. The bankers were confused, and could not get a good sense of all the relationships a customer might have with the bank (such as which services the customer used or a history of complaints the customer had). They had to flip screens constantly. The relationships were organized in a manner inconvenient to the bankers. A consultant that specializes in CRM systems observed that Siebel's system had everything, which is typically too much for small businesses. These clients, he said, usually lose the forest for the trees.

Another challenge was integrating Siebel's software with Citizens' banking software. Like many small and medium size banks, it uses Kirchman Bankway. The software helps process and track deposits, loans, and trust accounts. While the Kirchman software keeps customer last and first name in a single field in its database, Siebel's systems keeps them in two separate fields. This and other differences made integration of the systems time-consuming. The bankers did not expect the integration time to be so long. After three years, Citizens' management decided to abandon Siebel's system. The bank's consulting firm was committed to automating CRM at the bank.

As shown in the previous example, information technology is not always a successful initiative for business organizations. The goal of customer relationship management software (CRM) is to find, attract, and convert prospects to business customers of an organization. In addition, it must be able to retain its current customers as well as attempt to win back customers it may have lost. Ultimately, this software application can leverage its functionality to achieve its goal while reducing marketing costs and maintain quality customer service.

Investments in information technology for effective customer relationship management must focus on its ability to target the right customers to prospect and encouraging these customers to adopt a set of principles and actions to retain them for a lifecycle of profitability. Notice that it is not simply to "win" customers, but to gain profitable customers. An intensive approach to gain these customers is imperative. Research has shown that customers will open 73 percent of their accounts within the first 90 days of the relationship. To gain wallet share and customer loyalty, it's important to tailor the "pitch" based on their expectations. An effective CRM will provide that guidance to offer the best products to a prospective customer at the correct time.

An article focused on information technology solutions for financial institutions (credit unions) suggests three important considerations for CRM implementations:

1) The solution must fit your banking-specific needs.
2) The software must be easy to use.
3) The software should be integrated with your core system.

The article states that businesses are set in an environment exhibiting constant change. CRM software, along with sales force automation software, are evolving along with the changes in business strategy and operations. The suggestions above provide insight that the software solution must allow customization to the business needs. While the goal of CRM is to maximize the wallet and market share, a system which is complex or challenging to use will not achieve its purpose. The human factor associated with the ability to use the system is always a significant factor on how its users interact with a new system.

The data maintained by CRM systems needs to maintain a "360-degree view" of your relationship with your customers. Ultimately, data gathered from third-party sources as well as your core information system must all remain synchronized and integrated for your employees to develop an accurate relationship with customers.

Sources: Bartholomew, D., "Why Citizens National Bank Threw Out Siebel in Favor of Intuit's QuickBase," Baseline, February 26, 2007 (www.cnbwax.com), April 2007; Buhler, A., "CRM Selection," Credit Union Management, April 2012.

Thinking About the Case

1. What were the goals of installing CRM software?

2. A Siebel executive commented that the company's CRM system does not fit the needs of all clients. He noted that the clients need to decide if they want an application or a tool kit. Research the term "tool kit." Is Siebel's CRM system an application or a tool kit? Explain why.

3. The bank's president said that management learned a lesson, and that the $500,000 spent on the abandoned CRM system was tuition for that education. What would you have done in the first place to avoid this "tuition"? Use the three considerations as the foundation of your analysis.

Investing in Automation for Efficiency

In turbulent economic times and competitive markets, businesses that can reduce operating costs and increase resource productivity are the corporate version of an Olympic silver medalist. If a business expands its market share and/or sales revenue as well, they should be awarded a gold medal. Medco and Staples are two such organizations, gaining positive achievements through investment in automation and software. In businesses that distribute or manufacture hard goods, it is important to move products from distribution centers as efficiently and economically as possible. New strategies and tactics are needed to realize these goals.

One of the largest health-care companies in the United States, Medco was a spin-off of Merck with $60 billion in revenues in 2009. Its managed pharmacy benefits product provides services to about 20 percent of Americans. Various employers, unions, and governmental agencies contract with Medco to fulfill prescriptions for employees to keep them healthy while reducing costs. Not a simple goal.

Medco knew that they could not expand their business simply by hiring more pharmacy technicians to fulfill prescriptions. These employees are highly paid and are capable of providing more value than just counting pills and closing a cap. Management knew that a strategy capable of scalability was an important component of their expansion. The company embarked on an initiative to automate the prescription fulfillment process from order to shipment.

Their new system was developed with over 1 million lines of software code, capable of processing 1,500 database transactions per second. The confluence between the patient database management system and automated pharmacy dispensing formed the strategy for the information technology infrastructure. Their two fulfillment centers handle approximately 2,000 stock-keeping units (SKUs), focusing on high-volume and most-prescribed drugs. In 2007, their successful automated fulfillment system and expanding business created the need for a third fulfillment center.

In 2009, Medco fulfilled 103 million prescriptions annually. However, the success story does not revolve solely on the revenue and transactions, but on the astonishingly little time that Medco requires to process an order. Prescription transactions (received, dispensed, packed, and loaded for shipment) are completed in less than 25 minutes. Each order is required to pass through 100 automated control checkpoints during the lifecycle of the fulfillment process. Efficiency and speed without quality controls for prescription orders would create both liability and loss of business. Their engineering chief noted "The worst thing we could do would be to automate an error."

Staples has become the world's largest office products company, growing from $2 billion to $24 billion in annual sales over 15 years. Their management and operational successes have led the industry in profitability and are one of only three top office products companies to realize a profit.

Customer satisfaction with Staples's delivery business became problematic in 2005. Their analysis of the issues determined a direct correlation between orders with errors and loss of customers. The cost of new customer acquisition was lost with the inaccurate or late delivery of customer orders. Ultimately, the cost of rework and fulfilling an order correctly has "significant economic value."

A complete "out of the box" method was considered. Instead of the fulfillment personnel moving toward the product, why not have the product be brought toward the fulfillment personnel? The operators were placed at stations at the perimeter of the warehouse. Control software transports the products to the operators using mobile robots. The cycle times and labor requirements were reduced through the entire warehouse activity process, from receiving to shipping. Their pilot implementation was extremely successful, reducing the order fulfillment time by half and lowering the picking error rate.

Like Medco, Staples's new system can be adjusted according to demand and capacity assigned to jobs based on need. In addition, the new system is less demanding on its workers, with less walking and lifting necessary to complete an order.

Source: Manrodt, K. B., Ogle, M., & Harrington, L. (2011). The Case for Infrastructure Investment: Lessons from Medco and Staples. Supply Chain Management Review, 15(5), 40–46.

Thinking About the Case

1. Each of these systems needed significant investment in resources and capital. What do you believe was the rationale to justify the costs of these systems? What types of quantitative savings can be documented to support this rationale?

2. It is rather simplistic to conceive the benefits to automating business operations. What would be the subjective factors and risks associated with these initiatives?

3. The competitive pressures have become more prominent. How would initiatives such as those implemented by Medco and Staples change the competitive environment in their respective industries?

References

Anonymous. (2011). TCO for Open-Source Social Publishing. Burlington, MA.

Anonymous. (2012). BearingPoint Study Updates on Use of Free and Open Source Software in Automotive Industry. *Manufacturing Close-Up*, Mar 31.

Anonymous. (2013a). New to WebSphere. Retrieved June 8, 2013, from www.ibm.com/developerworks/websphere/newto/

Anonymous. (2013b). OS Platform Statistics. Retrieved June 10, 2013, from www.w3schools.com/browsers/browsers_os.asp

Anonymous. (2013c). WebSphere Software. Retrieved June 8, 2013, from www-01.ibm.com/software/websphere/

Collett, S. (2011). Open Source Unchecked, *Computerworld*, May 23, pp. 26, 28, 30.

Geoghegan, S. (2013). Fleet Management Software. *Law & Order*, 61(4), 52-55.

Yeaton, T. (2013). Beyond Cost-Cutting: Why Open Source Software Is Gaining Traction on Wall Street, *Wall Street & Technology - Online*, Feb 8.

SIX

BUSINESS NETWORKS AND TELECOMMUNICATIONS

Learning Objectives

Modern telecommunications technology allows businesses to send and receive information in seconds. Except when a physical transfer of goods or performance of a local service is involved, geographical distances are becoming insignificant in business transactions. When using computers and other digital devices, people can now work together as if they were sitting next to each other, even when they are thousands of miles apart. Financial transactions and information retrieval take seconds, and wireless technology enables us to perform these activities from almost anywhere and while on the go. Understanding the technology underlying telecommunications—its strengths, weaknesses, and available options—is essential in any professional career.

When you finish this chapter, you will be able to:

- Describe business and home applications of digital telecommunications.

- Identify the major media and devices used in telecommunications.

- Explain the concept of network protocols.

- Compare and contrast various networking and Internet services.

- List networking technologies and trends that are likely to have an impact on businesses and information management in the near future.

- Discuss the pros and cons of telecommuting.

KIMBALL'S RESTAURANT: A New Look at Customer Service and Technology

Tyler knew that the opening of the new location was quickly approaching. The renovations were going well and expected to be completed on time. The upgrade of the computer system was installed at the current location and functioned without any issues. The servers were entering orders using the touch screen monitor installed on a workstation in the restaurant. Michael and Tyler observed the servers as they used the new system. The servers seemed to readily accept the new technology and used it to enter customer orders. Tyler asked the servers for feedback.

They provided positive comments on how easy the system was to use. They still had to take notes at the table, although some were trying to remember the orders and then enter them into the system. They thought that the customers were impressed with the quality of service without writing the orders on a pad. One of the servers, Rick, said that when he placed the meals at the correct customer without asking, it showed superior customer service and saved time delivering the meals. At first, Rick did not think the new system would work well, but now sees its benefits.

Liz also saw the benefits. She noticed that the servers did not seem to be returning very many meals for mistakes after they were served. That reduced the number of "rush" meal reorders that caused chaos in the kitchen. The cooks have been pleased that they can prepare a meal once and eliminate additional effort to re-prepare a meal. Liz also noticed that she did not see any order changes with the new system. She wondered why. Customers could not suddenly stop changing their minds about orders. She asked one of the servers about this. Harriet, the most experienced server, said that customers often changed their meal details. However, from her experience, she said that these changes almost always happened within a short period of time after the server placed the order. Harriet believed that the change was entered into the system so that the kitchen staff probably was not aware of the change. Previously, she had to go into the kitchen and change the guest check.

Clark, from PosiDining, contacted Tyler about a new offering. They just completed the development of a software application that allows servers to enter orders on a tablet. Tyler thought that using tablets would be awesome, but wondered what it would cost. They already purchased a touch screen workstation that they are using in the current location and which would be installed at the new location.

Clark said, "You'll need additional workstations for two reasons. First, because the size of your new location is larger, you'll have too many servers trying to enter orders on one computer. Second, you should have at least one additional unit in the event of a hardware failure." Tyler thought that was reasonable. Clark explained that the hardware cost of the tablet is less than the touch screen hardware unit. He suggested that Tyler might want to use a combination of tablets and the traditional entry units. This system would require a simple router capable of both wired and wireless access connected to the current server. The PosiDining software would work with both Android and Apple tablets.

Serving the Technology Infrastructure

The new location was built over 50 years ago, when the only networks anyone knew about were TV networks. The building structure was not suited to adding network cabling throughout the building, but Tyler was thinking about where they would need networking and cabling. In the old location, his parents had not invested in an Internet connection for the restaurant. They used a small POS unit connected to a phone line to process credit transactions. Tyler knew that their new business model required some more general connections to the Internet.

In the renovation design, Tyler slipped in some additional networking specifications just before the contractors began their work. Using the floor plans, he was able to identify specific locations that needed network connectivity. These locations included the serving workstations, host station, bar, office, kitchen, banquet room, and dining room.

In the final month of renovations, Michael questioned the cost of these additions. Michael asked, "Tyler, why do we need network connections in the walls of the dining and banquet rooms? We only need it at the workstations for the servers. People are not going to be doing Internet work at their tables, are they?" Tyler sighed. "Dad, people want to be connected to the Internet for their smartphones. Look in coffee shops and other restaurants. They advertise it as something the establishment provides." Michael started to understand, and Tyler continued, "Think about it, Dad. If you book presentations and business meetings, the customer may need Internet for their meeting. We could either charge them for it or bundle it as an added service." Michael once again was grateful for Tyler's young perspective and recent business education, and how they would help Kimball's. He knew that the networking would add more cost to the renovation, but it would be worth it.

It is your first visit to Barcelona. You are standing at a bus stop, waiting for the bus that will take you on the next leg of your vacation tour. You pull out your mobile phone, send a short text message to a four-digit number, and receive a message with an accurate time when your bus will arrive. You then use the device to receive directions and maps describing how to get from one point to another. You use the time until the bus arrives to view a local TV program on your phone. On the bus, you use the device to check your email. When you arrive at your destination you use the phone to find one of the many hotspots where you can connect to the Internet. You use the phone to email and call home. Since the call uses the Internet, it is free.

Telecommunications, which is essential to smooth operations in today's business world, is the transmittal of data and information from one point to another. The Greek word *tele*, which means "distance," is part of such words as "telephone," "teleconference," and other words referring to technologies that allow communications over a distance. Thus, telecommunications is communications over a distance. When considering telephone, email, the web—none of these essential business services would be available without fast, reliable telecommunications. Telecommunications, made possible by networking technologies, has brought several improvements to business processes:

- *Better business communication.* When no physical objects need to be transferred from one place to another, telecommunications technology can make geographical distance irrelevant. Email, voice mail, instant messaging (IM), faxing, file transfer, mobile telephony, and teleconferencing enable detailed and instant communication, within and between organizations. Telecommunications can also be used by one person to monitor another person's performance in real time. The use of email, IM, and voice mail has brought some secondary benefits to business communications by establishing a permanent written or electronic record of, and accountability for, ideas. Web-based instant messaging is used to support online shoppers in real time. The result is more accurate business communications and reduced need for manual recording.

- *Greater efficiency.* Telecommunications has made business processes more efficient. Any information that is recorded electronically can become immediately available to anyone involved in a business process, even when the business units are located far apart. For example, as soon as an order is placed, anyone in the organization who will be involved with it at any stage can view the order: from the marketing people, to purchasing officers, to manufacturing managers, to shipping workers, to billing and collection clerks. For example, if a store lacks a certain item, a clerk can check the entire chain's inventory and tell the customer the nearest store that has the item available. If a customer wishes to return an item, she can do so at any store of the chain because a sales associate can easily verify the purchase details. This may also help retail chains discover "serial returners."

- *Better distribution of data.* Organizations that can transmit vital data quickly from one computer to another can choose not to have centralized databases. Business units that need certain data frequently might store it locally, while others can access it remotely. Only fast, reliable transfer of data makes this efficient arrangement possible.

- *Instant transactions.* The availability of the Internet to millions of businesses and consumers has shifted a significant volume of business transactions to the web. Both businesses and consumers can shop, purchase, and pay instantly online. Wireless technology has also made possible instant payment and data collection using small radio devices, such as electronic toll collection tags. In addition to commercial activities, people can use telecommunications for online education and entertainment.

- *Flexible and mobile workforce.* Employees do not have to come to the office to carry out their work as long as their jobs only involve the use and creation of information. They can telecommute using Internet connections. Salespeople, support personnel, and field workers are more mobile with wireless communication.

- *Alternative channels.* Services that used to be conducted through specialized dedicated channels can be conducted through alternative channels. For example, voice communication used to be conducted only through proprietary telephone networks but is now also conducted through the Internet using Voice over Internet Protocol (VoIP), which decreased its cost. Radio and television broadcasts were conducted through radio frequencies and company-owned cables. Newer technologies enable organizations to broadcast over the Internet and provide telephone services over the Internet as well. Furthermore, Internet technologies allow individuals to broadcast text, sound, and video to subscribers' computers or to web-capable mobile devices. (We discuss these technologies in Chapter 8, "The Web-Enabled Enterprise.")

At the same time you enjoy the opportunities created by telecommunications technology, you must recognize that it poses some risks. Once an organization connects its information systems to a public network, security becomes a challenge. Unauthorized access and data destruction are constant threats. Thus, organizations must establish proper security controls as preventive measures. We discuss the risks and security measures in Chapter 14, "Risks, Security, and Disaster Recovery."

Telecommunications in Daily Use

We have grown so accustomed to telecommunications networks that we no longer think much about them in daily life; however, they are pervasive. The most widespread telecommunications uses are described in the following sections.

Cellular Phones

Cellular phones derive their name from the territories of service providers, which are divided into areas known as cells. Each cell has at its center a computerized transceiver (transmitter-receiver), which both transmits signals to another receiver and receives signals from another transmitter. When a call is placed on a cellular phone, the signal is first transmitted to the closest transceiver, which sends a signal through landlines that dial the desired phone number. If the receiving phone is also mobile, the call is communicated to the transceiver closest to the receiving phone. As the user moves from one area, or cell, to another, other transceivers pick up the transmission and receiving tasks.

Using cellular phone networks, people can transmit and receive calls almost anywhere, freeing them from a fixed office location. Many mobile phones today are "smartphones"; they can access the Internet and web and include applications or "apps" to perform thousands of different functions. People use their mobile phones for email, web surfing, online banking, shopping, and keeping up with their friends. Many mobile phones include digital cameras, contact lists and calendars, and GPS (global positioning system) circuitry. "My car is my office" is a reality for many professionals who spend much of their time traveling. As technology advances and more capabilities are squeezed into smaller casings, some professionals can say, "My pocket is my office."

The major advantage of mobile phones is that they are attached to people, not offices. This is why many companies have decided to discard landlines in favor of either mobile phones or Internet-based (VoIP) phone services. In the U.S., people are replacing residential landline telephone service with cell phones. According to the National Center for Health Statistics, in 2011, 32 percent of all households consisted of wireless only service (Zager, 2012).

Some companies make the switch to mobile phones when they move their offices. Moving electronic switchboards and telephone lines to its new offices in Hawaii would have cost NovaSol, a scientific research firm, $30,000. The company decided to equip its 80 employees with cell phones. Other companies make the switch because so many employees already have both landline phones in the office and a cell phone for their time with customers or on manufacturing lines. For this reason, Dana Corp., a manufacturer of auto parts, removed most of the phones from its offices in Auburn Hills, Michigan. The lines left are used mainly for teleconferencing.

Videoconferencing

People sitting in conference rooms thousands of miles apart are brought together by their transmitted images and speech in what is called **videoconferencing**. Businesses use videoconferencing to save on travel costs and lodging, car fleets, and the time of highly salaried employees, whether they work in different organizations or at different sites of the same organization. From national and global perspectives, videoconferencing also reduces traffic congestion and air pollution. The increasing speed of Internet connections makes it easy for anyone with a high-speed link to establish videoconferences by using a peer-to-peer link or the services of a third party, a company that specializes in maintaining videoconferencing hardware and software. In the latter case, businesses pay a monthly fee for unlimited conferences or pay a per-use fee.

Videoconferencing saves time and travel expenses while increasing organizational productivity

Comstock/Photos.com

The popularity of video-conferencing has created several new application software pro-ducts used by individuals and businesses. Some examples are Citrix GoToMeeting, Cisco WebEx, Adobe Connect, ooVoo, and Skype. The increasing popularity of telecommuting has increased the adoption of videoconferencing. In addition to being a cost-effective alternative to travel, web-based meetings can be set up on an impromptu basis and can be made more productive with the tools provided in video-conferencing software.

Wireless Payments and Warehousing

Radio frequency identification (RFID) technology, mentioned in Chapter 3, "Business Functions and Supply Chains," and covered in more detail later in this chapter, enables us to conduct transactions and to make payments quickly. An increasing number of drivers never approach a cash register or swipe credit cards when paying for fuel at gasoline stations. If you use a speed payment device such as ExxonMobil's Speedpass™, an RFID tag communicates with a device on the pump to record the details of the transaction. An antenna dish on the rooftop of the gas station communicates these details and checks your credit through a link to a large database located hundreds or even thousands of miles away and operated by the bank authorizing the charge. In this transaction, you use telecommunications twice: once between the device and the pump, and once between the gas station's antenna and the database. Wireless toll payment systems use a similar technology. A special transceiver installed at the toll plaza sends a signal that prompts the tag installed in your car to send back its own signal, including the unique owner's code, entry location, and time the vehicle passes by. The information is used to charge the account associated with the owner's number, and the information captured is transmitted to a large database of account information.

RFID technology is also used in warehouses where employees can use handheld units to check a central system for availability and location of items to be picked up from and stored in shelves or bins. When storing, the handhelds are used to update inventory databases. Such systems have made the work of "untethered employees" more efficient compared with older systems that require physical access to a computer. Wireless communications have many other uses, some of which are discussed in detail later in the chapter.

Another form of wireless payment that is becoming increasingly popular is mobile payment/ electronic wallet apps for mobile devices. Mobile payments have received mixed reviews due to security concerns however; early investments from large banking institutions say otherwise. One product gaining traction in a few U.S. cities is Isis™. Isis™ is more than just a mobile payment app for a smartphone; it is a complete electronic wallet. Included in the wallet are payment cards, promotional offers, and loyalty cards. The app uses near-field communication to contact checkout terminals at Isis Ready™ merchants. **Near-field communication (NFC)** is a standard communication protocol to create a radio connection between two devices. The connection can be completed either by making contact between the two devices or by bringing the devices into close proximity (within a few centimeters). Currently, Isis is compatible with only American Express, Capital One, and Chase payment cards. Mobile payment and electronic wallet innovations capitalize on the convergence of two items that most people have on them at all times: their wallet and smartphone. (Leber, 2012; Anonymous, 2012b)

Peer-to-Peer File Sharing

One of the most exciting features in worldwide telecommunications is **peer-to-peer (P2P) file sharing** through the Internet: anyone with access to the Internet can download one of several free applications that help locate and download files from any online computer. You might have heard of some of these applications, such as LimeWire, BitTorrent, and Vuze. While the concept has effectively served scientists who share scientific text files and application developers who exchange code, the most extensive use has been in downloading artistic files, such as music and video files. Because unauthorized duplication and use of such files violates copyright laws and deprives recording and film companies of revenue, these industries have sued some violators in court, and the U.S. Supreme Court ruled against organizations that provide file-sharing services. Security is also a significant concern with peer-to-peer file sharing. Shared files may contain viruses and other malware.

Web-Empowered Commerce

Increasingly fast digital communication enables millions of organizations to conduct business and individuals to research, market, educate, train, shop, purchase, and pay online. Entire industries, such as online exchanges and auctions, have been created thanks to the web. Web-based commerce is covered in detail in Chapter 8, "The Web-Enabled Enterprise" and is illustrated with many examples throughout the book.

While people can enjoy technologies without understanding how they work, educated professionals often do need to understand some fundamental concepts to be able to participate in decision making when selecting networking equipment and services. This section introduces bandwidth and networking media.

Bandwidth

A communications *medium* is the physical means that transports the signal, such as a copper wire telephone line, a television cable, or radio waves. The **bandwidth** of the medium is the speed at which data is communicated, which is also called the **transmission rate** or simply the bit rate. It is measured as **bits per second (bps)**. Figure 6.1 shows common bit rate measurements. Bandwidth is a limited resource. Usually, the greater the bandwidth, the higher the cost associated with the communications service. Thus, determining the type of communications lines to install or subscribe to may be an important business decision.

FIGURE **6.1**

Transmission speed
measurement units

bps	=	Bits per second
Kbps	=	Thousand bps
Mbps	=	Million bps (mega bps)
Gbps	=	Billion bps (giga bps)
Tbps	=	Trillion bps (tera bps)

© Cengage Learning 2015

When a line is capable of carrying multiple transmissions simultaneously, it is said to be **broadband**. Cable television, DSL (digital subscriber line), fiber-optic cables, and most wireless connections are broadband. In general, broadband offers greater bandwidth and faster throughput, and in common usage the term "broadband" is associated with a high-speed networking connection, which is required for fast transmission of large files and multimedia material. In contrast, the term *narrowband* refers to lower speeds, although the speed under which communication is considered narrowband has constantly increased. Dial-up connections are generally considered to be narrowband.

Media

Communications media—the means through which bits are transmitted—come in several types. Media can be tangible, such as cables, or intangible, such as radio waves. The most available tangible media are twisted pair cable, coaxial cable, and optical fiber (see Figure 6.2). Intangible media include all microwave radio technologies, which support wireless communication. The electric power grid has also been added as a medium for communications. All can be used to link a business or household to the Internet. Later in the chapter we discuss the various Internet connection services and also refer to typical periodic cost of the services.

FIGURE 6.2

Networking media

Medium	Availability	Bandwidth	Vulnerability to Electromagnetic Interference
Twisted pair cable	High	Low to medium	High
Radio waves	High	Medium to high	Low (but vulnerable to radio frequency interference)
Microwave	Low	High	Low
Coaxial (TV) cable	High	High	Low
Optical fiber	Moderate but growing	Highest	Nonexistent
Electric power lines (BPL)	Very High	High	High

© Cengage Learning 2015

Twisted pair cables use an RJ-45 connector similar to the RJ-11 telephone connector

Василий Тороус/Photos.com

Twisted Pair Cable

Twisted pair cable is a popular medium for connecting computers and networking devices because it is relatively flexible, reliable, and low cost. The most common types of twisted pair network cable today are Category 5 or Category 6 (Cat 5 or Cat 6), named for the cable standards they follow. Twisted pair cable connects to network devices with RJ-45 plug-in connectors, which resemble the RJ-11 connectors used on telephone wire, but are slightly larger.

Twisted pair cable is also used in telephone networks, but in the United States and many other countries, twisted copper wires are now used only between the telephone jack and the central office of the company providing the telephone service. The typical distance of this link is 1.5–6 kilometers (about 1–4 miles), and is often referred to as "the last mile." The central offices themselves are connected with fiber optic cables, but it is often the "last mile" media that determine the overall speed of the connection. In recent years many "last mile" connections have also been converted to optical cables. Most new buildings, including residential ones, are equipped with fiber optic cables rather than copper wires.

Coaxial Cable

Coaxial cable is sometimes called TV cable or simply "cable" because of its common use for cable television transmission. It is widely used for links to the Internet. Television companies use the same networks they employ to transmit television programming to link households and businesses to the Internet. Since telephone services can be offered on any broadband Internet link, cable companies also offer telephone service through this medium.

Optical Fiber

Fiber optic technology uses light instead of electricity to represent bits. Fiber optic lines are made of thin fiberglass filaments. A transmitter sends tiny bursts of light using a laser or a light-emitting diode (LED) device. The receiver detects the period of light and no-light to receive the data bits. Optical fiber systems operate in the infrared and visible light frequencies. Because light is not susceptible to **EMI (electromagnetic interference)** and **RFI (radio frequency interference)**, fiber optic communication is much less prone to error than twisted pair and radio transmission. Optical fibers can also carry signals over relatively longer distances than other media.

Optical fibers (left) and coaxial cable (right)

Stockbyte/Photos.com

KATARZYNA ZWOLSKA/Photos.com

The maximum speed attained with optical fibers has been 25.6 terabits per second (Tbps), enough to transmit the content of 600 DVDs in one second. Some optical carriers support bit rates of up to several Tbps. Such great bandwidth enables multiple streams of both Internet and television transmission. Some telecommunications companies, such as Verizon, have laid optical fiber lines to offer households both services, directly competing with TV cable companies such as Comcast. In other countries, such as Japan and South Korea, a greater percentage of households are offered broadband over optical fibers, and the bandwidth that subscribers can receive is significantly higher than that in the United States. However, an increasing number of U.S. communities are served with optical fibers, with speeds of several tens of megabits per second (Mbps). Such speeds permit the telecommunications company to offer television service on the same fiber that provides telephone and Internet service. The potential of optical fibers is usually much greater than telecommunications companies actually provide.

Radio and Satellite Transmission

Microwave transceivers are used by businesses

© WIANGYA/Shutterstock.com

Radio frequency (RF) technologies use radio waves to carry bits. Several wireless technologies can transmit through air or space. Some of the most popular for personal and business networking, such as Wi-Fi and Bluetooth, are discussed later in this chapter. **Microwaves** are high-frequency radio waves that can carry signals over long distances with high accuracy. You have probably noticed the parabolic antennas on the roofs of some buildings. They are so numerous on rooftops and high antenna towers because microwave communication is effective only if the line of sight between the transmitter and receiver is unobstructed. Clusters of microwave antennas are often installed on high buildings and the tops of mountains to obtain a clear line of sight. Terrestrial microwave communication—so-called because signals are sent from and received by stations on the earth—is good for long-distance telecommunications but can also be used in local networks in and among buildings. It is commonly used for voice and television communications. When radio communication is used outside buildings, it is vulnerable to weather conditions—thunderstorms, fog, and snow might degrade communication quality.

Signals can also be transmitted using microwaves via satellite links. The two major types of satellites are geostationary, also called GEO, and low earth orbit, called LEO. Both types serve as radio relay stations in orbit above the earth that receive, amplify, and redirect signals. Microwave transceiver dishes are aimed at the satellite, which has antennas, amplifiers, and transmitters. The satellite receives a signal, amplifies it, and retransmits it to the destination.

Large companies lease communication satellite frequencies to transmit data around the globe

Comstock Images/Photos.com

GEO satellites are placed in orbit 35,784 kilometers (about 22,282 miles) above earth. At this distance the satellite is geosynchronized (synchronized with the earth); that is, once it starts orbiting, the satellite stays above the same point on earth at all times, without being propelled. Thus, a GEO satellite is stationary relative to earth. Because they orbit at such a great distance above the earth, three GEO satellites can provide service for every point on earth by relaying signals among themselves before transmitting them back down to their destinations.

Because of the distance from earth to satellites, the communication is fine for transmitting data because delays of a few seconds make no significant difference. However, a delay of even 2 or 3 seconds (due to the trip to and from the satellite and the time of processing the data) might be disturbing in interactive communication, such as when voice and pictures are communicated in real time. You might have noticed such delays when reporters use devices that communicate to a television station. When an anchorperson asks a question, the reporter on location receives the question with a noticeable delay.

LEO satellites minimize this shortcoming. These lower-cost satellites are placed about 650–2500 kilometers (400–1600 miles) above earth. The signals' round-trip is short enough for mobile telephone and interactive computer applications. Unlike GEOs, LEO satellites revolve around the globe every few hours. Multiple LEOs are required to maintain continuous coverage for uninterrupted communication.

Electrical Power Lines

One medium that had been available for years but has only recently been tapped for telecommunications is the electric power grid. The bits in an electric power grid are represented by electric impulses, but they must be distinct from the regular power that flows through the grid. Engineers have succeeded in overcoming this technical challenge. In some regions of the United States, broadband service is offered through power lines. The service is referred to as **Broadband over Power Lines (BPL)** or Power Line Communication (PLC). BPL is covered in more detail later in the chapter.

From the point of view of organizations, among the important factors in choosing a networking medium are availability, current and potential bandwidth, and vulnerability to electromagnetic interference (EMI) or radio frequency interference (RFI). Your business's current and future needs for data security, as well as compatibility with an already installed network, are also factors. Cost is another important consideration. For example, one of the benefits of optical fiber is that it is practically immune to EMI. However, it is more expensive than other options. Another point to consider is the availability of a specific service on an available medium. For instance, you might have a telephone line on a remote farm, but no company offers broadband service to it.

Networks

In the context of data communications, a **network** is a combination of devices or **nodes** (computers or communication devices) connected to each other through one of the communication media previously discussed. We will often use the word "computer" for a device that is networked, but this is only for convenience. Any compatible device that can transmit and receive on a network is part of it.

Types of Networks

Computer networks are classified according to their reach and complexity. The three basic types of networks are LANs (local area networks), which connect computers, printers, and other computer equipment for an office, several adjacent offices, an entire building or a campus; MANs (metropolitan area networks), which span a greater distance than LANs and usually have more complicated networking equipment for midrange communications; and WANs (wide area networks), which connect systems in an entire nation, continent, or worldwide. Some people also include a fourth category: PANs (personal area networks), which encompass connections between personal digital devices such as a computer and its keyboard or mouse, or a mobile phone and a hands-free headset.

LANs

A computer network within a building, or a campus of adjacent buildings, is called a **local area network**, or **LAN**. LANs are usually established by a single organization with offices within a radius of roughly 5–6 kilometers (3–4 miles). LANs are set up by organizations to enhance communications among employees and to share IT resources. Households might set up LANs to share a broadband link to the Internet and to transmit digital music, pictures, and video from one part of a home to another.

In office LANs, one computer is often used as a central repository of programs and files that all connected computers can use; this computer is called a **server**. Connected computers can store documents on their own disks or on the server, can share hardware such as printers, and can exchange email. When a LAN has a server, the server usually has centralized control of communications among the connected computers and between the computers and the server itself. Another computer or special communications device can also exercise this control, or control can be distributed among several servers. A **peer-to-peer LAN** is one in which no central device controls communications.

In recent years the cost of wireless devices has decreased significantly, and many offices as well as households now network their computers wirelessly, or create networks in which some of the computers are wired and some are not. **Wireless LANs (WLANs)** offer significant benefits: installation is easy because there is no need to drill through walls to install wires, and equipment can be moved to wherever it is needed. Wireless LANs are less costly to maintain when the network spans two or more buildings. They are also more scalable. **Scalability** is the ease of expanding a system. It is easy to add more nodes, or clients, to a WLAN, because all that is needed is wireless circuitry in any device that comes within range of a wireless network.

However, wireless LANs have a significant drawback: they are not as secure as wired LANs unless some measures are taken. On a wired network, one needs to physically connect a device to access the network resources. On a wireless network, security measures must be taken to prevent connection by unauthorized wireless devices within range of the network. Some of these measures are covered later in the chapter.

MANs

A **metropolitan area network (MAN)** usually links multiple LANs within a large city or metropolitan region and typically spans a distance of up to 50 kilometers (about 30 miles). For example, the LAN in a chemistry lab might be linked to a research hospital's LAN and to a pharmaceutical company's LAN several miles away in the same city to form a MAN. The individual LANs that compose a MAN might belong to the same organization or to several different organizations. The high-speed links between LANs within a MAN typically use fiber optic or wireless broadband connections.

WANs

A **wide area network (WAN)** is a far-reaching system of networks. One WAN is composed of multiple LANs or MANs that are connected across a distance of more than approximately 48 kilometers (or 30 miles). Large WANs might have many constituent LANs and MANs on different continents. The simplest WAN is a dial-up connection to a network provider's services over basic telephone lines. A more complex WAN is a satellite linkup between LANs in two different countries. The most well-known WAN is the Internet.

WANs can be public or private. The telephone network and the Internet are examples of public WANs. A private WAN might use either dedicated lines or satellite connections. Many organizations cannot afford to maintain a private WAN. They pay to use existing networks, which are provided in two basic formats: common carriers or value-added networks.

A common carrier provides public telephone lines that anyone can access or dial up, and leased lines, which are dedicated to the leasing organization's exclusive use. The user pays for public lines based on time used and distance called. Verizon and AT&T are common carriers. Leased lines are dedicated to the leaseholder and have a lower error rate than dial-up lines, because they are not switched among many different subscribers.

Value-added networks (VANs) provide enhanced network services. VANs fulfill organizational needs for reliable data communications while relieving the organization of the burden of providing its own network management and maintenance. Many businesses use VANs for their electronic data interchange (EDI) with other businesses, suppliers, and buyers. However, due to cost considerations, an increasing number of organizations prefer to conduct commerce via the Internet rather than through VANs. VAN services cost much more than those offered by **Internet service providers (ISPs)**. (Many VAN providers also provide Internet links.) This issue is discussed in Chapter 8, "The Web-Enabled Enterprise."

PANs

A **personal area network (PAN)** is a wireless network designed for handheld and portable devices such as smartphones and tablet or laptop computers, and is intended for use by only one or two people. Transmission speed is slow to moderate, and the maximum distance between devices is generally 10 meters (33 feet). For example, Maria and Simon meet at a conference and exchange electronic business cards using their Bluetooth-enabled smartphones. Maria's device automatically synchronizes her office notebook computer and/or contact databases, updating her address book on both devices to maintain accurate timely information. (Bluetooth and other wireless technologies are covered later in the chapter.)

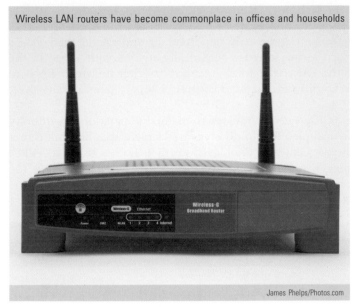
Wireless LAN routers have become commonplace in offices and households

James Phelps/Photos.com

Networking Hardware

Networks use a variety of devices to connect computers and peripheral devices (such as printers) to each other, and to connect networks to each other. Each computer or device connected to a network must have a **network interface card (NIC)** or proper networking circuitry, which connects through a cable or a wireless antenna to a switch, bridge, or router, which in turn connects to a LAN or WAN. A **switch** is a common device often used as a central location to connect computers or devices to a local network. A **bridge** is a device that connects two networks, such as a LAN, to the Internet. A **router** routes data packets to the next node on their way to the final destination. It can connect dissimilar networks and can be programmed to also act as a firewall to filter communications. Routers keep tables of network addresses, known as Internet Protocol (IP) addresses, which identify each computer on the network, along with the best routes to other network addresses. You are not likely to see a WAN router, but you might have seen a router used to support a LAN in a small office or in a household. Cable providers usually provide a router for wireless and wired Internet access in a household environment. A **repeater** amplifies or regenerates signals so that they do not become weak or distorted.

Another type of networking hardware that might be familiar to home computer users is the modem. A **modem**—a word contracted from *mod*ulator-*dem*odulator—in traditional usage is a device whose purpose is to translate communications signals from analog to digital, and vice versa. For many years the only way to link to the Internet was to dial up, meaning connecting over regular telephone lines. These lines were originally designed for analog—continuous—signals rather than for digital signals, which consist of discrete bursts. An analog modem turns the digital signal from your computer into an analog signal that can go out over the phone lines. A modem on the receiving computer transforms the analog signal back into a digital signal the computer can understand. The former transformation is called modulation and the latter is called demodulation.

A **dial-up connection** with a modem is very slow (usually no faster than 56 Kbps), so most users and small businesses have turned to faster connections that use digital signals throughout the connection, such as DSL and cable connections. Even though the medium transfers digital signals, the word "modem" is now used for the devices that connect computers to the Internet with these technologies. Thus, for example, if you use a cable company to link to the Internet, the device connecting your computer's network card to the cable is called a cable modem. If you use a DSL service, the device used is called a DSL modem, and if you use a power line, the device is called a BPL modem.

Virtual Private Networks

A LAN is a private network, because it only provides access to members of an organization. Though a firm does not own the lines it leases, the network of leased lines might be considered a private network, because only members authorized by the organization can use it. Many companies cannot afford or do not wish to pay for a private network. By implementing special software (and sometimes also hardware) they can create a **virtual private network (VPN)**. Although the Internet is discussed in Chapter 8, "The Web-Enabled Enterprise," VPNs are important in the context of the current discussion.

A virtual private network (VPN) can be thought of as a "tunnel" through the Internet or other public network that allows only authorized users to access company resources. The "virtual" in VPN refers to the illusion that the user is accessing a private network directly, rather than through a public network. VPNs enable the use of intranets and extranets. An intranet is a network that uses web technologies to serve an organization's employees who are located in several sites that might be many miles apart; an extranet serves both the employees and other enterprises that do business with the organization. It is important to understand that once a LAN is linked to a public network, such as the Internet, technically anyone with access to the public network can obtain access to the LAN. Therefore, organizations that link their LANs to the Internet implement sophisticated security measures to control or totally deny public access to their resources.

AT&T's Customer Service Centers utilize VPN technology to maintain operational continuity for their call centers. If operations are disrupted due to disaster or inclement weather, call center employees are able to access their contact center technology from their homes using the VPN. They are able to access all of the tools, data, and applications as if they were working at the service centers. VPN technology allows AT&T to establish business continuity for its customers while maintaining employee safety (Read, 2011).

Protocols

A communications **protocol** is a set of rules that govern communication between computers or between computers and other computer-related devices that exchange data. When these rules govern a network of devices, the rule set is often referred to as a *network protocol*. If a device does not know what the network's agreed-upon protocol is, or cannot comply with it, the device cannot communicate on the network.

Some protocols are designed for WANs, others are designed for LANs, and some are designed specifically for wireless communications. This discussion addresses only some of these protocols. Protocols, often called "standards," do not necessarily compete with each other. They often work together or serve different purposes. The most important and pervasive set of protocols for telecommunications and networks today is called TCP/IP.

TCP/IP

Communication on the Internet follows mainly **TCP/IP (Transmission Control Protocol/Internet Protocol)**, which is actually a set of related protocols. TCP ensures that the packets arrive accurately and in the proper order, while IP ensures delivery of packets from node to node in the most efficient manner.

A computer connected directly to the Internet **backbone**—the highest speed communication channels—is called a **host**. IP controls the delivery from one host to another until the message is received by the destination host. The host forwards messages to devices connected to it. Often, we call hosts servers. For example, your school has at least one email server; it forwards to your computer email messages addressed to you.

Every device on the Internet is uniquely identified with a numerical label known as an Internet protocol address, or **IP address**. There are currently two versions of IP addresses. Internet Protocol version 4 (IPv4) addresses consist of a 32-bit numeric address, presented in four parts separated by periods, such as 146.186.87.220. Each of these parts can be a number between 0 and 255. This structure allows for 4.3 billion unique IP addresses. However, with the explosive growth in Internet-connected devices such as smartphones, home security devices, tablets, and home computers, it became obvious that IPv4 was reaching its limits. The Internet Engineering Task Force (IETF) deployed Internet Protocol version 6 (IPv6) in June 2012. IPv6 uses a 128-bit address consisting of eight groups of four hexadecimal digits separated by colons. An example of the IPv6 address is 2001:0bc8:85f3:0042:6334:7a2a:0360:5025. The new structure supports 340 trillion trillion trillion (yes, you read that right) unique addresses, a number that should not run out anytime in the foreseeable future (Captain, 2012).

If you know the IP address of a website, you can enter those numbers in the address box of a web browser. However, it is easier to remember names and words, and therefore most organizations associate their IP addresses with names. The process of associating a character-based name such as *cengage.com* with an IP address is called domain name resolution, and the domain name resolution service is **DNS (Domain Name System)**. DNS servers are maintained by Internet service providers (ISPs) and other organizations. In large organizations, a server can be dedicated as a DNS server.

If a LAN is linked to the Internet through a router, the entire network has an IP address unique on the Internet. This number is stored in the router. To uniquely identify devices on the LAN, the router assigns local IP addresses to individual computers and devices. These IP addresses identify the computers only within the LAN. Only the router is identified uniquely on the Internet.

Servers and many other computers and devices are assigned permanent IP addresses, called a **static IP address**. A computer connected to the Internet intermittently might be assigned a temporary IP address for the duration of its connection only. Such a number is called a **dynamic IP address**. It is assigned by the host through which that computer is connecting to the Internet. Dynamic IP addresses give an organization flexibility with its limited number of assigned IP addresses: only devices seeking a connection to the Internet are assigned IP addresses. The number is disassociated from a device that logs off, and the server can then reassign the IP address to another device that has just logged on. Some broadband providers assign static IP addresses; others assign only dynamic IP addresses.

Ethernet

The Institute of Electrical and Electronics Engineers (IEEE) sets standards for communication protocols. IEEE 802.3, known as **Ethernet**, is the only LAN protocol of significance. Ethernet uses either coaxial cable or Cat 5 or 6 twisted pair cable. Different generations of Ethernet support speeds from 10 Mbps (10Base-T) to 100 Mbps (100Base-T or Fast Ethernet) to over 1 Gbps (**Gigabit Ethernet** and 10 Gigabit Ethernet).

Wireless Protocols

All wireless devices use radio transceivers (transmitter-receivers). The radio waves carry the digital signal, the bits. Depending on the protocol followed, the devices use different radio frequencies for their work.

IEEE 802.11 Wi-Fi

IEEE 802.11 is a family of wireless protocols, collectively known as **Wi-Fi** (for Wireless Fidelity). The term originally applied to the IEEE 802.11b standard that supports wireless communication within about 100 meters (300 feet) of a wireless router at a maximum speed of 11 Mbps. The later 802.11g standard supports speeds of up to 54 Mbps for the same range. The 802.11a standard supports similar speeds to 802.11g, but in a different frequency range that is less susceptible to interference from cell phones and microwave devices. The 802.11n standard was approved in 2009. 802.11n supports maximum speeds of 248 Mbps and has about twice the range of 802.11b and g, about 70 meters (230 feet) indoors and 160 meters (525 feet) outdoors. The g standard is backward-compatible with the b standard, meaning that you can add b devices to a g network. The n standard is backward-compatible with the b, g, and a standards. However, in a mixed network, throughput will likely be at the speed of the lowest-speed device. The b and g standards use a radio frequency in the 2.4–2.5 GHz range, the 802.11a standard operates in the 5 GHz frequency, while the n standard can operate in either frequency. These radio frequency ranges do not require government licenses (referred to as "unlicensed"), and therefore are used for wireless communication. A new protocol, 802.11ac, has been developed and was released in late 2012. Broadcom has stated that its 802.11ac chip structure provides faster throughput, higher capacity, broader coverage and longer battery life (Anonymous, 2012).

A single Wi-Fi router can be connected to an **access point (AP)**, which in turn is connected to a wired network and usually to the Internet, allowing tens to hundreds of Wi-Fi-equipped devices to share the Internet link. A direct link to a wireless router or AP creates a **hotspot**. Hotspots allow Internet access to anyone within range who uses a wireless-equipped device, provided logging in is not limited by controlled access codes. Figure 6.3 illustrates a home wireless LAN (WLAN).

FIGURE 6.3

An example of a home
using a wireless network

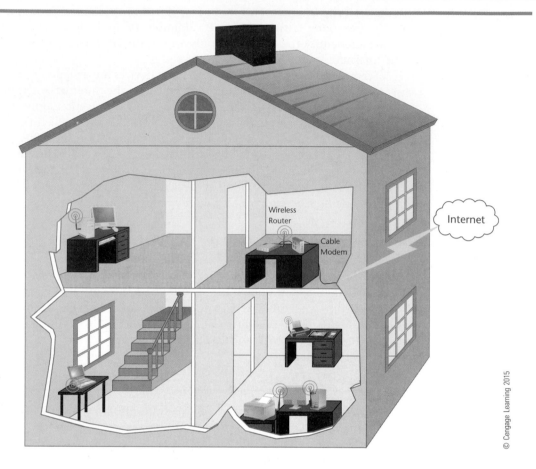

Wireless
Router

Cable
Modem

Internet

© Cengage Learning 2015

As mentioned earlier, security has been a concern for Wi-Fi networks. The earliest 802.11 standards had serious security flaws; 802.11n has improved security by offering the Wi-Fi Protected Access (WPA) and WPA2 security protocols. These protocols offer **encryption**, the ability to scramble and code messages through encryption keys that are shared only between the sender and receiver. Of course, to receive the protection of these protocols, they must be enabled on your wireless computer or device. Experienced "hackers" can break the codes of WPA. WPA2 is a preferred measure.

Wi-Fi hotspots are appearing everywhere, from airports and restaurant chains to the local library and barbershop. Businesses also use wireless LANs for many types of operations. You will find a WLAN in almost every warehouse. Workers holding smartphones or specialized electronic units communicate with each other and receive information about the location of items by section, shelf, and bin. For example, General Motors equipped the forklifts in all its warehouses with Wi-Fi transceivers to help their operators locate parts. On sunny days retailers place merchandise and cash registers on sidewalks. The cash registers are linked to a central system through a WLAN. Airports, conference centers and schools use WLANs to help guests, students, and staff to communicate as well as link to the Internet through a hotspot.

Many new airplanes are equipped with WLANs. Boeing started equipping its large airplanes with Wi-Fi in 2003. Lufthansa, British Airways, Japan Airlines, Scandinavian Airlines System, and other airlines have equipped their long-range jetliners with the technology to allow paying passengers to use a hotspot 12 kilometers (7.5 miles) above ground. Gogo provides Internet access on nine commercial airlines. Customers can purchase passes to access the Internet to work on their laptop or watch a feature movie on their tablet.

Utility companies have converted manually read electric, gas, and water meters to wireless meters. An employee need only pass by the client's building in a motor vehicle to record the reading. Newer meters use networks that relay the signal to the utility company's office and automatically update each customer's account in the company's computers. Wireless meters save millions of labor hours and overcome common problems, such as meters enclosed in locked places, inaccurate readings, and, occasionally, an aggressive dog.

A growing number of electronic devices, such as smartphones, digital cameras, and video game consoles, are equipped with wireless circuitry. This rids their owners of the need to physically connect a device to a computer or a router for communication. For example, with a wireless-enabled digital camera you can send digital pictures from your camera to your PC, or directly to a friend via a hotspot over the Internet.

Bluetooth technology supports a personal network enabling the hands-free use of mobile phones

Stockbyte/Photos.com

IEEE 802.15 Bluetooth

Named after a Scandinavian king who unified many tribes, the **Bluetooth** standard was developed for devices that communicate with each other within a short range of up to 10 meters (33 feet) in the office, at home, and in motor vehicles. It transmits voice and data. Bluetooth was later adopted by IEEE as its 802.15 standard. Typical Bluetooth devices include wireless keyboards and mice, wireless headsets for hands-free mobile phone use, and increasingly, digital entertainment devices. For example, you can purchase a wrist-worn MP3 player that uses Bluetooth to transmit the music to earbuds or headphones, avoiding the wires that typically connect a portable player to headphones. Bluetooth is considered a personal area network (PAN) technology, because it typically supports a network used by only one person. Bluetooth uses the 2.4–2.5 GHz radio frequency to transmit bits at a rate of 1 Mbps.

IEEE 802.16 WiMAX

IEEE 802.16, Worldwide Interoperability for Microwave Access (**WiMAX**), increases the range and speed of wireless communication. It might potentially reach up to 110 kilometers (about 70 miles) with a speed of 100 Mbps; however, it typically reaches 13–16 kilometers (8–10 miles). Experts say that with an investment of no more than $3 billion, WiMAX can cover 98 percent of American homes. This is a much lower investment than required for laying fiber optic cables. WiMAX uses licensed radio frequencies of 2–11 GHz. This standard can cover entire metropolitan areas and provide Internet access to hundreds of thousands of households that either cannot afford an Internet service or for some reason cannot obtain access. Many municipal governments wanted to establish such service for a fee or for free. However, this has created a threat to the business of ISPs, who count on subscriber fees for revenue, because an entire metropolitan area can become one huge hotspot, and the fees, if any, are collected by the local government rather than an ISP. Therefore, several states in the United States legislated against municipality-sponsored networks. However, some cities are using the technology, which enables households that cannot afford Internet connectivity to have access to this important resource. Philadelphia was the first American metropolis to do so. The city was exempt from a Pennsylvania law forbidding municipal networks.

WiMAX is a metropolitan area network (MAN) technology. Figure 6.4 shows how WiMAX works. A household, office, or public hotspot can use a router to link multiple devices either by linking directly to a WiMAX base antenna that is linked to the Internet, or by using a relay antenna that receives the signal and retransmits it to the Internet-linked antenna. If a mobile user's equipment included the proper WiMAX communication device, the user could communicate with the Internet moving at speeds of up to 150 Km/H (about 94 MPH), which enables convenient use of the Internet while sitting in a moving vehicle (though the driver should not be going that fast!). An extension of this standard, 802.16e, supports mobile Internet communication.

FIGURE 6.4

How a WiMAX network works

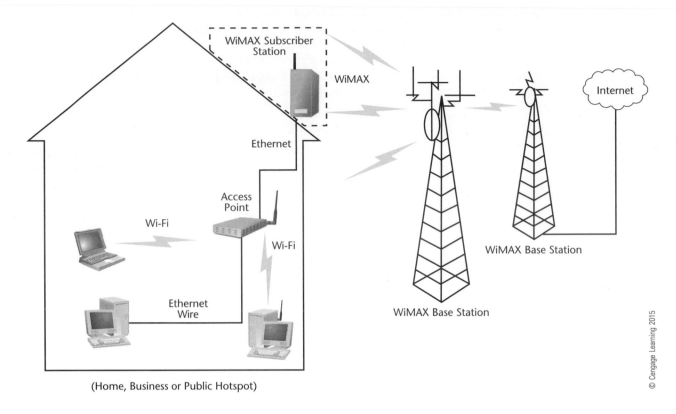

(Home, Business or Public Hotspot)

© Cengage Learning 2015

Long-Term Evolution

Long-Term Evolution (LTE), also known as 4G LTE, is a standard method of wireless communications, specifically for high-speed data transmission for mobile phones. It was developed through the 3rd Generation Partnership Project (3GPP), a collaborative effort of six telecommunication associations (referred to as the Organizational Partners) from various continents (Anonymous, 2013a). In 2010, the first organization to fully implement an LTE network in North America was Verizon Wireless. As an evolution of GSM (global system for mobile communications) standards, the objective of the new communication standard was to increase the speed and capacity of data transmission. It is currently capable of high upload and download transmission speeds, up to 170 and 300 Mbit/s respectively (Anonymous, 2013b).

Figure 6.5 summarizes relevant features of the various 802.xx wireless protocols.

FIGURE 6.5

Wireless networking protocols

Protocol	Max. Range	Max. Speed	Main Use
802.11a	75 meters (250 feet)	54 Mbps	LAN
802.11b	100 meters (330 feet)	11 Mbps	LAN
802.11g	100 meters (330 feet)	54 Mbps	LAN
802.11n	160 meters (530 feet)	248 Mbps	LAN
802.15 Bluetooth	10 meters (33 feet)	1 Mbps	PAN
802.16 WiMax	50 km (31 miles)	100 Mbps	MAN
802.11ac	90 meters (300 feet)	349 Mbps	LAN

© Cengage Learning 2015

Generations in Mobile Communications

Networking professionals often refer to generations of mobile communication technologies. Each generation refers to a communication protocol or a combination of protocols. The differences among generations are mainly in capabilities (e.g., enabling a mobile phone to access additional resources) and transmission speed. The first generation, 1G, was analog and used circuit switching. Then 2G protocols became the first to provide digital voice encoding, and they worked at faster transmission rates. They include the GSM (Global System for Mobile) and CDMA (Code Division Multiple Access) protocols, the details of which are outside the scope of this discussion.

The 3G protocols support transmission rates of 1 Mbps. The protocols support video, videoconferencing, and full Internet access. 4G protocol devices operate only digitally and with packet switching, increased at bandwidths, and include tighter security measures. In the U.S., Sprint, AT&T, Virgin Mobile and Verizon all have adopted LTE technology. The high speed of the technology enables mobile phone users to watch a video, listen to music files, browse the web, and make a telephone call at the same time.

POINT OF INTEREST   We Want It Now!

The increased demand for and reliance on the Internet, no matter one's location, has driven the improvement of mobile networks in past years. Internet providers have continuously responded by releasing generation after generation of mobile networks, each faster than the previous. Near the end of 2012, AT&T, one of the United States' top service providers, released the fastest wireless technology yet: 4G LTE. 4G LTE coverage is capable of delivering Internet speeds up to 10 times faster than 3G. Devices can upload, download, game, and stream faster than ever. People want Internet access, they want it now, and they want it faster. That's what 4G LTE does.

Source: Anonymous. (2012, Dec 13). AT&T 4G LTE Expands in Little Rock; More customers to benefit from ultra-fast mobile Internet on the latest LTE devices, M2 Presswire.

In a way, 3G and 4G cellular technologies compete with Wi-Fi, but it seems that generally the technologies complement each other: we use 3G and 4G on the go and Wi-Fi in stationary locations. Wi-Fi is significantly less expensive to use than 3G and 4G, because mobile phone services involve a monthly fee for each phone, while using the Internet through a hotspot is sometimes offered at no cost. In addition, most cellular service providers have changed their data plans to meter data service. To eliminate over-limit smartphone data charges, customers may be required to use Wi-Fi networks at their home and office.

Internet Networking Services

Both organizations and individuals can choose from a variety of options when subscribing to networking services. Figure 6.6 summarizes the major services offered by telecommunications companies. Note that the bit rates shown are for **downstream**, which is the speed of receiving from the network; **upstream** speeds, the speeds of transmitting into the network, are usually much lower. Also be aware that these are typical speeds in the United States. They might be different in other countries. Monthly costs, too, are typical but vary from region to region. For some services, such as T1 and T3, companies also offer fractions of the speeds for lower fees.

FIGURE 6.6

Typical features and costs of Internet services

Service	Downstream Speed	Availability	Monthly Fee
Dial-up	56 Kbps	Universal	$9–11
BPL	0.25–3 Mbps	Limited availability	$20–40
Cable	0.5–3 Mbps	Widespread; available nearly everywhere where cable TV service is offered	$30–50
DSL	0.25–1.5 Mbps	More limited than cable, but spreading faster; speed depends on distance from telco office	$30–50
T1	1.544 Mbps	Widespread	$250–500
T3	45 Mbps	Widespread	$4,000–16,000
Satellite	0.5–10 Mbps	Widespread; practical only with view to the southern sky	$50–70
Fixed Wireless	100 Mbps	Limited, but spreading	$30–50
Fiber to the Premises	5–30 Mbps	Limited, but spreading	$350
OC-3	155.52 Mbps	Limited availability	$20,000–45,000K $10,000–30,000K
OC-12	622.08 Mbps	Limited availability	Several hundred thousand dollars
OC-48	2.488 Gbps	Limited availability	Several hundred thousand dollars
OC-192	9.952 Gbps	Limited availability	Several hundred thousand dollars
OC-255	13.21 Gbps	Limited availability	Several hundred thousand dollars

For most individuals and businesses, a service that provides a much lower transmission rate (upstream speed) than reception rate (downstream speed) is suitable. This is because they rarely upload large files to websites or transmit large amounts of email that must arrive at its destination in a fraction of a second. However, organizations such as online businesses and media companies that must upload large files quickly must also have high upstream speeds. Such organizations may opt for Internet communication lines that allow high speeds both downstream and upstream.

The proliferation of high-speed connection services, also called broadband services, is mainly the result of businesses' and individuals' rush to the Internet. Some of the services, such as cable, DSL, and satellite links, are offered both to businesses and residences. Others, such as T1 and T3 lines and the OC class, are offered only to businesses, largely because of their high cost. Note that some of the services are actually groups of services that differ in speeds. For example, some DSL services designed for businesses provide the same speed downstream and upstream, while options for households (see later discussion of ADSL) always provide a greater downstream speed than upstream speed.

Cable

Internet service is also provided by television cable firms, mostly to residential customers. The medium is the same as for television reception, but the firms connect the cable to an Internet server. At the subscriber's residence, the cable is split—one part is connected to the television set, and the other is connected to the computer via a bridge that is often called a cable modem. Both television transmission and data are transmitted through the same line. The cable link is always on, so the computer is constantly connected to the Internet. More than 90 percent of cable operators in the United States offer Internet access.

The major downside of cable is that cable nodes are shared by all the subscribers connected to the node. Therefore, at peak times, such as television prime time (7–11 p.m.), communication speed slows down. The speed also slows down as more subscribers join the service in a given territory.

POINT OF INTEREST   Broadband at Home

A 2012 poll conducted by the Leichtman Research Group concluded that 90 percent of those with a personal computer at home subscribe to broadband service. Three percent were unsatisfied while 65 percent are very satisfied. The poll also noticed a direct correlation between increased income levels and having a computer at home. Of those households polled with an income of less than $30,000, 41 percent do not have a computer at home. On the contrary, 97 percent of those with incomes over $50,000 do have a computer at home. It was also noted that 1.3 percent of those who would like to receive broadband service cannot because the service is not available in their location.

Source: Krey, M. (2012, Sep 04). Broadband In 90% Of U.S. Homes With Computers: Poll, Investor's Business Daily.

Digital Subscriber Line (DSL)

With normal landline telephone service, the telephone company filters information that arrives in digital form and then transforms it to analog form; thus, it requires a modem to transform the signal back to digital form. This conversion constrains the capacity of the link between your telephone (or computer) and the telephone company's switching center to a low speed of 56 Kbps.

With **digital subscriber line (DSL)**, data remains digital throughout the entire transmission; it is never transformed into analog signals. So, the telephone company can transmit to subscribers' computers at significantly higher speeds of up to 300 Mbps depending on distance (Quick, 2010). To provide DSL service, the telecommunications company connects your telephone line to a DSL bridge (often called a DSL modem). At the telephone company's regional central office, DSL traffic is aggregated and forwarded to the ISP or data network provider with which the subscriber has a contract. Often, the telephone company is also the ISP.

The bit rates of DSL lines are closely related to the distance of the subscriber's computer from the regional central office of the telephone company. Telecommunications companies might offer the service to subscribers as far as 6,100 meters (20,000 feet) from the central office, but the speed then is usually no faster than 144 Kbps, unless the company has installed a DSL repeater on the line. Some companies do not offer the service if the subscriber's address is not within 4,500 meters (15,000 feet) of the central office.

T1 and T3 Lines

T1 and T3 lines are point-to-point dedicated digital circuits provided by telephone companies. A T1 line is made up of 24 channels (groups of wires) of 64 Kbps each. T3 lines are made up of 672 channels of 64 Kbps. T1 and T3 lines are expensive. Therefore, only businesses that must rely on high speeds are willing to accept the high cost of subscribing to the service. Most universities, as well as large companies, use T1 or T3 lines for their backbone and Internet connections.

Satellite

Businesses and households in rural areas and other regions that do not have access to cable or DSL might be able to obtain satellite services, which use microwave radio transmission. In fact, satellite service providers target these households. The service provider installs a dish antenna that is tuned to a communications satellite. Satellite connections might reach a speed of 45 Mbps. The antenna for satellite communication can be fixed, as the ones you can see installed in the yards of private houses, or mobile, such as those installed on the roofs of large trucks. Most of the subscribers of fixed satellite dishes are households; most mobile dish users are shipping and trucking businesses. Subscribers to fixed satellite service must purchase the dish antenna, with a typical cost of $400, and pay a monthly fee of about $50. Trucking companies must have an antenna installed on each truck.

Many people use a free satellite service, the global positioning system (GPS). While a proper device is required to enable reception from the satellites (which were launched into orbit by the U.S. government), anyone can communicate free of charge. The satellite transmits back to any GPS device its location on earth by longitude and latitude.

Fixed Wireless

Another alternative for households and small businesses that cannot obtain cable or DSL connections to the Internet is fixed wireless. **Fixed wireless** is point-to-point transmission between two stationary devices, usually between two buildings, as opposed to mobile wireless, in which people carry a mobile device. Companies such as Sprint, AT&T, and many ISPs offer the service. ISPs that specialize in fixed wireless services are often referred to as WISPs, wireless ISPs. They install microwave transceivers on rooftops instead of laying physical wires and cables. Subscribers connect their computers to the rooftop transceiver. They can communicate at speeds up to 2 Mbps. Repeaters are installed close to each other to enhance the signal, which can deteriorate in the presence of buildings, trees, and foul weather. Transmission rates depend on the distance between the receiver and the base station. Up to 14 kilometers (9 miles) from the base station, the speed is 100 Mbps; speeds drop to about 2 Mbps at about 56 kilometers (35 miles) from the base.

Fixed wireless is highly modular—the telecommunications company can add as many transceivers as it needs to serve a growing number of subscribers. Unlike cable service, the company does not need franchise licenses. The technology is suitable for both urban and rural areas.

Fiber to the Premises

Fiber to the premises connects a building to the Internet via optical fiber. The service is widely available in the United States and other countries, but at varying speeds. In Hong Kong and South Korea, the maximum speed the providers of this service allow is 100 Mbps. In the United States, Verizon provides the service, which it calls FiOS (Fiber Optic Service), but limits the speed to 30 Mbps. While Verizon has deployed the service on a large scale, other companies such as AT&T provide similar service to some communities. When the optical fiber reaches the subscriber's living or work space, it is referred to as **Fiber to the Home (FTTH)**. Subscribers simply connect their computer, or LAN's router, to the optical fiber socket in the wall. In some communities, Verizon has also provided television programming on the same optical lines.

Optical Carrier

Companies willing to pay high fees can enjoy very high connection speeds. These services are denoted with **OC**, the acronym for **optical carrier**, because they are provided through optical fiber lines. The number next to OC refers to data speed in multiples of 51.84 Mbps, considered the base rate bandwidth. Thus, when available, the services are denoted as C-1, C-3, C-9, C-12, C-18, C-48, and so on through C-3072. For illustration, OC-768 (40 Gbps) enables you to transmit the content of seven CDs in 1 second. Typical businesses that purchase the services are ISPs, providers of search engines, and businesses that wish to support content-rich websites and

When you are introduced to people, you usually mention your occupation, and then you might be asked, "Where do you work?" Many employed people now answer, "At home." They do not commute; they *telecommute*, or, as some prefer to call it, they *telework*. They have the shortest commute to work: from the bedroom to another room in the home that is equipped with a PC and a broadband Internet link. For an increasing number of workers, IT provides all that's needed to create the goods their employers sell: software, analysis reports, literature, tax returns, and many other types of output. If they need data from the office, they can connect to their office intranet using VPN software and retrieve the required information. If they need to talk to supervisors or coworkers, they use their computers to conduct videoconferencing. When they complete their product, they can simply email it or place it on a remote server.

- **Telecommuting on the Rise.** Depending on whom you count as a telecommuter, the number could range from 2.9 million to 33.7 million. A special tabulation calculated by the U.S. Census Bureau's annual American Community Survey put the 2009 U.S. telecommuter total at 2.9 million. This is a 61 percent increase from 2005. Most of the growth is due to teleworking federal and state workers. President of the Families and Work Institute, Ellen Galinsky, counts telecommuters as employees who work from home at least occasionally. This number is staked at 13.7 million, 10 percent of the nation's waged and salaried employees, and has not significantly altered from 2002-2008. At the highest point, 33.7 million, a 2009 report from WorldatWork's Telework Trendlines counts all employees, contractors, and business owners who work from home at least one day per month. This statistic is 17 percent higher than the 28.7 million tabulated in 2006. According to the 2011 Workplace Forecast by the Society for Human Resource Management (SHRM), 43 percent of HR professionals believe that the demand for workplace flexibility will have strategic impact on operations in future years (Meinert, 2011).

- **Employment Opportunities.** Telecommuting offers employment alternatives to those who wish to spend more time with their families. Some employees value spending time raising their children more than money. Eliminating the morning and afternoon commutes can reduce stress levels, giving employees a better work/life balance. In addition, reduced stress levels increase employees' quality of life and productivity levels. Offering telecommuting to potential employees serves as an incentive in acquiring the best talent for the firm. Eighty-two employers on Fortune's 2011 list of "100 Best Companies to Work For" offered telecommuting as an employment option for employees (Meinert, 2011).

- **Saving Time and Money.** Organizations offer telecommuting because it saves the cost of office space. Deloitte

LLP has offered most of its 45,000 nationwide employees the option to telecommute up to five days a week for the past 15 years. Deloitte has reduced office space as leases expired and has saved an additional 30 percent on energy costs. In 2008, they saved $30 million after redesigning their facilities to eliminate permanent office spaces for mobile employees who no longer needed a permanent desk.

As an alternative, Deloitte offers "hoteling" where employees who usually telecommute can reserve a workstation when they come into the office. Instead of traveling on a plane to meet with a client, employees can save their time and the company's money by using a "telesuite." Employees can use these to hold a videoconference with clients and fellow employees in different locations. Eighty-six percent of Deloitte's workers telecommute at minimum 20 percent of the workweek, according to Fortune (Meinert, 2011).

Telecommuters like their arrangement because they save the time and money they would spend on commuting. Telecommuting reduces millions of tons of pollutants, saves billions of gallons of gasoline, and frees billions of personal hours for leisure time.

- **The Downside.** However, not everyone is so enthusiastic about telecommuting. Sociologists have mixed opinions about the phenomenon. On one hand, telecommuting allows people to work who would otherwise remain outside the workforce, such as older professionals and many disabled people. On the other hand, it has been found that employers tend to pressure telecommuters to work harder than office workers. In the office an employee works a set number of hours, but the home worker has no defined workday; his or her workday is, the employer often assumes, 24 hours per day. In addition, telecommuters are more estranged from their fellow workers. Some business cultures are built on hallway conversations, and for employees working at home, they are left out of the loop. There is no office in which to foster new social ties and camaraderie.

Telecommuting might also foster isolation. Teleworkers share fewer experiences with other people. In addition, leaving the workplace behind means leaving behind one more community that gives many people a sense of belonging, even if this belonging amounts only to having a sandwich together at lunchtime and complaining about the boss. At the same time, some managers might prefer to see their employees in the office and keep them in their "line of sight."

From another standpoint, not all companies have the appropriate technology systems to allow employees to work seamlessly from their homes. As gas prices have flirted between three and four dollars per gallon within the last three years, more and more companies have tried offering telecommuting to their employees. Tech Data Corp. began offering telecommuting to 530 of their 1,500 employees in 2008. What they found out, however, was that they did not possess an adequate telephone system to route calls to the next available employee working at home.

On a national level, telecommuting could severely affect some segments of the economy. Imagine the huge drop in revenue of New York City restaurants during lunchtime if only half of the 3 million or so commuters did not rush to grab lunch between 12 and 2 p.m. Some cities' dining industries could crumble if the telecommuting trend continues at the current pace. Many people live in cities mainly because of proximity to their offices, thus further movement to suburbs and remote residential areas would gut many other industries in central cities.

Many workers, given the option to work at home, have decided to return to the office. Interestingly, this also happens in the very industries that are so amenable to telecommuting, such as software development. These returning workers claim they missed social interaction with their peers, hallway chats, lunches with friends, and direct communication with fellow workers and supervisors. But telecommuting has grown, and will probably continue

to grow, especially thanks to greater availability of broadband services and their declining monthly fees. Fewer than half of all Americans have broadband service at home. Among telecommuters, the proportion is greater than 90 percent. If the trend continues, offices occupied by organizations will be significantly smaller than they are now and will serve as the symbolic rather than physical centers of the organizations' activities.

While many employers are now offering telecommuting, in order for them to experience a return on investment, they must be able to reduce space and energy costs. Taking Deloitte as an example, they eliminated office spaces for workers who did not need a permanent desk and allowed them to reserve space for the days they were coming into the office. If employees only telecommute one or two days per week and still require a permanent desk, the employer will not be able to experience that ROI, says Jack Phillips, chairman of ROI Institute. Fifty-five percent of employers allow employees to work from home but only 17 percent offer it full-time. In years to come, look for strategic advancements in the evolution of telecommuting in order to reduce space and energy costs while increasing employee productivity (Meinert, 2011).

high-volume traffic. However, media companies have also purchased such services because the high speeds support streaming video. Among companies that use OC-768, for instance, are Deutsche Telecom, NBC, Disney, the U.S. Department of Defense Advanced Research Projects Agency (the agency that developed the Internet), NASA, and Nippon TV.

Broadband Over Power Lines (BPL)

As mentioned in the discussion of communications media, electric power lines are capable of carrying digital signals. Subscribers simply plug their BPL modem into standard electrical wall outlets. Usually, utility companies partner with telecommunications companies to provide Broadband over Power Lines (BPL). For example, Cinergy, a Cincinnati-based utility company that serves customers in Ohio, Kentucky, and Indiana, partnered with Current Communications to provide broadband service. The service is offered for a monthly fee of $20–40, based on transmission speed desired by the subscriber. Some experts estimate that the BPL market in the United States will grow, while others expect only households that currently use dial-up to link to the Internet to adopt this type of service. Dial-up service is still being used by 6 percent of homes. AOL has more than 3.5 million dial-up subscriber accounts (Todd, 2012).

The Impact of Networking Technologies

This section takes a look at networking technologies and trends that are likely to have a significant impact on businesses and the management of information in the near future: broadband telephony, radio frequency identification, and the convergence of digital technologies.

Broadband Telephony

While regular long-distance telephone companies charge according to the number of minutes a call lasts, Internet service providers (ISPs) charge customers a flat monthly fee for connection to the Internet. With the proper software and microphones attached to their computers, Internet users can conduct long-distance and international conversations via their Internet connection for a fraction of regular calling costs. The technology is called Internet telephony, IP telephony, or **VoIP (Voice over Internet Protocol)**. VoIP is a standard for software that digitizes and compresses voice signals and transmits the bits via the Internet link. Organizations can purchase the proper software or use the services of companies that specialize in providing IP telephony. Companies such as Vonage, Comcast, and many others offer inexpensive use of their VoIP telephone-to-telephone voice communication.

Computer-to-computer calls can be conducted free of charge by using the service of a company such as Skype or iCall. Phone-to-phone service requires an additional modem, but it does not require a new phone or phone number, and it does not require routing calls through a home computer. iCall offers two methods of free phone calling. You may initiate a call to any telephone in the U.S. or Canada or call other iCall users for no charge.

VoIP provides flexibility for business organizations with multiple locations as well as mobile employees. VoIP can include several services such as text translation that can be read through email, instant messaging, virtual meetings and videoconferencing.

Google Voice provides telecommunication services by assigning a phone number that is not linked to a device or location, but to a person. Their product allows the user to manage all of their phones (mobile, home, office or VoIP lines) using the Google Voice phone number. For example, you can specify that when someone calls your Google Voice number, your cell phone, office, and home phones ring simultaneously. The service can also send email or text message notifications when a voice mail is received, as well as call screening to listen to the caller's voice before deciding whether to accept the call or send it to voice mail.

PC-to-PC conversations can be conducted over the Internet at no cost using services such as Skype

VoIP can save companies and households money. Businesses are converting to VoIP systems from conventional PBXs (private branch exchanges). According to the research firm In-Stat, 20 percent of U.S. firms used VoIP in 2006, and 80 percent were expected to use VoIP by 2010 (Wenzel, 2011). The global market for VoIP solutions is expected to grow to over $18.1 billion by 2014 (Anonymous, 2011b).

JIG/MUIR, of Oakland California, used an aging PBX phone system. After implementing a new system from Boxfl, it saved $1,200 per month while increasing the bandwidth of its system by 300 percent. The system provided many of the features described above (Wenzel, 2011). LA Fitness needed to find a solution to link its 20,000 employees at over 370 clubs around the country. Their expansion across the United States complicated its ability to interact, share information, and provide customer service. LA Fitness deployed an enterprise-level communication system using VoIP that was more cost effective and productive (Anonymous, 2011a).

As some experts have predicted, the future of telephony is in the convergence of the cell phone and VoIP phone: you will use only one mobile phone. When outside the home or office, you will use the cell phone network; when back home or in the office, the phone will communicate through a VoIP service. This will reduce the higher cost of cell phone minutes.

Radio Frequency Identification

In Chapter 3, "Business Functions and Supply Chains," you learned about the expanded efficiency and business intelligence that companies, especially in manufacturing and retail, can gain from one particular type of communications technology: radio frequency identification (RFID). This section explains in more detail how RFID works. RFID tags can be very tiny, about the size of a rice grain, or several square inches, depending on the amount of information they need to contain and the environment in which they are used. They are not always flat; they can be cylindrical. The tags need very little power. Passive tags use power from the reader that queries them; active tags have their own tiny batteries, which increase the range of the reading range. These tiny batteries last a long time.

POINT OF INTEREST — Get Chipped

RFID chips have been utilized in many aspects of the business world including retail, transportation, and pharmaceuticals. But want to know the newest place you can find an RFID chip? You. At a 2012 hacker conference in northwest Washington, a do-it-yourselfer offered the chip installing service for only $30 and a signed waiver. The RFID chip was slipped underneath a layer of skin in the patients' hands between the thumb and forefinger. People with the RFID chip installed can use it to access their house, unlock their cell phone, or even start their car. Although some hold privacy concerns, others are eager to be on the forefront of RFID technology advancements.

Source: Greenburg, A. (2012). Want An RFID Chip Implanted Into Your Hand? Here's What The DIY Surgery Looks Like (Video). Forbes. Retrieved from http://www.forbes.com website: http://www.forbes.com/sites/andygreenberg/2012/08/13/want-an-rfid-chip-implanted-into-your-hand-heres-what-the-diy-surgery-looks-like-video/

An RFID system works as follows: objects are equipped, often embedded, with a tag that contains a transponder. A transponder is a radio transceiver (transmitter-receiver) that is activated for transmission by a signal transmitted to it. The tag is equipped with digital memory that is given a unique code. If the tag is used to identify a product, it contains an **EPC (electronic product code)**. The interrogator, a combination of an antenna, a transceiver, and a decoder, emits a signal activating the RFID tag so the interrogator can read data from it and write data to it. Although the interrogator also writes to the tag, it is often called a reader. When an RFID tag enters the reader's electromagnetic zone, it detects the reader's activation signal. The reader decodes the data stored in the tag's memory, and the data is passed to a host computer for processing.

Wal-Mart, British Tesco, and German Metro AG, three of the world's largest retailers, embarked on a project that might radically change supply chains. They required that suppliers use RFID. Hundreds complied, among them Procter & Gamble, the world's largest supplier of consumer products. The companies use microchips that are embedded in products to replace the ubiquitous bar codes for tracking and checkout at store registers. Each microchip holds a product identification number. The microchips communicate with wireless computers, including handheld and laptop computers, as they are moved in the production line, packed, picked, shipped, unloaded, shelved, and paid for by customers. As the item moves, the information about its location is communicated to a network of computers to which all businesses involved in the production and sale have access. This is often a Wi-Fi network. The benefits are a just-in-time (JIT) system that minimizes inventory throughout the supply chain to almost zero, and shelves that are always stocked. JIT, or a situation that is close to JIT, can be accomplished thanks to up-to-the-minute information about available inventory and when the next shipment from a supplier is needed. "Smart shelves," equipped with tiny wireless transceivers, alert employees whenever the shelf is running out of units, so they can put more units on the shelf immediately.

RFID is used for many other purposes as well, as Figure 6.7 shows. The investment in this technology yields efficiency rewards almost immediately to large companies, but is expensive for small suppliers. The average price of an EPC tag of the standard used by Wal-Mart, Tesco, Metro, and the U.S. Department of Defense was 5 cents in 2007.

FIGURE 6.7

Various examples of RFID applications in businesses

Use		Example
Access Control		Cards used to replace door keys.
People Tracking	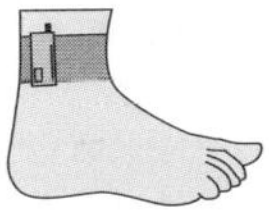	Keep children within school. Track prisoners on probation and prevent fleeing.
Animal Tracking		Track pets.
Livestock Management		Track life cycle of farm animals (e.g., feeding and immunization). Equip each cow with a unique ID to track diseases.
Antitheft Measures	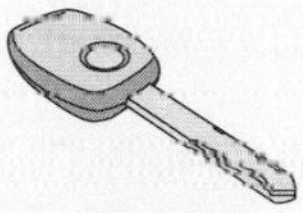	Transponders integrated into car keys. Only a legal key can start the engine.
Transportation		At airport, safety inspection of tagged luggage.
Retail		Tracking products in pallets and on shelves. Contactless payment.
Pharmaceuticals		Reduce drug counterfeiting.
Health Care		Tag people who enter and leave an epidemic zone.

© Cengage Learning 2015

Several retailers have announced plans to implement RFID technology. The RFID technology will provide EPC-enabled technology for the items sold by the retailers. Their adoption of RFID/EPC technology is heavily dependent on whether suppliers will cooperate by adopting the technology also. An October 2011 study by Accenture found that 58 suppliers and 56 retailers in North America believe that this technology needs to be adopted by more than 50 percent of retailers and suppliers. Item-level tagging is considered the most significant influence in increasing RFID/EPC adoption. Previously, apparel transported in cartons needed to be scanned manually, one item at a time. With the new technology, suppliers, distributors, and retailers can identify and capture item-level information for an entire carton immediately by reading the RFID tags (Napolitano, 2012).

The benefits of implementing RFID technology are clear. The American Productivity & Quality Center (APQC) believes that RFID implementation will improve distribution processes, reduce distribution center and warehouse costs, improve relationships with suppliers, and reduce inventory. The traceability at the item-level is believed to also increase the safety of consumer, pharmaceutical and food products (Partida, 2012).

The use of RFID can also improve the customer experience. Sibuya, a Japanese men's store, has tagged garment hangers. When a customer removes a garment from the rack, a display begins to show details about the product and recommend accessories for the product. In addition to providing customized advertising, it also tracks the number of times a garment is removed by customers (Liszewski, 2011).

It is expected that the price of RFID tags will continue to decrease to a cent or a fraction of a cent. When the price lowers sufficiently, you might begin to see many other uses of the technology as businesses continue to focus on employee productivity and operational efficiency.

Converging Technologies

Recall the discussion of converging hardware technologies in the previous chapter. Convergence occurs also in networking technologies. Cell phones used to be able to transmit and receive only through a dedicated network of analog or digital transceiver towers. Now many are constructed with dual technologies, so that they can serve both as a "traditional" cell phone and a wireless web phone. When the circuitry detects that the phone is within the range of a hotspot, calling switches to VoIP to save cost.

New home television sets are being designed to connect to cable, satellites, and the Internet, not only alternately, but concurrently. Thus, we will be able to watch a sports game and chat online about it at the same time through the same device, using two different networking technologies. Tablets and smartphones can already function as television sets and phones. For individuals, this means they can carry a single device that will connect them to any type of network, erasing the lines between radio, television, telephone, and Internet surfing. Appliance manufacturers are designing "smart appliances" that interact with their owners, alerting them to issues such as a refrigerator door left open for more than a few minutes, or enabling them to start a dryer remotely. Designers are working on a "smart fridge" that alerts the owner about expiration dates on perishable items (Barclay, 2012). For businesses, converging technologies offer an opportunity to provide new information services and manage a more effective and efficient salesforce.

POINT OF INTEREST | In the Future ...

We have seen cellphones evolve from the size of a briefcase to smaller than the size of a playing card. Their capabilities have expanded to the point where a smartphone may be the only device we need when we leave the house. Users can now talk, text, surf, video chat, email, stream, shop, read, game, tweet, navigate, take photos, and much more. So what's next in technology convergence? What other capabilities can be put in a smartphone to make our lives easier? Look for the screen quality and size to increase to allow users to rely solely on their smartphone to watch their favorite news, sports, weather, and TV shows. And why bring your camera or video camera when your smartphone will be able to take high-quality photos and videos with professional features? Smartphones will continue to add capabilities that will make us more reliant on them because they simplify and augment our busy day-to-day lives.

Source: Miles, S. (2012). What will your next mobile phone look like? Retrieved from http://articles.cnn. com website: http://articles.cnn.com/2012-02-28/tech/tech_mobile_mobile-trends-mwc_1_mobile-phone -qualcomm-phone-makers/2?_s=PM:TECH

Wireless technologies can be combined in the same device to enhance functionality. For example, a portable digital music and video player can use Wi-Fi to communicate with your PC or another Wi-Fi device (possibly another music/video player) to download files. It can then use Bluetooth to transmit the music to your wireless earphones. Local radio stations can broadcast to listeners everywhere over the Internet. With proper software you can then select from the songs to which you have just listened and downloaded to your portable player or home computer.

Currently, RFID technology can be used by your phone to read the electronic code of a product in a store and compare its price to the prices offered online by other retailers. Instead of asking for human help in finding an item in a supermarket, your phone may be able to guide you to the right aisle after it identifies the EPC of the product. And, as is already done in some countries, you will be able to pay for what you purchase by using your phone instead of a credit card.

Summary

- Telecommunications is communication over distance, primarily communication of bits representing many forms of data and information. In the past decade, telecommunications technology has driven the major developments in the dissemination and use of information.

- Telecommunications technology has changed the business environment. Businesspeople are increasingly more mobile; they can use cellular phones for greater availability to their employers and customers, using the phone for both voice and data communications. Videoconferencing brings together people who are thousands of miles apart. Peer-to-peer file sharing enables sharing of research, software code, and artistic works.

- Different media have different bandwidths, meaning that they are capable of carrying different numbers of bits per second (bps) without garbling messages. Wired media include twisted pair, coaxial cable, and optical fiber. Wireless media rely on radio waves, including terrestrial and satellite microwave.

- Networks are classified according to their reach and complexity. When computers are connected locally within an office, a campus, or a home, the arrangement is called a local area network (LAN). A metropolitan area network (MAN) connects LANs within a radius of about 50 kilometers (30 miles). When computers communicate over longer distances, the network is called a wide area network (WAN). Personal area networks (PANs) connect individual devices at short range.

- Although it uses the public Internet, a network can be turned into a virtual private network (VPN) by using advanced security measures.

- Network protocols are sets of rules to which all devices on a network must adhere. Communication on the Internet adheres to a set of protocols called TCP/IP. Ethernet has long been a popular protocol for wired LANs. Wireless protocols offer many opportunities for more people to enjoy Internet links and for mobility while communicating. The most important are the IEEE 802.xx protocols, which include the popular Wi-Fi, Bluetooth, and WiMAX standards.

- Wireless technologies make it easy and affordable to create wireless LANs (WLANs) and hotspots. They allow workers mobility while retrieving information in warehouses and other work environments. They enable airline and retail customers to link to the Internet with portable computers, and make the reading of utility meters much less labor intensive and more accurate.

- Organizations and individuals have a variety of choices when subscribing to networking services. They can choose among digital subscriber line (DSL), cable, T1 and T3 lines, satellite links, fixed wireless service, optical fiber to the premises, optical carriers (OC), and Broadband over Power Lines (BPL).

- As Internet links become faster, Internet telephony, also known as Voice over Internet Protocol (VoIP), is gaining in popularity. Several companies offer the service, which is significantly less expensive than a landline service while providing significant features to create flexibility and employee productivity.

- Wireless technologies support the increasingly popular RFID technologies. RFID supports a variety of noncontact identification and payment mechanisms, from quick toll and gas payment to cattle tracking to sophisticated supply chain management, and many future uses are anticipated. This adoption of this new technology has only begun to influence the processes of distributing, tracking and identifying hard good items. As the technology matures and business innovation develops, RFID will become part of everyday life.

- Much like hardware, telecommunications technologies are merging. The same device can now use several different networks simultaneously, such as cellular telephone networks, the Internet, and television broadcasts.

- Increasing numbers of employees now telecommute. Telecommuting has advantages, but it does not serve some basic human needs, such as socializing during lunch break and the clear separation between work and family obligations.

KIMBALL'S REVISITED

The contractors have installed the network cables to the places that Tyler has specified. Now they need to know what type of outlets to install. Tyler also needs to know what additional equipment and services need to be purchased. The number of server workstations that should be installed needs to be determined, especially if they are considering also using tablets. The restaurant's current use of the Internet and the web is not extremely high. Tyler anticipates that he will need to access the restaurant's webpages for redesign and maintenance as well as general web access for the restaurant for research and purchases. But he also wants to give Wi-Fi access to their customers, and wonders if they should do it now, and how that would affect the cost of equipment and Internet service. He also needs to consider phone equipment for the new location. What are their options?

What Is Your Advice?

1. What type of network equipment would be needed to provide wireless access for the servers' tablets as well as customers' smartphones?

2. Tyler has convinced his father that Internet services are needed for the new location. What options should he consider for Internet access for the new location?

3. What type of connections should Tyler tell the contractors to install for personal computer devices? Do you think they should install such connections? Why or why not?

New Perspectives

1. Should the use of tablets be phased in? Should the traditional workstations be used as backup? Should the workstations be used at the bar only? What advice would you provide to Tyler and Michael?

2. Michael is concerned about the cost of providing Wi-Fi access to customers, and about wireless security for the restaurant's operations. Would it be reasonable to purchase two routers, one for customer access and the other for server tablets?

3. Michael and Tyler discussed the need for a phone system for the new location. Tyler believed that an Internet connection could be used to provide phone service to the restaurant. What are the costs, hardware/software requirements and issues that they should consider?

Key Terms

access point (AP), 197
backbone, 196
bandwidth, 189
bits per second (bps), 189
Bluetooth, 199
bridge, 195
broadband, 189
Broadband over Power Lines (BPL), 192
coaxial cable, 190
dial-up connection, 195
digital subscriber line (DSL), 203
DNS (Domain Name System), 197
downstream, 201
dynamic IP address, 197
EMI (electromagnetic interference), 191
encryption, 198
EPC (Electronic Product Code), 208
Ethernet, 197
Fiber to the Home (FTTH), 204
fixed wireless, 204
Gigabit Ethernet, 197

host, 196
hotspot, 197
IEEE 802.11, 197
Internet service provider (ISP), 194
IP address, 196
local area network (LAN), 193
Long-Term Evolution (LTE), 200
metropolitan area network (MAN), 193
microwaves, 191
modem, 195
near-field communication (NFC), 188
network, 192
network interface card (NIC), 195
node, 192
OC (optical carrier), 204
peer-to-peer (P2P) file sharing, 188
peer-to-peer LAN, 193
personal area network (PAN), 194
protocol, 196
repeater, 195

RFI (radio frequency interference), 191
router, 195
scalability, 193
server, 193
static IP address, 197
switch, 195
T1 and T3 lines, 203
TCP/IP (Transmission Control Protocol/Internet Protocol), 196
telecommunications, 185
transmission rate, 189
twisted pair cable, 190
upstream, 201
value-added network (VAN), 194
videoconferencing, 187
virtual private network (VPN), 195
VoIP (Voice over Internet Protocol), 207
wide area network (WAN), 194
Wi-Fi, 197
WiMAX, 199
wireless LAN (WLAN), 193

Review Questions

1. If all the paths of data communications were visible to the human eye, we might be overwhelmed. Why? Give some examples.

2. What makes one medium capable of greater data communication speed than another?

3. Which medium currently enables the fastest data communications?

4. Repeaters are used on many communication lines. What is their purpose? What does a repeater do?

5. Networking professionals speak of "the last mile." What is "the last mile," and what is its significance?

6. Would an astronomy observatory 20 miles away from a city or town likely be able to get DSL service? Why?

7. What risks to organizations does the growing use of networks pose?

8. What is a virtual private network? Why is it called "virtual"?

9. What is a network protocol?

10. What are the technical advantages of optical fibers over other communications media?

11. The same communication medium can transport three different services. This is true of two media. Which media? What are the three services?

12. What do you believe are the security and privacy issues associated with placing RFID chips in clothing? How would you feel if the RFID chip remained in your clothing while you were wearing it?

13. What is VoIP? If you were a business owner, what factors would you consider to be important in order to switch to VoIP for your phone system?

14. What is BPL? Why is the technology potentially available to almost every home?

15. Explain the notions of WAN, LAN, MAN, and PAN.

16. What are hotspots, and how can they help businesspeople?

17. What is the purpose of municipally provided WiMAX, and why is it in competition with subscriber broadband services?

18. Cellular phones are already wireless. Why should companies be interested in equipping employees with Wi-Fi-enabled mobile phones?

Discussion Questions

19. Wi-Fi is all around us. Is there any downside to its pervasiveness?

20. People express themselves differently when they speak (either face to face or via the telephone) versus when they send and receive email. What are the differences? Which do you prefer when communicating with someone you don't know personally? Which do you prefer when you know the person?

21. Every home with access to the Internet can now inexpensively become a hotspot. How? Are there any risks in turning a home into a hotspot?

22. What are the implications of telecommunications for group work?

23. As broadband services cover larger regions and become less expensive, the number of small businesses and home businesses grows. What is the relationship?

24. Some organizations stopped allocating offices to their sales representatives. Why, and is this a wise move?

25. List and explain the benefits of videoconferencing to an organization. List and explain the benefits to society.

26. Anything that does not take space can be traded solely via telecommunications networks. Do you agree? Explain your answer.

27. Do you see any undesirable effects of humans communicating more and more via computer networks rather than in person or over the telephone? What don't you like and why? What do you like about it?

28. List several jobs in which telecommuting would be infeasible. Explain why.

29. Wi-Fi circuitry is now embedded in consumer electronic devices such as digital cameras and cell phones. Give an example of what you could do with the Wi-Fi capability of a digital camera.

30. If you were given the opportunity to telecommute, would you? Why or why not?

31. Suppose that you are a middle manager. Would you allow the people who report to you to telecommute? Why or why not?

32. As a supervisor, would you be more inclined to promote your telecommuting or nontelecommuting subordinates, or would you be egalitarian? Why?

Applying Concepts

33. James Marachio completed his book, *How to Become a Millionaire Upon Graduation*. He used a word processor to type the manuscript. He saved the book as a file of 8.8 MB. James lives in Charlotte. The publisher asked that he transmit the book via the Internet to the publisher's office in Boston. James can transmit the file at a guaranteed speed of 25 Mbps. Because each packet of data transmitted must also contain some non-data bits, assume the total number of bits to transmit is equivalent to 9 MB.

    How long (in minutes) does it take to transmit the book? Ignore the distance between the cities. Remember how many bytes make up 1 MB. Show your calculations clearly using a spreadsheet. Use measurement units throughout your calculation. Email the spreadsheet file to your professor.

34. You use a cable modem to transmit a report from your office to headquarters. Find a website capable of testing upload and download speed (like *www.speedtest.net*). Since the transmission protocol adds additional bits to data bytes, assume that, on average, there is 1 additional bit for each transmitted byte. On average, a page contains 3,000 characters, including spaces. You are allotted only 3 minutes for the transmission. How many pages can you transmit?

35. Of the residential telecommunications services listed in Figure 6.6, find out which are available where you live and how much they cost. You might find several DSL and cable services, and perhaps also satellite and BPL services. Calculate the ratio of maximum bit rate per dollar (downstream) to monthly fee for each service. Which service provides the "biggest bang for the buck," that is, the greatest speed per dollar of monthly fee?

Hands-On Activities

36. Broadband services provided in Japan, South Korea, and Canada are usually faster and less expensive than in the United States. Use the web to research why this is so. Write a one-page report discussing the reasons.

37. Search the web for a site that enables you to check your high-speed (broadband) link: DSL, cable, Fiber to the Premises, or (if you connect from school) T1 or T3 line. Follow the instructions. Usually, you simply have to click one button. Do so and wait for the response. Print out the response. Wait a minute, and repeat the process. The speeds are likely to be different. Why? Type up the answer, and submit with the two printouts analyzing the speed of your connection.

38. You are a telecommunications guru and love to help individuals and businesses. Assume that dial-up, cable, DSL, T3 line, and satellite links to the Internet are available everywhere unless the particular scenario indicates otherwise. Consider the following scenarios and suggest the best overall type of link (consider communication speed, cost, and any other factor you believe is relevant). Each scenario is independent of the others. For each scenario, explain why you selected the option.

a. An author works at home writing articles for a magazine. Once per week she must transmit an article to her editor. She rarely uses the link for any other purpose.

b. A large company maintains its own website for online catalogs and purchase transactions by its customers. Hundreds of customers visit the sites daily and make purchases.

c. A small business uses the Internet for daily research. Owners have heard that some links are shared by other subscribers in the same area, which might slow down the connection or even pose security threats. Thus, they would like to avoid such a service. They do need a speed of at least 200 Kbps.

d. A farm in New Mexico needs a link of at least 200 Kbps. People on the farm can receive television signals only through antennas. The closest telephone central office is 12 miles away.

e. An Internet service provider specializes in hosting websites of small businesses.

f. A cruise ship wants to provide Internet service to vacationers on the third deck. The ship cruises in the Caribbean. The link's speed must be at least 250 Kbps.

Team Activities

39. Team up with another student in class. Each team member needs to find a person they know who telecommutes and interview them. It could be a parent, family member, friend's parent, or a family friend. Ask them if they were offered telecommuting when they were hired, if not then, when was telecommuting offered? What made them want to telecommute? How often do they telecommute? What technology does their employer make available to them when working from home? Do they still have a permanent workspace at their office? Do they enjoy working from home? Do they miss the office or the people there? Do their colleagues telecommute as well? Ask other questions you believe are pertinent as well.

40. After conducting your respective interviews, download free videoconferencing software. Hold a videoconference with your partner, from separate locations, to compare answers and discuss the pros and cons of telecommuting from an employee standpoint, an employer's standpoint, and whether you would like to telecommute. After your videoconference, separately write a two-page reflection on your experience. Write the first page on the interview on telecommuting, whether you would like to telecommute, and why. Write the second page on your experience with videoconferencing with your partner and the benefits and takeaways of videoconferencing in a professional setting.

Food for Thought and Profit

People need food to survive. However, it is also a commodity. High volume. Razor thin gross margin. Aggressive competition. Food stores can gain market share and profitability with efficient operations and innovative, competent management. That's how Foley Food and Vending survives and also prospers.

A family-owned business based in Norwood, Massachusetts, they began their operations in 1973 and now maintain seven routes managed by its second generation. Similar to the "big players" in the food retail business, the integration of information technology is at the core of their profitability and operating efficiency. However, for a small organization such as Foley, it also allows them to carve out a market to remain competitive.

The company started its business by selling canned soft drinks in vending machines. Over the next six years, the company expanded its product line into snack foods, coffee, and food over three routes. During the 1980s, the business expanded enough that a 10,000 square foot building was needed as a warehouse. Their routes and operations grew through building new accounts as well as acquiring some business from competitors. In the mid-1990s with four routes, the owners decided to invest in vending machine software in order to support their growth. Their original software was developed by Rutherford and Associates. Their DOS-based (the pre-Windows, Disk Operating System for personal computers) software tracked product sales at the vending machine level.

A few years later, another technology company introduced new Windows-based vending machine management software. Streamware, also based in Massachusetts, agreed to an arrangement with Foley to track cash readings and item level sales from vending machines using DEX handheld units. Drivers used the DEX handheld units to transfer data from the vending machines on all of Foley's routes.

The early adoption of this vending machine technology provided the foundation for advanced products. In 2005, Foley implemented Internet-connected vending machines equipped with video touchscreens, named Quickstore24. Their successes with previous technology use allowed Foley to become one of the first to install these new advanced technology vending machines. These machines integrated the use of thumbprints to identify a customer initiating a form of payment for their purchases. In addition, the machines accepted other forms of payment and printed coupons from customers. The real-time reporting provided by these vending machines through network connections with the home office created another opportunity. Foley now could initiate pre-kitting the routes in the warehouse. This process allowed the preparation of accurate and efficient inventory restocking for the route drivers. Management believed that pre-kitting allowed the company to operate more efficiently, especially during the recession in 2008.

The use of Quickstore24 has also helped the company expand into a new model: self-checkout markets. This new business model allows the purchase of a large variety of products in open shelves and refrigeration units. Restocking these markets is much faster and more efficient than stocking vending machines. The self-checkout markets are equipped with a kiosk that allows the customer to scan UPC bar codes for each product they wish to purchase. The kiosk processes the payment for purchases through cash, credit card, or a stored-value card. The kiosk's video touchscreen also displays advertisements and offers promotions including a chance to win market credit.

Source: Maras, E. (2011, May). Foley Food & Vending strikes back hard in Boston with TECHNOLOGY SOLUTIONS. Automatic Merchandiser, 53, 58-60, 62-64.

Thinking About the Case

1. When management said that pre-kitting helped to support more efficient operations and inventory, discuss what you believe they found.

2. The vending machines capable of Internet connectivity are more expensive to purchase and operate for the company. Discuss how the new technology and connectivity benefit the organization.

3. Technology adoption is often called either "leading edge" or "bleeding edge." Do you believe that the pre-Quickstore24 technology implemented by Foley had any benefit to the organization? Or was it an inefficient use of funds and resources?

Networks Take Importance in Health Care

A study by The Leapfrog Group, a Washington, D.C. voluntary organization of healthcare product purchasers, concluded that better information technology could prevent more than 50 percent of erroneous drug prescriptions. IT in general, and networking technologies in particular, could save lives and morbidity in hospitals. Most hospitals have caught up with new networking technologies only in recent years.

Children's Memorial Hospital in Chicago was no exception until recently. The hospital is part of Northwestern University's Feinberg School of Medicine. It is now ranked as the best children's hospital in Illinois and one of the best in the United States. In 2006, the 1,100 pediatric specialists treated over 100,000 patients and had more than 365,000 outpatient visits.

For many years the hospital had a hodgepodge of communications technologies: landline phones, a local network to support cell phones, a wireless surveillance system, pagers, a radio frequency system for tracking the electronic tags that doctors wear, and a variety of patient-monitoring systems. It did not have a way to ensure accurate drug administration, and this was one reason to reconsider the hospital's communication infrastructure.

Often, one signal interfered with another, creating several areas where cell phones and pagers could not function. Structural challenges also presented problems. Hospitals are built from steel floors and many concrete walls. Thick concrete and lead walls are built around radiation rooms. All of these materials weaken radio signals or block them out altogether.

The hospital's Director of IT started to look for a comprehensive solution. This would include not only better communications, but also improved technologies for the bedside staff and computerized drug prescription entry. He preferred a single system that would address their many challenges. After an extensive search, he selected a company called InnerWireless to deploy a broadband system. InnerWireless produces a system it calls Medical-grade Wireless Utility.

The system uses passive wireless, which means that the devices the staff uses activate the networking circuitry. In active wireless, electronic devices must provide electric power to convert radio signals. Passive systems do not need to be powered. Therefore, with Medical-grade Wireless Utility, fewer access points had to be installed and maintained. Other systems would require more access points and still would not totally eliminate dead spots. The InnerWireless system requires few access points but still provides uninterrupted communications throughout the building. The technology also includes a distributed antenna system. This allows the same wireless systems to support cellular phones, pagers, Wi-Fi (IEEE 802.11), two-way radio for facilities management, and first-responder radio for fire, police, and emergency medical teams.

InnerWireless specializes in in-building wireless communication, and has installed its system in several hospitals. It customizes the deployment for every hospital to ensure that communication is available throughout each building. Typically, a wireless router is installed in the basement. From the router a cable is run up through the building's "spine," and a distribution system is located on each floor.

Now, physicians enter drug prescriptions into a database for each patient. The hospital's pharmacy receives the transmitted prescription and prepares the drug, then attaches the proper bar-code to it. Nurses use carts equipped with a small networked computer that is also equipped with a bar-code scanner. On their rounds, before they administer drugs to patients, they scan the bar-code. The data is automatically communicated to the pharmacy database, and the nurse can see if the drug and dosage are the right ones for the patient. Nurses can also use email through the same computers. The error rate of drug administration has decreased significantly.

Electronic medical records (EMRs), wireless devices, and mobile technology have increased the importance of hospital information technology networks. Wi-Fi allows wireless blood pressure cuffs to automatically store and transfer readings to a patient's records. Doctors can then view patient records on their iPads. Radiology images have also migrated from the use of film to electronic imaging. These images can now be stored, viewed, and distributed by medical personnel without having to find the traditional film images.

The reliance on technology networks becomes more imperative. CIO Cathy Bruno from Eastern Main Healthcare Systems says "To have a single unified electronic patient record across all our locations, so that information is available no matter where our patients access are, we need network connectivity." While it reduces the need for traditional hardcopy patient records, it also means that network connectivity must be available without downtimes or reduction in download speeds. The introduction of portable tablets has promoted the need for electronic patient recordkeeping. Medical personnel can now "carry" the technology with them. The availability of wireless medical devices such as blood pressure cuffs, must be able to ID a patient and transmit the data securely and accurately.

Sources: Anonymous. (2007). Children's Memorial Hospital, Chicago. from http://www.childrensmemorial.org; O'Connor, F. (2012). Hospital networks take key role in healthcare. Network World, 29(14), 11-11,16; Pettis, A. (2006). Patient Care Goes Wireless; Children's memorial Hospital, of Chicago, is like many of the facilities that serve the critically ill. eWeek, 23(15), 1-N1,N4.

Thinking About the Case

1. The hospital already had bar-coding before the new networking system was installed. What can be done now that could not be done before to reduce drug administration errors?

2. As the case explains, passive wireless ensures full coverage of communications in an entire building. Why is this so important in hospitals?

3. The new communication network is more than just an Internet hotspot. It supports several modes of communication. What does this mean from a maintenance perspective?

4. The benefits of EMRs are clearly positive for medical facilities. What are the challenges for maintaining patient care records electronically versus the traditional paper hardcopies?

References

Anonymous. (2011a, November 2011). LA Fitness Leverages Microsoft Lync Solution, *Entertainment Close-Up*.

Anonymous. (2011b). VoIP is the Next Wave to Ride On. *Communications Today*.

Anonymous (Producer). (2012a). World's First 5G WiFi 802.11ac SoC. Retrieved from http://www.broadcom.com/docs/press/80211ac_for_Enterprise.pdf

Anonymous. (2012b). What is Isis? Retrieved 12/13/2012, from http://www.paywithisis.com/whatis.xhtml

Anonymous. (2013a). About 3GPP. Retrieved June 14, 2013, from http://www.3gpp.org/About-3GPP

Anonymous. (2013b). LTE Keywords and Acronyms. Retrieved June 13, 2013, from http://www.3gpp.org/Technologies/Keywords-Acronyms/LTE

Barclay, E. (2012). The 'Smart Fridge' Finds The Lost Lettuce, For A Price. *the salt*. http://www.npr.org/blogs/thesalt/2012/05/03/151968878/the-smart-fridge-finds-the-lost-lettuce-for-a-price

Captain, S. (2012). Internet grows by trillions of addresses, as IPV6 rolls out worldwide. *Tech News Daily*. http://www.foxnews.com/tech/2012/06/06/internet-grows-by-trillions-addresses-as-ipv6-rolls-out-worldwide/

Children's Memorial Hospital, Chicago. (2007). from http://www.childrensmemorial.org

Inner Wireless. (2007). Retrieved April 2007, from http://www.innerwireless.com

Leber, J. (2012). A Banking Giant Makes a Mobile Payment Bet. *Technology Review*, 3. Retrieved from MIT Technology Review website: http://www.technologyreview.com/news/428453/a-banking-giant-makes-a-mobile-payment-bet/

Liszewski, A. (2011). RFID Clothing Hangers Sell Harder than Sales Clerks. *Gizmodo*. http://gizmodo.com/5850430/rfid-clothing-hangers-sell-harder-than-sales-clerks

Meinert, D. (2011). Make Telecommuting Pay Off. *HRMagazine*, *56*(6), 33-37.

Napolitano, M. (2012, Apr). RFID surges ahead. *Modern Materials Handling*, *67*, S48-S50.

O'Connor, F. (2012). Hospital networks take key role in healthcare. *Network World*, *29*(14), 11-11,16.

Partida, B. (2012). No Easy Answers on RFID Strategy. *Supply Chain Management Review*, *16*(2), 78-80.

Pettis, A. (2006). Patient Care Goes Wireless; Children's memorial Hospital, of Chicago, is like many of the facilities that serve the critically ill. *eWeek*, *23*(15), 1-N1,N4.

Quick, D. (2010). Transmission speeds of 100Mbps over 1km on existing copper networks. *Gizmag*. http://www.gizmag.com/alcatel-lucent-dsl-phantom-mode/14888/

Read, B. (2011). Continuing the Service. *Customer Inter@ction Solutions*, *30*(4), 18-20.

Todd, D. M. (2012). Plenty of Internet users cling to slow dial-up connections. *Post-Gazette.com*. http://www.post-gazette.com/stories/business/news/plenty-of-internet-users-cling to slow-dial-up-connections-85360/

Wenzel, E. (2011, Jun). VoIP Migration Leads to Savings and Employee Mobility. *PC World*, *29*, 30-30.

Zager, M. (2012). Courting Data Roaming Customers. *Rural Telecommunications*, *31*(5), 25-26,28.

seven

DATABASES AND DATA WAREHOUSES

Learning Objectives

As a professional, you will use databases and likely help design them. Understanding how to organize and use data is a way to gain responsibility and authority in a work environment. Data is usually collected in a way that does not make it immediately useful to professionals. Imagine building a model palace from a pile of building blocks. You have a good idea of what you want to build, but first you have to organize the blocks so it is easy for you to find and select only the blocks you need. Then you can combine them into substructures that eventually are integrated into your model. Similarly, data collected by organizations must be organized and stored so that useful information can be extracted from it in a flexible manner.

When you finish this chapter, you will be able to:

- Explain the difference between traditional file organization and the database approach to managing digital data.

- Explain how relational and object-oriented database management systems are used to construct databases, populate them with data, and manipulate the data to produce information.

- Enumerate the most important features and operations of a relational database, the most popular database model.

- Understand how data modeling and design creates a conceptual blueprint of a database.

- Discuss how databases are used on the web.

- List the operations involved in transferring data from transactional databases to data warehouses.

KIMBALL'S RESTAURANT: An Appetite for Data

Michael and Tyler visited the new location to look at the progress of the renovations. Michael was anxious about the grand opening that was only four weeks away. As they walked around the new location, they inspected the contractors' work. Michael inspected every detail to see if it fulfilled the plans and his requirements. Several times Michael asked, "Is this going to be fixed?" ... "Will this be finished in time?" ... "This does not look right, please fix it."

Tyler sensed his father's nervousness, so he sat down with him at a table overlooking the lake. "Dad, it will all be fine. The renovations are just about done. All we have to do is monitor its progress. The place looks great! Now we need to plan for the day when we open the doors."

Data Is the Main Course...

Tyler talked to his dad about two areas he thought they should focus on now. First, the restaurant needed data to help manage their food inventory and labor. They did not know which menu items were selling and at what levels. The new upgrades to the point-of-sale information system would help to track this data. Having the data, Tyler and Michael could work on reporting and analysis of the information maintained by the system. The system was operating at the current location and generating data. Tyler proposed prototyping some analyses of the current data that they could then use at the new location.

... With a Side of Promotion

The second area that Tyler wanted to focus on was promoting the new location. As they sat at a table overlooking the lake, Tyler said, "Dad, look out that window! What better promotion could we have than that?" He showed Michael some photos of the lake views at the new location. "I know that the renovations are not complete so we can't show interiors, but the lake is not being renovated!" He then showed his father the ads that he had designed with the new software he had purchased. Tyler had a list of each ad, where and when it would be published, as well as the cost. Michael was impressed with the thought and effort that his son had made. Tyler continued, saying that advertising was only one piece of the promotion strategy. Just as you have to have several items on the plate for a balanced meal, the print advertisements needed to be supplemented by other types of promotion, something more active. Tyler knew that the restaurant's current customers would be an "easy" sell and should be rewarded for their loyal patronage.

Tyler said, "Dad, what do you think about offering our current customers a special deal for the grand opening? Here is what I think we can do." He showed Michael a promotional campaign to invite current customers to the new location with an incentive in the next few weeks. However, Michael did not want to give discounts that would either cut deeply into their profits or did not gain the "word of mouth" advertising that was needed. Tyler said he was absolutely right. There had to be a reasonable balance of offering some goodwill to the steady customers that would also help promote the new location. Advertising is expensive, but needs to have a payback to the business. Tyler showed Michael some printed invitations that would be given to customers at the current location. The invitation to "Dine with Us on the Lake" would be given with guest checks to be redeemed over a two-week grand opening period. Capturing the data for marketing and operations would be crucial.

Tyler and Michael both knew that the challenge is always in the details. However, they thought that this initiative was a great step in the right direction. They were excited about implementing some new approaches to managing the restaurant in the new location.

Managing Digital Data

You use your web browser for all kinds of activities from searching for information, to communicating with others, to visiting your favorite online electronics store to search for high-definition television sets. When visiting the electronics store, you enter a price range and screen size. Within a few seconds, the screen is filled with details on available models complete with product photos and specifications. Where did this rich, well-organized information come from? It came from a database. A database management system responded almost instantly to your request.

Businesses collect and dissect data for a multitude of purposes. Digital data can be stored in a variety of ways on different types of media, as discussed in Chapter 4. Data can be stored in what can be called the traditional file format, in which the different pieces of information are not labeled and categorized, but are stored as continuous strings of bytes. The chief advantage of this format is the efficient use of space, but the data is nonetheless difficult to locate and manipulate. By contrast, the database format, in which each piece of data is labeled or categorized, provides a much more powerful information management tool. Data in this format can be easily accessed and manipulated in almost any way desired to create useful information for decision making.

The impact of database technology on business cannot be overstated. Not only has it changed the way almost every industry conducts business, but it has also created an information industry with far-reaching effects on both our business and personal lives. Databases are behind the successful use of automatic teller machines, increased efficiency in retail stores, almost every marketing effort, and the numerous online search engines and web-based businesses. Combined with interactive webpages on the Internet, databases have made an immense contribution to commerce. Without them, there would be no online banking, consumer catalogs, search engines, stock brokerages, or social media. Their impact on business has allowed fewer people to complete larger tasks, and their power has enabled organizations to learn more about us, as consumers, than we might realize. Imagine: every time you enter the address of a website, a special program performs a search in a huge database and matches your request with one of hundreds of millions of addresses. Every time you fill out an online form with details such as your address, phone number, or credit-card number, a program feeds the data into a database, where each item is recorded for further use.

POINT OF INTEREST — Smart Money in 2012 Presidential Election

Data management played a crucial role in the U.S. 2012 Presidential election. President Obama and his campaign strategy team had been collecting and analyzing data for the 2012 election since the 2008 election. One of the key advantages of their data collection was to distill information on the habits for specific demographic groups. Despite being outfunded by rival Mitt Romney, such data allowed Obama and his team to spend their campaign money 'smarter' than Romney and his team. Obama was able to run a more efficient campaign strategy and deliver the right information to the right people. Having access to crucial and well-organized data can be the strategic tool that separates candidates or businesses from their competitors.

Source: Rutenberg, J. (2012). Secret of the Obama Victory? Rerun Watchers, for One Thing, The New York Times. Retrieved from http://www.nytimes.com/2012/11/13/us/politics/obama-data-system-targeted-tv-viewers-for-support.html

In virtually every type of business today, you must understand the power of databases. The approaches to organizing and manipulating data presented in this chapter will help you gain this important knowledge.

WHY YOU SHOULD — Know About Databases

The amount of consumer data collected by direct marketers has increased exponentially, to the point that it is now considered "Big Data." With so much data at hand, it can be difficult to determine what is useful and what is not. As a data manager, you must know what data is necessary and what is not. In order to have data that adds value to your firm, you have to know what questions you want the data to answer—what trends you are looking for or what reports need to be generated. Big Data is useful to users only when they can maneuver in it and obtain desired outputs from it. Of the 500 billion marketing dollars spent each year worldwide, $200 billion are suboptimally invested (Kuehner-Hebert, 2012). Keeping only important data allows you to more easily see what the data is trying to tell you; who your top customers are, what trends you want to base your marketing plan on, or what marketing plan will yield the highest ROI.

You will also be a more productive professional if you know how databases and data warehouses are built and queried, and what types of information can be extracted from them. In any career you choose, you may be called to describe to database designers how data elements relate to each other, how you would like the data to be accessed, and what reports you may need.

The Traditional File Approach

Data can be maintained in one of two ways: the **traditional file approach**—which has no mechanism for tagging, retrieving, and manipulating data—and the **database approach**, which does have this mechanism. To appreciate the benefits of the database approach, you must keep in mind the inconvenience involved in accessing and manipulating data in the traditional file approach: program-data dependency, high data redundancy, and low data integrity.

Figure 7.1 illustrates an example of a human resource file structured in traditional file format.

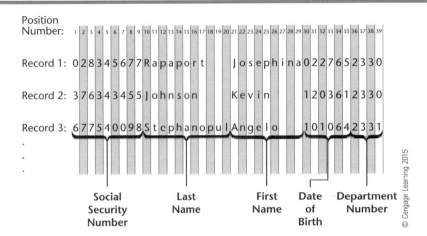

Other challenges with traditional file storage are high data redundancy and low data integrity, because in older file systems files were built, and are still maintained, for the use of specific organizational units. If your last and first name, as well as address and other details, appear in the files of the department where you work as well as in the payroll file of the Human Resource department, data can be duplicated. This **data redundancy** wastes storage space (and, consequently, money) and is inefficient. When corrections or modifications need to be performed, every change has to be made as many times as the number of locations where the data appears, which takes time and might introduce errors. If the same data was entered correctly in one place but incorrectly in another, your record is not only inaccurate, but might appear to represent a different person in each place. Inaccuracies affect **data integrity**—the characteristic that the data represents what it is supposed to represent and that it is complete and correct. Businesses need accurate and complete data in order to make effective decisions, operate efficiently, and provide value to its customers. Often, the traditional file approach to storing data leads to low data integrity. It is difficult to ensure that data is correct in all locations when there are myriads of places to insert data in files, as in the traditional approach.

The Database Approach

In the database approach, data pieces are organized about entities. An **entity** is any object about which an organization chooses to collect data. Entities can be types of people, such as employees, students, or members of fan clubs; events, such as sales transactions, sports events, or theatre shows; or inanimate objects, such as inventoried or for-sale products, buildings, or minerals. In the context of data management, "entity" refers to all the occurrences sharing the same types of data. Therefore, it does not matter if you maintain a record of one student or records of many students; the entity is "student." To understand how data is organized in a database, you must first understand the data hierarchy, described in Figure 7.2, which shows a compilation of information about students: their first names, last names, years of birth, student IDs, majors (department), and campus phone numbers. The smallest piece of data is a **character** (such as a letter in a first or last name, or a digit in a street address). Multiple characters make up a field. A **field** is one piece of information about an entity, such as the last name or first name of a student, or the student's street address. The fields related to the same entity make up a **record**. A collection of related records, such as all the records of a college's students, is called a **file**. Often, several related files must be kept together. A collection of such files is referred to as a database. However, the features of a database can be present even when a database consists of a single file.

FIGURE 7.2

The hierarchy of data

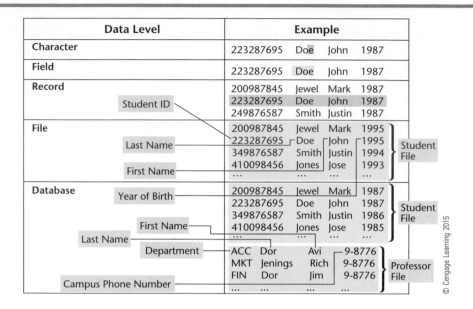

Once the fields are assigned names, including Last Name, First Name, ID, and the like, the data in each field carries a tag—a field name—and can be easily accessed by the field name, no matter where the data is physically stored. One of the greatest strengths of databases is their promotion of application-data independence. In other words, if an application is written to process data in a database, the application designer only needs to know the names of the fields, not their physical organization or their length.

Database fields are not limited to holding text and numbers. They can hold pictures, sounds, video clips, documents, and even spreadsheets. Fields can hold any content that can be digitized. For example, when you shop online, you can search for a product by its product name or code, and then retrieve its picture or a video clip about the product. When you select a video on YouTube, you retrieve a video clip from a database. The video media file itself is a field in the record stored in YouTube's database. The database example shows a real estate property record. The record includes several text fields as well as a picture of a home.

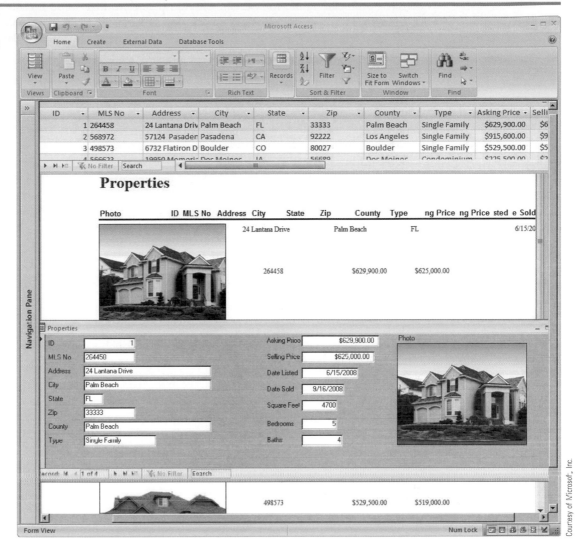

Courtesy of Microsoft, Inc.

While a database itself is a collection of several related files, the program used to build databases, populate them with data, and manipulate the data is called a **database management system (DBMS)**. The files themselves *are* the database, but DBMSs do all the work—structuring files, storing data, and linking records. As described previously, if you wanted to access data from files that were stored in a traditional file approach, you would have to know exactly how many characters were designated for each type of data. A DBMS, however, does much of this work (and a lot of other work) for you.

If you are using a database, you want to be able to move rapidly from one record to another, sort by different criteria, select certain records or fields, create different types of reports, and analyze the data in different ways. Because of these demands, databases are stored on and processed from direct access storage devices, such as magnetic disks or DVDs. They can be backed up to sequential storage devices such as magnetic or optical tapes, but cannot be efficiently processed off such media because it would take too long to access the records. Note that storing databases on any device that is non-writable, such as non-rewritable CDs or DVDs, may be suitable for a static database, such as a parts list used by car repair shops, but is unsuitable for a database that must be updated.

Gathering Organizational Data

Many business professionals consider assets in a financial or accounting context. A building is an asset that has a specific financial value. However, until recently, many business professionals did not view data as an asset because they could not assess or understand its value. While data does not have financial value, its use can provide organizational value for the decisions, strategies, and operations of a business. Data does not "magically" appear in corporate databases. There are several sources and methods that can be used to populate organizational databases:

- As outlined in Chapter 1, transaction processing systems record the basic activities of a business operation such as sales, payroll, expenses, and inventory. The data stored from these transactions provide context to both operational and strategic decisions for the organization.
- Source data input devices, discussed in Chapter 4, provide an accurate, efficient, and consistent approach to gathering data for storage. Hardware devices such as scanning and RFID provide the input to transaction processes.
- In the early days of information technology, all data was entered and gathered within the physical buildings of the business. Personnel entered data directly through internal systems such as payroll or order entry. However, the web and mobile revolution have created additional sources and methods of transacting business with the organization's stakeholders (suppliers, customers, etc.). Therefore, the information processed and stored by activities from these sources is a significant component of an organization's data infrastructure.
- External data can be purchased and stored by a business for use in its operations. Some examples of this category are credit reports, census data, or supplier information. For example, credit report information purchased from a credit agency can be stored in a bank's loan record for historical purposes.
- In recent years, nonoperational transaction data has increased significantly with the use of social media by businesses. This data, from sources such as Facebook and Twitter, can be gathered and analyzed to determine consumer behavior trends and patterns.

The source and storage of data for corporate databases is clearly a non-financial asset of a business. It is an important component of managing operations and strategy for an efficient and profitable business entity.

Queries and Reports

Data is accessed in a database by sending messages called **queries**, which request data from specific records and/or fields and direct the computer to display the results. Queries are also entered to manipulate data, including adding, deleting, and updating data. Queries can also support sorting the order of the records. Usually, the same software that is used to construct and populate the database, that is, the DBMS, is also used to present queries. Modern DBMSs provide fairly user-friendly means of querying a database.

DBMSs are usually bundled with a programming language or report generation module. Programmers can use this module to develop applications that facilitate queries and produce predesigned reports. Nontechnical personnel can use report generation software tools to develop ad-hoc reports based on their individual requirements. Reports that include data from organizational databases are an integral component to managing business operations. Various types of reports can provide data in a format and structure to assist management. For example, summary reporting can provide higher-level information showing the total sales by customer or sales representative. The detail sales transactions are omitted to focus on the activity by a particular group (customer, sales representative, or product). Alternatively, management can use exception reports to extract only those transactions and activities that are outside specified boundaries or norms. For example, a budget manager may want to see all expense accounts that have spent more than the budget allocation.

Security

The use of databases raises security and privacy issues. The fact that data is stored only once in a database for several different purposes does not mean that everyone with access to that database should have access to *all* the data in it. Restricting access is managed by customizing menus for different users and requiring users to enter codes that limit access to certain fields or records. As a result, users have different *views* of the database, as abstractly illustrated in Figure 7.3. The ability to limit users' views to only specific columns or records gives the **database administrator (DBA)** another advantage: the ability to implement security measures.

The measures are implemented once for the database, rather than multiple times for different files. For instance, in the database shown in Figure 7.4, while a human resource manager has access to all fields of the employee file (represented by the top table), the payroll personnel have access only to four fields of the employee file (middle part of the figure), and a project manager has access only to the Name and Hours Worked fields. Views can be limited to certain fields in a database, or certain records, or a combination of both. We discuss security issues in detail in Chapter 14, "Risks, Security, and Disaster Recovery."

FIGURE 7.3

Using database views, users may have different structural pictures of a database

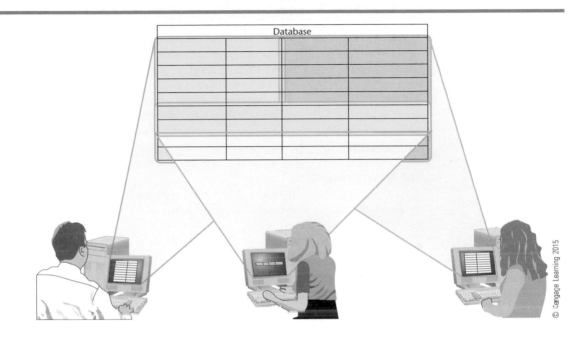

© Cengage Learning 2015

FIGURE 7.4

Different views from the same database

View of Human Resource Manager						
Hourly Rate	SSN	Name	D.O.B.	Hire Date	Marital Status	Benefits Code

View of Payroll Personnel			
SSN	Hourly Rate	Benefits Code	Hours Worked

View of Project Manager	
Name	Hours Worked

© Cengage Learning 2015

Backup and Recovery

Businesses must strive to maintain continuous and uninterrupted operations in order to serve their stakeholders (customers and suppliers) and preserve their financial well-being. With the increased reliance on information technology in businesses, the continuity of a business's technology infrastructure is a crucial factor for its operational activities. Imagine an airline's reservation system failing to operate due to a hardware malfunction accessing its databases. The entire operation would grind to a halt without the ability to reserve flights, check on flight status, or conduct boarding activities at airport gates. On a different scale, a clerk in a manufacturing company might accidentally delete some customers in its database. The need to create data backups and redundant storage of transactions in the event of a disruption in technology is required to resume and continue business activities. Several topics associated with technology continuity planning are covered in Chapter 14, "Risks, Security, and Disaster Recovery."

Database Models

A *database model* is the general logical structure in which records are stored within a database and the method used to establish relationships among the records. The several database models differ in the manner in which records are linked to each other, which in turn dictates the manner in which a user can navigate the database, retrieve desired records, and create reports. The oldest models, the hierarchical and network models, are still used in some databases that were built in the 1970s and 1980s, but are no longer used in newly constructed databases. Virtually all new databases are designed following the relational and object-oriented models.

The Relational Model

The **relational database model** consists of **tables**. Its roots are in relational algebra, but you do not have to know relational algebra to build and use relational databases. However, database experts still use relational algebra terminology: in a relational database, a record or row is called a *tuple*, a field—often referred to as a column—is called an *attribute*, and a table of records is called a *relation*. This text uses the simpler terms, as do the popular software packages: fields, records, and tables.

To design a relational database, you need a clear idea of the different entities and how they relate. For example, in a database for a book rental business, the entities might be Customer, Book, Rental, and Publisher. A single table is built for each entity (though each table can contain from only a few to potentially millions of records). Rental is an associative entity; you can see in Figure 7.5 that the Rental table associates data from the Customer and Book tables.

FIGURE 7.5

A structural representation of a relational database

Customer Table

CustID	CustName	CustPhone	CustAddr
33091	Jim Marasco	322-4907	121 Presidents Rd
35999	Marcia Belvadere	322-5577	32 Parentes Bl
36003	Betsy McCarthy	342-0071	9 Barrington St
36025	Rick Green	322-7299	84 Shopping Pl

Primary key

Composite primary key

Rental Table

CustID	BookID	Date Rented	Rental Cost	Date Returned
33091	456-3X	1/15/2013	50	
35999	632-7W	1/19/2013	55	
35999	854-4E	1/19/2013	45	
36003	854-4E	1/4/2013	45	
36025	115-5G	9/3/2012	60	12/19/2012

Part of composite key in Rental relates to the primary key in Book

Book Table

BookID	Title	PubID	Edition
115-5G	Marketing Research	412	1
747-8T	Investment Strategies	254	4
456-3X	IT Project Management	254	6
632-7W	Database Mgmt Concepts	254	7
854-4E	Business Communication	129	10

Primary key in Publisher relates to the foreign key in Book

Publisher Table

PubID	Pub Name	City
129	Alpha	Chicago
254	Cengage	Boston
412	Forrest	New York

© Cengage Learning 2015

Maintenance of a relational database is relatively easy because each table is independent of the others, although some tables are related to others. To add a customer record, the user accesses the Customer table. To delete a record of a Book, the user accesses the Book table. The advantages of this model make relational database management systems the most popular in the software market. Virtually all DBMSs currently on the market accommodate the relational model. This model is used in supply chain management (SCM) systems and many other enterprise applications as well as local, individual ISs.

To retrieve records from a relational database, or to sort them, you must use a *key*. A key is a field whose values identify records either for display or for processing. You can use any field as a key. For example, you could query the database for the record of Jim Marasco from the Customer table by using the CustName field as a key. That is, you enter a query, a condition that instructs the DBMS to retrieve a record with the value of CustName as "Jim Marasco." A key is *unique* if each value (content) in that field appears only in one record. Sometimes a key is composed of several fields, so that their combination provides a unique key.

As you can see, database design requires careful forethought. The designer must include fields for foreign keys from other tables so that join tables can be created in the future. A **join table** combines data from two or more tables. A table might include foreign keys from several tables, offering flexibility in creating reports with related data from several tables. The inclusion of foreign keys might cause considerable data redundancy. This complexity has not diminished the popularity of relational databases, however.

If a database has more than one record with "Jim Marasco" (because several customers happen to have that same name) in the CustName field, you might not retrieve the single record you desire. Depending on the application you use for the query, you might receive the first one that meets the condition, that is, a list of all the records with that value in the field. The only way to be sure you are retrieving the desired record is to use a unique key, such as a Social Security number, an employee ID, or, in our example, a customer ID (CustID). A unique key can serve as a **primary key**. A primary key is the field by which records in a table are uniquely identified. If your query specified that you wanted the record whose CustID value is 36003, the system would retrieve the record of Betsy McCarthy. It will be the Betsy McCarthy you wanted, even if there are more records of people with exactly the same name. Because the purpose of a primary key is to uniquely identify a record, each record must have a unique value in that field.

Usually, a table in a relational database must have a primary key, and most relational DBMSs enforce this rule; if the designer does not designate a field as a key, the DBMS creates its own serial number field as the primary key field for the table. Once the designer of the table determines the primary key when constructing the records' format, the DBMS does not allow a user to enter two records with the same value in that column. Note that there might be situations in which more than one field can be used as a primary key. Such is the case with motor vehicles, because three different fields can uniquely identify the record of a particular vehicle: the vehicle identification number (VIN), its title number, and its state license plate number. Thus, a database designer might establish one of these fields as a primary key to retrieve records.

For some business needs you must use a **composite key**, a combination of two or more fields that together serve as a primary key, because it is impractical to use a single field as a primary key. For example, consider flight records of a commercial airline. Flights of a certain route are the same every week or every day they are offered, so the daily FlySousa Airlines' flight from Boston to Honolulu—FS5025—for instance, cannot serve us well to retrieve a list of all the passengers who took this flight on May 3, 2013. However, we can use the combination of the flight number *and* date as a composite primary key. To check who sat in a particular seat, a composite key consisting of three fields is needed: flight number, date, and seat number.

To link records from one table with records of another table, the tables must have at least one field in common (i.e., one column in each table must contain the same type of data), and that field must be a primary key field for one of the tables. This repeated field is a primary key in one table, and a **foreign key** field in the other table. In the Book Rental example, if you will ever want to create a report showing the name of every distributor and all the books from that publisher, the primary key of the Publisher table, PubID, must also be included as a foreign key in the Book table. The resultant table (Figure 7.6) is a join table. Note that although PubID was used to create the join table, it does not have to be displayed in the join table, even though it could be.

FIGURE **7.6**

A representation of a join table from the Book and Publisher tables

Publisher	BookID	Title	Edition
Cengage	456-3X	IT Project Management	6
Alpha	854-4E	Business Communication	10
Cengage	747-8T	Investment Strategies	4
Forrest	115-5G	Marketing Research	1
Cengage	632-7W	Database Mgmt Concepts	7

© Cengage Learning 2015

Since the relationships between tables are created as part of manipulating the table, the relational model supports both one-to-many and many-to-many relationships between records of different tables. For example, a **one-to-many relationship** is created when a group of employees belongs to only one department. All would have the same department number as a foreign key in their records, and none will have more than one department key. There is *one* department, linked to *many* employees. A **many-to-many relationship** can be maintained, for instance, for professors and students in a college database. A professor might have many students, and a student might have many professors. This can be accomplished by creating a composite key of professor ID and student ID. In our example of the Book Rental store, there is a many-to-many relationship between customers and the books they have rented. The Rental table enables the bookstore manager to create a history report of customers and their rentals. It is clear that more than one customer has rented a certain book, and the same customer has rented many different books.

According to Gartner Research, the major vendors of relational DBMSs (RDBMSs) are Oracle, IBM, and Microsoft, with worldwide 2011 market share in licensing revenues of about one-half, one-fifth, and one-fifth, respectively (Fontecchio, 2012). IBM licenses DB2, Oracle licenses DBMSs by the company name, and Microsoft licenses SQL Server and Access. MySQL is the world's most popular open source DBMS (Bridgwater, 2012). MySQL is used by Facebook, Google, and Adobe to support their high-transaction volume websites. These DBMSs are an essential part of enterprise applications such as SCM and CRM systems.

The Object-Oriented Model

The **object-oriented database model** uses the object-oriented approach, described in Chapter 5, "Business Software," to maintaining records. In object-oriented technology, an object consists of both data and the procedures that manipulate the data. So, in addition to the attributes of an entity, an object also contains relationships with other entities and procedures to manipulate the data. The combined storage of both data and the procedures that manipulate them is referred to as **encapsulation**. Through encapsulation, an object can be "planted" in different data sets. The ability in object-oriented structures to create a new object automatically by replicating all or some of the characteristics of a previously developed object (called the parent object) is called **inheritance**. Figure 7.7 demonstrates how the same data maintained in a relational database at the DVD rental store would be stored and used in an object-oriented database. The relationships between data about entities are not managed by way of foreign keys, but through the relationships of one object with another. One advantage of this approach is the reduction of data redundancy.

FIGURE 7.7

An object-oriented database

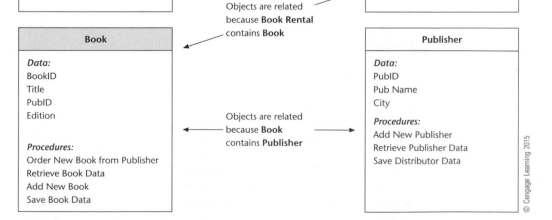

Some data and information cannot be organized as fields, but they can be handled as objects, such as drawings, maps, and webpages. All these capabilities make object-oriented DBMSs, also called object database management systems (ODBMSs) handy in computer-aided design (CAD), geographic information systems, and applications used to update thousands of webpages daily, because they can handle a wide range of data—such as graphics, voice, and text—more easily than the relational model.

Similar to relational DBMSs, ODBMSs provide a graphical user interface (GUI) to manage the DBMS. The user can choose objects from "classes," which are groups of objects that share similar characteristics. Elements of ODBMSs are often incorporated into relational databases, and such databases are sometimes known as *object-relational databases*.

Object-oriented databases (ODBs) do not store records, but data objects, which is an advantage for quick updates of data sets and the relationships among them. For instance, in the example of the DVD store, in the ODB the relationship between a DVD and its distributor is not established through a foreign key; it exists because the DVD class contains the Distributor class. However, object-oriented databases also have some disadvantages, compared with relational databases. For example, there is dependence between applications and data; they are simply "wrapped" together. Changing the structures of tables in a relational database does not require changes in applications that use the data in those tables, while it would require changes in applications in an object-oriented database. This dependence also limits the ability to enter *ad hoc* queries in an ODB, that is, to enter queries at will. While not as popular or as well understood as relational databases, ODBs are gaining adopters.

Several software companies have developed popular ODBMSs. Among them are Objectivity/DB (Objectivity, Inc.), ObjectStore (Versata), and Versant Object Database (Versant Corporation).

Relational Operations

As mentioned before, the most popular DBMSs are those that support the relational model. Therefore, you would benefit from becoming familiar with a widely used relational database, such as Access, Oracle, or SQL Server. To use the database, you should know how relational operations work. A **relational operation** creates a temporary table that is a subset of the original table or tables. It allows you to create a report containing records that satisfy a condition, create a list with only some fields about an entity, or produce a report from a join table, which combines relevant data from two or more tables. If so desired, the user can save the newly created table. Often, the temporary table is needed only for *ad hoc* reporting and is immediately discarded.

The three most important relational operations are *select*, *project*, and *join*. Select is the selection of records that meet certain conditions. For example, a human resources manager might need a report showing the entire record of every employee whose salary exceeds $60,000. *Project* is the selection of certain columns from a table, such as the salaries of all the employees. A query might specify a combination of selection and projection. In the preceding example, the manager might require only the ID number, last name (project), and salary of employees whose salaries are greater than $60,000 (select).

One of the most useful manipulations of a relational database is the creation of a new table from two or more other tables. As you might recall from our discussion of the relational model, the joining of data from multiple tables is called a *join*. We have already used a simple example from the book rental database (Figure 7.6). However, join queries can be much more complex. For example, a relational business database might have four tables: SalesRep, Catalog, Order, and Customer. A sales manager might wish to create a report showing, for each sales rep, a list of all customers who purchased anything last month, the items each customer purchased, and the total amount spent by each customer. The new table is created from a relational operation that draws data from all four tables.

The join operation is a powerful manipulation that can create very useful reports for decision making. A join table is created "on the fly" as a result of a query and exists only for the duration the user wishes to view it or to create a paper report from it. Design features allow the user to change the field headings (although the field names are kept the same in the internal table), place the output in different layouts on the screen or paper, and add graphics and text to the report. The new table might be saved as an additional table in the database.

Structured Query Language

Structured Query Language (SQL) has become the query language of choice for many developers of relational DBMSs. SQL is an international standard and is provided with most relational database management programs. Its strength is in its easy-to-remember intuitive commands. For example, assume the name of the entire database is DVD_Store. To create a list of all titles of thriller DVDs whose rental price is less than $5.00, the query would be:

```
SELECT TITLE, CATEGORY FROM DVD_STORE
WHERE CATEGORY 'Thriller' and RENTPRICE < 5
```

Statements like this can be used for *ad hoc* queries or integrated in a program that is saved for repeated use. Commands for updating the database are also easy to remember: INSERT, DELETE, and UPDATE.

Integrating SQL in a DBMS offers several advantages:

- With a standard language, users do not have to learn different sets of commands to create and manipulate databases in different DBMSs.
- SQL statements can be embedded in widely used programming languages such as COBOL or C and object-oriented languages such as C++ or Java, in which case these languages are called the "host language." The combination of highly tailored and efficient statements with SQL statements increases the efficiency and effectiveness of applications accessing relational databases.
- Because SQL statements are portable from one operating system to another, the programmer is not forced to rewrite statements.

Some relational DBMSs, such as Microsoft Access, provide GUIs to create SQL queries; SQL queries can be placed by clicking icons and selecting menu items, which are internally converted into SQL queries and executed. This capability allows relatively inexperienced database designers to use SQL.

The Schema and Metadata

When building a new database, users must first build a schema (from the Greek word for "plan"). The **schema** describes the structure of the database being designed: the names and types of fields in each record type and the general relationships among different sets of records or files. It includes a description of the database's structure, the names and sizes of fields, and details such as which field is a primary key. The number of records is never specified because it might change, and the maximum number of records is determined by the capacity of the storage media.

Fields can hold different types of data: numeric, alphanumeric, graphic, or time-related. Numeric fields hold numbers that can be manipulated by addition, multiplication, averaging, and the like. Alphanumeric fields hold textual values: words, numerals, and special symbols, which make up names, addresses, and identification numbers. Numerals entered in alphanumeric fields, such as Social Security numbers or zip codes, cannot be manipulated mathematically. The builder of a new database must also indicate which fields are to be used as primary keys. Many DBMSs also allow a builder to positively indicate when a field is not unique, meaning that the value in that field might be the same for more than one record.

Figure 7.8 presents the schema of a database table created with the Microsoft Access DBMS. The user is prompted to enter the names and types of fields. Access lets the user name the fields and determine the data types. The Description section allows the designer to describe the nature and function of the fields for people who maintain the database. In the lower part of the window the user is offered many options for each field, such as field size, format, and so on. In Access the primary key field is indicated by a little key icon to its left.

FIGURE 7.8

A schema of the Employee table in an Access 2010 database. The Field Properties area on the bottom shows the properties of the attribute (field) EmployeeID

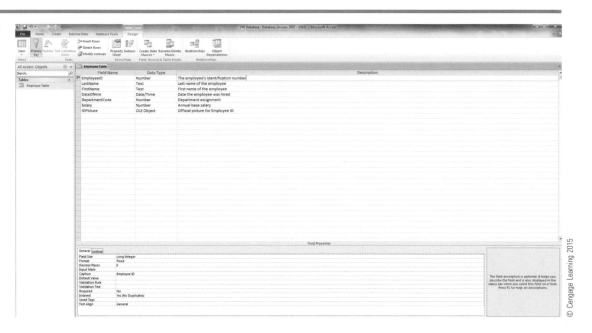

© Cengage Learning 2015

The description of each table structure and types of fields become part of a **data dictionary**, which is a repository of information about the data and their organization. Designers usually add more information about each field, such as where the data comes from (such as another system or entered manually); who owns the original data; who is allowed to add, delete, or update data in the field; and other details that help DBAs maintain the database and understand the meaning of the fields and their relationships. (Some people prefer to call this **metadata**, meaning "data about the data.") Metadata includes:

- The source of the data, including contact information.
- Tables that are related to the data.
- Field and index information, such as the size and type of the field (e.g., whether it is text or numeric), and the ways the data is sorted.
- Programs and processes that use the data.
- Population rules: what is inserted, or updated, and how often.

Databases must be carefully planned and designed to meet business goals. How they are designed enables or limits flexibility in use. Analyzing an organization's data and identifying the relationships among the data is called **data modeling**. Data modeling should first be done to decide which data should be collected and how it should be organized. Thus, data modeling should be proactive. Creating data models periodically is a good practice; it provides decision makers a clear picture of what data is available for reports, and what data the organization might need to start collecting for improved decision making. Managers can then ask experts to change the relationships and design new reports or applications that generate desired reports with a few keystrokes.

Many business databases consist of multiple tables with relationships among them. For example, a hospital might use a database that has a table holding the records of all its physicians, another one with all its nurses, another with all the current patients, and so on. The administrative staff must be able to create reports that link data from multiple tables. For example, one report might be about a doctor and all her patients during a certain period. Another might revolve around a patient, such as details of the patient, a list of all caregivers who were involved in his rehabilitation, and a list of medications. Thus, the database must be carefully planned to allow useful data manipulation and report generation.

Effective data modeling and design of each database involves the creation of a conceptual blueprint of the database. Such a blueprint is called an **entity relationship diagram (ERD)**. An ERD is a graphical representation of all entity relationships, an example of which is shown in Figure 7.9, and they are often consulted to determine a problem with a query or to implement changes. ERDs are a main tool for communication not only among professional DB designers, but also among users and between users and designers. Therefore it is important that professionals in all of these fields know how to create and read them.

FIGURE 7.9

An entity relationship diagram (ERD)

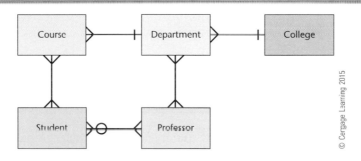

© Cengage Learning 2015

In an ERD, boxes are used to identify entities. Lines are used to indicate a relationship between entities. When lines shaped like crow's-feet are pointing to an object, there might be many instances of that object. When a link with a crow's-foot also includes a crossbar, then all instances of the object on the side of the crow's-foot are linked with a single instance of the object on the side of the crossbar. A second crossbar would denote "mandatory," which means that the relationship must occur, such as between a book title and author: a book title must have an author with which it is associated. A circle close to the box denotes "optional."

- In Figure 7.9, the crow's-foot on the Department end of the Department/College relationship indicates that there are several departments in one college, indicating a one-to-many relationship between College and Department. In addition, the crossbar at the College end of the College/Department link indicates that a department belongs to only one college.

- A department has many professors, but a professor might belong to more than one department; thus, the relationship between Professor and Department is many-to-many, represented by the crow's-feet at both ends of the link.

- A course is offered by a single department, indicated by the crossbar at the Department end of the Department/Course link.

- A professor might teach more than one student, and a student might have more than one professor, thus the crow's-feet at both the Professor and Student ends of the many-to-many relationship between Professor and Student.

- However, the circle at the Student end indicates that a professor does not have to have students at all. The circle means "optional," and is there for cases in which professors do not teach.

A diagram such as Figure 7.9 provides an initial ERD. The designers must also detail the fields of each object, which determines the fields for each record of that object. The attributes are listed in each object box, and the primary key attribute is underlined. Usually, the primary key field appears at the top of the field list in the box. Figure 7.10 is an example of possible attributes of a Professor entity. Database designers can use different notations; therefore, before you review an ER diagram, be sure you understand what each symbol means.

FIGURE 7.10

Fields of the Professor
entity

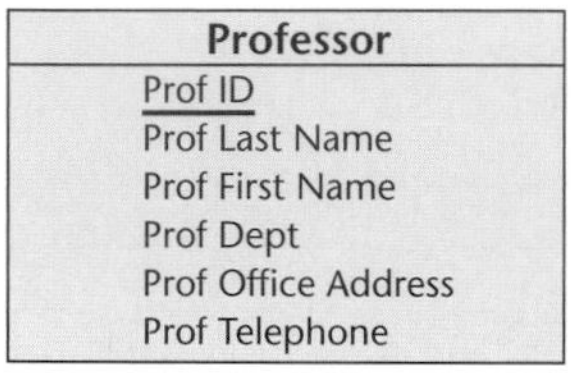

Professor
Prof ID
Prof Last Name
Prof First Name
Prof Dept
Prof Office Address
Prof Telephone

© Cengage Learning 2015

The examples given here are fairly simple. In reality, the reports that managers need to generate can be quite complex in terms of relationships among different data elements and the number of different tables from which they are assembled. Imagine the relationships among data maintained in libraries: a patron might borrow several titles; the library maintains several copies of each title; a title might be a book, a CD, DVD, or a media file; several authors might have published different books with the same title; librarians must be able to see availability and borrowed items by title, by author, and by patron; they should also be able to produce a history report of all the borrowing of each patron for a certain period of time; and so on. All of these relationships and the various needs for reports must be taken into account when designing the database.

Databases on the Web

The Internet and its user-friendly web would be practically useless if people could not access databases online. The premise of the web is that people can not only browse appealing webpages but also search for and find information. Most often, that information is stored in databases. When a shopper accesses an online store, he or she can look for information about any of thousands, or hundreds of thousands, of items offered for sale. For example, when you access websites such as Wal-Mart, Target, or Amazon, you can receive database information (such as an image of an electronics item, video, price, shipping time, and consumer evaluations) for hundreds of items offered for sale. Entering a keyword at YouTube results in a list of all video clips whose title or descriptive text contains the keyword. Many wholesalers make their catalogs available online. Applications at auction sites receive inquiries by category, price range, country of origin, color, date, and other attributes, and identify records of matching items, which often include pictures and detailed descriptions.

Behind each of these sites is a database. The only way for organizations to conduct these web-based businesses is to give people outside the organizations access to their databases. In other words, the organizations must link their databases to the Internet. The database provides a dynamic and organized collection of products and information to "report" back to the customer.

The Amazon.com webpage shown here, for example, displays several tablet products based on the customer's search criteria. The left of the webpage shows additional criteria (display size, operating system, etc.) that customers can select to further refine their searches.

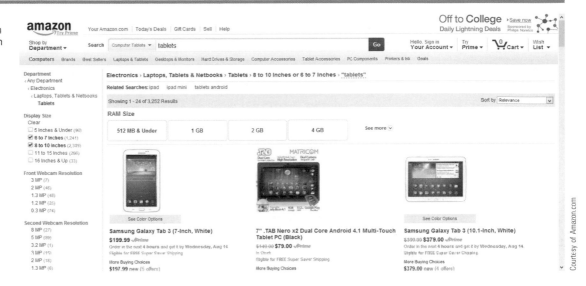

From a technical point of view, online databases that are used with web browsers are no different from other databases. However, they require an interface designed to work with the web. The user must see a form in which to enter queries or keywords to obtain information from the site's database. The interface designers must provide a mechanism to figure out data that users insert in the online forms so that they can be placed in the proper fields in the database. The system also needs a mechanism to pass queries and keywords from the user to the database. The interfaces can be programmed in one of several web programming languages, including Java servlets, active server pages (ASP), ASP.NET (the version of ASP processes within the .NET framework) and PHP (Hypertext Preprocessor), as well as by using web APIs (application program interfaces). The technical aspects of these applications are beyond the scope of this book. The process is diagrammed in Figure 7.11.

FIGURE 7.11

An example of how Active Server Page technology enables data queries and processing via the web

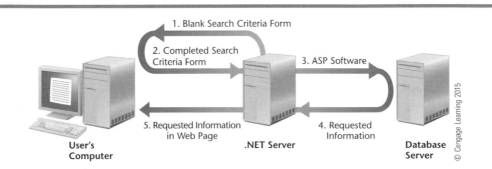

To ensure that their production databases are not vulnerable to attack via the Internet, organizations avoid linking their transaction databases to the Internet unless the databases are dedicated to online transactions, in which case the organization must apply proper security software through firewalls and authentication rules. Many organizational databases are used for online, web- and mobile-based transactions to ensure all transactions are processed and centralized in one database source. For example, a hotel must update the same reservation database regardless of whether it is processed through the web, mobile smartphone, or a customer service representative. They must also be careful when linking a data warehouse (discussed next) to the Internet.

Data Warehousing

The great majority of data collections in business are used for daily transactions and operations: records of customers and their purchases and information on employees, patients, and other parties for monitoring, collection, payment, and other business or legal purposes. The transactions do not stay in these databases long; usually only a few days or weeks. However, many organizations have found that if they accumulate transaction data, they can use it for important management decisions, such as researching market trends or tracking down fraud. Organizing and storing data for such purposes is called data warehousing.

A **data warehouse** is a large, typically relational, database that supports management decision making. The data warehouse is large because it contains data, or summaries of data, from millions of transactions over many years and/or from national or global transactions rather than from a short period or a single region. It might maintain records of individual transactions or summaries of transactions for predetermined periods, such as hourly, daily, or weekly. The purpose of data warehouses is to let managers produce reports or analyze large amounts of archival data and make decisions. Data-warehousing experts must be familiar with the types of business analyses that will be done with the data. They also have to design the data warehouse tables to be flexible enough for modifications in years to come, when business activities change or when different information must be extracted.

Data warehouses do not replace transactional databases, which are updated with daily transactions such as sales, billing, cash receipts, and returns. Instead, transactional data is copied into the data warehouse, which is a separate data repository. This large archive contains valuable information for the organization that might not be evident in the smaller amounts of data typically stored in transactional databases. For example, an insurance company might keep monthly tables of policy sales; it can then see trends in the types of policies customers prefer in general or by age group. Such trends are meaningful only if they are gleaned from data collected over several years. Data from transactional databases are added to the data warehouse at the end of each business day, week, or month, or it might be added automatically as soon as a transaction is recorded in a transactional database. While a transactional database contains current data, which is disposed of after some time, the data in data warehouses is accumulated and might reflect many years of business activities.

Organizations often set up their data warehouse as a collection of **data marts**, smaller collections of data that focus on a particular subject or department. If data marts need to be used as one large data warehouse, special software tools can unify data marts and make them appear as one large data warehouse.

From Database to Data Warehouse

Unlike data warehouses, transactional databases are usually not suitable for business analysis because they contain only current, not historical, data. Often, data in transactional databases are also scattered in different systems throughout an organization. The same data can be stored differently and under other names. For example, customer names might be recorded in a column called Name in one table and in two columns—First Name and Last Name—in another table. These discrepancies commonly occur when an organization uses both its own data and data it purchases from other organizations, or if it has developed more than one database that contains the same data under a different label. When management decides to build a data warehouse, the IT staff must carefully consider the hardware, software, and data involved in the effort.

The widespread use of database management systems coupled with web technologies allows organizations to collect, maintain, and sell vast amounts of private personal data fast and cheaply. Millions of credit-card transactions take place in the world, each consisting of private information. Millions of personal data items are routed daily to corporate databases through sales calls and credit checks. Millions of consumer records are collected and updated daily on the web. For businesses, such data is an important resource. But for individuals, such large data pools and the ways they are used threaten a fundamental human right: privacy.

- **Out of Hand—Out of Control.** You have just received a letter from John Doe Investments. In the letter, the president tells you that at your age, with a nice income like yours, the company could provide you with innovative investment services. How did the company know about your existence? About your annual income? Could it be that some time ago you applied for a credit card? The company receiving the information sold part of it, or all of it, to John Doe Investments. You now enjoy your credit card, but you paid a hidden cost for it.

- **The Web: A Source of Data Collection.** In the preceding example, you were at least aware that you gave somebody information. But many consumers provide information routinely without being aware of it. A huge amount of personal data is collected through the web. You might wonder why the home pages of so many websites ask you to register with them. When registering, you often provide your name, address, and other details. The site asks you to create a user ID and password. If the pages you are accessing contain private data such as your investment portfolio, a user ID and password protect you, but if you are accessing news or other non-personal pages, a user ID and password actually serve the site operator. From the moment you log on to the site, the server can collect data about every move you make: which pages you are visiting and for how long, which icons you click and in which order, and which advertising banners you click. In many cases, the organization that collects the data doesn't even own the site. The site owner hires a business such as DoubleClick, FastClick, and Avenue A to collect data. When you click an advertisement, that information is channeled into one of these organization's huge databases. What does the firm do with the database? It sells parts of it to other companies, or it slices and dices the information to help other companies target potential buyers belonging to certain demographic groups. And, no, it does not bother to tell you. While the software of such companies as DoubleClick can only identify the computer or IP number from which you logged on to a site and not you, personally, the information can be matched with you, personally, if you also use your personal ID and password.

In addition to web cookies, companies also use web bugs to track our web movements. A web bug, also known as a "web beacon" or "clear GIF," is a graphic image on a website used to monitor a surfer's activity. The image is usually undetectable because it usually consists of a single pixel. The bug links the webpage to the web server of a third party, such as DoubleClick. Much as other ads appear on a page you view from a server different from the site you accessed, a web bug comes from a different server, the server of a third party. This happens because the original site's page contains code that calls the bug (the same way as some ads) from the other server. The same technique is used in email. The third party's server obtains the URL (web address) of the user as well as the URL of the site from which the user views the page. As long as the bug is "displayed" by the user's computer, the third-party server can request session information from the user's web browser. Session information includes clickstream and other activities performed by the user while visiting the site.

- **Sharing What We Watch**. A 2012 bill passed by the U.S. House of Representatives enabled users of websites like Netflix to share information about what movies and shows they watch with their friends on social media sites like Facebook. It amended the Video Privacy Protection Act (VPPA), which previously prevented release of users' viewing history without written consent. Users must opt in to this sharing feature, will be asked to reconfirm their opt-in status automatically every two years, and can opt out of the sharing feature at any time.

The new wave of young consumers are more technologically involved than their parents and want to be able to share what they are watching with friends. Although the bill brings VPPA up to speed with technological advancements of the modern era, consumer privacy advocates were disgruntled that the bill did not include a provision to update the Electronic Communications Privacy Act of 1986 (ECPA). The update would have prevented law enforcement officials from accessing users' emails and online documents without a valid search warrant. Under the current ECPA, law enforcement can access citizens' files and communications stored by a third party for more than 180 days with only a subpoena. Despite these concerns, the bill was passed, fueled by the social-media-active youth whose desire to share more and more about themselves online superseded privacy issues (Couts, 2012). Bills such as this also receive support from businesses that wish to gain from the information that is generated by consumers.

- **Our Health Online.** Allowing medical staff and pharmacists to share patient medical information might help them help us. Imagine being injured on a trip thousands of miles from your home. If the doctor treating you can immediately receive information about your allergies to certain medications, it might save your life. However, any electronic record residing on a database that is connected to a public network is potentially exposed to unauthorized access by people who do not have a legitimate need to know.

The Health Insurance Portability and Accountability Act of 1996 (HIPAA) is the U.S. federal law that was enacted to—among other purposes—mandate how health-care providers and insurance firms are to maintain records and disclose information so that patient privacy is not violated. The law restricts who accesses your medical records. Yet, even this law recognizes the inability of organizations to ensure patient privacy. For example, you can ask your doctor not to share your medical record with other doctors or nurses in the clinic, but they do not have to agree to do what you ask.

- **The Upside.** In spite of the downside of collection of personal data, there is also a positive side. Database technology enables companies to provide us with better and faster services. It also makes the market more competitive. Small firms often cannot afford the great expense of data collection. For much less money, they can purchase sorted data —the same data that is available to the industry leader. So, the wide availability of data contributes to a more egalitarian and democratic business environment. The beneficiaries are not only vendors but also consumers, who can purchase new and cheaper products.

And while many of us complain that these huge databases add to the glut of junk mail and spam, better information in the hands of marketers might actually save consumers from such annoyances. After all, those annoying communications are for products and services you don't need. With more specific information, marketers can target only those individuals that might be interested in their offerings. While you shop, special tracking software can tell the online business, at least indirectly, what you do not like about the site. This enables businesses to improve their services. For example, many online retailers discovered that a hefty proportion of shoppers abandoned their virtual shopping carts just before the final purchase. Analysis of collected information discovered that some people wanted to know the handling and shipping charges before they charged their credit cards. Now, most online retailers provide clear shipping information and charges up front.

- **The Downside.** The potential benefits from online medical records could also create some challenges. The privacy, security, and access of medical records information is a paramount concern to consumers and health care providers. However, several additional challenges need to be considered and addressed such as data usability, fragmentation and ownership (Anonymous, 2013a). While some industries have achieved significant progress with technology adoption, health care has been primarily a paper-driven system. In addition, the fragmentation of data sources can cause the data sharing to be impeded, disrupting the benefits of sharing information for diagnosis. Lastly, the use of tablets can provide portable delivery of medical information in hospitals and offices. However, popularity of "bringing your own device" by health care professionals can pose security risks and privacy abuses (Yudkin, 2012).

At the time of this textbook's printing, the discussion, public scrutiny, and legislative inquiries into the transfer of data from telecommunication companies and storage by U.S. federal government agencies has become a topic of significant debate. It will be interesting to see the changes, if any, that occur in the future.

The larger the data warehouse, the larger the storage capacity, the greater the memory, and the greater the processing power of the computers that are needed. Because of capacity needs, organizations often choose mainframe computers with multiple CPUs to store and manage data warehouses. The computer memory must be large enough to allow processing of huge amounts of data at once. The amount of storage space and the access speed of disks are also important. Processing millions of records might take a long time, and variations in disk speed might mean the difference between hours or minutes in processing time. And since a data warehouse is considered a highly valuable asset, all data must be automatically backed up. Keep in mind that data warehouses grow continually, because their very purpose is to accumulate historical records. Retail chains such as Wal-Mart and Costco record millions of sales transactions daily, all of which are channeled into data warehouses. Some have data warehouses that hold tens or hundreds of terabytes of data. In addition to retailers, banks, credit-card issuers, health-care organizations, and other industries have augmented their hardware for large data warehouses. Many organizations accumulate not only sales transactions but also purchasing records, so they can produce information from which to make better purchasing decisions, such as which suppliers tend to offer lower prices for certain items at certain times of the year.

Data warehouses are gaining tremendous attention and popularity with businesses. The thirst for storing and analyzing data has become nearly unquenchable, as data warehouses become essential to the strategic and operational activities of many organizational activities and functions. A survey of 421 data managers affiliated with the Oracle Users Group determined that 66 percent of the companies use data warehouses as the foundation for business intelligence and analytics. However, most systems are developed in-house and used only by analysts and top decision makers. For example, only 33 percent of the respondents' companies enable access for marketing and sales personnel, which does not fully utilize data warehouses for a critical business function. Although the majority of data warehouse content is transactional data, the diversity of data is expanding into unstructured data at an escalating rate. Figure 7.12 illustrates the representative proportion of data types stored in data warehouses (McKendrick, 2011). While transactional data still remains the largest percentage of data warehouses, non-traditional data types such as video and images are growing.

FIGURE **7.12**

Data types in a data warehouse

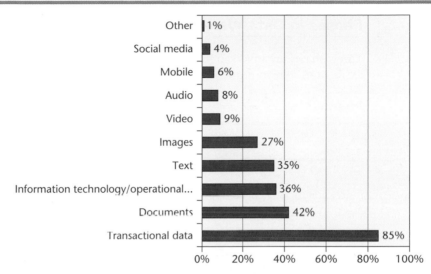

Source: McKendrick, J. (2011). Data Warehousing Reaches an Inflection Point. *Database Trends and Applications, 25*(4), 2–3.

POINT OF INTEREST   Cheaper and Faster Is Better

Many business organizations have decided to implement an analytics strategy, beginning sometimes with a scaled down initial capability. To implement these analytical capabilities, some businesses are opting for a new approach—the Cloud. While some people think that this technology is new, very often technology is a "remake" of something from a previous technology initiative. Remote access to applications software, platforms, data, and technology infrastructures has existed since the 1970s. By operating data analytics in the Cloud, businesses can have these applications managed and updated by a third party. The Cloud can also be used to implement a pilot project in a cost effective manner while testing its benefits and challenges.

Amazon Web Services (AWS) expanded their service offerings in late 2012 with their release of Amazon Redshift, a cloud-based warehousing service. Redshift decreases the cost of data storage from between $19,000 and $25,000 to only $1,000 per terabyte per year and promises query performance up to ten-times faster than conventional on-premise data warehousing. Amazon promises its managed service will stay on top of updates, tunings, and patches. Redshift is distinct from AWS's other cloud-based storage service, Amazon Relational Database Service (RDS), because Redshift is exclusively for warehousing and analytics, not transactional database use. In addition, Redshift is also capable of handling Big Data. The disruptive nature of the service combined with the vast improvements in cost and performance compared to previous services drew a lot of attention from the business/technology sector. If businesses can outsource data warehousing and save time and money, they can reallocate those resources to add value to their main line of business.

Sources: Griffin, J., & Danson, F. (2012, Nov). Analytics and the Cloud—the Future is Here, Financial Executive, pp. 97–98; Henschen, D. (2012). Amazon Debuts Low-Cost, Big Data Warehousing. InformationWeek. http://www.informationweek.com/software/information-management/amazon-debuts-low-cost-big-data-warehouse/240142712

The data from which data warehouses are built usually comes from within an organization, mainly from transactions, but it can also come from outside an organization. The latter might include national or regional demographic data, data from financial markets, and weather data. Similar to metadata in any database, data-warehouse designers create metadata for their large data pools. To uncover the valuable information contained in their data, organizations must use software that can effectively "mine" data warehouses. Data mining is covered in Chapter 11, "Business Intelligence and Knowledge Management."

Designers must keep in mind scalability: the ability of the data warehouse to grow as the amount of the data and the processing needs grow. Future growth needs require thoughtful planning in terms of both hardware and software.

Phases in Data Warehousing

Three phases are involved in transferring data from a transactional database to a data warehouse: extraction, transforming, and loading (ETL). Figure 7.13 describes the process.

FIGURE 7.13

Phases in preparing and using a data warehouse

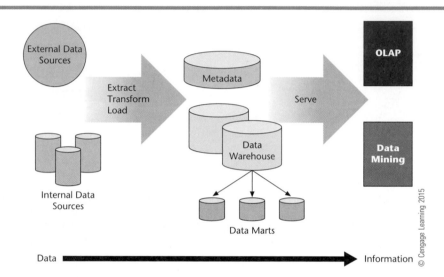

© Cengage Learning 2015

In the *extraction* phase, the builders create the files from transactional databases and save them on the server that holds the data warehouse. In the *transformation* phase, specialists "cleanse" the data and modify it into a form that allows insertion into the data warehouse. For example, they ascertain whether the data contains any spelling errors and fix them. They make sure that all data is consistent. For instance, Pennsylvania might be denoted as Pa., PA, Penna, or Pennsylvania. Only one form would be used in a data warehouse. The builders ensure that all addresses follow the same form, using uppercase or lowercase letters consistently and defining fields uniformly (such as one field for the entire street address and a separate field for zip codes). All the data that expresses the same type of quantities is "cleansed" to use the same measurement units.

In the *loading* phase, the specialists transfer the transformed files to the data warehouse. They then compare the data in the data warehouses with the original data to confirm completeness. As with any database, metadata helps the users know what they can find and analyze in the data warehouse.

A properly built data warehouse is a single source for all the data required for analysis. It is accessible to more users than the transactional databases (whose access is limited only to those who record transactions and some managers) and provides a "one-stop shopping" place for data. In fact, it is not unusual for a data warehouse to have large tables with fifty or more fields (attributes).

Much of the ETL activity can be automated. Depending on the needs of its users, the structure and content of the data warehouse might be changed occasionally. Techniques such as data mining and online analytical processing (OLAP) can be used to exploit it. Managers can then extract business intelligence for better decision making.

Data Warehousing and Big Data

Data warehousing has been an essential ingredient in the trend toward Big Data, specifically data collected about and from individuals. Although there are many definitions of Big Data, a common thread is that **Big Data** is a magnification or expansion of the amount, types, and level of detail of data that is collected and stored. Big Data involves high volumes of data compiled from traditional, ordinary business activities, as well as newer, nontraditional sources. With Big Data, instead of relying on aggregated data to populate data warehouses, the data is stored at a much more granular level: from detailed transactions received from point-of-sale (POS) terminals, automated teller machines (ATMs), webpages, and mobile phones. For example, each time you purchase groceries, Big Data would represent information about items you purchased: what you purchased (canned soup, apples, cheese, milk, etc.), what brands, at what price, and in which quantities. So, rather than one summary transaction that records the total paid for your groceries, Big Data would record possibly hundreds of more detailed data points. It's easy to see how this would create an "information explosion" and necessitate expanding data warehouse capabilities.

Big Data also includes data collected from nontraditional sources such as social media. As discussed previously, the collection of unstructured data in data warehouses has exploded over the last several years. However, the lack of a traditional data structure and format can make the data a challenge to analyze. For example, the textual data from a Twitter feed would be nearly impossible to analyze for patterns and trends using traditional statistical and database query tools. Sentiment analysis is a data mining method that uses a combination of natural language processing, computational linguistics, and text analytics to identify and extract subjective information in source materials (Anonymous, 2013b). It is primarily used to extract attitudes, opinions, and emotions contained in text-based data, specifically from the web. Sentiment analysis can be used to analyze data from a Twitter business account to understand how consumers feel about their product, customer service, or brand.

Aggregate, or summary, data can provide insight into many questions asked by business management and professionals. However, intense and detailed perspectives can only be gained with the granular transaction information compiled from the source of the business activity. While the sheer volume of data may be intimidating, it allows for a much greater depth of analysis. Consumer product companies will be able to understand the links, if any, for customers who purchase two or more of their product line and profile information (income, gender, household size, etc.). Without the detailed data on their purchases, it would be impossible to gather the necessary information to complete the analysis and determine these relationships. For example, using sentiment analysis, a consumer products company can determine the number of tweets which were categorized as positive or negative about a specific product or service. The summary values of this analysis can provide insight on the attitudes of consumers over time for a product.

Data mining, OLAP, and business intelligence are discussed in Chapter 11, "Business Intelligence and Knowledge Management."

Summary

- In their daily operations, organizations can collect vast amounts of data. This data is raw material for highly valuable information, but data is useless without tools to organize it, store it in an easily accessible manner, and manipulate it to produce that information. These functions are the strength of databases: collections of interrelated data that, within an organization and sometimes between organizations, are shared by many units and contribute to productivity and efficiency.

- The database approach has several advantages over the more traditional file approach: less data redundancy, application-data independence, and greater probability of data integrity.

- The smallest piece of data collected about an entity is a character. Multiple characters make up a field. Several fields make up a record. A collection of related records is a file, or in the relational model, a table. Databases usually contain several files, but the database approach can be applied to a single file.

- A database management system (DBMS) is a software tool that enables us to construct databases, populate them with data, and manipulate the data. Most DBMSs come with programming languages that can be used to develop applications that facilitate queries and produce reports. DBMSs are also a major part of enterprise applications.

- A database model is the general logical structure of records in a database. The various database models are: hierarchical, network, relational, and object-oriented. The most popular model is the relational model, which is used to build most new databases, although object-oriented databases are gaining popularity. Some vendors offer DBMSs that accommodate a combination of relational and object-oriented models, called object-relational.

- The links among entities in a relational database are maintained by the use of key fields. Primary keys are unique identifiers. Composite keys are combinations of two or more fields that are used as a primary key. Foreign keys link one table to another within the database.

- In an object-oriented database, data sets, along with the procedures that process them, are objects. The relationship between one set of data and another is established by one object containing the other, rather than by foreign keys.

- SQL has been adopted as an international standard language for querying relational databases. SQL statements can also be embedded in code that is produced using many programming languages.

- To construct a database, a designer first constructs a schema and prepares metadata, which is information about the data to be kept in the database.

- To plan databases, designers conduct data modeling. Before they design a database, they create entity relationship diagrams, which show the tables required for each data entity and the attributes (fields) it should hold, as well as the relationships between tables. Then they can move on to constructing a schema, which is the structure of all record structures of the entities, and the relationships among them.

- Many databases are linked to the web. This arrangement requires web server software, such as Active Server Pages and Java servlets, which allow users to enter queries or update databases over the Internet.

- Data warehouses are huge collections of historical transactions copied from transactional databases, often along with other data from outside sources. Managers use software tools to glean useful information from data warehouses to support their decision making. Some data warehouses are made up of several data marts, each focusing on an organizational unit or a subject.

- In each addition of data from a transactional database to a data warehouse, the data is extracted, transformed, and loaded, a process known by its acronym, ETL.

- The low price of efficient and effective database software exacerbates a societal problem of the Information Age: invasion of privacy. Because every transaction of an individual can be easily recorded and later combined with other personal data, it is inexpensive to produce large dossiers on individual consumers. This poses a threat to privacy. However, commercial organizations insist that they need personal information to improve their products and services and to target their marketing only to interested consumers.

- Big Data, the collection and storage of ever-more detailed quantities of data, has altered data gathering and analysis techniques. Big Data is also creating a new mindset by using nontraditional data sources, such as social media, to spot trends, attitudes, and patterns of consumers and the general public.

KIMBALL'S REVISITED

Tyler has begun to consider how to link the promotional strategy to the data needed to help his parents manage the new location. Although he is not sure exactly how to accomplish this, he is certain that collecting and storing the right data will help create a historical warehouse of information for operational, tactical, and strategic decisions.

What Is Your Advice?

1. Kimball's database from the order entry system is crucial to its operations. Information about the meals, drinks, and desserts ordered by customers can provide accurate insight to manage the restaurant's operations efficiently. What types of decisions are required to manage the daily operations? What decisions lead to managing costs? Is there any information that can provide assistance on their labor scheduling? Ordering? Compile a list of the critical success factors and decisions that management should review.

2. Should Kimball's maintain information on its suppliers? Would that level of detail be necessary, or would it overload the owners and Tyler? What information do they need to support their operational as well as tactical decisions? Is there any information that could help them with strategic decisions?

3. Where would you learn about the process of gathering data for management decisions? Consider some sources that would assist you with this important business process.

New Perspectives

1. Tyler wants to assemble a strategy to track the influence of their new customer loyalty program. What types of information should he consider tracking? How would it integrate with current information technology? Are new systems needed to track this data?

2. Nontraditional data is an important component of a data strategy. What types of nontraditional data sources should Tyler consider? How would it be analyzed? How might it relate with other systems at Kimball's?

Key Terms

Review Questions

1. It is easier to organize data and retrieve it when there is little or no dependence between programs and data. Why is there more dependence in a file approach and less in the database approach?

2. Spreadsheets have become quite powerful for data management. What can be done with database management systems that cannot be done with spreadsheet applications? Give several examples.

3. What is the difference between a database and a database management system?

4. DBMSs are usually bundled with powerful programming language modules. Why?

5. DBMSs are a component of every enterprise application, such as a supply chain management system. Why?

6. What are the advantages and disadvantages of object-oriented databases?

7. What is the relationship between a website's local search engines and online databases?

8. When constructing a database, the designer must know what types of relationships exist between records in different data sets, such as one-to-many or many-to-many. Give three examples for each of these relationships.

9. Give an example of a one-to-one relationship in a relational database.

10. What is SQL? In which database model does it operate? Why is it so popular?

11. What is a data warehouse? How is it different from a transactional database?

12. Why is it not advisable to query data from transactional databases for executive decision making the same way you do data warehouses?

13. What are the phases of adding data to a data warehouse?

14. What does it mean to cleanse data before it is stored in a data warehouse?

15. What are data marts? How do they differ from data warehouses?

Discussion Questions

16. Retail chains want to ensure that every time a customer returns to purchase something, the record of that purchase can be matched with previous data of that customer. What objects that consumers often use help the retailers in that regard?

17. Increasingly, corporate databases are updated by the corporations' customers rather than their employees. How so?

18. Can you think of an industry that would not benefit from the promise of a data warehouse? Explain.

19. Shouldn't those who build data warehouses trim the data before they load it to data warehouses? Why do they usually not cut any data from transactions?

20. The combination of RFID and database technology enables retailers to record data about consumers even when they have not purchased anything at the store. Can you think of an example and how the data could be used?

21. A retailer of household products maintains a data warehouse. In addition to data from sales transactions, the retailer also purchases and maintains in the warehouse daily weather data. What might be the reason?

22. Many organizations have posted privacy policies at their websites. Why do you think this is so? How is this related to databases and data warehouses?

23. Consider the following statement: Database management systems and data-warehousing techniques are the greatest threat to individual privacy in modern times. What do you believe are the issues associated with the consolidation and gathering of private-industry data (discussed in the Ethical & Societal section) by the federal government?

24. Privacy rights advocates demand that organizations ask individuals for permission to sell personal information about them. Some also demand that the subjects of the information be paid for their consent. Organizations have argued that they cannot practically comply with these demands and that the demands interfere with the free flow of information. What is your opinion?

25. Organizations whose websites offer visitors some control of how their personal information is

out" or "opt in." Explain each term.

26. Some people say that as long as the concept of "informed consent" is applied, individuals should not complain about invasion of their privacy. What is "informed consent"? Do you agree with the argument?

27. Businesses in the United States and many other countries rarely allow customers to scrutinize and correct records that the organizations keep about them. Technologically, does the web make it less expensive for organizations to allow that?

28. Big Data is gaining popularity in business organizations. How would the concept of Big Data alter the perspective of what type of data is stored and the challenges it poses? Consider the various sources outlined in the chapter for gathering data.

Applying Concepts

29. Direct your web browser to *www.zillow.com*. Enter a real address. What is displayed comes from at least one database. Prepare a short report answering these questions: What information elements must Zillow pull from databases to display what you see? (street address, town, etc.) Are all the data elements textual? Explain.

30. Acxiom is a data services firm. Browse this company's site and research its activities at its own site and at other websites. Write a two-page summary of the company's activity: What does the company sell? How does it obtain what it sells? Who are its customers, and how do they use what they purchase from Acxiom?

31. Research the business of DoubleClick, Inc. What type of data does the company collect and sell? How does it collect the data? Who are the company's customers, and how do they use the services or data they buy from DoubleClick? At the company's website, you may notice that the company presents a privacy policy *at this website*. Explain why only *at this website* and not a general privacy policy.

32. Research various cloud-based data warehouse services offered by businesses such as Amazon. Write a two to four page research paper for your management to provide insight and recommendations on using their service within your business.

Hands-On Activities

33. Mid-County Hospital holds data on doctors and patients in two tables in its database (see the following tables): DOCTOR and PATIENT.

Use your DBMS to build the appropriate schema, enter the records, and create the reports described in items a-c on the next page.

DOCTOR					
ID#	LIC#	Last Name	First Name	Ward	Salary
102	8234	Hogg	Yura	INT	187,000
104	4666	Tyme	Justin	INT	91,300
221	2908	Jones	Jane	OBG	189,650
243	7876	Anderson	Ralph	ONC	101,800
256	5676	Jones	Ernest	ORT	123,400
376	1909	Washington	Jaleel	INT	87,000
410	4531	Carrera	Carlos	ORT	97,000

PATIENT					
SSN	Last N	First N	Admission Date	Insurance	Doc ID
055675432	Hopkins	Jonathan	4/1/13	BlueCross	221
101234566	Bernstein	Miriam	4/28/14	HAP	243
111654456	McCole	John	3/31/13	Kemper	221
200987898	Meanny	Marc	2/27/14	HAP	221
367887654	Mornay	Rebecca	4/3/13	HAP	410
378626254	Blanchard	George	3/30/14	BlueCross	243
366511122	Rubin	David	4/1/13	Brook	243

a. A report showing the following details for each doctor in this order: Last Name, First Name, and Ward. Arrange the report by ascending alphabetical order of the last names.

b. A report showing the entire record with the original order of columns of all the doctors whose salary is greater than $100,000 who work for one of the following wards: Internal (INT), Obstetric-Gynecological (OBG), Oncology (ONC).

c. A report showing the following details for all of Dr. Anderson's patients: Dr. Anderson's first name, last name, and Doctor's ID, and ward (from the DOCTOR table) should appear once at the top of the report. Each record on the list should show the Patient's Last Name, First Name, and Date of Admission (from the PATIENT table).

34. Search for a video about databases on YouTube. Print the video that you found showing all the information associated with the video stored by YouTube. Identify all of the attributes (fields) in the printout that could be included in YouTube's database record structure. Compile a list of the attributes for YouTube's database.

35. Mr. Lawrence Husick is an inventor who, with other inventors, obtained several U.S. patents. Find the site of the U.S. Patent and Trademark Office. Conduct a patent search at the site's online patent database. Find all the patents that mention Lawrence Husick as an inventor. Type up the patent numbers along with their corresponding patent titles (what the invention is). Email the list to your professor. Find and print out the image of patent No. 6469. Who was the inventor and what was the invention?

Team Activities

36. Your team is to design a relational database for an online pizza service. Customers log on to the site and provide their first and last names, address, telephone number, and email address. They order pizza from a menu. Assume that each item on the menu has a unique number, a description, and a price. Assume there is one person per shift who receives orders and handles them, from giving the order to the kitchen to dispatching a delivery person. The system automatically records the time at which the server picked up the order. The business wants to maintain the details of customers, including their orders of the past six months. The following are reports that management might require: (1) a list of all the orders handled by a server over a period of time; (2) summaries of total sales, by item, for a period; and (3) a report showing all of the past week's deliveries by server, showing each individual order—customer last name and address, items ordered, time of order pickup, and last name of delivery person. (You can assume the last names of delivery people are unique, because if there is more than one with the same last name, a number is added to the name.)

a. Chart the table for each entity, including all its fields and the primary key.

b. Draw the entity relationship diagram.

37. Your team should contact a large organization, such as a bank, an insurance company, or a hospital. Interview the database administrator about the database he or she maintains on customers (or patients). What are the measures that the DBA has taken to protect the privacy of the subjects whose records are kept in the databases? Consider accuracy, timeliness, and appropriate access to personal records. Write a report on your findings. If you found loopholes in the procedures, list them and explain why they are loopholes and how they can be remedied. Alternatively, log on to the company website that has posted a detailed privacy policy and answer the same questions.

38. Use the YouTube exercise above for this exercise. Using Figure 7.5 as a guide, create a list of tables containing the attributes identified from a YouTube video entry. Compile a list of analysis questions that YouTube could use to determine various operational and tactical success factors to manage their business.

Filling the Shopping Bags with Data

Supermarkets compete in an industry with tight gross and profit margins. The operational and marketing challenges of this industry require disciplined inventory control as well as a focused eye on consumer market trends and product selection. Food retailers have a limited amount of shopping area and shelving space. Therefore, the decisions about which products to sell, their costs, and the available inventory are key success factors in supermarkets.

Lund Fund Holdings is a small, privately held retail organization selling food products in their 21 stores in the Minneapolis–St. Paul area. Their product line is high-end, similar to what is found at Whole Foods. Its family operated enterprise also includes catering services, online shopping, and pharmacies.

Lund's information technology infrastructure had a number of systems already installed and operational. Their point-of-sale system tracked sales, pricing, and inventory. Other systems provided necessary functions to its operations including an accounting system that maintained their financial transactions and reporting as well as a manufacturing system that provided functionality for in-store delicatessens and perishable goods. Although all of those systems were operating well for Lund, there was a problem. The various systems did not provide an integrated environment of corporate data. The "islands of technology" needed to be combined into one data warehouse populated from the various systems. Lund's manager of information systems clearly defined the issue: "We needed a [data] warehouse to pull data from all of those operational systems into a single spot."

Lund's needed the information technology and associated data to assist buyers with an important retail concept—to make sure that the appropriate products were available to the consumers at the right time. Easy to say, but challenging to accomplish. Their previous solution used Excel spreadsheets that were developed with requests to its information technology department. The time needed to fulfill these requests did not allow the buyers to make effective decisions. In addition, when the information was provided, the spreadsheets were not able to "drill down" into the data. The delays in the delivery of data and the limited functionality of the spreadsheet models limited Lund's ability to complete effective analysis and make timely purchasing decisions.

The goal was clear, but the journey needed to be constructed. They created a team that consisted of various resources and roles within the organization. The implementation team was to include both business and information technology personnel including store buyers (also called category managers), accounting, and store general managers lead by a project leader and a representative from Lund's business intelligence software provider and project consultant. They compiled a three-year plan to develop their data warehousing initiatives, looking for a phased-in approach rather than attempting to force the project's objectives too quickly. Once the objective was set, what specifically was needed to achieve that goal? Could everyone agree on what was required?

The team agreed that twelve key reports formed the foundation of the initial phase. Through a traditional business needs analysis, several interviews were completed to gather what information was needed to fulfill the organization's goals. The project team was able to extract data from its various application systems. The information system personnel's knowledge of the organization's data was invaluable to developing the data extraction process.

Once the data warehouse was created with the data from Lund's systems, they used MicroStrategy's BI product to interrogate the data warehouse. At this point, the benefits became more transparent and tangible. The category managers used their knowledge of the stores and market to complete the purchasing activities for each store. They received comprehensive sales information that they did not possess or have access to previously. The first benefit was that category managers were able to bargain more effectively with vendors, because they were equipped with timely and accurate information.

Lund's quickly realized that the newfound access to corporate data affected many levels of personnel, not just the category managers. Specifically, the store managers now received sales information early in the morning on their mobile devices. Decisions could be completed more effectively and timely by using accurate historical data contained in the data warehouse.

Corporate personnel could efficiently manage its sales forecasts and product shrinkage. Buyers were able to extract sales information on seasonal products from previous years. The buyer could now view product information on units sold, stock outs, and inventory overstocks. The buyers, equipped with accurate, objective information, compiled ordering forecasts that are required several months in advance. After implementing the data warehouse, sales increased 20 percent and after-holiday product overstocks that required discounting were reduced.

Product shrinkage has always plagued retail establishments. The new system collects data on what is discarded and no longer available for sale.

The shrinkage data, combined with sale and purchase data, has expanded the organization's data analysis capability. The result? Lund's gained a significant reduction of shrinkage for their perishable goods.

It is clear that this food retailer has checked out significant benefits by filling its cart with data.

Source: Briggs, L. L. (2010, First Quarter). Food Retailer Bags New Data Warehousing Solution. Business Intelligence Journal, 15, 39–41.

Thinking About the Case

1. Why was the knowledge of the IS department so valuable to the population of the data warehouse from Lund's various systems?

2. Consider the data that a supermarket tracks and maintains through its operations. Several new cracker products are being introduced in a few months. The buyers need to gather information to decide which new products should be approved for Lund's. Discuss what data should be extracted from their data warehouse to move this decision forward.

3. Lund's had several information technology systems already implemented in their organization. How influential were the depth and functionality of these systems on the success of the data warehouse project? Why?

Retailing Big Data

"Big Data" is getting big attention in many business organizations across various industries and markets. Any advantage that can be gained over your competitors is a plus. The challenge is that many business organizations are implementing similar technology initiatives. Therefore, the organization that crosses the technology "finish line" not only first, but more effectively, gains the most.

Retailing is a fragmented industry, ranging in size from the "big box" stores to local proprietors specializing in a particular product line. However, they all have the same issues: improving cost leadership, inventory efficiency, and revenue. One of the important "cogs" of the wheel is building customer loyalty. During challenging economic times, customers are looking for bargains and increased value. How can these be achieved without compromising profit?

Sears Holding, the parent company of Sears and Kmart, has been experiencing challenges to their organizational, financial, and market success. Faced with the intense competition from giant "brick and mortar" and online retailers, Sears needed to improve customer loyalty to survive. Sales revenue declined from $50 billion in 2008 to $42 billion in 2011. In the same period, Amazon increased its revenue from $19 billion to $48 billion, surpassing Sears for the first time.

In 2009, Sears decided to begin an initiative to get closer to its customers. They wanted to achieve this objective by implementing Big Data technology. However, their IT capabilities were not up to the task. Responding to the challenge in 2011, Sears initiated the "A Shop Your Way Rewards" membership program as one of five tactics to gain a competitive advantage. Sears also wanted to alter its reputation as lagging in technology adoption.

Their implementation of Apache Hadoop, a "high-scale, open source data processing platform," focusing on Big Data, was announced. Sears' past process for analyzing loyalty club memberships needed six weeks to complete on their mainframe systems using Teradata and SAS products. Their new Big Data product has reduced the turnaround to weekly. For some situations involving their mobile and online commerce applications, Sears can complete daily analyses–a radical difference from past practices. The level of data granularity was increased to view details down to the customer level if necessary. The size of data warehouses can become unwieldy and cumbersome with the increasing timeframe of stored data. However, Sears has found that maintaining all data "was crucial because we don't want to archive or delete meaningful data."

A significant component of their Big Data project's success focuses on the technology infrastructure. Their specific decision to implement Apache Hadoop, an open-source database platform, has been at the cornerstone of its initiative. With the Apache system, storing 200 terabytes costs about one-third what it would cost with a commercial relational database product. Therefore, the scalability as the system expands does not present a cost challenge to the organization. The new product also enables parallel processing computing power to reduce the time necessary to process records. To emphasize that gain, Sears states that the difference between processing 100 million and 2 billion records requires only a "little more than a minute." This fact must bring a smile to the faces of the Big Data miners.

Although Sears has struggled, it still remains the largest appliance retailer and service provider in the United States. Therefore, it is imperative for Sears to understand the needs of its appliance customers. They do not believe that they have realized the full potential of using Big Data with their appliance business. The various data elements associated with customer preferences, service trends, and warranty problems can provide more gains in this important product area.

Sears has populated its nearly 300 nodes with 2 petabytes of data including customer transactions, point-of-sale, and supply chain data. Though it might be easier to maintain only aggregate data in the data warehouse, Sears stores its transactions at the individual activity level. This approach allows the organization to analyze and report about their supply chain, logistics, and financial reporting as well as product and customer sales. It uses Datameer, which supports their data extraction and presentation in a spreadsheet-style environment. Using the Big Data initiative, Sears can be more proactive about its promotional tactics. It offers direct promotions to customers, personalized based on the data warehouse analysis. Previously, Sears would analyze only 10 percent of its customer data to determine what promotional offers would be successful. Now, with the new system, they can analyze all data faster and more efficiently.

As far as tangible results, in the quarter ended July 2012, earnings (before interest, taxes, depreciation and amortization) were up 163 percent, to $153 million. This impressive increase was accomplished while same-store sales decreased 2.9 percent and 4.7 percent at Sears and Kmart respectively. Sears suggests that their financial performance indicates more intelligent targeted marketing and promotion.

Sears has decided to leverage its Big Data project success. It has begun to market its Big Data technology infrastructure and expertise to other businesses through its new subsidiary, MetaScale. Its new business venture offers its Hadoop data center clusters either directly or remotely for customers needing Big Data applications. In addition, MetaScale provides consulting services to assist the implementation of data analytics initiatives.

Sears has one advantage over the giant retailer Amazon. Sears offers a marketing channel that Amazon does not, retail storefronts. While Amazon continually is redefining the customer's online experience, Sears like other "brick and mortar" retailers must determine how to improve the in-store environment. For traditional retailing, the challenge continues to reinvent the storefront, specifically how to serve its technologically savvy customers who use the web and mobile platforms. It is clear that Sears must focus its resources on leveraging technology to regain retail market share.

Sears' Chairman, Edward Lampert has indicated that technology will provide a strong influence for the business to succeed. Some of his five "pillars" include building brand awareness and creating value through information-sharing for store employees. He has stated that he spends more time on one pillar, "reinventing the company continuously through technology and innovation." He believes that the new customers will tend to use their smartphones simultaneously as they shop in stores. Therefore, defining and branding the cross-channel experience will be a major focus as new technology initiatives are considered.

Source: Henschen/Doug, Big Data, Big Questions; Henschen, D. (2012). Big Data, Big Questions. InformationWeek (1349), 18–22.

Thinking About the Case

1. Consider that Sears is maintaining their data warehouse to the individual transaction level. What are the advantages and disadvantages of this data storage strategy? If you were CTO, what data analyses could you accomplish with detail data as compared with aggregated data? Be specific.

2. The adoption of smartphone technology and mobile applications are expanding. Think about your experience of using your smartphones in a retail environment. What functions and features would you consider important for retailers to implement for cross-channel marketing?

3. The airline industry has used historical information for decades in order to determine pricing for airfares. Could the availability of historical data and price point modeling create dynamic price changes? Discuss the pros and cons of this initiative.

References

Anonymous. (2013a). 5 Challenges for Using Data in Healthcare. *Medical Economics*, 90(7), 13.

Anonymous. (2013b). Sentiment Analysis *Wikipedia*. San Francisco, CA.

Bridgwater, A. (2012). MySQL is "world's most popular" open source database. Retrieved January 8, 2013, from http://www.computerweekly.com/blogs/open-source-insider/2012/10/mysql-is-worlds-most-popular-open-source-database.html

Couts, A. (2012). Netflix-Facebook bill passes U.S. House withour email privacy protections. Retrieved from Digital Trends website: http://www.digitaltrends.com/social-media/netflix-facebook-bill-house-vppa-ecpa/

Fontecchio, M. (2012). Oracle the clear leader in $24 billion RDBMS market. Retrieved from http://itknowledgeexchange.techtarget.com/eye-on-oracle/oracle-the-clear-leader-in-24-billion-rdbms-market/

Kuehner-Hebert, K. (2012). Are You Ready for Big Data? *Target Marketing*, 35(7), 18-20, 22-23.

McKendrick, J. (2011). Data Warehousing Reaches an Inflection Point. *Database Trends and Applications*, 25(4), 2-3.

Rutenberg, J. (2012). Secret of the Obama Victory? Rerun Watchers, for One Thing, *The New York Times*. Retrieved from http://www.nytimes.com/2012/11/13/us/politics/obama-data-system-targeted-tv-viewers-for-support.html?nl=us&emc=edit_cn_20121113&_r=0

Yudkin, R. (2012). Popularity of mobile devices brings risk. *Health Management Technology*, 33(4), 32.

NetPhotos/Alamy

PART three

WEB-ENABLED COMMERCE

BUSINESS CHALLENGES

Early information technology enabled commerce through telephone calls, paper forms, and entering data at terminals connected to computer systems. Today, businesses of all sizes are integrating web-based technology and applications, and sharing information globally to transform how they interact and process transactions with their stakeholders. In these two chapters, you will explore how Kimball's Restaurant and other businesses can integrate web-based technologies and global information systems into their strategies and operations.

- In Chapter 8, "The Web-Enabled Enterprise," you learn how businesses use the Internet to achieve

strategic advantage and how they can use the Internet to extend their reach. Various information technology strategies such as websites, mobile computing and social media can help their business develop and become more efficient.

- In Chapter 9, "Challenges of Global Information Systems," you learn how sharing electronic information and operations among companies and across international boundaries can bring tremendous efficiencies—and challenges—to operations from small businesses to multinational corporations.

eight

THE WEB-ENABLED ENTERPRISE

Learning Objectives

The web continues to be the most exciting development in the field of information systems and telecommunications. The combination of advanced telecommunications technology, innovative software, and mobile hardware such as tablets and smartphones is revolutionizing the way people communicate, shop, process contracts and payments, educate, learn, and conduct business. Numerous companies throughout the world have been established thanks to the enabling power of the web, and existing businesses have used the web to extend their operations. Firms conduct business electronically with each other and directly with consumers, using a variety of business models. This chapter focuses on web technologies and businesses on the web.

When you finish this chapter, you will be able to:

- Describe how the web, high-speed Internet connections, and mobile technologies have changed business operations.

- Explain the functionality of various web technologies.

- Compare and contrast options for web servers.

- Explain basic business-to-business and business-to-consumer practices on the web.

- Explain the relationship between web technologies and supply chain management.

- Give examples of features and services that successful business websites offer.

- Explain how businesses use social media as part of their web strategies.

- Learn about online annoyances such as spam and adware, and how to protect against online identity theft.

KIMBALL'S RESTAURANT: Using the Internet

The new location was just about complete and would be ready to open within a month. Tyler worked with Justin, a local promotion consultant, to develop the final graphics for the Lakeside location's print promotions.

Serving a Full Plate of Websites

With the print campaign ready, Tyler wanted to focus on Kimball's web presence. Although he had some college courses on website design, and was familiar with social media through his personal Facebook, Instagram, and Twitter accounts, he asked Justin to consult with him on building a professional website and using social media to promote the restaurant.

Luckily, the domain name KimballsLakeside.com was available. Tyler registered the name immediately to ensure that customers could easily access the restaurant's website with an intuitive address. He discussed the content for the new website with Justin. What would be its purpose? How could the website promote the new location as well as drive more business to the restaurant? Could they integrate social media into their promotions?

Justin and Tyler discussed how to proceed with the web and social media strategy. Justin pointed out that websites should evolve over time as needs change. A website should reflect the short-term needs of the business, rather than hypothetical and perhaps ill-conceived ideas more than six months in the future. With the grand opening only a few weeks away, Justin felt the website's scope should be limited to what needs to be done to prepare for the opening.

Justin asked Tyler about his immediate objectives for the website. Tyler thought for a second and responded, "What I'd like right now is to create a buzz about the new location with two main thrusts: (1) to inform our loyal patrons about the new location and (2) to introduce new customers who would enjoy lakeside dining." Then he added, "We also need to include business meetings and social occasions as another market category. This would be an excellent source of

new business. Social occasions like wedding and baby showers, birthdays, and anniversaries could be a terrific market for our function room." Justin agreed.

Having a Social Meal

Tyler was excited about using social media as part of their marketing strategy. Justin warned that although social media can provide many benefits, its use needs to be planned with specific goals in mind for each "campaign" and outcome desired. "You can't just post things on Twitter and Facebook on a whim. Sure, some things can be sent such as 'Our Grand Opening is Rocking the World Tonight!' But in terms of promotions and marketing strategies, we need an overall plan for integrating social media." Justin cautioned that many businesses lose profit by over-promoting without a strategy to increase market, revenue, and customer base. They both knew that a well-constructed plan for the website and social media was important.

Even with the tight timeframe before the opening, Justin believed that the website and social media platforms could be constructed and ready to implement two weeks prior to the opening. Tyler created accounts for Twitter, Instagram, and Facebook to reserve the restaurant name. Justin and Tyler placed some initial general entries into the new accounts to begin the dialogue. Justin said the initial dialogue was important so that when the website "goes live" and the web address is included in advertisements, the social media accounts will already show activity. It is important for customers and potential customers to see action rather than a blank social media stream.

Tyler agreed to post something each day on the social networking accounts to inform customers of the restaurant's progress and get them excited about the grand opening. He also would upload some pictures to create interest in the new location. Then, he and Justin would focus on the structure of the website and integrating social media.

Web Business: Growing and Changing

Ford Motor Company is a world leader in automobile manufacturing based in Dearborn, Michigan. It employs about 176,000 people in 80 plants across the globe. Although manufacturing companies are not known for their social media or for their marketing departments in general, when Ford rolled out the Fiesta in 2010, it also rolled out an innovative social media package with it. The Fiesta Project was a social media marketing campaign that took a micro-targeting approach. The campaign used real people to share the Fiesta experience in a series of eight YouTube videos. The videos sparked over 1,000,000 views and 5,000 conversations across Facebook, Twitter, and YouTube. Ford chose social media for their rollout because it wanted to connect with and engage a specific market: a younger, tech-savvy audience. By targeting a specific group of people with a custom message, Ford made viewers feel understood and thus the message gained more traction. Ford's social media strategy gave them widespread online awareness of the Fiesta, as well as the ability to gauge the online response to their product. Ford acknowledged that the online attitude toward them was positive. With social media, if you aren't using, you're losing (Anonymous, 2010).

The web has been a great enabler for conducting business within organizations, between organizations, and between organizations and consumers. Vanguard, one of the world's largest mutual fund management companies, receives over 80 percent of its new clients through the web. Social networking on sites like Facebook and Twitter has exploded over the past few years, and content delivery of video clips and feature-length movies has boomed. The spread of broadband links, new ideas of web use for commerce, and continued development of web technologies help business on the web to grow and change all the time.

Web Technologies: A Review

Several standards and technologies enable the web to deliver rich information. The following is a review of some nonproprietary standards and technologies.

HTTP

In Chapter 6, "Business Networks and Telecommunications," you learned about protocols. The protocol used to transfer and download web information is **Hypertext Transfer Protocol**, or **HTTP**. A secure version of the protocol for confidential transactions is **HTTPS (HTTP Secure)**. Under these protocols, each web server is designated a **Uniform Resource Locator (URL)**, which is a unique address for a website. The address is the IP address assigned to the site, but in most cases the site also has a **domain name** made up from letters. The term "URL" also refers to the domain name. Domain names are used for convenience, because it is easier to remember domain names than IP addresses. Each webpage has its own URL, which contains the IP address or domain name of the site. Because the domain name must be unique, when an owner of a website reserves a domain name to be associated with an IP address, no other site can be associated with that domain name. Note that domain names often start with—but do not have to include—*www*.

The last part of a URL, such as the ".com" in www.pinzale.com, is the **top-level domain (TLD)**. In addition to .com, .org, and .edu, many other TLDs can be requested for a domain name, some of which are reserved for certain types of organizations and professions, and some that are not. Country codes such as .ca for Canada or .uk for the United Kingdom can also serve as TLDs. The only organization that is authorized to approve new TLDs is the Internet Corporation for Assigned Names and Numbers (ICANN), a not-for-profit organization established specifically for this purpose. Usually, a website with any TLD can be viewed in the same way regardless of technology. Recently, ICANN has expanded the portfolio of TLDs significantly to include names such as .museum, .name, .post, .travel, .jobs, .info, and .coop ("Top Level Domain Name List," 2013).

HTML and XML

Hypertext Markup Language (HTML) is the most common programming language for creating webpages and other information viewable in a web browser. It determines the look and location of text, pictures, animations, and other elements on a webpage. Extensible Markup Language (**XML**) enables the creation of various types of data. It is most often used not for determining the *appearance* of visual elements on a webpage but to convey the *meaning* or content of the data. The World Wide Web Consortium (W3C), the organization responsible for web standards, combined the two markup languages HTML and XML into a standard called Extensible Hypertext Markup Language (**XHTML**). **HTML5** is the newest version of HTML/XML. HTML5 includes support for the latest multimedia and mobile devices, and is rapidly becoming the standard for webpage development. The W3C is expected to publish the final HTML5 standard in 2014.

Every file displayed on the web is coded with a markup language such as HTML or XML. Simply put, markup languages provide a system of standardized "tags" that format elements of a document, including text, graphics, and sound. Formatting includes opening and closing tags preceding and following a part of the document, such as <b> at the start of bold text, and </b> at the end of bold text. Some tags are marked to link to another page either at the same site or another site, and others create links to email addresses. Browsers interpret HTML and XML tags and display the text in the fashion defined by the tags, or allow other software to pick up data from the page and process it or copy it into the proper place in a database.

As in HTML, tags are used in XML to mark data elements. However, XML tags define "what it is," as opposed to "how it looks." Figure 8.1 illustrates the difference between HTML and XML tags. XML tags can be used in the same page with HTML tags to indicate both what the data means (which is not visible to the user) and how each element should be displayed.

FIGURE 8.1

HTML and XML code: XML provides a method for describing or classifying data in a webpage

Visible Web Page Content	HTML code	XML code
Reebok® Classic Ace Tennis Shoe was $56.00; Now $38.99 Soft leather tennis shoe. Lightweight EVA molded midsole. Rubber outsole. China.	<strong><font face="Verdana, Arial, Helvetica, sans-serif">Reebok® Classic Ace Tennis Shoe </font></strong> <strong>Was $56.00; Now $38.99 </strong><table width="100%" border="1"><tr><td>Soft leather tennis shoe. Lightweight EVA molded midsole. Rubber outsole. China.</td></tr></table>	<product type="shoes"> <name> Reebok® Classics Ace Tennis Shoe </name> <price>$38.99</price> <description> Soft leather tennis shoe. Lightweight EVA molded midsole. Rubber outsole. China. </description> </product?

File Transfer

File Transfer Protocol (FTP) is a common way of transmitting files from one computer to another. Every time you download a file from a website or attach files to email, you are using an FTP application. The file transmitted can be of any type: text, graphics, animation, or sound. FTP is embedded in browsers and therefore is "transparent" to the users. You can also use a separate FTP utility, with many available as shareware, to manage transmitting files.

Businesses use FTP to place files on a server for sharing among professionals. FTP is also useful for placing files on a server that hosts a website. It's also convenient for retrieving large files that might exceed an email system's size limits. For example, authors can place large chapter and figure files in a folder on a server maintained by their publisher. Manufacturers often place full assembly and maintenance manuals or videos at their website so customers can download them any time. New methods have replaced FTP sites such as cloud drives, online backup tools (such as Carbonite), and groupware productivity products (such as Wiggio). However, FTP sites still remain popular due to the inexpensive and simple nature of file transfers.

Blogs

A **blog** (a contraction of "web log") is a webpage that invites surfers to post opinions and artistic work as well as links to sites of interest. Blog sites focus on a topic or a set of related topics, and provide an easy way to post webpages or update existing ones. Most blogs contain commentaries and humorous content. Users can simply click a button to open a window in which they type text, and click another button to post it. The text is added to the webpage either automatically or after a review by the blog's operators. Some blog sites simply let "bloggers" add comments on a topic, with the most recent comment appearing at the top. Many companies have established blogs, and invite employees to use them for self-expression. The policy might encourage new ideas from which the company can benefit. Some, however, shun the idea, because management believes blogs are too informal and uncontrolled. Users can easily set up a blog using websites such as WordPress, Typepad, Squarespace, and LiveJournal. Several blogging software vendors, such as WordPress and LiveJournal, offer blog hosting and software use at no cost.

One interesting feature of some blogs is **trackback**. Trackback software notifies bloggers when their posts have been mentioned elsewhere on the web, so they and their readers can extend the discussion beyond the original blog. Below each post there is a TrackBack button or similar option. When it is clicked, a new window pops up listing the sites mentioning the post.

The commercial potential of blogs has not escaped businesspeople. As traffic grows at some popular blogs, entrepreneurs have started selling advertising space at the sites. The popularity of blogs drives revenue to blog sponsors. A reader "clicking through" to a blog from a sponsored link becomes a source of revenue and increases the popularity rating of the blog. The old rule on the web is still much in force: the greater the number of eyeballs, the greater the commercial potential of the site.

The importance of blogs to commercial organizations is primarily to find out what blog participants think and say about the organizations. Many organizations use special software that combs blogs for postings that mention the organizations' names. PR people then read the content and relay feedback to others in the organization as needed. For example, an anonymous blogger boasted that he could break Kryptonite bicycle locks with a pen. Within a week the posted item was mentioned in *The New York Times*, and Kryptonite recalled the locks. Some companies offer blog mining applications, which is software that combs blogs, identifies company names, and automatically tracks discussions. Such tools can turn blog data into useful market research information.

Wikis

Many websites invite visitors or subscribers not only to read, view, and listen to their content, but also participate in the site building and editing process. In the past, to do so would require access codes and at least some knowledge of web editing software. Now, wikis make the process easy and fast.

A **wiki** (from Hawaiian: quick) is a web application that enables users to add to and edit the content of webpages. The term also refers to software that enables collaborative software used to create and revise websites. All the software required to edit the pages is embedded in the pages. Visitors do not need any software of their own, and do not need to upload saved pages. The additions and revisions are performed on the page, using tool icons that are provided at the site. The popular online encyclopedia Wikipedia, as shown in the screenshot, demonstrates the concept well. For example, if you enter the term "telecommuting," you will notice the disclaimer that alerts users that the page needs revisions. In addition, at the top of the page you can click on "Edit." When you click the edit link, a new window opens, displaying both the text and a set of tool icons to help you edit the text. Except for some protected entries, anyone with web access can participate in improving Wikipedia.

A wiki is a collaborative website where users can enter and edit content; Wikipedia.org is one of the best known

Courtesy of Wikipedia

Popular wiki applications include the free MediaWiki, Corendal Wiki, Wikiversity, and XWiki. The WikiMedia Foundation (*www.wikimedia.org*) provides information and links to sites that teach how to install and use wikis. The features of wiki technology make it a popular ingredient in groupware, software that helps groups collaborate on projects.

Podcasting

While blogging is publishing text and other visual material, podcasting is publishing sound and video. To **podcast** is to make a digital audio recording, usually of voice, and post the file on the web so that people can download it and listen to it. RSS software called an *aggregator* or *feed reader* automatically checks for new content and downloads files from a designated site in the same way as is done for text files from online newspapers. Users can subscribe to a podcast site to receive the latest audio files. The files are usually in MP3 format, which can be played on any portable player or smartphone, including the Apple iPod, from which the word "podcast" was born. However, one does not need this specific player to enjoy podcasts.

Podcasting has several potential uses. It already serves as "time-shifted" broadcast of radio stations that post their programs for later listening. It is used by some museums for audio tours. Some schools have experimented with the concept to deliver lessons to remote students or to post recordings of lessons for students to review. Whatever the use, people can listen to their favorite content wherever they can obtain a link to the Internet, without paying radio license fees.

Podcasting creates opportunities for businesses to communicate and promote their business, products, and services. Apple's iTunes product serves as a source to offer a variety of content consisting of training, lectures, television episodes, movies, and music. Many of these podcast media content files are free to download.

The web has changed the economics and delivery of many products and services in many industries, education being no different. Education and training have been transformed by podcasting. Recently, podcasting has evolved into a new concept distributed via the web called a **massive open online course (MOOC)**. This new education delivery combines the traditional course materials (readings, exercises, and so on) with interactive forums for educators and students. These forums can be conducted in a fully interactive, live setting or as stored video content to be played later. A form of distance learning, a MOOC extends an educational environment to various participants with a desire to learn a subject and expand their knowledge. This method is an excellent alternative for people in homebound situations, residents in areas geographically distant from educational institutions, and professionals with heavy travel commitments.

POINT OF INTEREST — Do You MOOC Much?

In February 2013, a study conducted by the Chronicle of Higher Education surveyed 184 professors that have taught a massive open online course; 56 percent responded to the survey. One professor after teaching his first MOOC believed that it was a full-time job to prepare for the session, but was astounded that his online course was attended by 28,000 students. After finishing the six-week class, he was "enthusiastic" and believed that "every person's education will have a significant online component."

The enrollment size of the courses was substantial ranging from hundreds to thousands; with the median enrollment 33,000. The professors leading these courses believe that some type of free online courses would be incorporated into a traditional delivery degree program and reduce the overall cost of providing classes at their home institution. The study found that the reason for engaging in this new education delivery method was both altruistic as well as increasing their visibility in the education community and general public.

However, there are consequences. Professors believed that the preparation time was overwhelming and required considerable hours in preparation and video recording. They conveyed that it reduced their ability for their on-campus responsibilities. The study found that the average pass rate for MOOCs are 7.5 percent; far below traditional education methods. Instead of offering traditional college credit, professors are offering certificates of completion. It is unclear how recruiters and employers would view the completion of MOOCs as compared to traditional college courses.

Source: Kolowich, S. (2013). The Professors Behind the MOOC Hype. The Chronicle of Higher Education.

Interactive Communication Technology

People communicate in various ways. Several years ago, **instant messaging (IM)** offered users real-time online interactivity. It might be thought of as "real-time email," because, unlike email, it is synchronous. IM allows a user to detect whether another person who uses the service is currently online, and the user can then exchange information with an entire group (referred to as a "chat room"), or with only one other "chatter" in privacy. Some IM applications include two-way video, which turns the chat into a video conference, and most also include FTP to allow sending and receiving files.

Over the last few years, instant messaging software has evolved from text-based communication to an expanded range of communication tools, including video chat. Many software applications provide text, video, and audio-based methods to communicate with other participants. Products such as Skype, ooVoo, and Wiggio provide a portfolio of tools to communicate with other people.

Free IM applications are operated through a server, or a group of connected servers, which provides a directory and functions as the hub for all callers. Some IM setups, such as AOL Instant Messenger (AIM), Yahoo! Messenger, MSN Messenger, and ICQ, have become the electronic meeting places for millions of people, making them an attractive target for online advertisers. To overcome the need to use multiple IM applications, some software developers produced universal IM applications that allow, for example, an AIM user to chat with an MSN Messenger user. Trillian and Pidgin are two of these applications.

While interactive messaging serves social purposes, it also can serve an important business purpose. Many online retailers post a special button on their webpages that lets shoppers establish real-time communication with a sales representative. This instant access fosters more personal service and saves telephone costs. For example, Venus Swimwear, a company that specializes in direct mail junior bathing suits, uses InstantService, a chat application that enables employees to answer customer questions in real time online. Venus's director of e-commerce marketing added this option to the three sites operated by the company because customers often abandoned the site when they could not get answers while shopping. Using the telephone was a bad option for those who used their telephone line for a dial-up Internet connection, and email was inefficient and time-consuming. IM enables sales agents to handle up to five inquiring customers at a time. The application also enables the company to "push" answers from a library of answers such as a sizing chart, instead of typing them. The live chat reduced the amount of email employees have to handle and decreased the customer abandonment rate by 15 percent despite the increasing traffic at the sites. As shown in the illustration, many businesses have added "Chat Online" options to the mail, telephone, and email contact information listed on their websites. Some companies have implemented an online callback function that allows customers to enter their contact information through a website to queue a callback.

Many business organizations integrate online chat into their contact options on the website

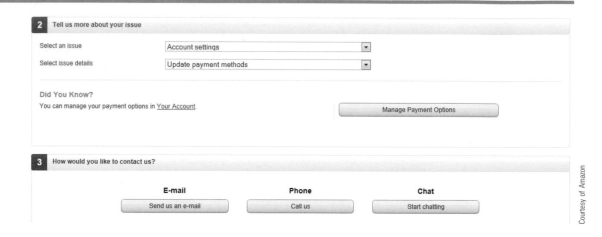

Courtesy of Amazon

Cookies

If you have surfed the web, your computer probably contains cookies. A **cookie** is a small file that a website places on a visitor's hard disk so that the website can remember something about the surfer later. Typically, a cookie records the surfer's ID or some other unique identifier. Combined with data collected from previous visits, the site can figure out the visitor's preferences. The user can opt to allow cookies; the option is exercised by checking a box in the browser's configuration window. On the user's hard disk, the cookie subdirectory (folder) contains a cookie file for each cookie-using website that the surfer has visited. Cookies might hold server URLs. When you instruct the browser to reach a URL from which you have a cookie, the browser transmits the information from the cookie to the server.

Cookies have an important function in web-based commerce, especially between businesses and consumers. They provide convenience to consumers; if the cookie contains your username and password for accessing a certain resource at the site (e.g., your bank account), you do not have to reenter the information. Cookies often help ensure that a user does not receive the same unsolicited information multiple times. For example, cookies are commonly used to rotate banner ads that a site sends so that a surfer receives different advertisements in a series of requested pages. They also help sites to customize other elements for customers. For example, when a retailer's site identifies a returning customer, it can build a page showing a list of items and information in which the customer might be interested based on previous purchases.

Some cookies are temporary; they are installed only for one session, and are removed when the user leaves the site. Others are persistent and stay on the hard disk unless the user deletes them. Many cookies are installed to serve only first parties, which are the businesses with which the user interacts directly. Others serve third parties, which are organizations that collect information about the user whenever the user visits a site that subscribes to the service of these organizations. These organizations include DoubleClick, ValueClick, and Avenue A.

While cookies can make online shopping, investing, and reading more convenient, they also open the door for intrusion into a person's privacy. Remember that every piece of information you provide while your browser is configured to permit cookies can be recorded and kept for further use—use over which you have no control. Choices you make when selecting menu items, clicking buttons, and moving from one page to another are also recorded. Such activities are called **clickstream tracking**. Although some organizations post privacy policies at their websites and tell you what they will or will not do with the information they gather, you cannot see what information they have compiled by using cookies and how they use it. Especially worrisome are third-party cookies, which collect your browsing and shopping habits across many websites. This is akin to a spy who follows you from one store to another. Software designed to trace and report your online behavior without your knowledge is called **spyware**. It includes cookies and other, more sophisticated applications that are installed on your computer unbeknownst to you and transmit information about you while you are online. As shown in the illustration, users can configure their browser's privacy settings to control the storage and use of cookies.

Cookies enable a site to identify a user and provide useful individualized service, but users can control the use of cookies in their browser

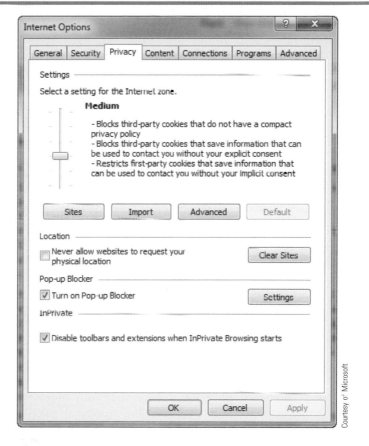

It seems that the public has become more aware of cookies and how companies use them. In January 2011, Valued Opinions disclosed the results of a study showing that 74 percent of users were uncomfortable with companies collecting private data. At the same time, people (53 percent) want to gain benefits from online activity and are willing to provide what is required to do so. Interestingly enough, 62 percent of the opinion panel does not clearly understand what data companies are collecting about them (Anonymous, 2011).

Proprietary Technologies

In addition to these and other widely used and usually free web technologies, many companies offer proprietary technologies. A proprietary technology is the intellectual property of its developer and is not free for all to use. These software packages include local search engines for finding information about specific items; shopping cart applications for purchase, including selection of items to place in a virtual cart and credit-card charging; wish lists, which allow shoppers to create lists of items they would like others to purchase for them; video streaming tools; and a host of software packages that are invisible to visitors but help the site owner to analyze and predict visitor behavior, especially shopper behavior. The latter technologies might not be considered web technologies per se, but they analyze data that is collected from visitors accessing websites. For example, Amazon.com uses software that follows the estimated age of those for whom a shopper purchases items, and offers new items that fit the progressing age of the shopper's family and friends.

Web-Enabled Business

Web-enabled business is often classified by the parties involved in the interaction: business-to-business (**B2B**), business-to-consumer (**B2C**), and business-to-government (**B2G**). Some people also add government-to-consumer and government-to-business. Auction sites are sometimes referred to as consumer-to-consumer (**C2C**) sites, but we consider them B2C, because the business does intervene in several parts of the transaction and also charges the parties commissions. The following sections describe the business models of the most pervasive types of web-based business.

B2B Trading

Business-to-business (B2B) trading takes place only between businesses. Consumers of the final goods and services are not involved. In general, the volume of e-commerce between businesses is about 10 times as great as that of business-to-consumer e-commerce. And although not all electronic B2B transactions take place on the Internet, most do. U.S. Census data estimates approximately US$300 billion of B2B revenue are transacted online, which does not include electronic data interchange (EDI) (Oracle, 2012). According to a B2B online survey, only 25 percent of B2B companies have an e-commerce site that indicates a projected growth in B2B e-commerce (Oracle, 2012). This section discusses the major forms of B2B e-commerce.

Advertising

Online advertising is done mainly in two ways: through search engines and through banners. Although advertising on the web is not aimed just at consumers, most of it is directed to them. However, selling and buying web ads occurs between businesses: the website operators sell advertising "real estate" to another business. Regardless of media, advertisers are interested in reaching as many people who might buy their goods or services as possible. On the web, advertisers are interested in what they call "traffic volume," that is, the number of people who come across their messages. As the number of people who log on to the web increases, so does advertiser interest in this medium. Internet World Stats estimated that of the 7 billion people in the world today, 2.4 billion—34.3 percent—used the Internet in 2012 ("Internet Usage Statistics," 2012). With this traffic volume, advertisers are willing to spend a lot of money on web advertising. The research firm GroupM estimated that about $84.8 billion was spent on web advertising in 2011, a 16 percent increase from 2010 (Hof, 2012; O'Leary, 2012). They also predicted web advertising spending will grow to $98.2 billion in 2012, accounting for 19 percent of all measured media spending (O'Leary, 2012).

Search advertising, which is any form of advertising through an online search site, is regarded by businesses as highly effective. Shoppers have discovered that the fastest way to find a business that can sell them the product or service they need is by looking up the product or service on the web, and the most effective searches are through the best-known services and those that identify the largest number of webpages: Google, Yahoo!, and Bing (see Figure 8.2). All of these sites have the same advertising patterns. Whenever you search for an item, the top and right-side links are, "Ads" or "sponsored" which are paid for by advertisers.

FIGURE 8.2

Businesses have their names and links displayed as an ad at the top or right in a search engine

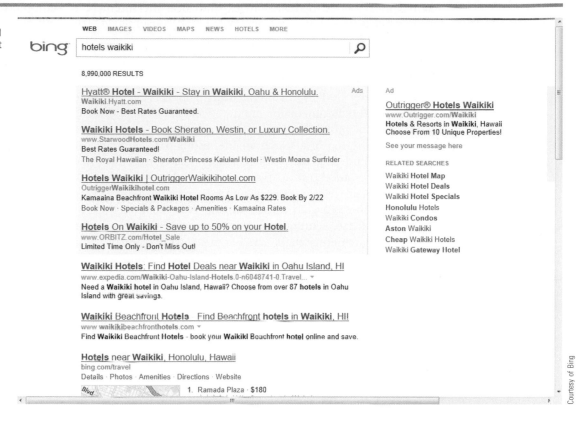

Courtesy of Bing

Banners are images placed on a website that link to the site of the company selling the product or service. In the early days of the web, the ads were shaped like a banner at the top of the page. However, any image placed for advertising is now referred to as a banner.

How does a potential advertiser know how much traffic a site attracts? The most basic metric that can be measured at a site is the number of impressions. An **impression** occurs whenever a browser downloads the page containing the banner. More useful metrics are provided by several companies that rate website visits similar to rating television viewing. For instance, comScore, an online rating firm, maintains a panel of more than 2 million English-speaking online consumers whom the firm polls periodically. The companies produce several metrics for subscribing companies. Usually, subscribers of online rating firms are high-traffic sites that generate large revenues from advertising.

In addition to impressions, rating companies measure other metrics. One is *unique visitors per month*. If the same person visited a site several times during a given month, the person is counted only once. The reason? Advertisers are interested in reaching many people, not the same people with many visits. Another metric is *unique visitor pages*, which is the number of different pages at the site that a single visitor accessed. The reason for this metric is that the same visitor is exposed to different ads at the site. **Reach percentage** is the percentage of web users who have visited the site in the past month, namely, the ratio of visitors to total web population.

As in print advertising, the site owner charges the advertiser by the ad's size (so many pixels by so many pixels) and by the amount of traffic, usually measured in number of impressions. Using the IP address of computers accessing the pages with the banners, the advertiser can easily count impressions. The charge is per month. Placing a banner at a heavily trafficked site may cost hundreds of thousands of dollars.

To find out which sites engage visitors more than others, advertisers count on the ranking of two main competing measurement firms: Nielsen and comScore. Prior to July 2007, both companies ranked sites by the number of pages viewed by visitors. In July 2007, Nielsen decided to rank sites by the amount of time visitors spend at sites.

The newest player in the market research industry is Kantar Group, a subsidiary of WPP PLC. Through a series of mergers executed in order to expand their service offerings, Kantar has become the second-largest market research firm in the United States, behind Nielsen. In 2011 Kantar and Nielsen partnered to expand local measurement of set-top-box data. In addition, Kantar tracks purchase data from 200 million consumers globally and processes 20 million new posts and articles from over 20 million new websites (Son, 2012).

Search Engine Optimization

The popularity and use of online search engines by consumers and businesses has created a competitive environment for online advertising; an online "capture the flag" battlefield. It is imperative for businesses to gain a competitive advantage by displaying their advertising entry as close to the top of a search engine results page. Most online users do not navigate past the second or third page in a search listing. Therefore, businesses with an online presence spend significant resources on a series of methodologies and techniques to increase the number of visitors to their website. **Search engine optimization (SEO)** implements a series of tactics to allow a business to gain a high-ranking placement of their online entry in the search results page. Using these techniques will optimize your website to influence the major search engines to rank your search entry higher. The higher the entry in the results list will increase the likelihood of generating a greater volume of qualified online traffic to your website.

An effective search engine optimization effort can directly lead to increased traffic to a website including visits to websites and improved returning visitors. As traffic and the popularity of the website expand, the increase of sales and profits also follows the same path. For example, the St. Petersburg Times implemented an SEO strategy for its website, tampabay.com. Using these techniques, their website reached 1.5 million hits a month and an increase of 22 percent in digital advertising reviewing from 2009 to 2010. The growth has continued in 2011 with a 14 percent increase in the first quarter from the same period in 2010. The most significant source of the website traffic growth was from search engines, a direct impact on their revenue success (Fletcher, 2011).

POINT OF INTEREST — Sales Tax for Everyone

Tax breaks for online shoppers could be coming to an end as states are strapped for revenue. According to the National Conference of State Legislatures, states could be flooded with $23 billion in new annual revenue if all states begin imposing sales tax for online purchases. Online retailers such as Amazon and Overstock.com have relied on a 1992 Supreme Court ruling stating companies who lacked a physical presence in the state where the customer lived did not have to charge sales tax. From the late 1990s onward, Amazon implemented a revenue-building program to milk the value of their massive reach called the "Affiliate Program." Other retailers could advertise their products on Amazon's website for a commission fee. However, by 2009 Amazon began cutting the affiliate program because some of their affiliates did have a physical presence and thus, states wanted their tax revenues. The retail giant Amazon no longer opposes the proposed taxes for online shopping. It plans to begin offering same-day delivery by having more warehouses in more locations, thus, paying more in state sales taxes. By 2014, Amazon claims it will pay sales tax in 13 states covering almost half of the U.S. population, but some state governors believe all states will collect sales tax for online purchases as early as 2013.

Sources: Chang, A. (2009, Jun 30). Amazon cuts affiliates to avoid taxes: The retailer severs ties with websites in two states so it won't have to collect sales tax on customers there, Los Angeles Times, p. B.4; Langley, M. (2012, Jul 16). Tax Break Nears End For Online Shoppers; Republican Governors, in Need of Revenue, Drop Opposition, Wall Street Journal (Online).

Exchanges and Auctions

In the old days, a meeting place of buyers and sellers had to be tangible: a marketplace, an annual fair, or a store building. Finding a buyer for scrap metal, used scientific equipment, or any other commodity might have taken a long time. Also, the buyer and seller had to pay high finder's fees to individuals and firms that specialized in such intermediary trade. On the web, the marketplace can include as many sellers and as many buyers as wish to participate, as long as they have access to the Internet.

An **intranet** is a network used only by the employees of an organization. An **extranet** limits site access to the employees of particular organizations, usually business partners. An extranet might be viewed as connecting intranets of business partners.

An exchange is an extranet for organizations that offer for sale and bid on products and services of a particular type. Unlike a public auction site, such as eBay or uBid, access is usually limited to subscribers who often pay a periodic fee to the site's operator. Auction sites whose purpose is to serve as a meeting place of buyers and sellers in a particular industry are sometimes operated by an industrial association. Others, like askart.com, are established by entrepreneurs for the sole purpose of making profit. When the purpose is only to provide a place where sellers compete for the business of a single buyer, the buyer operates the site.

When the site is established by a private business as a meeting place for multiple buyers and sellers, the operator is impartial and profits from transaction fees paid either by one party or both—the seller and buyer—whenever a sales transaction is signed. The advantages of businesses using auction sites to purchase materials are clear. In the past, purchasing agents had to spend a day to research sellers of a particular product. Then, using the research, the buyer would need to call a list of sellers for a single purchase or sale. Using an online auction site, the buyer can post the information on what they need online for sellers to view and respond. Different than the consumer-to-consumer purchases posted to eBay, B2B purchases require larger quantities of product and are more sensitive to price, quality, and delivery of materials to the buyer.

Very often, auction sites sell a great variety of items to reach a larger market of business buyers. Proxibid, located in Nebraska, is an example of an online auction site offering a wide portfolio of product categories. Proxibid has developed relationships with over 2,500 auction companies and thousands of bidders worldwide. Their product categories range from antiques, memorabilia to heavy construction equipment, farm machinery, and livestock.

Some electronic markets are established by a single buyer or by an organization that represents many buyers. For example, ChoiceBuys.com is a site operated by Choice Hotels International, a company that franchises the hotels Comfort Inn, Comfort Suites, Quality, Clarion, Sleep Inn, Econo Lodge, Rodeway Inn, Cambria Suites, Suburban Extended Stay Hotel, and MainStay Suites. The company franchises over 6,000 establishments in the United States and around the world. In 1999, the company established the website so it could concentrate all purchases for the hotels through a single channel. The site invites sellers to offer their products. For the sellers, this is an opportunity to obtain big contracts. For the hotels, this is a way to enjoy substantial discounts, which ChoiceBuys.com obtains through its buying power. For Choice Hotels, it is a way to generate revenue from the transaction fees that the bidders pay, and indirectly a way to attract more franchisees that, of course, pay the company franchise fees. Independent hotels are allowed to make their own purchases, but an increasing number of purchases are made through the Choice's procurement services site. Processing orders through the site not only saved money for the hotel operators but also enriched Choice Hotels. Since all transactions are electronic, they are automatically recorded and provide valuable data from which useful information can be gleaned. As shown in the illustration, Choice Hotels provides a comprehensive website forum for vendor information as well as other information for franchisees.

Online websites can provide a portal of services for purchasing, such as this site for Choice Hotels

Many exchanges require businesses to register as members and to pay an annual fee. Many guarantee sellers that they will receive payment even if the buyer defaults, an important and attractive consideration for sellers. Electronic marketplaces bring markets closer to what economists call perfect markets. In a perfect market, no single buyer or seller can affect the price of a product. On the Internet, all buyers and sellers have access to the same information at the same time. Thus, no single buyer or seller has an information advantage over competitors.

Online Business Alliances

Companies in the same industry—competitors—often collaborate in establishing a website for one or several purposes. One major purpose might be to create buying power by consolidating purchases. Another might be to create a single place for customers, assuming that expanded choice will benefit the group. The concept is not new: real estate agents have collaborated in the Multiple Listing Service (MLS), whereby multiple agencies have access to real estate that is registered for sale with one of them. This system, which was in place many years before the web, is now managed on the web.

Interestingly, real estate agents are now under competitive pressure from operators of websites. Sellers who wish to reduce the traditional 6 percent agent commission increasingly turn to online real estate markets. Many sellers are willing to do much of the work done by agents, and list their property with sites such as Redfin.com and ziprealty.com instead of with an agent who is a member of the National Association of Realtors® (NAR), the organization that operates MLS. Many buyers prefer to search for houses on their own. They can use a site such as Zillow.com to estimate house prices in an area of interest. They may save thousands of dollars when purchasing from a seller who pays a low flat fee instead of a high percentage commission to a real estate agent. In other words, the web is removing the expensive middleperson in this industry also.

In some cases, the purpose of an alliance site is the same as an auction site operated by a single company, but the operator is a business that works for the allied companies. The purpose of such a site is to set the prices of purchased products and services. Big players in an industry, such as airlines or automakers, establish a shared company that operates the site. Suppliers are invited to sell through the site and compete among themselves. The competition drives prices down. The allies may enjoy lower costs and greater profit margins. A grand attempt by the auto industry to use this method through an alliance called Covisint failed because suppliers refused to compete against each other online. The Covisint software was sold to Compuware, a software development company in Detroit. However, Star Alliance, an alliance of 27 airlines, has done well with its online joint purchasing.

Star Alliance is one of several airline alliances, such as OneWorld and SkyTeam Star Alliance that established an extranet for two purposes: to concentrate purchases from parts and service providers, and to represent the group to its clients, airline passengers. The Star Alliance includes Air Canada, Air New Zealand, Austrian Airlines, Lufthansa, Scandinavian Airlines, United, US Airways, and other companies. On the consumer side, the airlines collaborate in frequent flier programs: you can fly with any of them and accrue miles with the entire alliance rather than with a single airline. The Star Alliance site provides several useful services for travelers of all member airlines. On the B2B side, the alliance solicits bids from suppliers of aircraft parts and maintenance services, food, ground equipment, office supplies, and other products and services. The allies use the extranet to share information about inventory levels, facilitate joint planning and forecasting for material requirements, and facilitate communication and business transactions between the airlines and suppliers. The hub for joint purchasing has saved the allies millions of dollars annually.

In 2001, Orbitz was established by United Airlines, Delta Air Lines, Continental Airlines, Northwest Airlines, and American Airlines to serve customers through a single website. The allies wanted to establish a site that "would provide comprehensive and unbiased travel information" as well as one that would make planning and buying travel on the Internet easy and hassle free instead of the usual "scavenger hunt." The site provides a comprehensive search engine, a list of flights by lowest price and number of stops without favoring any airline, and special Internet-only fares with over 455 airlines. By using their own website, airlines can stop paying the $5 to $10 commission they usually pay to online brokers such as Expedia, Travelocity, and Priceline.com. They can also eliminate fees to online database companies that link travel agencies, airlines, and other travel companies. In addition to the airlines, the site serves 22 rental car companies, cruise lines, and tens of thousands of lodging establishments. After the approval of an initial public offering, in July 2007 Orbitz began trading on the NYSE.

Similar alliance sites have been established by firms in the general retail industry, the food industry, and the hospitality industry (hotels).

B2C Trading

Although business-to-business trading on the Internet is much larger in volume, online business-to-consumer (B2C) trading is more visible to the general public. Online consumer shopping and buying has become a daily activity for many consumers. In addition to e-retailing, also known as "e-tailing," B2C activities include reading an online newspaper and paying bills online. Figure 8.3 illustrates the growth in online consumer spending in the United States.

FIGURE **8.3**

Online consumer spending continues to grow in the United States

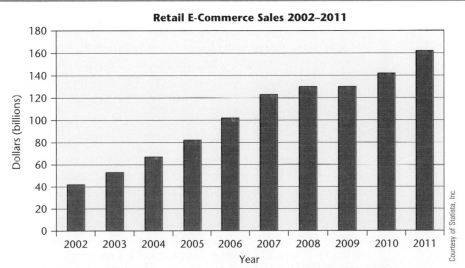

Source: Richter, Felix. (2012). [Graph illustration of e-commerce sales in the United States from 2002-2011]. E-Commerce in the United States. Retrieved from http://www.statista.com/topics/871/online-shopping/chart/683/e-commerce-in-the-united-states/

E-Tailing

You can shop the web for virtually any item you want, from collectibles to automobiles, order these items online, and receive them at your door. As Figure 8.3 indicates, e-commerce sales in the United States have steadily increased over the past 10 years, peaking in 2011 at $162 billion. At various retail sites, shoppers can use sophisticated search applications to find information on desired items, read other shoppers' reviews of items, post their own opinions, drop an item in a virtual shopping cart, change their minds and remove the item, or decide to buy the item and pay by providing a credit-card number or through a debit service such as PayPal. Online retailing—e-tailing—continues to grow throughout the world for several reasons: greater availability of faster communication lines to households, growing confidence in online purchases, and the increasing ability to find the item one searches for and rich information about it.

While e-tailing targets shoppers on PCs, "m-tailing" captures shoppers through their smartphones or tablets. U.S. mobile commerce revenue in 2010 was only $3 billion however; that number is expected to dramatically rise to $31 billion by 2016 (Richter, 2012).

In the new world of the web, there are several models associated with retail businesses. Traditional retailers, often called **brick-and-mortar** businesses, have extended their "storefront" by launching an e-tailing arm. Companies such as Target, Home Depot, and Walmart have created an online version of their retail operations. Businesses such as Amazon.com and Buy.com that transact business only through an online environment are called **pure play** retailers. Online sites combine user-friendly and enticing webpages, database management systems, and transaction software to provide shopping and buying convenience. Companies that sell online have smaller expenses than those selling from stores because they do not have to buy or rent store buildings and use labor to operate cash registers. They do, however, maintain large warehouses and pay for picking, packing, and shipping, three activities known as **fulfillment**. In some cases, however, they do not even need to maintain their entire inventory because they can simply route orders directly to manufacturers, who ship the items directly to the customer.

POINT OF INTEREST Buy Online. Pickup Offline.

Three major retailers, Nordstrom, Walmart, and Lowes, all offer ordering online with in-store pickups. Customers shop online just as they normally would except at checkout, they select "In store pickup" as the shipping option. They then go to the brick-and-mortar retail location to pick it up. This option allows customers to shop from the convenience of their own homes or from a mobile device and conduct research on alternative products. They also can avoid busy times at the mall and the bustling crowds. Customers benefit because they simply have to pay for the item when they arrive at the store without spending time trying to find it first. From the store's perspective, this is a negative aspect, because ordering online eliminates impulse purchases. Brick-and-mortar stores want people to walk around and see all the items for sale. The stores do benefit, however, because they get the sales of people who strictly shop online and would otherwise order products from large online retailers instead of brick-and-mortar stores.

Sources: Lowes (2012). Buy Online. Pick Up In Store. from http://www.lowes.com; Nordstrom (2013). Buy Online, Pick-Up in Store. from http://www.nordstrom.com; Walmart (2013). Help: Pick Up Today. from http://www.walmart.com

An important element of online retailing is selection. Compare the variety of products that can be offered at a web storefront with the selection offered by a brick-and-mortar store: a typical DVD store offers about 25,000 different titles, while Amazon offers 500,000 titles, which is the total number of titles offered for sale in the United States. E-tailers also experience fewer returns because shoppers have more information at hand before they make their purchases. So, shoppers are more satisfied with their buying decisions, and web businesses save the costs of dealing with returns. Another explanation for fewer returns is the creation of what marketers call one-to-one relationships. Using cookies, the website software can track the clickstreams of shoppers who browse the site and track their interests. When the same shopper logs on again, the software offers new items that fall within his or her interest area. And with every visit, the software learns more about visitors and their preferences.

As Figure 8.4 summarizes, consumers find several advantages to shopping online: convenience, time-savings, wide selection, search mechanisms, comparative shopping, and product reviews. E-tailers face mounting challenges, however. The competition is just a click away, so it is critical to offer a wide selection and excellent service, in addition to low price. E-tailers provide easy-to-use online tools to track shipments, and many make returns easy. Some brick-and-mortar retail chains allow purchases made on their websites to be returned to physical stores.

FIGURE 8.4

Online shopping benefits

Benefit	Because shoppers can...
Convenience	Shop from anywhere at any time of the day.
Time-saver	Visit numerous online stores in a few minutes; it would take hours to do so at shopping malls.
Wide selection	Choose from a selection of products that no shopping mall can offer.
Search mechanism	Find who sells a specific item within seconds by using search engines.
Comparative shopping	Quickly compare quality and price across multiple sellers.
Product reviews	Read product reviews by independent experts and other shoppers, often on the same webpage that describes the item.

© Cengage Learning 2015

The greatest challenge for e-tailers is turning shoppers into buyers, and then turning the buyers into repeat buyers. To this end, many e-tailers have linked their customer relationship management (CRM) applications, discussed in Chapter 3, "Business Functions and Supply Chains," to their websites. Using cookies and other software, they not only collect large amounts of information about individual shoppers but also constantly update their profiles. The purpose of **consumer profiling** is to know the consumers better so the business can serve them better, while also streamlining its marketing and sales operations.

While consumer profiling might sound benign, many privacy advocates claim that it violates privacy rights. Imagine that every time you log on to a site, this fact is recorded. Then, when you click on an icon, it is recorded, too. The software at the server side also records the time you spent at each specific page, assuming the longer you spent, the more interested you are. Chances are the site will send you promotional email about the items displayed on that carefully viewed page. Also, the next time you log on to the site, you might find that this particular page appears on your computer monitor faster than before. These subtle changes result from intelligent analysis of the information you provided knowingly or unknowingly to the site—and perhaps other sites that forwarded the information to this retailer. Many retailers also sell the information they collect to data brokers such as ChoicePoint and Acxiom, who combine personal data and sell the records to other companies. Privacy advocates object to such observation and sales of data without the user's consent.

Affiliate Programs Many online businesses offer affiliate programs to website owners. The affiliate, the website owner, places a link, usually a banner, to the e-tailer at the site. Affiliates are compensated in one of several ways: *pay per sale*, in which only if a visitor ended up purchasing something is the affiliate paid a fee; *pay per click*, in which the affiliate is paid a small fee (usually a few cents) whenever a visitor clicks the banner; or *pay per lead*, whereby a lead means that the visitor clicked through to the advertiser's site and filled out a registration form to receive periodic information. Retailers usually use the pay per sale model.

Some companies make money by being affiliate aggregators. LinkShare (www.linkshare.com) and Commission Junction (www.cj.com) let you choose from hundreds of affiliate advertisers, some offering reduced commissions. You can pick the ones you want to mention at your website.

Coopetition Amazon.com has taken a step beyond affiliate programs to cooperate with competitors, a model we may call "coopetition": Amazon includes its competitors on its own site. When you use the search engine at the company's site for a certain item, it brings up the product description and price from Amazon.com's database and also the same type of information from other companies' databases. Although these companies are direct competitors, Amazon benefits from this cooperation in two ways: it attracts more shoppers to visit its site first, because they know there is a high probability that they will find the item they want at the site, even if they end up buying from another company; and it receives a fee from these affiliated companies whenever they sell through Amazon's site. Recently, Amazon announced a virtual currency for its Android application store called Amazon Coins (Spence, 2013). They are targeting the new currency at buying applications online. Other e-tailers also give web presence to competitors.

Mobile Advertising

Smartphone and tablet screens are the frontier of advertising. The mobile advertising industry is rapidly growing, mostly due to smartphone and network adoption. Estimates put North American smartphone users in 2008 at about 60 million and growing to 239 million by 2013. 3G network data plans will reach 95 percent penetration by 2013 in the United States and 70 percent penetration in Canada by that time. In 2009, mobile advertising revenues in the United States and Canada were $208 million but by 2012 they were predicted to hit $1.5 billion, according to Parks Associates' report, Mobile Advertising: Analysis and Forecasts (Anonymous, 2009). One of the main types of mobile advertising is advertising in apps. Many applications on smartphones allow users to download a free version or purchase an ad-free version. Ads can be full-page displays that go away after an allotted period of time, or a smaller box on the screen. Advertisers charge per impression (view) or per click. Businesses can purchase ads to be seen on mobile devices through Google or Apple. Mobile ad spending is already estimated to be between $550 and $650 million (Gobry, 2011).

Auctions and Reverse Auctions

Similar to auctions among companies, some websites serve as auction hubs for individuals. The most prominent of the sites is eBay, but there are many other smaller and independent online auction sites such as uBid. The business model is simple: sellers list information about the items or services they offer for sale, and if a sale is executed, the site owner collects a fee. Because the sites provide only a platform for a transaction that eventually takes place between two consumers, some people like to call online auctions consumer-to-consumer e-business. To participate in auctions, one needs to register as a member. To help bidders know to what extent they can count on the sellers' integrity, eBay publishes the number of feedback comments it received on a member, and the number and percentage of positive feedbacks. (However, eBay's feedback may be abused. For example, a seller may earn positive feedback on many small sales, then use the high rating to cheat buyers on large sales.)

eBay is the world's largest online auction place with 108.3 million active users globally. In 2011, the total value of goods sold on eBay was $68.6 billion; that's $2,100 per second! The following stats are from 2012:

- A passenger vehicle sold every 2 minutes
- More than 4.69 million passenger vehicles have been sold to date on eBay Motors
- An RV or camper sold every 33 minutes
- A boat sold every 19 minutes
- A pair of shoes sold every 3 seconds
- A cell phone sold every 5 seconds
- An MP3 player sold every 26 seconds including Apple iPod, Creative Zen, and others
- A GPS device sold every minute
- An Apple iPad, laptop, or notebook sold every 2 minutes

Because eBay has such a massive global reach, more and more people go there first to buy or sell just about anything.

Sources: eBay (2012). eBay Marketplaces Fast Facts At-A-Glance (Q3 2012); eBay (2012). eBay Motors Fast Facts (Q3 2012); eBay (2012). Who We Are Overview. from http://www.ebayinc.com/who

The ability of websites to serve as prompt exchanges of information has supported another popular business model, the **reverse auction** or **name-your-own-price auction**. Consumers at Priceline.com are invited to post requests for services and name the prices they are willing to pay. Although they also deal in home mortgages, the services are mostly for travel, such as flights, cruises, lodging, and car rentals. Customers can post the destination, day, and time of a flight as well as the maximum price they are willing to pay. Then, airlines are invited to consider the requests. The first airline to accept the terms wins the offer. Shoppers are required to transmit a credit-card account number. The account is charged as soon as an airline accepts the deal. Priceline's revenue comes from the fees that airlines and other businesses pay to use the service.

Content Providers

On the web, content means information, such as news, research results, statistics, and other useful information as well as artistic works such as music, pictures, and video clips. Some place this category within classified ads, including job postings and online dating services. Over the years, individuals and organizations have spent increasing amounts of money on content. Although most news can be obtained free of charge, many articles cannot. Some audiences welcome for-fee content, especially if it is highly specialized. Given a choice, many people prefer to read the same information online rather than on paper because they can use search operations to quickly find specific articles. This might be one reason why many prefer to subscribe to the electronic version of a newspaper. Content revenues also have grown since companies such as Amazon, Apple, and Walmart started selling individual songs and books online.

In recent years, video has become a popular type of content. Several sites enable anyone to upload video clips. Some of the sites, such as YouTube, have attracted millions of people daily. The high volume of traffic translates into dollars through advertisements, as the site owners provide the content free of charge. While many YouTube users are individuals, YouTube has also become an integral component of the marketing strategy for business organizations for advertising, promotions, and contests. The no-fee, popularity, and high adoption rate of YouTube accounts provides a "win-win" value proposition for businesses. Companies can upload commercials aired on television as well as other corporate videos. For example, Frito-Lay uploaded a video with an intern to promote their internship program. This media promotion can provide significant value over traditional outlets, such as magazines or newspapers, to reach people with an interest in working for Frito-Lay.

Bill Presentment and Payment

Because it is so easy to transfer funds online from one bank account to another, and it is so easy to send information, including bills, by email, many utility companies try to convince customers to accept electronic bills and pay them online. Some customers accept the option of electronic bill presentment but refuse to sign an agreement that would enable the company to automatically charge their bank account. Obviously, banks are always a participant in electronic payment if the charge is to a bank account (which is how most utility and mortgage companies want to be paid), but some banks, for their own reasons, refuse to join such trilateral initiatives.

Electronic bill presentment and payment (EBPP) saves utility companies and financial institutions that bill customers regularly—mainly for loan payments—millions of dollars. The bills are presented automatically, directly from the companies' information systems to payers' email addresses, and therefore save labor, paper, and postage. Direct charge to a bank account saves the labor involved in receiving and depositing checks. Yet, EBPP is spreading slowly. Most people still prefer to pay their bills by check and through the mail, partly because fraud on the Internet has increased in recent years, especially through a practice called **phishing**, discussed in this chapter's Ethical & Societal Issues feature. Figure 8.5 illustrates the practice. Note that the link does not link directly to Barclays, but to a fictitious site that is also not secure. A legitimate website is secure when it includes an "s" in https:// URL. Also note the bank warnings to customers. This particular email was sent to a person who does not even have an account with the bank. Many banks have adopted a new technique to impede phishing. This technique requires the customer to select a personal image that is displayed with any forms that request a password. Customers of a bank's online services are advised to enter a password only when they see the image they originally selected.

FIGURE 8.5

Phishing plagues financial
institutions through fake
emails prompting
unsuspecting consumers
to click links and enter
personal information

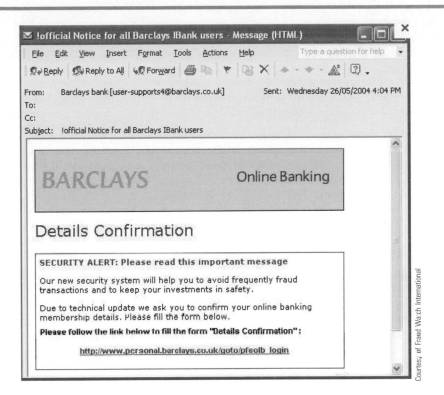

A recent study conducted at a Microsoft TechEd conference states that despite the public's growing awareness, phishing still remains a serious threat (Anonymous, 2012d). Large organizations continue to be targeted by phishing attacks that often lead to a security breach. The survey found that the number of organizations targeted by phishing incidents has risen to 58 percent in 2012 from 48 percent in 2010.

POINT OF INTEREST   Banks Fending Off Phishing

Phishing is a cyberattack tactic used to trick Internet users into giving up personal information such as PINs and account numbers. Nearly half of all "phishing" attacks in 2011 targeted the financial-services industry. Some of the biggest players in the industry such as American Express Co., J.P. Morgan Chase & Co., and Barclays PLC are taking steps to make life harder for Internet scammers by buying new exclusive domain extensions. Firms have put out at minimum $3.3 million or $185,000 per address to the Internet Corporation for Assigned Names and Numbers (ICANN), the nonprofit organization that oversees the Internet, to secure the extensions. Examples of the new extensions include .citi, .bofa, and .barclays. These firms hope the new extensions will assure their online customers that they are dealing with the bank's real site and not a scam website. The new domain extensions, which could be approved by ICANN as early as 2013, will help combat the large amount of Internet fraud in the financial industry by preventing customers from being tricked into dealing out confidential information to fake websites.

Source: Seidman, A. (2012, Aug 16). No 'Phishing': Banks Try to Sink Scammers; Financial Firms Apply for Own Internet Domain Names, Wall Street Journal (Online).

The web provides excellent opportunities but its wide availability combined with ingenuity have created some practices that range from mildly annoying to criminally dangerous.

- **Email Spam.** Spam is the term for any unsolicited commercial email. The reason for spam is simple: it is the most cost-effective marketing method. Even if a fraction of a percent of the recipients end up purchasing the product or service touted, the spammer profits. Both individuals and organizations dislike spam. Individuals have to wade through a long list of unsolicited email to get to useful email. Organizations face an increasingly costly burden. Consider that if spam makes up half of the email the organization receives, the organization must employ twice the bandwidth it really needs for communications and twice the space on email servers. Obviously, it will pay twice as much as necessary to operate an email system. Spam-filter software has helped to some extent, but spam is still on the rise and still wastes resources. In 2009, about 80 to 85 percent of all email traffic was spam (Radicati, 2009).

  The Direct Marketing Association (DMA) defends the right of businesses to send unsolicited commercial email as a legitimate and cost-effective way of doing business. Indeed, the method gives small, entrepreneurial businesses a chance to compete. The DMA sees no difference between junk "snail" mail, which most of us reluctantly tolerate, and spam.

  In May of 2009, a federal judge in California ordered convicted spammer Sanford Wallace and two other men to stay away from Facebook after they were found guilty for spamming on the site. Sanford was found guilty under the CAN-SPAM act a year prior for phishing and spamming MySpace users. The judge awarded MySpace $230 million in damages (McMillan, 2009). According to this law, spam is a crime only if the sending party hides its true identity or does not provide an opt-out option.

  Is unsolicited commercial email a legitimate marketing tool, or is it a nuisance that should be eradicated by strictly enforced laws? Would it be fair to outlaw an efficient way for businesses, especially entrepreneurial businesses, to approach potential customers?

- **Mobile Spam.** With 89.6 million Americans using their smartphones to access their email, according to comScore research, the threat of mobile spam arises (Pimanova, 11 September 2012). The problems and difficulties associated with mobile spam are different from those originating from email spam. For one, people with BlackBerries, iPhones, or other smartphones believe that because of the device's limited use, compared to a PC, they are more secure. That is a false assumption that can lead to smartphone users not being able to identify spam when they receive it. Additionally, clearing spam from inboxes on a smartphone with limited screen space takes considerably more time than

on a PC. Pay attention to fonts, headers, images, text, and links that appear skewed from the norm; those are usually good hints for picking out spam (Brown, 2009).

- **Pop-Up Windows.** You browse the web, stop to read an interesting article, and a few seconds later a window pops up, partially covering the text you were reading. The pop-up contains an advertisement. You look for the icon to close the window. It is not in its normal location. You finally manage to close the window, but as soon as you do, another one pops up. And so on, and so forth, more and more windows. When you finally close the main site's window, you discover that several other windows popped up *behind* the window. The site owner is paid by advertisers to run these pesky windows, which is legitimate. However, many people are quite annoyed by the practice. Some employ special applications or turn on a browser option that prevents pop-up windows. Is this a good solution? Not always. Many sites have links that open a little window to provide further information, such as a window with help or explanation of a term. If you block all pop-up windows, such useful windows do not open. If you use a selective pop-up "killer," you have to program it to allow pop-up windows for individual sites. Thus, even with a solution, pop-up windows waste surfers' time. Web surfers might not like pop-up windows, but advertisers love them, because they are an effective marketing tool.

- **Adware.** A growing number of organizations use adware, software that delivers ad banners or pop-up advertising windows on the web. Often, the banners hide large parts of the information on the page. Adware is often tailored to users, based on their profiles, such as previous interests. Some companies use adware that pops up deliberately to cover banners of competing companies that paid to advertise at the site a user visits. The visitor might not even know that the ad is not originating from the website or its legitimate advertising clients, but from another one.

- **Spyware.** A more disturbing "ware" is spyware. As discussed in this chapter, spyware is software that uses the Internet connection of a computer to transmit information about the user without the user's knowledge or permission. Usually, the software transmits information about users' activities with their computers, including their every move on the Internet. It sits on the computer's hard disk, secretly collects information, and transmits it to the computer of a company, usually for marketing purposes, but also for industrial espionage. Some surreptitious software is also designed to pop up windows. Some countries have criminalized adware and spyware, but in much of the world the software does not violate any law.

- **Phishing.** A growing number of web users receive a special kind of spam that intends not to sway them to buy something but to defraud them. The practice is called phishing, a play on "fishing." Criminals send thousands of messages that look as if they were sent from a bank, a credit-card company, or any other financial institution or an organization where the recipient has authority to withdraw funds. The email provides a web link where the recipient is urged to go and supply personal information, including codes that are used to withdraw or transfer funds. One of many "reasons" is "explained" in the message: your account must be renewed, the bank lost your details, you should verify your personal information or the account will be revoked, and many others. Thousands of people have fallen prey to the con artists, who used the information to withdraw funds. The most obvious sign that an email message tries to phish is a message from an institution with which you have never transacted, such as a bank where you do not have an account. A more subtle sign is the URL that appears when you move your mouse to the link provided: the domain name is not the one of the legitimate organization. Suspect every email message that asks you to update your personal information online. Call the organization using the legitimate number you have on file and ask if the message is genuine. Banks and other institutions rarely use email to ask for "account information update." Phishing continues to grow. According to a 2012 Symantec Intelligence Report, August of 2012 showed a jump in email phishing activity. While email phishing attacks averaged one out of every 500 emails in the previous four months, August showed a rate of one phishing email out of every 312 emails. In addition, the two most "phished" countries were the Netherlands at one phishing email in 94.4 emails (1.06 percent) and South Africa at one in 171.2 emails (0.58 percent) (Pimanova, 11 September 2012).

Extra-Organizational Workforce

The web enables companies to purchase labor from many more people than their own employees. **Crowdsourcing** is a process for outsourcing a variety of tasks to a distributed group of people, both online or offline. Different than traditional outsourcing, crowdsourcing is a task or problem that is outsourced to the public rather than a specific company contracted for a defined purpose. For example, companies can augment their intellectual pool by using the web to employ talent beyond their own employees. They can enjoy more labor for less money by offering cash for research and development (R&D) solutions provided by researchers outside their organizations.

InnoCentive, Inc., originally formed as a subsidiary of the pharmaceutical company Eli Lilly and Company, operates a website connecting companies ("seekers") with scientists ("solvers"). Companies whose R&D staffs cannot find a solution to a biological or chemical problem can post the challenge at the site and offer a cash reward for a practical solution. Scientists and researchers from around the world can register with the site and work on solutions. The site is operated in seven languages to accommodate scientists and organizations from all over the world. As of 2012, InnoCentive is a privately held, venture backed firm. Many companies, including Eli Lilly, Booz Allen Hamilton, Dow Chemical Co. and the giant consumer product company Procter & Gamble, have worked with InnoCentive. The company has more than 270,000 registered problem solvers in nearly 200 countries. With over 1,300 awards approved totaling $37 million, they have received over 34,000 solutions submissions. InnoCentive provides an online forum to connect problem solvers and cloud-based technology to create rapid solutions for innovative projects ("Innocentive Corporate Website—About Us," 2013).

When a company employs a staff of researchers it must pay them regardless of how fruitful their efforts are. When offering cash for solutions, many more scientists might work for the company, but the company pays only the scientist who solves the problem. This enables the company to tap many more creative minds and to reduce the high risk involved in R&D. The solution to a scientific or technological problem may arrive sooner, and the cost savings can be huge.

Mobile Commerce

In Chapter 6, "Business Networks and Telecommunications," you learned about the many wireless technologies that enable people to access the web while away from the office or home. Wireless technologies enable what some people call **mobile commerce**, sometimes referred to as m-commerce. Mobile devices already let users log on to the Internet, but they can also provide an additional benefit to businesses: a device can be located with an accuracy of several feet, much like locating a cellular phone. As soon as you come within a few blocks of a store, your handheld computer or phone could beep and display a promotional message on its monitor.

Mobile commerce allows people to use their mobile devices to experience an event and react immediately. For example, they might view a horse race and place bets from their seat. Or, they can see a demonstration of a product at a public place and order it online. Impulse shopping will no longer be limited to shopping malls. Recall our discussion in Chapter 6 of future uses of RFID. Mobile devices might be equipped with RFID readers so their owners can use a product's electronic product code (EPC) to download information about it from the web.

Smart mobile devices might be helpful in salesforce automation. Traveling salespeople are able to access data through the mobile device almost anywhere. They are able to access corporate databases through their company's intranet. Both traveling salespeople and consumers already practice mobile commerce whenever they transact while using a hotspot or a web-capable cell phone.

Maintaining information on travel itineraries can be tedious. Tripit is a mobile app that can track various travel reservations (hotel, airfare, rental car) and combine them into a travel plan for a particular trip. Users can build their travel plans through the application by forwarding an email confirmation from a travel provider to a Tripit email address. The user's app will read the email containing the travel information and automatically add it to the user's travel plan.

Mobile applications such as Tripit provide consumers with information about their travel itineraries

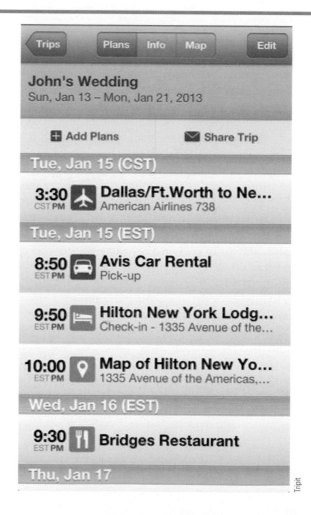

Some people believe that the most attractive mobile application might not be online buying, but the delivery of highly relevant information, custom-tailored to the user's current location and activity. Location-based services include downloading coupons at the store in which the consumer has just entered, finding out about nearby restaurants, or reading product reviews while shopping at an appliance store.

In the United States, cell phones must, by law, include global positioning system (GPS) capability, so that people can be located in case of emergency. As telephoning and other technologies are merged into a single device that can also link to the web, the potential for marketing and pushing information might be too tempting for businesses.

Most experts believe that exponential growth in mobile applications available on smartphones and tablets will continue. A recent survey by ClickZ reports more than three out of four people believed that all business organizations and brands should offer a mobile application (Klotz-Young, 2012). An excellent example of mobile computing and branding is Dunkin' Donuts. In April 2012, they announced the availability of a mobile application to "connect" guests to their brand. Customers can use the new app to complete many activities including paying for purchases at their franchises, adding funds to their account, sending gifts to friends, and locating the nearest location. In addition, their application links to Dunkin' Donuts social media communities consisting of 6.8 million Facebook fans (Anonymous, 2012b).

Privacy proponents have already voiced concerns about mobile commerce. Some people are unaware that commercial organizations can track them down anytime when their mobile device is on. These devices not only allow consumer profiling, as already practiced by many online retailers, but can also tell retailers and other organizations your exact location at any given time. The result might be "we know who you are, what you have done on the web, and where you are now." While some users are not comfortable about tracking, others are not concerned about privacy and security issues. In fact, many social media sites such as Twitter and Foursquare use location services to report where the user is located as they provide information through their site. However, a recent research study completed by Veracode notes that as more applications are web- and mobile-enabled, testing and security issues will need increased attention (Anonymous, 2012e).

The concerns over privacy are only one issue relating to security in mobile computing. As in the Dunkin' Donuts example, an increasing number of customers are paying for purchases with mobile devices. Mobile payment systems such as PayPal, Square, Google Wallet, and Apple Passbook have been developed to complete payments on mobile devices. It will be important to protect the consumer's identity and provide trust that purchasing information will not be sold (Purewal, 2013).

POINT OF INTEREST — Thou Shalt Not Steal ... My Identity!

The adoption of various information technology applications by consumers has increased over the last several years. The Bureau of Justice Statistics estimates that 8.6 million households with at least one child over 12 years old has been a victim of identity theft, a rise from 6.4 million in 2005. A significant proportion of the increase was due to the unauthorized use of an existing credit-card account between 2005 and 2010. The issue of identity theft has heightened the need for consumer caution. Although the number of households experiencing the fraudulent use of an existing account other than a credit card (checking, savings, utility) held stable at 35 percent, and the number of new accounts opened illegally decreased from 23 percent to 14 percent in the same period, the total financial losses due to identify theft were over $13 billion. Protecting your personal and financial account information needs to be a continued effort on the part of consumers.

Source: Anonymous (December 17, 2011). Bureau of Justice Statistics; Identity Theft Reported by Households Rose 33 Percent From 2005 to 2010. Investment Weekly News, 469.

Social Media on the Web

Social media have had a widespread influence on consumers and business organizations alike in recent years. More than 900 million people check their Facebook accounts on a monthly basis (Aquino, 2012). The adoption and use of social media is also generating advertising revenue. A recent study by BIA/Kelsey forecasts that social media ad revenues in the United States will reach $9.2 billion in 2016, up 100 percent from 2012 (Anonymous, 2012a). Popular social media sites such as Facebook, Twitter, Instagram, and Foursquare create a "buzz" about a variety of subjects and topics. Businesses can leverage additional advertising and exposure to their brand and products through well-planned social media strategies. Organizations can leverage social media to communicate with consumers immediately, instead of the longer timeframe of response for traditional communications mediums (newspapers, radio, television, etc.). Organizations are finding that using social media is even more effective for disseminating information than posting press releases and information on their websites. For example, a micro-blog message on Twitter can alert customers to a new promotion, product, or location. Like traditional marketing sourcing techniques, social media messages can link directly to an organization's website for more information, boosting web traffic to their site at no cost.

The challenges associated with social media mirror the challenges of any business strategy. An effective social media strategy must be well-organized and coordinated, focusing on objectives to communicate, promote, and market to an organization's customers and stakeholders. As with any information technology initiative, it is imperative for the business to drive the use of social media rather than the other way around. Information technology and business leaders must collaborate to focus on a common goal and approach, and then plan how to use social media to communicate this. Ford Motor Company, for example, has embraced the use of social media for its marketing and customer support activities. Its approach is to encourage employees to become advocates to share company content in social media environments (Donston-Miller & Carr, 2012).

One of the most frequent criticisms of social media is to question whether any value is gained from the resources devoted to its implementation. It is important to gather and compile data to determine the influence and value gained by your organization's social media efforts. Social media analytics can be used to calculate the returns, if any, to the business. Data analytic tools such as sentiment and content analysis can provide quantifiable metrics to track the value of social media initiatives. In a recent survey of business executives, over 60 percent of the companies using social media and data analytics allocated between 1 and 2.9 percent of their marketing budget to social analytics (Aquino, 2012).

Although there are challenges in integrating of social media, the benefits of doing so are becoming clear. A recent study posits that the social media interaction between a brand and its customers influences long-term sales increases. When implemented systematically, the realized benefits of social media interactions are seen in increased transactions, profits, and return on investment (Anonymous, 2012c). Social media not only increases business, but also has been influential in the area of learning. ASTD and the Institute for Corporate Productivity found that there is a clear relationship between how people learn and their age or generation. When asked for the context on how social media tools assist in accomplishing learning and accomplishing work, the millennial generation outpaces previous generations (Generation X and Baby Boomers) in every respect (Patel, 2010).

Social media also influences the dialogue with stakeholders outside of the products organizations sell. Sodexho implemented a recruitment campaign using Twitter. With a relatively small investment ($50K), recruiters searched Twitter to find food-related and job-searching tweets. Selected Twitter users were referred to Sodexho's recruiting webpage. Within six months, Sodexho's recruiters were able to fill enough open jobs to save $350,000 in recruiting ads targeted for Monster.com (Paine, 2011).

Supply Chains on the Web

Supply chains extend from commercial organizations to both suppliers and buyers. Organizations connect their supply chain management (SCM) systems to their suppliers at one end, and to their buyers at the other end. Thus, an organization might be a participant among other buyers in an extranet managed by one of its suppliers, and a participant among several sellers in an extranet of a buyer. Large retailers manage extranets through which their suppliers' SCM systems can provide useful information to their own, so they can track orders and shipments as well as collect useful information for decision making on which supplier to select for which order. In this regard, a large retailer's extranet becomes a marketplace for many sellers and a single buyer.

In the years before the Internet opened to commercial activities, many companies invested in Electronic Data Interchange (EDI) systems to exchange documents electronically with business partners. EDI consists of certain standards for formatting documents such as orders and invoices, software that translates the data properly, and the networks through which the information flows between subscribing organizations. The networks are owned and managed by value-added network (VAN) companies, telecommunications companies that manage the traffic of EDI between the business partners. Subscribers pay for this service. However, EDI can also be executed on the Internet. Although EDI provides some advantages, such as a high degree of data security and nonrepudiation (inability to deny sent messages), companies that want to connect to establish similar data exchange with business partners can use the web technologies on the Internet. XML and its descendants, in particular, enable business partners to set standards for data formats in webpages. Dynamic page technologies, the software that links webpages with databases, automate much of the business activity with business partners. Orders can automatically trigger notices to warehouse personnel on their stationery or handheld computers to pick and pack items for shipping. The information automatically flows into the accounting ISs as well as SCM systems of both the buyer and seller. Figure 8.6 illustrates how information flows between organizations.

FIGURE **8.6**

Online supply chain management

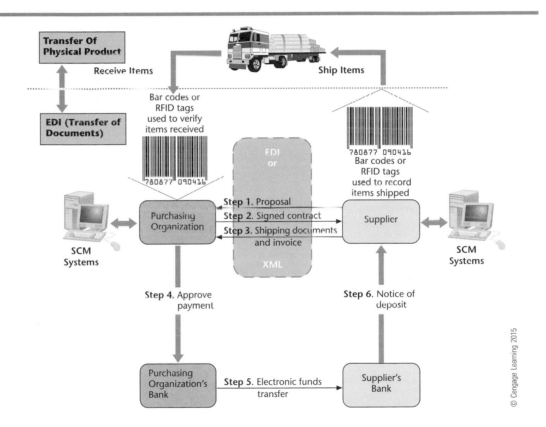

Companies encourage their suppliers to join their extranets. For example, the bookstore chain Barnes & Noble uses an extranet to do business with thousands of its suppliers. So does Office Depot, one of the world's largest retailers of office supplies. It uses an extranet to order billions of items annually. The extranet saves the company much paper and administrative labor. Walmart, the world's largest retailer, uses an extranet with Procter & Gamble and hundreds of other manufacturers. In addition to saving both labor and paper, the results are smaller inventory and greater in-stock availability of products. As shown in their webpage, Staples provides an online venue where suppliers can log in to transact business electronically.

Large retailers invite suppliers to join their extranets as trading partners

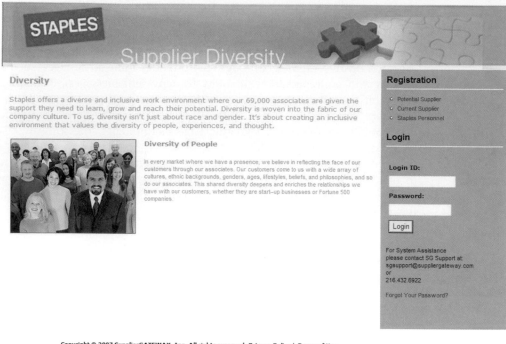

XML is used extensively in web technologies so that the SCM systems of two organizations can "speak to one another." This ensures that the meaning of data exchanged between the organizations can not only be displayed for employee eyes through web browsers, but that the received data can be interpreted correctly by systems that automatically capture and store it in a database for further processing.

Options in Establishing a Website

A website is, practically speaking, the webpages that make up the information and links to web technologies that the site provides. To establish a web business, an organization must have access to an Internet server and the ability to control its content. Recall that an Internet server is a computer that is connected to the Internet backbone. Businesses have two options when establishing a website: installing and maintaining their own servers, or contracting with a web hosting service.

Owning and Maintaining a Server

Installing and maintaining a server at the business's own facility is a costly option, but it gives the business the greatest degree of control. Setting up a server requires expertise, which may or may not be available within the business. The business must obtain a high-speed physical link to the Internet backbone. It must also employ specialists to maintain the server or many servers on which the website resides. In large organizations, these specialists might be employees of the company; in smaller ones, they might be contract personnel whose services the company hires. The specialists purchase a server (or multiple servers) for the company, connect it to the Internet through a high-speed dedicated line, register a domain name for the site, and install the proper software for managing the server and creating webpages. The specialists "scale up" the server system when the business grows and handle issues such as load balancing to ensure quick response and to minimize the probability of site crashing. A site crashes when too many people try to log on and the software stops responding to anyone. **Load balancing** transfers visitor inquiries from a busy server to a less busy server for identical information and services. Thus, the specialists often must connect **mirror servers**—servers on which the same content and applications are duplicated—to speed up and back up the process.

A large company that uses the web for much or all of its business usually has its own servers and manages them fully. This may be a company whose entire business is conducted online, or a brick-and-mortar company that owns stores but also offers the same, many of the same, or additional items for sale online. These companies employ crews that manage Internet networking, the hardware and software of the site, and the people responsible for updating the webpages.

Using a Hosting Service

A majority of organizations that have a commercial presence online either do not own servers or own servers but let someone else manage at least some aspect of the site. These organizations use **web hosting** services. Web hosting companies specialize in one or several types of web hosting: shared hosting, virtual private server hosting, dedicated hosting, or co-location.

In **shared hosting**, the client's website is stored on the host's same physical server along with the sites of other clients. The hosting company owns the server and the server management software. It offers space on the servers for hosting websites. This is a relatively inexpensive option. The client can use templates provided by the hosts for building pages, or, for an extra fee, have the host's designer design the website. However, many clients prefer to design and upload their own webpages. The service includes transaction and payment software for use by the subscribing businesses' clients. If the server is shared, the host might not be able to allow a client to maintain its own domain name, such as *www.myownco.com*, but only a subdomain that contains the host's domain name, such as *myownco.myhost.com*. However, special software employed by many hosts allows clients to use their own domain names, and although the server has only one IP address, the software directs traffic to the proper site on the server. If an independent domain name is important, this is a factor that a business must consider before selecting a hosting service.

Small businesses with a limited number of products to sell can select a host such as aplusnet for shared hosting. The company invites you to "create an online business" for $19.95 per month. When your business grows and has more products to sell, the company promises to "grow with you" by providing more disk space. Large search engine and portal companies, such as Yahoo!, offer similar services. Yahoo!, for example, offers to build and host a fully functioning online store for a monthly fee. Clients have access to easy-to-use web design software tools to create the pages of their new site. This type of option is often a "turnkey" solution for a small business that wishes to go online almost overnight. In addition to disk space and help with website design, the hosting company typically also provides a number of email addresses and a control "dashboard," a mechanism for the client business to have remote control over content and other aspects of the site. Many hosting services offer WordPress or Blogger which can be used to design websites using templates, or third-party software tools such as Artisteer. Some hosts also offer to list the new site on frequently used search sites, such as Yahoo! and Google. Many of the hosts also help with domain name registration.

In shared hosting, hundreds of businesses might share the same server and storage space. Therefore, the host often limits the storage space allotted to each client, the number of transactions performed per month, or simply the amount of data, in megabytes, that the site transmits per month. Also, a technical problem in one site could affect the functionality of the other sites residing on the server.

The purpose of a **virtual private server** is to create the impression that the client maintains its own server. Virtual private server technology enables one server to be virtually split into many addressable servers, each for a different client and with its own domain name. This option is usually less expensive than renting a dedicated server, while enjoying the same benefits, including full control of the content of the virtual server.

Some companies might want to use entire physical servers all for themselves, and therefore opt for dedicated hosting. In **dedicated hosting**, the host dedicates a server to the client, and the client can fully control the content on the server's disks. The host is responsible for networking management. For example, 1&1 (see illustration), Acenet, and InMotionHosting offer such a service and allow the client to select from several servers. The greater the server's power, the higher the monthly fee. This service is more expensive than shared hosting, but it comes with several advantages. Dedicated hosting has fewer restrictions on storage space and transactions, and since only one site resides on the disks, no other site can affect its functionality. Renters of dedicated servers usually have *root access*, which means they act as unrestricted administrators of that computer. The greater control of the dedicated server option comes with a price: this option is more expensive than shared hosting or a virtual private server. The web hosting service 1&1 is one of many organizations providing various features and services for a business's website.

Shared hosting services offer website hosting with many services for a reasonable monthly fee

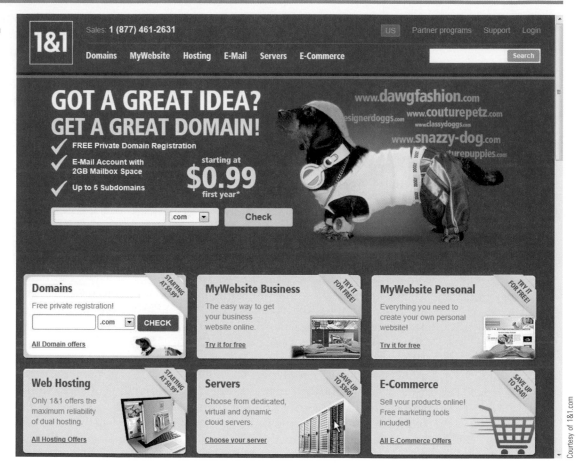

Courtesy of 1&1.com

In some cases, a company might want to fully manage its own web servers but prefers the expertise of a hosting company in managing networking and security. Some hosting services accommodate such demand by offering a **co-location** service. The client owns the servers and manages their content, but the servers are co-located with the servers of other clients as well as those of the host's in a secure (physical) site. This approach has been taken by some online retailers, such as Overstock.com, because it affords some advantages: the client does not have to employ hardware and network specialists, spend money on building a special secure location for the server, or ensure power supply. All these concerns are transferred to the hosting company. Co-location is usually the most expensive of hosting options. The client must purchase and run the servers, as well as pay for the co-location.

Selecting the proper host may determine the difference between a faltering site and a thriving one. ClawfootCollection.com was operated by an online retailer Vintage Tub & Bath. It was spun off from VintageTubs.com. The site offered reproduction antique bathtubs and bathroom fixtures. The site sold to no more than a dozen buyers in its first year online. Vintage decided to hire the services of a new hosting company, Demandware, Inc. Demandware not only hosted the site, but also redesigned it. It maintains the site's "back end"—the connections to software such as billing, accounting, and other business functions invisible to shoppers—and ensures the shopping cart works. Within a few months the site was listed as number one for the keywords 'acrylic clawfoot tub' and sales increased. Interestingly, Demandware charges its clients by the number of site visitors.

Considerations in Selecting a Web Host

A majority of businesses do not maintain their own web servers or co-locate them; they use host services. When a decision is made to use such a service, managers must consider several factors. Figure 8.7 lists the major factors. Hosts can be compared using points, for example, on a scale of 1 for the best and 5 for the worst. A simple evaluation method is for managers to compare each factor for the prospective host, compare the total scores, and then make a decision. The evaluators might wish to assign different weights to the various items based on how important each item is to the business.

FIGURE 8.7

Factors to consider when evaluating a web hosting service

Evaluation Criteria	Points
Type and quality of applications provided (Shopping carts, credit-card processing, blogs, Wikis)	_____
Storage space limitations	_____
Traffic/bandwidth limits	_____
Quality and availability of technical support	_____
Email accounts (number and features)	_____
Scalability	_____
Control panel and user interface	_____
Support and templates for website design	_____
Security	_____
Uptime ratio	_____
Setup	_____
Monthly fees	_____
Customer reviews	_____

The business should be able to use a database management system (DBMS) for cataloging its products and enable online shoppers to perform searches. Thus, the DBMS offered is important. It also might need to use **dynamic webpages**, pages that enable communication between the shopper's browser and the database. Such pages can be built with several programming tools: CGI, Java servlets, PHP, and ASP (Active Server Pages). Since the functionality of databases and dynamic pages, as well as some features on the pages, depend on the operating system that the hosts use, all this software must be considered. For example, if the client elects to build and maintain the webpages and prefers to use ASP, they should be aware that such software will run only on a server running Microsoft Windows.

Most hosting companies offer the use of a combination of software popularly called LAMP, which is an acronym: Linux for operating system, Apache for server management software, MySQL for DBMS, and PHP or Python or Perl for developing dynamic webpages. All of these resources are open source software, and therefore do not require license fees for the host, who can thus make the service more affordable. However, many hosts also offer other software, including Windows, for higher fees. In addition to these issues, the client should ensure satisfactory shopping cart, credit-card processing, and other applications at the site. If the client business needs integration of the web software to its back end systems, it must ensure that the hosting company can execute and maintain the integration.

Content management systems have become popular as a means of building and maintaining websites. Joomla! is popular content management software that allows users to publish, edit, and update website content. This product also provides procedures to manage the workflow of website maintenance in a collaborative environment.

Storage space limitations might become a serious inhibitor, especially if the business expects to offer a growing number of products and augment the information provided through the site. The client should enquire about options to increase storage space on demand and its cost.

Most hosts provide technical support 24 hours per day, 7 days per week throughout the year, known as 24/7/365. The client should ensure such service is provided and know exactly what support services are included in the contract.

You should be informed about the quality of the equipment that the hosting company provides, security measures it maintains, the sophistication of server and load management, and the technical skills of its personnel. Companies should inquire about past downtimes and recovery timeframes for the hosting company because they are an important part of technical support. If the client needs help in developing and updating webpages, the evaluators should explore the appearance and functionality of current clients of the hosting company.

Some hosting companies charge extra fees for shared hosting if the site experiences activity above a predetermined amount of data that is transferred (downloaded from the site or uploaded to it) or number of visits from web surfers, known as *hits*. In such arrangements, additional fees are charged for over-the-limit data transfer or hits. Web hosting companies price their services this way because the greater the number of hits, the more bandwidth they must allocate. The size of every file that is downloaded or uploaded is recorded, and if the limit—say 200 GB—has been exceeded, additional fees are charged. If the client's business grows, the cost might end up much greater than planned.

All hosting firms provide subscribers with several email addresses. Some also provide forwarding to other email addresses. Clients should examine these factors as well as the size of email boxes, autoresponding (automating email reply), and access to mailing lists.

Scalability is the ability of an organization to modify the capabilities of IT to accommodate growing needs. In this context, it is the ability for a website to grow—an important factor for most businesses. It is best to select a hosting company that has the hardware, software, and expertise to accommodate varying traffic levels and that can demonstrate its ability to develop a site from a simple, static one (one that does not require interactivity) to a heavily trafficked, interactive one. This applies to disk space, growing sophistication of software used, faster backup mechanisms, and other resources.

Smaller businesses often need help with the design of their webpages. They need to discover whether the hosting company maintains experienced and available web design personnel.

The host's physical site must be well secured against physical entry as well as intrusion through the Internet. Clients should ask for information about security measures. Some hosts are so careful as to not even advertise where they keep servers. Yahoo! is one such host.

Businesses want their websites available to users all the time. Downtime denies them business and damages their reputation. Hosting companies usually advertise their uptime as a percentage. For example, they might say they guarantee 99 percent uptime. This means that the client should expect the site to be down 1 percent (87.6 hours) of every year. Companies that need a higher uptime, such as 99.9 or 99.99 percent, should take notice of this and ensure that the host has the resources to claim such a high number of "nines." Such resources often include subscriptions to the services of two electric power companies or the availability of gas generators or other type of power backup. Redundancy, placing the site on two or more servers, is also a measure to ensure uptime.

Setup and monthly fees are self-explanatory. Monthly fees can range from several tens of dollars to several hundred dollars. Some hosting companies offer large discounts to clients that sign multiyear contracts. As in any purchase, customer reviews and independent evaluations should also be considered.

More than Meets the Eye

However a business chooses to run its website, several elements must be present to conduct business, which are illustrated in Figure 8.8. While the shopper (a consumer or corporate purchasing officer) sees only webpages, several applications and databases actually support online shopping and purchasing: an application that provides an inquiry interface for the shopper, which is connected to a catalog that is actually a database consisting of visual and text product descriptions; an application that takes the order, which is connected to an inventory application that is also connected to the product catalog database; a credit-card application that verifies authenticity of credit-card details and balance; and, in many cases, an order-fulfillment system that displays on monitors located in warehouses which items are to be picked off shelves and where they should be shipped. The latter system might include an automated conveyor system that picks the items with little human labor.

FIGURE **8.8**

The components of a web-based retailing operation

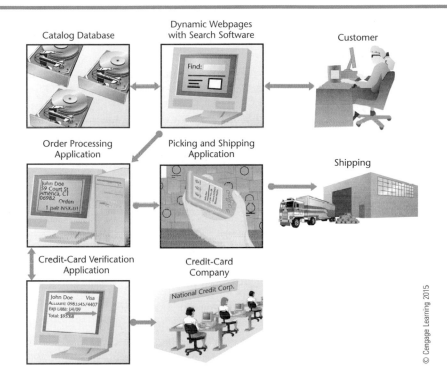

© Cengage Learning 2015

Rules for Successful Web-Based Business

Most organizations that operate a website do so to sell either products or services. Web software and the ability to connect web servers to organizational information systems open numerous opportunities. Often, whether an online business succeeds depends not only on availability of the proper software but how it is used. Several elements must be considered, especially if the site is to support B2C commerce.

Target the Right Customers

Targeting the people or organizations that are most likely to need the products and services you offer has always been the most important effort in marketing, with or without the web. On the web, targeting includes identifying the sites your audience frequently visits. For instance, a business that sells sporting goods should create clickable links at sites that cover sporting events and provide sports statistics. Banks that offer mortgage loans should create links at realtors' sites. And any business that targets its products to young people should do so at popular music sites. This principle should also apply to blogs and popular podcasts. Podcasting can include visual advertisements displayed by the player software.

Capture the Customer's Total Experience

By using cookies and recording shoppers' movements, CRM software can create electronic consumer profiles for each shopper and buyer. The shopper's experience with the site then becomes an asset of the business. Such marketing research fine-tunes the portfolio of products that the business offers and tailors webpages for individual customers. It also can be used to "market to one" by emailing the shopper about special deals on items in which he or she has shown an interest.

Personalize the Service

CRM software and webpage customization software can be combined to enable customers to personalize the pages and the service they receive when they log on to the site. Letting shoppers and readers select the type of email content they want is welcome, but sites should respect privacy by letting customers opt in rather than opt out. Opting in means that the customer can actively check options to receive email and other promotions, while opting out requires the customer to select *not* to receive such information—an annoyance to many customers.

The web also enables companies to let consumers tailor products. Land's End's website invites men to dress a virtual model with a build like theirs and order pants online. Although a pair costs significantly more than one a customer would purchase in a store, Land's End has been very successful with the concept. It has acquired many loyal customers because there is little reason to return a pair of pants that is made to order, although the company's policy allows returns.

Shorten the Business Cycle

One reason people like to do business on the web is that it saves them time. Businesses should keep looking for opportunities to shorten the business cycle for their customers, from shopping to paying to receiving the items they ordered. Fulfillment, the activities taking place after customers place orders online, is one of the greatest challenges for online businesses.

Those who can ship the ordered products fastest are likely to sustain or increase their market shares. Some have decided to outsource the entire fulfillment task to organizations that specialize in fulfillment, such as UPS's e-Logistics and FedEx's Supply Chain Services. E-Logistics, for example, offers to receive and store the business's merchandise in its warehouses, receive orders online, and then pick, pack, and ship them to the online business's customers. It also offers a product return service. A shorter business cycle is not only important for customer satisfaction but also enables the company to collect payments faster because credit cards are usually charged upon shipping.

Let Customers Help Themselves

Customers often need information from a web-enabled organization. Such information includes the status of an order, the status of a shipped item, and after-sale information such as installation of add-on components and troubleshooting. Placing useful information and downloadable software at the site not only encourages customer loyalty but also saves labor. This concept is often referred to as **self-service**—the customer's ability to determine the timing and services of their needs from a business organization through a website.

Practically every online business now sends email messages with the status of the order, a tracking number, and a link to the shipping company for checking the shipping status. Hardware companies can post online assembly instructions for their "assembly required" products. In addition to including Frequently Asked Questions (FAQs) information, some companies have used knowledge management software (discussed in Chapter 11, "Business Intelligence and Knowledge Management") that can answer open-ended questions.

Be Proactive and De-Commoditize

Expecting customers to visit your website every time they need your service might not be enough in today's competitive marketplace. Customers now demand not only prompt email replies to their queries but also proactive alerts. For example, the travel websites Orbitz and Travelocity email or text message airline customer's gate and time information if a customer's flight is delayed or if gates change. Some manufacturers email customers about product recalls or to schedule periodic service appointments. Online drugstores invite customers who regularly take a certain medication to register for automatic replenishment of their drugs. The company's software calculates when the next lot is to be shipped and ensures that it arrives in time.

All these initiatives, as well as many others, are efforts to *de-commoditize* what companies sell. A commodity is any product that is sold for about the same price by a multitude of vendors in a highly competitive market, usually with a thin margin of profit. By adding a special service or additional information, the company keeps the products it sells from becoming a commodity. Adding an original service or information to the product differentiates the "package" that online shoppers purchase from the "package" sold by competitors.

E-Commerce Is Every Commerce

You might have noticed that the title of this chapter does not contain the term "e-commerce." You might have also noticed that this is not the only chapter in which web-enabled business activities are discussed. In fact, every chapter in this book gives examples of what is popularly referred to as e-commerce. Web technologies have been integrated into the business world to a degree that makes it difficult at times to realize which activities take place inside the organization and which involve information flowing from other places through the Internet. We have become so accustomed to the integration of the web into our daily activities, especially the commercial ones, that the lines between commerce and e-commerce have been blurred. We will eventually stop using the term "e-commerce" and simply consider the web another means of supporting business, much the way we consider technologies like the telephone and computer.

Summary

- Some industries have changed dramatically and continue to change thanks to web technologies. This includes activities between and within organizations.

- HTTP is an Internet standard that enables addressing of web servers with domain names. HTTPS is a secure version of the protocol and is used for confidential transactions. HTML is a markup language for presentation of webpages. XML is a markup language for delivery of information about data communicated through webpages. XHTML combines features of HTML and XML. HTML5 is the most recent version of HTML, and integrates features of XML. FTP is a protocol for uploading and downloading files. Blogs enable people to conveniently create discussion webpages by posting comments and responding to them. Instant messaging online chat services enable people to correspond in real time and help businesses serve online customers. Cookies help websites to personalize the experience of visitors. Along with other software that spies on unwitting web surfers, they might provide detailed information about web users.

- In addition to a large number of nonproprietary web technologies, many more are developed and licensed to organizations by software vendors.

- An organization has two options when deciding to do commerce online: own and maintain its own web servers at its own facilities, or contract with a web hosting company. When contracting with a web host, there are several degrees of service: shared hosting, virtual private servers, dedicated hosting, and co-location.

- When selecting a web hosting company, organizations should consider several factors: type and quality of application provided, storage space, bandwidth, quality of technical support, traffic limits, availability of email accounts and services, scalability, user interface, support of webpage design, security, uptime ratio, setup fee, monthly fee, and customer reviews.

- Web-enabled commerce can generally be classified as business-to-business (B2B) or business-to-consumer (B2C). In the former, businesses use networks to trade with other businesses, possibly through an extranet. In the latter, businesses advertise and sell goods and services to consumers via the web. The higher volume of e-commerce is conducted between businesses.

- Business-to-business trading often relies on electronic data interchange (EDI), which is conducted over value-added networks. XML facilitates interorganizational online trading similar to EDI. When linked to internal ISs, web technologies enhance supply chain management. Online interorganizational commerce often takes place through an extranet.

- With the proliferation of mobile smartphones and wireless handheld computers, mobile commerce is increasingly important and needs to be considered in any online business strategy.

- To be successful, an online business must target the right customers, capture the customer's total experience, personalize the service, shorten the business cycle, let customers help themselves, and be proactive.

- Spam, and to a lesser degree spyware, adware, and pop-up windows, have become online annoyances. Society is trying to strike a balance between allowing these phenomena to continue as a form of commercial promotion and free speech, and curbing them to reduce the public's waste of resources. Phishing has become a pervasive crime, defrauding people and stealing their identities.

KIMBALL'S REVISITED

It quickly became evident to Tyler that creating a website was more difficult than he remembered from his college courses. Any website could be developed "on the fly." But would the design, layout, and format of the site match the Lakeside's setting and atmosphere? Just as the website for an elegant jewelry store should promote elegance and distinctiveness, he wanted the Kimball's Lakeside website to reflect its special features. And how was he going to channel his enthusiasm for social media into a plan that would really support his goals for Kimball's Lakeside?

What Is Your Advice?

1. If you were Justin, what advice would you give Tyler on the functions of the new website? What types of functions and information should the website provide to customers and prospective customers?

2. How would you recommend that Tyler use social media in the period leading up to the grand opening? What types of messages would you post?

3. What type of software would you need to build and maintain the website? What type of hosting service should Tyler purchase to host the initial website?

New Perspectives

1. Consider the concepts and discussion from Chapter 7 relating to data requirements that the owners need in order to manage the restaurant more effectively and efficiently. How would you integrate website and social media functions into those data requirements?

2. How could the restaurant use social media promotions like Groupon and Restaurant.com to integrate into their social media strategy? What are the advantages and disadvantages of this strategy?

3. What features of a website hosting service would be important to consider in planning for the potential future growth of Kimball's website?

Key Terms

B2B, 264
B2C, 264
B2G, 264
banner, 265
blog, 258
brick-and-mortar, 270
C2C, 264
clickstream tracking, 263
co-location, 284
consumer profiling, 271
content management
    system, 286
cookie, 262
crowdsourcing, 277
dedicated hosting, 283
domain name, 256
dynamic webpage, 285
extranet, 267
File Transfer Protocol (FTP), 258

fulfillment, 270
HTML5, 257
Hypertext Markup Language
    (HTML), 257
Hypertext Transfer Protocol
    (HTTP), 256
Hypertext Transfer Protocol
    Secure (HTTPS), 256
impression, 265
instant messaging (IM), 261
intranet, 267
load balancing, 282
massive open online course
    (MOOC), 260
mirror server, 283
mobile commerce, 277
phishing, 274
podcast, 260
pure play, 270

reach percentage, 265
reverse auction (name-your-own-
    price auction), 273
search advertising, 264
search engine optimization
    (SEO), 266
self-service, 288
shared hosting, 283
spyware, 263
top-level domain (TLD), 256
trackback, 259
Uniform Resource
    Locator (URL), 256
virtual private server, 283
web hosting, 283
wiki, 259
XHTML, 257
XML, 257

Review Questions

1. The web has been an enabler of new business methods. What does "enabler" mean in this context? Give an example of a business activity that is enabled by the web and that would not be possible without the web.

2. What is HTML, and why is it needed to use the web? What is HTML5 and how does it differ from previous versions?

3. What is XML? How is it different from HTML, and what purpose does it fulfill in web commerce?

4. What is the relationship between a domain name and an IP address?

5. When you visit a website and click a Download button, you activate software that adheres to a certain protocol. What protocol is that?

6. What is instant messaging (IM), and how can it support business operations? Which technology does IM replace or augment in online retailing?

7. What is blogging, and what potential does it have for businesses?

8. What is podcasting, and how is it different from radio broadcasting?

9. In the context of the web, what is a cookie? What is the benefit of cookies for online shoppers? What is the risk?

10. What is an intranet, and what purposes does it serve?

11. What is an extranet, and what purpose does it serve?

12. When contracting with a web hosting company, what is the difference between a shared server and a dedicated server?

13. When selecting a web hosting company, one of the important factors to consider is uptime ratio. What is it, and why is it important?

14. What does "unique monthly visitors" mean in online lingo? Who uses this metric and for what purpose?

15. What is phishing? How do people get "phished"?

16. What are the various issues and strategies to develop and implement a social media strategy?

Discussion Questions

17. Recall our discussion in Chapter 6, "Business Networks and Telecommunications." What is the single most important factor enabling streaming video on the web?

18. Some top-level domains (TLDs) are reserved for certain organizations. Why is this important? Would you prefer that anyone could register a TLD of his or her choice?

19. Podcasting is said to allow subscribers to "time-shift." What does this mean, and does this give listeners a benefit they do not have with radio programs?

20. E-tailers can use their software to charge different shoppers different prices. This is called price discrimination, and it is legal. Some observers say that shoppers discriminate based on price when they decide from whom to buy, and therefore it is ethical for e-tailers to price-discriminate. Do you agree?

21. Do you see blogging and podcasting as a threat to the written and broadcast media? Explain.

22. One of the most frustrating types of events to an e-tailer is shopping cart abandonment. From your own online shopping experience, what are the things that would cause you to abandon an online shopping cart?

23. Mobile commerce gives organizations the opportunity to send location-related advertising, that is, they can send advertising to our mobile devices based on where we are. What are the positives and negatives of this capability?

24. If you were giving advice to a business on using social media, what would you list as advantages and disadvantages? Can it be done "wrong"?

25. You have a new home business. You sell a consumer product for which you have a patent. You believe there will be much demand for it. To promote it, you decide to purchase a list of 2,000,000 email addresses of people who fall in the demographic groups that are likely to purchase the product. The seller told you that these were only addresses of people who did not opt out from

receiving messages from businesses. After you emailed the promotional message, you received hundreds of angry email messages, including one from the Coalition Against Unsolicited Commercial Email (CAUCE). Was there anything wrong in what you did? Why or why not?

26. The owners of a small business tell you that they would not be able to reach enough customers to survive if they couldn't use mass, unsolicited email. You strongly object to spamming. How do you respond to them?

27. Scott McNealy, former CEO of Sun Microsystems, said: "You already have zero privacy. Get over it!" Some observers say that expecting privacy when using the Internet is ridiculous; the Internet is a public network, and no one should expect privacy in a public network. Do you agree? Why or why not?

28. A student established a website that serves as an exchange of term papers. Students are invited to contribute their graded work and to search for term papers that other students contributed. When criticized, the student claims that this, too, is a way to do research. He argues that the moral responsibility rests with those who access his site, not with him. Do you agree? Why or why not?

29. There have been international efforts to harmonize laws addressing free speech on the web. Do you think such efforts can succeed? Why or why not?

30. What do you think makes social networking websites so popular?

31. Web advertising is directed mostly at consumers, yet the topic is discussed in this chapter as a business-to-business commercial interaction. What could be the reason for this?

Applying Concepts

32. Find three commercial sites that operate in three different markets and offer affiliate programs. Write up a summary: What do they sell? What do their affiliate programs promise, and in return for what? Classify each program as pay per sale, pay per click, pay per lead, or another type, and explain why you classified the way you did.

33. Choose a topic in which you are interested. Select three different search engines (e.g., Google, Yahoo!, and Bing) and use them to look for information about the subject. Rank the performance of each site. A long list of sites that provide too broad a range of information is bad; a shorter list of sites that provide more narrowly defined information is good. Explain your ranking.

34. You have been hired by a pizza delivery service to design a website. The site should be attractive to families and young professionals and should allow them to order home delivery. Use a webpage development application to build the home page of the business. Submit your page to your instructor.

35. A local health club wants to implement a website for its new opening. The listing below is an initial selection of their needs for the website. Compile a matrix of three shared hosting services including the various features and services offered by each service for comparison.

Included Domains	3
Web Space	250 GB
Monthly Transfer Volume	12,500 GB
Email Accounts	40
Mailbox Size	5 GB
Search Engine Submission	Yes
Website Builder	28 Pages
Blog	Yes
Mailing Lists	Yes, 3,000 customers
Content Management	Yes
Form Builder	Yes
Client Management	Yes
Support	24/7 Toll-free, Email

Hands-On Activities

36. Prepare your résumé as an HTML document. (*Hint:* You can use the File, Save As feature of your word processor to save a document as a webpage or .html file.) If you wish, include your scanned photograph. Submit your work by email, or post it to your website and email the website link to your professor.

37. Consider the following options for a business that wishes to use a website: (1) maintaining their own server at their facility, (2) using a host for a shared server, (3) using a host for a virtual private server, (4) using a host for a dedicated server. You are a consultant. Consider each of the following scenarios independently of the others, and recommend the best hosting option to the business. Consider all the relevant factors, such as purpose and cost.
    a. *A family-owned jewelry store at a shopping mall.* The owners want to make the public aware of what the store offers. They want to pay as little as possible for this web presence.
    b. *A large retail company.* Management wants to be able to execute purchases from suppliers through the new website, and to allow their own customers to shop and buy through the site. It is willing to employ its own team and facility for the servers.
    c. *A small printing business.* The owners insist on having their own domain name. They wish

visitors to have every sense that the site is run and controlled by the owners.
    d. *A small home business.* Management does not want to register and pay for its own domain name.
    e. *A large Internet-only e-tailer.* It needs to change the list of products daily. Its web design team might want to change the DBMS, shopping cart application, and other applications when the need arises. It already owns the servers but no longer wants to manage networking, backup, redundancy, and security.
    f. *A brick-and-mortar retailer that wants to extend its sales operations to the web.* It has a web design crew that is capable of changing content and is expert at using and modifying web applications such as dynamic pages and shopping cart applications. However, management does not want to purchase servers or manage their networking and security.

38. Devote one day as "Low Technology Day" and express your experience. For one full day (24 hours) do not use the Internet, do not use a mobile phone or any other communication device. Write a 1–2 page report on how this affected your mood, social experiences, time management, and any other aspect of your life during that 24-hour period.

Team Activities

39. Social media is being used by many companies to promote, sell, and market their products and services as well as reduce costs of operations. Research the use of social media by three business organizations and document (a) the details of their social media effort, (b) the return on its investment and benefits to its business, and (c) the critical factors that led to their success.

40. Team up with another student to analyze the privacy policies of three companies that specialize in collecting consumer information on the web. All must be companies that install third-party cookies. There are at least 10 such companies. List the common factors of the three companies. Then list the factors in which they differ. For each of the differing elements, which company treats consumers better, in terms of less invasion of privacy and more

disclosure of its activities? Among other factors, see if the companies offer opt-in or opt-out options.

41. With two other team members, prepare a rationale for an original business idea that could generate revenue on the web. Prepare the rationale in a way that would convince a venture capitalist to invest money in this new business.

42. You are the owner of the pizza delivery business with minimal understanding and skills to develop a website. Your team has been assigned to use a shared hosting service to design and implement a website using WordPress. Find two software packages compatible with WordPress that will automate the design with templates. What are the costs and issues associated with this website development approach?

Building a Home Lending Operation

Buying a home is a complex and detailed process. A consumer has to gather and consider so many details and data points in order to make an informed decision, and it is hard to know if you're getting the best deal and if it's in your best long-term interests. The various options and suppliers involved in the process only tend to magnify the complexity and time needed. Even for a buyer who has been through the process previously, it is time consuming. For a beginner, it can be terrifying.

Some people may believe that the depth and complexity of a home purchase and financing may not lend itself to a web-based solution. Think so? That's not what Wells Fargo believes.

Even with economic challenges, the market for first-time homebuyers is strong. A survey completed by Wells Fargo in 2011 found that the most significant opportunities in the housing industry were for the millennial generation (born between the early 1980s and early 2000s). Even considering the large Baby Boomer generation (born between 1946 and 1964), the millennials consist of more than 77 million people. This new generation is eager and able to find information, especially online. This foundation of information builds confidence and knowledge. Although there were many different options to collect information about home ownership, Wells Fargo also believed the market lacked a "comprehensive, one-stop, self-directed resource" for home buyers. It was clear that a market existed for the new initiative, but how should it be fulfilled? Would you build a home without a plan? Drawings? No.

Websites, like any other software development, need to be planned, designed, and implemented with careful thought and research. For a variety of reasons, sometimes website development is not well planned. Wells Fargo instituted a methodical approach. From the beginning of this initiative, they defined the goals of the project and remained focused on the mission of the project. Their guiding metaphor for design was a "roadmap" to assist consumers in the process of gathering information and making choices toward their goal of obtaining a mortgage. Many consumers have a "full plate" of complicated economic and financial challenges. The key to success was to assemble a website to get essential information to consumers and add value to their online experience. Like the sales cycle, the home lending process has a similar cycle from researching, application, approval, and servicing. Again, the roadmap was important to the design process. In addition, Wells Fargo also compiled data on how consumers gained access to their current website as well as what they did (tools, functions) once they arrived. This information provided the bank with insight on consumer preferences associated with an online experience.

Their goal was to "serve customers the way they wanted to be served." This goal would be defined in three strategies: (1) focus on consumers' financial needs, (2) deliver and provide educational value, and (3) humanize the online channel. Although the goal is important, specific tactics would be needed to clearly frame the building of the website. For example, while the website would "perform" based on a consumer's preferences, they could always decide to connect with a mortgage consultant at Wells Fargo to supplement the online experience. The online experience is crucial to deliver information and education in a timeframe and environment that the consumer chooses. However, when the process requires a personal touch, they can elect to have a consultant intervene, again, based on their choice.

Wells Fargo believed that careful thought to design conquers the complexity of the entire process. This mentality centers on the principles of simplicity and not overcomplicating initiatives. To embed these principles in the website, the design stage included several characteristics, including: (1) delivering information tailored to the customer's individual needs, (2) providing comprehensive, but consumable information, (3) protecting the consumer's anonymity during the process, (4) allowing consumers to speak with a representative when needed, (5) offering transparency to information and the process, and (6) providing easy access to information. These six characteristics help to clearly frame the process of building the website.

As Wells Fargo drilled deeper into the project, they began to define the essential elements of the proposed website. These elements included a learning center, glossary of terms, tools/tips, online application forms, checklists to guide the consumer through the process, and home ownership guides. These features were developed to satisfy the objectives of the website project as well as clearly define how those objectives would be accomplished in the new product.

The self-service nature of the website provides a flexible environment for consumers with various levels of financing knowledge, at purchasing stages, and with different preferences to be informed about Wells Fargo financing products and home buying in general. Business relationships, even in an area as complicated as home financing, can be developed through a self-service, online environment. Building those relationships through a free website product can build affinity and ultimately increase the customer base of a bank's mortgage portfolio.

Source: Slaughter, P. (2012). Playing Online. Home Furnishings Business, 7(9), 14-19.

Thinking About the Case

1. Some websites are not very useful, functional, or well organized. Why do you believe that websites are approached differently than other software development initiatives? What did Wells Fargo do differently?

2. Consider the feature that the consumer could remain anonymous for as long as they wished. Why would it be beneficial to have the prospective home financing customer anonymous? Why would Wells Fargo encourage (or require) the consumer to contact a representative? Would this interaction increase the likelihood of closing the sale?

3. Wells Fargo said that "We also were mindful that each consumer comes to the transaction with a different level of understanding and with different styles of learning." What challenges does that create for the bank and its website design? Is the marketing of home financing different than marketing other service products?

Furnishing Dollars with Online Initiatives

With the early adoption and use of websites, there were certain items that businesspeople and consumers believed were "off limits" for online purchasing. Who would have thought you could have purchased shoes online? Cars? Clothes? How about furniture?

According to an IBISWorld study released in 2012, online furniture sales amounted to $6.3 billion in 2011, a 7.5-percent increase from 2010. With the estimate that 2012 online furniture sales will increase by 9.9 percent. While they predict that the growth will increase to $10.8 billion by 2017, these sales are not just for small items, but all types of furniture. The original thought was that people needed to "touch and feel" furniture in order to complete the sale. However, with the growing number of furniture sales being completed online, that attitude and culture is changing. Here is a tale of three companies that set up their furniture businesses in an online environment.

Gardiners, an 80-year-old company with five stores in the Baltimore area, has leveraged website technology for its business. They launched their online business with help from a website development and Internet consulting firm that specialized in the furniture industry. Their transition into the online environment was planned with the "walk before you run" mindset. They began by selling online only those products that were stocked at their stores. Because their original online system did not directly interface with their in-house systems, they were required to update the online system nightly with accurate product information based on what was sold in their stores each day.

Can social media have a positive influence on furniture sales? La-Z-Boy believed the answer to that question was "Yes." They used the social media site Pinterest in a recent marketing campaign. Pinterest, a popular social media site, was conceived to create a platform where users can upload images of what they enjoy in their lives in an online "bulletin board" format. In 2012, La-Z-Boy's Hammary division developed a marketing campaign using Pinterest to increase its consumer and retailer participation, along with its current social media channels (Facebook and Twitter). Consumers participated in a contest by posting images on Pinterest of Hammary's products that they would like to win. After uploading images to Pinterest, the contestant then "pinned" their submission to Hammary's Facebook or Twitter account. The contest winner, chosen based on the largest total number of Twitter followers, Pinterest re-pins, and Facebook "likes," would be given $2,000 worth of furniture. La-Z-Boy is leveraging the success of this campaign to target retailers. Their marketing executive stated, "We'll use Pinterest to get retailers into the showroom. This interior design community we built definitely helped position us."

The concept of online shopping carts can be transformed with social media. Carl's Furniture City in Utica NY has attempted the integration of a shopping cart with Facebook. In one month, they received three sales totaling $2,100 sourced from Facebook. Data like this, compiled by Web4Retail, can provide a measureable, objective payback for retailers to support social media strategies. However, could the use of an online site draw shopping away from stores? Web4Retail executives believe that "retailers that commit to doing business on the Internet are giving their stores more protection against getting shopped than those who don't." They believe that customers visit the store to view items which were once created by an online shopping cart. Customers do not have the time to re-visit the store, but then rely on the shopping cart to purchase products at home. Sales personnel at the store can properly log the visit and then gain credit for the online sale, protecting their commission.

Source: Zakrajsek, L., & McGee, K. (2012). Wells Fargo's New Home Lending Site. Mortgage Banking, 72(9), 88–91.

Thinking About the Case

1. Do you think that the more gradual implementation of online sales implemented by Gardiners is too safe? Is there a benefit to this careful, planned approach? Are there any risks to the delayed updates to Gardiners online system?

2. How did the Pinterest campaign using social media increase interest for La-Z-Boy's retail channel? When the marketing executive

discussed the "community we built," what do you believe he meant?

3. Are retail stores being used by consumers to "touch and feel" products and then purchase them online from other online retailers?

Do you believe this practice is widespread? Do you believe that social media and an intelligent strategy can create synergy between a retailer's online and "brick and mortar" channels?

References

Anonymous. (2009, Jun 16). Smartphones, Data Plans, New Apps to Drive Mobile Advertising Revenues to $1.5 Billion in 2013, *PR Newswire*.

Anonymous. (2010, Jul 22). Ford Launches Second Chapter of The Fiesta Project; Eight New Web-isodes Hit YouTube for Ford Fiesta's 2011 Social Media Campaign, *PR Newswire*.

Anonymous. (2011, Jan 19). Valued Opinions Online Survey Shows Concern Over Internet Security, *PR Newswire*.

Anonymous. (2012a). BIA/Kelsey; BIA/Kelsey Forecasts U.S. Social Media Ad Revenues to Grow from $4.6B in 2012 to $9.2B in 2016. *Marketing Weekly News*, 68.

Anonymous. (2012b). Dunkin' Donuts Unveils Mobile App for Payment and Gifting of Dunkin' Products. *Entertainment Close-Up*.

Anonymous. (2012c). LoyaltyOne; Consumer Social Media Engagement with Brands Leads to Increased Sales, Study Reveals. *Marketing Weekly News*, 134.

Anonymous. (2012d). Spear Phishing Statistics: 2012 Findings from Microsoft TechEd, RSA Security Conference Surveys. Retrieved from http://blog .proofpoint.com/2012/07/spear-phishing -statistics-2012-findings-from-teched-rsa-security -conference-surveys.html

Anonymous. (2012e). Veracode, Inc.; Growth in SaaS and Mobile Applications Increases Requirement for Software Security Testing at Scale. *Investment Weekly News*, 521.

Aquino, J. (2012, Nov). TRANSFORMING SOCIAL MEDIA DATA INTO PREDICTIVE ANALYTICS. *Customer Relationship Management*, 16, 38-42.

Brown, C. (2009). Fighting mobile phone spam. *Network World*, 26(27), 25-25.

Donston-Miller, D., & Carr, D. F. (2012). 7 Lessons In Social Business. *InformationWeek* (1350), 22-27.

Fletcher, H. (2011). Finding 'Things To Do'. *Target Marketing*, 34(6), 16-18, 20.

Gobry, P.-E. (2011). The Online Ad Market Comes Roaring Back With A Record $26 Billion In 2010. From http://www.businessinsider.com/internet-advertising-report-2011-4?op=1

Hof, R. (2012). Internet Ad Spending Bucks Economy to Grow 12% in Q1. Retrieved from www.Forbes .com website: http://www.forbes.com/sites/ roberthof/2012/07/10/internet-ad-spending-bucks-economy-to-grow-12-in-q1/

Innocentive Corporate Website – About Us. (2013). Retrieved January 18, 2013, from https://www .innocentive.com/contact-innocentive

Internet Usage Statistics. (January 1, 2013). Retrieved January 2, 2013, from http://internetworldstats .com/stats.htm

Klotz-Young, H. (2012). Staying Connected Via Apps. *SDM*, 42(9), 57-60, 62.

McMillan, R. (2009, May). Judge Kicks Notorious Spammer off Facebook. *PC World*, 27, 20-20.

O'Leary, N. (2012). GroupM: Global Web Ad Spend Up in 2011. http://www.adweek.com/news/advertising-branding/groupm-global-web-ad-spend-16-percent-2011-139483

Oracle. (2012). *2012 B2B E-Commerce Survey: Results and Trends*. [White Paper]. http://www.oracle.com/ us/products/applications/b2b-ecommerce-trends-2012-1503041.pdf

Paine, K. D. (2011). Measuring the real ROI of social media. *Communication World*, 28(1), 20-23.

Patel, L. (2010). THE RISE OF SOCIAL MEDIA. *T + D*, 64(7), 60-61, 68.

Pimanova, J. (11 September 2012). Summer 2012: Email Phishing Trends Heat Up. From http://www .emailtray.com/blog/category/email-trends-and-stats/

Purewal, S. J. (2013, Jan). The Privacy and Security Implications of a Cashless Society. *PC World*, 31, 33-34.

Radicati, S. (2009). Email Statistics Report, 2009-2013: The Radicati Group, Inc.

Richter, F. (2012). e-Commerce in the United States: Statista.

Son, A. (2012). Industry Report 54191 Market Research in the US. *IBISWorld*, 25-27. http://0-clients1 .ibisworld.com.helin.uri.edu/reports/us/industry/ default.aspx?entid=1442

Spence, E. (2013). Amazon Coins Will Be A Welcome Disruption To Android Developers. *Forbes.com*. http://www.forbes.com/sites/ewanspence/2013/ 02/05/amazon-coins-will-be-a-welcome-disruption-to-android-developers/

Top Level Domain Name List. (2013). Retrieved January 16, 2013, from http://data.iana.org/TLD/ tlds-alpha-by-domain.txt

CHAPTER nine

CHALLENGES OF GLOBAL INFORMATION SYSTEMS

Learning Objectives

A growing number of organizations operate globally or, at least, in more than one geographic market. These organizations face some challenges that have a considerable impact on their information systems. The organizations have to meet the demands of global operations by providing international ISs designed to accommodate the free flow of information both within a single company's divisions and between multinational corporations. These issues are important because so many companies operate a website, and websites are accessible globally. For professionals, this means a growing focus to understand other cultures, standards, and legal systems when applying and using information systems in a global business community.

When you finish this chapter, you will be able to:

- Explain why multinational corporations must use global information systems.

- Provide elementary advice for designing websites for an international audience.

- Cite the cultural, legal, and other challenges to implementing international information systems.

KIMBALL'S RESTAURANT: Long Distance Recipes

While Michael and Tyler were planning the operational and marketing aspects of the Lakeside location, Liz began to consider some details of the kitchen operations and menu. The family's plan was to maintain the "hometown" meals and reasonable cost in the new location. However, she also thought that the menu needed some "upgrades" for the new location. She believed it was important to maintain their core menu choices, but to also set a slightly different tone with additional menu choices for the Lakeside. Because their plan was to offer the Lakeside function room for business meetings, social functions, and special occasions for groups, a broader array of menu choices could give them a competitive advantage.

Michael and Liz enjoyed traveling to places outside of the United States. When they traveled, Liz explored the local restaurants and food stores to get inspiration for new recipes and ingredients. She found interesting items in countries such as Spain, Italy, Portugal, and France. She wondered how Kimball's could stimulate their current menu choices as well as build new choices to rebrand the new location. Using the current menu along with her travel notes on various meals and ingredients, she was excited about developing a winning menu for their Lakeside location.

New View, New Menu

Liz began to develop new appetizers, entrees, and side dishes that used various imported spices and condiments. Whether it was imported olive oil, pasta, or roasted peppers, the imported ingredients could add great value to the menu. Now, what would be the cost and availability for such items? She searched on the Internet for foreign suppliers to purchase items that she would need. There were several suppliers who sold and shipped products to the United States. She also researched several U.S. food suppliers to compare costs and shipping logistics. Michael and Liz then met to review her ideas and what she found.

Michael liked Liz's additions to the menu. For example, an appetizer tray of various imported cheeses, olives, and roasted peppers could appeal to groups as well as individual patrons. Michael agreed with Liz that they were not abandoning their "old" menu selection, just expanding it to appeal to a broader range of customers. The upgraded appetizers could be marketed to a late-night crowd along with drinks and light fare. Michael also thought that these additional menu items could be offered on certain nights as a special promotion or for "after work" gatherings.

Michael, being the numbers fanatic, evaluated the costs of purchasing these items through a local supplier or overseas. He found the costs were very similar; probably balanced between the local supplier's markup versus dealing with the overseas manufacturer/supplier directly. Purchasing from a foreign supplier did not seem outrageous.

Liz and Michael were pleased with the newly redesigned menu and its potential to brand The Lakeside a little differently than their current location.

Multinational Organizations

Consider this: An American software development firm sends out an annual brochure to its global investors to include the state of the company, some brief statistics, and a compacted S.W.O.T. (Strengths, Weaknesses, Opportunities, and Threats) analysis. Under the heading "Future External Threats," the company put a picture of a red flag, which is a symbol of 'danger' in the United States. The company was bombarded with emails and letters from global investors who were upset and confused as to why a socialist revolution, symbolized by the red flag, threatened the future of the company. In addition, after company representatives finished writing and designing the brochure, it was sent to a translator to be converted to the native languages of the company's global investors. The brochure's wording included terms and phrases that were untranslatable, such as 'FAQs' and 'wrap-up.' Some of the software development firm's largest international investors were perturbed that although the brochure they received was translated to the right language, it was in the wrong local dialect. Being some of the company's biggest investors, they were dismayed that the company did not take the time to cater to this seemingly minor detail. International corporations regularly encounter these types of problems, and realize that they need to overcome cultural, legal, and other challenges.

An increasing number of the world's corporations have branched into countries all over the globe, becoming true multinationals. While they might have headquarters in a single country, they operate divisions and subsidiaries in different countries to take advantage of local benefits. For instance, a company might establish engineering facilities in countries that offer large pools of qualified engineers, build production lines in countries that can supply inexpensive labor, and open sales offices in countries that are strategically situated for effective marketing.

Because of these dispersed operations, a company's nationality is not always obvious. 3M, which stands for Minnesota Mining and Manufacturing, is headquartered in St. Paul, Minnesota but has about 44,000 international employees in 60 different countries (3M, n.d.; Amari, 2012). For 3M to become as successful as it is today, it had to establish an international presence in order to gain access to new materials. To create a beachhead into foreign markets, 3M merged with other companies in similar industries who are headquartered abroad. Facebook is another example of an American company that went global for multiple reasons. First, Facebook expanded its reach and connected more people by making its services available in 50 different languages. Second, it has established subsidiaries in other countries such as Ireland in order to ease the funneling of profits in and out and to take advantage of tax benefits (Drucker, Oct 21, 2010). Subsidiaries like this are registered and operate under the laws of the respective host countries, and they employ local workers.

One hundred of the 500 largest Canadian companies have majority U.S. ownership, and 90 percent of U.S. multinational companies have Canadian offices. Most large international companies have a subsidiary in Canada such as Walmart, Ford, Hewlett-Packard, and TJX (Post, 2010). Japanese companies own U.S. subsidiaries in every imaginable industry. British companies have the largest foreign investment in the United States (Jackson, 2012). Thanks to the North American Free Trade Agreement (NAFTA) and agreements between the United States and the European Union, we might witness the internationalization of many more American, Canadian, Mexican, and European corporations.

Multinational corporations must use **global information systems**, which are systems that serve organizations and individuals in multiple countries. These companies might have unified policies throughout their organizations, but they still have to abide by the laws of the countries in which each unit operates, and be sensitive to other local aspects of their interaction with businesses as well as consumers. Therefore, unlike organizations that operate in a single country, multinational companies have the burden of ensuring that their information systems and the information flowing through the systems conform to laws, cultures, standards, and other elements that are specific to countries or regions.

The Web and International Commerce

The emergence of the web as a global medium for information exchange has made it an important vehicle for both business-to-business (B2B) and business-to-consumer (B2C) commerce. As of June 2012, more than 2.4 billion people logged on to the Internet across the globe (Anonymous, 2012). Over 70 percent of them come from non-English-speaking countries, as Figure 9.1 shows, and more than half of all e-commerce revenues come from these countries. The ratio of non-English speakers to English speakers has steadily grown over the years. As Figure 9.2 indicates, a growing number of web users come from regions other than North America.

FIGURE 9.1

Over 70 percent of
Internet users reside in
non-English-speaking
countries

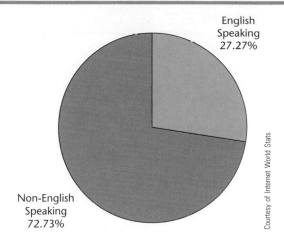

English
Speaking
27.27%

Non-English
Speaking
72.73%

Courtesy of Internet World Stats

FIGURE 9.2

Internet users by global
region

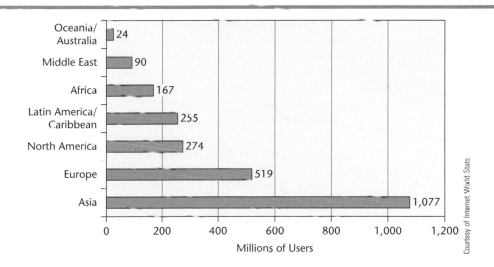

Courtesy of Internet World Stats

The spread of Internet use opens enormous opportunities for businesses the world over. Some of the countries with current low participation rates have the greatest potential for expanding accessibility to the Internet, such as China. About 1 billion citizens of the People's Republic of China logged on as of June 2012, but that represents only 27 percent of the population. The Chinese market is expected one day to be the world's largest in terms of consumer spending. For some regions, the trajectory in growth from 2000 to 2012 has been astounding. For example, the Middle East, Latin America, and Africa have all increased over 1,300 percent in 12 years (Anonymous, 2012).

The web offers opportunities not only to increase revenue but also to save on costs. Consider, for example, how much money is saved when instead of printing product and service manuals on paper and shipping them to customers, companies publish them on the web, ready to be downloaded at a user's convenience. Furthermore, imagine the convenience if the manuals were prepared not only using hypertext and graphics but also animation for easier and more informative use. Some companies place video clips to instruct buyers how to assemble the products they purchased. Many companies have stopped enclosing manuals with their retail products. They invite you to log on to their website and peruse the product's manual in your own language. This saves not only paper and printing but also much of the labor involved in customer service. By placing maintenance manuals in multiple languages on their websites, some companies cut as much as 50 percent of their customer service costs.

Organizations that wish to do business globally through their websites must be sensitive to local audiences. Thus websites should be tailored to the audiences they are meant to reach. A majority of web users prefer to access the web using a language other than English, so organizations must provide their online information and services in other languages, as well as English. As Figure 9.3 shows, organizations must plan and carefully design their global sites so that they also cater to local needs and preferences, a process sometimes called **glocalization**.

FIGURE 9.3

Imperatives to consider when designing websites for an international audience	**Plan**	Plan the site before you develop it. A site for an international audience requires more planning than a national one.
	Learn the Preferences	Learn the cultural preferences, convention differences, and legal issues, or use experts who know these preferences. Tailor each local site (or the local section of your site) to the way in which the local people prefer to shop, buy, and pay.
	Translate Properly	Use local interpreters to translate content for local audiences. Do not use software or other automated methods, unless humans review the translated material. Experienced translators are attentive to contemporary nuances and connotations.
	Be Egalitarian	Do not let any audience feel as if it is less important than other audiences. Keep all local sections of your site updated and with the same level of information and services.
	Avoid Cultural Imperialism	If the local language or culture has a word or picture for communicating an idea, use it; do not use those of your own country. Give the local audience a homey experience.

© Cengage Learning 2015

Glocalization is a combination of universal business models and management philosophy with some adaptations for local audiences. One example of an organization that glocalizes is McDonald's. While the restaurant chain's logo and many other features are the same throughout the world, it makes some menu changes to appeal to local palates. Sometimes, other elements are changed. For example, in France, the restaurant chain replaced its familiar Ronald McDonald mascot with Asterix the Gaul, a popular French comic book character. Much like the presence of a global restaurant chain, websites are present everywhere someone can link to the web. Therefore, website designers must keep glocalization in mind. The design and implementation of information technology must support an organization's deployment of glocalization.

Think Globally, Act Locally

Marketing experts often advise companies that operate internationally to "think globally, act locally." Acting locally means being sensitive to regional customs and language nuances. When interest in the company's business increases, especially from consumers, it is advisable to open a local office and let a local team handle both the website and fulfillment operations. Recall that fulfillment in online business includes picking, packing, and shipping. When most of the business comes from one country or region, the business, its website, and its information systems are managed centrally, but when a growing proportion of transactions are completed in other regions, businesses find that they must decentralize control.

Thinking globally and acting locally might sound like contradictory ideas, but they are not. Recall our discussion of strategies in Chapter 2, "Strategic Uses of Information Systems." Thinking globally has to do with the company's strategic planning. It involves decisions such as product lines and business alliances. However, the same strategy can be followed with a local flavor. For example, the same product, in whose design and production the company holds a competitive advantage, can be packaged and advertised with local motifs. The local branch of the company might still recruit engineers with the same excellent qualifications as those of their peers in other countries, but apply different interview tactics and social benefits suited to the customs and holidays of that country.

WHY YOU SHOULD | Learn About Challenges of Global ISs

The growing globalization of business means that chances are high you will be employed by a company that operates outside your country. Even if your employer does not have offices in another country, you may be involved in global business. Being aware of the challenges involved in global business and the information systems supporting the business may determine your professional success. One does not have to work for a multinational corporation to need to be aware of the challenges discussed in this chapter. One only has to work for any organization that has a multilingual workforce or which operates in multicultural markets to have to care about these issues. And there is a high probability that you will work for such an organization.

By default, every business that establishes a website in some way uses a global information system. Many organizations use additional types of global ISs. All face challenges. Neglecting to pay attention to such issues as different cultures, language nuances, conflicting national laws, and different standards can hurt the business's reputation and cause loss of revenue. As a professional who is knowledgeable about these issues, you can be a valuable asset to your organization.

Challenges of Global Information Systems

While the web offers tremendous opportunities for establishing international ISs, global ISs are not without their challenges, both for B2B and B2C commerce. Some of the challenges that businesses must address are technological barriers, regulations and tariffs, electronic payment mechanisms, different languages and cultures, economic and political considerations, different measurement and notation standards, legal barriers, and different time zones. These challenges are discussed in the following sections.

Note that we discuss differences among world regions and among countries, but much of the discussion applies to regions within the same country. For example, there are legal and cultural differences among states in the United States, Germany, India, and Brazil, as well as legal, cultural, and linguistic differences among provinces in Canada and cantons in Switzerland.

Technological Challenges

Not all countries have adequate information technology infrastructure to allow resident companies to build an international information system. International ISs, especially those using the web, often incorporate graphics to convey technical or business information, and those applications, as well as interactive software, require increasingly fast (broadband) communication lines. The bandwidth available in some countries is too narrow for high-volume transmission of graphically and animation-rich webpages. Thus, companies might have to offer two versions of their sites, one for wide bandwidth and another for narrow bandwidth. Often, companies use one website but provide the same content in using both graphically rich and text-only pages, or use the same video for download at different speeds.

POINT OF INTEREST   Translation Troubles

Multicultural businesses face two main types of translation issues. The first occurs when there is no direct word in the target language and the word must be described rather than translated. The second issue arises when the word appears to have an appropriate match in the targeted language but the meaning or importance is lost in translation. Translation issues like these are troublesome for multicultural businesses who seek to get their messages across accurately without being inconsiderate or insulting to other cultures.

Source: Blenkinsopp, J., & Maryam Shademan, P. (2010). Lost in translation? Culture, language and the role of the translator in international business. Critical Perspectives on International Business, 6(1), 38–52.

Language issues present another technological challenge. You might recall the earlier discussion of how characters are represented by bytes in computers. This setup is fine for languages with up to 256 (2^8) characters, such as English and other languages whose alphabetic root is Latin, and for other languages whose characters represent individual phonemes rather than words, such as Cyrillic, Hebrew, and Arabic. But eight-bit bytes are not sufficient for languages with larger numbers of characters, such as Chinese, in which characters represent whole words. The solution for this obstacle is to ensure that computers can use Unicode, with double-byte characters—allowing for up to 65,536 (2^{16}) characters. However, if only the servers are programmed to accommodate Unicode, while the other systems (such as databases and applications on computers interacting with the servers) work with single-byte characters, then these back-end systems will record and display gibberish. Thus, entire systems must be reprogrammed or use special conversion software. As computers convert to operating systems that support Unicode, displaying different character sets should be less of a problem. As shown in the illustration, Amazon has designed its website to include differences based on the targeted country. It not only includes language differences, but changes the advertisements specific for the country.

Businesses that cater to an international audience must "glocalize" their websites

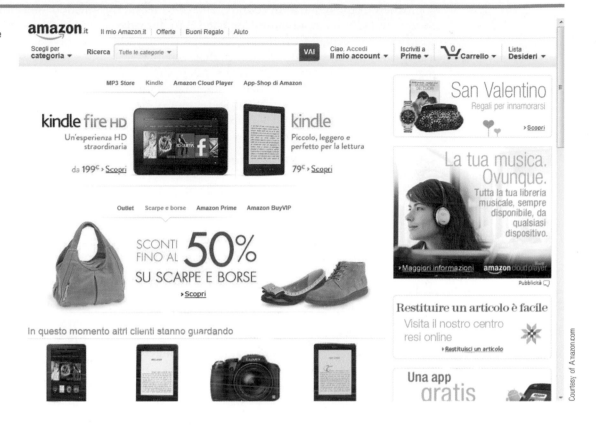

Other points that might sound trivial can also wreak havoc in international ISs or prevent individuals and companies in some world regions from transacting with companies that did not make their websites and applications flexible. For example, fields such as telephone numbers should be set for variable length, because the number of digits in telephone numbers varies by country. Many sites still offer forms that limit telephone numbers to 10 digits and do not accept shorter or longer numbers even when they are meant for audiences outside the United States and Canada. Similarly, postal codes are organized differently in different countries and are not called zip codes, and yet some U.S. sites are still designed with only a 5-digit (or extended 9-digit) postal code field.

In some cases, no elegant solution can be found even if every effort is made to localize information systems. AES Corp. generates and distributes electric power to 27 countries on five continents. It uses SAP's ERP system on servers that connect all of its sites. When AES originally installed SAP, it did not support the Ukrainian language, so the company decided to use Russian in its Ukrainian office. As of 2013, it does support the Ukrainian language.

Regulations and Tariffs

Countries have different regulations on what may or may not be imported and which tariff applies to which imported product. While many executives know they might be missing out on lucrative deals with overseas businesses, they are afraid that exploring international opportunities would entail too many hassles. They are also afraid that even with the proper research, employees might not know how to comply with the laws of destination countries, let alone calculate how much the organization would have to pay in taxes, tariffs, custom duties, and other levies on exported or imported goods.

Companies such as NextLinx, operating as a subsidiary of Amber Road, help exporters and importers who use the web for commerce. The NextLinx software is integrated with a company's ERP systems and website. When a business from another country places an order, the information—such as type of item and destination country—is captured by the software, and an export manager can see how much the company will have to pay in tariffs, receive an estimate of how long the goods will stay in the seaport or airport before they are released from customs, and, if the manager wishes, also receive information on regulations, license required, shipping companies in the destination country, and other useful information. Since the software is linked to the web, it is continuously updated and provides useful information immediately. The software also calculates, on the fly, the total cost of delivering the goods to the buyer's door. It also provides more than 100 forms that exporters can fill out and save electronically. The logistics component of the application offers shipping options with land, sea, and air carriers; books shipping space; and tracks shipping status. Several studies have shown that U.S. companies have turned away about 80 percent of online orders that come from other countries because they are not familiar with export regulations. This service can expedite the process.

Differences in Payment Mechanisms

One of the greatest expectations of e-commerce is easy payment for what we buy online. Credit cards are very common in North America and are the way businesses prefer to be paid online. However, this practice is not widespread in other regions of the world. The high rate of stolen credit cards, especially in Eastern Europe, attaches risk to such payments and deters potential online customers. Also, most Europeans prefer to use debit cards rather than credit cards. (The holder of a debit card must maintain a bank account from which the purchase is immediately deducted; the holder of a credit-card receives a grace period of up to a month and pays the credit-card issuer in any way he or she prefers. The holder of a credit-card is subject to fees and interest charges while a debit card holder may receive interest on their account balance.) Americans are more willing to give credit-card details via the web than people from other nations. Until citizens of other countries become willing to do so, payment through the web, and therefore B2C trade, will not reach its full potential.

In 2008, there were 176.8 million credit-card holders holding 1.49 billion credit cards in America (Woolsey, 2012). By 2011, there were 183 million credit-card holders with only 1.28 billion credit cards (Anonymous, n.d.-b). Americans pay with credit cards in 20 percent of all transactions and in almost all online transactions. In Japan, on the other hand, only 8 percent of transactions involve credit cards, and most Japanese are reluctant to use credit cards for online purchases. This calls for a different mechanism of payment. In Japan, many people who order merchandise online prefer to pick it up at convenience stores called "konbini," and pay there for what they purchase. Since shipping companies are reluctant to leave parcels unattended when the recipient is not home, the alliance of e-tailers and konbini affords not only payment confidence but also convenience. The British and French prefer to use debit cards, while in Germany, online bank transfers and the PayPal online payment service are most popular (Holmes, 2011). (See the table illustration for credit-card expenditures by country.) E-tailers from other countries who want to operate internationally in Japan must be aware of these regional preferences. The following diagram shows the various countries and their respective credit-card transaction amounts.

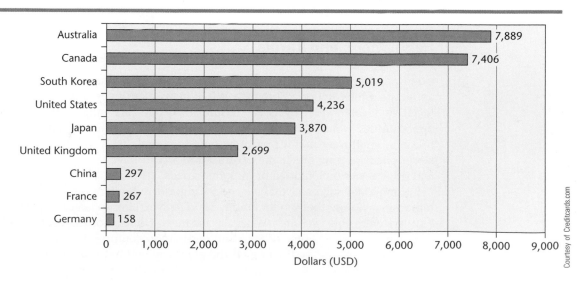

Average spent on credit-card transactions in 2012

Country	Dollars (USD)
Australia	7,889
Canada	7,406
South Korea	5,019
United States	4,236
Japan	3,870
United Kingdom	2,699
China	297
France	267
Germany	158

Courtesy of Creditcards.com

Contactless payments and digital wallets are growing in popularity globally although they have not overtaken traditional forms of payment. Google Wallet and Isis are "virtual wallets" on your smartphone. The customer creates an account with a payment provider linked to a financial account such as a checking or credit-card. Then, when purchasing goods or services with a business that accepts the provider's payment system, the customer authorizes payment immediately as opposed to providing a credit-card number directly.

At this writing, Google Wallet is only available in the United States and Isis is only available in Salt Lake City, Utah and Austin, Texas (Anonymous, n.d.-a; n.d.-c). Contactless payments, using near-field-communication (NFC) in physical cards, have existed in London, UK since 2007, primarily in coffee and sandwich shops. Contactless cards were introduced in Ireland in 2011 (Anonymous, 2011). The use of mobile payments is increasing steadily. In 2012, Adyen processed more than $10 billion globally through online, mobile, and point-of-sale payment transactions (Lomas, 2013). Europe leads the world with 15.3 percent of all payment transactions using a mobile device, followed by North America and Asia with 12.4 and 11.2 percent, respectively.

Security concerns are the main reason behind the slow adoption of new forms of electronic payments. In 2011, Citi's security was hacked and credit data of some of its North American cardholders was stolen. Such events make consumers question the security of their personal information and may delay the transition to e-payment as a primary means of payment in some societies.

Language Differences

To communicate internationally, parties must agree on a common language, and that can create problems. For instance, data might not be transmittable internationally in real time because the information must first be translated (usually by human beings). Although some computer applications can translate "on the fly," they are far from perfect. Another hurdle is that national laws usually forbid businesses to run accounting and other systems in a foreign language, leading to an awkward and expensive solution: running these systems in two languages, the local one and English, which is the *de facto* international language.

Companies that are in the forefront of web-based e-commerce have translated their original websites into local languages. They localize their sites by creating a dedicated site for each national audience. But translation can be tricky. For instance, the Taiwanese use the traditional set of Chinese characters, but people in the People's Republic of China prefer the simplified character set. Spanish terms in Spain might be different from those in Latin America, and even within Latin America. In some parts of South America people do not even call the language Español (Spanish) but Castellano (Castilian). In addition, mere linguistic translation might not capture cultural sensitivities. Therefore, some companies prefer to leave web design and translation to their local overseas offices.

Several companies, such as TRADOS, Inc., offer translation software and services to companies involved in global commerce. TRADOS' software package by the same name translates webpages into many languages, including those requiring special characters such as Hindi, Chinese, Greek, and Hebrew, but also ensures consistency of terms and sentence structure in different languages. When webpages are translated, the software ensures that the XML tags and statements are retained from the original languages, so that the company maintaining the website can continue to use the same XML code for online transactions with companies and shoppers in its new markets. Other tools translate MS-Word documents to multiple languages. One such tool is Wordfast. Google also offers a translation service for text as well as being able to translate websites into different languages.

Cultural Differences

XL Group is a global insurance firm operating 60 offices in 21 countries and branding itself as "one company without borders." At one point, the company had seven different email addressing standards at local offices. When the company's CIO decided to adopt a single universal naming format, he faced resistance. In South America, for instance, a person might use five names: his first and middle names, and his parent's middle and last names. That caused some people to have long email addresses. The CIO's suggestion to use employee ID numbers as their email addresses (with the company's suffix) was received with resentment in South America and Europe because it was impersonal. To mitigate these unexpected cultural differences, the CIO established a system that greets each employee by name in a personal manner as soon as the employee logs on to a computer.

Cultural differences refer in general to the many ways in which people from different countries vary in their tastes, gestures, preferred colors, treatment of people of certain gender or age, attitudes about work, opinions about different ethical issues, and the like. ISs might challenge cultural traditions by imposing the culture of one nation upon another (cultural imperialism). Conservative groups in some countries have complained about the "Americanization" of their young generations. Governments might be inclined to forbid the reception of some information for reasons of undesirable cultural influence. An example of such fear is the French directive against use of foreign words in government-supported mass media and official communications. A similar example is the ban by the Canadian province of Quebec on the use of non-French words in business signs. These fears have intensified with the growth of the Internet and use of the web. Because the Internet was invented and first developed in the United States and is still used by a greater percentage of Americans compared with any other single nation, its predominant culture is American.

As mentioned previously, companies that use the web for business must learn cultural differences and design their sites accordingly. Web designers need to be sensitive to cultural differences. People might be offended by the use of certain images, colors, and words. For example, black has sinister connotations in Europe, Asia, and Latin America; the index-finger-to-thumb sign of approval is a rude gesture meaning "jackass" in Brazil; the thumbs-up sign is a rude gesture in Latin America, as is the waving hand in Arab countries; and pictures of women with exposed arms or legs are offensive in many Muslim countries.

Conflicting Economic, Scientific, and Security Interests

The goal of corporate management is to seize a large market share and maximize its organization's profits. The goal of a national government is to protect the economic, scientific, and security interests of its people. Scientific information is an important national resource and a great source of income for foreign corporations, so occasionally those interests conflict.

For instance, companies that design and manufacture weapons have technical drawings and specifications that are financially valuable to the company but also valuable to the security of their country. Hence, many governments, including the U.S. federal government, do not allow the exchange of weapon designs. Transfer of military information to another country, even if the receiving party is part of an American business, is prohibited. Often, products whose purpose has nothing to do with the military are included in the list of prohibited trade items, because of the fear that they could be converted for use against the country of origin. In recent years, the list has included some software packages. The result is that, although American divisions of a company can use such software, their sister divisions in other countries cannot.

The U.S. Customs and Border Protection (CBP) requires a license for the permanent export, temporary import, or temporary export of classified or unclassified items that have military application that are considered defense articles. These items can include software or technology, blueprints, design plans, and retail software packages and technical information. Items that have been temporarily imported/exported or permanently exported without a license are subject to detention and possible seizure. Items that have dual-use (commercial and military applications) may be subject to an export license depending on the specifications of the commodity. Because some software applications and technologies designed in the United States can be used against the U.S. in times of warfare or in acts of terrorism, the CBP strictly regulates the exportation of these commodities (Anonymous, 2012).

Another problem that arises with international information interchange is that countries treat trade secrets, patents, and copyrights differently. Sometimes business partners are reluctant to transfer documents when one partner is in a country that restricts intellectual property rights, while another is in a country that has laws to protect intellectual property. On the other hand, the employees of a division of a multinational corporation might be able to divulge information locally with impunity. Intellectual property is tightly protected in the United States and Western Europe, and American trade negotiators and diplomats have pressured some countries to pass and enforce similar laws. Reportedly, the legislatures of several Asian nations have passed such laws or have revised existing laws in response to U.S. pressure.

Political Challenges

Information is power. Some countries fear that a policy of free access to information could threaten their sovereignty. For instance, a nation's government might believe that access to certain data, such as the location and quantity of natural resources, might give other nations an opportunity to control an indigenous resource, thereby gaining a business advantage that would adversely affect the resource-rich country's political interests.

As mentioned in Chapter 5, "Business Software," however, the recent trend in less rich countries is to adopt free open source software to avoid high costs. National governments in South America as well as local governments in Asia and Europe have adopted policies of using only open source software whenever it is available. Global corporations must ensure compatibility with the software adopted by governments and corporations in such locales.

Companies must also be aware of limits that some governments impose on Internet use. China, Singapore, and many Arab countries impose restrictions on what their citizens can download, view, and read. Free speech is not a universal principle. In practical terms, this means that executives might want to rephrase or cut out some content from their websites or risk their sites being blocked by some governments. This is an especially sensitive issue if a company enables employees or customers to use blogs at its website, in which they express their personal opinions.

Some corporations have found themselves in uneasy positions in countries that have limited civil rights. Microsoft, Yahoo, and Google were warned that they could not do business in China unless they collaborated with the government. This collaboration started by blocking certain search terms (e.g., "Taiwan" and "Falun Gong"), but were extended to providing the government the identities of people who searched for certain information, which the government took as a sign that they were dissidents. In some cases, individuals were imprisoned and tortured. The ethical dilemma for these companies is how to balance the business interest of their shareholders with moral principles of privacy, serving all web users equitably, and not helping dictatorships to violate civil rights.

Different Standards

Differences in standards must be considered when integrating ISs internationally, even within the same company. Because nations use different standards and rules in their daily business operations, sometimes records within one company are incompatible. For instance, the bookkeeping records of one division of a multinational company might be incompatible with the records of other divisions and headquarters. As another example, the United States still uses the English system of length and weight measures (inches, feet, miles, quarts, pounds, and so on), while the rest of the world (including England) officially uses the metric system (centimeters, meters, liters, kilograms, and the like). There are also different standards for communicating dates, times, temperatures, and addresses. The United States uses the format of month, day, year, while the rest of the world records dates in the format of day, month, year—so a date recorded as 10/12/14 might be misinterpreted. The United States uses a 12-hour time notation with the addition of a.m. or p.m., while other parts of the world use a 24-hour notation (called "military time" in the United States because the U.S. military uses this notation). The United States uses Fahrenheit temperatures, while other countries use Celsius temperatures. Americans communicate addresses in the format of street number, street name, and city name. Citizens of some other countries communicate addresses in the format of street name, street number, and city name.

Not resolving different standards can be extremely costly. In 1999, NASA lost track of a spacecraft that it sent to Mars. Reportedly, an investigation found that an error in a transfer of information between the Mars Climate Orbiter team in Colorado and the mission navigation team in California led to the spacecraft's loss. Apparently, one team used English units and the other used metric units for a key spacecraft operation. The information was critical to the maneuvers required to place the spacecraft in the proper Mars orbit. The cost to U.S. taxpayers was $125 million.

Companies that want to operate globally must adapt their ISs to changing formal or *de facto* standards. In recent years the growing number of countries joining the European Union (EU) imparted significant power to this bloc. Corporations in non-EU countries have grown accustomed to adapting their systems to those of the EU. For example, in 1976, Europeans adopted the 13-digit **European Article Number (EAN)**, while American companies used the 12-digit **Universal Product Code (UPC)**. The additional bar in the EAN bar code identifies the product's country of origin. For seven years, the American **Uniform Code Council (UCC)** promoted the use of the European standard. In 2004, the organization officially adopted it. Retailers embarked on a hectic effort to modify information systems to recognize, record, and process UPCs of 13 bars instead of 12 bars so they could meet the January 2005 deadline. Most bar-code readers could already read the extra bar, but the software in back-office systems—such as sales, shipping, receiving, and accounting systems—had to be modified. Best Buy, the large electronics and appliance retailer, spent 25,000 hours of staff and consultant time to ensure that cash registers, software applications, and databases could process and store the extra digit.

The GTIN-14 bar code is capable of storing 14 digits to identify trade items, products, or services

GTIN-14
(GS1-128 or ITF-14)

0 00 12345 60001 2

Courtesy of gtin

The UCC has developed the 14-digit **Global Trade Item Numbers (GTINs)**. This code is large enough to identify more than 100 times the number of products and manufacturers that the 12-digit UPCs could. An example of the GTIN-14 bar code is shown on the previous page. GTINs are designed to support global supply chains. Eventually, manufacturers and retailers might have to use either GTINs or another standard of larger codes embedded in RFID tags. RFID tags are heavily used in the United States, and American standards could expand to Europe and the rest of the world.

ETHICAL & SOCIETAL ISSUES: Legal Jurisdictions in Cyberspace

Imagine you are surfing the web and come across a virulent site that preaches hatred and violence. You file a complaint in court, but the court cannot do anything because the site is maintained in another country that does not uphold your country's law. Or, you shop on the web and purchase an item from a site that is physically maintained on a server in another country. When you receive the item, you discover that it is of a lower quality than promised. When you contact the site, the owners are rude and unresponsive. You decide to sue, but under which country's laws? These problems are two examples of the legal challenges in today's electronic global markets.

- **Offshore Websites.** Dawn Thompson overcame an accident that left her a paraplegic and became an award-winning romance writer. When she died in 2008, she hoped that the ongoing royalties from her books would be put toward caring for her disabled sister. The good news is that her books are still widely read. The bad news is that readers have downloaded Thompson's works over 4800 times from a single offshore website for free. These 'rogue' sites operate from outside the United States and offer copyrighted material such as books, movies, and music for free (Aistars, 2011).

In early 2012, one of the Internet's most popular file-sharing websites, Megaupload, was busted by the U.S. Federal Bureau of Investigation. Megaupload, Ltd. and its collection of websites, based in Hong Kong, was responsible for generating over $175 million in illegal profits and was responsible for over a half a billion dollars in damages to copyright owners. Sites like Megaupload are considered 'cyberlockers' because they are a virtual storage space for files that can be downloaded from any web browser. These sites are usually littered with a smorgasbord of pirated movies, TV shows, music, e-books, and software that can be downloaded with ease (Fowler, 20 January 2012).

American consumers, through their overwhelming Internet presence, indirectly ask American authors, publishers, producers, and musicians to participate in e-commerce to share their works. Their works need to be protected to ensure fair business practices. Although the U.S. Congress was presented with the 'Stop Online Piracy Act' bill in early 2012, it was met with heavy opposition and soon afterwards was shelved by Congress (MacCullagh, 30 March 2012). Web censorship is a tricky issue because it can be seen as infringing on the U.S. First Amendment right to freedom of speech.

- **Consumer Protection by Whom?** Where can consumers sue for e-commerce transactions gone wrong? Suppose you purchased an item from a site located in another country, and the item has a defect or arrived after the time promised. Because your request for compensation or another remedy has not been answered satisfactorily, you decide to sue the e-tailer. Where do you file the lawsuit? Your own country? The e-tailer's country? The venue of e-commerce lawsuits is still undecided in many parts of the world.

In November 2000, the European Union (EU) passed a law that lets consumers file lawsuits against an online business in any of the member countries composing the EU. Before the amendment to the 1968 Brussels Convention (which regulates commercial-legal issues in the EU), consumers could sue an online business only in courts in the country of the online business. If a website has directed its business at consumers in a certain country, the consumers can sue the website's owner in their own national courts. Businesses vehemently opposed the move, but consumer advocates said people would be more confident about online shopping if they knew they could get redress in their local courts.

- **Two Approaches to Jurisdiction.** As you have seen, the issue of e-commerce jurisdiction is broad. The U.S. Federal Trade Commission and European government organizations have examined the issue in an attempt to reach an international agreement such as the one reached within the EU.

There are two approaches to such an agreement. One approach is the country-of-origin principle, whereby all legal matters are confined to the country from which the site operates. Under this principle, the laws of that country apply to the operations and conduct of the site and whoever interacts with the site, regardless of their own location. Therefore, a lawsuit could be brought only in the country of the website and would be adjudicated according to that country's laws. Under this principle it is likely many firms would opt to establish websites in countries with lax consumer protection laws.

The other approach is the country-of-destination principle, whereby dealings with the site, regardless of the site's country of operation, are guided by the laws of the country to which the site caters. The EU adopted this approach within its territory, however achieving broad international agreement on e-commerce jurisdiction might take several years.

Legal Barriers

The fact that countries have different laws has a significant impact on global business in general, and on e-commerce in particular. The differing laws can pose serious challenges to international transfer of data, free speech, and the location of legal proceedings when disputes arise between buyer and seller.

Privacy Laws

Although many of the challenges involved in cross-border data transfer have been resolved through international agreements, one remains unresolved: respect for individual privacy in the conduct of international business. Interestingly, despite the importance attached to privacy, its value is not even mentioned in the constitutions of the United States and many other countries. Nonetheless, a majority of the democratic nations try to protect individual privacy.

POINT OF INTEREST International Hall of Shame

Privacy International (PI) is an international organization that is essentially a counter-attack to the 'Big Brother' effect. Their mission is to protect the global right to privacy and fight intrusive surveillance from governments and corporations. In the European Privacy and Human Rights report conducted by PI, The Electronic Privacy Information Center (EPIC), and Center for Media and Communications Studies (CMCS), assessments ruled European democracies were generally in good standing although some countries faltered with preserving privacy. In Croatia there was found to be no direct method for reviewing or auditing the actions of security services and medical databases were emerging with centralized registries. Additionally, in Croatia and Bulgaria, there was direct access to information held by third parties without warrants or proper legal documentation, by unaccountable organizations. The report's final conclusion on the EU: for a world leader, the privacy provisions were sub-par while surveillance intrusions went too far. The security risks and the extent of government surveillance which exist in some foreign countries can deter businesses from setting up shop there.

Source: European Privacy and Human Rights (EPHR) 2010. (26 January 2011): Privacy International, the Electronic Privacy Information Center (EPIC), and the Center for Media and Communications Studies (CMCS).

Countries differ in their approaches to the issue of privacy, as reflected in their laws. Some are willing to forgo some privacy for the sake of a more free flow of information and better marketing. Others restrict any collection of personal data without the consent of the individual.

The European Union enforces a privacy law called the Directive on Data Privacy. Member countries have crafted their laws according to the Directive. Usually the law is titled "Data Protection Law." The EU defines personal data as "any information relating to an identified or identifiable natural person; an identifiable person is one who can be identified, directly or indirectly, in particular by reference to an identification number or to one or more factors specific to his physical, physiological, mental, economic, cultural, or social identity." Some of the principles of the directive are in stark contrast to the practices of U.S. businesses and therefore limit the free flow of personal data between the United States and the EU. For example, consider the following provisions and how they conflict with U.S. practices:

- Personal data can be collected only for specified, explicit, and legitimate purposes and not further processed in a way incompatible with those purposes. However, in the United States, businesses often collect data from people without having to tell them how the data will be used. Many U.S. corporations use personal data for purposes other than the original one, and many organizations purchase personal data from other organizations, so subjects do not even know that the data is used, let alone for what purpose. Obviously, these activities would not be allowed under the EU directive.

- Personal data can be processed only if the subject has given unambiguous consent or under other specific circumstances that the directive provides. Such circumstances are not required by American laws. In the United States, private organizations are allowed to process personal data without the subject's consent, and for practically any purpose.

- Individuals or organizations that receive personal data (the directive calls them "controllers") not directly from the subject must identify themselves to the subject. In the United States, many organizations purchase personal data from third parties and never notify the subject.

- People have the right to obtain from controllers "without constraint at reasonable intervals and without excessive delay or expense" confirmation that data about them is processed, to whom the data is disclosed, and the source that provided the data. They are also entitled to receive information on the "logic involved in any automatic processing of data concerning" them, at least in the case of automated decision making. Decision making, practically speaking, means using decision-support systems and expert systems to make decisions on hiring, credit extension, admittance to educational institutions, and so forth. None of these rights is mandated by any U.S. law.

- People have the right to object, "on request and free of charge," to the processing of personal data for the purpose of direct marketing, or to be informed before personal data is disclosed for the first time to third parties or used for direct marketing. Furthermore, controllers must expressly offer the right to object free of charge to disclosure of personal data to others. American companies use personal data *especially* for direct marketing, never tell subjects that they obtain data about them from third parties, and rarely offer subjects the right to object to disclosure of such data to other parties.

American companies are very busy collecting, buying, and selling personal data for decision-making and marketing purposes. The American view is that such practices are essential to efficient business operations, especially in marketing and extension of credit. Thus, this huge discrepancy between the European and American approaches does not allow unrestricted flow of information.

Applicable Law

As discussed in the Ethical & Societal Issues box in this chapter, countries have differing laws regarding free speech, which can significantly impact what a company may or may not display from its servers. Other laws affecting online business include those that address gambling, auctioning, sales of alcoholic beverages and drugs, and other areas. After establishing online business in another country, some companies discovered that their practice was not in compliance with a local law. For example, eBay discovered that Dutch and Italian laws required that a certified auctioneer be present at any auction. This made its online auctions illegal in these countries. Some countries have changed their laws to accommodate online business, but others have not. Such legal discrepancy among jurisdictions should not come as a surprise to executives; they must research the legal environment in every jurisdiction where they intend to do business. The lessons of Yahoo!, eBay, and other online pioneers prompted many companies to employ legal research experts before they start business in a new jurisdiction. Often, this effort is part of a larger effort to research the local culture and practices. Some companies have hired local experts to help them in assessing local considerations, and in some cases executives decided to avoid doing online business in certain countries altogether.

As mentioned before, legal barriers to online business often exist within a country. For example, states in the United States have different laws regarding the purchase and delivery of alcoholic beverages. A company selling wine online to individual consumers must ensure that the buyer's state allows home delivery of wine. Shipping to a state forbidding such a transaction is criminal.

Different Time Zones

Companies that operate in many global regions, especially multinational corporations, must craft policies for the work of both their employees and information systems. Teleconferencing systems must be available much of the day, and in many cases 24 hours per day, so that employees many

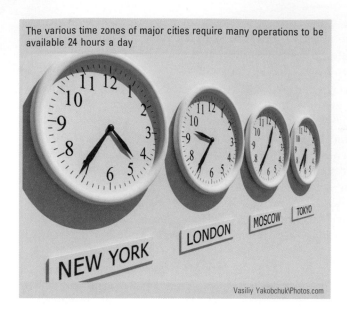
The various time zones of major cities require many operations to be available 24 hours a day

Vasiliy Yakobchuk\Photos.com

time zones apart can communicate to discuss problems that need immediate resolution. Teams in support centers might have to work in shifts to accommodate clients worldwide. When scheduling teleconferencing sessions, managers in North America should remember, for instance, that scheduling a session for Friday afternoon with their Australian counterparts will force the Australians to come to the office on Saturday morning.

In their global supply chain management systems, managers must be aware of what might seem to be incorrect time stamping in shipments and payment records. For example, consider interaction between a corporation's Pennsylvania manufacturing plant and its South Korean assembly plant. Because South Korea is 14 hours ahead of Pennsylvania, shipping records could show that subassemblies were shipped from Pennsylvania a day before they were ordered in South Korea. To eliminate confusion, the systems at both locations can be designed to record the local times of both locations, or only that of a single location, such as the company headquarters' time.

Summary

- As more companies use the web for both B2C and B2B business, they must accommodate non-English-speaking audiences and tailor their sites to local preferences. They also must be carefully attuned to the cultural differences and payment preferences of different world regions as well as be aware of legal and tariff issues.

- Organizations that engage in international trade, especially through the web, must also be aware of the linguistic, cultural, economic, and political challenges involved in such trade.

- One important unresolved issue is the discrepancy between the laws governing the collection and manipulation of personal data in two economic powers, the United States and the European Union, which have incompatible data privacy laws. This difference restricts the flow of personal data between the United States and the EU.

- Several cases have demonstrated that the old legal approach of territorial jurisdiction is inadequate when so much information is communicated and so much business is conducted on the Internet. Issues such as free speech and consumer litigation of e-tailers have brought to light the need for an international legal reform for cyberspace.

KIMBALL'S REVISITED

Liz considered the advice from Michael when evaluating suppliers. She refined her list of overseas suppliers and developed an inventory list and associated prices. The list included the name of the company, website URL, contact number, and the products that would be purchased from the company. She knows that the suppliers need to be linked to the food items in the new point-of-sale system.

What Is Your Advice?

1. Contracting with supplier partners in other countries can offer challenges compared with dealing with onshore partners. What issues do you believe Liz and Michael should address when ordering from suppliers overseas? Should they order online, or off-line?

2. How should Liz address the interaction with the point-of-sale system information in relation to the food supplies that are purchased overseas?

New Perspectives

1. When Liz and Michael were in Europe a few summers ago, Liz made a few of her sauces and appetizers for a local restaurant in Spain. She received positive comments on these items from the chef at the restaurant. Tyler and Michael thought that they could sell these items both in the U.S. and overseas. What advice would you give them to consider when developing a website for onshore (U.S.) sales, as well as some European countries (Italy, Spain, Portugal, and France)?

Key Terms

European Article Number (EAN), 310
global information system, 300

Global Trade Item Number (GTIN), 311
glocalization, 302

Uniform Code Council (UCC), 310
Universal Product Code (UPC), 310

Review Questions

1. What is meant by the term "global information systems"?

2. Executives of multinational corporations are advised to think globally and act locally. What does this mean?

3. Manufacturers and retailers have used product bar codes for many years. What information does the 13-digit European Article Number (EAN) contain that the 12-digit Universal Product Code (UPC) did not, and why is this information important?

4. Is every website a form of global IS? Why or why not?

5. Using software for automatic translation of webpages into other languages for local audiences saves much labor cost and time. If you were an executive for a company that maintains a multilingual website, would you settle for software-based translation only? Why or why not?

6. Many organizations, especially multinational corporations, must consolidate reports to ensure smooth operations. These reports include currency, measurements, and dates. How would you help them receive reports "on the fly" that are in the desired currency and format?

7. Many European countries have stricter privacy laws than the United States. What is the impact of this discrepancy on multinational corporations with offices on both continents? In terms of business functions, which activities, in particular, are affected?

8. Give three examples of cultural imperialism. Why do you think your examples reflect cultural imperialism?

9. American companies whose main business is web search have encountered political challenges in some countries. Give two examples of such challenges.

10. What are the implications of different time zones for global supply chain management systems?

11. Countries can adopt either a country-of-origin law or a country-of-destination law. What is the difference between the two approaches? Which is more helpful to consumers and which is more helpful to e-tailers? Explain.

Discussion Questions

12. Ask yourself: what are the "nationalities" of the following corporations? Consider nationality to be the country where the corporation is registered: SAP (software), BP (gasoline), CheckPoint (security software), LG (electronics), Corona (beer), Heineken (beer), Goodyear (tires), JVC (electronics), Braun (small appliances), Siemens (electronics), Nokia (mobile telephones), Business Objects (software). In your opinion, if a company has its headquarters in Bermuda, is it a "Bermudan" company? If so, in what respect? If not, explain why not.

13. Several technologies have been practically given away by the United States to the world. Name at least two such technologies. Do you think that this was "charity" or that the United States reaps some benefits from having made the technologies widely available? Explain.

14. The U.S. Department of Commerce has relaxed restrictions on the export of encryption (scrambling) software for communications, but it still bans the export of many such applications. Do you agree with such bans? Why or why not?

15. Almost all of the European Union countries use the Euro as their common currency. Does this help or hinder international ISs? Does it foster the use of information systems and the web? Explain.

16. Consider sensitivity to privacy in the United States. Are Americans more sensitive to *government* handling of private information or to *business* handling of private information? Now answer the question regarding Western European countries.

17. Apparently, the European Union has stricter privacy laws than the United States, and not many U.S. companies are willing to comply with the EU Directive on Data Protection. How would *you* resolve the conflict?

18. If a non-English-speaking country had established the Internet, do you think that country would impose its own "cultural imperialism" on the web? Why or why not?

19. Which legal approach do you prefer for e-commerce: country of origin or country of destination? Answer the question as a business-person, then answer it as a consumer.

20. If some countries clearly adopt the country-of-origin approach for legal issues of e-commerce, online retailers might relocate to operate from those countries. Why?

21. An American company employs engineers in California and in several Asian and European countries. The engineers exchange email and communicate via VoIP, teleconferencing, and collaborative project management tools. The Americans often use phrases such as "Let's touch base in a week," "Right off the bat...," and "...all the way to the end zone." An executive instructs them to avoid such phrases in communication with colleagues from other countries, and per-haps even with any colleague. Why?

Applying Concepts

22. You are an executive for Bidway.com, an auction site that has successfully competed with eBay and Yahoo! in the United States. Management decided to open use of the site to residents of all countries. You were given an important assign-ment: collect intelligence that will help ensure a smooth transition from a national business to an international business. If you envision that there might be too many difficulties in certain coun-tries, management will accept your recommen-dation to block bidding by residents of those countries, but you must be careful not to miss potentially profitable markets. Prepare an outline of all the aspects about which you will collect intelligence for each country, and explain why this item is important.

23. Why does the United States still use the English system? When was the last attempt to officially move to the metric system? Does the use of English measurement units put U.S. companies at a disadvantage when competing on international contracts? How has software solved the chal-lenge? Give examples of engineering software that resolves this challenge. Research on the web and summarize your findings in two pages.

Hands-On Activities

24. You are the international sales manager for Aladdin Rugs, Inc., a multinational company headquartered in the United States. At the end of every month, you receive reports from the national sales managers on your company's operations in England, Germany, and Japan. The products are sold by area. The managers report the units sold and income from sales in their national currencies: pounds sterling (£), euros (€), yens (¥), and U.S. dollars (US$). Use your spreadsheet program to consolidate the sales reports you received, as follows.
    a. Under "Totals," enter formulas to convert square yards to square meters and enter another formula to total the area in square meters for all four countries.
    b. In a financial newspaper such as the *Wall Street Journal* or on the web, find the rates of exchange for the three currencies against the US$ on the last business day of last month. Enter a formula that will convert all non-U.S. currencies to US$. (Extra challenge: program a macro to do the calculations.)
    c. Test all formulas with actual numbers.

25. Google and other sites offer web-based transla-tion services. Test the quality of such tools. Write a message of 50 words in English. Use the tool to translate it to German or another language with which you might be familiar. Copy the translated text, paste it to be translated, and use the tool to translate it back to English. Compare the original and translated English messages. Write a short

report and email it to your professor. How good is the translation tool? About how much of the text in the translated version came out identical to the original? Was the *spirit* of the message accurate (even if in different words)? Did you find anything funny in the back-translated text?

Team Activities

26. Team up with three other students. Decide on three keywords with which the team will conduct a web search. All of you should use the same search engine. One team member should record the number of sites found in the United States, another in Germany, another in France, and another in the Netherlands. Also, record the sites the team found whose domain name is non-U.S. but that used English rather than, or in addition to, the local language. (Note that many non-U.S. companies use the .com and .org top-level domains. Before you start this assignment, research the web for ways to determine the location of websites by their IP address rather than the TLD.) Prepare a brief report detailing what you recorded. Write your own conclusion. How dominant is English on the web? Do you think the web is "Americanized"? Do you consider what you found to be cultural imperialism?

27. "Electronic immigrants" are residents of one country who are employed by a company in another country. They are the result of what some people call "offshoring" of jobs. They deliver the results of their work through the Internet or private communications networks. Your team should conduct research with two companies in four different industries, one of which is in software development. The title of your research is "The Electronic Immigrant: Economic and Political Implications." Contact the human resource managers of the two companies, present the issue, and ask for the managers' opinions on the following issues. Can the company use "electronic immigrants"? Can it be hurt if competitors use them? Do the HR managers think the national economy can gain or lose from the phenomenon? Do they foresee any political ramifications? Your team should prepare a report starting with half a page of background on each company.

From Ideas to Application: Real Cases

Unilever Goes Streamlined

Unilever is an international company that owns brands in the food, beverage, cleaning agent, and personal care product industries. With 4 million consumer connections across all of North America, the volume of Unilever's data is enormous. Consider this for Dove, one of Unilever's many brands. Depending on what country the product is being shipped to, it must have different packaging with a different language and adhere to different countries' regulations. Production managers must work together with sales managers from different parts of the globe to ensure that the right order gets to the right destination with the right labeling. One can only imagine the amount of data Unilever accumulates from transactions for Dove and their additional 90 brands.

Accessing Unilever's large, complex product information database was slowing response times to customer inquiries and affecting sales negatively because the sales team did not have adequate access to organized, pertinent information. Managers were challenged because the data they needed was not on their desk until it was too late or the information was unable to be found at all. Over a period of years, Unilever had been building its database with product, health, and ingredient information and made the database accessible to agents. Agents, whose responsibility is to engage with customers, are the faces and voices of brands. It is easy to see why agents need access to the right information at the right time. The problem was that because the database had been built up over time by many different contributors, the organization of the database was lacking. Some information was in the database multiple times, sometimes under different titles. Some information was not there at all. The internal product information database was extremely user unfriendly. In order for the customer relations employees to run a search, they had to go through a 'trees' system in which the only way to exit was to back out, requiring six clicks. This was a time-consuming process with a customer on the phone. The database's disorganization and processing method were costly for Unilever on two levels. The first being an internal support team costs time and money. The second issue is that the unorganized database was hurting the sales of the agents who had to muck through the trees system while a customer waited on the line for an answer to their inquiry. The telephony system was another aspect that needed to be updated to become more centralized. Needless to say, Unilever's database system had many areas for improvement.

Unilever turned to Astute Solutions to streamline their product information. They implemented a 'one-click' approach to database navigation which made it much easier to navigate the database and thus to accurately respond to customer inquiries in a timely fashion. Visual images of labels and web links were also available to inform employees of ingredients, some of which had unpronounceable names. Not having to leave a desk to retrieve a bottle or label information saved a lot of time. As elementary as it may sound, one of the most useful aspects of Astute's solutions was the natural language screen that caught common misspellings. The telephony system was upgraded to a single system with multiple contact centers with call controls embedded with ePowerCenter Customer Relationship Management (CRM) applications. All calls were recorded to prevent any 'he said/she said' scenarios. The Astute system they chose to install was a "learn-by-use" system, saving the company money in training costs that are associated with a traditional "babysitting" system, which requires much more over-the-shoulder training.

Although the changes were not welcomed by Unilever employees, the changes did pay off. The results of the changes made by Astute Solutions led to a 50 percent reduction in calls made to the internal help desk, a sign of a user-friendly database. Unilever has also achieved a 95 percent web self-service accuracy rate and has experienced a 90 percent reduction in e-mail volume as a result of effective online self-service. How do these results affect the bottom line? Unilever has received an annual savings of $4.4 million in addition to a sales impact of about $9 million.

In addition to those statistical results, an organized and streamlined approach to product information that is accessible across all company fields can add predictive value to a company's data. Unilever's streamlined approach to data management has reduced response times and saved the company millions in reduced support costs. Unilever's next step is to move more into social CRM.

Sources: Beck, K. (2011). Information Overload. Customer Relationship Management, 15, 38–38. Sherlock, A. (2012). Managing Information Overload. Pharmaceutical Executive, 32(5), 58, 60.

Thinking About the Case

1. Why is it important for an international company to have clear lines of communication between regional managers and manufacturing/distribution? How can this directly impact sales?

2. List the different areas in which Unilever saved money by implementing the changes made by

Astute Solutions. As an agent, why do you believe that they had a positive impact?

3. What are the benefits of having all product information visible to all fields of a company in an organized, central location? What are the risks?

4. What can Unilever's agents do to become more engaged with their customers through social CRM?

Abercrombie & Fitch Centralizes and Expands

Abercrombie & Fitch is an international clothing retailer that learned the importance of efficient data management when expanding internationally. Because of the lower promotional costs and higher profits, international expansion was attractive to A&F. After launching their international strategy in Canada and the U.K. in 2006 and 2007, respectively, A&F could see further international growth on the horizon. However, it knew its data management was not capable of handling the level of growth that was expected.

A&F's financial visibility of merchandising was dismal. A&F managers were using spreadsheets of data to plan future merchandise levels, making any conclusions as to whether they were over- or under-buying merchandise virtually inconceivable. Floor space layouts were designed based on merchandise allocations assigned by merchandising managers. If the merchandise allocation was inaccurate or became delayed, the floor space had to be redesigned because the merchandise that was planned to go on display was not at the store in time. Store managers began to overstock merchandise to prevent these occurrences. All merchandise was shipped to the A&F distribution base in Columbus, Ohio and stayed there until it was called upon by an individual store. This made it difficult to efficiently restock inventory in overseas locations. The previously stated flaws in A&F's merchandising system and adjoining distribution system were too great to sustain the international growth they wanted to pursue.

To support the data influx that comes with international growth like A&F experienced, they needed an open operating platform and integrated point-of-sale (POS) infrastructure in order to keep the closest eye on transactional data. For an international retail company, the data accessible today is used to make decisions that have impacts far into the future. Without the appropriate data at the appropriate time, the wrong decisions can easily be made and the

company can suffer severe consequences. A&F chose to install the Oracle Retail Merchandising system in its headquarters in Columbus, Ohio. Transactional data from all store locations, domestic and international, is centrally managed there. A&F also implemented changes to the front lines. They used Oracle's Retail Point-of-Sale Software System (ORPOS) to collect real-time data from their 1,100 store locations across the globe. Each store was connected to a regional database that manages up to 30 stores. With all data visible to headquarters in Ohio, A&F's merchandising managers had all the information they needed to make educated decisions, in one location. Transactional data from all departments including supply chain, inventory management, and POS processing are now all visible on an international scale.

Since installing the platform, inventory order accuracy has increased from 94 percent to 100 percent. Additionally, A&F's international stores have brought in close to $1 billion in sales.

Air shipments have decreased from 25 percent of all shipments to only 8 percent, a huge expense savings. A&F's software gives them a real-time view of transactions occurring in stores globally. The new POS software provides benefits for many different departments of the company including inventory management and logistics, and store managers who need access to this information can plan future merchandising levels. If store managers have accurate merchandise levels, they can design the most effective floor layouts without worrying about having to change the layout at the last minute. A&F saves money by not overstocking and does not lose sales due to under-stocking. The improved data management software adds predictive value to A&F and also allows it to use data to draw conclusions on purchasing patterns that determine future merchandise levels.

Source: Amato-McCoy, D. (2012). Mobility 101. *Chain Store Age, 88*(3), 24.

Thinking About the Case

1. Why is it important for a company that operates internationally to have centrally located information visible to multiple departments?

2. What are the challenges a global clothing retailer faces in regards to maintaining proper inventory levels?

3. How did efficient transactional data management lead to a decrease in air shipment costs of A&F?

References

3M. (n.d.). History. from http://solutions.3m.com/wps/portal/3M/en_US/3M-Company/Information/Resources/History/#

Aistars, S. (2011, Nov 17). Rogue Websites Stifling American Entrepreneurs, *Roll Call*.

Amari, R. (2012). IBISWorld Journal Industry Report 32552 Adhesive Manufacturing in the US.

Anonymous. (5 April 2012). Prohibited and Restricted Items. Retrieved January 31, 2013, from http://www.cbp.gov/xp/cgov/travel/vacation/kbyg/prohibited_restricted.xml

Anonymous. (2011, Aug 01). Empty wallet is no problem in this electronic age, *Irish Times*, p. 14.

Anonymous. (2012). Internet Usage Statistics. Retrieved January 2, 2013, from http://internetworldstats.com/stats.htm

Anonymous. (n.d.-a). Google Wallet Overview. Retrieved June 29, 2013, from http://www.google.com/wallet/

Anonymous. (n.d.-b). Number of Credit Cards and Credit Card Holders. from http://www.cardhub.com/edu/number-of-credit-cards/

Anonymous. (n.d.-c). Where can I use it? 2013, from http://www.paywithisis.com/where-to-use.xhtml

Drucker, J. (Oct 21, 2010). Google 2.4% rate shows how $60 billion lost to tax loopholes. from http://www.bloomberg.com/news/2010-10-21/google-2-4-rate-shows-how-60-billion-u-s-revenue-lost-to-tax-loopholes.html/

Fowler, G. A., Barrett, Devlin, and Schechner, Sam (20 January 2012). U.S. Shuts Offshore Fileshare 'Locker'. http://online.wsj.com/article/SB10001424052970204616504577171060611948408.html

Holmes, T. (5 January 2011). How different cultures handle credit cards. http://www.creditcards.com/credit-card-news/credit-cards-in-different-cultures-1267.php#globalcreditcarduse

Jackson, J. K. (2012). Foreign Direct Investment in the United States: An Economic Analysis.

Lomas, N. (2013). Tablets Continue To Build Momentum As A Place To Pay, Android & iPad Up 5% In 10 Months. *Techcrunch.com*. http://techcrunch.com/2013/06/06/adyen-m-commerce-index/

MacCullagh, D. (30 March 2012). White House calls for new law targeting 'offshore' Web sites. http://news.cnet.com/8301-31921_3-57407356-281/white-house-calls-for-new-law-targeting-offshore-web-sites/

Post, F. (2010). FP 500 Foreign Controlled. from http://www.financialpost.com/news/FP500/2011/foreign-controlled.html?sort=rank&page=1

Woolsey, B. a. S. M. (28 February 2012). Credit card statistics, industry facts, debt statistics. http://www.creditcards.com/credit-card-news/credit-card-industry-facts-personal-debt-statistics-1276.php

DECISION SUPPORT AND BUSINESS INTELLIGENCE

BUSINESS CHALLENGES

New restaurants open every year. However, restaurants can be challenging to manage effectively and profitably. Liz and Michael want to succeed in the new location by making accurate and timely decisions. Although their past business and cooking experience is useful, it will be important to manage the business efficiently as well as anticipate trends in their operations and financial status. These important strategic and operational decisions should be based, in part, on their analysis of the data processed and maintained by their business.

- In Chapter 10, "*Decision Support and Expert Systems,*" you learn how to determine the characteristics of businesses and decisions that can benefit from decision support systems and what is involved in creating and using them.

- In Chapter 11, "*Business Intelligence and Knowledge Management,*" you learn how knowledge management systems support the business process and how data mining can be used to establish strategic advantage.

CHAPTER ten

DECISION SUPPORT AND EXPERT SYSTEMS

Learning Objectives

Decision making plays a key role in managerial work. Managers often have to consider large amounts of data, extract and synthesize only relevant information, and make decisions that will benefit the organization. As the amount of available data grows, so does the need for computer-based aids to assist managers in their decision-making process.

When you finish this chapter, you will be able to:

- List and explain the phases in decision making.

- Articulate the difference between structured and unstructured decision making.

- Describe the typical software components that decision support systems and expert systems comprise.

- Give examples of how decision support systems and expert systems are used in various domains.

- Describe the typical elements and uses of geographic information systems.

- List the benefits and risks of automated decision making.

KIMBALL'S RESTAURANT: Preparing to Serve

Michael and Liz were finalizing the new menus for The Lakeside. They decided to add several seatings to begin branding the new location differently. They wanted to add a Sunday breakfast/brunch, happy hour bar appetizers, and late night dining on Fridays and Saturdays. To create more traffic as well as gain new customers, Tyler developed a targeted marketing campaign to local businesses for after-work informal gatherings at the bar. After the first few weeks, they would begin to offer the late-night menu on weekends to target customers who attended movies, theatre, and other events. Liz hoped to start Sunday breakfast/brunch within a month. There were only two restaurants offering breakfast: a local small diner and a restaurant about five miles away.

Decisions at the Dinner Table

With the expanded meal offerings at the new location, Liz and Michael knew that using some forecasting would help them with the ordering decisions. The new system could provide them with historical data on meals and number of guests. However, they needed some type of standard process to order the food necessary to support the estimated meals. Liz said she could take an educated guess. But Michael said, "Liz, we can't be making guesses. Also, the more time you are spending on calculating the orders, the less time you are managing the kitchen operations. We need to focus our time on important operational and management issues, not

guessing on orders." Michael was hoping that she would accept that. Luckily, Liz agreed.

Michael asked Liz to make a list of items that she needed to prepare the meals for all menus. He created a small spreadsheet page for Liz to compile those items. She asked him, "Michael, would it be beneficial to break down each menu item using the recipe to identify the food needed to create the item?" Michael smiled and conveyed to Liz that she really understood the issue. However, she did not have the time or technical expertise to accomplish it. She could compile the food items and recipes, but didn't know how to integrate it all together to develop the order list.

Michael also knew that managing their suppliers as well as their orders would be a key factor in their success. Focusing on one supplier for specific products would gain the lowest cost. Conversely, relying on just a few suppliers would build a competitive environment as well as ensure a backup supplier in case of problems. However, he needed a standard process to calculate the quantity and frequency of deliveries to increase his leverage with the suppliers.

Michael has decided to ask Jim, one of Tyler's friends with a great deal of experience in information technology, to build a spreadsheet model to help with this task. Michael asked Tyler to explain the ordering process to Jim, so Jim can develop an iterative decision making model to help with ordering and purchasing. Michael knows that the challenges will be to gather the necessary data and to set up the calculations to make efficient purchasing decisions.

Decision Support

The success of an organization largely depends on the quality of the decisions that its employees make. When decision making involves large amounts of information and a lot of processing, computer-based systems can make the process efficient and effective. This chapter discusses two types of decision support aids: decision support systems (DSSs) and expert systems (ESs). In recent years applications have been developed to combine several features and methods of these aids. Also, decision support modules are often part of larger enterprise applications. For example, ERP (enterprise resource planning) systems support decision making in such areas as production capacity planning, logistics, and inventory replenishment.

Furthermore, many vendors of computer-based decision support tools, such as Pilot Software and Cognos, Inc., no longer call their applications decision support systems. (Pilot Software was acquired by SAP in 2007. Cognos was acquired by IBM in 2008. These acquisitions may be an indication of how decision support software is becoming an integral part of enterprise software and information technology applications.) These firms prefer to call them business analysis tools, business intelligence applications, or other names. In a way, almost any system that produces useful information is a decision aid. Decision support systems and expert systems are especially designed to streamline the decision-making process by providing either a single optimal solution to a question or problem, or a narrow set of solutions from which decision makers can select.

The emergence of data warehouses and online processing (OLAP) technologies has enhanced the abilities of employees at all levels to effectively use data for decision making. We discuss OLAP in Chapter 11, "Business Intelligence and Knowledge Management." The pervasive use of the web prompted software developers to make practically all decision support applications accessible through web browsers.

The Decision-Making Process

When do you have to make a decision? When you drive your car to a certain destination and there is only one road, you do not have to make a decision. The road will take you there. But if you come to a fork, you have to decide which way to go. In fact, whenever more than one possible action is available, a decision must be made. If you have to decide based only on distance, making a decision is easy. If you have to choose between a short but heavily trafficked road and a longer road with lighter traffic, the decision is a bit more difficult.

A decision is easy to make when one option will clearly bring about a better outcome than any other. Decisions become more difficult when more than one alternative seems reasonable and when the number of alternatives is great. In business, there can be dozens, hundreds, or even millions of different courses of action available to achieve a desired result. The problem is deciding on the best alternative. You can see why problem solving and decision making are so closely related.

Herbert Simon, a researcher of management and decision making, described decision making as a three-phase process (Simon, 1960). As shown in Figure 10.1, in the *intelligence* phase, decision makers collect facts, beliefs, and ideas. In business, the facts might be millions of pieces of data. Second, in the *design* phase, the method for considering the data is designed. The methods are sequences of steps, formulas, models, and other tools that systematically reduce the alternatives to a manageable number. Third, in the *choice* phase, when there is a reduced number of alternatives, decision makers make a choice; that is, they select the most promising alternative. After the choice phase, the business implements and executes the selected course of action.

FIGURE **10.1**

The three phrases of decision making

Intelligence	• Collect data from inside the organization. • Collect data from outside the organization. • Collect information on possible ways to solve the problem.
Design	• Organize the data; select a model to process the data. • Produce reasonable, potential courses of action.
Choice	• Select a course of action.

Businesses collect data internally (from within the organization) and externally (from outside sources). They use models to analyze data. Generally speaking, a **model** is an abstraction of reality. For instance, in architecture, a tabletop representation of a building or a city block is a model of the full-sized structure. A map is a small-scale representation—a model—of a particular geographic area that can include topographic information and political boundaries. And in business, mathematical equations that represent the relationships among variables can be models for how businesses respond to changes, such as: what happens to profits when sales and expenses go up or down? Decision makers either use universal models, such as certain statistical models, or design their own models to analyze data. Then they select what they perceive as the best course of action.

A **structured problem** is one in which an optimal solution can be reached through a single set of steps. Since the one set of steps is known, and since the steps must be followed in a known sequence, solving a structured problem with the same data always yields the same solution. Mathematicians call a sequence of steps an **algorithm** and the categories of data that are considered when following those steps **parameters**. For instance, when considering the problem of the shortest route for picking up and delivering shipments, the parameters are shipment size, the time when shipments are ready for pickup, the time when shipments are needed at their destinations, the distance of existing vehicles from the various destinations, the mandatory rest times of the drivers, the capacities of the trucks, and so on.

Most mathematical and physical problems are structured. Finding the roots of a quadratic equation is a structured problem: there is a formula (an algorithm) you can use to solve the problem. For the same equation the roots are always the same. Predicting how hot a liquid will get in a particular setting is a structured problem: if you know the properties of the liquid, the size of its container, the properties of the energy source heating the liquid, and the exact length of time the energy will be applied, you can figure out what temperature the liquid will reach. Unfortunately, most problems in the business world cannot be solved so easily.

An **unstructured problem** is one for which there is no algorithm to follow to reach an optimal solution—either because there is not enough information about the factors that might affect the solution or because there are so many potential factors that no algorithm can be formulated to guarantee a unique optimal solution. An unstructured situation is closely related to uncertainty. You cannot be sure what the weather will be tomorrow, let alone two months from now; nobody can guarantee what an investment in a certain portfolio of stocks will yield by year's end; and two physicians might diagnose the same symptoms differently. These are all areas where unstructured problems predominate.

Some management scientists refer to semi-structured problems. A **semi-structured problem** is one that is neither fully structured nor totally unstructured. The problem "Should I invest for two years $100,000 in municipal bonds that pay 3 percent per annum tax free or should I invest in CDs (certificates of deposit) with 4 percent taxable interest?" is structured. To find the solution you have to follow a simple algorithm that takes as parameters your $100,000, the two years, and the 3 percent interest rate. Unless the city that issued the bonds goes bankrupt, your calculated income is guaranteed. Similarly, it is easy to calculate the after-tax yield of the same amount invested in the CDs. However, the problem "Should I invest $100,000 in the stock of XYZ, Inc. and sell the stock after two years?" is semi-structured. Too many factors must be taken into account for it to be considered structured: the demand for the company's products, entrance of competitors into its market, the market of its products in this country and overseas, and so on. So many factors affecting the price of the stocks might change over the next two years that the problem is semi-structured at best and totally unstructured at worst. Professionals encounter semi-structured problems almost daily in many different industries and in many different business functions (see Figure 10.2).

FIGURE **10.2**

Examples of structured
and semi-structured
problems in business

Structured Problems

How many workers are needed to fully
staff production line A?

What is our optimal order quantity for raw
material Z, based on our production?

How many turbines are needed to supply
power to Hickstown?

Which of our regions yields the highest
revenue per salesperson?

Which money market fund currently yields
the highest return?

How much would the implementation of
pollution-preventing devices cost us?

Semi-structured Problems

What are the benefits of merging with XYZ, Inc.?

Where should we deploy the next five stores of
our retail chain?

How will the consumer react if we lower the
price of our product by 10 percent?

What is the best advertisement campaign to
launch our new financial service?

What are the benefits of opening an office in
Paris, France?

Which stock will yield the highest return by
the end of the year?

© Cengage Learning 2015

A manager solving a typical semi-structured problem faces multiple courses of action. The
task is to choose the one alternative that will bring about the best outcome. For example:

- In manufacturing, managers must provide solutions to semi-structured problems such as:
  (1) Which supplier should we use to receive the best price for purchased raw materials while
  guaranteeing on-time delivery? (2) Assembly line B has a stoppage; should we transfer workers
  to another assembly line or wait for B to be fixed? (3) The demand for product X has
  decreased. Should we dismantle one of the production lines, or should we continue to manufacture at the current rate, stock the finished products, and wait for an upswing in demand?

- Managers of investment portfolios must face semi-structured decision making when they
  decide which securities to sell and which to buy so they can maximize the overall return on
  investment. The purpose of research in stock investing is to minimize uncertainties by trying
  to find patterns of behavior of stocks, among other trends. Managers of mutual funds spend
  much of their time in semi-structured decision making.

- Human resource managers are faced with semi-structured problems when they have to decide
  whom to recommend for a new position, considering a person's qualifications and his or her
  ability to learn and assume new responsibilities.

- Marketing professionals face semi-structured problems constantly: should they spend money
  on print, television, web, email, or direct-mail advertisements? Which sector of the population should they target?

Stock investment, position
recruiting, and marketing
promotion are domains for
unstructured and semi-
structured decision
making

Comstock/Photos.com   Alex Slobodkin/Photos.com   Brian Jackson/Photos.com

Because of the complexities of the problems they face, managers in many functional areas
often rely on decision support applications to select the best course of action.

The terms "decision support systems" and "expert systems" are mentioned less frequently these days. However, the concepts of modeling decision-making processes and automating them and the transformation of human expertise into software are alive and thriving. While many situations exist in which only an experienced professional can make good decisions, much of the decision-making process can be automated through use of computer-based decision aids. The raw materials for many decisions are already in corporate databases and data warehouses, and they can be accessed through ISs such as supply chain management systems. Your ideas of how to automate routine decisions can save much labor and time for your organization. Knowing how expert systems and geographic information systems work might stimulate fresh ideas in your mind for implementation of new ISs, which can not only save labor and time but also be a competitive tool for your organization.

Decision Support Systems

To save time and effort in their decision making, knowledge workers use several types of decision support applications. One such type, a **decision support system (DSS)**, is a computer-based information system designed to help knowledge workers select one of many alternative solutions to a problem. DSSs can help corporations increase market share, reduce costs, increase profitability, and enhance product quality. By automating some of the decision-making process, the systems give knowledge workers access to previously unavailable analyses. Technically, certain analyses could be performed by managers, but it would be prohibitively time-consuming and would render late, and therefore bad, decisions. DSSs provide sophisticated and fast analysis of vast amounts of data and information. Although the use of DSSs typically increases with the level of management, the systems are used at all levels, and often by non-managerial staff.

The definition of a DSS has been changing over the years. The following sections discuss the components of stand-alone DSSs: either self-contained applications or applications that are designed to address a rather narrow decision-making domain. You should realize that some components of a computer-based decision aid, such as databases, might already be in place when a new DSS is developed. Therefore, consider the following discussion a general framework and not a rigid recipe for the development of all DSSs.

The majority of DSSs comprise three major components: a data management module, a model management module, and a dialog module (see Figure 10.3). Together, these modules (1) help the user enter a request in a convenient manner, (2) search vast amounts of data to focus on the relevant facts, (3) process the data through desired models, and (4) present the results in one or several formats so the output can be easily understood. These steps follow the decision-making sequence described by Herbert Simon.

FIGURE **10.3**

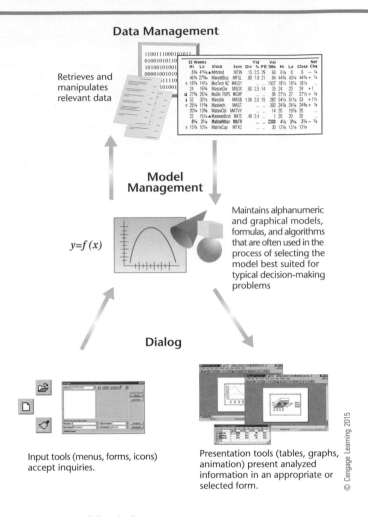

Data Management

Retrieves and manipulates relevant data

Model Management

$y=f(x)$

Maintains alphanumeric and graphical models, formulas, and algorithms that are often used in the process of selecting the model best suited for typical decision-making problems

Dialog

Input tools (menus, forms, icons) accept inquiries.

Presentation tools (tables, graphs, animation) present analyzed information in an appropriate or selected form.

© Cengage Learning 2015

The Data Management Module

A DSS's **data management module** is a database or data warehouse that provides the data for the intelligence phase of decision making. For example, an investment consultant always needs access to current stock prices and those from at least the preceding few years. A data management module accesses the data and provides a means for the DSS to select data according to certain criteria: type of stock, range of years, and so on.

A DSS might use a database created specifically for that system, but DSSs are usually linked to databases used for other purposes as well, such as purchasing, shipping, billing, and other daily transactions. When organizations use a supply chain management (SCM) or customer relationship management (CRM) system, the databases of such systems provide the data for the DSS. In fact, the DSS itself might be part of that system. Companies prefer their DSSs to access the data warehouse rather than the transactional database, to provide substantially more historical data than is available in transactional databases. This enables the DSS to consider data that covers a longer time period and/or a larger geographic area. Indeed, the major reason for building data warehouses is to enhance decision making.

Many DSSs are now closely intertwined with other organizational systems, including data warehouses, data marts, and ERP systems, from which they draw relevant data. For example, Rapt, Inc. offers a decision support application that helps optimize purchasing decisions of goods, especially for high-volume purchasers. Rapt Buy, acquired by Microsoft in 2008, is a web-based application that captures business variables in data marts through an SAP or Oracle supply chain management (SCM) system. The application's analytical software builds models that identify various elements of risk and then recommends purchasing strategies. It considers dozens of economic variables, including demand for the raw materials and yield (the percentage of the materials that are actually used in the final products). The system suggests how many units of each component the company should purchase to avoid carrying too much or too little inventory. In addition, the system provides multi-period plans for optimizing procurement into the future. Within minutes, the application analyzes the potential effect of various procurement and negotiation strategies. At Sun Microsystems Corp., forecasting demand for new products can be off by up to 70 percent. Before implementing this system, procurement officers at this large manufacturer of servers spent many hours of manual analytical work. Now, they use this system to calculate forecasts faster and more accurately.

POINT OF INTEREST — DSSs in Auditing

Auditing is the financial evaluation of a company conducted by accountants, similar to a check-up or a physical at the doctor's office. Accountants frequently use DSSs in auditing to speed up decision making and reduce the amount of manual input needed to come up with those outputs. Auditing involves an increasingly large amount of data and thus the automation of decision making can provide users of financial statements with significantly more accurate and timely outputs. Additionally, auditing DSSs can train rookies to produce expert-like findings. Shareholders' desire for real-time information drives the evolution of continuous monitoring. In the future, data mining systems could continuously input information into an automated auditing system. This step would lead to more effective and efficient auditing.

Source: Hunton, J. E., & Rose, J. M. (2010). 21st Century Auditing: Advancing Decision Support Systems to Achieve Continuous Auditing. Accounting Horizons, 24(2), 297–312.

The Model Management Module

To turn data into useful information, the system utilizes its **model management module**, which offers a single fixed model, a dynamically modified model, or a collection of models from which either the DSS or the user selects the most appropriate one. A fixed variable model does not change. A dynamically modified model is one that is automatically adjusted based on changing relationships among variables.

A sequence of events or a pattern of behavior might become a useful model when the relationships among its inputs, outputs, and conditions can be established well enough that they can be used to analyze different parameters. Models are used to predict output on the basis of different input or different conditions or to estimate what combination of conditions and input might lead to a desired output. Models are often based on mathematical research or on experience. A model might be a widely used method to predict performance, such as best-fit linear analysis, or it might be built by the organization, using the experience that employees in the firm have accumulated over time. Many companies will not divulge details of the models they have programmed because they view them as important trade secrets and valuable assets that could give them competitive advantages. Patterns or models might be unique to a certain industry or even to an individual business. For example:

- In trying to serve bank customers better, operations research experts create a model that predicts the most efficient positioning and scheduling of tellers.
- In the trucking business, models are developed to minimize the total mileage trucks must travel and maximize the trucks' loads, while maintaining satisfactory delivery times. Similar models are developed in the airline industry to maximize revenue.
- Another model for revenue maximization in the airline industry will automatically price tickets according to the parameters the user enters: date of the flight, day of the week of the flight, departure and destination points, and the length of stay if the ticket is for a round-trip flight.
- Car rental companies use similar models to price their services by car class, rental period, and drop-off options in different countries.
- A model can help to provide a decision on whether to purchase land (as illustrated on the next page with Vanguard Software's Business Analytics Suite).

Decision support systems can process collected data and suggest a solution for a land investment problem

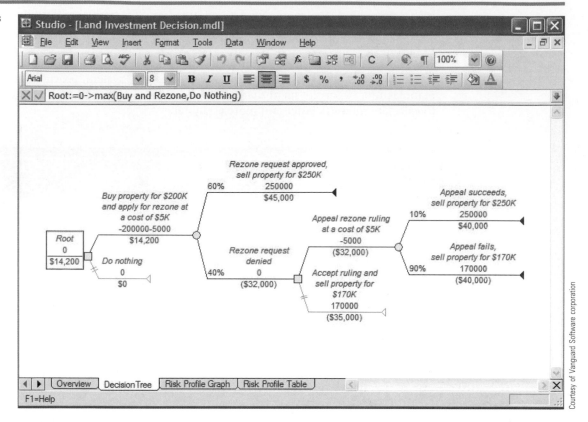

Among the general statistical models, a linear regression model is the best-fit linear relationship between two variables, such as sales and the money spent on marketing. A private business might develop a linear regression model to estimate future sales based on past experience. For example, the marketing department of a shoe store chain might apply linear regression to the relationship between the dollar amount spent on search website advertising and change in sales volume. This linear relationship can be translated into a program in a DSS. Then the user can enter the total amount to be spent on search website advertising for the next year into the DSS, and the program will enter that figure into the model and find the estimated change in the sales volume. The relationship between the two variables can be plotted, as shown in Figure 10.4.

FIGURE 10.4

A linear regression model for predicting sales volume as a function of dollars spent on web advertising

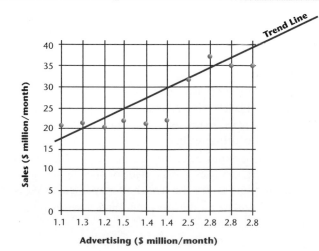

Advertising ($M/month)	Sales ($M/month)
1.1	20.3
1.3	21
1.2	20.1
1.5	22.7
1.4	21.9
1.4	22
2.5	32
2.8	36
2.8	35
2.8	34.8

© Cengage Learning 2015

Note that the actual data points rarely lie on the regression line produced from the data. This illustrates the uncertainty involved in many models. For instance, in Figure 10.4, if the marketing managers tried to estimate the sales volume resulting from spending $1.4 million per month on web advertising, their estimates for both months plotted on the graph would be more than the actual sales. In spite of these discrepancies, the regression line might be adequate in general for modeling, with the understanding that results are not necessarily precise. Also note that models often describe relationships among more than two variables and that some models can be expressed as a curve, rather than a straight line.

Usually, models are not so simple. In this advertising and sales example, for instance, many more factors might play a role: the number of salespeople, the location of the stores, the types of shoes offered for sale, the search keywords with which the advertising is associated, and many more parameters. Therefore, before models are programmed to become part of a DSS, the environment in which the decision will be executed must be carefully considered.

Not all DSS models are business-oriented. In some areas, especially engineering, DSS models might simulate physical rather than business environments. For example, aeronautical engineers use computer models of wind tunnels to view how a computer model of an aircraft with a new wing design might behave. It is significantly less expensive to construct a software model than to build a physical model. The simulation provides valuable information on vibrations, drag, metal fatigue, and other factors in relation to various speeds and weather conditions. The output, in the form of both animated pictures and numerical tables, enables engineers to make important decisions before spending huge amounts of money to actually build aircraft— decisions such as the angle in which the aircraft wings are swept, the shape of the fuselage's cross section, the spreading of weight over different parts of the plane, and so forth. When using this type of model, engineers base part of their decision on visual examination of the behavior of the simulation model.

The Dialog Module

For the user to glean information from the DSS, the system must provide an easy way to interact with the program. The part of the DSS that allows the user to interact with it is called the **dialog module**. It prompts the user to select a model, allowing the user to access the database and select data for the decision process or to set criteria for selecting such data. It lets the user enter parameters and change them to see how the change affects the result of the analysis. The dialog might be in the form of commands, pull-down menus, icons, dialog boxes, or any other approach. In essence, the dialog module is not much different from the user interfaces of other types of applications. As an increasing number of DSSs are available for use through the Internet, some dialog modules are especially designed to be compatible with web browsers. Many such DSSs are accessed through corporate intranets.

The dialog module is also responsible for displaying the results of the analysis. DSSs use various textual, tabular, and graphical displays from which the decision maker can choose. Take the previous advertising effort scenario, for example, where the company's marketing manager is trying to decide how to spend promotional dollars. The dialog component of the DSS presents a menu allowing the marketing executive to select web search advertising from a variety of promotional choices and to choose the amount to be spent in that channel (see Figure 10.5). Now the dialog module calls up the part of the database that holds current data on advertising expenditures and sales volumes for the corresponding months. At this point, the system might either present a list of models for analyzing the data from which the user can choose or, if it is sophisticated enough, select a model automatically, based on the problem at hand. The model projects sales figures based on the data from the database, and the dialog component presents the results of the analysis. The output helps the executive make a decision by answering the question, "Will the proposed amount to be spent on web ads yield a large enough boost in sales?"

FIGURE 10.5

A DSS can help marketers make decisions on how to spend promotion resources

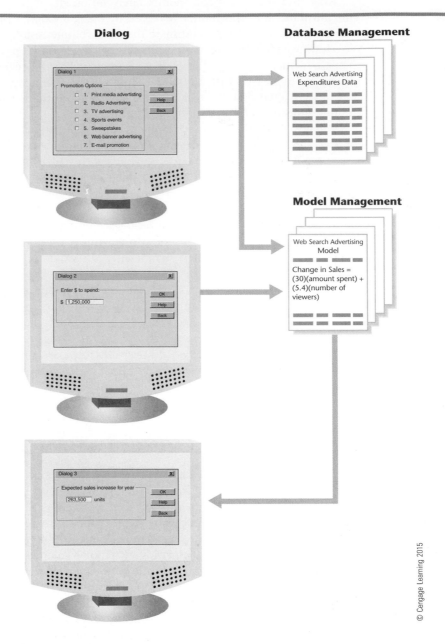

Dialog

Dialog 1

Promotion Options

☐ 1. Print media advertising
☐ 2. Radio Advertising
☐ 3. TV advertising
☐ 4. Sports events
☐ 5. Sweepstakes
   6. Web banner advertising
   7. E-mail promotion

OK | Help | Back

Dialog 2

Enter $ to spend:
$ 1,250,000

OK | Help | Back

Dialog 3

Expected sales increase for year
263,500 units

OK | Help | Back

Database Management

Web Search Advertising
Expenditures Data

Model Management

Web Search Advertising
Model

Change in Sales =
(30)(amount spent) +
(5.4)(number of
viewers)

© Cengage Learning 2015

Sensitivity Analysis

An outcome is almost always affected by more than one parameter; for instance, the sales volume of a product is affected by the number of salespeople, the number of regional sales representatives, the amount spent on national and local television advertising, price, competition, and so on. However, outcomes rarely respond in equal measure to changes in parameters. For instance, a small change in price per unit might result in a dramatic increase in sales, which means sales volume has a high sensitivity to product price. However, the same sales might increase only slightly in response to a huge investment in advertising dollars, which means that sales have a low sensitivity to advertising expenditure. It is important to pinpoint the parameters to which the outcome is highly sensitive, so that an organization can focus efforts where they are most effective. Sometimes the parameters to which an outcome is most sensitive also affect other parameters, so these interactions must be carefully tracked as well.

If a company wishes to maximize profit, managers must find the optimal combination of many factors. To equip a DSS to help achieve this goal, an approximate mathematical formula that expresses the relationship between each factor and the total profit is built into the DSS.

Then a **sensitivity analysis** is conducted to test the degree to which the total profit grows or shrinks if one or more of the factors is increased or decreased. The results indicate the relative sensitivity of the profit to the changes. If the outcome is affected significantly even when the parameter is changed only a little, then the sensitivity of the outcome to the parameter is said to be high. The opposite is also true: if the outcome is affected only a little, even when the parameter is varied widely, the outcome is said to be insensitive to the parameter. For instance, a manager might ask, "What is the impact on total quarterly profits if television advertising is decreased by 10 percent and the number of commissioned sales representatives is increased by 5 percent?" Because questions typically are phrased in this format, sensitivity analysis is often referred to as **what-if analysis**. Note that you can use a DSS to perform what if analyses on multiple parameters at the same time.

Equally important is the use of sensitivity tests to learn which parameters do *not* make a difference. For example, based on data collected during a promotion via coupons, marketing analysts might learn that discounts did not increase sales and/or did not bring in new customers. The obvious decision would be not to conduct similar promotions in the near future.

You might be familiar with sensitivity analysis from using electronic spreadsheets. Spreadsheets enable you to enter both data and formulas in cells. Thus, they are an excellent tool for building both the data and the models that decision support systems need, and therefore they make excellent tools for building decision support software. Changing data in one or several cells will result in a different solution to a problem. This allows you to see the effect that a change in one parameter has on the calculated outcome.

Decision Support Systems in Action

DSSs can be used on demand, when a manager needs help in making an occasional decision, or they might be integrated into a scheme that enforces corporate policy. In either case, DSSs help maintain standard criteria in decision making throughout the organization. A growing number of organizations implement software applications that produce decisions automatically and in real time. The only labor involved is the entry of relevant parameters, and when the DSS is linked to the organization's website, even this activity might not be performed by employees but by clients. Following are some examples of how DSSs are used for various purposes.

Book Sales and Food Production

The retail bookselling industry is rapidly evolving, moving away from traditional brick-and-mortar stores and toward e-readers and online libraries. Large bookstore retailers are adjusting and adapting to the new challenges put upon them by attempting to lure customers into their stores and keep them coming back. Barnes & Noble (B&N) reacted to the increasing competition of online sales by implementing a warehousing system and attached analytical capabilities allowed employees to see trends and patterns with remarkable timing value. The new system with its wide array of out-of-the box analytical tools and tiered-access portal allowed B&N merchandising employees to make crucial stocking and promotional decisions immediately instead of wasting precious weeks. With only one chance to make a first impression on a customer who enters a B&N location, it is essential that the shelves are stocked with the right reads. The implementation of B&N's smarter analytical system reduced the analytical query run time by over 95 percent and the time it took for an employee to administer the business intelligence solution was reduced by more than 70 percent. By capitalizing on the opportunity to predict customer demands, B&N optimized its inventory through efficiently utilizing the full potential of their stored transactional data (Anonymous, 2012a).

In the restaurant industry, managers have to forecast the number of patrons and the amount of ingredients to purchase, as well as where to purchase it to minimize cost. FoodPro, a DSS developed and sold by Aurora Information Systems, helps make such decisions. Based on the historical data restaurants accumulate, the system helps with these decisions. A recipe database is used to propose decisions on ingredients, quantities, and consolidated purchases from specific vendors. Other components of the system include financial forecasting, invoicing, accounting, and practically every other aspect of managing restaurants.

Tax Planning

Some applications that people may not think of as DSSs actually are. TurboTax, TaxCut, and other tax-preparation applications have been developed over the years to do much more than help fill out forms. They come with sophisticated formulas to help taxpayers plan the best strategy in selecting options, with the final purpose of minimizing the tax paid. For example, the applications compare filing status and deduction options: which approach would result in a lower combined tax, filing as two individuals or joint filing as husband and wife? Itemizing deductions, or taking a standard deduction? Taking a smaller education credit, or a larger education deduction? Based on the taxable income and the combination of deductions taken, the applications warn users about their chances of being audited by the Internal Revenue Service and give them a chance to modify deductions. The applications also remind users of optional deductions, tell them what the deductions entail (e.g., if you take deduction X you may not take deduction Y or you increase the probability of being audited) and thereby make it easy for filers to make decisions. And when users complete their tax preparation for the past year, they can plan their tax for next year—based on their total income and type of income (wages, business, capital gains, and so forth)—and make decisions on how much to contribute to pension funds, charity, and other purposes that serve as tax shields to reduce the tax owed next year.

Website Planning and Adjustment

Because so many companies use the web for marketing, selling, and customer support, decisions on how to design websites are extremely important. Some companies offer DSSs specifically designed to analyze shoppers' behavior at their sites based on captured data such as pages, how visitors found the site, and which search engines and keywords brought the most traffic. iWebTrack offers web traffic analytical services to a wide array of customers that include individual webmasters, universities, Fortune 500 companies, and private-label resellers.

iWebTrack monitors and records visitor trends, geographic data of website visitors, website activity by date and time, and how visitors find the site. By extracting trends and patterns from this data, iWebTrack customers can monitor the success of their website in real time, measure the return on investment of their online marketing campaign, and pinpoint high-traffic times to create an optimal promotional strategy (Anonymous, 2013d). Another company, WebCEO (see illustration), sells decision tools that help decide which keywords to use for improved listing on search engines, how to optimize webpages for greater conversion, submit URLs to search engines, and analyze conversions.

Web analysis tools help recommend decisions to increase popularity in searches

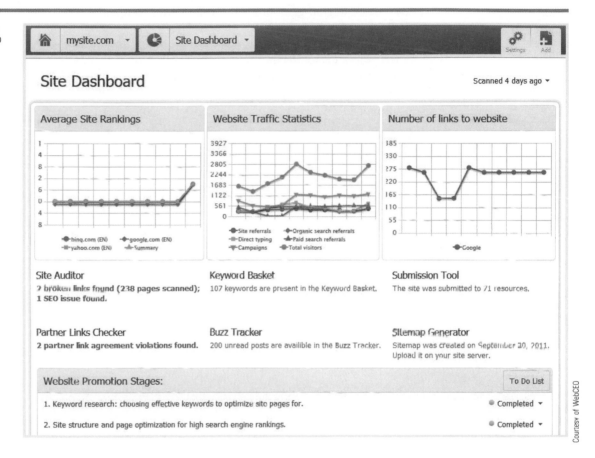

Courtesy of WebCEO

Yield Management

You might be surprised to learn that the passenger sitting next to you on an airplane paid a third of what you paid for the same flight. This is the result of recommendations the airline receives from a DSS whose purpose is to maximize revenue. The concept is called **yield management** or *revenue management*. For each flight, revenue managers enter a myriad of data, including departure point and time, destination point and time of arrival, the number of airports in which the airplane stops, the airplane capacity, and information on utilized capacity from previous operations of the particular flight. They change pricing, or let the system change prices, according to the time a ticket is purchased, and how long before the passenger flies back. The dilemma is between offering low prices to fill up the plane, or upping the price and risking flying with some empty seats.

The purpose of yield management DSSs is to find the proper pricing to maximize the overall revenue from selling seats for each flight. The result is often price discrimination, which is legal and a common practice in the airline industry: you might pay a different price depending on how far in advance you purchased the ticket, the fact that a companion flies with you, the number of days between departure and return, and several other variables. Typically, airlines double or triple the price of a ticket when it is purchased only a few days before departure, because usually the availability of seats on competitors' flights is limited. Also, late purchasers tend to be business people who are reimbursed for their travel and therefore are less price-sensitive. Airlines take advantage of these facts and the expectation that customers who make a late reservation usually do so because they have little flexibility in selecting the flight date. Other variables are less obvious, and therefore DSSs are used to model demand and sensitivity to prices.

Similar decision aids are used in the hospitality industry. For example, Harrah's Entertainment, the operators of a chain of hotels and casinos, uses such a system to set room rates for its hotels and for offering different rates to different levels of members in its customer loyalty programs. Room rates might be lower, or even free, for customers who regularly spend a great deal of money on gambling. Like many other companies, the chain has a customer loyalty program called Total Rewards. Harrah's data analysis program, called Revenue Management System, recognizes a Total Rewards member's telephone number and allows reservation agents to offer lower prices for rooms during a busy weekend for a high-value customer—one who usually spends a lot—or to raise the price of a Saturday night stay for customers who don't yield much profit.

Financial Services

Manually deciding how much money to loan to which customer at what interest rate could delay the decision process to a point of losing the potential customer. Loan applicants are reluctant to wait more than a day or even a few hours for the bank's response. Automated decision aids can produce offers within minutes after a customer enters data. The DSS combines this data with data retrieved from credit history databases and preprogrammed rule models to create a rapid response.

Quicken Loans has become an industry leader in online retail mortgage lending. Potential borrowers initiate the process by calling or submitting a request online at www.quickenloans.com. Quicken Loans then runs a credit check that produces a report in seconds. If the applicant is accepted, Quicken Loans creates an account that allows borrowers to access their account information online or even with a mobile phone app. Quicken Loans takes the responsibility of ordering an appraisal from a state certified appraiser on the borrower's behalf and will meet anywhere to close the deal (Anonymous, 2013a). Their step-by-step process is easy to follow and focused on simplifying the complexity of receiving a home mortgage. In September of 2010, Quicken Loans set a record by closing about 15,500 home loans totaling $3.4 billion in loan volume. This mark surpassed the previous record set the previous month of 14,000 closed for a total of $3.15 billion in loan volume (Anonymous, 2010). An increasing amount of decision making in the financial services and many other industries are made this way: automatically and in real time. This saves many hours of labor and ensures speedy service for customers.

Benefits Selection

Employers can save labor costs and provide convenience to their employees by helping them make decisions. One area where this can occur is selection of benefits, especially health care plans. ADP, Inc., a company known for its payroll processing services, teamed with Subimo LLC to offer an online application to help employees evaluate health care plan costs. The analysis is based on individual medical needs. The tool uses an individual's age, gender, geographic region, and health condition to estimate several costs of a family's health care. It predicts the health services the individual or family would most likely need. The tool's modeling is based on the demographic data and experience of over 60 million U.S. patients. Employees can use the predictions to select plans and to decide how to fund a flexible spending account, a health saving account, or health reimbursement arrangement.

Similar decision support tools are offered by other companies, including some of the largest health care management organizations (HMOs) in the United States. A tool called MyHealthcareAdvisor.com, also offered by Subimo, serves small businesses that wish to augment their employee coverage. It is estimated that about 60 million Americans have access to tools that help make decisions on health care plans and options within plans. Interestingly, about 95 percent of enrollment transactions are executed online.

Every year thousands of people are denied credit not because they are bad credit risks, but because of errors that lending institutions make. For example, a newly married woman might be denied credit because her credit history is still only under her maiden name. Errors in recording monthly payments are also a common reason for denying credit; it's possible for one late payment to deduct many points from one's credit score. For some banks, if your credit score is in the 500s or even 600s on a scale of 350–850, you are not considered a good credit risk. Some banks might agree to give you a loan with an interest rate that is higher than most people get.

A single late credit-card or mortgage payment could lower your credit score severely, but you might never know that, because the law does not require anyone to notify you. Many people do not even know that a credit score system exists, and that it is shared by all banks and other lenders. Chances are you will find out about your too-low score only when you apply for a loan and only if you ask for the reason of denial or higher offered interest rate. And when you find out and try to explain that there was a mitigating circumstance for the late payment, your explanation might not help you much. That's because American banks use computers for credit decisions. It is often a computer program that decides who will or will not receive credit. And the decision is final.

Every consumer in the U.S. has the right to one free credit check per 12 months in accordance with the Fair and Accurate Credit Transactions Act (FACT Act). www.AnnualCreditReport.com provides these credit checks and is run by the three nationwide consumer credit reporting companies: Equifax, Experian, and TransUnion. The website has strict fraud prevention measures enacted to ensure consumers their information is safe (www.AnnualCreditReport.com, 2013). It is important to review your credit at least annually to make sure there are no mistakes or issues that you did not know of. Sometimes mistakes can be simple data-entry errors or they could be more serious computer-related issues. According to a study conducted by the University of Missouri-St. Louis, 12 percent of credit reports they examined contained errors such as wrong birthdates, ages, or addresses. Although it may be impossible to determine how the errors occurred, it is not hard at all however, to correct the mistakes. The three major consumer credit reporting companies listed above all have a "Disputes" link on their pages. In their research, after errors were corrected, participants' scores increased as much as 40 points, enough to help them qualify for a large loan or a better interest rate. To keep the best credit score possible, it is important to pay bills on time, keep balances as low as possible, and apply for new credit only when absolutely necessary. 35 percent of your credit score is based on paying bills on time and another 30 percent is based on your debt in relation to your debt capacity (Stroud, 2008).

- **Who Needs Protection?** To what extent should organizations rely on computer-based decision aids to make business decisions about individuals? Automated decision making is used routinely in the United States by banks, credit-card companies, mortgage companies, employers, and, to some extent, educational institutions. The affected individuals might be consumers, credit applicants, employees, job applicants, prospective students, applicants for membership in associations, and people who are evaluated by organizations in other capacities.

Creditworthiness is determined by processing personal financial data in models that have been developed specifically to sort the good risks from the bad risks. A bad risk is a person or institution that is likely to default on a loan. Should credit-card companies, for instance, ask their officers to open a manila folder for every American adult and make a decision on creditworthiness only after leafing through the filed documents in it? Should they be banned from using an automated process that makes the decision for them based on the same criteria that the officers would use manually? And when employers sift through hundreds and thousands of digitized résumés of job applicants, should they be banned from using software that retrieves the résumés with keywords that suggest a good fit for the job, while eliminating those without them? Would it be practical for Google not to use software to sift through the 1.5 million job applications the company receives every year?

The use of automated decision making offers not only added efficiency but also enhanced effectiveness. When using a DSS or an expert system, the user enjoys the knowledge and experience that have been accumulated by other people over many years. Thus, in addition to efficiency, automated decision making might be more effective than manual decision making.

- **Hidden Injustice.** On the other hand, shifting decision making to a machine might create injustices. Suppose your record is among several hundred records of applicants considered for a position. The records were obtained from a third party, a company that sells personal information. Your qualifications are excellent, but your record also indicates a law violation. The system removes you from the pool of eligible candidates, and you do not get the job. Had you seen your record before its processing, you could have told the company that this entry was an error: you were charged once but acquitted in court. If the company had contacted you, you could have ironed out the misunderstanding and possibly have gotten the job.

Do American organizations overuse automated decision making? Is it practical, in the digital age, to give up the efficiency of automated decision making to determine an individual's creditworthiness or job performance? Does a little more justice in credit and employment justify giving up the greater efficiencies of automated decision making?

It is not always possible to exploit expertise by coupling quantitative data from a database with decision models. In such cases, an expert system might be required. An **expert system (ES)** is developed to emulate the knowledge of an expert to solve problems and make decisions in a relatively narrow domain. A *domain* is a specific area of knowledge. For example, in medicine a domain is often a diagnosis of a specific disease or a family of related diseases, such as bacterial diseases. The purpose of ESs is to replicate the unstructured and undocumented knowledge of the few (the experts), and put it at the disposal of the many other people who need the knowledge, often novices or professionals in the same domain but with far less expertise. Advanced programs might include **neural networks** (computer programs that emulate the way the human brain works) which can learn from new situations and formulate new rules in their knowledge bases to address events not originally considered in their development. Expert systems and neural networks are two techniques researched and implemented in a field called **artificial intelligence (AI)**. The field is so called because it focuses on methods and technologies to emulate how humans learn and solve problems.

POINT OF
INTEREST   The Turing Test

Scientists continue the quest for software that will be at least as smart as humans, so that expertise can be enhanced and delivered through information technology. In 1950, Alan Turing, a British mathematician, published an article titled "Can Machines Think?" His own answer was yes. Today the Turing test is this: An interrogator is connected to a person and to a machine via a terminal and cannot see either. The interrogator asks both the person and the machines questions and is to determine by their answers which is a human and which is a machine. If the machine can fool the interrogator, it is considered intelligent. In 1990, Hugh Loebner offered to grant a gold medal and $100,000 to the first person who could build such a machine. At the annual competition, judges present the same questions to computers and people, but cannot see either. The communication is by text, similar to online chat. Competitors try to build software whose answers would be indistinguishable from those of humans. So far nobody has won. You can find information about the competition at www.loebner.net/Prizef/loebner-prize.html.

Source: Oppy, G., & Dowe, D. (2011). The Turing Test. Stanford Encyclopedia of Philosophy: Stanford University.

As Figure 10.6 illustrates, the major difference between DSSs and ESs is in the "base" they use and how it is structured. DSSs use data from databases. An ES uses a **knowledge base**, which is a collection of facts and the relationships among them. An ES does not use a model module but an inference engine. The **inference engine** is software that combines data that is input by the user with the data relationships stored in the knowledge base. The result is a diagnosis or suggestion for the best course of action. In most ESs, the knowledge base is built as a series of IF-THEN rules.

FIGURE **10.6**

Components of an expert
system; numbers indicate
the order of processes

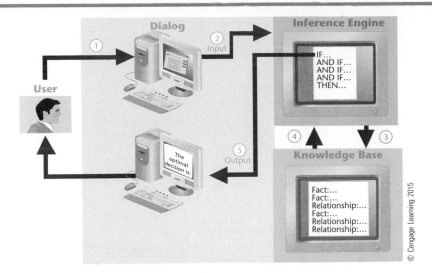

Figure 10.7 provides a simple illustration of how such rules are used to conclude which disease is infecting a tree. If the humidity is low, the average air temperature is higher than 60 degrees Fahrenheit, the tree leaves are dark green, and the tree's age is 0-2 years, then the tree has disease A at a probability of 90 percent. However, if the humidity is low, the temperature is between 40 and 65 degrees Fahrenheit, the tree leaves are green, and the tree's age is 0-2, there is a 40 percent probability that the disease is A and 50 percent that the disease is B. The diagnosis helps reach a decision on proper treatment to stop the disease. A real expert system for such diagnosis would consist of many more rules, usually hundreds or thousands, because there are many more conditions—antecedents—and combinations of factors that may cause a disease; and there are more diseases that a particular tree may have.

FIGURE **10.7**

In IF-THEN rules,
different combinations
of conditions lead to
different conclusions

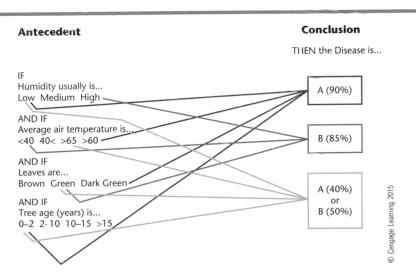

In a mineral exploration, for example, such rules can be: IF the drilling depth is so many meters, AND IF the sample includes a certain percentage of carbon (and so forth), THEN there is a 90-percent probability that so many meters further down there is oil of commercial quality and quantity. Such rules are often not quantitative but qualitative, and therefore can only be stored as a knowledge base rather than a database.

ES researchers continue to look for ways to better capture knowledge and represent it. They test the results of such efforts in highly unstructured problem-solving domains, including games. One such game that has intrigued both researchers and laypeople is chess. The game is a highly unstructured environment in which the number of possible moves is enormous, and hence, the player must be an expert to select the best move for every board configuration.

Rather than containing a set of IF-THEN rules, more sophisticated ESs use neural networks (neural nets), programs that are designed to mimic the way a human brain learns. An ES is constructed with a set of rules, but as data on real successes and failures of decisions is accumulated and fed into the system, the neural network refines the rules to accomplish a higher success rate.

Business applications have increasingly combined neural nets and ES technologies in software that monitors business processes and supply chain management. An example of this application is Finch Paper's implementation of Honeywell's Process Knowledge System. Finch, a pulp and paper mill in Glen Falls, NY, needed to focus more attention on the quality of its products while reducing costs. Unfortunately, Finch had a variety of obsolete systems to track and report on the quality of products manufactured. They needed key plant data in order to increase efficiency and performance while maintaining employee safety. Through the implementation of Honeywell's product, Finch was able to improve plant efficiency by 1 percent for a savings of $100,000 per year. In addition, consolidating the organization's older systems gained increased connectivity and sharing of information through the mill. In addition, Finch improved plant productivity by allowing operators to "make faster, more informed decisions" (Anonymous, 2011).

Expert systems often provide intelligent agents to alert someone of a situation. An **intelligent agent** is software that is "dormant" until it detects a certain event, at which time it performs a prescribed action. For example, in a retail business, it is important to maintain enough quantity on the shelf for consumers to purchase the product and avoid any stock-outs. A stock-out is a loss of a sale as well as a potential loss in customer satisfaction. Therefore, an information system designed with an intelligent agent could automatically reorder a product when the shelf quantity falls below some threshold (safety stock) to eliminate a stock out. The agent would send an order to the manufacturer or distributor for a shipment.

POINT OF INTEREST   Who's In Control?

Oregon State University (OSU) researchers believe that air traffic controllers (ATCs) should be aided by smart computers to reduce congestion and avoid bottlenecks. The proposed system developed at OSU over a five-year span would still leave the decision making aspect in the hands of experienced ATC but they would basically receive suggestions from the computer system. After being adapted to be more flexible for voluntary use by ATCs, developers believe it should be able to improve ATC system-wide performance by as much as 20 percent. Computers are able to compute algorithms quicker and more efficient that humans. It may not make sense for an air traffic controller landing a plane in Chicago to be worrying about thunderstorms in Miami and a bottleneck growing at LAX. However, computers can handle all of these scenarios and produce data that human ATCs can use to improve air traffic efficiency.

Source: Anonymous. (2010). Smart Computers Should Assist Controllers. Air Safety Week, 24(13).

Neural nets have been very effective in detecting fraud of many types. For example, Falcon Fraud Manager, owned by FICO, allows financial institutions to identify credit card transactions that do not correspond with customers' spending profiles. Under normal procedures, banks usually call the member to verify the charge, and if it is fraudulent, deny the charge and reissue a new credit card. However, the institution takes the loss for fraudulent transactions. CO-OP Financial Services purchased FICO's product to deny fraudulent transactions in real time. Using the new expert system software, point-of-sale transactions are processed through a series of rules and stopped immediately if they don't successfully meet the rule criteria; Falcon or the credit institution's fraud team follows up on stopped transactions. The new real-time system has reduced their losses by $940,000 for 2009 and 2010 (Rapport, 2012).

Insurance companies use neural nets to detect fraudulent claims both from the insured party and from health-care providers. Empire Blue Cross Blue Shield has used the technology for many years and has saved millions of dollars. In one case, it caught a doctor who allegedly provided an annual respiratory test that normally is provided no more than twice per lifetime. In another case, it caught a doctor who filed a claim for a pregnancy test, but the software detected that the test was given to a man.

Another technique to use expertise is **case-based reasoning**; a methodology of solving a new problem established on the solutions of similar problems. The software that supports the technique is often called case-based ESs. The important parameters of a case to be analyzed are compared to many cases until one or a small number of them are found highly similar to the analyzed case. The system then brings up the decision made in those cases, and a successful decision is applied. The knowledge base is a database of cases. Instead of an inference engine, the system uses software that searches key parameters in the archival case reports.

Case-based reasoning is useful especially in medical decision making. Comparison with previous, similar cases helps to diagnose a symptom and recommend remedial action such as medication and other treatments.

Expert Systems in Action

ESs have been implemented to help professionals in many different industries, such as health care, telecommunications, financial services, and agriculture. The following is a small sample.

Medical expert systems help diagnose patients and suggest treatments

Alexander Raths/Photos.com

Medical Diagnosis

Because medicine is one of the most unstructured domains, it is not surprising that many of the early ESs were developed to help doctors with the diagnosis of symptoms and treatment advice, as mentioned earlier. MYCIN (diagnosis of bacterial diseases), CADUCEUS (internal medicine diagnostics), and PUFF (diagnosis of pulmonary diseases) are only a few of these systems. PUFF includes instrumentation that connects to the patient's body and feeds various data about the patient's condition into the ES to be analyzed for pulmonary diseases. As shown in the picture, doctors can utilize expert systems for patient medical diagnosis.

German scientists developed an ES that enhances the accuracy in diagnoses of Alzheimer's disease, which gradually destroys memory. The system examines positron emission tomography scans of the patient's brain. The scans provide images that can be reliably interpreted only by experienced physicians. Based on the expertise of such experts, the ES can detect Alzheimer's before the appearance of behavior typical of the disease. More than 5 million Americans suffer from Alzheimer's, and the proportion of the U.S. population that suffers from this yet incurable disease is growing. An early, accurate diagnosis helps patients and their families plan and gives them time to discuss care while the patient can still take part in decision making. When tested on 150 suspected patients, the ES performed as well as the experts. Now it can serve any doctor in early diagnosis of the disease.

Medical Management

In addition to diagnostic ESs, some hospitals use systems that help discern which tests or other initial treatment a patient should receive. Some of the decisions might be administrative. For example, The University of Illinois at Chicago Medical Center uses an application called Discern Expert. It monitors patient data and events and recommends action, such as admission, transfer to another ward or hospital, discharge, or order of tests or treatments. For instance, a set of rules in the system can look like this:

```
IF: An order for a contrast-enhanced CAT SCAN is received
AND: The patient's BUN level is HIGH
AND: The patient's CREATININE level is HIGH
THEN: Send a message to the patient's physician via electronic
mail indicating a possible adverse effect of contrast agent use in
this setting.
```

Blood urea nitrogen (BUN) is caused by the breakdown of blood, muscle, and protein. High levels of it might indicate kidney disease. Creatinine is a protein produced by muscle tissue and released into the blood. High levels of it might indicate kidney failure. Discern Expert helps staff members prevent complications or unnecessary testing. Once a medical ES is composed, it can be used anywhere, bringing expertise to poor regions of the world, where expert doctors are in dire shortage.

In addition to testing, health information management (HIM) solutions are being adopted by healthcare providers. With an increased focus on reducing the skyrocketing costs in health care, the integration of reimbursement for healthcare services and the delivery of quality health care will continue to dominate the dialogue. In addition the U.S. federal government is placing more emphasis on electronic health records and exchange of health information. The exchange of information and compliance with new regulations will determine how much healthcare providers will receive for reimbursement. To assist with health information management, it is clear that several technologies will be used including natural-language processing, and expert systems will provide an important role (Klein, 2010).

POINT OF INTEREST — ES, You're Practicing Medicine!

IBM software development experts have teamed up with doctors to develop new technology that will aid doctors in saving the lives of premature babies. First used in an ICU unit in Canada, the early warning system alerts healthcare professionals at the first sign premature babies could be developing potentially life-threatening complications. The revolutionary advancement in computing software will be capable of processing 512 readings per second including heart rate, temperature, respiration, and more, and will provide clinicians with the most real-time analytical data possible. This way, when an infant's condition suddenly changes, clinicians and doctors will have the best data possible to make difficult decisions.

Source: Frean, A. (2011, Jun 16). Big Blue and the endless pursuit of blue sky thinking, The Times, p. 53.

Credit Evaluation

Holders of American Express (AmEx) credit cards can potentially charge the card for hundreds of thousands of dollars per purchase. Obviously, most retailers and restaurateurs will not process a charge before they contact AmEx for approval. The AmEx clerk who considers the request uses an ES. The system requests data such as account number, location of the establishment, and amount of the purchase. Coupled with information from a database that contains previous data on the account, and a knowledge base with criteria for approving or denying credit, the ES provides a response.

Another expert system called RiskAnalyst, developed by Moody's Analytics, provides data storage and credit analysis (Anonymous, 2013c). The system is used by asset managers, banks and insurers worldwide. It consolidates into one software platform the ability to collect, analyze and store credit information coupled with assessment tools for risk and credit evaluation (Anonymous, 2013c).

The system provides complex analysis of the data contained in applicants' financial reports. The expert system not only provides English-language interpretation of the historical financial output but also prepares the assumptions for annual projections and produces text output linkable to word-processing software. It eliminates much of the tedious writing of analytical reports, producing standard financial statement reviews.

Loan officers periodically update the knowledge base to customize it for a bank's current loan policy, as well as national and local economic forecasts and interest rate projections. The system consistently and reliably interprets the relationship of these variable factors and the levels of sensitivity that the loan officers associate with a particular financial statement.

Detection of Insider Securities Trading

Like other similar institutions, the American Stock Exchange (AMEX) has a special department to prevent insider trading of the securities under its supervision. Insider trading is the trading of stocks based on information available only to those affiliated with a company, not to the general public. This practice is a serious breach of U.S. federal law. To detect insider trading, the department receives information from several sources on unusual trading activity and uses this information to identify a stock it might want to investigate. Using an ES, the department's analysts access a large database of the stock's history and choose a time period of interest. The system provides questions that the analysts can answer with the information they received from the database. The questions are formulated to reflect the experience of expert investigators. After the analysts finish answering all the questions, the system provides two numbers: the probability that a further investigation is warranted, and the probability that it is not.

Detection of Common Metals

Metallurgists are experts, and their time is expensive. Also, they usually work in laboratories, which are expensive, too. General Electric Corp. developed an expert system that helps nonexperts to identify common metals and alloys outside laboratories. The user provides information on density, color, and hardness of the metal and results of simple chemical tests that can be performed by novices outside the laboratory setting. If the user provides sufficient information, the system will positively identify the metal or alloy. If the information is insufficient, the system will provide a list of possible metals in order of likelihood. Even such a list can be helpful in some situations, saving much time, labor cost, and the need to wait for lab testing.

Diagnosis and Prediction of Mechanical Failure

A vehicle that can diagnose its own mechanical failures has obvious benefits. But what about vehicles that can alert you to an approaching traffic jam, entertain passengers, and diagnose its own mechanical failures? Now that is more like it. For example, the Haw'lai Bu sedan and the Geely EC825 car are the first two mass-produced Chinese cars with in-vehicle infotainment systems. The systems, run by Intel Atom processors, support a fully connected driving experience including navigation, entertainment, and Internet services. The system can recognize traffic maps in real time and recommend alternative travel routes. These features build on the basic diagnostic system that is found in most vehicles. Owners can even receive alerts while away from the car, which provides surveillance video of the situation (Hoffmann, 2011).

POINT OF INTEREST — **A Tweet from Your Car?**

In the future, cars may be able to "tweet" their mechanical issues to their drivers. The technology already partially exists. GM's telematics system has been around for over a decade and Ford has technology that allows the car to read incoming text messages from the driver's mobile phone. The potential exists, therefore, for a vehicle's system to be able to check diagnostics and alert the driver via tweet such as, 'check brakes' or 'change oil.' Although it would be a revolutionary step for a car to specifically diagnose its own mechanical issues, it would still be the responsibility of the owner/driver to actually get the car fixed.

Source: Howell, D. (2010, June 23). Your Car Could Soon Tweet You With Its Latest Diagnostics Report, Investor's Business Daily.

The remote diagnostics increasingly found in some Toyota and Ford vehicles goes beyond being a core safety and security feature. Interaction with the car in the form of vehicle self-diagnostics is becoming a method for car companies to develop customer relationship management (CRM). The interaction, communication, and experience of the car are just as important as the physical features of the car itself. In the future, look for vehicles' intelligence to evolve, just as the cell phone has (Anonymous, 2012b).

When a team of people are to make decisions, a **group decision support system (GDSS)** can be useful. The systems are often named group intelligence systems, collaborative systems, or simply group systems. Their purpose is to facilitate the contribution of ideas, brainstorming, and choosing promising solutions. Often, one person serves as a facilitator of the entire process. Typically, a session starts by defining a problem to be resolved or a decision to be made; followed by contribution of ideas, evaluation of the ideas (such as pros and cons of each idea), and some method of voting on the ideas. The voting determines the ranking of ideas to solve the problem or make a decision. The entire list of suggested decisions is then submitted to the final decision maker. If the group is authorized to make the decision, then the top-ranked offered decision is adopted. FacilitatePro, offered by Facilitate.com (see illustration), is a typical example of such application software. Electrogrid, a company that manages electrical power grids, used FacilitatePro to deal with challenging organization dynamics to enable and implement a strategic planning process (Anonymous, 2009).

FacilitatePro, a group decision support system, enables decision makers to brainstorm, evaluate ideas, and vote to reach a decision

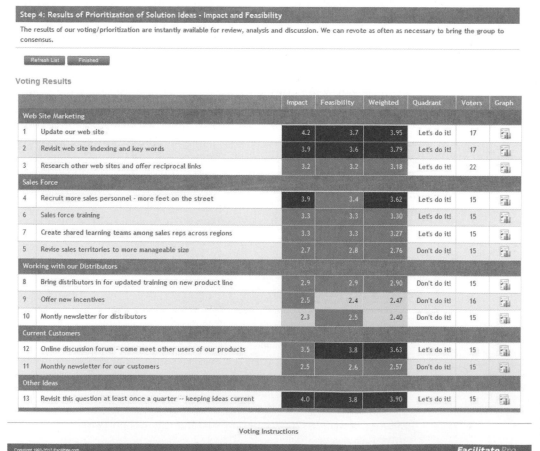

Like many other application software systems, group decision support systems have also migrated to the cloud. For example, Analytica Cloud Player (ACP) from Lumina Decision Systems, combines the advantages of GDDSs while eliminating the need to update software as changes are available (Anonymous, 2013b).

The process not only helps in structuring the group decision-making process, it also creates an environment different from sitting around a table. GDSSs allow participants to maintain anonymity during the entire session or parts of it. This removes the fear of putting forth ideas that might be dismissed or ridiculed. It also puts all the participants on equal footing regardless of rank or seniority. Anonymity helps elicit more creative ideas and a more open and thorough decision-making process. It also results in a consensus or at least a decision by a majority. Such decisions are less politically motivated and therefore garner more support when implemented.

Geographic Information Systems

As mentioned in Chapter 5, "Business Software," some decisions can be made only when examining information on a map. Many business decisions concern geographic locations—as input, output, or both. For example, consider the process of choosing the best locations for new stores or determining how to deploy police forces optimally. For map-related decisions, **geographic information systems (GISs)** are often the best decision aids. GISs process location data and provide output. For instance, a GIS could be used to help a housing developer determine where to invest by tracking and displaying population changes on a map, highlighting in color increases of more than 10 percent over the past three years. With this information, a developer could easily decide where to invest on the basis of population growth trends. Other examples include the following:

- Delivery managers looking for the shortest distance a truck can travel to deliver ordered goods at the lowest cost.
- School district officials looking for the most efficient routes for busing school children to and from their homes.
- A retailer gathering information on population and demographics to locate a new store.
- City planners looking to deploy services to better serve residents, which might include police officers deciding how to deploy their forces on the basis of precinct maps indicating levels of criminal activity.
- Healthcare agencies analyzing which areas of a community need more or less attention and resources for treatment of certain diseases or injuries that result from criminal violence.
- Oil companies looking to determine drilling locations on the basis of geological tests.
- Mapping concentrations of people at work and in shopping centers to help banks decide where to install new ATMs.

In Springfield, Massachusetts, for instance, healthcare professionals integrated data collected for Hampden County with information from the area's two major medical centers and the city's health, planning, and police departments to use in combination with the region's map. They use models that help identify geographic areas and population groups that need health-care intervention in youth violence and late-stage breast cancer detection. Healthcare provider Kaiser Permanente utilizes a GIS to gather data that will impact the delivery of their services. Their enterprise-level GIS uses data about the location of its members to better understand where to locate new medical offices. The GIS integrates demographic and socioeconomic information provided by the U.S. Census Bureau (Kehoe, 2011).

A typical GIS consists of (1) a database of quantitative and qualitative data from which information is extracted for display, (2) a database of maps, and (3) a program that displays the information on the maps. The digitized maps are produced from satellite and aerial photography. Displays might be in the form of easily understood symbols and colors or even moving images. For instance, an oil exploration map might show different concentrations of expected crude oil deposits in different hues of red. Or, population density might be similarly displayed on a map using different hues of blue. A more sophisticated GIS might display, in colors or icons, concentrations of specific consumer groups by age, income, and other characteristics. As shown in the following illustration, Microsoft MapPoint integrates sales data into a mapping, geographic context.

Microsoft MapPoint shows an example of a GIS integrating sales data by state

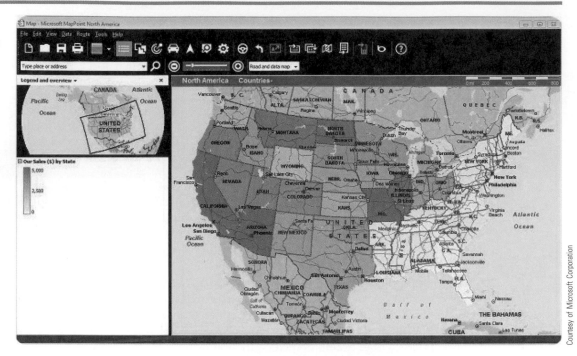

Courtesy of Microsoft Corporation

Web technology helps promote the use of GISs by private organizations and governments alike. Intranets allow employees to bring up thousands of maps from a central repository on their own PCs. HTML and XML, the primary languages used to compose and retrieve webpages, support the presentation of pictures with marked areas, which makes them ideal for retrieval of marked maps. Clicking different areas of a map can zoom in and out as well as bring up related information in the form of other maps or text, utilizing the multimedia capabilities of the web to the fullest.

For example, sales managers can bring up maps of continents and see how past sales have performed over different territories. They can zoom in and zoom out on a territory. With the touch of a finger or click of a mouse they can receive detailed information on who serves the territory and other pertinent information. Indeed, more and more retail chains are adopting GISs for decision making. Pollo Tropical, a Hispanic-Caribbean restaurant chain, operates 125 restaurants throughout the southeastern U.S. and abroad. Its managers used "gut feeling" to determine where to open new restaurants. Now they use a GIS with geo-demographic data purchased from MapInfo (now a division of Pitney Bowes), a leader in location intelligence software. The system helps them pinpoint where their best customers live and work in the company's effort to expand outside Florida.

In government work, a city clerk can bring up a map of the neighborhood of a resident, zoom in on the resident's house pictured on the map, click on the picture, and receive information such as real-estate taxes owed and paid over the past several years. Further information, such as whether a neighborhood uses septic tanks or a sewage system, might be rendered by different colors. The map can also show different zoning codes, such as land designated for residential, industrial, or commercial purposes. GISs could also be used to assist law-enforcement officials to analyze crime statistics.

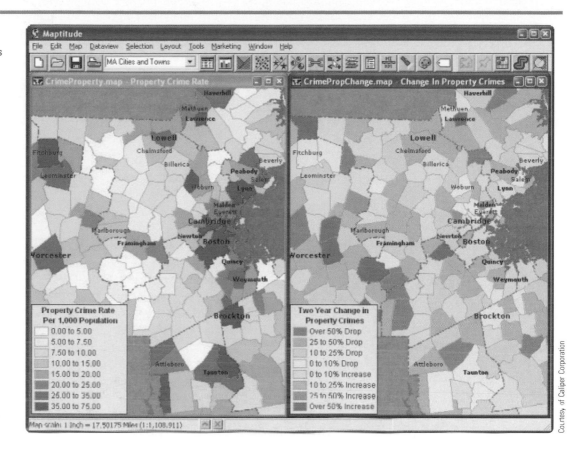

You may be familiar with some popular web-based GISs: Google Earth, Mapquest, Yahoo Maps, and others. Some of the companies that own these applications have opened the software for anyone to create specialized GISs through mashups. Recall our discussion of mashups in Chapter 5, "Business Software." Mashups are applications that combine features of two or more online applications. Often, one of these applications shows maps. Combining the maps with data such as the location of certain information—events, clubs, real estate for sale—creates a specialized GIS. For example, www.zillow.com mashes a map with up-to-date estimates of real estate prices. The web has hundreds of similar mashups involving maps. One site where you can see over a hundred of such mashups is www.programmableweb.com/mashups.

Summary

- Decision aids include decision support systems, expert systems, group decision support systems, geographic information systems, and any other software tool that helps with decision making automatically or on demand. Some are stand-alone systems, and others are part of larger systems. Most are accessible through a web browser.

- The decision-making process combines three major phases: intelligence, design, and choice. In the first phase, data is collected from which relevant information will be gleaned. In the design phase, the data is organized into useful information and processed by models to analyze it and produce potential courses of action. In the final stage, the decision maker selects an alternative, that is, makes the decision.

- Problems span a continuum between two extremes: structured and unstructured. A structured problem is one for whose solution there is a proven algorithm. An unstructured problem is one for which there are multiple potential solutions. A semi-structured problem is one that is neither fully structured nor totally unstructured.

- Most DSSs have three components. The data management module gives the user access to databases from which relevant information can be retrieved. The model management module selects, or lets the user select, an appropriate model through which the data are analyzed. The dialog module serves as an interface between the user and the other two modules. It allows the user to enter queries and parameters, and then presents the result in an appropriate or selected form, such as tabular or graphical.

- DSSs provide a quick way to perform sensitivity analysis. The user can change one or several parameters in the model and answer "what if" questions, called what-if analysis.

- Powerful software tools such as electronic spreadsheets let users with little expertise in systems development create their own DSSs.

- Expert systems are developed to emulate the knowledge of an expert. Developers use artificial intelligence techniques. An expert system consists of a knowledge base, inference engine, and a dialog module.

- Neural network software is often integrated into an expert system to enable the system to learn and refine decision rules based on success or failure.

- Expert systems are used in narrow domains in which typical diagnosis and decisions are unstructured, such as health care, mineral exploration, stock investment, and weather forecasting.

- When decisions involve locations and routes, professionals can use geographic information systems (GISs). GISs provide maps with icons and colors to represent measurable variables such as population concentrations, potential natural resources, deployment of police forces, pinpointing concentrations of diseases, and other factors that involve locations and routes.

- Computerized decision aids practically leave decision making to machines. When machines determine whom to hire, whom to accept for higher education, or to whom to extend credit, the decision-making process could overlook important circumstances, in which case the decisions might not be accurate or fair.

KIMBALL'S REVISITED

Michael found the Simon model helpful to organize developing the ordering process; intelligence, design, and choice. Michael knows that the point-of-sale system for the restaurant collected data from the dining sales. He can identify the data maintained by the system and has exported it several times. At the same time, he also is aware that external data was needed from the suppliers: products sold, order quantity, price and product number. All of this data is the intelligence. The restaurant had several suppliers that they purchased various categories of food products; vegetables, meats, fish, beverages, condiments and cooking spices.

When Jim and Michael brainstormed some ideas, it was clear that data from a variety of sources needed to be consolidated to form a warehouse of data. The consolidated data was one of two elements of the design phase. The second element would then use the consolidated data that would form the basis of the algorithms and process to report the products needed. The various courses of action could then be developed to ultimately lead to the third phase, choosing a course of action; determining the actual orders to suppliers for various quantities and products. With this process, Michael hoped to provide Kimball's with an accurate, timely purchasing decision making process.

What Is Your Advice?

1. What are the various sources of the data maintained internally? Externally? Some data may need to be gathered and entered manually into the system. Identify these sources also.

2. From these sources, what data fields would then be needed from these sources to form the warehouse of data? List what would be needed to use as input to the design process.

3. What types of calculations and decisions could you recommend to help Michael and Jim with this new model?

New Perspectives

1. Do you believe that this decision making process could be completed using a spreadsheet? Or is there a pre-developed software product that could help with this function?

2. Could you recommend any types of hardware and software you learned about in earlier chapters to allow more efficient data entry?

Key Terms

algorithm, 327
artificial intelligence (AI), 340
case-based reasoning, 343
data management module, 330
decision support system (DSS), 329
dialog module, 333
expert system (ES), 340

geographic information system (GIS), 347
group decision support system (GDSS), 346
inference engine, 340
intelligent agent, 342
knowledge base, 340
model, 326
model management module, 331

neural networks, 340
parameter, 327
semi-structured problem, 327
sensitivity analysis, 335
structured problem, 327
unstructured problem, 327
what-if analysis, 335
yield management, 337

1. What is a decision? When does a person have to make a decision?

2. DSSs use models to process data. Explain what a model is. Give an example that is not mentioned in the chapter.

3. Many DSSs are not stand-alone anymore, but are embedded in other ISs. What are those ISs?

4. What is a sensitivity test? Give three examples.

5. The travel industry uses DSSs for yield management. What is yield management, and what is the output of a yield management DSS? How does it affect revenue and operations?

6. What is the purpose of an expert system? How can it serve as a competitive tool?

7. Explain how expert systems can distribute expertise.

8. How could an ES be used to detect probable fraud committed by a bank employee?

9. What is the advantage of combining ES and neural net technologies?

10. What is a GIS? What purpose does it serve?

11. Name the three major elements that are combined to make up a GIS.

12. DSSs and ESs give structure to an often unstructured decision-making process. Explain this statement.

13. Bank officers use DSSs to make decisions on extending or denying credit. Universities might use DSSs to decide which applicant to admit and which applicant to reject. Would you agree to use DSSs for such decisions without human intervention?

14. Some companies use DSSs to make decisions for their knowledge workers. The decisions are based on previous experience and on corporate policy. Would you prefer to work for a company that requires you to use a DSS for the decisions you have to execute, or would you rather work for a company that lets you make decisions on your own? Explain.

15. Some managers say that you should never accept the output of any computer-based decision aid without scrutiny. Do you agree? Explain.

16. Give three examples of a business decision for which you would not use a decision support system or any other software. Give three nonbusiness examples. Explain your choices.

17. Think of executives in human resources, finance, marketing, and information systems. In which of these areas could executives benefit the most from using GIS technologies? Explain.

18. Some DSSs allow the user to select a model for an analysis. Would you like to have the final say in determining which model would be used, or would you prefer to let the software use whatever model it chose for the analysis, and then produce a decision? Why?

19. Credit scoring firms such as Fair Isaac base their scoring only on electronic data collected from financial sources. A low credit score may significantly affect a person's or a family's life. What information that may be relevant is not considered in the scoring?

20. How could you use a GIS for scheduling your classes? What would be the likely sources of data for such a system?

21. Some GISs are used for very small geographic areas, such as a campus or a single building. Can you think of how a GIS could help the maintenance department of a university campus?

22. As an increasing amount of decision making is carried out by software, do you think the demand for college-educated workers will diminish?

23. You noticed that the family doctor and the specialists that you see consult their PC and hand-held computers for practically every diagnosis they make and for every prescription they give you. Does this make you trust these physicians less than physicians who do not consult their computers?

24. Many software packages offer expertise in a multitude of areas, such as investment, nutrition, and writing your own will. Do you trust the advice of such software?

25. "The more professionals use ESs, the less expertise they accumulate, because the less actual

hands-on experience they gain. This is akin to a pilot who spends most of his flying time watching an autopilot system rather than flying the airplane with his own hands." Do you think that ESs can *decrease* real expertise for its users? Why or why not?

Applying Concepts

26. Make a list of six daily activities you perform. They might include preparing homework assignments, shopping, and other activities. Ensure that three of the activities call for decision making that is unstructured (or semi-structured) and that three involve structured decision making. Prepare a one-page report listing the activities, stating what decision making is required, and explaining why the decision making is unstructured or structured.

27. Prepare a one-page report on the career you intend to pursue. Give at least four examples of activities involved in such a career that call for problem solving. Explain which problem solving is structured and which is unstructured.

28. You are the head of a medical team that wants to learn about the spread of a new disease in your state. You decide to engage a company that designs GISs. List the types of data that would be needed for the system and which agencies are likely to have collected the data. Suggest visual effects to make it easy to identify concentrations of sick people and the spread of the disease.

Hands-On Activities

29. Use an electronic spreadsheet such as Excel to design a DSS for solving the following problem. A publisher makes and sells books that have different titles but have the same format and are made of the same materials (paper, ink, binding, and so forth). Three types of costs are involved in the process:

    Fixed cost per title: $15,000 for setting up the press, regardless of how many pages a title has or how many copies will be made of that title.

    Fixed cost per page: Setting the plates for printing costs $2.00 per page, regardless of the number of books. (Thus, for a book of 324 pages, the per-page fixed cost would be $648.)

    Variable cost per page: The printing and binding of each page of each copy of a title costs 7 cents.

    Assume that no other costs are involved (such as shipping and handling). Prepare a decision model that allows the publisher to decide the following:
    a. For a given number of copies, what should be the book's minimum retail price per copy to break even?
    b. For a given retail price, what is the break-even quantity of copies?
    Test your decision tool for a title that has 250 pages. If the publisher intends to sell 40,000 copies, what is the break-even price? If the publisher decides to price the book at $18.00, what is the break-even quantity that must be sold?

    Email your spreadsheet to your professor, attached to a message in which you answer the two test questions.

30. Use a spreadsheet or download a free ES shell for this assignment. Build a simple ES that determines the eligibility of an applicant for a bank loan of $50,000 for 30 years. Eligibility is determined by the number of points the applicant accumulates in several risk categories, based on the following:

    Loan size

    No points are deducted for a $10,000 loan. Henceforth, 2 points are deducted from the total score for each additional $10,000 of the requested loan.

    Loan life

    No points are deducted for the first 5 years of the loan's life (years to repay the loan). Henceforth, 1 point is deducted for every 5 years.

    Rule

    If the applicant's total number of points is equal to or exceeds 60, grant the loan.

31. For a small business with an Internet presence, the data capturing technology they need to maximize web exposure and thus profits may be financially unfeasible. However, with the creation of Google Analytics, small businesses now have access to the big data they need to monitor vital site data. Google Analytics includes many tools

such as Content Analytics, which shows which parts of your website are performing well, and Conversion Analytics to display how many visitors your site is attracting. Go to the Google Analytics site and browse its features. Then, use what you have learned in this chapter to make some insights into the artificial intelligence behind Google Analytics. Explain what systems drive analytics, what the outputs are, and how small businesses use the outputs.

32. Even if you don't have a credit card, you probably still have a credit report. If you have any bills in your name such as a telephone or cell phone bill or have a savings account or checking account at a bank, you have a credit report. Banks use your credit report to determine if they will lend you money or issue you a line of credit. In reality, the time when people often find out they have a poor credit report is when they try to apply for a loan or credit card. Even if there are mistakes in your credit report, it may take months or even a year to fix the mistakes. The delay in accessing credit has obvious consequences. Additionally, clearing up any mistakes in your report could enhance your borrowing capacity or decrease your borrowing interest rate. Go to www.AnnualCreditReport.com, select your state, input your information, and request your free credit report. Review your report for errors and see which companies inquired about you. Print it out and bring it into class. Lead a discussion with a small group on what computer intelligence systems are behind collecting all of the personal information that makes up your credit report. Does reviewing your credit report increase or decrease worries about identity theft or fraud?

Team Activities

33. Team up with two other students. Contact a local stockbroker. Ask the broker to give you a list of the most important points he or she considers when predicting appreciation of a stock. Ask how each point (such as last year's earnings per share, percentage of appreciation/depreciation over the past six months, and the like) affects the net result, as a percentage. Use the input to formalize the model in a spreadsheet application. Select a portfolio of 100 units of 10 traded stocks. Use the model to predict the increase in the price of each stock and the value of the entire portfolio a year into the future. If you know how to use macros, embellish your new DSS with a user-friendly dialog module.

34. Team up with another student. Obtain a digitized map of your campus. If you cannot copy one, you can use a scanner to digitize a paper map. Use a web design application to create a simple GIS. On the map page, mark 10 areas so that when clicked, another page comes up with additional information about the building or part of a building you marked. Examples of marked areas that you could include: registrar's office, school of business building, the student union, and the computer lab. Email your GIS to your professor.

Transporting a Transparent and Nimble Cash Flow Forecasting System

The Kansas Department of Transportation (KDOT) was facing one of the most basic financial dilemmas: can current obligations be fulfilled with available resources? Facing a ten-year, $6 billion highway maintenance and restoration project, the KDOT needed to be able to have clear visibility over the impact of declining cash balances, budget cuts, and weather-related expenditures. Their old data system consisted of a plethora of spreadsheets requiring manual inputs and changing data could take up to six weeks. All signs pointed to a redesigned system that could respond to cash flow shifts quickly, accurately, and easily. Their dilemma led to the creation of the Cash Availability and Forecasting Environment (CAFE) and the overhaul of their project managing system.

The KDOT needed a cash flow forecasting system that could provide the agency with transparent management of cash forecasting models and assumptions and produce timely forecasts to increase visibility across multiple departments. Due to the large number of variables affecting future cash flows, the necessity to quickly realize the impact of a change to any one of those variables required a system that could run extensive contingency plans. Additionally, the CAFE system would have to be connected to the updated project management system, which was being updated to enhance and streamline the communication of interrelated data between adjacent departments.

KDOT's first step was to hire an independent consultant to guide the process of transforming their project management and forecasting systems. The project managers and cash flow forecasters collaborated to determine the needs for the new system. The two sides ensured the success of the new system by recognizing the "big picture" that the two divisions had to be separate yet connected. The agency selected a vendor that had complex statistical process that took into consideration curvilinear data rather than just linear data, which means data could be more precise. The vendor could create complex models that could incorporate external factors automatically. The vendor worked with KDOT administrators to ensure that the project management system was compatible with the CAFE cash forecasting system. Additionally, it was important that the new system included an intuitive user interface for model builders and users and have great analytics. Because CAFE is accessible through a web browser, the vendor could easily make adjustments, upload the new system for agency to critique, and let the agency provide feedback. This refining process was ideal for the back-and-forth exchanges necessary to create the finished product.

KDOT's success relates to their future cash payouts, thus signifying the importance that the models representing these payouts are accurate and timely. Payout curve models determine the sum of the KDOTs cash needs. The original system had 13 different curves with tables and lacked uniformity, making drawing conclusions difficult. The new models had to be able to accommodate fluctuations in variables and adjust for changing biases. The payout model used today in CAFE was made by using historical data from every payout scenario available to KDOT. CAFE automatically applies the payout model to every project and managers can alter variables such as delayed start time or cost estimates to see how the scenarios play out.

The culture of KDOT's communication prior to the implementation of CAFE was ancient. Project data used for cash flow forecasting was distributed on CDs only once a month and that was after the bids were in place. The manual requirements of the previous system significantly reduced the data sharing that was even possible. CAFE automatically updates when changes are made with project data.

Changes made to the project management system (PMS) automatically change in the cash flow system and are changed in all forecast models thus, eliminating the tedious manual inputting of data, which only slows response time and leads to errors. Managers can instantly see future cash flow reports produced for any cash payout over the lifetime of a project or just one day. They can also test contingency models and create payout curve adjusted for biases, seasonality, project length, and other variables. CAFE can also help the municipality determine when a bond issuance would yield the highest payout.

The implementation of CAFE allows project managers to understand their impact on the KDOT's cash balance. Although under the prior system project managers acknowledged their actions had consequences on the cash flow, it is difficult to comprehend the capacity of those consequences without the right data system in place. Now when project managers ask KDOT cash flow analysts if they can change the start time of a project for example, CAFE can make that decision instantly. CAFE has proven to efficiently handle cash and predict future cash availability for KDOT. Without

CAFE, the state agency would not have been able to plan and support the 10-year $8 billion program for highway maintenance and preservation.

Source: Ferrill, M., Malcom, K., & Suggs, R. (2012). The Kansas Department of Transportation Builds a Transparent and Nimble Cash Flow Forecasting System. *Government Finance Review,* 28(6), 14–18.

Thinking About the Case

1. The planning stage of creating a new ES may be the most important stage. What did KDOT do in the planning stage that led them to success in the long run?

2. Comment on the flaws in the communication practices of KDOT's previous system. What was the issue with distributing the cash flow information after the bids had already been placed?

3. Explain why the payout curve models in today's CAFE use historical data from every KDOT project available.

4. Why was the integration of CAFE to KDOT's project management system important?

Decisions to Support Health Care and Patients

Decision support systems can provide many benefits and efficiencies for operational and tactical decision making. From marketing to employees during open enrollment for health insurance to the delivery of quality patient care, decision support tools can add value to health care.

The cost of delivering health care in the U.S. is a topic receiving a lot of attention and national dialogue. This issue is complex and widespread, both economically and personally. It affects every individual, family, and business in the U.S. and probably will require many solutions and approaches to address the problem. The effect of "consumerism" has influenced the debate associated with the costs and delivery of health care.

In some industries such as education and health care, the word "sales" has never been a term used in operations and management, probably because the connotation would not be appropriate to identify with customers and their transfer of funds. However, revenue into a business organization still remains as a sale. In an increasingly competitive marketplace for many industries, it is important to attract and retain customers in a long-term, profitable relationship. The integration of business process management (BPM) methodologies and decision support systems can provide the methods for developing relationships with customers.

When businesses offer their employees the selection of benefits alternatives during open enrollment, it is important that health insurers promote a personalized environment. Considering that the consumer has the power of the purchase, communicating effective choices to the prospective employee may heavily influence the enrollment (or the sale) in the health plan. BPM systems can collect crucial data on the consumer, such as demographics and past claims, to personalize the process. Using decision support systems and predictive analytics, "the best sales experience for the consumer, including portal designs, product offerings and transactional navigation tailored for the best fit." (Hart, 2011) The system could compile a low-cost product offering and highlight gym memberships for a young adult employee. The demographics and lower claims potential would target their need for a reduced-benefit insurance plan. In a similar manner to Amazon's recommendations, the personalization of product offerings based on data and a structured decision-making process can increase the lead-to-close ratio and increase sales.

After the marketing and enrollment is done, decision support systems can also gain positive benefits also for the actual delivery of health care while maintaining the quality of care and safety of patients. The "first step" of the process is to provide the appropriate and accurate data to the nurses and doctors treating the patient in a timely manner. Carle Foundation Hospital, in Urbana, IL, has implemented a system to "put tools into physicians' and nurses' hands to provide the right information at the right time." (Page, 2011) Carle installed an inpatient, emergency department, and pharmacy electronic medical record system.

A crucial component of the implementation related to how the project was managed and approached. Rather than branding the new initiative as an IT project, Carle managed the project as a "clinical transformation initiative." Improving medical care was the objective, rather than improving efficiency. Tools were developed that focused on clinical decision support methodologies and best practices became the "core measures" of the new system. A series of data points are analyzed by the decision support tools to assess patients' need for medical attention.

Sources: Hart, E. (2011). A new era promises better outcomes. *Health Management Technology,* 32(11), 14–15; Page, D. (2011). 'Most Improved' Take Similar Steps to Reach New Heights. *Hospitals & Health Networks,* 85(1), 42–42, 44.

Thinking About the Case

1. Consider the various data elements that would be gathered for prospective health insurance customers. Think about other approaches that could be developed to target customers and the associated structured decisions.

2. Why did Carle Foundation Hospital's approach of implementing the new system create a successful project? Why would the approach of "improving efficiency" have altered the implementation of this project?

3. Are there any risks of integrating DSS tools to help diagnose patient health care? If so, how could these risks be minimized?

4. Can DSS tools have a positive effect on the delivery of health care? How?

References

Anonymous. RiskAnalyst. Retrieved July 8, 2013, from http://www.moodys.com/sites/products/Product Attachments/RiskAnalyst%20Fact%20Sheet% 20English.pdf

Anonymous. (2009). Electrogrid Uses FacilitatePro to Spark Collaborative Strategic Planning. http://facilitate.com/solutions/case-studies/electrogrid-corporation.html

Anonymous. (2010, Oct 14). Quicken Loans Reports 25-Year All-Time Record Closed Loan Production of $3.4 Billion in September 2010, *U.S. Newswire*.

Anonymous. (2011). FACING UP TO THE CHALLENGE. *PPI, 53*(11), 29–30.

Anonymous. (2012a). Barnes & Noble (White Paper). Retrieved 12 Feb, 2012, from http://www-01.ibm.com/software/success/cssdb.nsf/CS/JHUD-92JRDT?OpenDocument&Site=corp&cty=en_us

Anonymous. (2012b, Sep 24). Remote Diagnostics Springboard for Car OEMs to Full CRM Service Approach, Toyota and Ford Leading the Way, Says ABI Research, *Business Wire*.

Anonymous. (2013a). Amazing Mortgage Process. Retrieved Feb 14, 2013, from http://www.quickenloans.com/about/amazing-mortgage-process

Anonymous. (2013b). Analytica Cloud Player. Retrieved July 9, 2013, from http://www.lumina.com/products/analytica-cloud-player/

Anonymous. (2013c). RiskAnalyst. Retrieved July 8, 2013, from http://www.moodys.com/sites/products/ProductAttachments/RiskAnalyst%20Fact%20Sheet%20English.pdf

Anonymous. (2013d). Why iWebTrack. Retrieved 12 Feb, 2013, from http://www.iwebtrack.com/why.asp

Hart, E. (2011). A new era promises better outcomes. *Health Management Technology, 32*(11), 14–15.

Hoffmann, J. (2011). In-vehicle infotainment evolves for safe, efficient connectivity on wheels. *Electronic Engineering Times*(1607), 37–38, 40, 42, 44.

Kehoe, B. (2011). BENDING the Cost Curve. *Hospitals & Health Networks, 85*(8), 42–43, 42.

Klein, J. (2010). The Year of HIM. *Health Management Technology, 31*(1), 17–17.

Page, D. (2011). 'Most Improved' Take Similar Steps to Reach New Heights. *Hospitals & Health Networks, 85*(1), 42–42, 44.

Rapport, M. (2012). CO-OP Shifts to Real-Time Fraud Monitoring. *Credit Union Times*, n/a.

Simon, H. A. (1960). *The new science of management decision*: Harper & Brothers.

Stroud, J. (2008). Study shows importance of checking your credit report, *St. Louis Post - Dispatch*, p. F.3.

www.AnnualCreditReport.com. (2013). About Us. Retrieved Feb 14, 2013, from https://www.annualcreditreport.com/cra/helpabout

eleven

BUSINESS INTELLIGENCE AND KNOWLEDGE MANAGEMENT

Learning Objectives

As more and more business operations are managed using information from information systems and sometimes automatically *by* information systems, large amounts of data are collected and stored electronically. With proper software tools, data stored in databases and data warehouses enables executives to glean business intelligence—information that helps them know more about customers and suppliers—and therefore helps them make better decisions. Information technology also makes it possible to organize stored knowledge and garner knowledge from vast amounts of unstructured data.

When you finish this chapter, you will be able to:

- Explain the concepts of data mining and online analytical processing.

- Explain the notion of business intelligence and its benefits to organizations.

- Identify needs for knowledge storage and management in organizations.

- Explain the challenges in knowledge management and its benefits to organizations.

- Identify possible ethical and societal issues arising from the increasing globalization of information technology.

KIMBALL'S RESTAURANT: Building and Developing Loyalty

Michael and Tyler have discussed a customer loyalty program for the new location. They believe that a solid program can be a crucial component in the new location's success. Kimball's will need additional clientele to be profitable. A well-designed loyalty program will incentivize customers to patronize the new location and increase customer retention. Dining out is heavily dependent on disposable income. In a difficult economy, Kimball's must build affinity with new customers while encouraging current customers. However, Michael also noted that their focus should include multiple revenue streams for the new location.

Takeout for Success

Tyler was visiting the current location to get some paperwork. He decided to sit at a table and have some breakfast, knowing that it might be the only meal he would have that day. He remembered what his father said about multiple revenue streams for the new operation. He started to jot down some ideas on his tablet while he ate. Michael and Tyler had already developed a series of menus and advertising for group events targeted for special occasions, banquets, and business meetings. He was pondering if there were any other revenue sources that Kimball's could develop. As he sat there, he overheard a customer talking. The customer, Brooke, was a frequent customer of the restaurant. She is a busy professional with a husband and two children. Tyler heard her say, "Gee, these pastries are delicious. I never have time to bake anymore. Maybe I should take a few home for the kids."

Brooke's comment started Tyler thinking. He knew his mother was an excellent baker as well as a cook. He remembers how often Liz was complimented during the holidays and parties about her cakes and pastries. Could the extra kitchen space at the new location be used to offer fresh-baked pastries and cakes? If Brooke enjoyed the pastries, it is reasonable to conclude that other customers also enjoyed the baked goods. Why couldn't they market the new location to take orders for baked goods?

Always the conversationalist, Tyler decided to sit with Brooke and ask her those questions. He asked Brooke if he could join her and her husband Randy. The conversation quickly developed into something interesting. With their busy schedules, they did not have the time to make baked goods. They also entertained a great deal and would love to be able to order cakes for special events or holidays. Brooke said, "It would be great to order great food like this to pick up. The closest bakery is about six miles from here–and your mom is a much better cook than I am!" Tyler laughed. But then he had an interesting thought. She used the words "great food" in her conversation. Why focus just on baked goods? Would a family meal to go be something they were interested in? Brooke and Randy thought it was a great idea. They said that the convenience of quality food at a reasonable price would help them a lot. Fast food can be convenient, but a family style meal for takeout would be a nice alternative. Also, they were excited about the possibility of ordering special items when they were entertaining friends.

What an idea ... Kimball's on the Go! This would create a new revenue stream and leverage the expanded capabilities of the new location. Liz's food and baked goods were already very popular at the current location; why not offer takeout food for customers?

The breakfast break was worth Tyler's time. It also proved that sometimes you have to be a good listener and remain attentive to customers' needs. The new location would have multiple "products" to join into a loyalty program—lunch, dinner, late-night dining, after-work gatherings, group events, Sunday brunch, and now, take out. These various products could be covered in one loyalty program and create significant cross-marketing strategies. He could not wait to discuss his idea with his parents.

Data Mining and Online Analysis

Recall from our discussion in Chapter 7, "Databases and Data Warehouses," that data warehouses are large databases containing historical transactions and other data. However, data warehouses in themselves are useless. To make data warehouses useful, organizations must use software tools to process data from these huge databases into meaningful information. Because executives can obtain significantly more information about their customers, suppliers, and their own organizations, they like to call information gleaned with such tools **business intelligence (BI)** or **business analytics**. The two main uses of these databases are data mining and online analytical processing. These terms are often used interchangeably.

Data Mining

Data warehouses could be regarded as a type of mine, where the data is the ore, and new useful information is the precious find. **Data mining** is the process of selecting, exploring, and modeling large amounts of data to discover previously unknown relationships that can support decision making. Data-mining software searches through large amounts of data for meaningful patterns of information.

Some data-mining tools are complex statistical analysis applications, and others use additional tools that go beyond statistical analysis and hypothesis testing. While some tools help find predefined relationships and ratios, they do not answer the question that more powerful data-mining tools can answer: "What are the relationships we do not yet know?" This is because the investigator must determine which relationships the software should look for in the first place. To answer this question, other techniques are used in data mining, including artificial intelligence techniques, described in Chapter 10, "Decision Support and Expert Systems."

To illustrate the difference between traditional queries and data-mining queries, consider the following examples. A typical traditional query would be: "What is the relationship between the amount of product X and the amount of product Y that we sold over the past quarter?" A typical data-mining query would be: "Discover two products most likely to sell well together on a weekend." The latter query lets the software find patterns that would otherwise not be detected through observation. Although data has traditionally been used to see whether this or that pattern exists, data mining allows you to ask *what* patterns exist. Thus, some experts say that in data mining you let the computer answer questions that you do not know to ask. The combination of data-warehousing techniques and data-mining software makes it easier to predict future outcomes based on patterns discovered within historical data.

Data mining has four main objectives:

- *Sequence* or *path analysis*: Finding patterns where one event leads to another, later event.
- *Classification*: Finding whether certain facts fall into predefined groups.
- *Clustering*: Finding groups of related facts not previously known.
- *Forecasting*: Discovering patterns in data that can lead to reasonable predictions.

These techniques can be used in marketing, fraud detection, and other areas (see Figure 11.1). Of the four types of analysis, you may be most familiar with clustering. When you search for a certain item, you often see a list of other items with a message similar to "Customers who purchased this item also bought...". Data mining is most often used by marketing managers, who are constantly analyzing purchasing patterns so that potential buyers can be targeted more efficiently through special sales, product displays, or direct mail and email campaigns. Data mining is an especially powerful tool in an environment in which businesses are shifting from mass-marketing a product to targeting the individual consumer with a variety of products that are likely to satisfy that person. Some observers call this approach "marketing to one."

FIGURE 11.1

Potential applications of
data mining

DATA-MINING APPLICATION	DESCRIPTION
Consumer clustering	Identify the common characteristics of customers who tend to buy the same products and services from your company.
Customer churn	Identify the reason customers switch to competitors; predict which customers are likely to do so.
Fraud detection	Identify characteristics of transactions that are most likely to be fraudulent.
Direct marketing	Identify which prospective clients should be included in a mailing or email list to obtain the highest response rate.
Interactive marketing	Predict what each individual accessing a website is most likely to be interested in seeing.
Market basket analysis	Understand what products or services are commonly purchased together, and on what days of the week.
Trend analysis	Reveal the difference between a typical customer this month and a typical customer last month.

© Cengage Learning 2015

WHY YOU SHOULD   Learn About BI and KM Tools

Information technology has advanced from fast calculation machines to systems that produce useful information using structured data and then to software that turns unstructured information into knowledge. Knowing how to use BI tools will help you to independently produce highly useful information from data warehouses and other large data sources. In your work you will also need to use other peoples' knowledge. Much of this knowledge exists in the recorded work and in the minds of coworkers and experts outside your organization. Knowing how to use these tools will help you as well as others perform better. As a knowledge worker you will be able not only to use your own, limited knowledge but also augment it with the experiences of other people.

Predicting Customer Behavior

In banking, data mining is employed to find profitable customers and patterns of fraud. It is also used to predict bankruptcies and loan payment defaults. For example, when Bank of America looked for new approaches to retain customers, it used data-mining techniques. It merged various behavior patterns into finely tuned customer profiles. The data was clustered into smaller groups of individuals who were using banking services that didn't best support their activities. Bank employees contacted these customers and offered advice on services that would serve them better. The result was greater customer loyalty (measured in fewer accounts closed and fewer moves to other banks).

Businesses are continually implementing technology initiatives to approach strategic, tactical, and operational effectiveness. The compilation of accurate, timely, and relevant information to analyze using data mining techniques is gaining significant attention in the marketplace. A recent McKinsey & Co. study estimates that the amount of global digital data increased by 40 percent in 2012 alone (Holm, 2012). The key is how to harness and analyze the growing amount of data gathered from business activities. The American International Group (AIG) has invested heavily in data mining techniques to realize benefits to their insurance operations. AIG's initiatives have created an analytics team of approximately 100 professionals. The team studies its information about marketing efforts, customer-service practices, underwriting assumptions, and fraud-detection programs by "digging" through their mountains of data in search of knowledge. It is all about revealing the knowledge hidden in their data. The benefit? From increasing customer loyalty through decreasing the number of telephone rings before answering to more competitive pricing to increase sales (Holm, 2012).

To ensure a steady flow of customer data into their data warehouses, companies in almost every industry—from airlines to lodging, dining, and gambling—operate customer loyalty programs similar to the original frequent-flier programs. Membership is often free, and customers leave a record every time they make a purchase even if they do not use a credit card to pay. In many cases, mining such data provides business intelligence to target individual customers.

A large U.S. airline collects every possible piece of data on passengers in a central data warehouse, from frequent-flyer numbers through reservations and flight details. The airline uses data-mining tools to extract information that helps retain frequent flyers. For example, the executives can query the data warehouse to see how many flight disruptions, cancellations, or delayed arrivals its best customers experience in a given month. This helps the airline to proactively contact these customers and offer them incentives to ensure their continued business.

UPS has an organizational unit called Customer Intelligence Group. The group analyzes patterns of customer behavior so it can make predictions that help the company enhance services and retain customers. For example, the group is able to accurately predict customer defections by examining usage patterns and complaints. When the data of a specific customer indicates that the customer might defect, a salesperson contacts that customer to review and resolve any problems. The software helped to significantly reduce the loss of customers.

Identifying Profitable Customer Groups

Financial institutions, especially insurance companies, often dismiss high-risk customers. Better analysis of such customers can yield good business, as Progressive Casualty Insurance Company has proven. Progressive uses proprietary analytical software and widely available insurance industry data. The company defines narrow groups or "cells" of customers, for example, college-educated motorcycle riders ages 35 and older whose credit scores are above 650 and who have no accidents recorded. For each cell, the company performs a statistical regression analysis to identify factors that most closely correlate with the losses that this particular group causes. For each cell, the company then sets premiums that should enable the company to earn a profit on its portfolio of customer groups. The company uses simulation software to test the financial implications of accepting the analyzed groups as customers. This way, Progressive can profitably insure customers in traditionally high-risk categories. Other insurance companies reject such applicants and refuse to renew the contracts of customers who became high-risk because of claims such as for car accidents. These companies do so without bothering to analyze the data more deeply.

Utilizing Loyalty Programs

Loyalty programs such as frequent flier, travel, and consumer clubs help organizations collect a significant amount of data about their customers. Some grocery chains, for example, issue discount coupons only to the most loyal customers. Loyalty programs such as frequent flier, travel, and consumer clubs help organizations collect a significant amount of data about their customers. Some grocery chains, for example, issue discount coupons only to the most loyal customers. The Marriott Corporation, the hotel and resort chain, uses data from its rewards program (see illustration on the next page) to develop customized email newsletters targeted to individual customers, rather than to groups. Marriott believes that a "well-designed email newsletter keeps its audience interested and engaged" in order to increase customers' response to its offers. Their system customizes content including targeted special offers and partner specials based on customer interaction with Marriott (Anonymous, 2011). Ultimately, this initiative provides Marriott with a low-cost strategy using technology and data warehouses to increase revenue at their properties. Customers who are Marriott rewards program members also get a customized webpage for discounted rates and special deals at Marriott properties.

Collecting and mining data though its customer loyalty program has helped Marriott Corporation customize customer offers and increase revenue

Courtesy of Marriott Corporation

Inferring Demographics

Some companies use data-mining techniques to try to predict what customers are likely to purchase in the future. As mentioned in previous chapters, Amazon.com is a leader in exploiting customer data. The company registered U.S. Patent Number 6,865,546, titled "Methods and systems of assisting users in purchasing items." The software developed by Amazon determines the age of the recipient of an item purchased by a customer. The age range is estimated based at least in part on a customer order history of gifts purchased for the recipient. The first gift is associated with the first "age appropriateness designation." The second gift is associated with a second age appropriateness designation. An age range associated with the recipient is estimated. The software also captures and analyzes any data that may indicate the recipient's gender. The recipient's age progression is calculated, and the company uses it to offer the customer gifts for that person when the customer logs on to the site. So, if you purchase gifts from Amazon.com for your baby niece, do not be surprised if Amazon entices you to purchase items for a young girl, a young woman, and an older woman over the next few decades. Here is another example of what this data-mining tool can do: if you purchased perfume a week before Valentine's Day, it will infer that you bought the item as a Valentine's gift for a woman and offer certain colors for the wrapping paper.

Online Analytical Processing

Online analytical processing (OLAP) is another type of application used to exploit data warehouses. Although OLAP might not be as sophisticated in terms of the analysis conducted, it has extremely fast response time and enables executives to make timely decisions. Tables, even if joining data from several sources, limit the review of information. Often, executives need to view information in multiple combinations of two dimensions. For example, an executive might want to see a summary of the quantity of each product sold in each region. Then, she might want to view the total quantities of each product sold within each city of a region. And she might also want to view quantities sold of a specific product in all cities of all regions. OLAP is specially designed to answer queries such as these. OLAP applications let a user rotate virtual "cubes" of information, whereby each side of the cube provides another two dimensions of relevant information.

The Power of OLAP

Figure 11.2 on the next page shows the interface of a web-based OLAP application whose purpose is to provide information about federal employees. You can go to www.fedscope.opm.gov and receive information about federal personnel in almost any imaginable dimension for several years. Dimensions include region of employment, level of service, occupation, salary range, and many more. The middle table shows number of employees by department and region. Clicking the Cabinet Level Agencies link produces more detailed information for all cabinet-level departments, using the same dimension as before, but only for this department (bottom table). You could also view similar data for a specific cabinet-level agency such as the Department of Education. This would be an example of **drilling down**, a process by which one starts with a table that shows broad information and successively retrieves tables of more specific information. The OLAP application lets you receive the information in numbers of employees or as their percentages in each region, department, or organizational units within the department.

OLAP applications operate on data organized especially for such use or process data from relational databases. A dynamic OLAP application responds to commands by composing tables "on the fly." To speed up response, databases can be organized in the first place as dimensional. In **dimensional databases**—also called **multidimensional databases**—the raw data is organized in tables that show information in summaries and ratios so that the inquirer does not have to wait for processing raw data. Many firms organize data in relational databases and data warehouses but also employ applications that automatically summarize that data and organize the information in dimensional databases for OLAP. Cognos (a subsidiary of Oracle) and many other companies sell multidimensional database packages and OLAP tools to use them.

OLAP applications can easily answer questions such as, "What products are selling well?" or "Where are my weakest-performing sales offices?" Note that although the word "cube" is used to illustrate the multidimensionality of OLAP tables, the number of tables is not limited to six, which is the number of sides of a real cube. It is possible to produce tables showing relationships of any two related variables contained in the database, as long as the data exists in the database. OLAP enables managers to see summaries and ratios of the intersection of any two dimensions. As mentioned in Chapter 7, "Databases and Data Warehouses," the data used by OLAP applications usually comes from a data warehouse.

OLAP applications are powerful tools for executives. For example, consider Figure 11.3 on page 367. Executives of a manufacturing company want to know how the three models of their product have sold over the past quarter in three world regions. They can see sales in dollar terms (top table) and then in unit terms (second table). They can then drill down into summaries of a particular region, in this case North America, and see the number of units sold not only by model but by model and color, because each model is sold in three colors. This information might lead them to recommend to the dealer to stop selling Model 3 in blue in North America, because sales of blue units of this model are quite low in this region. While still investigating last quarter's sales in North America, the executives might want to examine the sales performance of each dealer in this region. It seems that Dealer 3 enjoyed brisk sales of Model 1, but not of Models 2 and 3. If the sales picture is the same for another quarter or two, they might decide to stop sales of these models through Dealer 3 and increase the number of Model 1 units they provide to that dealer.

FIGURE **11.2**

FedScope is an online OLAP application maintained by the U.S. government's Office of Personnel Management

U.S. OFFICE OF PERSONNEL MANAGEMENT
Ensuring the Federal Government has an effective civilian workforce

[ ] Go
Advanced Search

FedScope
Federal Human Resources Data   Main | Data Definitions | Help | Employment Statistics | Join our ListServ

Employment Cubes

Latest Available Quarter: September 2012
Enhanced Interface

Quick Description

Cube Interfaces:
↳ Enhanced →
↳ Generic

Main

March	June	September	December
2012	2012	2012	2011
2011	2011	2011	2010
2010	2010	2010	2009
		2009	
		2008	
		2007	
		2006	
		2005	
		2004	
		2003	
		2002	
		2001	
		2000	
		1999	
		1998	

U.S. Office of Personnel Management 1900 E Street NW, Washington, DC 20415 | (202) 606-1800 | TTY (202) 606-2532

Employment as values	United States	U.S. Territories	Foreign Countries	Unspecified	Location - All
Cabinet Level Agencies	1,870,535	14,443	35,378	1,208	1,921,564
Large Independent Agencies (1000 or more employees)	164,366	660	1,770	71	166,867
Medium Independent Agencies (100-999 employees)	12,027	7	234	3	12,271
Small Independent Agencies (less than 100 employees)	1,539	0	28	0	1,567
Agency - All	**2,048,467**	**15,110**	**37,410**	**1,282**	**2,102,269**

Employment as values	United States	U.S. Territories	Foreign Countries	Unspecified	Location - All
AF-DEPARTMENT OF THE AIR FORCE	169,115	393	3,155	219	172,882
AG-DEPARTMENT OF AGRICULTURE	91,501	715	177	137	92,530
AR-DEPARTMENT OF THE ARMY	266,723	1,364	12,705	0	280,792
CM-DEPARTMENT OF COMMERCE	44,000	127	194	51	44,372
DD-DEPARTMENT OF DEFENSE	98,308	1,356	13,384	0	113,048
DJ-DEPARTMENT OF JUSTICE	115,009	509	95	8	115,621
DL-DEPARTMENT OF LABOR	16,390	44	1	0	16,435
DN-DEPARTMENT OF ENERGY	15,937	0	23	0	15,960
ED-DEPARTMENT OF EDUCATION	4,508	6	0	0	4,514
HE-DEPARTMENT OF HEALTH AND HUMAN SERVICES	85,038	224	253	8	85,523
HS-DEPARTMENT OF HOMELAND SECURITY	193,524	2,989	978	315	197,806
HU-DEPARTMENT OF HOUSING AND URBAN DEVELOPMENT	9,299	75	0	3	9,377
IN-DEPARTMENT OF THE INTERIOR	70,444	364	4	5	70,817
NV-DEPARTMENT OF THE NAVY	192,270	1,441	4,249	0	197,960
ST-DEPARTMENT OF STATE	12,629	1	19	1	12,650
TD-DEPARTMENT OF TRANSPORTATION	56,899	270	62	25	57,256
TR-DEPARTMENT OF THE TREASURY	114,785	707	62	323	115,877
VA-DEPARTMENT OF VETERANS AFFAIRS	314,156	3,858	17	113	318,144
Cabinet Level Agencies	**1,870,535**	**14,443**	**35,378**	**1,208**	**1,921,564**

FIGURE 11.3

Using OLAP tables to compare the sales of three product models by continent

Sales ($ 000)			
	Model 1	Model 2	Model 3
North America	115800	136941	53550
South America	72550	63021	25236
Asia	65875	53781	17136
Total	254225	253743	95922

Sales (Units)			
	Model 1	Model 2	Model 3
North America	4632	6521	2975
South America	2902	3001	1402
Asia	2635	2561	952
Total	10169	12083	5329

North America (Units)			
	Model 1	Model 2	Model 3
Red	2401	1785	2512
Blue	1766	527	52
White	465	4209	411
Total	4632	6521	2975

North America Dealerships (Units)			
	Model 1	Model 2	Model 3
Dealer 1	102	556	2011
Dealer 2	1578	2450	108
Dealer 3	2358	0	10
Dealer 4	20	520	57
Dealer 5	574	2995	789
Total	4632	6521	2975

© Cengage Learning 2015

In a similar manner, Ruby Tuesday, the restaurant chain, solved a problem at one of its restaurants. Managers who examined performance by location discovered that a restaurant in Knoxville, Tennessee, was performing well below the chain's average in terms of sales and profit. Analyzing the store's information revealed that customers were waiting longer than normally for tables, and for their food after they were seated. There could be many reasons for this: an inexperienced cook, understaffing, or slow waiters, to name a few.

Managers at headquarters decided to take a look at the average time between when a check was opened at the cash register and the time the customer paid. In the restaurant industry this is an indication of an important factor: how long it takes to move from one party to another at a given table. The shorter the time, the better. The average time "to close a check" at Ruby Tuesday's restaurants is 45 minutes. At this particular location it was 55–60 minutes. Examining additional information, management concluded that the reason for the longer wait was increased demand thanks to an economic boom in the region. The company sent people to change the layout of the kitchen, positions of the cooks, and the placement of food. Cooking took less time, serving was faster, and the wait time decreased by 10 percent. More customers could be served, and revenue went up.

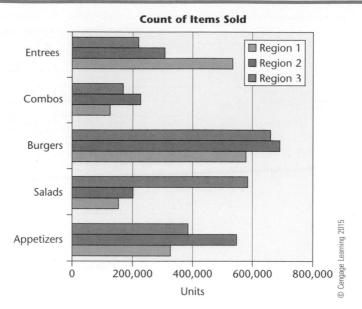

Restaurants can use business intelligence software to improve service and increase revenue

Count of Items Sold

Legend:
- Region 1
- Region 2
- Region 3

Categories (top to bottom): Entrees, Combos, Burgers, Salads, Appetizers

X-axis: Units (0, 200,000, 400,000, 600,000, 800,000)

© Cengage Learning 2015

OLAP applications are usually installed on a special server that communicates with both the user's computer and the server or servers that contain a data warehouse or dimensional databases (although OLAP might also process data from a transactional database). Since OLAP applications are designed to process large amounts of records and produce summaries, they are usually significantly faster than relational applications such as those using SQL (Structured Query Language) queries. OLAP applications can process 20,000 records per second. As mentioned before, when using preorganized dimensional tables, the only processing involved is finding the table that corresponds to the dimensions and mode of presentation (such as values or percentages) that the user specified.

POINT OF INTEREST   Meet Your New Co-Worker, BI

Experts have made predictions on the advancements and evolution of business intelligence (BI) in the workplace by 2020. A growing commonality among a majority of Americans and people across the globe is their degree of hyperconnectedness. People no longer just retrieve information while sitting alone at a desktop computer. They are on the go and in contact with a network of communication channels through mobile devices. BI comes into play in delivering that information in an interpretable manner. Screen sizes of mobile devices vary and mobile BI will be a key player in ensuring mobile users can receive personalized content in formats designed for their connection methods. In other words, BI will be responsible for making a 'one size fits all' format for personalized connection methods. Another influence of BI that is expected to be seen in the workplace by 2020 is de-routinization. The routine work currently performed by humans on an everyday basis will soon be a daily automated function of BI. It is predicted that by 2017 the amount of non-routine work will increase from 25 to 40 percent of an employee's day. This leaves humans more time for innovating, teaming, selling, and leading; tasks that can't be easily automated.

Source: Henry, H., & Hiltbrand, T. (2012, First Quarter). The 2020 Workplace and the Evolution of Business Intelligence. Business Intelligence Journal, 17, 13-19.

OLAP in Action

OLAP is increasingly used by corporations to gain efficiencies. For example, executives at Office Depot, Inc. wanted to know how successful sales clerks and stores were at cross-selling certain items. A store succeeds in cross-selling when it convinces customers to buy paper when they buy pens, or to purchase computer peripherals when they purchase a computer. The company used

OLAP on its data warehouse, which saves transactions from 1,629 stores and by more than 38,000 employees in 59 countries. During its first use of OLAP software, Office Depot compiled the proper conclusions to help the company increase annual sales revenues by $117 million. Management now knows better which items cross-sell with other items and therefore makes better decisions on placing items on shelves in proximity.

Managers in some companies now track information about their products from the purchasing of raw materials to the receipt of payment, not only for operations but so they can learn more about their clients and their own business. For example, Ben & Jerry's, one of the largest U.S. ice cream makers, collects data about every container of ice cream it sells, starting with the ingredients. Each container is stamped with a tracking number, which is stored in a relational database. Using OLAP software, salespeople can track how fast new types of ice cream gain popularity, and which remain stagnant, on an hourly basis. Matching such information with about 200 telephone calls and email messages the company receives weekly, managers can figure out which supplier's ingredients might have caused dissatisfaction with a certain product.

Employees who know very little about programming and report design are discovering that BI software is becoming easier to use. Intelligent interfaces allow them to enter questions in free form or close to free form. A part of the application that is called the semantic layer parses the question, which has been written as if you were speaking to a person, translates it into instructions to the computer to access the appropriate data mart or the proper columns of a data warehouse, and produces the answer, which is a number of charts showing trends. In a few seconds, a manager at Lands' End can find out which type of denim pants was the company's best-seller over the past six months. BI software has become so popular in large companies that Microsoft has integrated such software into its popular database management system, SQL Server.

More Customer Intelligence

We have discussed customer relationship management (CRM) in several previous chapters. A major effort of most businesses, especially retail businesses, in using such systems is to collect business intelligence about customers. Both data-mining and OLAP software are often integrated into CRM systems for this purpose. Since an increasing number of transactions are executed through the web, managers can use data that is already in electronic form to analyze and strategize. The challenge is to address the right customer, at the right time, with the right offer, instead of spending millions of dollars in mass marketing or covering numerous websites with ads.

Clickstream software has become almost a standard feature of the server management software used by many companies. Clickstream software tracks and stores data about every visit to a site, including the site from which the visitor has come, which pages have been viewed, how long each page has been viewed, which items have been clicked, and so on. The data can then be analyzed to help redesign the site to make visits of all or certain demographic groups more attractive. The purpose may be to have the visitors spend more time at the site so its potential for advertising revenue from other companies grows, and/or to entice visitors to make more purchases.

Many companies find that using only the data collected directly from consumers does not provide a full picture. They approach third parties, companies that specialize in collection and analysis of consumer data. The companies, such as Razorfish, DoubleClick, and Engage Software, use cookies and spyware (explained in Chapter 8, "The Web-Enabled Enterprise") to collect consumer data, which can be combined with the individual's clickstream data.

By compiling billions of consumer clickstreams and creating behavioral models, these companies can determine individual consumers' interests from the sites they visited (what do they like?), the frequency of visits (are they loyal?), the times they surf (are they at work or at home?), and the number of times they click on ads or complete a transaction. Then, sites can display ads that match the typical interests at sites where the likely customers tend to visit. They can use software that will change the ad for each visitor by using cookies that identify the user. OpenTracker is software that analyzes clickstream data. In the illustration on the next page, a business can analyze from what countries (or states) visitors gained access to their website.

Using OpenTracker can help businesses track the geographic location of website visitors

	No.		country / region / city	code	visitors	visits	visitors graph
⊖	1	🇺🇸	United States	US	101	116	
⊕			California		21	24	
⊕			New Jersey		7	7	
⊕			New York		6	8	
⊖			Texas		6	8	
			Austin		2	4	
			Dallas		2	2	
			Houston		2	2	
⊕			Illinois		5	5	
⊕			Connecticut		5	5	
⊕	2	🇬🇧	United Kingdom	GB	19	24	

Courtesy of OpenTracker.net

Consider the challenge that was facing Drugstore.com, a web-based drugstore headquartered in Bellevue, Washington. Management wanted to reach more customers who were likely to purchase its products, but they did not have the tools to discover who those people were. While Drugstore.com had plenty of information about customers—including name, address, and a list of past purchases—the company still did not know where exactly to find those customers on the web or where to find more people who have the same buying habits. Management hired Razorfish, Inc., a firm that specializes in consumer profiling. Razorfish managers say they know where 100 million web users visit, shop, and buy. This information comes from data they have collected for several years, not for any specific client. During a previous marketing campaign for Drugstore.com, Razorfish had compiled anonymous information about every Drugstore.com customer who made a purchase during the campaign. Razorfish knew what specific ad or promotion a given customer had responded to, what that customer had browsed for on the Drugstore.com site, whether the customer had made a purchase, and how many times the customer had returned to purchase.

POINT OF INTEREST
Amazon's Tablet May Infringe on Privacy

Amazon has grown from an online bookstore to an Internet retailing giant in a short period of time. One aspect of Amazon's business that is not regularly visible is their Amazon Web Services division, which stores and delivers Amazon's massive base of online books, movies, and songs, as well as rents out computing storage and power. This is known as Amazon Cloud Drive. Amazon's newest tablet, the Kindle Fire, uses its web browser, Amazon Silk, to access the web through the Amazon Cloud Drive. Cloud Drive is used for the grunt work of loading the page and then the information is zapped back to the tablet. The issue? Every site the tablet user goes to is sent to the Cloud, a massive storage base. Amazon can record unthinkable amounts of consumer web browsing data, more than the average tablet user might feel comfortable with. Privacy advocates have already raised concerns because Amazon can see what customers are looking at and where they are looking.

Sources: Woo, S., & Fowler, G. A. (2011, Sep 30). Amazon Cloud Boosts Fire; Computing Network Cuts Costs, Adds Power to Tablet, but Stirs Privacy Concerns, Wall Street Journal (Online).

Using its Web Affinity Analysis software, Razorfish could track Drugstore.com's individual customers across more than 3000 websites. Razorfish then constructed common themes in the customers' online behavior, such as the general websites they visited, visits to competing online drug retailers, and the likelihood that those individuals would click on ads. The company gave Drugstore.com a list of 1.45 million "high-quality prospects," shoppers with a high potential of purchasing from Drustore.com. Drugstore.com managers used the information to build a marketing strategy, assuming that those common characteristics and habits would be shared by as-yet-unconverted customers. A converted customer is a shopper that is convinced to buy.

Using similar software helped Eddie Bauer, Inc. to decrease its marketing cost per sale by 74 percent over three months, and the Expedia, Inc. travel site to cut its cost per sale by 91 percent over eight months.

Dashboards

To make the use of BI tools convenient for executives, companies that develop BI tools create interfaces that help the executives and other employees to quickly grasp business situations. In the early 1990s, these systems were called executive information systems (EISs) and were used only sporadically. However, with the contemporary popularity of Big Data and analytics, EISs transformed into a more contemporary interface. The popular name of such an interface is **dashboard**, because it looks something like a car dashboard. Car dashboards provide information in the form of clock-like indicators and scales. BI dashboards use similar visual images. They include speedometer-like indicators for periodic revenues, profits, and other financial information; plus bar charts, line graphs, and other graphical presentations whenever the information can be presented graphically. Figure 11.4 shows a dashboard from MicroStrategy, a provider of BI software. Similar dashboards are parts of BI tools offered by other vendors, including Cognos and SAS. ERP vendors, such as SAP and Oracle, also include dashboards in their applications.

FIGURE **11.4**

BI dashboards like this one from MicroStrategy help executives quickly view organizational metrics, ratios, and trends on one screen

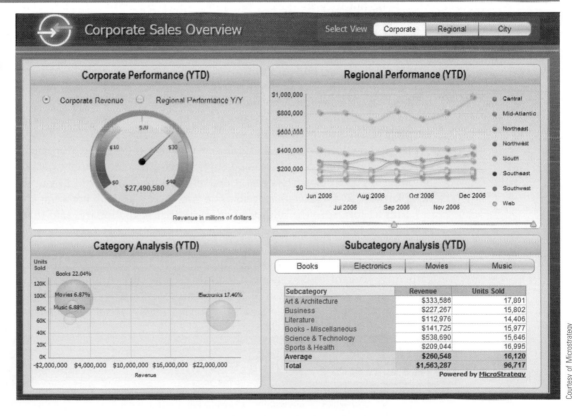

Courtesy of Microstrategy

One of the most important responsibilities of any organization's senior management is to develop, guide, and monitor the strategic initiatives of their business. These initiatives are evaluated to determine the costs, savings, and benefits to be derived from their implementation. Since these factors are developed prior to implementation, they are estimated based on a series of assumptions and calculations. When implemented, it is important to view these **key performance indicators (KPIs)** as real data is captured, comparing the data to benchmark or historical values. Dashboards are designed to quickly present predefined KPIs. Sometimes called metrics, some examples of KPIs are occupancy ratios in hotels and hospitals, inventory turns in retail, or customer phone hold time in customer relations. The dashboard in the figure shows a "speedometer" and other graphs to illustrate KPIs such as performance and analysis by categories and subcategories. These graphic indicators often use corporate-defined zones to show whether the current value is acceptable (or not) by color, in an easy-to-read environment.

GCAN Insurance Company, based in Toronto, sells casualty and property insurance to businesses in Canada. The insurer wanted to provide management with current data in order to make more effective decisions. Using Microsoft SharePoint Server, GCAN built a business intelligence dashboard. The entire development and implementation process, from prototype to product delivery, was completed in only one month. The dashboard provides 25 managers access to the dashboard through a browser with real-time data from their financial systems. The project created one repository of data so that all managers were viewing the same data. Previously, managers needed about four hours to assemble and validate data across several data sources. The BI dashboard provides the data to managers proactively rather than having to compile and wait for the information (Anonymous, 2010).

Knowledge Management

Imagine you work for a consulting firm. Your supervisor assigns you to a new client. As a smart professional, the first thing you want to check is whether your firm has had previous experience with this client and what knowledge has been accumulated about the experience. You heard that two ex-employees had contact with this client several years ago. It would be great to discuss it with them, but they are gone. Their knowledge is no longer available to the firm, because it is not recorded anywhere. The data recorded about the financial transactions with this client cannot provide the knowledge you are seeking: How easy or difficult was the interaction with the client's executives? What are the strengths and weaknesses of that organization? In engineering companies, engineers might want to see if colleagues have already encountered a problem they are trying to solve, and what the solution to that problem was. IT professionals might want to know if their colleagues have encountered a similar repeating failure with a network management system.

An organization can learn much about its customers, sellers, and itself by mining data warehouses and using OLAP software, but such techniques still do not satisfy another important challenge: how to manage knowledge, expertise that is created within and outside the organization. As discussed in Chapter 10, "Decision Support and Expert Systems," expertise in narrow domains can be programmed in expert systems. However, organizations would like to garner and manage much more knowledge. Effective management of knowledge can help both employees and customers.

Samuel Johnson, the author of an early English dictionary, said that one type of knowledge is what we know about a subject, and the other type is knowing where to find information about the subject. The purpose of knowledge management is mainly to gain the second type of knowledge. **Knowledge management (KM)** is the combination of activities involved in gathering, organizing, sharing, analyzing, and disseminating knowledge to improve an organization's performance.

POINT OF INTEREST   With Age Comes Wisdom

There are two kinds of knowledge: knowing what and knowing how. The former can be taught; the latter can only be learned. As the large number of baby boomers continues to punch their tickets for retirement on the green golf courses of Florida, they take their years of expertise with them. Knowledge-driven organizations that rely and operate on their expertise and on-the-job acquired knowledge are scrambling to mine that human information and store it for future use. The importance of knowledge management can be seen in a parable. One day at a factory, the production line came to a screeching halt. The manager called in his trusty technician. The technician walked around the machine line a bit, tapped it once with a hammer, and the production line jumped back to life. The technician handed the manager an invoice that read $1,000. The manager called out, "$1,000? But all you did was tap it once!" The technician took the invoice and revised to read, "Tapping with hammer—$10; knowing where to tap—$990."

Source: Tryon, C. (2010). Employers must bridge knowledge gap, Tulsa World, Aug 05.

Information that can be gleaned from stored data is knowledge, but there is much more knowledge that organizations would like to store that they currently do not. The knowledge that is not maintained in information systems is typically of the type that cannot be extracted from readily captured data at websites or other electronic means of transactions. It is accumulated through experience. Much of it is kept in people's minds, on paper notes, on discussion transcripts, and in other places that are not readily accessible to a company's employees. Therefore, knowledge management is a great challenge. Knowledge management is the attempt by organizations to put procedures and technologies in place to do the following:

- Transfer individual knowledge into databases.
- Filter and separate the most relevant knowledge.
- Organize that knowledge in databases that allow employees easy access to it or that "push" specific knowledge to employees based on pre-specified needs.

Knowledge management software facilitates these activities. As the cost of storage media continues to decrease and database management packages are increasingly more sophisticated and affordable, storage and organization of unstructured information have been less of a challenge. The more difficult issue is development of tools that address the third challenge: quickly finding the most relevant information for solving problems.

Capturing and Sorting Organizational Knowledge

The research company IDC argues that almost half of the work that **knowledge workers** do in organizations has already been done, at least partially. This work includes researching a certain subject, preparing a report, and providing information as part of a consulting contract. It estimates that labor worth $3,000–5,000 per knowledge worker is wasted annually because workers try to solve the same problem that other workers have already solved. Organizations could save this duplication, or replication, by collecting and organizing knowledge that is gained by members of the organization.

To transfer knowledge into manageable online resources, some companies require workers to create reports of their finding. Others, especially consulting firms, require their employees to create reports about sessions with clients. However organizations collect information, the results might be several terabytes of potential knowledge, but the challenge for employees is to know how to find answers to specific questions. Some software tools have been developed to help.

For example, the Bank of Montreal needed to provide more information to its corporate credit card managers and sales force. In its old system, the credit card division created spreadsheets to consolidate data gathered from approximately 60 reports. As you can imagine, the effort required for this process was cumbersome and time-consuming. New application software replaced over a hundred reports with only a few dashboards. Bank managers need to understand which types of credit cards are most active and gauge their performance. The new application provides purchase volume and number of transactions over a series of months by region and city (within region). The user can view a different location's data on the graph by simply clicking on a region and then "drilling down" into a city within that region. A manager can view the purchases both in dollars as well as the number of transactions as the region and city is changed. Further analysis can be viewed by selecting a specific zone of a city. A smaller graph illustrates the volume within a city zone filtered from the city volume data. In addition, the user can "slide" a marker to customize the time range displayed by the graph (Howson, 2012).

Employee Knowledge Networks

While some tools build knowledge bases and help employees access them, others put the emphasis on directing employees to other employees who have a certain expertise. The advantage of this approach is that an expert can provide expertise that has not been captured in information systems (see Figure 11.5). Large companies, especially multisite ones, often waste money because employees in one organizational unit are not aware of the experience of employees in another unit. For example, one energy company spent $1 million on a product designed to work on oil rigs to prevent sediment from falling into wells. When the equipment was installed, it failed. The executives of another unit decided to purchase the same equipment, which, not surprisingly, failed in the other location. Then a third unit, elsewhere, purchased the equipment, which also failed. While one can justify the loss of the first $1 million as legitimate business expense in the course of trying a product, the other $2 million was lost because decision makers did not know that the equipment had already been tried and failed. To alleviate similar problems, some software companies, such as Tacit Systems (acquired by Oracle), Hivemine (currently owns AskMe software) and Safeharbor Knowledge Solutions have developed **employee knowledge networks**, tools that facilitate knowledge sharing through intranets. Recall that an intranet uses web technologies to link employees of the same organization.

FIGURE **11.5**

An employee knowledge network can capture information and distribute information not captured in an information system

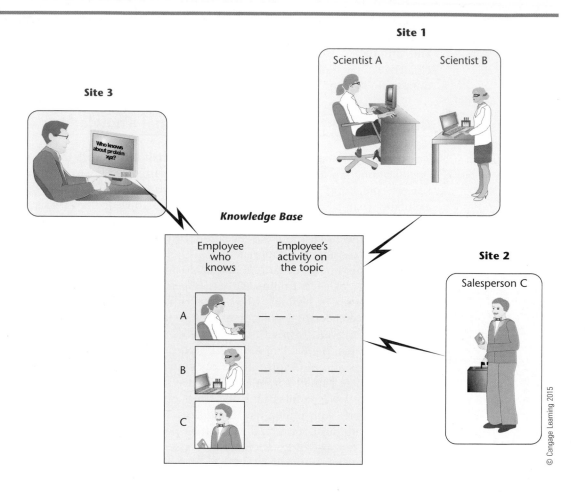

Tacit Systems' ActiveNet tool continuously processes email, documents, and other business communications and automatically "discovers" each employee's work focus, expertise, and business relationships. The tool "mines" this unstructured data to build a profile of each employee in terms of topics and interests. The goal is to ensure that two people who might benefit from creating a connection in a workplace do so, so that one can learn from the experience of another about a specific issue. By analyzing email and documents, the tool extracts the employee's interests and solutions to problems, and that information is added to the employee's profile. Other employees who seek advice can access the profile, but they cannot see the original email or document created by the employee. This ensures uninhibited brainstorming and communication.

AskMe's software also detects and captures keywords from email and documents created by employees. It creates a knowledge base that holds the names of employees and their interests.

In the Middle Ages, Venice considered its expertise in making glassware not only a business trade secret but also a state secret. Divulging glassmaking knowledge to anyone outside the republic of Venice was punishable by death, because much of the state's economy depended on excluding other states and countries from such knowledge. Venice, like other states in that era, would never "offshore" any of the work to another country. Nowadays, matters are completely different. What was expertise a year ago has become routine work this year and may become automated next year. At that point, the expertise value in the product will have diminished, and to make a profit the organization that once had a comparative advantage in producing the product will have to use the least expensive labor available. Then, the business will offshore manufacturing to a factory in a country where labor is cheaper. The industry in the original country will lose jobs.

Information technology helps create knowledge but also expedites the turning of knowledge into routine, automated processes that can be carried out elsewhere. IT also expedites the transfer of knowledge from countries that created it to countries that can quickly use it. Software used to be developed almost exclusively in the United States. Much of the software that the world uses now has been developed in Germany, India, Ireland, Israel, and Russia. A growing amount of the software developed for U.S. companies is created in India and China. The programmers' expertise is similar, but the wages earned by programmers in those two countries are a fraction of what American programmers would be paid for the same work. This is a pivotal element in what is called *globalization*—moving from national economies to a global economy. Is this bad for countries such as the United States and good only for countries such as India and China?

BI and KM software is developed mainly in the United States, Germany, and the United Kingdom. However, these systems are sold anywhere and can help companies in other countries compete with companies in those "developed" countries. This puts developing countries in position to gain knowledge much faster than before and compete better. Now, the competition is not only in the manufacturing and service areas but also in R&D.

In the United States, some observers view the issue in the following light: America used to be a world leader in manufacturing, but other countries now have a comparative advantage in manufacturing, and their workers have taken the jobs that American laborers used to perform. For some time Americans had an advantage in providing services, but many of these services are now provided over the Internet and telephone lines by workers in other countries, so the service sector's advantage has diminished. The United States is still ahead in terms of innovation and creation of know-how, they say, but we are starting to see this advantage slipping away, too. And when other countries beat us in creation of knowledge, they ask, what's left with which to compete?

Should governments take measures—legal or otherwise—that protect their economic advantages? Should they penalize companies that offshore manufacturing jobs? Should they forbid the sale of know-how to other countries? Should they adopt the Venetian model? Or, should we look at the world as one large economy where each worker and each organization should compete for a piece of the pie regardless of national borders, so that consumers everywhere can enjoy products of the highest quality for the lowest price possible?

An employee can access a webpage at which the employee enters a free-form question. The software responds by listing the names of other employees who have created email, text documents, or presentations on the subject, and the topics of their work. The employee can view the activity profiles of these people, and then contact them via the website, email, instant messages, or paging. The responder can use the same website to respond and attach documents that might help the inquirer. AskMe's tool captures the communication, including attached documents, and adds them to the knowledge base. (Note that in this context the knowledge base is not organized as the knowledge bases in expert systems are.)

Knowledge from the Web

Consumers keep posting their opinions on products and services on the web. Some do so at the site of the seller, others at general product evaluation sites such as epinions.com, and some on blogs. Consumer opinions are expressed in billions of webpages. This information is difficult to locate and highly unstructured. If organizations could distill knowledge from it they could learn much more than they do from conducting market research studies, such as focus groups, both about their own products and those sold by competitors.

Factiva, a subsidiary of Dow Jones, promotes a software tool by the same name. Factiva is accessible through a website and gathers information online from over 10,000 sources—newspapers, journals, market data, and newswires—information that amounts to millions of documents. About 60 percent of the information is not accessible to the general public. It screens every piece of new information that is posted at any of these websites for information specified by a subscribing organization. The search can be more tailored and specific than searches performed through free search engines such as Google or Yahoo! The software helps organizations add to their knowledge base, especially in terms of what others say about their products and services. The tool takes into account factors such as the industry and context in which an inquirer works to select and deliver the proper information. For example, a key word such as "apple" means one thing to an employee of a hardware or software organization and something completely different to an employee in agriculture or a supermarket chain. The Factiva illustration shows a consolidation of technology publications and web news content summarized by companies and executives for reading and review.

KM tools like Factiva help to extract and consolidate knowledge from millions of web documents

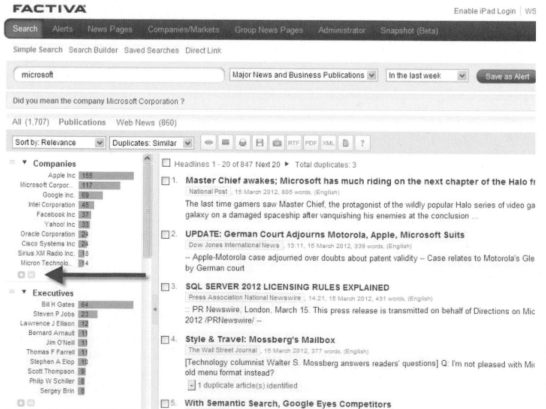

Courtesy of DowJones.com

Autocategorization

To categorize knowledge into manageable data, companies use autocategorization software. **Autocategorization** or **automatic taxonomy** automates the classification (taxonomy) of data into categories for future retrieval. Practically all search engine sites, such as Google and Yahoo!, use autocategorization software, and continue to improve the software to provide more precise and faster responses to queries. Many companies have installed such software at their corporate websites.

For example, U.S. Robotics (USR), a large manufacturer of networking devices, operates in a market with narrow profit margins, and thus one call to the support personnel about a purchased item might wipe out the profit on that sale. Therefore, reducing support personnel labor is important. The firm's surveys showed that 90 percent of clients calling technical support had visited the USR website before calling. USR purchased autocategorization software from iPhrase Technologies, Inc. (a subsidiary of IBM) to help customers help themselves in searching for answers to their questions at the website so that customers would not have to telephone the support staff. The software can help interpret customer queries even if the queries are misspelled. The software improved the accuracy and responsiveness of the support database at USR's website. Consequently, support calls decreased by a third, saving the company more than $135,000 monthly.

Google, Yahoo!, and other companies in the search engine industry have developed applications that sift through documents both online and offline, categorize them, and help users bring up only links to the most relevant documents. These companies sell their products to corporations to use at their websites, intranets, and extranets.

Summary

- Business intelligence (BI) or business analytics is any information about the organization, its customers, and its suppliers that can help firms make decisions. In recent years organizations have implemented a growing number of increasingly sophisticated BI software tools.

- Data mining is the process of selecting, exploring, and modeling large amounts of data to discover previously unknown relationships that can support decision making. Data mining helps sequence analysis, classification, clustering, and forecasting.

- Data mining is useful in such activities as predicting customer behavior and detecting fraud.

- Online analytical processing (OLAP) helps users peruse two-dimensional tables created from data that is usually stored in data warehouses. OLAP applications are said to provide a virtual cube that the user can rotate from one table to another.

- OLAP either uses dimensional databases or calculates desired tables on the fly.

- OLAP facilitates drilling down, moving from a broad view of information to increasingly detailed information about a narrow aspect of the business.

- Dashboards interface with BI software tools to help users quickly receive information such as business metrics.

- Knowledge management involves gathering, organizing, sharing, analyzing, and disseminating knowledge that can improve an organization's performance.

- The main challenge in knowledge management is identifying and classifying useful information to be gleaned from unstructured sources.

- Most unstructured knowledge is textual, both inside an organization and in files available to the public on the web.

- Employee knowledge networks are software tools that help employees find other employees who have expertise in certain areas of inquiry.

- Autocategorization (automatic taxonomy), the automatic classification of information, is one important element of knowledge management. Autocategorization has been used in online customer support webpages to reduce the labor involved in helping customers solve problems.

KIMBALL'S REVISITED

Tyler thought of a loyalty program that would integrate the various dining options and takeout business. And he knows that there is a tight balance between offering promotions and benefits with a loyalty program, but it cannot erode profits without gaining sustainable business.

The point-of-sale system stores a great deal of data from the daily activities of the business. Tyler is aware that the system can process takeout orders as well as advance food orders. He needs to understand the data stored by the system. From this research, the system maintains data on each table with the number of diners, the day and time of their seating, how long they were seated, the total check and the individual items ordered; all the normal data points associated with dining.

What Is Your Advice?

1. What other data elements do you believe would assist Kimball's to implement a successful customer loyalty program? Define these data elements and give a rationale for their use.

2. The best analysis to develop a successful business intelligence strategy is to compile a series of questions. The answers to these questions will provide a foundation to develop the data elements, reporting, and presentation of data to monitor business operations and strategies. What questions can be developed for Tyler to build an effective customer loyalty program?

3. What data mining techniques or examples could be designed for a business intelligence system at Kimball's?

New Perspectives

1. What types of strategies can Tyler implement to integrate the social media and advertising programs?

2. How can Tyler evaluate the effectiveness of their social media and advertising efforts?

autocategorization, 377
automatic taxonomy, 377
business analytics, 360
business intelligence (BI), 360
clickstream software, 369
dashboard, 371
data mining, 360

dimensional database, 365
drilling down, 365
employee knowledge
    network, 374
key performance
    indicator (KPI), 371

knowledge management
    (KM), 372
knowledge worker, 373
multidimensional database, 365
Online analytical processing
    (OLAP), 364

Review Questions

1. What is business intelligence?

2. What is OLAP, and why is it often associated with visual cubes?

3. What is the advantage of using a dimensional database rather than on-the-fly processing in OLAP?

4. Why is online analytical processing usually conducted on warehoused data or dimensional databases rather than on data in transactional databases?

5. What is "drilling down"?

6. What are data-mining techniques expected to find in the huge data warehouses that they scour?

7. Explain dimensional databases and the rationale behind their name. What is their use?

8. What is knowledge, and how does it differ from other information?

9. In general, what is the purpose of knowledge management in organizations?

10. What is the purpose of employee knowledge networks?

11. What is the benefit of tools that direct employees to experts rather than to stored knowledge?

12. What is autocategorization (automatic taxonomy)? How can autocategorization software help companies to serve customers and employees?

13. Context is a major factor when using tools to glean knowledge from web sources. How so?

14. Data mining helps mainly in four ways: sequence analysis, classification, clustering, and forecasting. Data mining helps determine whether a person has committed fraud. Which of the four types of analysis help do that? Explain why.

15. The web is a huge resource from which almost any organization could derive knowledge, yet few do. What is the major challenge?

Discussion Questions

16. What does intelligence mean? Do you accept the use of the word in "business intelligence software tools," or do you think the use of this word is exaggerated compared with what these tools provide?

17. You are an executive for a large retail chain. Your IT professionals use data-mining software. They tell you of the following relationship the software found: middle-aged single men tend to purchase personal grooming products and light bulbs together. Should you assign employees to research the reason for this? How will you use this information?

18. Employee knowledge network software keeps tabs of much of what employees create on their computers and all the email they send. As an employee, would you be comfortable with such software? Why or why not?

19. The term "business intelligence" has been used by IT professionals to mean many different things. What might be the reason for this?

20. Can businesses use free search engines, such as those provided by Google, Bing, and Yahoo!, to efficiently gather useful knowledge for better decision making?

21. Recall the discussion of expert systems in Chapter 10, "Decision Support and Expert Systems." In what sense are employee knowledge networks similar to expert systems and in what sense are they different?

22. Consider data-mining software, which infers demographic information about the recipients of gifts. Is letting software infer demographics less of an invasion of privacy than questionnaires or other forms of direct questioning? Is such inference more effective in obtaining customer information? Why or why not?

23. Consider the discussion of autocategorization and smart search engines, like the one used by US Robotics. Suppose you purchased an electronic device and have a problem with it. You turn to the company's website and find either a FAQ (frequently asked questions) section or a webpage that invites you to enter a free-form question about your problem. Which option do you prefer, and why?

24. Companies would like to have systems that would allow them to store all the business-related knowledge that their employees have accumulated. Do you expect that such systems will exist in your lifetime? Why or why not?

Applying Concepts

25. Search the web for a story on an organization that successfully used data-mining techniques. Write a two to three-page paper in which you describe what the software was able to do for the organization and how the results benefited the organization. Emphasize what information the organization now has that could not be obtained without data-mining techniques.

26. Write a one-page report explaining what one can do with a business intelligence application that cannot be done with the same data in a spreadsheet or a relational database. Give at least two examples. Discuss why a BI application or dashboard would be more effective.

Hands-On Activities

27. Go to *www.fedscope.opm.gov*. Produce the following tables for the latest year for which data is available:
    a. Number of U.S. federal employees by category size (large, medium, small) by country of service.
    b. Number of U.S. federal employees by category size, only for employees working in Australia.
    c. Number of U.S. federal employees by department within the *large* agency category, only for employees working in Australia.

    Is the sequence in which you produced the three tables considered drilling down? Explain why or why not.

28. Select an organization and research what it produces and where and how it operates. Using a pen and paper or graphical software, design three to six dashboards that the senior executives (vice president level) could use to receive up-to-date information to improve the organization's performance. Explain the purpose of each indicator.

Team Activities

29. Team up with another student. Select a specific company and write a report about its knowledge management needs. Start with a description of the activities that take place. List the types of employees who could benefit from access to documented expertise. Say which expertise you would take from internal sources and which from external sources. Give examples of knowledge that the company could use.

30. Team up with two other students. The team is to prepare a plan for The Researcher Connection, an employee knowledge network, to help the professors at your institution develop research ideas and conduct their research. List the elements of your proposed system and convince potential users in your report how it will help them (1) find relevant literature on a research subject, (2) learn who in the institution has done a similar study, (3) learn who in the institution would be interested in collaborating in the research, and (4) perform any other activity that is involved in conducting research and publishing the resultant article. Explain which of the resources to be used in the system already exist and will only need to be tapped (and how).

From Ideas to Application: Real Cases

No Guessing: Dressing for Decisions

The apparel company Guess?, Inc. is constantly striving to be on the forefront of the fashion world. This mission requires members from several branches of the company to have easy and immediate access to influential, decision-making information. To solve this issue, Guess used Apple iPads and mobile BI software from MicroStrategy to create a BI app that provided Guess buyers and executives with vital information from any location. The project, headed by the innovative director of BI, Bruce Yen, and his team, focused on content, ease-of-use, and the visual aspect of the app. Content is always the main focus when developing BI, but they also wanted their app to be easy to use and visually appealing.

Guess needed a better method to provide its buyers and executives with crucial information that could influence buying activities. Excel spreadsheets were too bulky and were not useful when trying to quickly locate specific details. Starting in 2008, Guess began using RIM Blackberry devices to provide info to executives and corporate directors at headquarters and to regional directors in the field. In 2009, they added dashboards to mobile BI offerings and supplied the information to nontraditional BI users such as buyers and planners. This was the first attempt at increasing the emphasis placed on visual layout. In 2010, Bruce Yen attended a MicroStrategy conference. Guess had already used some software from MicroStrategy, a BI company, but Yen noticed MicroStrategy's mobile app for the iPad and thought he could use it to solve existing business problems. The problem Yen aimed to solve with this technology was helping Guess buyers, who are constantly on the road traveling to retail locations, gain the information necessary to make purchasing decisions. The information-sharing power and high degree of intuitiveness of the project would make it a tremendous asset to the company.

Software Application

Although Yen initially thought the app would be used by buyers at Guess retail locations, it was discovered that some store locations did not have wireless connectivity. While traveling, buyers were using the iPad app more frequently before they arrived at the store, at hotspots in hotels and restaurants where they would brief themselves for their upcoming meetings. They would surf the app prior to arriving at store locations to get up-to-date information on sales patterns and store management history. The app was also widely used in the office, as it was much easier to snag specific snippets of information via the app than from a full-blown report.

They did run into many issues throughout the designing and launching process. Once, they submitted over 50 enhancements and issues to MicroStrategy to refine the software! The popularity and increasing use of the app spurred an inquiry of how Yen and management could access and use the BI app on personal iPads. This raised security risks for Yen and his team. To solve the issue, Yen turned to third-party mobile device management that can close off access to the app if the iPad is reported stolen or lost, in addition to using traditional security passcodes. The security system encourages app use on personal iPads without jeopardizing corporate assets.

It was no surprise that this fashion leader placed heavy focus on the design of the app. Every pixel on every slide of every page was scrutinized. The app provides users with so much different information from so many different angles that it can be used by a wide range of users, from top-level executives to buyers in the field. Besides the fact that the app runs on an already intuitive device, the final result is an app that can be picked up and used by almost anyone in the company. Bruce Yen conducted informal test-runs with the software simply by asking some of his design-savvy colleagues to play with it for ten minutes. Yen even followed buyers around as they visited Guess retail locations to see if they had any visible performance or connectivity problems. Most likely due to his arduous research and first-hand testing, he has not received any requests for formal training on how to use the app. While content was a key focus throughout the app's development, aesthetics and visual layout were a close second.

Yen constructed a BI mobile app that is intuitive, visually appealing, and content efficient. Through collaboration, communication, and extreme fine-point critiquing, the app surpassed expectations and has successfully aided Guess in maintaining its leadership in the fashion industry, even in hard economic times. What started out as a solution to existing problems turned into a staple of Guess's technological assets.

Source: Briggs, L. L. (2011, Fourth Quarter). BI Case Study: Apparel Company App Melds Fashion, Mobile BI. *Business Intelligence Journal, 16,* 39-41.

Thinking About the Case

1. Some app planners may use second-hand research to fuel their system planning. List at least three instances in which Yen used hands-on experience to gain insight on how to alter the product. Why is that first-hand experience so valuable? Explain how a buyer's access to

real-time sales patterns of a specific retail location can influence their purchasing decisions.

2. To what other branches of Guess?, Inc. could the app be useful besides top-level executives and buyers?

Monkeying Around with Business Intelligence

Zoos, parks, aquariums, and museums are known for their cultural and educational value. They provide a wealth of information and knowledge about animals, artifacts, history, religion, and sciences. But what about the information on their business operations? Marketing? Increasing visitors? With the reductions of government grants, this industry needed to be more proactive on expanding their revenue sources.

The Cincinnati Zoo (CZ) draws 1.3 million visitors and $26 million in revenue annually with about 400 full and part-time employees. After reviewing their current systems, they found that their information technology infrastructure was preventing revenue growth and service to customers. Over the years, their systems became isolated islands of technology processing ticketing, retail and food service on separate systems. Their entire multi-million sales operation was operated though non-networked cash registers. The information source for retail and ticketing sales were gained from register tapes. Therefore, it sometimes required two weeks to generate sales report for food and beverage sales. The Zoo knew a change was needed.

Ultimately, they developed two objectives: (1) increase attendance and (2) increase spending per guest. Using some incentives, CZ's management believed that they could increase revenue per guest. However, the key was to understand "what types of customers were spending, how much and on what." These questions would provide the data points that would provide a foundation to create these incentives and promotions.

The Zoo embarked to implement several point-of-sales systems to integrate ticketing, retail and food services. One of the systems, Gateway Ticket Systems, offered a ticketing system specific for their industry. After this system was fully implemented, the Zoo then purchased IBM's Cognos business analytics software for the data analysis. Instead of providing information about the various animals in their property, they focused on compiling data on their visitors.

The next step was to create a customer loyalty program. Management began to analyze customer purchasing transaction data at every point in the zoo. The customers' buying patterns were identified by collecting visitors' zip codes. Using this data, the Zoo could identify specific geographic areas having low spenders. At this point, specific geographical areas could be targeted with loyalty promotions to increase their spending patterns. The availability and scope of the data collected from these new systems have created new questions. They can "drill down" to very detailed data such as how many members are buying a hot dog. Or management can identify who is *not* visiting the zoo. Targeted mailings and offers could then be sent to incentivize them to visit the zoo.

Segments of their visiting population can also achieve benefits. The transactional data can be categorized into season pass holders and non-pass holders. The season pass customers clearly indicate that they attend evening events and purchase food while not purchasing from the Zoo's retail venues. Therefore, coupons and sales could be offered to season pass holders to promote additional purchases in the retail stores. The historical data can also provide some insight on the items that they may be more inclined to purchase, hopefully increasing the likelihood of increased retail sales and reducing unwanted promotions.

Additional features have been integrated into the customer loyalty program. Bar-coded membership cards can be scanned in at every venue. Member discounts and benefits can then be applied to purchases. This process encourages member visitors to use their membership cards for purchases and creates the "linkages" in the data warehouse to identify customers' purchases. Text alerts are now integrated into the systems based on specific triggers. For example, when a large donor or VIP enters the Zoo, a text message is sent to specific personnel to alert the Zoo of the visit. When supplies are running low at concessions, another text message can identify actions to be taken.

Dashboards and reports are accessed using a simple web browser so that the data can be accessed on any technology device. The Zoo's staff uses Apple iPhones so that text messages can maintain communication and a connection to operations. The reporting and dashboards help to integrate a variety of data sources, including budget information, in order to analyze and synthesize the real-time information.

Within a few months after implementation, the Zoo reported an additional 50,000 annual visitors to the Zoo along with an additional $350K in revenue. They believe that the return on their investment in the technology initiatives has been positive for the Zoo. Business intelligence has turned the attention from visitors looking at the Zoo's animals to the Zoo looking at customers.

Sources: Briggs, L. L. (2011). BI Case Study: Business Analytics Helps Tame Data at Cincinnati Zoo. Business Intelligence Journal, 16, 36-38; Klie, L. (2011). Cincy's Zoo Goes Ape for IBM. Customer Relationship Management, 15, 37-38.

Thinking About the Case

1. Do you believe that many companies use an isolated information technology infrastructure such as the Cincinnati Zoo? How does this structure hinder efficient operations? Why would businesses continue to operate in this environment?

2. The convergence of business intelligence data and texting can provide several creative operational and strategic initiatives. What other examples of integrating text messaging with technology solutions could the Zoo implement?

3. What types of business intelligence analysis could be done with food, retail, and ticketing data to increase the value of the data? What type of OLAP analysis could be accomplished?

References

Anonymous. (2010). Insurer Builds Business Intelligence Tool in One Month, Enables Better Decisions. *Microsoft Case Studies*. http://www.microsoft.com/casestudies/Case_Study_Detail.aspx?CaseStudyID=4000006733

Anonymous. (2011). Lodging Companies; Marriott Rewards Marketing Gets the Gold at Marketing-Sherpa Email Awards. *Marketing Weekly News*, 1231.

Briggs, L. L. (2011). BI Case Study: Business Analytics Helps Tame Data at Cincinnati Zoo. *Business Intelligence Journal, 16*, 36-38.

Holm, E. (2012). Hoping to Strike Profit Gold, AIG Ramps Up in Data Mining, *Wall Street Journal (Online)*.

Howson, C. (2012). Dashboards and Visual Discovery: More than Just Pretty BI. Tyson Corner, VA.

PART five

PLANNING, ACQUISITION, AND CONTROLS

BUSINESS CHALLENGES

After studying the next three chapters, you will know the basics of systems development efforts. You'll explore the issues of planning, systems development and alternatives for acquiring systems, and security and disaster recovery. The owners of Kimball's believe that they need to implement additional information technology initiatives to operate more efficiently and strategically. However, it is important for businesses to plan and analyze the various methods of acquiring technology.

- In Chapter 12, "Systems Planning and Development," you learn the steps to creating a plan for a new system, and what steps to follow to develop new systems, including feasibility studies and defining the essential functions of the new system.

- In Chapter 13, "Choices in Systems Acquisition," you learn how to evaluate the benefits and risks of alternative methods of acquiring an information system, including purchasing or leasing a program to create an integrated system.

- In Chapter 14, "Risks, Security, and Disaster Recovery," you learn about the risks threatening information systems, especially those dealing with financial transactions on the web, and ways to protect systems against attack.

SYSTEMS PLANNING AND DEVELOPMENT

Learning Objectives

Planning and developing new information systems can be complex. Systems planning often requires creating or adjusting strategic plans because of the great impact of IT on business models and operations. Those involved in development have to translate a business opportunity, a solution to a problem, or a directive into a working set of hardware, software, and networking components. Once a development project is under way, many people from different disciplines are usually involved in the effort. Communications skills are extremely important for successful results.

When you finish this chapter, you will be able to:

- Explain the importance of and steps in IT planning.

- Describe the systems development life cycle, which is the traditional approach to systems development.

- Explain the challenges involved in systems development.

- List the advantages and disadvantages of different system conversion strategies.

- Enumerate and explain the principles of agile systems development methods.

- Be able to contribute a meaningful set of requirements when serving on a project development team for a new or modified IS.

- Explain the concept of systems integration.

- Discuss whether IT professionals should be certified.

KIMBALL'S RESTAURANT: Planning Loyalty

After discussing the customer loyalty program for the new location with his parents, Tyler wanted to investigate the implementation of an information system to fulfill this strategy. He knows that the strategy has two major objectives: (1) give customers incentive to visit the new location and (2) build customer loyalty, which would lead to an increase in sales. Tyler researched area competitors and found that no other restaurant within 20 miles had implemented such a program. He was convinced that this initiative would help "lock in" customers to patronize the restaurant when they wanted to dine out.

Tyler told his father about his research on the restaurant's competitors and their lack of customer loyalty programs. He explained that while there were both operational and start-up costs from this new initiative, he believed that it could add positive dividends to the new location. Michael thought he was right, but he said that he was a "numbers guy" and that he needed more details to make an informed decision. Tyler explained, "Dad, I learned in school that when you provide incentives to customers, it alters their approach to buying something. Once you have successfully altered their buying decision, it will encourage repeat business." Michael asked for some examples. Tyler gave examples including gambling casinos, hotels, airlines, and credit cards.

Michael said, "Go for it, but I need additional details on the costs against potential increase in sales."

Failure to Plan Is a Plan to Fail

Tyler researched the point-of-sale system that the restaurant has installed to see if he could use it to help implement the loyalty program. His investigation of the POS's features was disappointing; the system did not have any ability to track and maintain customer activity and incentives. A dead end! He felt a bit deflated. He realized that he should have done this research prior to discussing the loyalty program with his family. While the concept was great, he now either had to admit that the current system could not do this function and abandon this initiative or find another way to implement the program. Both options had down sides. He was embarrassed that his parents would know he did not analyze this properly. At the same time, implementing a totally new system would have additional costs in money and time. He did not want to admit failure, but he also needed to present a more comprehensive proposal to his family in order to move forward.

He contacted one of his college friends, Becky, who majored in information technology. She had graduated one year before him and could provide some advice on how to approach this task. He scheduled a meeting with Becky and compiled some notes and ideas that would help the discussion.

Planning Information Systems

In recent years, a growing number of corporations have implemented enterprise ISs such as ERP systems, mobile systems, CRM systems, or other systems that serve the entire organization or many of its units. The investment of resources in such systems, both in financial and other terms, is substantial, as is the risk in implementing such large systems. If the implementation is successful, the new system can significantly change the manner in which the organization conducts business and even the products or services it sells. For all these reasons it is necessary to plan the implementation of information systems, whether they are developed in-house, made to order by another company, or purchased and adapted for the organization. When planning, it is important to align IT strategies with the overall strategies of the organization. (In this discussion, the terms "IT planning" and "IS planning" are used interchangeably.)

Steps in Planning Information Systems

IT planning includes a few key steps that are a part of any successful planning process:

- Creating a corporate and IT mission statement.
- Articulating the vision for IT within the organization.
- Creating IT strategic and tactical plans.

- Creating a plan for operations to achieve the mission and vision.
- Creating a budget to ensure that resources are available to achieve the mission and vision (see Figure 12.1).

The steps associated with information systems planning

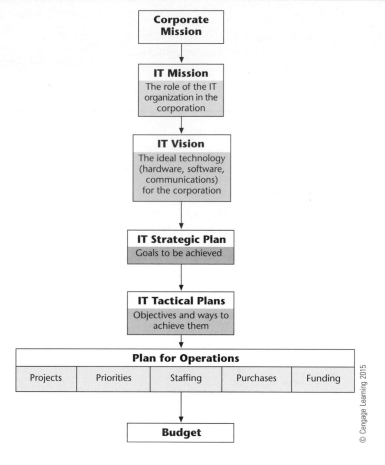

A **mission statement** is a paragraph that communicates the most important overarching goal of the organization for the next few years. Although the ultimate mission of any organization is to survive and—if it is a for-profit organization—to produce profit for its owners, mission statements are rarely limited to these points. Rather, they say how the organization intends to survive and thrive. For example, in Amazon.com's early years, its mission was to brand itself as the most recognized retailer on the web and to create the largest possible market share. Management pursued this mission, though it resulted in years of financial loss.

An important part of an organization's overall mission statement is an IT mission statement that is compatible with the larger mission. It is usually a paragraph, or several paragraphs, describing the role of IT in the organization. Often, the IT mission and IT vision are combined into one statement. The IT vision includes the ideal combination of hardware, software, and networking to support the overarching mission. For example, Amazon.com's management continues to recognize that innovative IT, especially web and fulfillment technologies, is the most important resource for the organization's success.

At its founding, Amazon was known for selling products in physical form (books, music CDs, computer software, and DVDs). Over the years, however, their strategy has shifted to providing electronic-based media content and services to its customers in direct competition with Apple's iTunes, as well as providing cloud storage for individuals and businesses. Amazon has accumulated the distribution rights for a collection of mobile/tablet apps, books, videos, audio, and music for its customers to purchase and download directly. Through its Amazon Prime program, customers pay an annual subscription fee and receive free two-day shipping as well as access to its electronic media library for free or paid ebooks, video, and audio. Their Kindle product line of tablets and e-readers uses the "razor and blade" strategy. This common strategy, named for shaving holder and blade replacements, involves two co-dependent products. The initial product is highly discounted or sold at cost while the second dependent product is not discounted. Amazon sets Kindle prices at cost in order to "lock in" customers, who purchase Amazon's electronic media offerings using their web-based technology distribution already in place. Printer manufacturers often sell the hardware at cost in order to build a "lock-in" customer for the purchase of replacement ink cartridges.

The CIO, with cooperation of senior management as well as managers in the IT unit, devises a strategic plan for implementation of IT in the organization. The plan addresses what technology will be used and how employees, customers, and suppliers will use it over the next several years. Since IT advances so quickly, strategic IT plans are typically prepared for no longer than five years.

The goals laid out in the strategic plan are broken down into objectives, which are concrete details of how to accomplish those goals. The objectives typically include resources to be purchased or developed; timetables for purchasing, developing, adapting, and implementing those resources; training of employees to use the new resources; and other details to ensure timely implementation and transition.

The objectives are further broken down into specific operational details. For each project, management assigns a project manager and a team; vendors are selected from whom available components of hardware, software, and services will be purchased; and funding is requested. When the financial requests are approved, the corporate budget includes the money to be spent over several months or years on these projects.

IT planning is not much different from planning any other acquisition of resources—starting with a vision of how the resources will be used to accomplish goals and breaking those ideas down into projects and the resources to be allocated to carry the projects to successful completion. In recent years, a growing proportion of IT funds have been spent on software, with most of the funds going to purchase and adapt software, rather than developing it in-house or assigning development to another company.

Inspiration for development and/or implementation of new information technologies comes from several sources, including users like you. Figure 12.2 displays typical sources for new systems. Competitive pressure inspires many members of the organization, not only senior managers, to come up with creative ideas. Often, such ideas are included in IT planning. In many organizations a steering committee oversees IT planning and the execution of IT projects. Steering committees are composed of users, IT professionals, and senior managers. There is high probability that in your career you will find yourself on such a committee.

Information technology projects often involve redefining organizational processes and procedures. IT systems are usually developed in response to changes in the competitive, economic, and industry environments, and can require employees, suppliers, customers, and other stakeholders to change their operational tasks. **Change management** is a structured, disciplined approach that facilitates the adoption of new or modified systems by various groups and individuals within an organization. Change management increasingly is being implemented on a global scale by businesses, governmental entities, and nonprofit organizations.

FIGURE 12.2

IT planning can be driven by a variety of sources in the marketplace

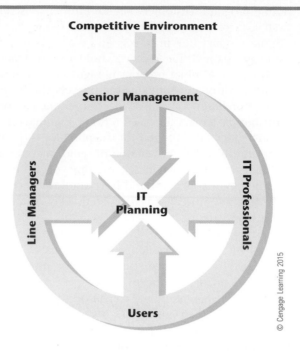

WHY YOU SHOULD — Understand the Principles of Systems Development

By and large, organizations have recognized the need to let non-IT professionals play major roles in systems development. You might be called on to participate in this process, not just to provide input here and there but as a member of a development team. The IT professionals on the team need your insight into the business processes in which you participate. They need your advice on ways to improve these processes through the use of new or improved ISs. One approach to development, agile methods, actually views the users as sharing at least half of the responsibility for the effort.

Software developers count on you and your coworkers to provide them with proper requirements and feedback. You should be knowledgeable, active, and assertive in software development projects, because you will have to live with the products of these efforts. Also, when your organization decides to discard one IS and adopt a new one, your understanding of the implementation process and your proper cooperation will be highly valuable. Your knowledge will be solicited regularly and will play a valuable role in decision making if you work for a small organization.

The Benefits of Standardization in Planning

One major goal—and advantage—of planning is standardization. When management decides to adopt a certain IT resource for all its units, regardless of function or location, it standardizes its IT. Standardization results in several benefits:

- *Cost savings.* When the organization decides to purchase the same hardware or software for all its units, it has better bargaining power and therefore can obtain lower prices from vendors. This applies to purchasing or leasing computers of all classes—mainframe, midrange, and personal computers—as well as licensing software.

- *Efficient training.* It is easier to train employees how to use a small variety of software than to train them how to use a large variety. Less training time is required, and—more importantly—employees spend less time on training and more time on their regular assignments. This also saves cost in the form of fewer labor hours spent on training. Even if each employee only uses a single application, but the organization maintains several applications for the same purpose, training time is extended.

- *Efficient support.* Standardizing for a small number of computer models and software applications enables the IT staff to specialize in the hardware and software they have to support. The more focused skills required for a standard suite of hardware and applications make it easier for the organization to recruit support personnel, and results in more satisfactory service to users.

Hewlett-Packard's IT services division decided to consolidate and modernize its offerings to be more attractive to existing and potential customers. From 2010 to 2013 it planned to invest $1 billion to standardize its enterprise data centers, build modernized facilities to wean clients away from the old services that are expensive to run and maintain, and lure them into using its ultramodern, highly secure, highly dense, green, sustainable infrastructure. HP planned to cut service management platforms from nine to just one and cut 9,000 jobs (but add 6,000 jobs as part of the services restructuring). The standardization of HP's IT services division cost HP up front but will save them money down the road through the efficiencies of using fewer man-hours and resources to achieve a higher output (Yeo, 2010). Another example of standardized planning is the use of one aircraft model (Boeing 737) for Southwest Airlines' fleet. This decision allows Southwest to focus its training efforts for mechanical, maintenance, and inflight operations on one aircraft, and to reduce parts inventory, labor, and costs. They can implement economies of scale as well as specialize on one type of aircraft to deploy their operations. In addition, their central reservation system is simplified by having just one seating structure, for the Boeing 737.

From Planning to Development

After planning a new IS or a set of ISs, management decides how to obtain the systems. In a great majority of cases, "systems" means software. For example, CRM and SCM systems rarely require specialized hardware (although they may require more, or more powerful, hardware). An increasing number of new systems are purchased and adapted for an organization's needs rather than developed in-house, although in-house development still takes place in many organizations. The approaches to systems development are the same regardless of who develops the system—the organization or its vendor.

Systems development generally is conducted in two approaches: the systems development life cycle (SDLC) and nontraditional methods, among which are many gathered under the umbrella of agile methods. SDLC is the more traditional approach and has been used for several decades. In certain circumstances, it should still be used. Agile methods developed out of prototyping, an application development approach that emerged in the 1980s aimed at cutting costs and time. **Prototyping** involves fast development of an application based on initial user requirements and several cycles of user input and developer improvements. Practicing the philosophy of prototyping—that coding should start as soon as possible and that users should be involved throughout the process—led to several methods of software development called agile methods. The two development approaches are not necessarily mutually exclusive. System development projects can begin using an agile method, such as prototyping, to either develop a working system model to gain knowledge about an evolving initiative or develop a subset of a larger system that may involve more end-user involvement. Systems development often involves **progressive elaboration**, where a vision of an initiative continually develops and influences the final product over time as more information and knowledge is available. In this respect, agile methods may have an advantage over traditional development approaches. The following sections discuss both approaches.

The Systems Development Life Cycle

Large ISs that address structured problems, such as accounting and payroll systems and enterprise software applications, are usually conceived, planned, developed, and maintained within a framework called the **systems development life cycle (SDLC)**. The SDLC approach is also called "waterfall" development, because it consists of several distinct phases that are followed methodically, and the developers complete the phases sequentially. Described graphically, the phases look like a waterfall from the side. The developers do not deliver pieces of the system before the entire system is fully completed. Although textbooks might refer to the various phases and subphases of the SDLC by different names, or organize them slightly differently, in general, the process follows the same steps. While the SDLC is a powerful methodology for systems development, organizations are sometimes forced to take shortcuts, skipping a step here or there. Occasionally, time pressures, funding constraints, or other factors lead developers to use different approaches to systems development.

The SDLC approach assumes that the life of an IS starts with a need, followed by an assessment of the functions that a system must have to fulfill that need, and ends when the benefits of the system no longer outweigh its maintenance costs, or when the net benefit of a new system would exceed the net benefits of the current system. At this point the life of a new system begins. Hence, the process is called a *life cycle*. After the planning phase, the SDLC includes four major phases: analysis, design, implementation, and support. Figure 12.3 depicts the cycle and the conditions that can trigger a return to a previous phase. The analysis and design phases are broken down into several steps, as described in the following discussion.

FIGURE **12.3**

The systems development life cycle

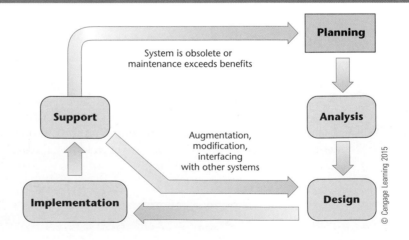

Analysis

The **systems analysis** phase is a five-step process (summarized in Figure 12.4) that is designed to answer these questions:

FIGURE **12.4**

Phases in systems
analysis

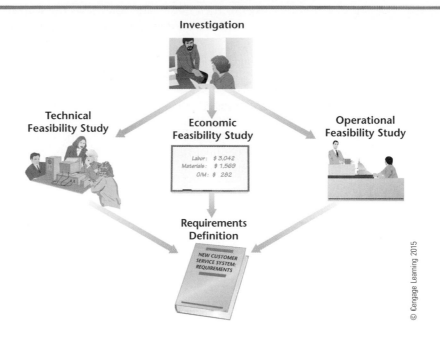

Investigation

- What is the business process or functions that the system is to support?
- What business opportunity do you want the system to seize, what problems do you want it to solve, or what directive must you fulfill?

Technical Feasibility Study

- Is technology available to create the system and result you want?
- Which of the available technologies should we use? Are these technologies mature enough to provide stability to the system?

Economic Feasibility Study

- What resources do you need to implement the system?
- Will the system's benefits outweigh its costs? Will the system provide specific value to the organization and its stakeholders?

Operational Feasibility Study

- Will the system be used appropriately by its intended users (employees, customers, suppliers)?
- Will the system be used to its full capacity?

Requirements Definition

- What features do you want the system to have?
- What interfaces will the system have with other systems, and how should the systems interface?
- Can it support other systems such as web and mobile technologies?

Investigation

The first step in systems analysis is investigation, which determines whether there is a real need for a system and whether the system as conceived is feasible. Usually, a small *ad hoc* team—consisting of a representative of the sponsoring executive, one or two systems analysts, and representatives of business units that would use the new system or be affected by it—is put together to perform a quick preliminary investigation.

The team spends time with employees at their workstations to learn firsthand about the way they currently carry out their duties, and interviews the workers about problems with the current system. This direct contact with users gives workers the opportunity to express their ideas about the way they would like a new IS to function and to improve their work. The investigative team prepares a written report summarizing the information gathered. The team members also forward their own opinions on the need for a new system. They will not necessarily agree that a new system is justified.

If the preliminary report concludes that the business situation warrants investment in a new IS, a more comprehensive investigation might be authorized. The sponsoring executive selects members for a larger analysis team. Usually, members of the original team are included in this augmented group to conduct **feasibility studies**. The objective of the larger investigation team is to determine whether the proposed system is feasible technically, economically, and operationally.

The Technical Feasibility Study

A new IS is technically feasible if its components exist or can be developed with available tools. The team must also consider the organization's existing investment in hardware, software, and telecommunications equipment. For example, if the company recently purchased hundreds of units of a certain computer, it is unlikely that management will approve the purchase of computers of another model for a single new application. Thus, the investigators must find out whether the proposed system can run properly on existing hardware.

The Economic Feasibility Study

Like any project, the development of a new IS must be economically justified, so organizations conduct an economic feasibility study. That is, over the life of the system, the benefits must outweigh the costs. To this end, the analysts prepare a **cost/benefit analysis**, which can be a spreadsheet showing all the costs to be incurred by the system and all the benefits that are expected from its operation.

The most accurate method of economic analysis is the fully quantitative **return on investment (ROI)**, which is a calculation of the difference between the stream of benefits and the stream of costs over the life of the system, discounted by the applicable interest rate, as shown in Figure 12.5. To find the ROI, the net present value of the system is calculated by combining the net present value of the costs of the system with the net present value of the benefits of the system, using calculations based on annual costs and benefits and using the appropriate interest rate. If the ROI is positive, the system is economically feasible, or cost justified. Remember that during the time the system is developed, which might be several years, there are no benefits, only development costs. Operational costs during the system's life include software license fees, maintenance personnel, telecommunications, power, and computer-related supplies (such as hardware replacement, software upgrades, and paper and toner purchases). If the system involves a website, the cost of revising and enhancing the site by webmasters and other professionals must also be included.

Figure 12.5 presents a simplified example of a cost/benefit spreadsheet and analysis for a small system. Since the net present value of the system is positive ($45.18 million), and therefore the benefits exceed the investment, the development effort is economically justified. In the figure, in the year 2020, the net present value decreases significantly. As this value continues to diminish, the organization should reconsider the value of the system. If the system is not replaced or significantly upgraded, the existing system will become a drain on the organization over time. The analysis shown in the figure represents the **total cost of ownership (TCO)** for a new information system implementation. TCO is a financial estimate for business leaders to objectively and accurately evaluate the direct and indirect costs of a new organizational project. Many business organizations evaluate the short-term and long-term financial, operational, and other effects of a new IT initiative prior to its approval. Just as you must consider the entire cost and savings when purchasing an automobile (insurance, maintenance, taxes, and so on), the total costs and savings of an IT initiative must be considered in addition to the simple "purchase" price.

FIGURE 12.5

Estimated benefits and costs of an information system (in thousands)

Year	2015	2016	2017	2018	2019	2020
Benefits						
Increase in sales			60,000	40,000	40,000	20,000
Reduction in costs			30,000	20,000	20,000	10,000
Total Benefits	0	0	90,000	60,000	60,000	30,000
Costs						
Analysis	20,000					
Design	40,000					
Implementation		60,000				
Hardware		25,000				
Operation/ maintenance costs		0	5,000	5,200	5,400	5,700
Total Costs	60,000	85,000	5,000	5,200	5,400	5,700
Difference	(60,000)	(85,000)	85,000	54,800	54,600	24,300
Discounted at 5%	(57,143)	(77,098)	73,426	45,084	42,781	18,133
Net present value (6 years)	45,183					

Often, it is difficult to justify the cost of a new IS because too many of the benefits are *intangible*, that is, they cannot be quantified in dollar terms. Improved customer service, better decision making, and a more enjoyable workplace are all benefits that might eventually increase profit but are very difficult to estimate in dollar amounts. This inability to measure benefits is especially true when the new IS is intended not merely to automate a manual process but to support a new business initiative or improve intellectual activities such as decision making. For example, it is difficult to quantify the benefits of business intelligence (BI) and knowledge management (KM) systems. Software vendors often promote "fast ROI" as a selling point, and express it in terms of the short period of time over which the adopting organization can recoup the investment. Still, such claims are difficult, if not impossible, to demonstrate. Therefore, the economic incentive for investing in a new IS is often "we must use it because our competitors use it" and a general expectation that the new IS will benefit the organization in at least one way.

When laws or regulations dictate the implementation of a new IS, no ROI analysis is carried out. For example, when companies implement software to comply with the record keeping and financial procedures of the Sarbanes-Oxley Act, the question is not whether to implement the system. The economic analysis becomes which software is the least expensive and which personnel—internal or hired from consulting firms—would implement the system for the least cost while maintaining the required standards.

In recent years the World Health Organization (WHO) has determined that the economic cost of road crashes in low-income, middle-income, and upper-income countries accounts for 1, 1.5, and 2 percent, respectively, of their gross national products, making road crashes a significant global economic issue. WHO is looking at a potential information-systems-based solution called intelligent transportation systems (ITS). ITS collects and analyzes data on people, roads, and vehicles in ways that are far superior to the existing system, which relies on motion sensors. ITS can also use artificial vision systems to analyze traffic. The ITS uses the Internet as the communication link and provides digitally enhanced connectivity using Bluetooth technology as well as embedded systems built into cars, bridges, tunnels, and roads. However, the artificial vision system in road-traffic analysis is yet to be highly implemented because of feasibility concerns. Because the ITS requires Internet connectivity, the infrastructure is not universally established and currently is not economically feasible. With further research and testing, ITS may reach a stage in which the benefits outweigh the costs and it will replace the current system.

Source: Barrero, F., Toral, S., Vargas, M., Cortés, F., & Milla, J. M. (2010). Internet in the development of future road-traffic control systems. Internet Research, 20(2), 154–168.

The Operational Feasibility Study

The purpose of the operational feasibility study is to determine whether the new system will be used as intended. More specifically, this analysis answers the following questions:

- Will the system fit into the culture of this organization?
- Will all the intended users use the system to its full capacity?
- Will the system interfere with company policies or statutory laws?

Organizational culture is an umbrella term referring to the general tone of the corporate environment. This includes issues such as tendency to share or not to share information among units and people, willingness to team-play, and the proclivity of employees to experiment with new ideas and technologies. The development team must consider culture to ensure that the new system will fit the organization. For example, if the system will be used by telecommuters, the organization must be open to telecommunications via the Internet. The analysts must find out whether this need would compromise information security and confidentiality, and implement the proper security measures.

Another point the team considers is compliance with statutory regulations and company policy. For example, the record-keeping system the staff wants to use might violate customer privacy or risk the confidentiality of government contracts with the company. If these issues cannot be overcome at the outset, then the proposed system is not operationally feasible.

Requirements Definition

When the analysts determine that the proposed system is feasible, the project team is assembled. Management or the consulting firm nominates a project leader who puts together a project team to develop the system until it is ready for delivery. The team includes systems analysts, programmers, and, often, representatives from the prospective groups of users.

One of the first pieces of information the analysts need to know is the system requirements. **System requirements** are the functions that the system is expected to fulfill and the features through which it will perform its tasks. In other words, system requirements are what the system should be able to do and the means by which it will fulfill its stated goal. This can be done through interviews, questionnaires, examination of documents, and on-the-job observations. Once facts are gathered, they are organized into a document detailing the system requirements.

The managers of the business unit, or business units, for which the system is to be developed often sign the document as a contract between them and the developers. This formal sign-off is a crucial milestone in the analysis process; if the requirements are not well defined, resources will be wasted or under-budgeted, and the completion of the project will be delayed.

Design

With a comprehensive list of requirements, the project team can begin the next step in systems development, designing the new system. The purpose of this phase is to devise the means to meet all the business requirements detailed in the requirements report. As indicated in Figure 12.6, **systems design** comprises three steps: a description of the components and how they will work, construction, and testing. If the decision is to purchase ready-made software, the description of components details how certain components will be adapted for the particular needs of the purchasing organization, and construction is the actual changes in programming code.

FIGURE **12.6**

Phases in systems design

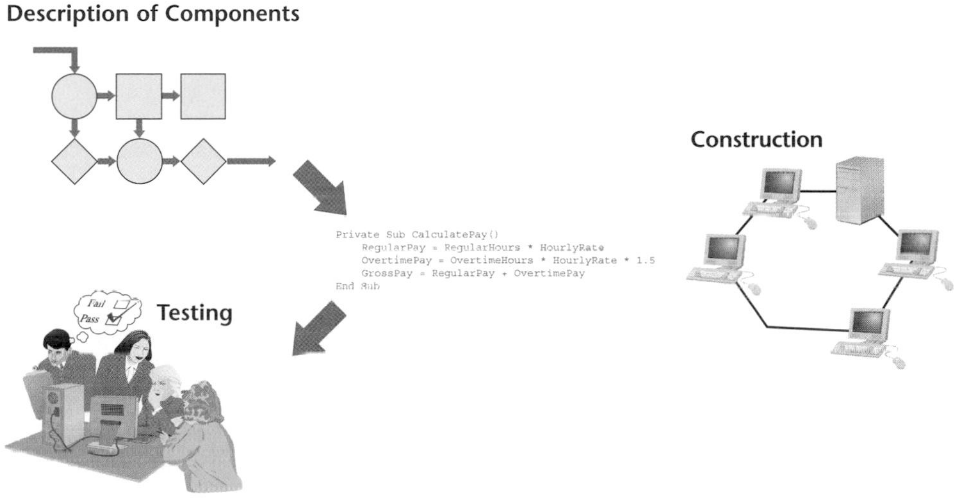

Description of Components

Construction

```
Private Sub CalculatePay()
    RegularPay = RegularHours * HourlyRate
    OvertimePay = OvertimeHours * HourlyRate * 1.5
    GrossPay = RegularPay + OvertimePay
End Sub
```

Testing

Fail
Pass

© Cengage Learning 2015

To communicate ideas about data, processes, and information gleaned from data, systems analysts and programmers use conventional symbols. The advantage of such conventions is that visual information can be grasped much faster and more accurately than text, much as a blueprint for a building conveys specifications more efficiently than the equivalent text. One such convention is the data flow diagram.

Data Flow Diagrams

A **data flow diagram (DFD)** is used to describe the flow of data in a business operation, using only four symbols for these elements: external entities, processes, data stores, and the direction in which data flows (see Figure 12.7). *External entities* include individuals and groups of people who are external to the system, such as customers, employees, other departments in the organization, or other organizations. A *process* is any event or sequence of events in which data is either changed or acted on, such as the processing of data into information or the application of data to decision making. A *data store* is any form of data at rest, such as a filing cabinet or a database. Data flows from an external entity to a process, from a process to a data store, from a data store to a process, and so on. Thus, a carefully drawn DFD can provide a useful representation of a system, whether existing or planned.

FIGURE **12.7**

Data flow diagram (DFD) symbols

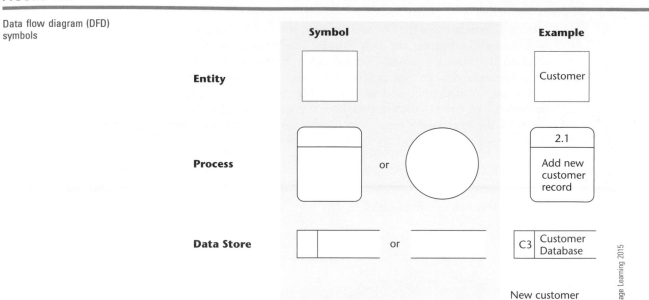

Symbol		Example

The use of only four symbols and the simplicity of DFDs are their great advantage. Often, systems analysts produce several levels of DFDs for a system. The highest level contains the least number of symbols and is the least detailed. A lower level is more detailed; what might be represented only as a general process in the higher level is exploded into several sub-processes and several databases. The lowest-level diagram explodes some processes further and is the most detailed; it shows every possible process, data store, and entity involved. Usually, the first- and second-level diagrams are presented to non-IS executives, and the lowest-level DFD is considered by the IS professionals while they analyze or develop the system.

The DFD in Figure 12.8 shows a process of calculating a sales bonus. A salesclerk is an entity entering data (in this case, salespeople's ID numbers), which flows into a process, namely, the bonus calculation, which also receives data from the salespeople database (in this case, the dollar amount each salesperson sold over the past year). The result of the process, the bonus amount for each salesperson, is information that flows into a bonus file. Later, the company's controller will use the information to generate bonus checks.

FIGURE **12.8**

A data flow diagram to represent a sales bonus system

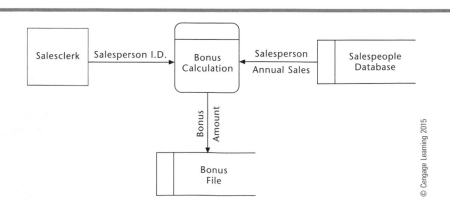

DFD symbols are suitable for describing any IS, even if it is not computer-based. A DFD of the existing system helps pinpoint its weaknesses by describing the flow of data graphically and allowing analysts to pinpoint which processes and databases can be automated, shared by different processes, or otherwise changed to strengthen the IS. If a new IS is needed, a DFD of the conceptualized new system is drawn to provide the logical blueprint for its construction.

While DFDs are easy to learn and use, they have shortcomings—like any diagramming method—and cannot describe a system completely. For example, they do not specify computations within a process or timing relationships among data flows. A payroll DFD, for instance, cannot specify whether employee time sheets are checked as they are submitted or at the end of the week. Such details usually accompany DFDs as text comments.

Unified Modeling Language (UML)

As an increasing number of developed applications became object oriented, a new way to describe desired software was needed. Several diagramming sets were developed by the 1970s, but in the late 1990s a *de facto* standard emerged: **Unified Modeling Language (UML)**. UML is a graphical standard for visualizing, specifying, and documenting software. It helps developers to communicate and logically validate desired features in the design phases of software development projects. It is independent of particular programming languages, but it does provide standard visual symbols and notations for specifying object-oriented elements, such as classes and procedures. It also provides symbols to communicate software that is used for constructing websites and web-based activities, such as selecting items from an online catalog and executing online payments.

UML consists of diagrams that describe the following types of software: use case, class, interaction, state, activity, and physical components. A *use case* is an activity that the system executes in response to a user. A user is referred to as an *actor*. Use case diagrams communicate the relationships between actors and use cases. *Class diagrams* describe class structure and contents and use the three-part symbol for class: name, attributes, and methods (see the example in Chapter 5, Figure 5.4). *Interaction diagrams* describe interactions of objects and the sequence of their activities. *State charts* communicate the states through which objects pass, as well as the objects' responses to signals (called stimuli) they receive. *Activity diagrams* represent highly active states that are triggered by completion of the actions of other states; therefore, they focus on internal processing. *Physical diagrams* are high-level descriptions of software modules. They consist of components diagrams, which describe the software, including source code, compilation, and execution, and deployment diagrams, which describe the configuration of software components when they are executed. Figure 12.9 shows an example of modeling in UML.

© Cengage Learning 2015

FIGURE **12.9**

A sample Unified Modeling Language diagram and its explanation

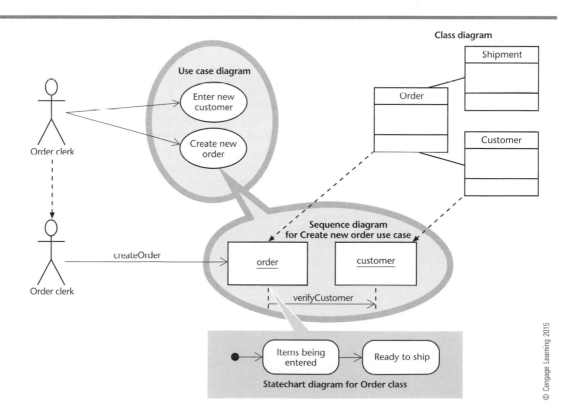

Construction

Once the software development tools are chosen, construction of the system begins. System construction is predominantly programming. Professional programmers translate input, output, and processes, as described in data flow diagrams, into programs. The effort often takes months or even years (in which case the users might not be served well due to changes in business needs). When a program module is completed, it is tested. Testing is performed by way of walk-through and simulation.

In a walk-through, the systems analysts and programmers follow the logic of the program, conduct processes that the system is programmed to execute when running, produce output, and compare output with what they know the results should be. In simulation, the team actually runs the program with the data. When all the modules of the application are completed and successfully tested, the modules are integrated into one coherent program.

System Testing

Although simulation with each module provides some testing, it is important to test the entire integrated system. The system is checked against the system requirements originally defined in the analysis phase by running typical data through the system. The quality of the output is examined, and processing times are measured to ensure that the original requirements are met.

Testing should include attempts to get the system to fail, by violating processing and security controls. The testers should try to "outsmart" the system, entering unreasonable data and trying to access files that should not be accessed directly by some users or—under certain circumstances—by any user. This violation of typical operating rules is a crucial step in the development effort, because many unforeseen snags can be discovered and fixed before the system is introduced for daily use. If the new system passes the tests, it is ready for implementation in the business units that will use it.

Testing tends to be the least respected phase in systems development. Too often project managers who are under time pressure to deliver a new IS either hasten testing or forgo it altogether. Because it is the last phase before delivery of the new system, it is the natural "victim" when time and budget have run out. This rush has caused many failures and, eventually, longer delays than if the system had undergone comprehensive testing. A thorough testing phase might delay delivery, but it drastically reduces the probability that flaws will be discovered only after the new system is delivered.

Implementation

The **implementation** of a new IS, also called delivery, consists of two steps: conversion and training. Although training might precede conversion, if training is done on the job it can occur after conversion. **Conversion** takes place when an operation switches from using an old system to using a new system. Conversion can be a difficult time for an organization. Operators need to get used to new systems, and even though the system might have been thoroughly tested, conversion can hold some unpleasant surprises if bugs or problems have not been discovered earlier. Services to other departments and to customers might be delayed, and data might be lost. Four basic conversion strategies can be employed to manage the transition (see Figure 12.10).

FIGURE **12.10**

Strategies for converting
one IS to another

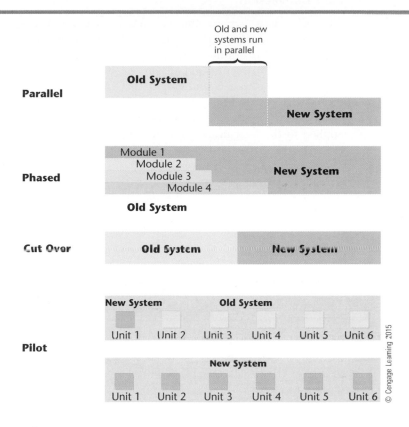

Parallel Conversion

In **parallel conversion**, the old system is used along with the new system for a prede-termined period of time. This duplication minimizes risk because if the new system fails, operations are not stopped and no damage is caused to the organization. However, parallel conversion is costly because of the expenses, especially labor costs, associated with running two systems. It is also labor intensive because users must enter data twice, into the new and old systems. By and large, parallel conversion is rarely used nowadays. When it is, parallel conversion is used for internal applications used only by employees, not customer or business partners.

Phased Conversion

ISs, especially large ones, can often be broken into functional modules and phased into operation one at a time, a process called **phased conversion**. For example, conversion of an accounting IS can be phased, with the accounts receivable module converted first, then the accounts payable, then the general ledger, and so on. A supply chain management system might be implemented one module at a time: first, the customer order module, then the shipment module, then the inventory control module, and so on, up to the collection module. This phased approach also reduces risk, although the benefits of using the entire integrated system are delayed. Also, users can learn how to use one module at a time, which is easier than learning the entire system at once. However, when parts of both systems are used, there might be data inconsistencies between the two.

Cut-Over Conversion

In a **cut-over conversion**—also called **flash cut conversion** or direct conversion, or direct cut-over—the old system is discarded and the new one takes over the entire business operation for which it was developed. This strategy is highly risky, but it can be inexpensive, if successful, because no resources are spent on running two systems in parallel, and the benefits of the entire new system are immediately realized.

Pilot Conversion

In a **pilot conversion**, the new system is introduced for a period of time in a single unit or limited arena, where problems can be addressed and the system can be polished before implementing it in other business units. This trial conversion is also possible for systems shared by many departments and disparate sites, as is increasingly the case due to the growing popularity of intranets and extranets. Obviously, piloting reduces risks because it confines any problems to fewer units. It is especially useful for determining how comfortable staff members and other users, such as suppliers and customers, are with a new system—a lesson that can be applied to the later units. As with the parallel strategy, the pilot strategy means that benefits of the full implementation of the system are delayed.

When a system is developed by a software vendor for a wide market rather than for a specific client, conversion often takes place at beta sites. A **beta site** is an organization whose management agrees to test the new system for several months and provide feedback. (In the Greek alphabet, beta is the second letter. Alpha, the first letter, is used for an Alpha site, the developing organization.)

POINT OF INTEREST   Out of this World Auditing

Training for auditing information systems has reached a whole new level. In one case study, a virtual data center was constructed in the online 3-D world of Second Life and populated with multiple risks and exposures for an organization. Auditing information systems students were to conduct a site visit in Second Life and apply what they had learned about auditing principles to discover these faults and weaknesses. The exercise fulfilled several learning objectives: The students were to be able to demonstrate their general knowledge of physical security of information systems, implement basic principles of IS auditing, demonstrate their knowledge of Institute of Internal Auditors' (IIA) guidelines, develop skill and practice in accessing exposures and their potential consequences on an organization, and more. Afterwards, students were required to present their results in a professional manner as specified by the IIA. Because of their training in the virtual world, students entering this field could be better equipped with the skills and tools they need to be successful in protecting organizations and seeking out threats.

Source: Moscato, D. R., & Boekman, D. M. E. (2010). Using 3-D Virtual Worlds as a Platform for an Experiential Case Study in Information Systems Auditing. Communications of the IIMA, 10(1), 19–26.

Support

The role of IT professionals does not end with delivery of the new system. They must support the system and ensure that users can operate it satisfactorily. **Application systems support** includes two main responsibilities: maintenance and user help. Maintenance consists of post-implementation debugging and updating (making changes and additions), including adding features that were originally desired but later postponed so budget and time limits could be met. Usually, updating is the greater effort.

Debugging is the correction of bugs or problems in programs that were not discovered during tests. Updating is revising the system to comply with changing business needs that occur after the implementation phase. For example, if a company collects personal data for market analysis, managers might want to use the new IS to collect more data, which might require new fields in the databases.

Although maintenance is viewed by IS professionals as lacking in glamour, it should not be taken lightly or left to less-experienced professionals. Company surveys show that up to 80 percent of IS budgets is spent on maintenance, the cost of which varies widely from system to system. The major reason for this huge proportion is that support is the longest phase in a system's life cycle. While development takes several months to about three years, the system is expected to yield benefits over many years.

Efficient and effective system maintenance is possible only if good documentation is created while the system is being developed, and if the code is written in a structured, easy-to-follow manner. Documentation consists of three main types: paper books, electronic documents, and in-program documentation. The latter covers non-executable comments in the code, seen only when reviewing the application's source code. You can see this type of documentation when you retrieve the source code of many webpages. In-program documentation briefly describes what each module of the program does and sometimes who developed it. Printed and electronic documentation is prepared both for programmers, who can better understand how to revise code, and for users who want to learn about the various features of the application.

Agile Methods

While the full approach of the SDLC or similar waterfall methods are used to develop ISs, it is widely recognized that these methods are lengthy, expensive, and inflexible. Systems developed on the SDLC model are often unable to adapt to vague or rapidly changing user requirements. To overcome these challenges, alternative methods have emerged that are collectively called **agile methods**. As Figure 12.11 illustrates, agile methods treat software development as a series of contacts with users, with the goal of fast development of software to satisfy user requirements, and then improving the software shortly after users request modifications. Agile methods make extensive use of iterative programming, involving users often, and keeping programmers open to modifications while development is still under way. The better known methods are Extreme Programming (XP), Adaptive Software Development (ASD), Lean Development (LD), Rational Unified Process (RUP), Feature Driven Development (FDD), Dynamic Systems Development Method (DSDM), Scrum, and Crystal Clear. FDD and DSDM are more structured than other agile methods.

FIGURE **12.11**

Agile methods emphasize continuous improvement based on user requirements

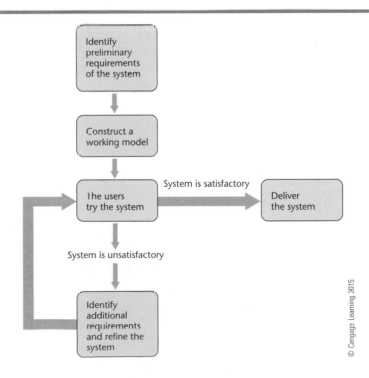

The differences among the methods are outside the scope of this discussion. However, the major advantage of all agile methods is that they result in fast development of applications so that users can have them within weeks rather than months or years. Users do not have to wait long for system modifications, whether they are required because of programmer errors or because users have second thoughts about some features.

However, the benefits of agile methods do not come without risks. First, the analysis phase is minimal or is sometimes eliminated completely. Reducing or skipping a thorough formal analysis increases the risk of incompatibilities and other unforeseen mishaps. Also, the developers devote most of their time to construction and little time to documentation, so modification at a later date can be extremely time consuming, if not impossible. Because of the inherent risks, there are times when agile methods are appropriate and others when they are not (see the discussion later in this section).

Software developers who espouse the approach usually subscribe to the *Manifesto for Agile Software Development* (Anonymous, 2001), which expresses the following priorities: individuals and interactions over processes and tools; working software over comprehensive documentation; customer collaboration over contract negotiation; and responding to change over following a plan. You can find the full Manifesto at *http://agilemanifesto.org/principles.html*. The software developed should primarily satisfy users, not business processes, because users must be satisfied with the applications they use even if that means changing processes. While program documentation is important, it should not come at the expense of well-functioning software, especially when time is limited and the programmers must decide how to allot their time—on better software or on better documentation. The customers of software development, the users, are not an adverse party and should not be negotiated with but regarded as co-developers and co-owners of the software. Plans are good but might stand in the way of necessary changes. Responding to changing user requirements is more important than following a plan. If there is a development plan at all, it is fine to change it often.

All agile methods aim to have "light but sufficient" development processes. Therefore, project teams avoid use of formal project management plans, financial spreadsheets for budgeting, task lists, or any other activity that does not directly contribute to development of a functioning application.

While the SDLC or any other waterfall approach requires users to sign off on their requirements and then wait for the system to be completed, agile methods encourage users' involvement throughout the process and encourage developers to change requirements in response to user input if needed. The purpose of agile methods is not to conform to a static contract with the users but to ensure that the users receive an application with which they are happy. To avoid costly redesign, agile methods encourage developers to test each module as soon as it is complete.

For example, Extreme Programming (XP) includes the following principles: produce the initial software within weeks (rather than months) to receive rapid feedback from users; invent simple solutions so there is less to change and necessary changes are easy to make; improve design quality continually, so that the next "story" is less costly to implement; and test constantly to accomplish earlier, less expensive defect detection. (A *story* is a requirement or set of requirements delivered by the users.) Instead of formal requirements, developers encourage the users to give examples of how they would like to use the application in a certain business situation. Communication with users is highly informal and takes place on a daily basis.

POINT OF INTEREST Participation: the Path to Success

The Copenhagen Business School of Frederiksberg, Denmark conducted an investigative study on the role of the users and customers in an agile software development project. The research was performed as a semi-structured case study and interviews were administered to an assortment of key players including future users and a third of the development team. The findings concluded that the direct and indirect customer and user participation in a structured form of planning games, user stories, and story cards contributed to the success of the final software project. In the planning stages of agile software development, the participation of users and customers is important because they will be the end users of the software and thus, know what the software needs to accomplish to be successful.

Source: Kautz, K. (2011). Investigating the design process: participatory design in agile software development. Information Technology & People, 24(3), 217–235.

Unlike more traditional methods, XP encourages two programmers to work on the same module of code on the same computer. This fosters constructive criticism and feedback. The constant communication between the two coders is meant to ensure cross-fertilization of ideas and high-quality software. The idea is that two minds, working on the same code, create synergy. Two people are more likely to identify bugs than a single person.

Critics of agile programming in general and XP in particular argue that the relaxed approach to planning as well as ceding decision making and accountability to clients (users) might result in disasters, especially if such methods are applied to large, complex projects. The critics cite the DaimlerChrysler payroll system (Chrysler Comprehensive Compensation, known as C3). C3 was the first large application developed with the XP method and was eventually canceled. The software never delivered more than one-fourth of the features it was supposed to have.

On the other hand, supporters give examples of success. One is a system developed by British Airways. The airline believed that information about passengers could be used by in-flight personnel. Instead of relying on paper reports, they developed an iPad app to relay information about club status, ticket class, and dietary requirements to the in-flight crew, which they hoped would increase the level of customer service. Using the agile software development methodology, they deployed iPads to its senior crew members on their routes and released software updates about once a month (Zetlin, 2012).

When to Use Agile Methods

Agile methods are an efficient approach to development when a system is small, when it deals with unstructured problems, and when the users cannot specify all the requirements at the start of the project. They are also useful when developing a user interface: the developers can save time by quickly developing the screens, icons, and menus for users to evaluate instead of forcing the users to provide specifications.

When a system to be developed is small in scale, the risk involved in the lack of thorough analysis is minimal, partly because the investment of resources is small. (A small system is one that serves one person or a small group of employees. A large system is one that serves many employees, who might be accessing the system via a network from different sites.) If the small-system development takes longer than planned, the overall cost is still likely to be smaller than if a full SDLC were performed.

When users cannot communicate their requirements, either because they are not familiar with technological developments or because they find it hard to conceptualize the system's input and output files, processes, and user interface, developers have no choice but to use agile methods. In this case the users are often able to communicate their requirements as the development proceeds. For example, it is easier for marketing personnel to evaluate webpages designed for a new electronic catalog and promotion site than to describe in detail what they want before seeing anything. Without being shown actual examples, users often can offer little guidance beyond "I will know it when I see it." It is easier for future users to respond to screens, menus, procedures, and other features developed by IT professionals than to provide a list of requirements for them.

When Not to Use Agile Methods

Agile methods might not be appropriate for all systems development. If a system is large or complex, or if it is designed to interface with other systems, using agile methods might pose too great a risk because the methods skip feasibility studies. Some experts do not recommend the use of agile methods for large systems (with the possible exception of Crystal, which accommodates scalable software development) because such systems require a significant investment of resources; therefore, system failure could entail considerable financial loss. The systematic approach of the SDLC is recommended if the system is complex and consists of many modules, because extra care must be applied in documenting requirements and the manner in which components will be integrated, to ensure smooth and successful development.

For the same reasons, use of agile methods should be avoided when a system is to be interfaced with other systems. The system requirements and integration must be analyzed carefully, documented, and carried out according to a plan agreed on by the users and developers before the design and construction phases start. This early consensus reduces the risk of incompatibility and damage to other, existing systems. Therefore, accounting ISs, large order-entry systems, and payroll systems as whole systems are rarely developed under agile methods. Other factors that should encourage use of waterfall methods are the size of the development team, how often the application is expected to be modified, how critical it is in terms of affecting people's lives and key organizational goals, and how tight the development budget is.

An additional risk with any type of prototyping is the difference between visible and nonvisible features of the software. Users tend to judge software by its visible elements and be less concerned about features such as database integrity, security measures, and other invisible but important elements. They may discover too late that some features are either missing or do not function to their satisfaction.

Figure 12.12 summarizes factors in deciding when and when not to use agile methods.

FIGURE **12.12**

Characteristics for deciding to use (or not use) agile methods

When to use agile methods	When not to use agile methods
Small-scale system	Large-scale system
System solving unstructured problems	Complex system
When it's difficult for users to specify system requirements	System with interfaces to other systems
When the development team is small and co-located	When the team is large or distributed in multiple sites
System requirements are dynamic	System requirements are fairly static
System will not put people and critical organization goals at risk	System will significantly affect people's well-being and critical organizational goals
Development project budget is tight	Development is well-funded

© Cengage Learning 2015

Outsourcing

Outsourcing is steadily being used by organizations to maximize their value as well as reduce costs. **Outsourcing** is the formal business relationship to transfer internal business processes and functions to a third-party business. IDC expects that the business process outsourcing market will reach $202 billion worldwide by 2016, with the U.S market reaching $92 billion (Anonymous, 2012a). IDC has found that many of the vendors providing these services will focus on process solutions relating to information technology such as business analytics, bid data, and cloud delivery. At the same time, IDC also found that the expansion of outsourcing services has created extreme competition, causing some businesses to reduce the number of service providers that they use (Anonymous, 2012b).

Many industries and businesses seek third-party outsourcing vendors to create efficiencies. Ferro Corporation, a supplier of performance materials and chemicals, wanted to improve operational efficiencies, reduce costs while creating value (Anonymous, 2013). Ferro contracted with Capgemini to provide a variety of information technology and business process outsourcing services expected to return $70 million of operational cost savings through 2014. Capgemini will support Ferro's enterprise-wide SAP environment as well as oversee its global finance and accounting processes.

Universities and even governments have followed the private sector to embrace outsourcing processes and functions. Accenture is helping the University of Michigan by analyzing its finance and human resource operations to develop a business case for a shared services delivery model. Yale University is also receiving assistance from Accenture to expand its shared services organization's various institutional functions as well as create a grant management function for its College of Arts and Sciences (Anonymous, 2011).

Outsourcing initiatives can fail. In 2010, UBS Global Asset Management found it was relying on older technology (Steinert-Threlkeld, 2012). They did not want to develop a new system, and replacing the system with a purchased alternative was estimated to take five years, so they considered outsourcing with the appealing "no cost" (incremental) approach. They requested information from a variety of outsourcing companies. They believed that the annual operating costs, even including the outsourcer's fee, would result in a cost-neutral proposal. Even with these benefits, however, UBS never announced their choice for outsourcing the system. The reason for the reversal? UBS realized the importance of retaining the privacy of their data, and the control of storing it internally. When they realized they needed to design a method of anonymizing the data so that no client information would be maintained by outsourced systems, they found that the business case "started to deteriorate" and was simply not worth it.

POINT OF INTEREST — Smart IT Outsourcing

Although outsourcing may sound engaging and simplistic, it must be approached with proper planning and analysis. Sometimes outsourcing IT functions is not a good idea. Some industry experts contend that businesses can, and should consider, outsourcing functions that are not associated with their core competencies. The authors of *The Discipline of Market Leaders* believe that organizations must establish their competency in one of three areas: product and innovation leadership, customer service and intimacy, or operational excellence; and should not try to excel at all three.

Some, like J. Ditmore, believe that information technology is crucial to all three areas. The tight and fundamental integration to these competencies should not be compared to other organizational functions such as security or legal. Business organizations must retain control over their intellectual properties and business functions that provide strategic value for their stakeholders. Even when outsourcing, businesses should always retain and develop the key design and management internally.

Sources: Ditmore, J. (2012). Why IT Outsourcing Often Fails. InformationWeek(1339), 5–6; Treacy, M., & Wiersema, F. (1997). The Discipline of Market Leaders: Choose Your Customers, Narrow Your Focus, Dominate Your Market. Jackson, TN: Basic Books.

Project Planning and Management Tools

Several tools exist to help plan and manage development projects. Some of the tools encompass planning and managing the development of many ISs. IBM's Rational Project Coordinator is software that helps organizations plan investment in a new system, and then plan and manage the development project and delivery. All who are involved in the projects can track the progress and the sums spent on resources. Similarly, Oracle's Primavera P6 provides integrated **project portfolio management** (PPM) software. Project portfolio management is a set of processes and methods used by project managers to determine which projects will meet the organization's operational and financial goals in relation to its strategic objectives as well as the needs of its customers. As discussed in Chapter 2, organizations strive to find that perfect mix of projects that fulfill their strategic and tactical goals.

While some tools, such as Rational Project Coordinator, are geared to help with software development projects, others, such as Clarizen, Project Insight, AtTask, Microsoft Project, and many others, are designed to accommodate planning and management of any type of project. These software products plan and track the progress of project execution in order to reduce or eliminate time and cost overruns. As shown in the illustration of AtTask project management software on the next page, a Gantt chart depicts the effort, schedule, and status of a series of tasks on a project. A Gantt chart is an efficient and visual method of understanding the interrelationships between tasks (predecessors and successors) and the effort required to complete the task.

AtTask project
management software
helps plan and control the
costs, schedule, and
resources of projects

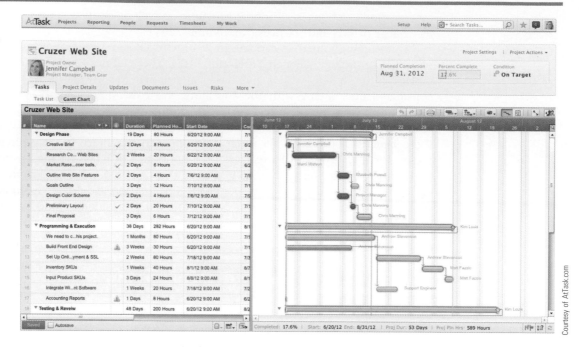

Courtesy of AtTask.com

Systems Integration

Firms often must wrestle with highly distributed, heterogeneous environments populated with applications for special tasks, which cannot be accessed by systems used for other tasks. Often, the disparate systems cannot "talk to each other" because they run on different operating systems (or, as IS professionals say, on different platforms).

Much of what IT professionals do is systems integration, rather than analysis and development of a stand-alone IS. **Systems integration** looks at the information needs of an entire organization, or at least of a major division of it. The analysts consider the existing, but often disparate, ISs and then produce a plan to integrate them so that data can flow more easily among different units of the organization and users can access different types of data via a single interface. Consequently, many IS service companies call themselves systems integrators. Systems integration has become increasingly important mainly because more and more ISs are linked to websites, because more legacy databases are integrated into new enterprise applications such as SCM and ERP systems, and because of the growing linking of ISs between organizations (see Figure 12.13). *Legacy systems* are older systems that organizations decide to continue to use because the investment in a new system would not justify the improved features, or because the old systems have some advantage that cannot be obtained from newer systems. In addition, with the rapid adoption of smartphones, social media, and tablets, existing legacy systems need to be integrated into these new customer-centric systems.

FIGURE **12.13**

Organizational initiatives requiring system integration

- Linking existing ISs to websites, smartphones, and tablet applications
- Linking databases to websites, smartphones, and tablet applications
- Linking legacy databases with enterprise applications
- Integrating legacy systems with new systems
- Integrating media content (videos) and social media into existing websites
- Sharing information systems and data among organizations and trading partners

© Cengage Learning 2015

Systems integration is often more challenging than systems development. In fact, some IT professionals regard systems development as a subspecialty of systems integration because the integrator must develop systems with an understanding of how data maintained in disparate systems can be efficiently retrieved and used for effective business processes, and because legacy systems must often be interfaced with recently acquired systems.

For example, marketing managers can have richer information for decision making if they have easy access to accounting and financial data through their own marketing IS. The better the integration, the better they can incorporate this information into their marketing information.

POINT OF INTEREST   Want to Be Certified?

If you are willing to take the test, you can add one or several of the following titles to your name: CCP, CBIP, CSIH, CDMP, ISA, ACP, CITC, CITCP, CITGP ISP. The Institute for Certification of Computer Professionals tests IT professionals and provides them with certificates. To see the goals of this not-for-profit organization and how the certification process is carried out, as well as what these acronyms stand for, visit www.iccp.org. Similarly, those interested in achieving the Project Management Professional (PMP) credential should investigate more on the Project Management Institute's site: *http://www.pmi.org/default .aspx* or computer security certification (CSIH) at *http://www.cert.org/certification/*.

Sources: Anonymous. (2012). Eligibility for Certification. Retrieved March 28, 2013, from http://iccp. org/certification/becoming-certified/eligibility; Anonymous. (2013). Project Management Professional (PMP). Retrieved March 28, 2013, from http://www.pmi.org/Certification/Project-Management-Professional-PMP.aspx

Systems integrators must also be well-versed in hardware and software issues, because different ISs often use incompatible hardware and software. Often, overcoming incompatibility issues is one of the most difficult aspects of integration. Consider business intelligence systems, which were discussed in Chapter 11, "Business Intelligence and Knowledge Management." The concept of extracting business intelligence from large data warehouses often involves integration of several ISs. The challenges are significant, and by some estimates more than half of all BI projects are never completed or fail to deliver all the expected features and benefits.

Systems integration has become increasingly complex because it now involves the ISs not only of a single organization but of several organizations. In the era of extranets, the challenge is many times more difficult because IT professionals must integrate systems of several different companies so that they can communicate and work well using telecommunications. Imagine how difficult it is to integrate disparate legacy systems of several companies. For this reason, companies often contract with highly experienced experts for such projects.

When organizations commit millions of dollars to developing systems, they count on IT professionals to provide high-quality systems that will fulfill their intended purposes without harming their businesses, their employees, or their consumers. But the products of IT professionals often fail and cause serious damage. Some people argue that because of the high investment and high risk usually associated with systems development and operation, IT professionals, like other professionals, should be certified. These people argue that certification would minimize problems caused by ISs. Others argue that certification might stifle free competition and innovation, or even create a profession whose members will make it difficult to pass certification examinations so that current members can continue to enjoy high income.

Certification is meant to guarantee that the experts have passed tests that ensure their skills. The government or other authorized bodies are expected to license experts, thereby certifying which people have knowledge and skills in a particular discipline that are significantly greater than those of a layperson. Proponents of the measure argue that certification could reduce the malfunctioning of ISs.

Certification Pros. Some experts say certification could minimize the number and severity of IS malfunctions. Civil engineers must be certified to plan buildings and bridges. Doctors pass rigorous exams before they receive their licenses and begin to practice without supervision. Public accountants must be licensed to perform audits. Lawyers must pass the bar exams to practice. Why, these people ask, should IS professionals be allowed to practice without licensing?

Software experts do possess all the characteristics of professionals. They work in a field that requires expertise, and the public and their clients usually are not qualified to evaluate their skills. Certification could help the following groups in their relationships with IT specialists:

- *Employers* often hire software professionals without knowing what they are getting. They count on the information included in the candidate's résumé and, sometimes, on letters of recommendation. Mandatory certification might protect potential employers against charlatans. Also, certification would provide potential employers with information on a candidate's suitability for different levels of performance. For example, a professional might be qualified to participate in a systems development team but not to head the project team.

- *Clients* could realize even greater benefit from mandatory certification. While employers can learn, in time, of the real capabilities of their personnel, businesses that hire consultants have no previous employment experience on which to rely.

- *Society* might enjoy fewer software-related failures. Only those who are qualified would be allowed to engage in development and maintenance of information systems, thereby improving the overall integrity of ISs. Certification is especially needed for those holding key development positions for systems whose impact on society is significant, such as medical ISs and software embedded in weapons systems.

Certification Cons. Three arguments are raised against mandatory certification:

- It is difficult, if not impossible, to devise a way to measure software development competence. For instance, there are many different methods for developing applications, and there is no proven advantage of one over another. A computer professional might be very experienced in one method but not in others. It would be unfair to disqualify that individual merely on this basis.

- Some argue that mandatory certification might create a "closed shop" by using a single entry exam designed to admit very few people. In such a scenario, the status and income of those admitted would be enhanced at the expense of those excluded. With little fear of competition within the closed group, there is often little incentive to improve skills.

- IT progresses very fast, faster than many other fields. Ensuring that a specialist knows how to use certain information technologies and methods today does not ensure that this person will know how to use technologies and methods two years from now. This person's knowledge may be obsolete and render the certificate useless.

Where We Operate Now. Mandatory certification or licensing of IT professionals is rare. Only Texas, British Columbia, and Ontario require licensing of software development professionals. In fact, the industry cannot reach agreement about who should be considered an IT professional. Some organizations, such as the Institute for Certification of Computer Professionals (ICCP), test and certify people who voluntarily take their tests. (About 55,000 people have been certified by ICCP globally, out of millions who consider themselves IT professionals.) Some software companies certify analysts and programmers to install their companies' tools. However, there are no certification regulations for IT professionals in the United States or anywhere else that are similar to those for many other professions.

The increasing issues and challenges associated with computer security have also created related certifications for

IT professionals. The CERT program (at Carnegie Mellon) offers the computer security incident handler (CSIH) certification to help security, system, and network administrators to gain knowledge and training to avert security intrusions and other malicious acts.

Importance of Certifications. A study completed by CompTIA finds that certifications are important when hiring information technology professionals. A significant number of hiring managers (64 percent) consider certifications as a "high value" to validate information technology skills. The study posits that these certifications will continue to grow as employers recruit technology professionals. However, the study also reports that human resources departments do not completely understand technology-based certifications. IT hiring managers believe that education and certifications rank high when reviewing applicants for information technology positions.

Source: Anonymous. (2011, Feb 07). IT Certifications Grow in Importance in Hiring Process, but Employers Challenged by Evaluation, Validation Issues, CompTIA Study Finds, Business Wire.

Summary

- IT planning is important especially because investing in IT is typically substantial and because of the high risk in implementing enterprise applications.

- Standardization is often an important part of IT planning. Standardization helps save costs, provides efficient training, and results in efficient support.

- The systems development life cycle (SDLC) and other waterfall methods consist of well-defined and carefully followed phases: analysis, design, implementation, and support.

- The purpose of systems analysis is to determine what needs the system will satisfy.

- Feasibility studies determine whether developing the system is possible and desirable from a number of viewpoints. The technical feasibility study examines the technical state of the art to ensure that the hardware and software exist to build the system. The economic feasibility study weighs the benefits of the system against its cost. The operational feasibility study determines whether the system will fit the organizational culture and be used to full capacity.

- System requirements detail the features the users need in the new system.

- In systems design, developers outline the systems components graphically and construct the software. Tools such as data flow diagrams and the Unified Modeling Language (UML) are used to create a model of the desired system.

- When the system is completed, it is implemented. Implementation includes training and conversion from the old system to the new system. Conversion can take place by one of several strategies: parallel, phased, cut-over, or piloting.

- The systems life cycle continues in the form of support. The system is maintained to ensure operability without fault and satisfaction of changing business needs.

- Agile methods are a popular alternative to the traditional systems development life cycle. Agile methods place considerable emphasis on flexible requirements and frequent interaction with users. These methods skip detailed systems analysis and aim at delivering a new application in the shortest possible time.

- Several applications help plan and manage development projects. Some are geared toward planning and management of software development. Some are web-based, allowing remote access.

- Systems integration is often much more complicated than systems development, because it requires the IT professionals to make different applications communicate with each other seamlessly. The complexity is multiplied when integrating ISs of several organizations that must work together over the web.

- Because of the major responsibility of IS professionals, the question of whether certification is needed has come up. If doctors, civil engineers, lawyers, and public accountants are subject to mandatory certification, many people argue that IS professionals should be, too.

KIMBALL'S REVISITED

Tyler met with Becky at the new location. He explained his vision of the new loyalty program. After listening to him, she began to convey her thoughts and questions. She separated the issues and challenges of the new program into two categories: functional and technological.

Functional

- How would the structure of the program work? How would it incentivize or create loyalty?
- Would customers be incentivized by dining only? What about takeout? Bakery?
- What could customers receive for their loyalty?
- What data is needed to support the structure of the program?

Technological

- For the data needed to support the new system, what is already processed and stored by the current POS?
- Does the POS system support data access by external systems? Does the database support open access or is it proprietary?
- For the data not maintained by the POS system, how would it be created and updated?

Tyler was fairly overwhelmed by the questions, even though he knew they were all reasonable. He said "Geez, I didn't realize planning an information system was so complex. I thought that you could just build it with 'wizards'. I thought it was more technical. I now know it isn't." However, he was pleased that he took a "step back" to analyze the problem first. Becky said, "Look Tyler, this is not rocket science. But you need the answers to these questions to build a solid system, fulfill what you want to achieve, and reduce your risk."

What Is Your Advice?

1. Using the information on structuring data (marketing, financial, and operational) from Chapter 11, define how the structure and functional issues would frame the design of the Kimball's information system.

2. It is clear that the POS system does not maintain enough customer information to support the new loyalty system. Analyze this challenge and provide a recommendation to overcome it.

New Perspectives

1. Consider the various hardware components from Chapter 4. What types of hardware devices could be used to implement this system?

2. If the POS system allowed for open access to its database, how would this affect the design of the new system and minimize data entry on the part of the wait staff?

Key Terms

agile methods, 403
application systems support, 402
beta site, 402
change management, 389
conversion, 400
cost/benefit analysis, 394
cut-over conversion (flash cut conversion), 401
data flow diagram (DFD), 397
feasibility studies, 394
implementation, 400

mission statement, 388
organizational culture, 396
outsourcing, 406
parallel conversion, 401
phased conversion, 401
pilot conversion, 402
progressive elaboration, 391
project portfolio management, 407
prototyping, 391
return on investment (ROI), 394

system requirements, 396
systems analysis, 392
systems design, 397
systems development life cycle (SDLC), 391
systems integration, 408
total cost of ownership (TCO), 394
Unified Modeling Language (UML), 399

Review Questions

1. Why is IT planning so important?

2. As part of their IT planning, many organizations decide to standardize. What does standardization mean in this context, and what are its potential benefits?

3. Why is traditional systems development referred to as a "cycle"? What determines the cycle's end?

4. Systems developers often use the term "application development" rather than "systems development." Why?

5. What are the benefits of using data flow diagrams? Who benefits from DFDs?

6. SDLC is usually recommended for developing an IS that interfaces with other ISs. Give two examples of an IS that is interfaced with at least two other ISs.

7. Recall the discussion of IT professionals in Chapter 1, "Business Information Systems: An Overview." Of the following professionals, who does the majority of the systems construction job: the CIO, systems analyst, database administrator (DBA), or programmer? Why?

8. What are the advantages of agile methods over waterfall development methods, such as the traditional SDLC? What are the risks?

9. Are agile methods more important in today's business environment? Why or why not?

10. Why are agile methods so helpful when users cannot define system requirements?

11. An increasing number of IS professionals prefer to call the end users of their creations "customers," even if the developers and users are employees of the same organization. Why?

12. What is systems integration?

13. Why is systems integration more complicated when the systems involve the web than when they do not? Smartphones? Tablets?

14. The emergence of the web, social media, and mobile devices as vehicles for business increased the need for systems integration. How so?

Discussion Questions

15. The modern view of systems development is that it should be a continuation of IS planning. Why?

16. Consider a new chain of shoe stores. The marketing department of the corporation would like to know the customers and their preferences. What questions would you ask before developing an IS for data collection and analysis?

17. The analysis phase of systems development includes fact finding. Suggest ways to find facts, other than the ways mentioned in this chapter.

18. In data flow diagrams, a process is always labeled with an action, while entities and data stores are labeled with nouns. Why? Give two examples for each of these elements.

19. You are asked to recommend a conversion strategy for a new accounts receivable system. The system will be used only by the controller's office. Which strategy will you recommend, and why?

20. You are asked to recommend a conversion strategy for a new ERP system that includes accounting, sales, purchasing, and payroll modules. Which strategy will you recommend, and why?

21. What are the elements that make the responsibilities of IT professionals similar to those of other professionals, such as engineers and financial analysts?

22. Many software companies (such as Microsoft, Oracle, and SAP) certify people as consultants for their products. For instance, you might become a certified SAP R/3 Technical Consultant. Is this type of certification the same, in principle, as the certification of a physician, lawyer, or certified public accountant (CPA)? Explain.

23. Suppose you are the IT director for a hospital. You have a small crew that helps the medical and administrative staffs with their computers and applications, but when a new system must be developed, you must hire IT professionals. How would you conduct your search for reliable IS developers? Whom would you contact, and what questions would you ask?

24. You are the CIO for a large university hospital. The medical staff of the cardiac ward would like to build an expert system for diagnosis. Your preliminary review shows that the financial

investment would be considerable. What questions do you ask (of both the doctors and your staff) to decide whether to use a thorough SDLC or agile methods to develop the system? List and explain your questions.

25. You are trying to explain to your supervisor the general details of a proposed IS. The IS involves a server connecting many PCs. Your supervisor is not an IS professional and has no idea what a DFD is. How would you prefer to communicate your ideas: verbally; in writing, but without diagrams; with a DFD; or with a combination of some or all of these means? Explain your choice.

26. During development of a new IS, professional jargon might facilitate communication among IS professionals, but it might be detrimental when used to communicate with users. Explain.

Applying Concepts

27. Prepare a 10-minute software-based presentation (use PowerPoint or another application) to make a presentation on the topic: "Factors that have made IS planning difficult over the past five years." Include in your presentation developments in hardware, software, and telecommunications; globalization; the Internet; the IT labor force; and any other area that has had an impact on IT planning.

28. You were hired as an IS consultant by a small chain of stores that rents domestic appliances. Partly because operations are run with paper records, one store does not know what is going on in the other stores. The president of this small company thinks that the chain doesn't utilize its inventory efficiently. For example, if a customer needs a lawnmower and the appliance is not available in store A, the salespeople cannot tell the customer if the mower is available at another outlet or offer to bring it for the customer from

another outlet. The president would like an IS that would allow the chain to serve the customers better and that would help with tracking and billing, too. She would like to take advantage of the web to help both employees and customers. Both should know what is available for rent and at which store at any given time. List the questions you would ask in your fact-finding effort and indicate who in the organization would be asked each question.

29. Assume you are the leader of a team that has just completed construction of a website that provides information but also allows online purchasing of your company's products. Enumerate and explain the steps you would take to test the system. Prepare a software-based presentation (using PowerPoint or a similar application) to explain all the testing steps and why each must be taken. (*Hint*: Keep in mind different operating systems, web browsers, screen sizes, and so forth.)

Hands-On Activities

30. Prepare a DFD that describes the following application: Gadgets, Inc. sells its items through traveling salespeople. When a salesperson receives a signed contract from a client, he or she enters the details into a notebook computer. The salesperson later transmits the record to the company's mainframe computer at its headquarters. The program records the details in four files: sales, shipping, accounts receivable, and commissions. If the buyer is a new customer (one who is not yet in the customer database), the program enters

the customer's record into the customer database and generates a thank-you letter. The program also calculates the 4 percent commission, which is recorded in the commission file with the salesperson's code. At the end of the month, the program produces a paper report with the records of all the new customers. In addition, if the total monthly sales of the salesperson exceed $300,000, the program generates a congratulatory letter showing that total. If the total is less than $10,000, the program produces a letter showing the total and the sentence: "Try harder next month."

31. Find a business organization that provides a multi-level (in-house, mobile, web, tablet, social media) approach to the delivery of information systems. Compile some research to outline the various activities and functions that this organization provides to its customers. Create a diagram illustrating all of the various components of the organization's information technology offerings and how they interact with the "central" information system (data, functions, etc.). Compile a report describing the integration.

Team Activities

32. Team up with another student. Each of you should select a different agile method from the list appearing in this chapter. Each should write a one-page summary of the principles, benefits, and shortcomings of the method. Then, sit together and write a one-page summary of the differences between the two methods along the three points.

33. Team up with another student to search the web for tools that facilitate software development, and choose three tools. List the features provided in each of the tools. Assume that the vendors' claims are true. Which phases and activities of the systems development life cycle does each tool support? Which would you prefer to use in systems development? Why? Prepare a 5-minute software-based presentation (using PowerPoint or a similar application) to present your findings and explain your recommendations.

Change for the Sake of Change?

The word *change* does not usually evoke comfortable feelings or create a warm impression. When change is mentioned in business organizations, it often creates anxiety or, in its worst case, resentment or opposition. Change can be implemented in many ways: through imposition or edict; consensually or democratically; gradually or precipitously. The approach or tone of the execution of change is as important as the basis for change itself.

Consider the example of Chesterfield County, Virginia and employee timecard entry. The County, consisting of 3,000 employees and 600 supervisors, embarked on the implementation of a new online system for employees to enter their timecard data. The timecard entry process involved approximately 60 timekeepers.

The County replaced several legacy systems with the new online system. The new system combined two systems: an internally developed time and attendance system and an "off the shelf" payroll and human resources system. The challenges of the new information technology system extended beyond its technology components: Employees would have to learn a new process of entering their hours into the system and being paid. System developers often forget to assess how familiar the system's stakeholders are with the computer and other skills they would need to use the new system, but County administrators knew they needed a sensible and reasonable approach to manage the change. A well-developed information system without an appropriately planned implementation with its stakeholders can often fail.

The County created a team to manage the change to the new system and develop a change management strategy. The team used several methodologies to ensure that stakeholders were involved throughout the implementation, communicating with key department personnel to "build on existing processes, drawing up communication plans and creating a well-thought-out training plan." The team was comprised of several managers from the various financial, operational, and payroll functional departments as well as their local educational institution, Chesterfield University.

From this team, they established a communication process to connect with customer departments. This network was responsible for determining training needs, analyzing a security procedure, coordinating training, and gaining valuable input from the various stakeholders. Ultimately, the goal of this process was to maintain the lines of communication among the employees and other stakeholders. The process involved not simply words, but also actions. In addition, since quality training was an important component of the system rollout, the Information Systems department worked closely with Chesterfield University to develop and conduct training sessions as well as to provide technical assistance to support employees through the installation.

An essential component of change management is to gain acceptance by the system's stakeholders. The County understood that appropriate communication would help gain acceptance and reduce employee anxiety. The final version of the communication plan changed "substantially" from the initial version. As input was received and evaluated, so did the methods and approach to how and what they communicated. Constant and interactive communication through newsletters, emails, surveys, meetings and an intranet site provided timely and constant information flow.

Over 300 issues were reported and tracked during the first parallel test run of the new system. A total of four system changes were approved to be implemented, resolving 285 issues, with only seven issues unresolved before the second parallel test. At the final implementation, the employees successfully used the new timecard system with only six payroll checks processed in error for the first payroll period.

Sources: Brown, P. J. (2013). Change Management Makes the Difference in Chesterfield County. *Government Finance Review,* 29(1), 60–62.

Thinking About the Case

1. Consider the statement "A well-developed information system without an appropriately planned implementation with its stakeholders can often fail." Why? Provide examples and details.

2. The County's initial approach to assembling their plan for change was a critical factor to the success of the implementation. Taking the role of a County employee, discuss how the County's approach would reduce anxiety as well as create an environment for success with the new information system.

3. Communication is a critical factor to any new initiative and to change management. Does too much communication adversely affect an initiative? Why or why not?

4. Considering the 300 issues that arose during the parallel pilot, did the change management system work effectively? Should the number of issues have been less? Discuss your position.

Video Apps Changing the Status Quo of Television

Video app development has rapidly expanded in recent years due in great part to the explosive sales of mobile tablets and smartphones. In fact, the desire for video apps has spread and apps are being created for set-top-boxes and other connected devices. Three companies are making some noise with their newly developed and successful video applications. Their main mission: reach more people, on more devices, more quickly.

SyncTV is an online video streaming company backed by television manufacturers. It delivers a live and on-demand pay TV service to a connected device. Devices can include Macs, PCs, connected TVs, Blu-ray players, iPods, iPads, Android devices, Roku and Boxee boxes, and more. SyncTV has built the infrastructure to support as many Netflix-type channels as the market desires. They are a small company but have high output. Their automated workflow ingests and reformats content on the fly so it can be appropriately distributed to specified devices. SyncTV's initial purpose was to provide an option for TV watchers to get the content they desire while circumventing the traditional cable companies. An added benefit is that subscribers get access to their favorite shows wherever they are connected to the Internet, instead of just at their home. Users subscribe to only the channels they want from content providers. As long as users have a TV with an IP address, SyncTV will work. No cable or satellite connections are required–just TV when, where, and what you like.

Brightcove is a B2B video app that is similar to YouTube but includes additional expertise and analytics. Brightcove's app VideoCloud has device detection so it can format content to the screen size of a device whether it is a PC, Mac, tablet, or smartphone. Brightcove is a total platform for developing, deploying, and operating mobile content apps. Businesses can design an entire website and place their videos, connected to Brightcove VideoCloud, on the site. Businesses outsource video hosting to Brightcove and embed videos on their own page while Brightcove provides the specialized engineering to get their customers' content delivered to multiple devices. Brightcove has made its niche through providing this multi-platform service along with real-time analytics and data about clients' videos. VideoCloud was designed and built from the perspective of a web developer and includes the App Cloud Workshop app, so video developers can use tools with which they are already familiar. Brightcove's VideoCloud has become a relied upon asset to businesses with an online presence.

HBO GO is the mobile platform for HBO Premium and the baby of the HBO app family. The app is offered to all HBO subscribers at no extra cost. Released in April of 2011, the app was being used by only 10 percent of HBO's subscriber base. By the end of the month, 80 percent had begun using the app. HBO GO is accessible through mobile devices including laptops, iPads, iPhones, iPods, and Android devices, as well as Macs and PCs. HBO has huge brand recognition, premium content, and a large customer base, which is why offering a mobile app for their content was deemed a superior way to increase their bottom line. HBO makes it convenient for customers to watch what they want, when they want, and where they want. One challenge they faced was that content had to be suitable for a wide range of bandwidth—low-bandwidth to high-definition depending on the device on which the app was being used. By focusing on exceptional consumer experience and developing new platforms for delivering that experience, HBO has successfully built a video app that is attractive to new and existing users.

With the advances in video technology, what's in store for the future? The motivations that drove the technologies we have today include providing content to as many devices as possible and to as many people as possible. It is likely that this theme will expand in the future. More devices, like game consoles and Blu-ray players, will continue to be added as platforms to deliver video apps. App stores created by TV manufacturers such as Samsung, LG, and Vizio will become more popular platforms for video apps. It is also likely that the success of video apps such as SyncTV and HBO GO may force changes in traditional cable and satellite TV distribution models.

Sources: Anonymous. (2013a). Brightcove. Retrieved March 29, 2013, from http://www.synctv.com/; Anonymous. (2013c). SyncTv. Television. Unleashed; Klejna, T. (2011). The App's the Thing. Streaming Media Magazine, 40–42, 44, 46–47.

Thinking About the Case

1. How does the information technology development for video-based businesses differ from traditional businesses?

2. What challenges do these types of companies face in relation to the rapid changes in consumer adoption of hardware devices?

3. How do the technological changes to these devices affect the planning and development of these companies?

4. Discuss the changes to consumer media viewing patterns from video app technology. Will television be outdated? Will the Internet be able to support this technology if adoption increases?

References

Anonymous. (2001). Manifesto for Agile Software Development. Retrieved March 27, 2013, from http://agilemanifesto.org/iso/en/

Anonymous. (2011, Mar 28). Accenture Helping U.S. Universities Target Administrative Efficiency, *Business Wire*.

Anonymous. (2012a, May 16). Global Business Process Outsourcing Market to Reach $202.6 billion in 2016, *PR Newswire*.

Anonymous. (2012b, Nov 28). New IDC Report Analyzes Profitability Trends in the Worldwide Services Market, Assisting Service Vendors in Their Strategic Planning Process, *Business Wire*.

Anonymous. (2013). Ferro Chooses Capgemini for Global Delivery of Business Process and Information Technology Outsourcing Services. *Entertainment Close-Up*.

Steinert-Threlkeld, T. (2012). No Surefire Success When Outsourcing. *Money Management Executive*, *20*(23), 1-n/a.

Yeo, V. (2010, June 24). Standardization floats HP's next wave of services growth. http://www.zdnet.com/standardization-floats-hps-next-wave-of-services-growth-2062200998/

Zetlin, M. (2012). British Airway's iPad App Improves Customer Service. *Computerworld*, *46*(2), 16.

© ChameleonsEye/Shutterstock.com

CHOICES IN SYSTEMS ACQUISITION

Learning Objectives

Developing systems, in-house or hiring a software development firm, is the most expensive way to acquire ISs. Other alternatives might be less expensive and offer different benefits. Some of the alternatives have been mentioned in previous chapters, but they are discussed in more depth here and will provide a deeper understanding of systems acquisition.

When you finish this chapter, you will be able to:

- Explain the differences among the alternatives to tailored system development, which include outsourcing, licensing ready-made software, using software as a service, and encouraging users to develop their own applications.

- List the business trade-offs inherent in the various methods of acquiring systems.

- Describe which systems acquisition approach is appropriate for a particular set of circumstances.

- Discuss organizational policies on employee computer use.

KIMBALL'S RESTAURANT: Technology for Customer Loyalty

Tyler and Becky have met and made significant progress on the design of the customer loyalty system. They have explored many of the options associated with the hardware, data requirements, and any system integration that may be needed with the current point-of-sale system. They are confident that they have documented the requirements well in order to move forward.

Tyler believes strongly that the new system is crucial to the success of the Lakeside location to incentivize current customers to continue their loyalty as well as build a "buzz" for new customers. The new menu and expanded hours, as well as the picturesque location, are a solid foundation. Now Tyler believes the "word of mouth" approach needs to be expanded with a solid marketing promotion campaign coupled with a new logo for the Lakeside.

Being More Mobile

Becky and Tyler discussed how to proceed. Then, she thought of a related initiative. "Tyler, have you thought of how a mobile app would add to your new location?" He thought, "How could I have missed that?!" Then, he sighed. "Is this too much to accomplish too soon?" They took a piece of paper and started to plan out how these technology initiatives would work together with their existing plans for marketing, operations, and technology infrastructure.

After an hour, they had an initial diagram to show the various components of the plan. From this, they discussed the relationships between the components and how they would align with an overall strategy. They were unsure of how the various components should be sequenced for implementation. Tyler decided to apply a concept he had learned in school, about "hard logic" tasks that must be completed in a specific order. He and Becky continued to analyze and apply that principle to the initiatives.

She then thought and added, "Tyler, have you developed a mobile app before?" He said "No, but I use them a lot!" She replied, "Then if you really want the restaurant to have a mobile app, we have to look at the options."

Options and Priorities

In Chapter 12, "Systems Planning and Development," you learned about software development and that few companies develop their own ISs in-house. Recall, also, that "systems" almost always means "applications," and therefore the terms will be used interchangeably in this chapter, as in Chapter 12. The four alternatives to in-house development by IT specialists, as illustrated in Figure 13.1, are outsourcing, licensing, using software as a service (SaaS), and having users develop the system. However, there are many tradeoffs to consider when analyzing the various development alternatives.

If an application of the desired features and quality can be obtained from more than one of these sources (and that's a big "If"), then several factors need to be weighed such as cost, impact on current technology infrastructure, and time to implement. The total cost of ownership should be determined to include total cost of design, development, implementation, and maintenance. Just as you must consider after-purchase costs such as gas, insurance, and maintenance when you purchase a car, businesses must document the costs after purchase to accurately compare the costs of various alternatives. Because so many organizational systems are integrated and rely on other systems, a thorough analysis of how each alternative would interface with all current systems, and appropriate costs, is also important. And, in today's economic and competitive environment, the ability for an organization to gain first mover status and a competitive advantage can potentially be a more important factor than the cost of the project. For example, a more costly development approach, with appropriate quality and functionality, might be implemented earlier to gain a strategic or operational advantage.

If the application cannot be licensed, the next choice would usually be to obtain use of the system as a service from an application service provider (ASP) because the system is immediately available for use and the organization does not have to lay out a large sum up front for such use. However, even with the increased use of ASPs, this alternative might not be the best fit for all organizations and development projects. If an ASP alternative would cause significant, complex, or widespread changes in an organization's operations, branding, or stakeholder branding, then in-house (or contracted) development could be more suitable.

FIGURE **13.1**

Alternative approaches to
the in-house development
of information systems

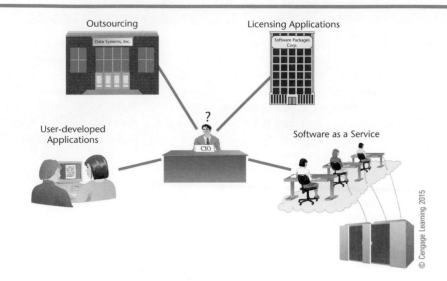

If ASPs do not offer the desired IS and it can be developed by non-IT employees, then this would usually be the chosen alternative. If non-IT employees cannot develop the IS, the choice might then be to outsource IS development. However, as you will see, outsourcing is a concept that might encompass more than just commissioning the development of an application.

Many factors must be considered in addition to quality and cost. Therefore, these alternatives are not fully comparable and often cannot be prioritized as simply as they have been here. The purpose of this discussion is to clarify the advantages and disadvantages of these options. As you will see, a variety of factors drive organizations to decide how they acquire ISs and the service that supports the maintenance and use of the systems.

Outsourcing

As discussed in Chapter 12, outsourcing in general means hiring the services of another organization or individual to perform some of the work that otherwise would be performed by you or your employees. In the IT arena, outsourcing has two meanings. One is to commission the development of an application to another organization, usually a company that specializes in the development of this type of application. The other is to hire the services of another company to manage all or parts of the services that otherwise would be rendered by an IT unit of the organization. The latter concept might not include development of new applications. However, the notion that "one size fits all" in IS development needs to be reconsidered. For any new implementation, a mixed approach can be an effective alternative when there are limitations as compressed implementation timeframes, lack of expertise, or limited resources. For example, senior management may require that a new system be deployed in a rapid timeframe for market and competitive reasons. After reviewing the resource requirements and organizational resources, the project may simply need more people. Or, in some cases, a project may require the use of new technology knowledge that current employees do not have. Outsourcing to a third party can provide that expertise directly as well as transfer that knowledge to in-house professionals. Each of these examples is an effective use of mixed-approach development methods.

POINT OF INTEREST The Death of Outsourcing

The outlook for traditional outsourcing is grim. A 2011 Forrester survey of 568 companies, mostly from the United States and some from France, Germany, and the U.K., found that the cost savings associated with outsourcing were lower than expected. Cloud-based technologies are emerging as a major competitor to traditional outsourcing. Cloud-based technologies provide customers with access to services and applications over the Internet, which are usually more cost-effective than traditional outsourcing. The decreased cost-savings associated with outsourcing combined with the rise of better technologies could lead to the extinction of outsourcing as we know it today.

Source: Anonymous. (2011, Jul 19). Forrester predicts death of traditional outsourcing, Mint Magazine.

Outsourcing Custom-Designed Applications

Often, an organization has a need that no existing software can satisfy. For example, if the cost-accounting procedures of a particular company are so specific that no commercially available software can perform them, the company must develop **custom-designed**, or **tailored**, **software**. In recent years, the number of companies developing applications in-house has declined. The majority of custom-designed applications are developed by companies that specialize in providing consulting and software development services to other businesses.

WHY YOU SHOULD Understand Alternative Avenues for the Acquisition of Information Systems

As an increasing number of business activities are supported and enhanced by ISs, it is extremely important for organizations to acquire systems that best fit their needs and are available as soon as possible, and to minimize the cost of systems acquisition and maintenance. As explained in Chapter 12, "Systems Planning and Development," employees should involve themselves in the process of deciding which ISs will be introduced into their business units and what features they will have. Since there are several ways to obtain ISs, professionals like you must understand the advantages and disadvantages of each. If you have a concern with a certain approach to acquire the system you need, you should voice it and be able to propose other options.

While custom-designed applications are more expensive than purchased ones, they have several advantages (see Figure 13.2).

- *Good fit to need*: The organization enjoys an application that meets its needs exactly, rather than settling for the near fit of a ready-made program.
- *Good fit to culture*: When custom-developing a system, developers are more sensitive to the organizational culture. Employees enjoy an application that fits their work. When licensing a packaged application, employees sometimes must change their work to accommodate the software.
- *Dedicated maintenance*: Because the programmers are easily accessible to the company, they are familiar with the programs and can provide customized software maintenance. Maintenance includes modification for business changes (including mergers with and acquisition of other organizations) and upgrading of the software when new technologies become available.
- *Seamless interface*: When a system is custom-made for an organization, special requirements can be implemented to ensure that it has proper interfaces with other systems. Specifically, it is important to transfer data between systems in an accurate and timely manner. New systems need to communicate seamlessly with other systems, eliminating any human intervention.
- *Specialized security*: Special security measures can be integrated into the application. Because the program is custom designed, security measures are known only to the organization.

- *Potential for strategic advantage*: Recall from the discussion in Chapter 2, "Strategic Uses of Information Systems," that companies gain a strategic advantage when they can employ an IS that their competitors do not have. A unique application might give a business a strategic advantage because it is the only business that can enjoy the application. For example, no CRM application can do for a business what an enterprise application that was developed specifically to serve its customers in a unique way can do.

FIGURE **13.2**

Advantages and disadvantages of custom-designed applications

Advantages

- Good fit of features to business needs
- Good fit of features to organizational culture
- Personnel available for maintenance
- Seamless interfaces with other information systems
- Availability of special security measures
- Potential for a strategic advantage

Disadvantages

- High cost
- Long wait for development if IS personnel are busy with other projects
- Application may be too organization-specific to interface with systems of other organizations

The greatest disadvantage of tailored applications is their high cost. Tailored software development requires an organization to fund all development costs; in contrast, costs of developing off-the-shelf and other ready applications are distributed over a larger number of expected purchasers. Another disadvantage of custom-designed development is that the production schedule can be delayed because IS personnel might not be available for long periods. Another important downside is that custom-designed software is less likely to be compatible with other organizations' systems. If organizations with different tailor-made systems decide to link their systems, they might incur significant cost to modify one or both of the systems.

Clients of outsourced software development should also be aware of an inherent conflict of this option: on one hand they want the developing firm to conform to a contract that includes specific requirements of the software. On the other hand, specific requirements may make the development effort inflexible and potentially costly: if the client company needs to change requirements as the development progresses, the developers might either refuse to deviate from the original requirements or might agree to make the changes for hefty additional charges. Contracts for outsourced software development might also be incompatible with some development methods, such as agile methods, discussed in Chapter 12, "Systems Planning and Development." The essence of such methods is the clients' ability to request modified or new features as the development moves forward, which might stand in stark contrast to the contract.

Many North American and European countries have outsourced development of well-defined applications to professionals in other countries, an act often referred to as **offshoring**. Gartner identified the top 30 offshoring countries including Costa Rica, Indonesia, and Columbia (Anonymous, 2010c). Programmers in India, China, and the Philippines earn a fraction of their colleagues in Western countries while often mastering the same level of skills. Hiring these programmers might reduce the cost of development significantly. Offshoring has caused layoffs of programmers in Western countries and created much bitterness among those professionals and supporters of local labor. However, this is apparently an inevitable result of the growing scope of economic globalization.

A study on outsourcing and offshore outsourcing of information technology in major corporations was conducted based on analyzing secondary data obtained from surveys of financial executives. The study differentiated itself from previous studies on the subject by avoiding the traditional standpoint of examining outsourcing from a theoretical standpoint and chose to view outsourcing from a top financial executive's standpoint. This study found evidence supporting the idea that outsourcing actually does not provide higher returns because of hidden costs and contract management. According to executives, the most important attribute of service provider preference was client loyalty. This result indicates that executives are more focused on quality, consistency, and support than strictly on cost. Another result of the study was that if IT was a core competency of the company, the company was less likely to outsource offshore. Companies with IT as a core competency would most likely want to have more control and power over such an influential and important business area. Outsourcing and offshore outsourcing of IT are options for many companies yet they may not be the right choice depending on the core competencies of the company.

Source: Peslak, A. R. (2012). Outsourcing and offshore outsourcing of information technology in major corporations. Management Research Review, 35(1), 14-31.

Outsourcing IT Services

A large number of businesses have turned to IT companies for long-term services: purchasing and maintaining hardware; developing, licensing, and maintaining software; installing and maintaining communications networks; developing, maintaining, and operating websites; staffing help desks; running IT daily operations; managing customer and supplier relations; developing and maintaining mobile applications; and so on. An organization might use a combination of in-house and outsourced services. It might outsource the development of an IS, but then put its own employees in charge of system operation, or it might outsource both the development and operation of the system. When a business outsources only routine business processes, such as customer order entry or human resource transactions, the practice is sometimes called *business process outsourcing*. Note, however, that this term refers to the outsourcing of many activities, whereas this discussion is limited to only IT services.

In considering whether to outsource IT services, management should ask the following questions:

- What are our core business competencies? Of the business we conduct, what specialties should we continue to practice and refine ourselves?
- What do we do outside our specialties that could be done better for us by organizations specializing in that area?
- Which of our activities could be improved if we created an alliance with IT organizations?
- Which of our activities should we work to improve internally?
- What are the risks to the organization's operations?
- Does our organization compromise our competitive advantage by outsourcing any activities?

Many companies have come to realize that IT is not their core competency and should not be a focus of their efforts. In addition, the pace of developments in IT might require more expertise than is available within many organizations. Some organizations also consider the loss of internal expertise and personnel development by outsourcing activities.

A growing portion of corporate IS budgets is allocated for purchased (outsourced) services. IT companies that made their reputation by providing hardware and software, such as IBM and Unisys, have seen revenue from the outsourcing service portion of their business grow faster than the revenue from hardware and software sales. Among the largest IT service providers are IBM, Fujitsu, Accenture, Computer Sciences Corp. (CSC), Northrop Grumman, Hitachi, Capgemini, Perot Systems, NEC, and Hewlett-Packard (Verberne, 2010). For the sake of simplicity and clarity here, such companies are called vendors, and the organizations to which they outsource are called clients. Some trade journals refer to vendors as outsourcers. Outsourcing is typically a long-term contractual relationship in which the vendor assumes the responsibilities over some or all of a client's IT functions. Businesses can also outsource transaction activities, such as credit-card processing, to reduce internal resources. Typical outsourced functions are listed in Figure 13.3.

FIGURE 13.3

Typical outsourced IT services

- Application development and software maintenance
- Hardware purchasing and hardware maintenance
- Telecommunications installation and maintenance
- Help desk services
- Website design and maintenance
- Staff training
- Data storage (cloud) and backup services
- Transaction processing

© Cengage Learning 2015

IT outsourcing contracts are typically signed for long periods of time, usually for 7 to 10 years. The sums of money involved are very large, some reaching billions of dollars. For example, Idea Cellular Ltd., India's fourth largest mobile phone operator by subscribers, extended its outsourcing contract with IBM in 2012 for an additional 8 years and $700 million. The contract was signed in 2007 and was initially expected to expire in 2017. The extension pushes back the end of the contract date to 2020. The reason behind the mid-contract extension is that IBM will avoid a formal bidding process when the contract was previously set to expire in 2017. IBM will provide Idea Cellular Ltd. with IT infrastructure and applications. IBM has also begun outsourcing contract extension negotiations with India's biggest telecom company, Bharti Airtel Ltd., which is currently set to expire in 2014. Negotiations with Indian telecos are complicated by revenues that are tied to subscribers yet the increase in costs has hindered profit margins (Anonymous, 2012c). In July 2010, CSC announced that MBDA, a world leader in missile systems, agreed to an outsourcing contract extension spanning until December of 2014 if all options are exercised. The agreement marks the continuation of a relationship between the two companies that began in the U.K. in 1994. Under the extended contract, CSC will provide MBDA with a full range of IT services including infrastructure and applications management. CSC was named in Fortune Magazine as one of the Most Admired Companies for Information Technology Services in 2010 (Anonymous, 2010b). In July 2012, IBM signed a 10-year, $1 billion outsourcing contract with Cemex to take care of the building supplier's IT operations in Monterrey, Mexico (McDougall, 2012). In January 2010, Perot Systems signed a 5-year, $42 million contract to provide network operations, desktop services, email and information assurance services for the U.S. Army (Mark, 2010).

There is a peculiar—and paradoxical—aspect to IT outsourcing: while contracts are signed for long periods of time, they typically involve rapidly changing technologies. Vendors often agree to sign outsourcing contracts only if the period is at least 5 years because of the human resource commitment they have to make, but strategic IT plans—as discussed in Chapter 12, "Systems Planning and Development"—are for only 3–5 years. As a result, clients sometimes find themselves bound by contracts that no longer satisfy their needs or believing that the contract services are not being fulfilled. Then litigation is the next step. For example, in 2012, the State of Indiana sued IBM for $437 million it paid for a failed welfare information system development. The State contended that IBM breached its 2006 contract originally valued at $1.6 billion. However, Indiana failed to convince the court that IBM breached its contractual responsibilities. It was a rare judgment in favor of an outsourcing provider. Very often, large service providers are not willing to endure the adverse publicity of litigation. In this situation, that was not the case. Cases such as these are very difficult to resolve through litigation in court due to complex contracts, various data points, and a multitude of documents to review. Various sources maintain that neither party "won" this litigation (Overby, 2012b).

In another example in April 2013, Walsh College of Troy, Michigan renewed its contract with CareTech Solutions, an information technology and web products service provider to hospitals and higher education institutions. The contract would expand CareTech's responsibilities to include providing all IT infrastructure operations and most of the application support services for the college. CareTech has been praised by Walsh College for its exceptional service in providing day-to-day IT operations and strategic insight into the future needs of the students, faculty, and staff. The 5-year outsourcing contract renewal extends the relationship between the partners until 2017 (Anonymous, 2013).

Renegotiation of outsourcing contracts is not unusual. Several companies that signed long-term contracts have found that the financial burden was too heavy or that the expected benefits had not materialized. In April 2004, Sears, Roebuck and Co. signed a 10-year, $1.6 billion outsourcing contract with CSC. Eleven months later, in May 2005, Sears terminated the agreement, claiming that CSC failed to perform some of its obligations. In late 2007, CSC and Sears, Roebuck, and Co. amicably reached an agreement to settle the contract dispute that they entered into in May 2004. Sears paid an undisclosed amount to CSC who did not expect any impairment costs to the assets associated with the Sears contract. The parent company of Sears, Roebuck, and Co., Sears Holdings Corporation, created a reserve for the foreseen settlement by Sears and thus did not expect the settlement to have a material impact on its 2007 financial statements (CSC, 2007).

Making educated decisions on outsourcing IT services has been a major success factor for organizations. However, trends in offshore outsourcing could mean a reduction in the success a business experiences with offshore outsourcing of IT services. Global IT outsourcers have been shrinking the number of onsite and onshore staff who act as liaisons between customers and service providers. To ensure that businesses continue receiving solid offshore IT services, they should follow these tips (Overby, 2012a):

- Conduct a process design review to make sure that essential onsite roles will still be filled, and possibly investigate bringing some IT roles back in-house.
- Reevaluate the possibility of near-shore alternatives. Due to the North American Free Trade Agreement (NAFTA), IT workers can be more easily transferred across borders than across oceans.

- Review the firm's infrastructure to make sure it is compatible with that of the offshore service provider.
- Revisit the price if the IT service provider is moving onsite roles overseas.

It is crucial for companies utilizing outsourced IT services to stay up to date with evolving technologies and the tactical actions of the service providers to ensure they are receiving the appropriate services at a reasonable price.

POINT OF INTEREST — Software for SOX

Since the Sarbanes-Oxley (SOX) Corporate Governance Act passed in 2005, some companies have made a living off of creating software that aids businesses manage risk and comply with the Act's corporate financial reporting requirements. OpenPages was one of those companies until they were bought out by information technology giant IBM in 2010. OpenPages' services were merged into IBM's SoftWare Group. With fines for noncompliance of financial reporting mandates soaring into the millions of dollars, there is a significant market opportunity to provide software solutions that help businesses avoid those hefty fines.

Source: Cody, T. (2010). OpenPages Sold to IBM. Mergers & Acquisitions Report, 23(38), p. 21.

Advantages of Outsourcing IT Services

Clients contract for IT services to offload in-house responsibility and to better manage risks. When a client outsources, management knows how much the outsourced services will cost; thus, the risk of miscalculation is eliminated. Additional advantages make the contracting option attractive:

- *Improved financial planning*: Outsourcing allows a client to know exactly what the cost of its IS functions will be over the period of the contract, which is usually several years. This allows for better financial planning.
- *Reduced license and maintenance fees*: Professional IS firms often pay discounted prices for CASE (computer-aided software engineering) tools and other resources, based on volume purchases; they can pass these savings on to their clients.
- *Increased attention to core business*: Letting outside experts manage IT frees executives from managing it. They can thus concentrate on the company's core business—including developing and marketing new products.
- *Shorter implementation cycles*: IT vendors can usually complete a new application project in less time than an in-house development team can, thanks to their experience with development projects of similar systems for other clients. (However, they are not likely to use less time if they lack experience with such systems, or if they insist on a waterfall development process rather than an agile method.)
- *Reduction of personnel and fixed costs*: In-house IS salaries and benefits and expensive capital expenditures for items such as CASE tools are paid whether or not the IS staff is productive. IS firms, on the other hand, spread their fixed and overhead costs (office space, furnishings, systems development software, and the like) over many projects and clients, thereby decreasing the expense absorbed by any single client.
- *Increased access to highly qualified know-how*: Outsourcing allows clients to tap into one of the greatest assets of an IT vendor: experience gained through work with many clients in different environments.
- *Availability of ongoing consulting as part of standard support*: Most outsourcing contracts allow client companies to consult the vendor for all types of IT advice, which would otherwise be unavailable (or only available from a highly paid consultant). Such advice might include guidance on how to use a feature of a recently purchased application or on how to move data from one application to another.

As you can see, cost savings is only one reason to outsource IS functions. In fact, studies show that saving money is not the most common reason for outsourcing. Surveys have shown that executives expect several benefits from an outsourcing relationship. Figure 13.4 shows the most cited expectations, such as access to technological skills and industry expertise. To many executives, these anticipated benefits are more important than cost savings, especially in light of reports that in many cases outsourcing did not save the client money.

FIGURE 13.4

Benefits to be gained from IT outsourcing

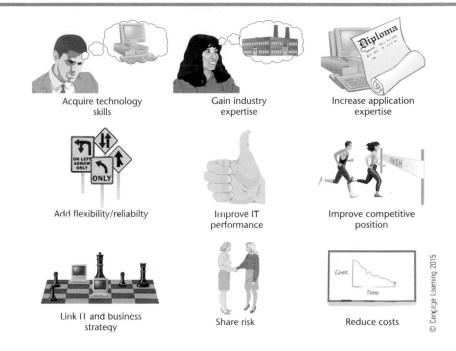

Acquire technology skills

Gain industry expertise

Increase application expertise

Add flexibility/reliabilty

Improve IT performance

Improve competitive position

Link IT and business strategy

Share risk

Reduce costs

© Cengage Learning 2015

Risks of Outsourcing IT Services

Despite its popularity, outsourcing is not a panacea and should be considered carefully before it is adopted. In some situations, organizations should avoid outsourcing. The major risks are as follows:

- *Loss of control*: A company that outsources a major part of its IT operations will probably be unable to regain control for a long time. The organization must evaluate the nature of the industry in which it operates. While outsourcing can be a good option in a relatively stable industry, it is highly risky in one that is quickly changing. Although the personnel of an IT service company might have the necessary IS technical skills, they might jeopardize the client's core business in the long run if they cannot adapt to constantly changing business realities in the client's industry. Sometimes when this problem becomes clear, the client might have disposed of all personnel who could react properly to such developments. Moreover, even if the client organization still employs qualified IT professionals, the vendor might object to their involvement in activities that, according to the outsourcing contract, are outside their jurisdiction.

- *Loss of experienced employees*: Outsourcing often involves transferring hundreds, or even thousands, of the organization's employees to the IS vendor. For example, as part of the outsourcing contract between Motorola and CSC in 2003, CSC absorbed 1300 of Motorola's IT employees, and when the Wall Street company JPMorgan outsourced its IT functions to IBM in 2003, IBM hired its client's 4000 IT employees. The organization that absorbs the workers can usually employ them with lower overhead expenses than their former employer and use their skills more productively. The client eliminates this overhead cost, but it also gives up well-trained personnel. In addition, if most of the vendor's personnel serving the client are the same employees that the client maintained until the outsourcing contract was signed, the company's ability to gain new expertise from outsourcing could be compromised.

- *Risks of losing a competitive advantage*: Innovative ISs, especially those intended to give their owners a competitive advantage, should not be outsourced. Outsourcing the development of strategic systems is a way of disclosing trade secrets. Confidentiality agreements can reduce, but never completely eliminate, the risk. A competitor might hire the same vendor to build an IS for the same purpose, thereby potentially eliminating the first client's advantage. In addition, assuming that these systems incorporate new business or technical concepts, vendors will bring less than their usual level of experience—and therefore fewer benefits—to the project. Outsourcing strategic or core business ISs incurs more risk than outsourcing the routine tasks of operational ISs (see Figure 13.5).

- *High price*: Despite careful pre-contract calculations, some companies find out that outsourcing costs them significantly more than they would have spent had they taken care of their own ISs or related services. Several clients have pressured vendors to renegotiate their outsourcing contracts or have found a way to terminate the contract because executives believed they could enjoy the same level of service, or higher-quality service, by maintaining a corporate IT staff. To minimize such unpleasant discoveries, the negotiating team must clearly define every service to be included in the arrangement, including the quality of personnel, service hours, and the scope and quality of services rendered when new hardware and software are adopted or when the client company decides to embark on new ventures, such as e-commerce initiatives or establishment of an intranet.

FIGURE 13.5

Risks of outsourcing are higher at higher levels of decision making

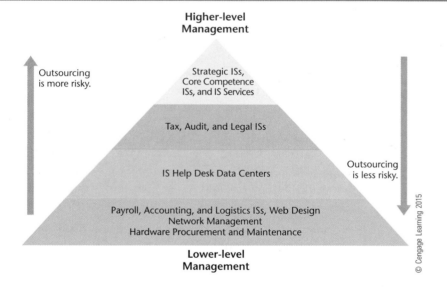

The most important element of an outsourcing agreement for both parties, but mostly for the client, is what professionals call the **service-level agreement**. The negotiators for the client must carefully list all the types of services expected of the vendor as well as the metrics to be used to measure the degree to which the vendor has met the level of promised services. Clients should not expect vendors to list the service level and metrics; the *clients* must do it. It is in the client's interest to have as specific a contract as possible, because any service that is not included in the contract, or is mentioned only in general terms, leaves the door open for the vendor not to render it, or not to render it to a level expected by the client.

Considering Outsourcing IT Services

When approaching outsourcing, review the following points to make sure that it is the appropriate choice for your organization and that you are prepared to deal with any issues that come up:

- *Research*: Review outsourcing contracts from other business organizations, especially those contracts for similar industries and services. It is important to consider and integrate lessons learned from other situations in order to eliminate faulty approaches and methodologies, and technology issues.

- *Contractual requirements and scope of services*: The single most important facet of executing a project or contract is its scope. When two parties engage in an outsourcing relationship, it is crucial to specifically outline the boundaries of the contractual requirements and the responsibilities of all parties. In some business situations, too many details or minutia can be ineffective. However, when compiling an IT outsourcing services contract, no detail should be overlooked or minimized. And as important as it is to define what is required, it is also crucial to define any exclusions that are outside the scope or responsibilities of either party.

- *Commitment and engagement in change*: As with any information technology initiative, change is inevitable. With the addition of an outside entity as a service provider, both parties should be engaged in a discussion of the issues involved in the outsourcing initiative. In many cases, business organizations do not outsource what is working well and efficiently. Patients do not visit a doctor when they are feeling well. Therefore, businesses outsource to gain the resources and expertise to assume the responsibility for activities that are currently being completed in a less than optimum fashion by organizational personnel and departments. It is important to discuss any issues or problems with the current environment clearly and honestly with the outsourcing company before beginning the contract. Additionally, make sure the service provider can document or show its ability to complete the services—do not take a simple "yes" as evidence of competence.

- *Monitoring and conflict resolution*: Any new initiative should not be viewed as a potential conflict or failure. At the same time, both parties must be invested in its success. It is crucial to monitor and track the progress with measureable performance measures for both parties. A frequent and consistent dialogue on these measures should be the focus during the term of the contract. When conflicts arise (and they will), the conflict is not the important issue. Both parties must "come to the table" in order to gain a resolution in a timely manner. This process is often easier said than done; however, agreement on monitoring and conflict resolution can avoid relationship issues and litigation.

- *Refrain from outsourcing the world*: Simply said, the more expensive the contract or the more services that are being provided, the greater the risk of contract failure. Contracts for outsourcing IT services that include a scope of services that are limited and well-defined have the best opportunity for success. Businesses should not view outsourcing IT services as a panacea that will rid management of responsibility. In some cases, businesses try to resolve organizational issues and costs with "quick" outsourcing solutions. Sometimes, the outsourcing contract is simply not feasible. Corporations often view outsourcing decisions to focus solely on the reduction of costs while not considering short- and long-term challenges.

Licensing Applications

Businesses can select from a growing list of high-quality packaged software, from office applications that fit on a CD to large enterprise applications. Therefore, purchasing prepackaged software should be the first alternative considered when a company needs to acquire a new system. Recall that "purchased" software is almost always *licensed* software. The purchaser actually purchases a license to use the software, not the software itself. Thus, here the term "licensing" means purchasing a license to use. Unless an IS must be tailored to unique needs in an organization, licensing a prepackaged system might well be the best option.

Ready-made software can be classified into two groups: one is the relatively inexpensive software that helps in the workplace, such as Microsoft Office and similar suites, including software that supports more specific tasks such as project management and tax preparation. Such software usually costs tens of dollars to several hundred dollars for a single user or thousands of dollars for a company with many employees. The other group includes large software applications that support entire organizational functions, such as human resource management and financial management, or enterprise applications that span the entire organization. Such packages include ERP, SCM, and CRM applications and typically cost millions of dollars.

Software as a service (SaaS; see more on this later in the chapter) is licensed as a recurring monthly or annual cost. In most cases, an SaaS application operates over the Internet using a standard browser and a cloud computing architecture. In addition, some software publishers are licensing both delivery models (installed vs. cloud computing) for their application software products. Intuit, for example, still markets its QuickBooks product to install on your local computer system for a one-time licensing cost as well as an online version with a monthly cost. The online version requires less up-front expense and does not require the purchase of updated software, as this is automatically included in the monthly licensing fee.

Software Licensing Benefits

When licensing a software package, the buyer gains several benefits: immediate system availability, high quality, low price (license fee), and available support. Immediate availability helps shorten the time from the decision to implement a new system and the actual implementation. If the company maintains an IT staff that develops applications, purchasing software frees the staff to develop the systems that must be specifically tailored to its business needs.

High-quality software is guaranteed through purchase partly because the software company specializes in developing its products and partly because its products would not survive on the market if they were not of high quality. Large developers often distribute prerelease versions, called **beta versions**, or simply betas, of software to be tested by companies (called beta sites) that agree to use the application with actual data for several months. The beta sites then report problems and propose improvements in return for receiving the fully developed software free or for a reduced license fee. By the time the software is released to the general market, it has been well tested.

Because software companies spread product development costs over many units, the price to a single customer is a fraction of what it would cost to develop a similar application in-house or to hire an outside company to develop it. Also, instead of devoting its own personnel to maintain the software, the buyer can usually contract for long-term service and be notified of new, advanced versions of the application. All software development companies provide after-the-sale support. Often, buyers enjoy a period of three months to one year of free service.

Even large companies that could afford to develop ISs on their own often elect to purchase when they can find suitable software. For example, CMS Energy, a $9 billion energy producer in Jackson, Michigan, decided to install a web-based supply chain management system to link with the company's equipment suppliers. The company's information technologists wanted to build the system themselves. The executive vice president and chief financial and administrative officer, whose professional background is in IT, nixed the idea. He estimated that the cost of a homegrown system—about $20 million—would be greater than the savings it would deliver in its first few years of operation. Instead, he suggested the company use packaged software. This alternative cut the cost of the system in half.

You might be more familiar with off-the-shelf applications than with larger, more complex packaged applications. However, in recent years, enterprise applications have constituted a far larger part of IT expenditures on packaged software. As mentioned earlier, enterprise applications are complex applications that serve many parts of an organization, often several departments. They consist of several modules, each of which can be interfaced with another module from the same vendor.

Organizations cannot simply purchase such large applications and install them; they must employ professionals who specialize in the installation of the software, which might take months. Within limits, the providers of these large applications agree to customize part of the applications to the specific needs of a client. However, such customization is very expensive and is often risky. In some cases, customization has taken significantly longer than planned and was not completed to the full satisfaction of the client.

Software Licensing Risks

Although licensing a ready-made application is attractive, it has its risks:

- *Loose fit between needs and features*: Ready-made software is developed for the widest common denominator of potential user organizations. It might be useful to many, but it will be optimal for few. Companies must take extra care to ensure that ready-made software truly complies with company needs, including organizational culture. Obtaining input from many potential users in the selection process reduces this risk. Therefore, it is important to clearly and completely define the functional, information and reporting requirements. Categorize and prioritize each of these requirements in order to evaluate and rate the various software products.

- *Difficulties in modifications*: Many companies find that they must have packaged software such as ERP and SCM applications modified to meet their specific needs, and too many of them find that the vendor does a poor job. For example, Nike spent $400 million to have i2 Technologies implement i2's SCM software. Nike claimed that the software did not work properly, causing shortages of high-demand products and overstocks of less popular items. Nike's management said that the software, which was supposed to lower operating costs and streamline communication with suppliers and buyers, failed both in performance and functionality. i2 blamed difficulties on customizing the software and Nike's inappropriate implementation of the software according to i2's suggested methods. Nike found the methods too rigid and did not implement them. The mishap reduced Nike's sales in the first quarter after implementation by $100 million. Apparently, "just do it" did not suffice. "Do it right" would have been a better approach.

- *Dissolution of the vendor*: If the vendor goes out of business, the purchaser is left without support, maintenance service, and the opportunity to purchase upgrades to an application to which it is committed. Except for checking the financial strength of potential vendors, there is not much the purchaser can do to reduce this risk.

- *High turnover of vendor personnel*: Turnover among IS professionals is significantly higher than in other occupations. If a substantial number of employees involved in application development and upgrading leave a vendor, support is likely to deteriorate, and upgrades will be of poor quality. Purchasers can do little to reduce this risk.

- *Custom modifications vs. vendor updates*: One of the benefits of acquiring pre-developed software is the broad functionality of the software. Contracting with a solid software developer can provide the opportunity to gain software updates including new features and functionality designed for a mass market. However, these updates may not be able to be implemented locally depending on the degree of the modifications to be applied. Any new updates could require tedious "weaving" into the current system with the local modifications. By implementing the unmodified software, software updates can be implemented without significant resources.

Steps in Licensing Ready-Made Software

When selecting a particular software package, companies invest a lot of money and make a long-term commitment to conducting their business in a particular manner. Factors such as the complexity of installation, cost of training, and quality and cost of after-sale service must be considered in addition to the demonstrable quality of the software (refer to Figure 5.9 in Chapter 5 for an example of a software evaluation checklist). Once a company decides that it will purchase a ready-made application, a project management team is formed to oversee system implementation and handle all vendor contact. The project management team has the following responsibilities (see Figure 13.6):

FIGURE **13.6**

Steps in licensing software

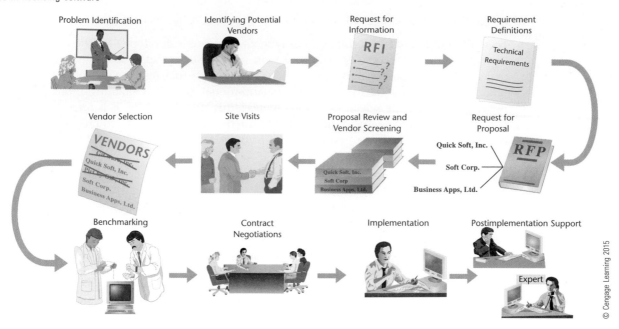

- *Identifying the problem or opportunity*: This step is similar to the initial inquiry and fact-finding step in the systems development life cycle (SDLC), discussed in Chapter 12, "Systems Planning and Development." The inquiry results in the identification of gross functional requirements and key integration points with other systems. The report generated often serves as a basis for a request for information from potential vendors.

- *Identifying potential vendors*: On the basis of information in trade journals (printed and on the web) and previously received promotional material, as well as client references, vendors who offer applications in the domain at hand are identified. In addition to these sources, IS people might gather information at trade shows, from other organizations that have used similar technology, and from colleagues.

- *Soliciting vendor information*: The project manager sends a **request for information (RFI)** to the vendors identified, requesting general, somewhat informal information about the product.

- *Defining system requirements*: The project manager lists a set of functional and technical requirements and identifies the functional and technical capabilities of all vendors, highlighting the items that are common to both lists as well as those that are not. The project management team involves the users in defining system requirements to ensure that the chosen application will integrate well with existing and planned systems.

- *Requesting vendor proposals*: The team prepares a **request for proposal (RFP)**, a document specifying all the system requirements and soliciting a proposal from each vendor contacted. The response should include not only technical requirements but also a detailed description of the implementation process as well as a timetable and budget that can be easily transformed into a contractual agreement. The team should strive to provide enough detail and vision to limit the amount of pre-contract clarification and negotiation.

- *Reviewing proposals and screening vendors*: The team reviews the proposals and identifies the most qualified vendors. Vendor selection criteria include functionality, architectural fit, price, services, and support.

- *Visiting sites*: The complexity of the RFP responses might make evaluation impossible without a visit to a client site where a copy of the application is in use. The team should discuss with other clients the pros and cons of the application.

- *Selecting the vendor*: The team should rank the remaining vendors. The selection factors are weighted, and the vendor with the highest total points is chosen for contract negotiation. Sometimes make-or-break factors are identified early in the process to eliminate vendors that cannot provide the essential service. By now, the team has gathered enough information on the functionality of the various systems.

- *Benchmarking*: Before finalizing the purchasing decision, the system should be tested using **benchmarking**, which is comparing actual performance against specific quantifiable criteria. If all other conditions are the same for all the bidders, the vendor whose application best meets or exceeds the benchmarks is selected.

- *Negotiating a contract*: The contract should clearly define performance expectations and include penalties if requirements are not met. Special attention should be given to the schedule, budget, responsibility for system support, and support response times. Some clients include a clause on keeping the source code in escrow. If the vendor goes out of business, the client will receive the source code, without which the system cannot be maintained. The client should tie all payments to completion of milestones by the vendor and acceptance of deliverables.

- *Implementing the new system*: The new system is introduced in the business units it will serve, and user training is conducted.

- *Managing post-implementation support*: Vendors expect buyers of their large applications to request extensive on-site post-implementation support. Unexpected lapses or unfamiliarity with the system might require fine-tuning, additional training, and modification of the software. It is best to develop an ongoing relationship with the vendor because a solid relationship will foster timely service and support.

When choosing a vendor, organizations look for the quality and reliability of the product, but several additional factors, such as quality of service and support, vendor's support for industry standards, and vendor financial soundness, are extremely important. In surveys, IS managers have almost invariably revealed the importance of factors considered in selecting a vendor, as shown in Figure 13.7 (in descending order). Product quality and reliability stand well ahead of the price/performance ratio.

FIGURE 13.7

How IT management can rank the importance of product purchase factors

FACTOR	RATING
Quality and reliability	_____
Product performance	_____
Quality of after-sale service and support	_____
Trustworthiness of vendor	_____
Price/performance ratio	_____
Ease of doing business with vendor	_____
Vendor's support for industry standards	_____
Openness of future strategies and plans	_____
Vendor financial stability	_____

Software as a Service

In an age when virtually every employee knows how to use a web browser and access applications online, why should companies install applications at all? Salesforce.com was founded by Mark Benioff and three partners in March 1999 in a one-bedroom apartment in San Francisco. The concept was simple: offer intuitive, easy-to-use customer relationship management (CRM) software on demand via the Internet, and charge customers per use, per month for access to the software. The company has 104,000 customers (as of July 2011) and 1.5 million subscribers (as of July 2009), the employees of these customers (Anonymous, 2011). Salesforce.com offers many more types of on-demand software than just CRM.

An organization that offers the use of software through a network (the Internet or private network) is called an **application service provider (ASP)**. The concept is called **software as a service (SaaS)** or *software on demand*. Salesforce.com, CSC, IBM Global Services, NetSuite, Inc., Oracle Corp., Microsoft Corp., and RightNow Technologies, Inc. (now owned by Oracle) are among the better known players in this industry, but many other companies offer such services. According to the IT research firm Gartner, SaaS revenues are expected to reach more than $22 billion by 2015 (Anonymous, 2012b).

An ASP does not install any software on a client's computers. Rather, the application is installed at the ASP's location, along with the databases and other files that the application processes for the client. However, clients can choose to save all the files produced by the application on their own local storage devices. The clients' employees access the application through the web. They call up the application, enter data, process the data, produce reports online and on paper, and in general use the application the same way they would had it been installed at their location. SaaS interface software enables thousands of users from multiple corporate clients to use the same application simultaneously.

ASPs do not necessarily offer their own software packages. They often offer software developed by other companies. For example, USinternetworking (a subsidiary of AT&T) provides on-demand software by Oracle, Microsoft, and Ariba. On-demand service may cost several tens or hundreds of dollars per month per user, depending on the software rented.

POINT OF INTEREST — IBM: Not Only Computers

IBM is the world's largest information technology services company. That's "services," not "computers." For several years the main stream of revenue for the company has been its software development, consulting services, and outsourcing services rather than sales of computers. Consider the company's revenue for the fourth quarter of 2012 by activity: Global Technology Services (outsourcing and software development): $10.28 billion; Global Business Services (business consulting): $4.72 billion; Systems and Technology (including sales of mainframe computers, servers, and microchips): $5.76 billion. IBM signed 22 outsourcing contracts worth over $100 billion in the first quarter of 2013.

Source: Anonymous. (2013). International Business Machines Corp. Brokerage Research Digest, 11. http://www.zacks.com/ZER/rd_get_pdf.php?r=IBM

As Figure 13.8 shows, renting and using software through the web has benefits as well as risks. As in any time-limited rental, the client does not have to commit large sums of money up front. No employees have to devote time to learning how to maintain the software, nor to maintaining it once it is installed. No storage hardware is required for the applications and associated data, because the vendor uses its own hardware. And the software is usually available significantly sooner than if installed at the client's location; while it might take years to install and test enterprise applications on-site, an online renter can use the same application within days after signing a contract. And even if an organization is willing to pay for the software, it might not find skilled personnel to install and maintain the software.

FIGURE **13.8**

Benefits and risks of
Software as a Service
(SaaS)

Benefits

- Eliminate the need to maintain the application software

- Eliminate the reliance on hired experts for installation and maintenance

- No need to purchase or maintain hardware for the installation

- Significant reduction of implementation time

- Low financial risk

- Support provided by SaaS vendor

Risks

- Possible long transaction response time through the Internet

- Information security, such as interception by competitors

- Potential integration issues between SaaS applications and other internal systems

© Cengage Learning 2015

For many small companies this option is clearly the best. Holden Humphrey Co. is a lumber wholesaler in Chicopee, Massachusetts. It has 24 employees. The company's president decided it made no financial sense to hire IT personnel or pay for licensed software. The company pays $1,000 per month to an ASP, which enables nine of the employees to remotely access inventory management, accounting, and CRM applications.

The "software on demand" approach is attracting a growing clientele. Clients are mainly small and medium corporations, but some large organizations also prefer this option. The obvious risk is that the client cedes control of the systems, the application, and possibly its related data to another party. Although some vendors are willing to make minor changes to suit the client's needs, they will not make all requested changes. Some experts argue that by using SaaS, clients have less control over their systems, and that it is better to retain the ability to modify applications in-house. Response time might become a problem as well, because neither the ASP nor the client has full control over traffic on the Internet. Also, as with all activities through a public network, there are security risks, such as interception of information by a competitor.

For this reason, some clients prefer to use a leased line rather than the Internet to connect to the ASP. For instance, Simpson Industries, a manufacturer of auto parts in Plymouth, Michigan, uses an ERP system offered by IBM Global Services. But employees use the application through a leased line (a network connection for their exclusive use) to connect directly to IBM's service center in Rochester, New York. When considering using a leased line, IT managers should consider the cost. While a DSL, cable, or optical fiber link costs $30 to $50 per month, a leased line with the same capacity costs $1000 to $2000 per month. Organizations should also consider the type of application and data their company is about to use.

Caveat Emptor: Buyer Beware

In recent years, faster links to the Internet and a more stable ASP industry have made SaaS an attractive option. However, even with reputable providers, some subscribers were disappointed because the scope of services and level of reliability were not what they had expected when they signed the contract. Managers in organizations considering ASPs should heed the following "commandments":

- *Research the ASP's history.* Ask the provider for a list of references, and contact these customers to ask about their experience. Ask how soon the provider switched to a new version of the application they rented. Talk to the references to gain detailed information on the vendor and its product.

- *Validate the ASP's financial strength.* Request copies of the ASP's financial reports. Ensure that it has enough funds or secured funding to stay in business for the duration of your planned contract.
- *Ensure you understand the price structure.* Ask whether the price changes when you decide to switch to another application. Ask whether the price includes help desk services.
- *Get a list of the provider's infrastructure.* Ask to see a list of the ASP's hardware, software, and telecommunication facilities. Ask the ASP to identify its business partners for hardware, software, and telecommunication services. Ask how data, including sensitive data such as credit-card account numbers, are stored and protected. Ask about security measures.
- *Craft the service contract carefully.* Ensure that the contract includes penalties the ASP will pay if services are not rendered fully. Ensure that your organization will not have to pay penalties for early termination.

One important point to check when examining the list of facilities is uptime. **Uptime** is the proportion of time that the ASP's systems and communication links are up and running. Since no provider can guarantee 100 percent uptime, ASPs often promise 99.9 percent ("three nines," in professional lingo) uptime, which sounds satisfactory, but it might not be. Three nines mean that downtime might reach 500 minutes per year. This is usually acceptable for customer relationship management systems. Human resource managers or sales representatives, who typically use ISs less than 50 hours per week, might settle even for two nines (99 percent guaranteed uptime). However, experts recommend that organizations look for ASPs that can guarantee five nines—99.999 percent uptime—for critical applications. This high percentage of uptime ensures downtime of no more than five minutes per year. Some firms specialize in monitoring the uptime of ASPs.

Who hires the services of ASPs? Although you will find a variety of companies among ASP clients, the majority of clients fall into four categories:

- Companies that are growing fast and rely on software for deployment of their operations.
- Small companies that do not have the cash to pay up front, but who must use office, telecommunications, and basic business operations applications.
- Medium-sized companies that need expensive software, such as enterprise applications, for their operations but cannot afford the immediate payment of large sums (examples are ERP applications from companies such as SAP and Oracle).
- Organizational units at geographical sites where it is difficult to obtain desired software or personnel to install and maintain the software. These sites are typically located far away from a regional headquarters in a less-developed country. The office at that site can then use applications from a more developed country.

Another type of service provider, similar to an ASP, started to catch the attention of businesses in need of IT services: the **storage service provider (SSP)**. An SSP does not rent software applications, but rents storage space. Instead of spending money on the purchase of data storage devices, a company can contract with an SSP and have all or some of its files stored remotely on the SSP's devices. The storage and retrieval are executed through communication lines, in most cases the Internet. SSPs charge by the number of terabytes used per month. Some of the leading SSPs are StorageNetworks, HP, and Amazon.com. Storage service providers for both consumer and commercial customers are expected to grow significantly over the next several years. Gartner believes that consumers will store more than a third of their digital files in the cloud by 2016, growing to 4.1 zettabytes in 2016 (Anonymous, 2012a).

User Application Development

If an adequate application is not available on the market, or if an organization does not wish to take the risks discussed earlier with purchasing or renting, and if the application is not too complex, another alternative to software development is available. In **user application development**, nonprogrammer users write their own business applications. Typically, user-developed software is fairly simple and limited in scope; it is unlikely that users could develop complex applications such as ERP systems. If end users do have the necessary skills, they should be allowed to develop small applications for immediate needs, and when they do, such applications can be maintained by the end users. They should be encouraged to develop applications that will be used for a brief time and then discarded. End users should not develop large or complex applications, applications that interface with other systems, or applications that are vital for the survival of the organization. They should also be discouraged from developing applications that might survive their own tenure in the organization (Figure 13.9).

FIGURE **13.9**

Guidelines for end-user
development of
information technology
applications

End users should develop if...	End users should not develop if...
End users have the necessary skills	The application is large or complex
The application is small	The application interfaces with other systems
The application is needed immediately	The application is vital for the organization's survival
The application can be maintained by the users	The application will survive the user-developer tenure
The application will be used briefly and discarded	

Managing User-Developed Applications

The proliferation of user-developed applications poses challenges to managers, both in IT units and other business units. In addition to the rules outlined in Figure 13.9, management must cope with the following challenges:

- *Managing the reaction of IT professionals*: IT professionals often react negatively to user development because they perceive it as undermining their own duties and authority. To solve this problem, management must set clear guidelines delineating what types of applications end users may and may not develop.
- *Providing support*: To encourage users to develop applications, IS managers must designate a single technical contact for users. It is difficult to provide IT support for user-developed applications, because the IT staff members are usually unfamiliar with an application developed without their involvement. Yet, IT staff should help solve problems or enhance such applications when end users think their own skills are not adequate.
- *Compatibility*: To ensure compatibility with other applications within an organization, the organization's IT professionals should adopt and supply standard development tools to interested users. Users should not be allowed to use nonstandard tools. Note that compatibility in this context is for the purpose of transferring data among end users; interfacing user-developed applications with other organizational systems should be discouraged.
- *Managing access*: Sometimes, users need to copy data from organizational databases to their own developed spreadsheets or databases. If access to organizational databases is granted for such a purpose, access should be tightly controlled by the IT staff to maintain data integrity and security. Users should be forewarned not to rely on such access when developing their own applications if this is against the organization's policy.

Advantages and Risks

User development of applications offers several important advantages:

- *Shortened lead times*: Users almost always develop applications more quickly than IS personnel, because they are highly motivated (they will benefit from the new system); their systems are usually simpler in design; and they have a head start by being totally familiar with the business domain for which they are developing the application.

- *Good fit to needs*: Nobody knows the users' specific business needs better than the users themselves. Thus, they are apt to develop an application that will satisfy all their needs.
- *Compliance with culture*: User-developed software closely conforms to an individual unit's subculture, which makes the transition to a new system easier for employees.
- *Efficient utilization of resources*: Developing software on computers that are already being used for many other purposes is an efficient use of IT resources.
- *Acquisition of skills*: The more employees there are who know how to develop applications, the greater an organization's skills inventory.
- *Freeing up IS staff time*: User-developers free IS staff to develop and maintain an organization's more complex and sophisticated systems.

However, with all the advantages, application development by users also has some drawbacks. They must be considered seriously. The risks are as follows:

- *Poorly developed applications*: User-developers are not as skilled as IS personnel. On average, the applications they develop are of lower quality than systems developed by professionals. Users are often tempted to develop applications that are too complex for their skills and tools, resulting in systems that are difficult to use and maintain.
- *Islands of information*: An organization that relies on user development runs the risk of creating islands of information and "private" databases not under the control of the organization's IS managers. This lack of control might make it difficult to achieve the benefits of integrated ISs.
- *Duplication*: User-developers often waste resources developing applications that are identical or similar to systems that already exist elsewhere within the organization.
- *Security problems*: Giving end users access to organizational databases for the purpose of creating systems might result in violations of security policies. This risk is especially true in client/server environments. The creation of "private databases" known only to the individual user is risky. The user might not be aware that the information he or she produces from the data is "classified" under an organization's policy.
- *Poor documentation*: Practically speaking, "poor documentation" might be a misnomer. Usually, users do not create any documentation at all because (1) they do not know how to write documentation, and (2) they develop the application on their own to have it ready as soon as possible, and they don't want to take the time to document it. Lack of documentation makes system maintenance difficult at best and impossible at worst. Often, applications are patched together by new users, and pretty soon nobody knows how to iron out bugs or modify programs.

The increasing numbers of PCs and the pervasive use of email and the web in businesses have exposed more people to ISs. In 2010, the U.S. Census Bureau found that over 50 percent of employed Americans could access a computer at their workplace (Anonymous, 2010a). Although computers enable workers to be more productive, they are often used for unproductive, or even destructive, activities. A study on workplace activity has found that 40 percent of Internet access is non-work-related while 60 percent of all purchases are completed during working hours (Griffiths, 2010). In another research study, over 50 percent of employees have accessed social media at work (Ashling, 2009). If an employee uses a company car without permission, the act is obviously wrong. But if an employee uses a company computer to store private files, is this wrong? Accessing a company's intranet is legitimate and encouraged. Accessing another employee's file might be wrong. However, some employees might not be aware of the differences. What are the appropriate personal uses of company computers? Is the answer to this question already covered in existing laws? Should companies have policies that define the appropriate uses of their IT resources? Do we need new laws to ensure a law-abiding workforce? The answers to these questions vary.

- **When There Is No Corporate Policy.** Although unauthorized use of computers might be considered theft, authorities usually do not deal with it as such. Perhaps this is why most state statutes do not specifically address unauthorized use of computers.

  If someone from outside a company accessed the company's computer without authorization and used it for any purpose whatsoever, the act would clearly be criminal under the laws of many countries and of every state in the United States. However, if an *employee* uses the same company computer after hours to prepare a homework assignment for a college class, the act might not be considered unethical, let alone criminal, unless the organization has a clear policy against such activity. What about creating a résumé or writing a letter as part of a job search? Without a company policy, the answer to this question is not clear.

  Widespread access to the web makes the issues even more complicated. Employees have been fired for surfing the web for their own personal purposes during work time. Some have been fired for surfing the web during lunch breaks or after work hours; while they did not waste company-paid time, management objected to the specific sites they accessed, mostly those displaying pornographic images.

- **Company Policies Work.** To avoid misunderstanding, employers should provide clear guidelines, stating that any computer use not for the company's direct benefit,

without the prior approval of the company, is forbidden. One simple measure that some organizations have taken is to have a written policy that is conspicuously posted, signed by employees upon hiring, or both. The notice could read as follows:

"Company policy forbids any employee, without prior authorization of the employee's supervisor, to (a) access or use any equipment or data unless such access is work-related and required to fulfill that employee's duties, or (b) alter, damage, or destroy any company computer resource or property, including any computer equipment, system, terminal, network, software, data, or documentation, including individual employee computer files. Any such act by an employee might result in civil and criminal liability under federal, state, and local laws."

Many companies do not object to recreational or educational use of their computers by employees outside of company time. If this is the case, the policy should say so. Without a policy, companies should not be surprised when their employees' interpretation of reasonable personal use differs from their employers'. However, if there is no clear policy, employees should always remember that a PC is a work tool that their employer put at their disposal for responsible use as part of their job. It is not there to help their own business, shop on the web, or entertain them either during or outside of paid time. Thus, for example, they should not use email or instant messaging to chat with their friends or browse the web for their enjoyment. Yet, is sending a personal email message during lunch break really much different from using a company pen to write a personal note during lunch break? Perhaps the best way to avoid misunderstanding is to simply ask your employer if what you intend to do is objectionable.

To enforce their policies—explicit or implicit—many companies resort to means that are, in some minds, questionable. They use surreptitious surveillance software to monitor employee use of IT. Consider BeAware, an application offered by Ascentive LLC. The software tracks all employee PC activity with live, real-time monitoring of emails, web surfing, chats, and program usage, recording screen shots, time used, and content (Anonymous, 2009).

Everything that you do with your computer can, at the same time, be tracked and recorded, and everything that you see on your monitor is also seen on the monitor of the person who tracks you. The same software is often used to monitor children's web surfing activities and spouses' suspected of infidelity. The question is, should employees be treated as undisciplined children or cheating spouses? An equally fair question is, should employers not have the right to monitor what's done with their equipment, especially on paid time?

Summary

- The alternatives to having applications developed in-house are outsourcing, licensing ready-made software, using software as a service, and user application development.

- Outsourcing has two meanings in IT: commissioning the development of a tailored application to an IT company, and assigning all or some of the IT services of the organization to a vendor of IT services.

- Outsourcing custom-designed applications might afford the organization good fit of the software to need, good fit to culture, dedicated maintenance, seamless interface, specialized security, and potential for strategic advantage.

- The potential advantages of outsourcing IT services include improving cost clarity and reducing license and maintenance fees, freeing the client to concentrate on its core businesses, shortening the time needed to implement new technologies, reducing personnel and fixed costs, gaining access to highly qualified know-how, and receiving ongoing consulting as part of standard support. However, outsourcing IT services has some potential risks: loss of control, loss of experienced employees, loss of competitive advantage, and high price. To ensure that the client enjoys all the expected services and their quality, a detailed service-level agreement must be signed with the IT service vendor.

- When an organization purchases a license to use ready-made software, it enjoys high-quality software that is immediately available at a low price (license fee). However, licensed ready-made software has some potential risks: loose fit between needs and the software features, difficulties in modifications, bankruptcy of the vendor, and high turnover of the vendor's employees.

- Using software as a service (SaaS) has become popular. The client pays monthly fees based on the type of application used and the number of users, and its employees use the applications via a network, mostly through the Internet. ASP clients enjoy availability of applications, avoid the costs of storage hardware and large IT staffs, and do not have to make a long-term commitment of capital to software that might become obsolete in two or three years. The downsides of using an ASP are the loss of control over applications, the potentially low speed of interaction, and the security risks associated with using an IS via a public network.

- The advantages to user application development include a short lead time, good fit of application capabilities to business needs, good compliance with organizational culture, efficient utilization of computing resources, acquisition of skills by users, and the freeing of IS staff to deal with the more complex challenges of the systems. Disadvantages of user-developed applications include the risk of poorly developed applications, undesirable islands of information and private databases, duplications of effort, security problems, and poor documentation. Thus, user development of applications needs to be managed. IS managers need to determine the applications that users should and should not develop and dictate the tools that should be used.

- A majority of America's office workers now have rich computer resources at the tips of their fingers. Often, employees do not know which activities are welcomed and which are not. If an organization lacks a clear policy, employees are not discouraged from abusing computers. This abuse is especially true when employees access websites that are objectionable to their employer or when employees use email for purposes not intended by the employer. If no policy has been established, the simple rule is that employees should not use their computers for anything but work.

KIMBALL'S REVISITED

The initial advertising and promotional campaigns have been developed for the grand opening as well as a tentative schedule for implementation. However, Tyler was unsure how he should approach the development and implementation of the customer loyalty and mobile application technology projects. Becky discussed the various development approaches as well as potential suppliers of these applications. Tyler considered that each approach would include a different set of costs, time, benefits, and risks. How should he approach this important decision?

What Is Your Advice?

1. Tyler and Becky developed a detailed set of information and functional requirements for the customer loyalty system. They believe that they have prioritized their early needs as well as some "nice to haves" for the new system. List some of the advantages of each acquisition approach for this new system as well as the risks. What advice would you give to Tyler on how to continue?

2. Tyler and Becky also discussed the need for a mobile application for the Lakeside. Is the acquisition approach for this application different than the customer loyalty system? Compile a list of advantages and disadvantages of the various approaches, along with your recommendation.

New Perspectives

1. List some mobile application functions that would be helpful to a new restaurant. Establish a priority of the various functions to implement in various versions of the mobile application.

2. If you were Tyler, considering the customer loyalty system and mobile app along with limited resources, which initiative would you decide to implement first? Consider both the strategic and operational importance of each initiative along with the estimated complexity (time to implement, cost, etc.) and discuss your recommendations.

Key Terms

application service provider
(ASP), 436
benchmarking, 435
beta version, 432
custom-designed (tailored)
software, 423

offshoring, 424
request for information (RFI), 434
request for proposal (RFP), 434
service-level agreement, 430
software as a service (SaaS), 436

storage service provider (SSP),
438
uptime, 438
user application development,
438

1. List and explain all the various options now available for an organization to enjoy the services of an IS.

2. Few organizations would develop an application in-house or pay another company to develop it if a similar application can be licensed. Why?

3. What are the benefits and risks of outsourcing IT services?

4. The major hardware and software makers, such as IBM and Hewlett-Packard, derive an increasing portion of their revenue from outsourcing contracts. Analyze and explain why they focus more of their efforts in this direction.

5. What might cause a client to ask to renegotiate a long-term outsourcing contract?

6. You are the CIO of a large manufacturing company. A software vendor approaches you with an offer to have your company serve as a beta site for a new human resource application. What would you consider before making a decision?

7. What is an RFI? What is the difference between an RFI and an RFP? The ideal response to an RFP is one that can be easily transformed into a contract. Why?

8. What is the purpose of benchmarking? Often, benchmarking involves visiting other organizations that have applied the system under consideration. Why?

9. What would you benchmark in a system whose purpose is to enter customer orders and accept customer credit-card account numbers for payment at your web-based site?

10. When purchasing an off-the-shelf application, to which phase of the SDLC is the post-implementation support and service equivalent?

11. Some organizations charge the purchase price of an application that serves only a particular organizational unit back to the unit. Why does the existence of a charge-back arrangement create an incentive to have users develop their own applications?

12. Why don't users commonly document the applications they develop? Why is poor documentation a problem?

13. List and explain the benefits and risks of using the services of an on-demand software provider.

14. Some companies use software as a service (SaaS) because they want to concentrate on core competencies. What is a core competency? How would you determine what an organization's core competencies are?

15. What is a storage service provider (SSP)? How is it different from an ASP?

16. Some outsourcing clients have devised contracts that incentivize their vendors to develop new, innovative ISs for the client. What elements would you include in a contract like this if you were a manager for an outsourcing (client) company?

17. Vendors like to market themselves as "partners" with their outsourcing clients. Why?

18. Do you think that development of ISs by end users should be encouraged? Do the benefits of the practice outweigh its risks?

19. Will ready-made software applications ever meet all the needs of all businesses? Explain.

20. The volume of the software as a service (SaaS) market is growing and predicted to reach one-fourth of the software market. In addition to the benefits listed in the chapter, what are the technological developments that cause this growth?

21. One of Salesforce.com's slogans is *The End of Software*. Do you agree that the term describes the concept of SaaS? Why or why not? Do you think that SaaS will eventually become the only way in which corporations use software? Why or why not?

22. A CIO said that while he would not use a public network such as the Internet with an ASP for some types of ISs, he would allow employees to use the web for other types, such as an accounting application. Give three examples of applications that you would recommend and three that you would not recommend for use through the web. Explain your choices.

23. Except for Salesforce.com, the industry leaders in the SaaS market are companies that have been software leaders before the concept emerged. What do you think is the reason for this? Has this business environment suppressed innovation?

24. Explain why you agree or disagree with the following statement: "Employees are smart enough to know what they should and should not do with their computers. A conduct policy will not prevent wrongdoing."

25. When using the services of an ASP, the client gains an important element that is often overlooked: support service. Considering only support service, would you prefer to have the rented software installed on your own company's hardware or leave it installed at the vendor's site? Explain.

26. Should employees be allowed to use their employers' email for private communication at all? Should they be allowed to do so outside of paid time?

27. Assume that you are the CEO of a company that provides computers and access to email and the web to almost all of its employees. You are about to circulate a new IT use policy in the company. List and explain your "ten commandments" (or fewer, or more) for employees' use of software, email, and the web.

Applying Concepts

28. You are a manager for a new company that is about to start selling textbooks to college bookstores via the web. Several firms specialize in software that supports transactions and data collection on the web. Prepare an RFI for an application to support your new company's effort on the web, including posted catalogs, orders, shipment tracking, payment, and data collection for future marketing.

    Submit the list of questions you want prospective bidders to answer, and be ready to provide an explanation for including each of the questions.

29. A small company considering three storage service providers (SSPs) has asked for your advice. Research the various SSPs mentioned in this chapter and compile your recommendations to the company. Consider cost, flexibility, length of client commitment, communication speed, security, reputation, and any other relevant information. Base your recommendation on your analysis of all the relevant strengths and weaknesses of each provider.

Hands-On Activities

30. In recent years several companies experienced either a total failure or major mishaps when trying to have vendors implement enterprise applications. Consider "failure" as inability to complete the project or a project that ended up costing the client significantly more than expected, including lost revenue. Find at least three sources about such a case. Synthesize, list, and explain what happened and why. Conclude with your own recommendations of what could be done to avoid or minimize the damage. The recommendations should be written so that potential clients of such projects could take proper precautions. Your report should be about 1,500 words long.

31. In recent years a growing amount of software has been outsourced by U.S. companies to other countries, such as India and China. Research the web and write a two-page paper that lists and explains the benefits and the disadvantages of offshoring application development. If you conclude that there are some benefits or advantages to offshoring of specific types of applications, say so and explain your conclusion.

32. Every online retailer (e-tailer) uses a virtual shopping cart application. Team up with another student, research the web for companies that sell such applications, and write a 1,500 to 2,000-word report that summarizes the following points: (a) Who are the major companies that sell these applications? (b) What are the prices of these packages? (c) How long does it take to install the applications? (d) How is the relationship with the bank processing the credit-card payments established? (e) Are there ASPs that offer the use of such systems over the Internet? (Namely, the e-tailer uses a shopping cart application installed at the ASP's location.) (f) If there are ASPs that rent such systems, what are the payment schemes? *Note*: Many web-hosting companies offer shopping carts as part of their packages. You may use these companies, but if you do, report whether the shopping cart service must be tied to the purchasing of other services.

33. Throughout this book, many organizations that provide information and advice on IT have been mentioned. Explore the websites of these organizations and the websites of IT-related magazines to find the latest statistics on the different alternatives for obtaining business applications or the use of business applications. Create a PowerPoint presentation to answer the following questions, and express your answers in pie charts:

    a. What was the dollar amount spent on IT in your country in each of the past three years, and what percentage of this amount was spent on software acquisition?

    b. How was the amount spent on software distributed among in-house development, purchased (or licensed) ready-made software, and outsourced development?

Outsourcing Call Centers

Contact centers have failed to keep up with the times. While most people have adapted to advancements in telephony technologies by forgetting that cellphones were the size of a briefcase only a short decade ago, some companies are still subjecting customers to virtually prehistoric call center technologies. The question which arises is, if the people who use contact centers are using the most modern technology, why aren't the call centers? Outsourcing call center duties to a reputable and distinguished company can make all the difference in customers' call center experience.

Businesses today know more about their customers than ever before. Through cookies, websites, and smartphone applications, companies have been able to acquire more customer data than was ever thought possible. However, while these internal channels are highly advanced, businesses still leave customers hanging out to dry with their lower-cost, self-service contact center systems. Customers hate calling a service provider for assistance, only to be directed to a self-service, voice automated system. Repeating information via website or smartphone app is continually among the top three most irritating attributes of call centers in most all customer feedback surveys. Yet executives are resistant to change their system for two main reasons. The first is cost, followed by risk. They assume that potential replacement solutions put their current telephony infrastructure and delivery capabilities at risk. This is false.

There are simple, low-risk, and cost-effective ways to modernize a contact center through outsourcing. Executives looking to do so should conduct a little research into what web callback and smartphone offerings are available. Fonolo, Radish, and Virtual Hold are three companies with reputable contact center solutions.

Fonolo improves call center experience for customers yet reduces the cost. In 2011, Sirius Canada, a leader in the country for audio entertainment, reached an agreement with Fonolo to provide improved calling services for their subscribers. Another large company using Fonolo is RBC. Fonolo connects the call center with a website, which is necessary for providing a satisfying experience. Customers can choose the link on the webpage that matches the reason for their call and they will be contacted back when the right agent is available. This technique addresses the issue of long wait times on the phone, which customers despise. Sirius Canada has praised Fonolo for its dedication to staying on the cutting edge of customer service.

Radish's ChoiceView is their new app, which allows callers to talk to ChoiceView-enabled businesses while receiving visual information on their smartphone, either from a human business representative or an interactive voice response system. The live visual communication during smartphone calls results in faster communication and thus faster and increased user comprehension. ChoiceView allows users to visually comprehend the process they are attempting to undertake while having the aid of a human voice on the line.

Virtual Hold, as the name implies, focuses on reducing hold time. Customers can skip the wait time by hanging up and receiving a call back when a representative is available. The recording the customers hear alerts them of estimated callback time, so the system has a 90 percent successful rate of connection. Virtual Hold service is cloud-based and thus does not require a severe upfront cost.

In addition to these companies, webcasts are offered on how to connect web presence and smartphone apps with CSRs. All of the previously listed offerings use the callback model for their smartphone and web-to-call offerings. Instead of talking to a computer, customers can get a callback from a fully briefed CSR and speak with a real human. Implementing these technologies can bring a contact center up to date with what customers want: human answers from humans.

Even short periods of time on hold can seem endless when customers have an urgent question. There are low-cost, low-risk outsourcing options available for renovating a business's call center. If executives would have to suffer like end-users of call centers do, they would call for change as well.

Sources: Anonymous. (2011, Mar 08). Sirius Canada Selects Fonolo to Enhance the Calling Experience for its Subscribers, Canada NewsWire; Anonymous. (2012b, May 10). Can We Talk* Verizon and Virtual Hold Technology Help Organizations Dial Down Hold Times; New Voice Call-Back Solution Improves Customer Experience, M2 Presswire; Brown, K. (2013). Raise Your Mobile Profile. Speech Technology, 18(1), 6-6; Thomas, J. (2011). Radish sprouts visual application for smartphones. Boulder County Business Report, 30(19), 1-5B.

Thinking About the Case

1. What are the consequences of having an outdated contact center?

2. How should executives decide on when to outsource a contact center? Which outsourced contact center solution should they choose?

3. What problems do some of the technological advances exhibited by Fonolo's, Radish's and Virtual Hold's new call center solutions solve?

Hearing the Sound of Cost Savings

Business organizations are focused on creating value for their customers, developing or refining their products and expanding their revenue sources. At the same time, management wants to reduce costs and labor resources and create operational efficiencies. While these are lofty and reasonable objectives, without careful and thoughtful planning, these goals are a challenge to implement collectively.

The reliance on custom-designed information technology applications is dwindling. Flat budgets and organizational pressures to achieve more with the same (or less) personnel continue to be the marquee headlines for most business organizations. Information technology is being asked to assess its operations and associated costs, especially with implementation of new application systems.

Information Week's recent State of the Data Center Survey (Marko, 2012) shows a shift from planning and renovating physical plants, including the traditional issues of heating, cooling, and maximizing processing power with existing space. The large-scale projects are more difficult to justify in today's economic and business environment. The "old days" where corporate application development projects that heavily influenced large hardware purchases appear to be disappearing.

The survey respondents, consisting of 256 people responsible for data center management and decision-making, are faced with guiding their organizations with a new data center strategy. Sixty percent of the respondents spend less than 30 percent of their total IT budget on their data center facilities, hardware, and operations; with 30 percent spending less than 20 percent. IT managers are taking a "best of the breed" approach by evaluating each request to find the appropriate software. However, less than 2 percent of the respondents develop applications in-house. The application development landscape is changing, and SaaS seems to be at the forefront of this change.

One such situation involves the American Society of Composers, Authors and Publishers (ASCAP). Founded in 1914, ASCAP chartered its founding with John Philip Sousa (no relation to this book's author) and Irving Berlin as a performing rights organization to maintain licensing agreements for its 435,000 members and individuals. Its licensing personnel negotiate music usage licenses, collect royalties, and pursue legal matters as necessary. Like many businesses in the beginning, ASCAP operated with ledger cards, migrated to a mainframe system, transitioned to SQL Server, and finally to Lotus Notes to process their operational transactions. Its deployment of Notes in 1993 was, at the time, the leading edge of technology. It allowed ASCAP to centralize its databases in the Nashville location for its 26 offices around the country. The implementation achieved its objective. However, over time, the system evolved into multiple Notes databases spread across several servers. So, like the evolution of music from vinyl records, to eight-track tapes, to CDs, to MP3s and now to Internet-streaming services, their technology needed to transition as well.

ASCAP decided to purchase Salesforce.com SaaS CRM service, purchasing about 200 licenses to interact into both the Sales Cloud as well as sales tools for maintaining its account and contact information. They also adopted the Sales Cloud to facilitate business collaboration similar to a "social networking-like customer service platform." Through the implementation of the Salesforce.com products, they were able to use tablet computers for users to generate documents in the cloud and integrate marketing with sales activities. As all of these functions were completed by its licensing personnel, the data was being maintained by the SaaS application with the data centralized in the cloud.

The use of the new product has realized cost savings by reducing the need for IT to maintain and administer the Notes system. The cost savings associated with that labor appears to have paid for the licensing cost of the Salesforce.com product. However, the cost savings has translated beyond the technology function. John Johnson, vice president of licensing operations conveys that the most significant cost savings is "...what it would have cost us to do business with the agility that we have now without having SaaS in the picture." The new "out of the box" functionality has altered the manner in which ASCAP does its business.

The implementation of Salesforce.com was not their only use of cloud technology. ASCAP has also utilized both Amazon and Google to consolidate a 2,000 square-foot warehouse of filing cabinets into a 130 GB database of scanned documents stored and maintained by Amazon's Simple Storage cloud for $20 per month, resulting in $100K in savings.

The transition from using in-house services and resources to cloud-based application software and document retention has been music to the ears of ASCAP.

Source: Anonymous. (2012a). ASCAP ROCKS THE CLOUD. Network World, 29(11), 27–28.

Thinking About the Case

1. Why would the use of a SaaS product provide more agility over an in-house developed product? What do you believe is meant by the increased agility by using Salesforce.com?

2. Do you believe that storing documents in the cloud can create any challenges for a business organization? What do you believe are the key points to consider and analyze before implementing a cloud approach?

3. Will the implementation of SaaS-based applications eliminate any in-house development? Will it allow companies to redeploy their information technology efforts to gain more value? Discuss your thoughts.

References

Anonymous. (2009). Ascentive BeAware Home Internet Monitoring Software Updated, from http://www.ascentive.com/about_us/ascentive/press090817_beawareupdate.html

Anonymous. (2010a). Computer and Internet Use in the United States. Washington, DC.

Anonymous. (2010b, Jul 12). CSC Signs IT Outsourcing Contract Extension with MBDA, *Business Wire*.

Anonymous. (2010c). Gartner Identifies Top 30 Countries for Offshore Services in 2010-2011 Retrieved April 9, 2013, from http://www.gartner.com/newsroom/id/1500514

Anonymous. (2011). Company Milestones Retrieved April 9, 2013, from http://www.salesforce.com/company/

Anonymous. (2012a). Gartner Says That Consumers Will Store More Than a Third of Their Digital Content in the Cloud by 2016 Retrieved April 9, 2013, from http://www.gartner.com/newsroom/id/2060215

Anonymous. (2012b). Gartner Says Worldwide Software-as-a-Service Revenue to Reach $14.5 Billion in 2012 Retrieved April 9, 2013, from http://www.gartner.com/newsroom/id/1963815

Anonymous. (2012c, Dec 13). Idea extends IT outsourcing contract with IBM, *Mint*.

Anonymous. (2013, Apr 09). Walsh College Renews IT Outsourcing Contract with CareTech Solutions, *Business Wire*.

Ashling, J. (2009). Internet Use: Analysis and Abuse. *Information Today*, 26(1), 22-23.

CSC. (2007). CSC and Sears Settle Contract Dispute Retrieved April 10, 2013, from http://www.csc.com/newsroom/press_releases/3285-csc_and_sears_settle_contract_dispute

Griffiths, M. (2010). Internet abuse and internet addiction in the workplace. *Journal of Workplace Learning, 22*(7), 463-472. doi: http://dx.doi.org/10.1108/13665621011071127

Mark, R. (2010). Dell Perot Systems Wins $42M Army Contract. *eWeek*. Retrieved from http://www.eweek.com/c/a/Government-IT/Dell-Perot-Systems-Wins-42M-Army-Contract-495610/

McDougall, P. (2012). IBM Cements $1 Billion Outsourcing Deal With Cemex. *InformationWeek.com*. Retrieved from http://www.informationweek.com/services/outsourcing/ibm-cements-1-billion-outsourcing-deal-w/240004580

Overby, S. (2012a). 5 Tips to Keep IT Outsourcing on Track as Global Providers Cut Staff. Retrieved from http://www.cio.com/article/698063/5_Tips_to_Keep_IT_Outsourcing_on_Track_as_Global_Providers_Cut_Staff?page=2&taxonomyId=3195

Overby, S. (2012b). IBM Beats Indiana in Outsourcing Case No One 'Deserves to Win'. *CIO.com*. Retrieved from http://www.cio.com/article/712259/IBM_Beats_Indiana_in_Outsourcing_Case_No_One_Deserves_to_Win

Verberne, B. (2010). Services Top 100: The World's Largest IT Services Companies (2009) Retrieved April 10, 2013, from http://www.servicestop100.org/services-top-100-the-world-s-largest-it-services-companies.php

CHAPTER fourteen

RISKS, SECURITY, AND DISASTER RECOVERY

Learning Objectives

As the use of computer-based information systems has spread, so has the threat to the integrity of data and the reliability of information. Organizations must deal seriously with the risks of both natural and human menaces. Alexander Dewdney once noted, "The only truly secure system is powered off, cast in a block of concrete, and sealed in a lead room with armed guards. And even then I have my doubts." (Dewdney, 1989) Indeed, there is no way to fully secure an information system against every potential mishap, but there are ways to significantly reduce risks and recover losses.

When you finish this chapter, you will be able to:

• Describe the primary goals of information security.

• Enumerate the main types of risks to information systems.

• List the various types of attacks on networked systems.

• Describe the types of controls required to ensure the integrity of data entry and processing and uninterrupted ecommerce.

• Describe the various kinds of security measures that can be implemented to protect data and ISs.

• Improve the security of your personal information system and the information it stores.

• Recognize online scams.

• Outline the principles of developing a recovery plan.

• Explain the economic aspects of information security.

KIMBALL'S RESTAURANT: Plating the Opening

Tyler visited the Lakeside location and found that all the renovations were done. His father was very pleased that all of the planning and expense for the move to the new location had worked well to make it a reality. Tyler asked his father to meet and review the final list of items that needed their attention in order to open the new location.

They first reviewed the marketing and promotion campaign for the opening. They agreed that the marketing was well planned and would help the opening to be successful. All of the branding for the location was developed strategically and integrated into the various media, web, and social media venues. Feeling comfortable with the marketing, they then reviewed the renovations and operations. They decided to walk through the restaurant and simulate the opening to see if they missed any operational issues.

As they were walking through, one of the contractors knocked over a water bottle on one of his electronic tools and it shorted out and sent sparks flying. Luckily no harm was done to the restaurant, but the tool no longer functioned. With all of the food and beverages at the restaurant, Michael wondered if they were properly prepared for any equipment malfunctions due to breakdown or accidental spills. At the same time, Tyler was talking to someone on his cell phone. In the middle of the conversation, the call was disrupted when his cell phone battery ran out; he was always forgetting to charge his phone. Tyler laughed it off at first, but then he thought of the business, "I have pictures and other files on my phone backed up to the cloud, but what would happen if our business data was destroyed or unavailable?"

Goals of Information Security

In 2009, hackers took over Twitter twice, allowing them to steal personal user information and infiltrate accounts to send out phony tweets. Among the Twitter accounts accessed by the hackers were those of President Barack Obama, Britney Spears, and then-CNN anchor Rick Sanchez (Sarno, 2011). On April 20, 2011, Sony Corp was forced to shut down its PlayStation Network, an online gaming network that allows console owners to compete against other players online. The company reported that a hacker had stolen names, birth dates, and possibly credit-card numbers from 77 million accounts on the PlayStation Network. Less than two weeks later, Sony's PC-Game service, Sony Online Entertainment, was also shut down due to hacker invasions in which the company believed names, birth dates, and addresses of users were stolen. Additionally, hackers acquired access to data from 12,700 non-U.S. credit card accounts and 10,700 bank account numbers (Sherr, 2011). In total, the cyber-attacks on Sony Corp resulted in data from over 100 million accounts being accessed by hackers in a period of only days. This is a small sample of what can happen to information systems and the data stored on them.

As you have already seen, the development, implementation, and maintenance of ISs constitute a large and growing part of the cost of doing business; protecting these resources is a primary concern. The increasing reliance on ISs—combined with their connection to the outside world through a public network, the Internet—makes securing corporate ISs increasingly challenging. Adding to the challenges is the increased tendency to store data on portable devices. The role of computer controls and security is to protect systems against accidental mishaps and intentional theft and corruption of data and applications. They also help organizations ensure that their IT operations comply with the law and with expectations of employees and customers for privacy. The major goals of information security are to:

- Reduce the risk of systems and organizations ceasing operations.
- Maintain information confidentiality.
- Ensure the integrity and reliability of data resources.
- Ensure the uninterrupted availability of data resources and online operations.
- Ensure compliance with policies and laws regarding security and privacy.

To plan measures to support these goals, organizations first must be aware of the possible risks to their information resources, which include hardware, applications, data, and networks; then, they must execute security measures to defend against those risks.

In recent years, the U.S. Congress passed several laws that set standards for the protection of patient, student, and customer privacy and compliance with corporate internal controls. They include the Health Insurance Portability and Accountability Act of 1996 (HIPAA) and Sarbanes-Oxley Act of 2002 (SOX). These laws have an important effect on securing information and, therefore, on securing information systems. Other countries have similar laws that have similar implications for information security. However, corporate concern should be focused not only on complying with the law, but also on ensuring that their information resources are secure. Organizations would then be able to minimize situations that might compromise their business operations.

One of the foundational concepts associated with information systems security is known as the **CIA triad**, defined as confidentiality, integrity, and availability (Chia, 2012):

- *Confidentiality*—Preventing the disclosure of information to unauthorized people, entities and systems. For example, maintaining the privacy of individual health care information would be an important characteristic of any newly developed information system.
- *Integrity*—Ensuring the accuracy and consistency of data throughout the life cycle of the data. The data should not be modified or deleted without authorization or detection. For example, a bill of $150 paid online should not be altered and processed for $1,500.
- *Availability*—Data must be accessible to authorized parties, entities, and systems when needed and at an appropriate time. A business might allow employees to access financial data only during business hours and through authorized workstations. These restrictions would prevent an employee from gaining access to data from an external location during off-hours.

The U.S. government, as well as many states, have adopted several laws that focus on the privacy and security of personal and corporate information. Some of the federal legislation passed includes: the Family Educational Rights and Privacy Act of 1974 (FERPA), HIPAA (see above), and the Gramm-Leach-Bliley Act of 1999 (GLBA). FERPA specifically protects the privacy of a student's educational records for all colleges receiving federal funds.

WHY YOU SHOULD   Understand Risks, Security, and Disaster Recovery Planning

Some time ago you started working for a small company. You love your new job. It's Monday 10:00 a.m., and the IS you use is down. Apparently, there's a blackout, and in a freak accident the backup generators don't work. Do you know what *you* are supposed to do? As explained and demonstrated throughout this book, information is the lifeblood of any modern organization. Practically every aspect of business depends on the currency of processed data and the timely provision of information. This fluent process can be achieved only if information systems are protected against threats. As a professional, you must be aware of what might happen to the ISs upon which you and your colleagues or subordinates depend. You must protect the systems against events that threaten their operation and make it impossible to carry out critical business activities. When a new system is developed, you should ask the developers to provide a system that not only supports the functions of your business unit but also incorporates controls that will minimize any potential system compromises. You also need to be prepared for a disaster, and should know how to implement your part of the business recovery plan to help restore operations as soon as possible.

Risks to Information Systems

Cloud computing and data storage are popular technology "buzzwords" with today's information technology and corporate executives. However, business organizations must evaluate the risks as well as the benefits of these technologies. On Christmas Eve 2012, Netflix's online system went down and remained unavailable for more than 12 hours (Finkle, 2012). The system outage for the popular video rental company was caused by Amazon Web Services (AWS), which operates systems to provide data storage and Internet services for businesses. AWS reported that the outage was from one of its operations in Virginia, which was also the cause of an outage to Netflix earlier that year in June (Bensinger, 2012; Finkle, 2012).

In recent years, especially because of the growth of online business, corporations have considered protection of their IS resources an increasingly important issue, for good reasons. **Downtime**, the time during which ISs or data are not available in the course of conducting business, has become a dreaded situation for almost every business worldwide. By some estimates, U.S. businesses lose $26 billion annually because of downtime (Harris, 2011). The organizational cost of a cloud outage can be significant. For example, according to Amazon.com's earnings report, the company posts $10.8 billion per quarter. Therefore, one hour of downtime can be estimated at about $5 million per hour (Linthicum, 2013). According to research by Gartner, the cost per hour of downtime to small or medium-sized businesses is approximately $42,000 (Anonymous, 2012d). The costs are averages and depend on industry, the size of the company, and other factors. These costs may be much larger in many cases. The following section discusses the most pervasive risks to IS operations. In addition to the threats discussed here, it is important to remember that terrorism has posed a serious threat to all aspects of ISs: hardware, software, and data.

Risks to Hardware

While stories about damage to ISs by malicious Internet attacks grab headlines, the truth about risks to ISs is simply this: the number one cause of systems downtime is hardware failure. Risks to hardware involve physical damage to computers, peripheral equipment, and communications media. The major causes of such damage are natural disasters, blackouts and brownouts, and vandalism.

Natural Disasters

Natural disasters that pose a risk to ISs include fires, floods, earthquakes, hurricanes, tornadoes, and lightning, which can destroy hardware, software, or both and cause total or partial paralysis of systems or communications lines. Floodwater can ruin storage media and cause short circuits that burn delicate components such as microchips. Floods, in this context, include those occurring as a result of plumbing problems inside buildings. Lightning and voltage surges cause tiny wires to melt and destroy circuitry. In addition, wildlife and human error occasionally destroy communications lines; animals gnaw cables, and farmers and construction workers occasionally cut cables inadvertently.

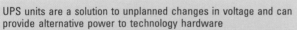
UPS units are a solution to unplanned changes in voltage and can provide alternative power to technology hardware

Mile Atanasov/Photos.com

Blackouts and Brownouts

Computers run on electricity. If power is disrupted, the computer and its peripheral devices cannot function, and the change in power supply can be very damaging to computer processes and storage. **Blackouts** are total losses of electrical power. In **brownouts**, the voltage of the power decreases, or very short interruptions occur in the flow of power. Power failure might not only disrupt operations, but it can also cause irreparable damage to hardware. Occasional surges in voltage are equally harmful, because their impact on equipment is similar to that of lightning.

The popular way of handling brownouts is to connect a voltage regulator between computers and the electric network. A voltage regulator boosts or decreases voltage to smooth out drops or surges and maintains voltage within an acceptable tolerance.

To ensure against interruptions in power supply, organizations use **uninterruptible power supply (UPS)** systems, which provide an alternative power supply for a short time, as soon as a power network fails. The only practical measure against prolonged blackouts in a public electrical network is to maintain an alternative source of power, such as a generator that uses diesel or another fuel. Once the main power stops, backup batteries provide power until the generator starts, gets up to speed, and produces the power needed for the computer system.

Vandalism

Vandalism occurs when human beings deliberately destroy computer systems. Bitter customers might damage ATMs, or disgruntled employees might destroy computer equipment out of fear that it will eliminate their jobs or simply to get even with their superiors. It is difficult to defend computers against vandalism. ATMs and other equipment that are accessible to the public are often encased in metal boxes, but someone with persistence can still cause severe damage. In the workplace, the best measure against vandalism is to allow access only to those who have a real need for the system. Sensitive equipment, such as servers, should be locked in a special room. Such rooms usually are well equipped with fire-suppression systems and are air-conditioned, and thus protect against environmental risks.

Risks to Data and Applications

The primary concern of any organization should be its data, because it is often a unique resource. Data collected over time can almost never be recollected the same way, and even when it can, the process would be too expensive and time consuming. The concern for applications, especially if the applications are not tailor-made, should come second. All data and applications are susceptible to disruption, damage, and theft. While the culprit in the destruction of hardware is often a natural disaster or power spike, the culprit in damage to software is almost always human.

Theft of Information and Identity Theft

Sometimes the negligence of corporations and the careless use of technology, especially on public links to the Internet, create security "holes" or vulnerabilities. A university student admitted to using software to capture his professors' passwords to gain access to the records system and change his grades. In another case, a young man installed a program called Invisible KeyLogger Stealth on public-use computers in 14 Kinko's stores, where customers can access the Internet. Personal computers connected to the Internet are widely available in hotels, public libraries and airports. Keystroke logging—or simply **keylogging**—software records individual keystrokes. For one year, his software secretly recorded more than 450 usernames and passwords, which he used to access existing bank accounts and create new ones. He was caught when he used an application called GoToMyPC. Subscribers to the GoToMyPC service can use an application by the same name to link to a PC from another PC and fully control the remote one as if they were sitting in front of it. Using the application, he remotely accessed and used one of his victims' PCs. Using the PC at home, this person noticed that the cursor was moving "by itself." The cursor opened files and subscribed to an online payment transfer service. The perpetrator pled guilty in court.

Keylogging has also been put to work on a much more massive scale by criminal rings. Computer users might click a link that appears innocent, but actually installs spyware and keyloggers on their computers. The keylogging application records communication with the victim's bank, insurance company, or other financial institutions. The collected data might include credit-card details, Social Security numbers, usernames, passwords, instant-messaging chat sessions, and search terms. This collected data is saved in a file hosted on a server that is likely not registered in the United States. This security threat continues to be a challenging issue that often goes undetected by antivirus software (Collins, 2012).

In some cases it is employees who unwittingly give away important information such as access codes. Con artists use tricks known as **social engineering**. They telephone an employee who has a password to access an application or a database, introduce themselves as service people from a telephone company or the organization's own IT unit, and say they must have the employee's password to fix a problem. Employees are often tempted to provide their password. The "social engineers" then steal valuable information.

Once criminals have a person's identifying details, such as a Social Security number, driver's license number, or credit-card number, they can pretend to be this person. This crime is called **identity theft**. The imposter can easily withdraw money from the victim's bank accounts, put charges on the victim's credit card, and apply for new credit cards. Since an increasing number of applications for such instruments as well as financial transactions are executed online, identity theft has become a serious problem. These thieves sift through your garbage or deceive you to obtain your personal information. The Federal Trade Commission put identify theft at the top of its consumer complaint list for a fifth year, logging over 2 million complaints in 2012 (Christman, 2013). According to research firm Javelin Strategy & Research, 8.1 million U.S. adults were identity-theft victims in 2011, and their combined financial loss was $37 billion (Anonymous, 2011). While the number of incidents declined in 2011, in 2010 the costs increased by 63 percent to about $631 per incident, compared to $387 per incident in the previous year (Anonymous, 2011). The National Health Care Anti-Fraud Association estimates that about 3 percent of all health care costs are attributed to fraud by providing false information (Turner, 2012).

Both social engineering and hacking to steal data from online databases have caused huge damage to corporations. Connecting databases to the Internet is necessary for proper operation of multisite organizations and organizations that must share data remotely with business partners. The only way to minimize hacking into such systems is to improve security measures.

POINT OF INTEREST — Like Handing Your Home Key to a Burglar

According to SplashData, a password management company, the three most common passwords that people use to access their computers, in descending order of frequency, are "password," "123456," and "12345678." The company published a list of the 25 worst passwords of the year. Their CEO reported that hacking tools are becoming more cutting-edge every year. A strong password is one that takes a long time to figure out by an unauthorized party, even if that party uses sophisticated software to crack it. Stronger passwords are longer, and contain a mix of letters, digits, and special characters (e.g., the characters +*&^%$#@!). Thus, a password such as hockeyGoalwins4now would be a strong password. Several websites provide tools to measure the strength of your password. Try Microsoft's Safety & Security Center at *http://www.microsoft.com/security/online-privacy/passwords-create.aspx*

Source: Ngak, C. (2012). The 25 most common passwords of 2012. April 25, 2013. Retrieved from http://www.cbsnews.com/8301-205_162-57539366/the-25-most-common-passwords-of-2012/

In recent years, identity theft has been more prevalent as part of *phishing*, a crime discussed in Chapter 8, "The Web-Enabled Enterprise." Crooks spam millions of recipients with bogus messages, supposedly from legitimate companies, directing them to a site where they are requested to "update" their personal data, including passwords. The sites are ones constructed by the criminals who steal the personal data and use it to charge the victim's credit account, apply for new credit cards, or—in the worst situations—also apply for other documents such as driver's licenses and online loans.

In a more recent form of phishing, *spear phishing*, criminals use personal information to attack organizational systems. The illustration on the next page shows a sample phishing email shown on PayPal's website with tips on how to recognize such emails. If you place your mouse pointer over the *"Please register here"* hyperlink, you would view a link to a web address not associated with PayPal. Not surprisingly, financial institutions are the most targeted sector. Spear phishers strive to steal money from online accounts.

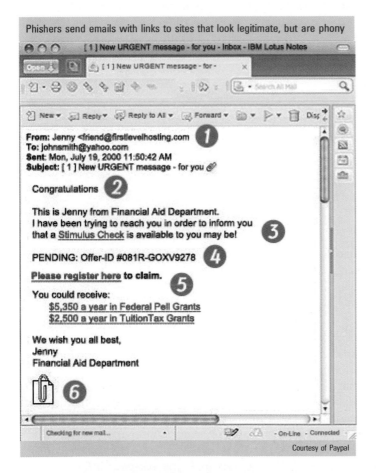

Phishers send emails with links to sites that look legitimate, but are phony

Courtesy of Paypal

Cyber Terrorism

In recent years, business organizations' information systems have been targeted for terrorist attacks, sometimes referred to as **cyber terrorism**. In 2003, a survey conducted by Dataquest found that most U.S. businesses were not prepared to respond appropriately when faced with a cyber attack on their technology infrastructure (Rapport, 2003). Since then, more attention has been focused on the topic by both government and business organizations. Research conducted by ABI Research estimates that worldwide spending on security technology will increase to $10 billion in 2016, compared to $6 billion in 2010 (Simpkins, 2011). The U.S. Defense Department alone will invest more than $3 billion to counter cyber terrorism threats. A security expert, Dr. Frank Umbach states, "for the first time, cyber-attacks have been listed ahead of international terrorism in the catalogue of dangers." (Anonymous, 2013b) Cyber attacks could be used to disrupt network communication, implement denial of service attacks, as well as destroy or steal corporate and government information. It is not a topic discussed in detail or highlighted in the media due to the secretive nature of the attacks, probably due to classified intelligence and federal government involvement.

Data Alteration, Data Destruction, and Web Defacement

Alteration or destruction of data is often an act of mischief. As mentioned before, an organization's data is often the most important asset it owns, even more important than its hardware and applications. Even if data is altered or destroyed as a prank, the damage to the organization is considerable. The effort to reinstate missing or altered records from a backup copy might entail expensive labor. Even if the actual damage is not substantial, IT staff must spend a lot of time scanning the data pools to ascertain the integrity of the entire resource, and they must also figure out how the perpetrator managed to circumvent security controls. This activity itself wastes the time of high-salaried employees.

Often, the target of online vandals is not data but the organization's website. Each day, some organizations find their websites defaced. Defacement causes several types of damage: first-time visitors are not likely to stay around long enough or revisit to learn about the true nature of the site, and they might associate the offensive material with the organization; frequent visitors might never come back; and shoppers who have had a good experience with the site might leave it forever because they no longer trust its security measures.

To deface a website, an intruder needs to know the site's access code or codes that enable the webmaster and other authorized people to work on the site's server and update its pages. The intruder might either obtain the codes from someone who knows them or use special "brute force" software that tries different codes until it succeeds in accessing the pages.

The best measure against defacement, of course, is software that protects against unauthorized access, or as it is more commonly known, hacking. However, since such software might fail, the public damage can be minimized by ensuring that members of the organization monitor the home page and other essential pages frequently. When the defacement is detected shortly after it occurs, the defaced pages can be replaced with backups before too many visitors have seen the rogue pages. An increasing number of websites are restored within hours or even minutes from the defacement.

The cure to any unauthorized entry to an IS is for the organization to find the weakness in its security software and fix it with the appropriate software. Such software is often called a "patch." Software companies that sell server management applications often produce patches and invite clients to download and install them.

To combat hackers, organizations use honeytokens. A **honeytoken** is a bogus record in a networked database that neither employees nor business partners would ever access for legitimate purposes. When the intruder copies the database or the part of the database that contains that record, a simple program alerts security personnel, who can start an investigation. The program that detects the incident might also reside on a router or another communications device that is programmed to send an alert as soon as it detects the honeytoken. To entice the intruder to retrieve the honeytoken when only searching for individual records, the honeytoken might be a bogus record of a famous person, such as a medical record of a celebrity in a medical database or the salary of the CEO in a payroll database.

To learn of security holes and methods of unauthorized access, organizations can establish honeypots. A **honeypot** is a server that contains a mirrored copy of a production database (a database that is used for business operations), or one with invalid records. It is set up to make intruders think they have accessed a production database. The traces they leave educate information security officers of vulnerable points in the configuration of servers that perform valid work. In some cases, security people have followed an intruder's "roaming" in the honeypot in real time. Note, however, that different sources have different definitions of the terms honeypot and honeytoken. For example, some define honeypot as any trap set for abusers, including a physical computer, and a honeytoken as a special case where the trap is only data.

POINT OF INTEREST   Sounds Vishy

Vishing is a method of stealing money or information from people over the telephone. It works like this. Typically the scammer will implement a technique called 'caller ID' spoofing to make it look like they are calling from a familiar or legitimate source. The caller is then directed by a recorded message to call a toll-free number, similar to how a phishing attack tells a person to go to a fraudulent website. The caller is asked to dial in personal information such as a credit card or Social Security number. In 2009, two tele-marketing firms in Florida were sued by the Federal Trade Commission for using this method of theft to sell bogus automobile warranties for between $2,000 and $3,000 each. In the two years they were in operation, they made approximately 1 billion calls and generated more than $10 billion. Until the Truth in Caller ID Act of 2009 (signed into law in 2010), caller ID spoofing was legal. The overdue FCC rules "prohibit any person or entity from transmitting misleading or inaccurate caller ID information with the intent to defraud, cause harm, or wrongfully obtain anything of value." The rules do however, provide exceptions that allow law enforcement officials to manipulate their caller ID with a court's permission.

Sources: Federal Communications Commission. (2013). Caller ID and Spoofing. Retrieved from http://www.fcc.gov/guides/caller-id-and-spoofing; Reardon, Marguerite. (19 May 2009). Protecting yourself from vishing attacks. Retrieved from http://news.cnet.com/8301-1035_3-10244200-94.html

Computer Viruses, Worms, and Logic Bombs

Computer **viruses** are so named because they act on programs and data in a fashion similar to the way viruses act on living tissue: computer viruses easily spread from computer to computer. Because so many computers are now connected to one another and many people share files, people unknowingly transmit to other computers viruses that have infected their own files. Once a virus reaches a computer, it damages applications and data files. In addition to destroying legitimate applications and data files, viruses might disrupt data communications: the presence of viruses causes data communications applications to process huge numbers of messages and files for no useful purpose, which detracts from the efficiency of transmitting and receiving legitimate messages and files. The only difference between a computer virus and a worm is that a **worm** spreads in a network without human intervention. A worm attacks computers without the need to send email or open any received files. Most people refer to both types of rogue code as viruses, as does this book.

Almost as soon as email became widespread, criminal minds used it to launch viruses. The Melissa virus of 1999 was an early demonstration of why you should be suspicious of email messages even when they seem to come from people or organizations you know. In the Melissa case, an innocent-looking email message contained an attached Microsoft Word document that, when opened, activated a macro that sent an infected message to the first 50 entries in the victim's Microsoft Outlook address book. Many other viruses spread in a similar way: the recipient is tempted to open—and thereby activate—a file that is attached to a message. The program in that file then destroys files, slows down operations, or does both, and uses vulnerabilities in the operating system and other applications to launch copies of itself to other computers linked to the Internet. Since Melissa, there have been thousands of virus and worm attacks, and millions of computers continue to be infected.

There are many more viruses waiting for victims. In April 2012, Kaspersky Labs estimated that 280 million malicious programs were detected, 134 million web-based infections were prevented, and more than 24 million malicious URLs were found (Anonymous, 2012b). According to the report, the two web-based applications with the greatest number of virus detections are Adobe's Acrobat Reader and Oracle's Java.

One way to protect against viruses is to use **antivirus software**, which is readily available on the market from companies that specialize in developing this kind of software, such as Kaspersky, Symantec, and McAfee (see figure), or the free AVG and free open source ClamWin. Subscribers can regularly update the software with code that identifies and deletes or quarantines new viruses, or choose automatic updates, in which virus definitions are updated automatically when the computer is connected to the Internet. However, if a new virus is designed to operate in a way not yet known, the software is unlikely to detect it. Most virus-detection applications allow the user to automatically or selectively destroy suspect programs. Another way to minimize virus threats is to program network software, especially email server software, to reject any messages that come with executable files that might be or contain viruses. Some email applications, such as Microsoft Outlook, are programmed to reject such files.

Some viruses are called **Trojan horses**, analogous to the destructive gift given to the ancient Trojans, as described in Greek mythology. In their war against Troy, the Greeks pretended they were abandoning the city's outskirts and left behind

Antivirus software is an important application for blocking computer viruses

McAfee | SecurityCenter

- Home
- Navigation
- About
- ? Help

Your computer is secure (no action required)

McAfee SECURE

- ✓ Real-Time Scanning: On >
- ✓ Updates: Current >
- ✓ Firewall: On >
- ✓ Subscription: Active >

0

Viruses and spyware detected in your last scan

View Reports
View Threat Map

Features

- Virus and Spyware Protection ⌄
- Web and Email Protection ⌄
- Data Protection ⌄
- PC and Home Network Tools ⌄
- Parental Controls ⌄

Courtesy of McAfee, Inc

a big wooden horse as a present. The Trojans pulled the horse into the city. When night fell, Greek soldiers hidden within the horse jumped out and opened the gates for thousands of their comrades, who conquered the city. In computer terms, a Trojan horse is any virus disguised as legitimate software or useful software that contains a virus. Many people also refer to spyware that comes with useful software as Trojan horse software.

A growing number of viruses and worms take advantage of vulnerable features of operating systems, most notably Microsoft Windows. Most attack this company's operating systems because the large majority of organizations worldwide use Microsoft operating systems to run their servers and computers. Software vendors provide patches against direct intrusion into computer systems and distribute security patches against viruses and worms. However, it is up to security professionals and network administrators to implement the patches as soon as they become available.

Some rogue computer programs do not spread immediately like a virus but are often significantly more damaging to the individual organization that is victimized. A **logic bomb** is software that is programmed to cause damage at a specified time to specific applications and data files. It lies dormant until a certain event takes place in the computer or until the computer's inner clock reaches the specified time; the event or time triggers the virus to start causing damage. Logic bombs are usually planted by insiders, that is, employees of the victimized organization. In one case, a former employee at the U.S. Transportation Security Administration (TSA)'s Colorado Springs Operations Center (CSOC) was convicted of planting a logic bomb in 2009 after he was given notice that his job was being terminated. The infected system was set to cause damage to data on CSOC's database, creating malfunctions in airline passenger screening. Fortunately, the disruption was found by TSA personnel and disabled before it manifested its damage (Zetter, 2011).

Non-malicious Mishaps

Unintentional damage to software occurs because of poor training, lack of adherence to backup procedures, or simple human error. Although unintentional damage rarely occurs in robust applications, poor training might result in inappropriate use of an application so that it ruins data, unbeknownst to the user. For instance, when faced with an instruction that might change or delete data, a robust application will pose a question such as: "Are you sure you want to delete the record?" or issue a warning such as "This might destroy the file." More common damage is caused by the failure to save all work and create a backup copy. Destruction of data often happens when using a word-processing program to create or change text files and when updating databases.

Unauthorized downloading and installation of software that might cause damage can be controlled by limiting administration rights to employees. Many organizations instruct operating systems to deny such rights to most employees. They program ISs to accept new software installation only when the proper access codes are entered.

Risks to Online Operations

The massive movement of operations to the Internet has attracted hackers who try to interrupt such operations daily. In addition to unauthorized access, data theft, and defacing of webpages, there has been a surge in denial-of-service attacks and hijacking of computers.

Denial of Service

In July 2011, Internet shoppers trying to access their PayPal accounts could not do so due to a denial-of-service attack (Bryan-Low, 2011). **Denial of Service (DoS)** occurs when a website receives an overwhelming number of information requests, such as merely logging on to a site. The intention of high-volume log-on requests is to slow down legitimate traffic on the site's server; business can slow to a halt. The server's frantic efforts to handle the massive amount of traffic denied legitimate visitors and business partners access to the site.

In most such attacks, the perpetrator launches software that uses other people's computers for the attack—unbeknownst to them; thus the attacks are sometimes known as distributed denial-of-service (DDoS) attacks. Professionals call the computers used in these attacks "zombies." Zombie computers not only exacerbate the volume of traffic but also make it impossible to track down the generator of the attack.

DoS attacks continue to be a major problem. These attacks affect every business and industry. In the annual reports to the Securities and Exchange Commission, at least 19 financial institutions have reported that they were targeted by DoS attacks. The SEC has asked that companies disclose "significant computerized theft or disruption" based on public knowledge of this issue (Nakashima & Douglas, 2013). In early 2013, Bank of America struggled to restore service to 40 million households without access to its electronic banking services (mobile, online and telephone) because of a DoS attack (Reckard, 2013). Citigroup's website was affected by a DoS attack where some customers had difficulty accessing their accounts (Browdie, 2012). It is clear from these and other examples that financial institutions continue to be the target of technology crimes to disrupt and deny services to their customers.

Because it is impossible to stop anyone from trying to log on to a website, there is no full cure for a DoS attack, but equipment is available that can filter most illegitimate traffic targeting a site. The equipment detects repeated requests that come from the same IP addresses at an abnormal frequency and blocks them, and it can be programmed to block all incoming communication from suspected servers. The equipment can filter about 99 percent of false requests, but using the equipment slows down communication, so the site's response is slowed. In addition, blocking requests might also deny access to legitimate visitors from suspected servers, especially if the server is used by an ISP that provides Internet access to thousands of people and organizations. One way to mitigate DoS attacks is for an organization to use multiple servers, which is a good idea anyway to handle periods of legitimate traffic increases.

No organization is immune to DoS. Some of the most visible websites have been attacked, including those of eBay, Amazon, CNN, and the U.S. Federal Bureau of Investigation (Bryan-Low, 2011). All had to shut down their sites for several hours. Amazon, eBay, and other commercial sites have lost revenue as a result. Neustar, Inc., a real-time information provider, reported that of the 1,000 North American IT professionals surveyed on DoS attacks, over 300 respondents reported their organizations had been attacked. Of those attacked, 35 percent reported attacks lasting longer than 24 hours and 11 percent lasting over a week (Anonymous, 2012c).

Computer Hijacking

You might not be aware of it, but there is a good chance your networked computer has been hijacked. No, nobody would remove it from your desk, but if it is connected to the Internet, it is used by other people. **Hijacking** a computer means using some or all of the resources of a computer linked to a public network without the consent of its owner. As you have seen, this has been done for DoS, but it is also done for other purposes.

Hijacking is carried out by surreptitiously installing a small program called a **bot** on a computer. Like many viruses, these programs are downloaded unwittingly by people who use chat rooms and file-sharing networks. When your computer is hijacked, your Internet connection might slow to a crawl. The damage to corporations in the form of reduced productivity can be great. The main purpose of hijacking computers is spamming: using hijacked computers to send unsolicited commercial email to large numbers of people, often millions of addresses. Spammers do so for two reasons: they hide the real source of the email so that they cannot be identified and pursued, and they take advantage of the hijacked machines' computer resources—CPU time, memory, and communications link—to expedite the distribution of spam.

Nobody knows how many computers are infected with bots. With the increased popularity of social media, companies like Facebook are experiencing the influence of bots, which impact their click statistics. Facebook believes that 1.5 percent of its monthly active users are there for the purpose of spamming and violating its terms. One of their accounts claimed that 80 percent of clicks on its Facebook ad campaign were initiated by bots (Darwell, 2012).

To hijack computers, spammers exploit security holes in operating systems and communications software, and then surreptitiously install email forwarding software, much as one would install a virus. Most users do not notice the extra work their computers do. One precaution is to check why a computer continues activity (such as hard disk work) when the owner does not use it. Computer owners can also install special software that detects email forwarding applications.

Computer hijacking is also done to turn computers into zombies to help a DoS. Instead of exploiting the computers to send email, they are used to send repeated service requests to web servers.

Controls

Controls are constraints and other restrictions imposed on a user or a system, and they can be used to secure systems against the risks just discussed or to reduce damage caused to systems, applications, and data. Figure 14.1 lists the most common controls. Controls are implemented not only for access but also to implement policies and ensure that nonsensical data is not entered into corporate databases.

FIGURE **14.1**

Common controls used to protect systems from risks

- ◆ Program robustness and data entry controls
- ◆ Backup
- ◆ Access controls
- ◆ Atomic transactions
- ◆ Audit trail

Application Reliability and Data Entry Controls

Apart from performing programmed functions, reliable applications can resist inappropriate usage, such as incorrect data entry or processing. The most reliable programs consider every possible misuse or abuse. A highly reliable program includes code that promptly produces a clear message if a user either makes an error or tries to circumvent a process. For example, a website invites users to select a username and password, and the operators demand passwords that are not easy to guess. The application should be programmed to reject any password that has fewer than a certain number of characters or does not include numerals. A clear message then must be presented, inviting the user to follow the guidelines.

Controls also translate business policies into system features. For example, businesses use their IS to implement a policy limiting debt for each customer to a certain level. When a customer reaches the debt limit and tries to purchase additional items, a message appears on the cash register screen alerting the sales associate of the issue. Thus, the policy is implemented by using a control at the point of sale. Similar systems do not allow any expenditure to be committed unless a certain budgetary item is first checked to ensure sufficient allocation. A spending policy has been implemented through the proper software. Information technology systems are highly effective in implementing and enforcing business policies and procedures.

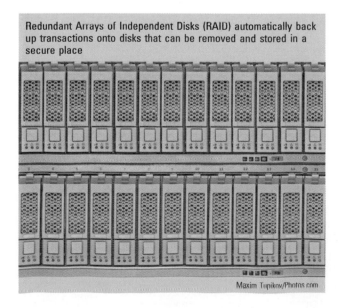

Redundant Arrays of Independent Disks (RAID) automatically back up transactions onto disks that can be removed and stored in a secure place

Maxim Tupikov/Photos.com

Backup

Probably the easiest way to protect against loss of data is to automatically duplicate all data periodically, a process referred to as data **backup**. Storage media suitable for routine backup were discussed in Chapter 4, "Business Hardware." Many systems have built-in automatic backup programs. The data might be duplicated on inexpensive storage devices such as magnetic tapes. Manufacturers of storage devices also offer Redundant Arrays of Independent Disks (RAID) for this purpose. As explained in Chapter 4, **RAID** is a set of disks that is programmed to replicate stored data, providing a higher degree of reliability. The figure on the previous page shows an example of RAID disk drives used in a business.

Of course, backing up data is not enough. The disks or tapes containing backed-up data must be routinely transported off-site, so that if a business site is damaged by a disaster, the remote storage can be used since it is likely to be spared. In the past, many companies had a truck haul backup disks and tapes to the storage location at the end of every business day, and some might still do so. However, due to developments in telecommunications in recent years, most corporations prefer to back up data at a remote site over a network. In fact, this approach is safer than transporting physical disks and tapes; on several occasions such media fell off vans or were stolen. Often, the backup disks or tapes reside thousands of miles away from the organization's business offices. For additional protection, backup disks or tapes are locked in safes that can withstand fire and floods.

Companies can also use the services of firms that specialize in providing backup facilities. The vendor maintains a site with huge amounts of storage space linked to the Internet. The online data backup service typically provides client organizations with an application that copies designated files from the client's systems to remote storage. The client's data is transmitted through the Internet and stored at the vendor's secure site. These vendors also use a variety of redundancy and multi-location platforms to increase the security of the client backup data in the event of a disaster at their facilities. These services, offered for a monthly or annual subscription fee, provide individuals and businesses with a service managed by professionals whose sole responsibility is the secure backup and access of important data. In addition, customers do not need to be concerned about increasing their storage capacity as their backup requirements increase. The vendor continues to provide scalability as the customer's storage needs change. These services are referred to as online backup, cloud backup, or e-vaulting. Several companies provide this service, such as Carbonite (see illustration), Backblaze, Mozy, and Crashplan+.

Businesses and individuals can subscribe to online backup services that automatically create a remote backup of data files

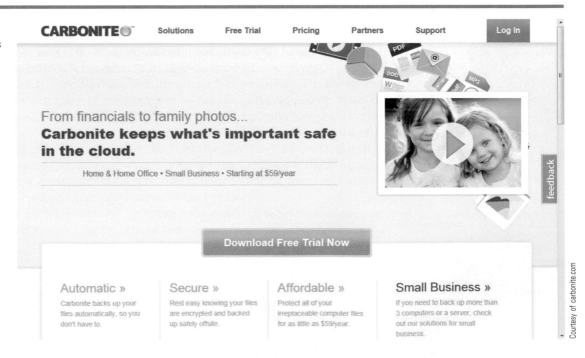

Courtesy of carbonite.com

Access Controls

Unauthorized access to information systems, usually via public networks such as the Internet, does not always damage IT resources. However, it is regarded as one of the most serious threats to security because it is often the prelude to the destruction of websites, databases, and other resources, or theft of valuable information.

Access controls are measures taken to ensure that only those who are authorized have access to a computer or network, or to certain applications or data. One way to block access to a computer is by physically locking it in a facility to which only authorized users have a key or by locking the computer itself with a physical key. However, in the age of networked computers, this solution is practical only for a limited number of servers and other computers. Therefore, these organizations must use other access controls, most of which rely on software.

Experts like to classify access controls into three groups: what you know, what you have, and who you are. "What you know" includes access codes such as user IDs, account numbers, and passwords. "What you have" is some kind of a device, such as a security card, which you use directly or which continuously changes coordinated access codes and displays them for you. "Who you are" includes your unique physical characteristics.

The most common way to control access is through the combination of a user ID and a password. While user IDs are usually not secret, passwords are. IS managers encourage users to change their passwords frequently, which most systems easily allow, so that others do not have time to figure them out and to limit the usefulness of stolen passwords. Some organizations have systems that force users to change their passwords at preset intervals, such as once a month or once every three months. Some systems also prevent users from selecting a password that they have used in the past, to minimize the chance that someone else might guess it, and many require a minimum length and mix of characters and numerals. Access codes and their related passwords are maintained either in a special list that becomes part of the operating system or in a database that the system searches to determine whether a user is authorized to access the requested resource.

Access controls include what you know (passwords), what you have (devices), and what you are (biometric characteristics)

Thinkstock Images/Photos.com

A more secure measure than passwords is security cards, such as RSA's SecureID. The device is distributed to employees who need access to confidential databases, usually remotely. Employees receive a small device that displays a 6-digit number. Special circuitry changes the number both at the server and the device to the same new number every minute. To gain access, employees enter at least one access code and the current number. The device is small enough to be carried on a key chain or in a wallet. This two-factor access control increases the probability that only authorized people gain access. This is an example of using both what you know and what you have.

In recent years, some companies have adopted physical access controls called biometrics. A **biometric** characteristic is a unique physical, measurable characteristic of a human being that is used to identify a person. Characteristics such as fingerprints, retinal scans, or voiceprints can be used in biometrics. They are in the class of "who you are." When a fingerprint is used, the user presses a finger on a scanner (see figure) or puts it before a digital camera. The fingerprint is compared against a database of digitized fingerprints of people with authorized access. A growing number of laptop computers have a built-in fingerprint scanner for the same purpose. The procedure is similar when the image of a person's retina is scanned. With voice recognition, the user is instructed to utter a word or several words. The intonation and accent are digitized and compared with a list of digitized voice samples.

POINT OF INTEREST   Scan a Hand

The Transportation Security Administration (TSA) has been one of the most heavily impacted federal organizations by the events of September 11, 2001. In the aftermath, the TSA exponentially tightened security. Proper human identification in airports is just one area that has seen an increase in applied security measures, and biometrics is the most common and upcoming form of security tool used to control highly secure areas. Biometrics can measure physical or behavioral traits such as body shape, fingerprints, facial characteristics, DNA, hand geometry, and iris recognition. For instance, a hand recognition system, which can be combined with a PIN or proximity card, can allow a system supervisor to immediately deny access to a user if necessary. Not only does biometrics provide a highly reliable and accurate form of security, a biometrics-recognition system can save an organization thousands in human security labor hours.

Source: Dubin, C. H. (2011). Biometrics: Hands down. Security, 48(2), 52–54.

Several manufacturers of computer equipment offer individual keyboard-embedded and mouse-embedded fingerprint devices. For example, SecuGen Corporation offers EyeD Mouse, a mouse that includes a fingerprint reader on the thumb side of the device. It verifies a fingerprint in less than a second. Using biometric access devices is the best way not only to prevent unauthorized access to computers but also to reduce the workload of Help desk personnel. Up to 50 percent of the calls Help desk personnel receive come from employees who have forgotten their passwords.

Atomic Transactions

As you know, in an efficient IS, a user enters data only once, and the data is recorded in different files for different purposes, according to the system's programmed instructions. For instance, in a typical order system, a sale is recorded in several files: the shipping file (so that the warehouse knows what to pack and ship), the invoice file (to produce an invoice and keep a copy in the system), the accounts receivable file (for accounting purposes), and the commission file (so that the salesperson can be compensated with the appropriate commission fee at the end of the month). As indicated in Figure 14.2, a system supports atomic transactions when its code only allows the recording of data if they successfully reach all their many destinations. An **atomic transaction** (from the Greek *atomos*, indivisible) is a set of indivisible transactions; either all transactions are executed or none are—never only some. Using atomic transactions ensures that only full entry occurs in all the appropriate files.

FIGURE 14.2

Atomic transactions ensure updating of all appropriate files accurately

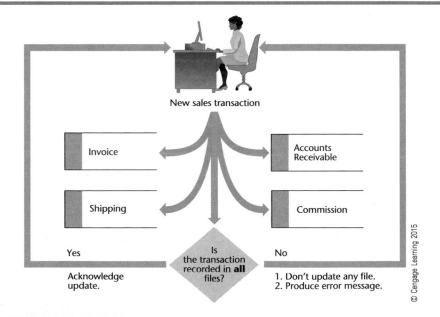

© Cengage Learning 2015

For instance, suppose the different files just mentioned reside on more than one disk, one of which is malfunctioning. When the clerk enters the sale transaction, the system tries to automatically record the appropriate data from the entry into each of the files. The shipping, accounts receivable, and invoice files are updated, but the malfunctioning commission file cannot accept the data. Without controls, the sale would be recorded, but unknown to anyone, the commission would not be updated, and the salesperson would be deprived of the commission on this deal. However, an atomic transaction control mechanism detects that not all four files have been updated with the transaction, and it doesn't update any of the files. The system might try to update again later, but if the update does not go through, the application produces an appropriate error message for the clerk, and remedial action can be taken.

Note that this is a control not only against a malfunction but also against fraud. Suppose the salesperson collaborates with the clerk to enter the sale only in the commission file, so he or she can be rewarded for a sale that has never taken place—and then plans to split the fee with the clerk. The atomic transaction control would not let this happen. Recall our discussion of relational database management systems. Virtually all current relational DBMSs have atomicity— the ability to make transactions atomic—as a required feature.

Audit Trail

In spite of the many steps taken to prevent system abuse, it nonetheless occurs. Consequently, further steps are needed to track transactions so that (1) when abuses are found, they can be traced, and (2) fear of detection indirectly discourages abuse. One popular tracking tool is the **audit trail**: a series of documented facts that help detect who recorded which transactions, at what time, and under whose approval. Whenever an employee records a transaction, the system prompts the employee to provide certain information: an invoice number, account number, salesperson ID number, and the like. Sometimes an audit trail is automatically created using data, such as the date and time of a transaction or the name or password of the user updating the file. This data is recorded directly from the computer—often unbeknownst to the user—and attached to the record of the transaction.

The laws and regulations of many countries require certain policy and audit trail controls, and since so many operations are performed using ISs, the controls must be programmed into software. In the United States, the Sarbanes-Oxley Act of 2002 requires corporations to implement audit trails and other measures in their systems.

Audit trail information helps uncover undesirable acts, from innocent mistakes to premeditated fraud. The information helps determine who authorized and who made the entries, the date and time of the transactions, and other identifying data that is essential in correcting mistakes or recovering losses. The audit trail is the most important tool of the **information systems auditor** (formerly known as the electronic data processing auditor), the professional whose job it is to find erroneous or fraudulent cases and investigate them.

POINT OF INTEREST   Costly Breaches

According to a Ponemon Institute survey of 850 executives, the average time required to restore an organization's reputation after a data breach is one year. Despite the time and effort necessary to rebuild a brand, severe losses in brand value can be incurred as well. Average losses in brand value ranged from $184 million to over $330 million for brands that averaged a brand value of $1.5 billion pre-breach. Thus, the loss in value was 12 percent but sometimes reached as high as 25 percent. No industry or individual company is immune to data breaches. Of companies surveyed, 43 percent had not implemented a data breach incident response plan prior to having a breach. To protect data and brand image, Experian Data Breach Resolution offers the following tips: plan, protect, and partner. Specifically, *plan* an outline for what steps a company should take in the event of a data breach. Companies should *protect* themselves by being proactive instead of reactive and assume that they will encounter a breach in the future. If a company does not have adequate resources to protect itself from breaches, *partner* with a third-party to get professional protection. It takes years to build a reputable brand image but only one breach to set it back years and millions of dollars.

Source: Ponemon institute survey: Data breaches can cause lasting and costly damage to the reputation of affected organizations. (2011). Entertainment Close-Up.

As you've seen so far in this chapter, the increase in the number of people and organizations using the Internet has provided fertile ground for unauthorized and destructive activity. This section describes several ways that organizations can protect themselves against such attacks, including using firewalls, authentication and encryption, digital signatures, and digital certificates.

Firewalls and Proxy Servers

The best defense against unauthorized access to systems over the Internet is a **firewall**, which is hardware and software that blocks access to computing resources. Firewalls are routinely integrated into the circuitry of routers, as discussed in Chapter 6, "Business Networks and Telecommunications." Firewall software screens the activities of a person who logs on to a website; it allows retrieval and viewing of certain material, but blocks attempts to change the information or to access other resources that reside on the same computer or computers connected to it.

It is important to note that while firewalls are used to keep unauthorized users out, they are also used to restrict unauthorized software or instructions, such as computer viruses and other rogue software. When an employee uses a company computer to access external websites, the firewall screens for viruses and active attempts to invade company resources through the open communications line. It might also be programmed to block employee access to sites that are suspected of launching rogue programs, or to sites that provide no useful resources. The firewall then prohibits the user from logging on to those sites.

Figure 14.3 illustrates how a firewall operates to protect network data, and shows the Windows 8 Firewall screen. As the figure illustrates, a firewall controls communication between a trusted network and the "untrusted" Internet. The firewall can be installed on a server or a router. Network professionals use firewall software to check which applications can access the Internet and which servers might be accessed from the organization's network. Systems administrators can configure the Windows firewall parameters to gain access to a trusted network when accessing an organization's network from an external network. In some cases, antivirus software, such as McAfee, maintains the firewall parameters as a function of its software. Therefore, the antivirus software will also monitor the firewall connections to prevent the transfer of viruses and malware and maintain a secure connection.

FIGURE **14.3**

Firewalls attempt to prevent unauthorized access through an open communications line

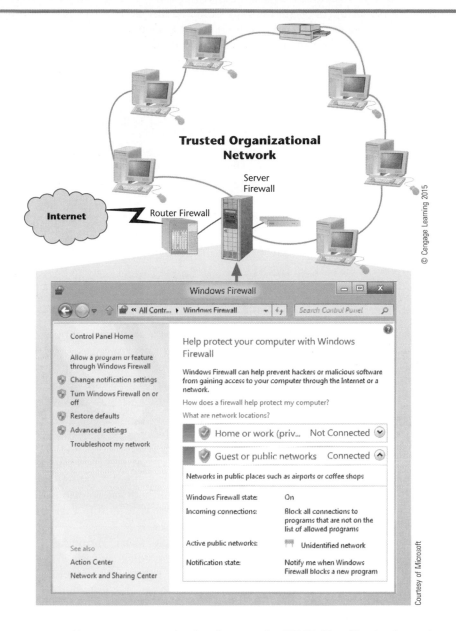

To increase security, some companies implement the **DMZ** (demilitarized zone) approach. The DMZ is a network of computers that are connected to the company's trusted network (such as an intranet) at one end and the untrusted network—the public Internet—at the other end. The DMZ includes resources to which the organization allows direct access from the Internet. It might include a website and computers from which people can download files. A DMZ provides a barrier between the Internet and a company's organizational network, which is usually an intranet. The connection between the DMZ and the organization's trusted network is established by using a proxy server.

A **proxy server** "represents" another server for all information requests from resources inside the trusted network. However, a proxy server can also be placed between the Internet and the organization's trusted network when there is no DMZ. For example, this might be the arrangement when the organization establishes its website as part of its trusted network. The proxy server then retrieves webpages for computers requesting them remotely through the Internet. Thus, external computers requesting webpages never come in direct contact with the computer hosting the webpages. When a business hires the services of an ISP, the proxy server is often the one operated by the ISP.

Both the organizational network server and proxy server employ firewalls. As shown in Figure 14.3, the firewalls would be installed on the server of the organizational network and the router. The router is often called a "boundary router." The double firewall architecture adds an extra measure of security for an intranet.

POINT OF **INTEREST**   **Behind Every Corner**

A *Consumer Reports* survey shows that over 5 million online U.S. households experienced some type of abuse on Facebook alone in the past year. This includes but is not limited to virus infections, identity theft, stalking, and for a million children, bullying. In 2010, estimated losses due to malware infection cost consumers $2.3 billion and were the reason for replacing 1.3 million PCs. The ubiquitous threats that lurk online make it essential to use some form of security software. Even free anti-malware programs should provide sufficient protection for most online users.

Source: Anonymous. (2011, June). Online Exposure. Consumer Reports.

Authentication and Encryption

With so much web-based commerce and other communication on the Internet, businesses and individuals must be able to authenticate messages. That is, they must be able to tell whether certain information, plain or encrypted, was sent to them by the party that was supposed to send it. Note that the word "message" is used here for any type of information, not only text. It might be images, sounds, or any other information in digital form.

Authentication is the process of ensuring that the person who sends a message to or receives a message from you is indeed that person. Authentication can be accomplished by senders and receivers exchanging codes known only to them. Once authentication is established, keeping a message secret can be accomplished by transforming it into a form that cannot be read by anyone who intercepts it. Coding a message into a form unreadable to an interceptor is called **encryption**. Authentication also often occurs when an encrypted message is received, because the recipient needs to ensure that the message was indeed encrypted and sent by a certain party.

Both authentication and secrecy are important when communicating confidential information such as financial and medical records. They are also essential when transacting business through a public network. For example, millions of people now buy and sell shares of stock and other financial products on the web, businesses and individuals make purchases through the web and use credit-card account numbers for payment, and medical clinics use the web to transmit patient records to insurance companies and prescriptions to pharmacies. All must authenticate the recipient and keep the entire communication confidential.

To authenticate the users and maintain secrecy, the parties can use encryption programs. Encryption programs scramble information transmitted over the network so that an interceptor only receives unintelligible data. The original message is called **plaintext**; the coded message is called **ciphertext**. Encryption uses a mathematical algorithm, which is a formula, combined with a key. The key is a unique combination of bits that must be used in the formula to decipher the ciphertext. As indicated in Figure 14.4, the receiving computer uses the key to decipher the ciphertext back into plaintext.

FIGURE **14.4**

Encrypting
communications
increases security

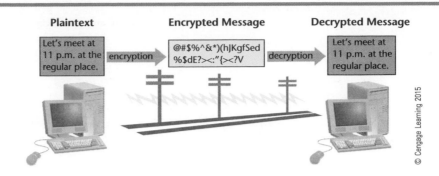

To illustrate the use of encryption algorithms and keys, here is a simple example. Suppose you send a secret message that you want the recipient to decipher. Remember that each character in your digital message is represented by a byte, which is a combination of eight bits. The byte can be expressed as a numeric value. For instance, the character represented by 00010101 has a decimal value of 21. So, each character in your message has a numeric value based on a specific algorithm embedded into the software on the sending and receiving computers. The result of any manipulation of text by this algorithm is a string of characters that makes no sense to anyone who cannot figure out the algorithm and the key. Note that this is an extremely simple example. In reality, encryption algorithms are significantly more complex. Also note that the key used in this example is a combination of eight bits, which is quite easy to figure out. It would be significantly more difficult to figure out a key consisting of 128, 256, 512, or 1024 bits, which are commonly used in Internet communication. When keys that long are used, even with the latest hardware and most sophisticated code-breaking software the average time to decipher an encrypted message is so long that the probability of success is extremely small.

Public-Key Encryption

As Figure 14.5 indicates, when both the sender and recipient use the same secret key (which is the case in the earlier example), the technique is called **symmetric encryption**. However, symmetric encryption requires that the recipient have the key before the encrypted text is received. Therefore, the key is referred to simply as a *secret key* or *private key*. While it is fairly simple to keep the secrecy of a message when the sender and recipient have the same key beforehand, it is impractical in daily transactions on the Internet. For example, a retail website would not be able to function if every buyer would require a secret key with each transaction to ensure confidentiality. Therefore, in such communication, there must be a way for the sender to communicate the key to the recipient before the message is sent. To this end, the parties use an **asymmetric encryption** comprising two keys: one is public, and the other is private. It is clear why this type of encryption is also called "public-key" encryption.

FIGURE **14.5**

Symmetric (secret key)
and asymmetric (public
key) encryption

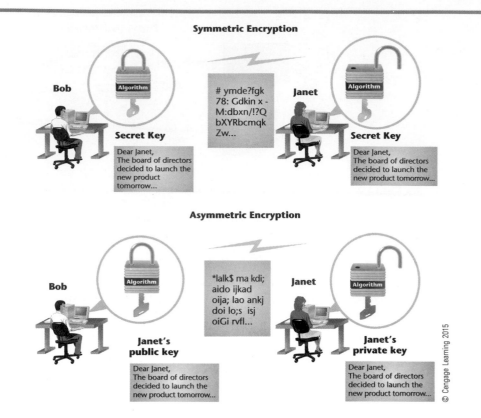

A public key is distributed widely and might be known to everyone; a private key is secret and known only to the recipient of the message. When the sender wants to send a secure message to the recipient, he uses the recipient's public key to encrypt the message. The recipient then uses her own private key to decrypt it. A mathematical relationship exists between the public and private keys. The public and private keys are related in such a way that only the public key can be used to encrypt messages, and only the corresponding private key can be used to decrypt them. It is virtually impossible to deduce the private key from the public key. All applications that use public keys and private keys use the same principles. What differentiates them from one another is the different encryption algorithm each uses.

Online businesses often switch site visitors to a secure server when they are asked to provide secret information such as credit-card account numbers or other personal data. The secure server provides the visitor's web browser with the site's public key. The browser uses it to encrypt the credit-card number and any other personal information. The secure server uses the private key to decrypt the information. Once an encrypted exchange is established, the server can send the visitor's browser a secret key that both can use. Moreover, the server can change the key often during the session to make decryption more difficult.

Transport Layer Security

A protocol called **Transport Layer Security (TLS)** is used for transactions on the web. TLS is the successor of Secure Sockets Layer (SSL) and works following the same principles as SSL, with some additional improvements that are outside the scope of this discussion. TLS is part of virtually all current web browsers. Current versions of browsers use TLS with a 128-bit key. TLS uses a combination of public key and symmetric key encryption. It works as follows:

1. When a visitor connects to an online site, the site's server sends the visitor's browser its public key.
2. The visitor's browser creates a temporary symmetric (secret) key of 128 bits. The key is transmitted to the site's server encrypted by using the site's public key. Now both the visitor's browser and the site's server know the same secret key and can use it for encryption.
3. The visitor can now safely transmit confidential information.

How safe is a 128-bit key? It would take 250 PCs working simultaneously around the clock an estimated average of 9 trillion times the age of the universe just to decrypt a single message. This is the reason why practically all financial institutions use 128-bit encryption, and if you want to bank online, you must use a browser that supports this key length. However, how long it takes an interceptor to decipher depends on current speed of hardware and sophistication of code-breaking software. As hardware becomes faster and software becomes more sophisticated, standard keys usually are set longer.

When you log on to secure servers, such as the PayPal website shown in the illustration, you might notice that the "HTTP://" or "http://" in the URL box at the top of the browser turns into an HTTPS:// (or https://), and a security icon, usually a little closed padlock, appears in the browser. In some browsers, as in the illustration, the address bar turns green if it is a secure site. It is advisable not to transfer any confidential information through the web if you don't see both https:// and the padlock icon. **HTTPS** is the secure version of HTTP, discussed in Chapter 8, "The Web-Enabled Enterprise." HTTPS encrypts communication using SSL or TLS. Fortunately, all this encryption and decryption is done by the browser. When you access a secure area of a website, the communication between the site's server and your web browser is encrypted. The information you view on your screen was encrypted by the software installed on the site's server and then decrypted by your browser.

The https://, padlock icon, and green color in the Address bar of this web browser indicate that you are communicating with a secure server

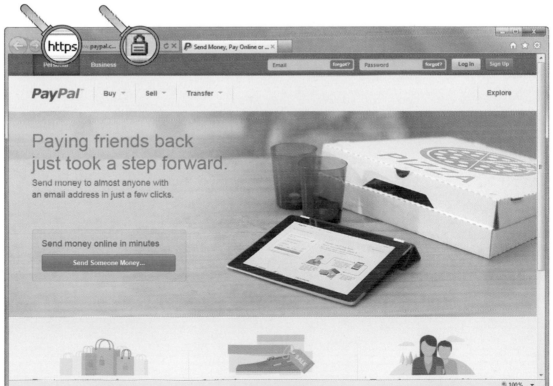

Digital Signatures

A **digital signature** is a way to authenticate online messages, analogous to a physical signature on a piece of paper, but implemented with public-key cryptography. The digital signature authenticates the identity of the sender of a message and also guarantees that no one has altered the sent document; it is as if the message were carried in an electronically sealed envelope.

When you send an encrypted message, two phases are involved in creating a digital signature. First, the encryption software uses a hashing algorithm (a mathematical formula) to create a message digest from the file you wish to transmit. A **message digest** is akin to the unique fingerprint of a file. Then, the software uses your private (secret) key to encrypt the message digest. The result is a digital signature for that specific file.

How does it work? Follow the flowchart in Figure 14.6. Suppose you want to send the draft of a detailed price proposal to your business partner. You want to be certain that the document you intend to send is indeed the one she receives. She wants the assurance that the document she receives is really from you.

1. You attach the price proposal file to an email message. The entire communication is essentially one message, indicated as "Plain message" in Figure 14.6.
2. Using the hashing software, your computer creates a message hash, the message digest, which is a mathematically manipulated file of the message and is not readily readable by a human.
3. You then use a private key that you have previously obtained from the public-key issuer, such as a certificate authority, to encrypt the message digest. Your computer uses your private key to turn the message digest into a digital signature.
4. The computer also uses your private key to encrypt the message in its plain (unhashed) form. Your computer sends off both files.
5. Your business partner receives the encrypted files: the digital signature (which is an encrypted message digest) and the encrypted message, which usually come as one file.
6. Your business partner's computer uses her private key (which is mathematically related to her public key, which you used) to decrypt both your digital signature and your encrypted unhashed message.
7. The decrypted digital signature becomes the message digest. Hashing the decrypted unhashed message turns this message into a digest, too.
8. If the two message digests are identical, the message received is, apparently, the one you sent, unchanged.

FIGURE **14.6**

How digital signatures
transmit data on the
Internet

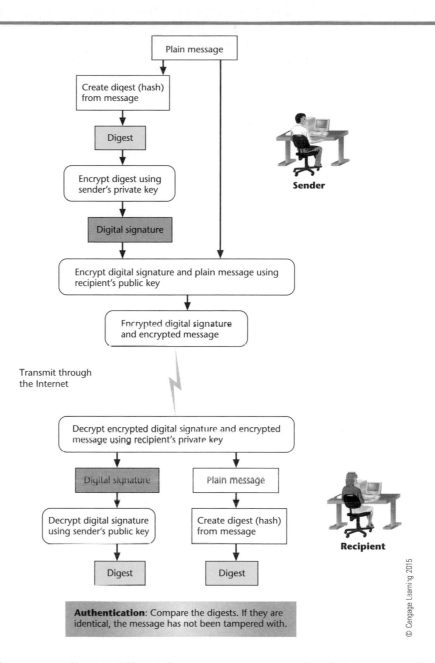

Since the message digest is different for every message, your digital signature is different each time you send a message. As described here, senders of encrypted messages obtain the public key of the recipient from an issuer of such keys. In most cases, the issuer is a certificate authority, and the recipient's public key is included in the recipient's digital certificate, which is discussed next.

Digital Certificates

To authenticate a digital signature, both buyers and sellers must use digital certificates (also known as digital IDs). **Digital certificates** are computer files that serve as the equivalent of ID cards by associating one's identity with one's public key. An issuer of digital certificates is called a **certificate authority (CA)**, an organization that serves as a trusted third party. A CA certifies the identity of anyone who inquires about a party communicating on the Internet. Some CAs are subsidiaries of banks and credit-card companies, and others are independent. Symantec Trust Network, GeoTrust, Inc., DigiCert, Inc., and GlobalSign are just a few of the numerous companies that sell digital certificates. To view a long list of CAs you can go to *http://www.sos.ca.gov/digsig/* (Anonymous, 2013a). A CA issues the public (and private) keys associated with a certificate.

A digital certificate contains its holder's name, a serial number, expiration dates, and a copy of the certificate holder's public key (used to encrypt messages and digital signatures). It also contains the digital signature of the certificate authority so that a recipient can verify that the certificate is real. To view the digital certificate of a secure online business, click the padlock icon in the address bar or status bar of your browser. Figure 14.7 shows the same certificate presented through two different web browsers, Google Chrome (left) and Microsoft Internet Explorer (right).

FIGURE 14.7

A digital certificate as shown in two different web browsers

Digital certificates are the equivalent of tamper-proof photo identification cards. They are based on public-key encryption techniques that verify the identities of the buyer and seller in electronic transactions and prevent documents from being altered after the transaction is completed.

POINT OF INTEREST   The Rise of IT Security Workers

In light of the increasing number and sophistication of data theft and other security issues, the demand for IT security workers has continued to grow. Most organizations are not looking for workers dedicated to IT security only, but for IT professionals who are security-savvy. Many organizations offer certification in the area of IT security. Among them are IBM, Cisco, Hewlett-Packard, Microsoft, Oracle, and the International Information Systems Security Certification Consortium (ISC[2]). Companies vie for systems administrators and database analysts who have a good blend of technical expertise and security knowledge. Additionally, a career as an IT Security Consultant is an attractive position as it ranked 15th on CNNMoney's 2012 list of Best Jobs in America. As news of security breaches keeps popping up in the media, organizations have increased the demand for such talent and have steadily increased such workers' salaries.

Sources: Barrett, L., "I.T. Security Specialists See Salaries Rise in First Half," Baseline, July 9, 2007; T.Z. (2012). Best Jobs in America. Retrieved from http://money.cnn.com/magazines/moneymag/bestjobs/2010/snapshots/17.html

The Downside of Security Measures

Security measures—especially passwords, encryption applications, and firewalls—have a price that relates to more than money: they slow down data communications, and they require user discipline, which is not always easy to maintain. Employees tend to forget their passwords, especially if they must replace them every 30 or 90 days.

Employees are especially annoyed when they have to remember a different password for every system they use; in some companies, there might be four or five different systems, each with its own access control. A simpler solution is an approach called **SSO (single sign-on)**. With SSO, users are required to identify themselves only once before accessing several different systems. However, SSO requires special software that interacts with all the systems in an organization, and the systems must be linked through a network. Not many organizations have installed such software.

CIOs often cite SSO as an effective way to decrease the amount of work their subordinates must do. In February 2013, SurePassID announced its technology solution to create a SSO for the hybrid cloud. It has developed a single sign-on to integrate with existing IT infrastructures and is compatible with many popular technology platforms including Apple's iPhone and iPad as well as Android and BlackBerry devices (Anonymous, 2013c). Wells Fargo has offered its commercial customers a new service, CEO Desktop Deposit. This new technology allows customers to deposit checks through their CEO Portal using a single sign-on (Anonymous, 2012a).

Encryption slows down communication because the software must encrypt and decrypt every message. Remember that when you use a secure website, much of the information you view on your screen is encrypted by the software installed on the site's server, and then decrypted by your browser. All this activity takes time, and the delay only exacerbates the Internet's low download speed during periods of heavy traffic. Firewalls have the same slowing effect; screening every download takes time, which affects anyone trying to access information, including employees, business partners, and consumers.

IT specialists must clearly explain to managers the implications of applying security measures, especially on systems connected to the Internet. The IT specialists and other managers must first determine which resource should be accessed only with passwords and which also require other screening methods, such as firewalls. They must tell employees what impact a new security measure will have on their daily work—and if the measure will adversely affect their work, the specialists must convince the employees that the inconvenience is the price for protecting data. The IT specialists should also continue to work on methods that minimize inconvenience and delays.

Recall the discussion of virtual private networks (VPNs), which enable employees to access ISs using special security software involving passwords and encryption. This approach allows employees to access an intranet only from computers equipped with the proper VPN software and only if they remember passwords. Wawa Corporation, a convenience store chain, implemented a new SAP ERP system. The new system implemented a one-time keyfob similar to SecurID®. The password changes frequently, and the user does not have to remember it because it appears automatically on the keyfob. There is no need to use VPN software. If someone steals a password, the thief cannot use it for more than a few seconds because it then changes. This enables Wawa employees to access the intranet from any computer in the world.

Recovery Measures

Security measures might reduce undesirable mishaps, but nobody can control all disasters. According to 2006 statistics of the Federal Emergency Management Agency (FEMA), the cost of weather and other disasters in the period 1986–2005 in the United States was $278 billion. Only $21.6 billion of this damage was caused by terrorism. The other causes were tropical storms, tornadoes, winter storms, earthquakes, and other events. To be prepared for disasters when they do occur, organizations must have recovery measures in place. Organizations that depend heavily on ISs for their daily business often use redundancy; that is, they run all systems and

Information technology can help track down criminals and terrorists, but it also helps criminals and terrorists in their efforts. The technology can help protect privacy and other civil rights, but it can also help violate such rights. The growing danger of terrorism and the continued effort of governments to reduce drug-related and other crimes led to controversial use, or abuse, of IT. In the United States, one particular law with a long name includes controversial provisions that have worried civil libertarians since October 2001. Uniting and Strengthening America by Providing Appropriate Tools Required to Intercept and Obstruct Terrorism Act of 2001, the PATRIOT Act, as it is popularly known, gives law enforcement agencies surveillance and wiretapping rights they did not have before that year. The law permits the FBI to read private files and personal Internet records without informing the suspected citizen and without need for a law enforcement agency to present to the court a probable cause. "Our constitutional freedoms are in jeopardy. Now is the time to restore real checks and balances to the worst sections of the Patriot Act" called a web posting of the American Civil Liberties Union (ACLU) in 2005, when the law was reconsidered by the U.S. Congress. On the contrary, said many members of Congress, the law should be enhanced to give the FBI even freer hand.

The Electronic Privacy Information Center (EPIC) explains the major concerns with the Act, which made changes to 15 existing laws. The Act gives more power than before to law enforcement agencies in installing pen registers and trap-and-trace devices. A pen register is any device that records outgoing phone numbers. A trap-and-trace device—a caller ID device, for instance—captures and records incoming telephone numbers. Similarly, the Act extends the government's authority to gain access to personal financial information and student information, even if the subject of the investigation is not suspected of wrongdoing. Agents only have to certify that the information likely to be obtained is relevant to an ongoing criminal investigation. In the past, the government had to show to a judge probable cause—a reasonable suspicion that the subject of an investigation is committing or is about to commit a crime. If a government attorney "certifies" that the information collected is likely to be relevant, the judge must grant permission to install the device and collect the information.

The previous federal law referred only to telephones, but the new Act expanded communication tapping to the Internet, because it redefined a pen register as "a device or process which records or decodes dialing, routing, addressing, or signaling information transmitted by an instrument or facility from which a wire or electronic communication is transmitted." This essentially allows law enforcement agencies to record, without probable cause and court supervision, email addresses and URLs. Some jurists opine that this actually allows the agencies to record not only email sender and recipient addresses and web addresses but also the content of email messages and webpages.

Even before adoption of the PATRIOT Act, the FBI used "packet sniffing" devices connected to the servers operated by Internet service providers (ISPs). Until 2002, the agency used a custom-built device known as Carnivore, and later started using commercial devices that reportedly perform the same way. The devices are supposed to monitor email traffic of suspects. However, millions of other subscribers use the same servers and therefore are subject to the same surveillance.

When tapping communications, law enforcement agencies need the cooperation of a third party, such as a telephone company or an ISP. In the past, the law limited the definition of such third parties. Now, there is no limitation. Therefore, if a university, public library, municipality, or an airport provides access to the Internet—such as through a hotspot—all users of these services are subject to surveillance. Furthermore, that third party is prohibited from notifying anyone, including unsuspected users, of the surveillance.

Proponents of the Act wanted to leave all its provisions in place and add two more. They would like to allow the FBI to demand records without first obtaining an approval from a prosecutor or a judge. Some would also amend the law to require the U.S. Postal Service to let FBI agents copy information from the outside of envelopes in the mail. The law was not changed, and its term was extended.

Again, we are faced with an old dilemma: How far should we allow our governments to go in their efforts to protect us against crime and terrorism? At what point do we start to pay too much in terms of privacy and civil rights for such protection? And when terrorists strike or threaten to strike, should we give up our liberties for more security?

---

transactions on two computers in parallel to protect against loss of data and business. If one computer is down, the work can continue on the other computer. Redundancy makes the system fault tolerant. However, in distributed systems, doubling every computing resource is extremely expensive, so other measures must be taken.

The Business Recovery Plan

To prepare for mishaps, whether natural or malicious, many organizations have well-planned programs in place, called **business recovery plans** (also called *disaster recovery plans*, *business* *resumption plans*, or *business continuity plans*). The plans detail what should be done and by whom if critical systems go down. In principle, the systems do not have to be ISs. However, most of the attention and resources in recovery plans are devoted to measures that should be taken when ISs go down or if IS operations become untrustworthy. The U.S. federal government regards business continuity planning as being in the national interest, and the Department of Homeland Security has established a website that includes useful information on this topic (*www.ready.gov*).

In business recovery planning, the emphasis should not be on the damage to the organization's assets but to its business. The estimates and measures taken should be to minimize damage to the organization's ability to resume business operations as well as to minimize the damage to operations from the disaster.

Hurricane Katrina, which hit the U.S. Gulf Coast in 2005, was a wake-up call for many executives, reminding them in terrible terms of the need for recovery planning. Concern about disaster recovery has spread beyond banks, insurance companies, and data centers, those traditionally concerned with disaster recovery. Many customer service and retail firms realize that they can easily lose customers if they don't deliver services and products in a timely manner, which is why the terms "business recovery," "business resumption," and "business continuity" have caught on in some circles. In interactive computing environments, when business systems are idle, so are the people who bring in revenue. Employees cannot do their work, customers cannot purchase, and suppliers cannot accept requests for raw materials and services. In addition, companies' reputations can be harmed, and competitive advantage and market share lost.

In 2012, hurricane Sandy hit the east coast of the United States. The New York Stock Exchange trading floor was not operational for two days, the longest weather delay for NYSE in over 100 years. Capital One Financial's Remote Deposit Capture (RDC) found that smartphones complemented the system and helped businesses that were without power deposit checks. Businesses that could not gain access to their offices used their mobile devices to scan checks instead of an office scanner. However, a mobile device depletes its battery and requires power. So backing up mobile devices is also important (Adams, 2012).

Experts propose nine steps to develop a business recovery plan:

1. *Obtain management's commitment to the plan.* Development of a recovery plan requires substantial resources. Top management must be convinced of the potential damages that paralysis of information systems might cause. Once management is committed, it should appoint a business recovery coordinator to develop the plan and execute the plan if disaster occurs.
2. *Establish a planning committee.* The coordinator establishes a planning committee comprising representatives from all business units that are dependent on computer-based ISs. The members serve as liaisons between the coordinator and their unit managers. The managers are authorized to establish emergency procedures for their own departments.
3. *Perform risk assessment and impact analysis.* The committee assesses which operations would be hurt by disasters, and how long the organization could continue to operate without the damaged resources. This analysis is carried out through interviews with managers of functional business areas. The committee compiles information regarding maximum allowable downtime, required backup information, and the financial, operational, and legal consequences of extended downtime.
4. *Prioritize recovery needs.* The disaster recovery coordinator ranks each IS application according to its effect on an organization's ability to achieve its mission. **Mission-critical applications**, those without which the business cannot conduct its operations, are given the highest priority. The largest or most widely used system might not be the most critical. Applications might be categorized into several classes, such as:
   - *Critical*: Applications that cannot be replaced with manual systems under any circumstances.
   - *Vital*: Applications that can be replaced with manual systems for a brief period, such as several days.
   - *Sensitive*: Applications that can be replaced with acceptable manual systems for an extended period of time, though at great cost.
   - *Noncritical*: Applications that can be interrupted for an extended period of time at little or no cost to the organization.

5. *Select a recovery plan.* Recovery plan alternatives are evaluated by considering advantages and disadvantages in terms of risk reduction, cost, and the speed at which employees can adjust to the alternative system.

6. *Select vendors.* If it is determined that an external vendor can better respond to a disaster than in-house staff and can provide a better alternative system, then the most cost-effective external vendor should be selected. Factors considered should include the vendor's ability to provide telecommunications alternatives, experience, and capacity to support current applications.

7. *Develop and implement the plan.* The plan includes organizational and vendor responsibilities and the sequence of events that will take place. Each business unit is informed of its responsibilities, who the key contacts are in each department, and the training programs available for personnel.

8. *Test the plan.* Testing includes a walk-through with each business unit, simulations as if a real disaster had occurred, and (if no damage will be caused) a deliberate interruption of the system and implementation of the plan. In mock disasters, the coordinator measures the time it takes to implement the plan and its effectiveness.

9. *Continually test and evaluate.* The staff must be aware of the plan at all times. Therefore, the plan must be tested periodically. It should be evaluated in light of new business practices and the addition of new applications. If necessary, the plan should be modified to accommodate these changes.

The plan should include the key personnel and their responsibilities as well as a procedure to reinstitute interactions with outside business partners and suppliers. Because an organization's priorities and environment change over time, the plan must be examined periodically and updated if necessary. There will be new business processes or changes in the relative importance of existing processes or tasks, new or different application software, changes in hardware, and new or different IS and end users. The plan must be modified to reflect the new environment, and the changes must be thoroughly tested. A copy of the plan should be kept off-site, because if a disaster occurs, an on-site copy might not be available. Many companies keep an electronic copy posted at a server many miles away, so that they can retrieve it from wherever their officer can have Internet access.

Although the threat of terrorism has increased awareness for the need of recovery plans, CIOs often find the tasks of earmarking funds for disaster recovery programs difficult because they cannot show the return on investment (ROI) of such planning. Most companies institute recovery programs only after a disaster or near-disaster occurs. Usually, the larger companies have such programs. Even at companies that do have recovery plans, experts estimate that most plans are never tested. Worse, some experts observed that one out of five recovery plans did not work well when tested.

Recovery Planning and Hot Site Providers

Companies that choose not to fully develop their own recovery plan can outsource it to companies that specialize in either disaster recovery planning or provision of alternative sites. Many companies provide both planning and software for disaster recovery. The software helps create and update records of key people and procedures. Fewer companies provide alternative sites—**hot sites**—chief among them IBM, Hewlett-Packard, and SunGard Availability Services, a division of SunGard. They provide backup and operation facilities to which a client's employees can move and continue operations in case of a disaster.

For example, IBM maintains a business continuity and recovery center in Sterling Forest, New York, 45 miles from midtown Manhattan. The center is equipped with desks, computer systems, and Internet links. Customers can use the duplicate databases and applications maintained for them. The company also provides hotel rooms and air mattresses for people who need to work long hours. As soon as the power went out one summer, the center's diesel-powered generators started up, and it was ready to take in clients' employees. Some clients had secured online systems but no light in the offices. These clients operated the systems from links at the center.

More than 90 percent of U.S. businesses are within 35 miles of a SunGard center. Worldwide, the company maintains redundant facilities totaling 279,000 square meters (3 million square feet), equipped with software and networking facilities to enable a client organization to resume business within hours.

Hewlett-Packard's Business Continuity & Availability Services division offers both hot sites and mobile facilities. When a disaster occurs, HP sends a mobile office within 24-48 hours to a place designated by the client. Each air-conditioned office includes up to 30 desks equipped with computers, telephones, a server, and power generators. Company technicians help load applications and data. The hot site can accommodate up to 1000 client employees. The company has established more than 50 recovery facilities worldwide to enable the resumption of business operations in less than four hours with a loss of less than 15 minutes of data.

POINT OF INTEREST — Seeing Security Differently

A 2011 Forrester Research report indicates businesses are getting the hint on the importance of IT security. The survey is based on the responses of 2,058 IT professionals in North American and European businesses of all sizes. In 2007, security only harnessed 8.2 percent of the total IT budget but that number grew to 14 percent in 2010. The more businesses rely on information security, the more difficult it is to keep up with evolving threats. More sophisticated attacks, heftier data breach cleanup costs, and businesses' increasing use of outsourced IT resources attributed to the increase in IT security budgets. Although the survey results show businesses are realizing the necessity for IT security, too many organizations are still applying their IT security resources reactively while they should be trying to predict and prevent the attacks of tomorrow.

Source: Schwartz, Mathew J. (2011, February 15). Security Spending Grabs Greater Share of IT Budgets. Retrieved from http://www.informationweek.com/security/management/security-spending-grabs-greater-share-of/229218689

The Economics of Information Security

Security measures should be dealt with in a manner similar to purchasing insurance. The spending on measures should be proportional to the potential damage. Organizations also need to assess the minimum acceptable rate of system downtime and ensure that they can financially sustain the downtime.

How Much Security Is Enough Security?

From a pure-cost point of view, how much should an organization spend on data security measures? Two types of costs must be considered to answer this question: the cost of the potential damage, and the cost of implementing a preventive measure. The cost of the damage is the aggregate of all the potential damages multiplied by their respective probabilities, as follows:

$$Cost\ of\ potential\ damage = \sum_{i=1}^{n} Cost\ of\ disruption_i \times Probability\ of\ disruption_i$$

where i is a probable event, and n is the number of events.

Experts are usually employed to estimate the cost and probabilities of damages as well as the cost of security measures. Obviously, the more extensive the preventive measures, the smaller the damage potential. So, as the cost of security measures goes up, the cost of potential damage goes down. Ideally, the enterprise places itself at the optimum point, which is the point at which the total of the two costs is minimized, as Figure 14.8 illustrates.

FIGURE **14.8**

Optimal spending on IT
security

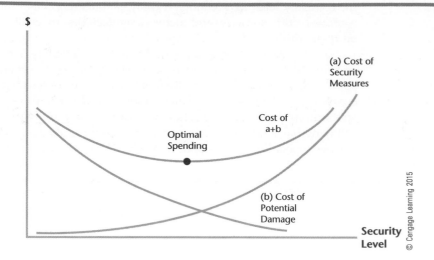

When budgeting for IT security, managers need to define what they want to protect. They should focus on the asset they must protect, which in most cases is information, not applications. Copies of applications are usually kept in a safe place to replace those that get damaged. They should also estimate the loss of revenue from downtime. Then, they should budget sums that do not exceed the value of what the measures protect—information and potential revenues. Even the most ardent IT security advocates agree that there is no point spending $100,000 to protect information that is worth $10,000.

Calculating Downtime

All other factors being equal, businesses should try to install ISs whose downtime is the lowest possible, but if obtaining a system with a higher uptime adds to the cost, they should consider the benefit of greater uptime against the added cost. Mission-critical systems must be connected to an alternative source of power, duplicated with a redundant system, or both. Often, such systems must be up 24 hours per day, 7 days per week.

When the service that the business provides depends on uninterrupted power, the systems are often connected to the grids of two utility companies and an alternative off-grid power source, such as generators. For example, Equinix, a company in Newark and Secaucus, New Jersey, that maintains data centers for large companies uses such an arrangement. Both facilities receive power from two power stations. Even if both utility companies stop supplying electricity, the company's systems are automatically powered by batteries, and shortly after that by diesel generators. Clients can continue to transmit and receive data as if nothing happened.

Recall the discussion of system uptime in Chapter 8, "The Web-Enabled Enterprise." Experts can provide good estimates of the probability that systems will fail, both in terms of power failure in a certain region and for particular applications. Experience in operating certain systems, such as ERP and SCM systems, can teach the IT staff for how many minutes or seconds per year the system is likely to fail. For example, if the uptime of a system is 99 percent ("two nines"), it should be expected to be down 1 percent of the time, and if "time" means 24 × 7, downtime expectancy is 87.6 hours per year (365 days × 24 hours × 0.01). This might be sufficient for a system supporting some human resources operations, but not an airline reservation system or an SCM system of a global company. For these systems, the number of nines must be greater, such as 99.999 percent, in which case there would be only 5.256 minutes of downtime expected per year (365 × 24 × 60 × 0.00001).

More and more ISs are now interfaced with other systems, which makes them a chain or cluster of several interdependent systems. For example, if system A is connected to system B, B depends on A, and the uptime of the systems are 99 percent and 99.5 percent, respectively; the probability of uptime for B is the multiplication of these probabilities, or 98.505 percent. Therefore, you could expect the systems to be down 0.01495 of the time, about 131 hours per year. This is a greater downtime than if system B operated independently. The greater the number of interdependent systems, the greater the expected downtime.

Redundancies, on the other hand, reduce expected downtime. For example, if two airline reservation systems operate in parallel, each can serve all the transactions, and the probabilities of their failures are 2 percent and 3 percent, the probability that the reservation service will be down is 0.06 percent (0.03×0.02), just 0.0006 of the time. This downtime is significantly smaller than the downtime of a service based on either system individually. This is why so many companies rely on redundant power sources and systems, such as duplicate databases, mirrored servers, and duplicate applications, especially when much of their operations are executed online, and even more so when the operations depend on constant online interaction with customers.

There might be no point in spending much money to increase the "nines" of uptime for every system. For example, if the only purpose of an IS is to help access a data warehouse to glean business intelligence (recall the discussions in Chapter 7, "Databases and Data Warehouses," and Chapter 11, "Business Intelligence and Knowledge Management"), spending thousands of dollars to increase its number of nines from 99 to 99.999 is probably not a wise choice. For a data warehouse, if an analysis cannot be performed immediately, it can usually be performed later without serious ramifications.

Summary

- The purpose of controls and security measures is to maintain the functionality of ISs, the confidentiality of information, the integrity and availability of data and computing resources, the uninterruptible availability of data resources and online operations, and compliance with security and privacy laws.

- Risks to ISs include risks to hardware, risks to data and applications, and risks to networks.

- Risks to hardware include natural disasters such as earthquakes, fires, floods, and power failures, as well as vandalism. Protective measures run the gamut from surge protectors to the maintenance of duplicate systems, which make ISs fault tolerant.

- Risks to data and applications include theft of information, identify theft, data alteration, data destruction, defacement of websites, computer viruses, worms, and logic bombs, as well as cyber terrorism and nonmalicious mishaps such as unauthorized downloading and installation of software.

- Risks to online operations include denial of service and computer hijacking.

- To minimize disruption, organizations use controls. Controls include program robustness and constraints on data entry, periodic backup of software and data files, access controls, atomic transactions, and audit trails.

- Access controls can be categorized into three groups: what you know, what you have, and who you are. Access controls also include information that must be entered before information resources can be used: passwords, security cards, and biometrics.

- Atomic transactions are an important control that ensures information integrity: either all files involved in a transaction are updated, or no files are updated.

- To protect resources that are linked to the Internet, organizations use firewalls, which are special hardware and software to control access to servers and their contents.

- Encryption schemes scramble messages at the sending end and descramble them at the receiving end. Encryption is also used to authenticate the sender or recipient of a message, verifying that the user is indeed the party he or she claims to be.

- To encrypt and decrypt messages the communicating parties must use a key. The larger the number of bits in the key, the longer it takes to break the encryption. In symmetric encryption, both users use a private, secret key. In asymmetric key encryption, the parties use a public and a private key.

- The public-private key method does not require both parties to have a common secret key before the communication starts. This system is a useful feature that lets consumers and organizations transact business confidentially on the web.

- SSL, TLS, and HTTPS are encryption standards specially designed for the web. They are embedded in web browsers.

- Organizations can purchase public and private keys along with an associated digital certificate from a certificate authority. Digital certificates contain the certificate holder's public key and other information, such as the issue and expiration date of the certificate.

- Many organizations have business recovery plans that are developed and periodically tested by a special committee. The plans identify mission-critical applications and prescribe steps that various employees should take in a disaster.

- A growing number of companies also use the services of organizations that specialize in providing alternative sites, known as hot sites, to continue operations in case of a debilitating event such as a terror attack, natural disaster, or power outage.

- When considering how much to invest in security measures, organizations should evaluate the dollar amounts of the potential damage on one hand, and the cost of security on the other hand. The more that is spent on security, the smaller the potential loss.

- A system that depends on other systems for input has a greater downtime probability than if it is used independently of other systems. Redundant systems significantly reduce downtime probability.

- Governments are obliged to protect citizens against crime and terrorism and therefore must be able to tap electronic communication of suspects. Such practices often collide with individuals' right to privacy.

After their walkthrough, Michael and Tyler realize that although the restaurant is heavily reliant on equipment and technology, they haven't made specific plans to safeguard their data and equipment. Michael has read many recent reports of retailers who had its databases hacked and customers' credit card information compromised. From his days working in human resources, he knows the liability issues associated with safekeeping organizational information.

They know that the fire department as well as the health and building inspectors have specific requirements for food, employee, and customer safety. However, there is no inspector for the technology. They quickly realized several points that they all missed.

What Is Your Advice?

1. In terms of the point-of-sale and other organizational data, what recommendations would you give to safeguard their data? Should they consider other alternatives if one of their server stations should malfunction?

2. The POS system requires the server to log in to the workstation. What advice on password safety would you suggest? What other elements of POS security should be pointed out?

3. Based on your knowledge of restaurant operations, what other security, access, and recovery issues need to be analyzed? What is your advice on implementing these issues?

New Perspectives

1. Connecting uninterruptible power supplies to servers is a common practice. However, if the restaurant's power were to be lost, the equipment in the kitchen would be inoperable. So since the operation of the restaurant would be inhibited, why does the point of sale server need to continue operating?

2. Should the restaurant consider any terms of use or privacy policy for their website? Social media? Affinity program? If so, what would you recommend?

Key Terms

access controls, 462
antivirus software, 458
asymmetric (public key)
    encryption, 469
atomic transaction, 464
audit trail, 465
authentication, 468
backup, 461
biometric, 463
blackout, 453
bot, 460
brownout, 453
business recovery plan, 476
certificate authority (CA), 473
CIA triad, 452
ciphertext, 468
controls, 461

cyber terrorism, 456
denial of service (DoS), 459
digital certificate, 473
digital signature, 472
DMZ, 467
downtime, 453
encryption, 468
firewall, 466
hijacking, 460
honeypot, 457
honeytoken, 457
hot site, 478
HTTPS, 471
identity theft, 455
information systems auditor, 465
keylogging, 454
logic bomb, 459

message digest, 472
mission-critical application, 477
plaintext, 468
proxy server, 467
RAID, 462
social engineering, 454
SSO (single sign-on), 475
symmetric (secret or private key)
    encryption, 469
Transport Layer Security (TLS),
    470
Trojan horses, 458
uninterruptible power supply
    (UPS), 453
virus, 458
worm, 458

1. What are the goals of security measures for ISs? Explain.

2. All the data of your company is concentrated in two databases. All employees use PCs or laptop computers, and all use a corporate network. You are to prioritize protection of the following elements of your company: PCs and laptops, the databases, the corporate network. Which is the element about which you should be most concerned, and why?

3. Data alteration and destruction are dreaded by many IS managers more than any other mishap. Why? Is the threat of website defacement as severe as data destruction or alteration? Why or why not?

4. Some companies still make a duplicate copy of disks or tapes and transport them to a remote site as a precaution against loss of data on the original storage media. What is the preferred method of keeping secured copies of data nowadays? Give at least two benefits and one possible drawback of the more recent approach.

5. Comment on the following statement: If your computer is connected to an external communication line, anyone with a similar link can potentially access your systems.

6. What is a honeytoken and how is it used by companies?

7. What is a honeypot and how is it used by businesses?

8. What is the difference between a virus and a worm? Which is potentially more dangerous and why?

9. Why is encryption that uses the public-key method so important in electronic commerce?

10. Assume that you are charged with developing an application to record basketball performance statistics. What limits would you include to ensure that the information entered is reasonable?

11. What is an audit trail? What audit trail information would you have for a shipping record?

12. This chapter gives an example of an atomic transaction. Give another example from any business area.

13. What is the difference between authentication and confidentiality?

14. What are biometric access controls? How are they better than passwords?

15. What is a firewall, and how does it work?

16. What is a DoS? How is it executed, and what is the purpose of zombies in a DoS? What can organizations do to prevent a DoS attack?

17. What is the purpose of business recovery plans?

18. A growing number of companies have implemented business recovery plans, but many still have not developed such plans. What may be the reasons for that?

19. Companies that process credit-card transactions for merchants have their computers vaulted behind concrete walls, iron bars, and heavy steel doors. Employees must enter a code into a keypad to enter the vaults. Yet, every so often information on millions of credit-card accounts is stolen without any physical break-in. How so?

20. A military officer in Colorado orders an item whose part number is 7954. The clerk at the supply center hundreds of miles away receives the order through his computer and ships the item: a ship's anchor, not realizing that Colorado is located hundreds of miles from any ocean. Apparently, the officer wanted to order item number 7945, a fuel tank for a fighter aircraft, but he erred when entering the item's number.

What controls would you implement both at the entry system and at the systems employed at the supply center to prevent such mistakes?

21. The average loss in a bank robbery is several thousand dollars, and the culprit has an 85 percent chance of being caught. The average damage in a "usual" white-collar fraud is several tens of thousands of dollars. The average amount stolen in computer fraud against organizations is several hundreds of thousands of dollars, and it is extremely hard to find the culprit. Why is the amount involved in computer fraud so high, and why is it difficult to find the culprits?

22. To prevent unauthorized people from copying data from a database, some companies forbid

their employees to come to work with USB flash memory devices and they subject the employees to body searches. Is this an effective measure? Why or why not?

23. The majority of criminals who commit computer fraud are insiders, that is, employees. What measures would you take to minimize insider fraud through ISs?

24. When accessing an information system, would you prefer that your identity be verified with a biometric (such as your palm or fingerprint, or your retinal scan), or with a password? Why?

25. Explain in an intuitive way why the downtime probability of a system that depends on another system is greater than if it were operating independently.

26. Employees often complain about the hurdles they have to pass whenever they need to access data and the slow response of ISs because of firewalls and encryption measures. As a CIO, how would you explain the need for such measures to employees? Would you give them any say in the decision of how to balance convenience and protection of data and applications?

27. Organizations often use firewalls to block employee access to certain websites. Do you agree with this practice, or do you think it violates employee privacy?

28. Special software might keep track of webpages that employees download to their PCs. Do you think this practice violates employee privacy?

29. When financial institutions discover that their ISs (especially databases) have been broken into, they often do not report the event to law enforcement officers. Even if they know who the hacker is, they do what they can to avoid publicity. Why? Should they be forced to report such events?

30. When hackers are caught, they often argue that they actually did a service to the organization whose system they accessed without permission; now, they say, the organization knows its system has a weak point, and it can take the proper steps to improve security. Do you agree with this claim? Why or why not?

31. A CIO tells you, "We regularly review all of the potential vulnerabilities of our information systems and networks. We implement hardware, software, and procedures against any potential event, no matter the cost." What do you say to this executive?

32. Is the potential for identity theft growing? Explain. (*Note*: The question is not about actual identity theft for any period of time; it is about the *potential* of identity theft.)

33. Encryption helps individuals and organizations to maintain privacy and confidentiality, thereby helping protect civil liberties. However, encryption also helps terrorists and criminals hide their intentions. Some governments have laws that forbid nongovernment organizations to use strong encryption software. The idea is to allow people to encrypt their communication, but not strongly enough to prevent the government from decrypting the communication in surveillance of suspected criminals and terrorists. Do you favor such laws, or do you advocate that everybody have access to the strongest encryption software available? Explain.

Applying Concepts

34. Search the web for the full text of HIPAA. Assume you are the CIO of a health insurance company. List and explain five controls that you must implement in your organization's ISs as a result of this law.

35. Research the impact of the Sarbanes-Oxley Act on ISs. Write a two-page report explaining the major controls corporations must incorporate in their ISs to satisfy the Act.

36. Log on to a secure website. Figure out which icon you have to click to receive information on the security measures used in the session. Send your professor an email message detailing the site's

URL and all the information you obtained: the length of the key that is used for encryption, the type of digital certificate used, the issuer of the digital certificate, the date it was issued and its expiration date, and so forth. Explain each item.

37. Some companies provide free software versions of their firewalls. Research three such firewall applications and compare their characteristics: options to block incoming communication, options to block outgoing communication, ease of learning, ease of use, etc. Make a recommendation for individuals based on your comparison.

38. Use Excel or another spreadsheet application to show your work when solving the following problem: A company uses three information systems that are linked sequentially: System A feeds System B, and System B feeds System C. Consider the following average uptimes: System A, 98 percent; System B, 97 percent; System C, 95 percent. What is the average expected downtime (as a percentage) of System C?

39. Use Excel or another spreadsheet application to show your work when solving the following problem: To reduce chances of failure, a company has connected all of its vital information systems to electric power from two different utility firms. The probability of failure of electric power from one utility firm is 2 percent. The probability of failure of electric power from the other utility firm is 1.5 percent. What is the probability that these information systems will receive no electric power at all?

40. A CIO states, "Our online transaction system has availability of five nines. However, we have a SaaS (software as a service) contract for using a human resources information system. The HR system has availability of only three nines."
   a. Calculate the minutes of downtime per week for each of these systems.
   b. Explain why the company must have such a high number of nines for one system but can settle for a significantly lower number of nines for the other system.

41. Team up with another student. Research the web for recovery planning expenditures in your country or worldwide over the past five years. Prepare a table showing the expenditure amounts for each year. Add an analysis that explains the reasons for changes in the expenditures from one year to another.

42. Your team should evaluate the business recovery plan of your school. If there is none, write a plan for the school. If there is one in place, evaluate its weaknesses and make suggestions for improvement. Prepare a 10-minute, software-based presentation of your findings and suggestions.

Biometrics Gives Healthcare a Hand

Correct identification (ID) of a patient, as elementary a task as it sounds, is the leading cause of medical errors as determined by the Joint Commission on the Accreditation of Healthcare Organizations (JCAHO). Misidentifying patients can lead to an array of unwanted events including medical identity theft and insurance fraud, where either patients share insurance cards or providers submit false claims. Sometimes misidentification can be due to simple clerical errors, technological failures, or even dishonest patients misrepresenting their identity. Whatever the cause, a positive patient identification (PPID) system is now the standard in healthcare facilities.

Multiple options are available to solve the healthcare industry's patient misidentification troubles. At the point of registration, patients need two key documents: a valid form of identification such as a driver's license and their insurance card. The information from these documents is crucial to the patient receiving the proper medical treatments and for insurance billing information. However, an issue arises when clerks must manually copy down all the information into the patient's electronic record, a time-consuming task that can result in human errors. The best solution for streamlining the digitalization of patient data is a dedicated, high-resolution card scanner. The best scanners take pictures of the cards and then upload them to the patient's electronic medical record (EMR). The technology is being used at IntraHealth Group where a scanner has turned recording patient data into a "scan-and-click operation."

High-resolution card scanners reduce patient registration times and allow staff members to focus more on the individual health concerns of the patient. The out-of-the-box systems require virtually no maintenance, set-up, or training. Additionally, the scanner prevents unsecured copies of important documents from having to be made. Dedicated, high-resolution scanners are one way to decrease patient misidentification and various associated forms of healthcare fraud.

The most advanced solutions implemented to combat patient misidentification are systems that rely on biometrics. At BayCare Health Systems in Tampa, Florida, palm-vein recognition technology is used to streamline and secure patient processing. Palm-vein biometrics work by shining a near-infrared light on the patient's hand which penetrates the outer layer of skin but reflects off deoxygenated blood. Simply put, the patient's veins are highlighted to present a pattern unique to that individual. Palm-vein technology has been proven to be just as accurate if not more accurate than iris-scanning technology. In comparative testing conducted by the International Biometrics Group (IBG), palm-vein technology exhibited significantly low rates of both false positive and false negative readings. By ensuring a near-zero enrollment failure, palm-vein technology is compatible with essentially all patients.

This technology is integrated with EMR and registration systems in order to address the patient identification issues. BayCare updated their electronic medical records system to make it compatible with the palm-vein biometric technology. When a palm-vein reading is taken, it is sent directly to a patient's EMR. The combined system is referred to as Patient Secure Identity (PSI) and offers several business and health-related benefits. First and foremost is patient safety. With the PSI system, duplicate medical records are eliminated and overlays prevented, thus ensuring doctors that the medical records in their hands are comprehensive, accurate, and not those of anyone else. On the front end, biometric readings forgo the need to transmit sensitive information at registration such as a Social Security number.

BayCare's PSI system was launched only 60 days after the project initiation and was fully implemented within six months at all BayCare hospitals, outpatient centers, and outreach lab locations. The PSI system is linked to all BayCare locations. Once a patient is in the system, that patient can be correctly identified at any one of BayCare's ten healthcare locations whether it is a hospital, clinic, or imaging center, just by scanning their hand. BayCare's PSI system with biometric palm-vein identification has successfully fulfilled BayCare Health System's concern about ensuring patient safety and preventing identity theft and fraud.

PPID is a difficult yet crucial task for healthcare facilities. In order for healthcare providers to best execute their responsibilities, they need to address the patient's medical issues in a timely fashion, know who they are treating, and know the patient's medical history. Dedicated, high-resolution card scanners and biometrics linked to patient health records address these concerns, as well as decrease the ability for fraud to be committed. PPID systems are now a much-needed staple to a reputable healthcare facility's IT portfolio.

Sources: Biometric technology verifies patients' identity. (2010). Health Management Technology, 31(3), 20-21; Cunningham, B. (2012). Positive patient identification begins at step one. Health Management Technology, 33(8), 10-11.

Thinking About the Case

1. Although biometrics at BayCare Health Systems helps reduce risk by properly identifying patients

at registration, what aspect of their system opens them up to a different area of risk?

2. Why would a "non-patient" want to enroll in the BayCare system?

3. Does BayCare's PSI system hold too much information? Does linking patient data to BayCare's 10 locations infringe on privacy?

4. What risk does BayCare run by collecting such a large amount of private patient information and transmitting it between their 10 locations?

A Tale of Two Attacks

Do you leave your office or business door open and unlocked? Or your home? Unless you live in a rural or country area, probably not. How many times have you closed a door and checked to see if it is locked and securely closed? Probably too many times to count. Have you left your personal records on the lawn or your deck? Again, you probably have never done that. Ultimately, securing your personal property and information is a constant and continuing process; one that requires vigilance and gaining knowledge of new approaches to remain secure.

LinkedIn found its organization embroiled in a customer privacy protection controversy. The issue involved password leaks that could have affected their organization's accounts. After several hours of blogging and tweeting postings, the company admitted the next day that several million LinkedIn passwords had been posted on a hacker forum. LinkedIn communicated that they had "enhanced our security measures through an additional layer of technical protection known as 'salting' to better secure your information." This interesting statement appears to suggest that some extraordinary tactics were implemented that "sealed" a gap that was not detected prior to the security compromise. The weakness had been found and an appropriate remedy was implemented. However, should this have happened? The organization was the focus of significant attention and scrutiny following the situation. Ultimately, the question centered on why the passwords were not subjected to technical processes (e.g. encryption) to eliminate the security weakness. Inevitably, a lawsuit was filed in June 2012 seeking $5 million in compensation, stating that LinkedIn did not adequately implement the appropriate technical practices and adhere to its privacy policy.

In the same week that LinkedIn was dealing with its situation, another well-known company was dealing with its own technology controversy. eHarmony, an online dating service, implemented new security methodologies when 1.5 million customer passwords were compromised. eHarmony posted a blog which conveyed that "After investigating reports of compromised passwords, we have found that a small fraction of our user base has been affected. We are continuing to investigate but would like to provide the following actions we are taking to protect our members." The blog entry explained that eHarmony took action to resolve the issue and provided advice on how to create a strong password.

The issues of data breaches and security gaps continue to make headlines. The Federal Trade Commission (FTC) has reported that identity theft cost Americans $1.52 million in 2011 and appears on the rise. According to a 2012 report by The Ponemon Institute, the average annual cost of cybercrime is $8.9 million, ranging from $1.4 million to $46 million. The impact of the various cybercrime approaches, including denial of service, viruses and malicious code, continue to cause disruption to business operations and pirating of organizational and personal data. A recent report found that 43 percent of the companies surveyed had not implemented a data breach response plan prior to experiencing a violation. The Internet as well as the increasing popularity of connected devices (smartphones, tablets, etc.) continues to make computer crimes more profitable and widespread.

The issues of stolen data and cybercrimes have increased importance when considering an organization's mission-critical applications. The importance of these network-enabled devices to gain access to applications is woven into the daily activities of both businesses and individuals. Various organizational applications cannot be compromised by downtime due to the loss of revenue. It is important that these applications serve both employees needing to gain information from a corporate system as well as customers completing daily transactions. For example, it is important for an organization with significant online sales to maintain 100 percent uptime for its website.

There is no magic technology wand that will resolve all of these issues and eliminate cybercrimes and technology attacks. Business, government, and individuals need to continue the battle against criminals and groups whose intention is to compromise the security and well-being of individuals and businesses. Legislators and government agencies need to continue to be vigilant by providing laws and guidance on how to counteract these challenges.

Sources: Anonymous. (2011). Ponemon Institute Survey: Data Breaches Can Cause Lasting and Costly Damage to the Reputation of Affected Organizations. Entertainment Close-Up; Anonymous. (2012). 2012 Cost of Cyber Crime Study: United States. Traverse City, MI; Liyakasa, K. (2012). Cracking the Code on Cyber Crimes. Customer Relationship Management, 16, 36-40; McTigue, J. (2012). Application Early Warning System. InformationWeek (1347), 6-11; Teroka, B. (2012). Update on Compromised Passwords. Retrieved from http://www.eharmony.com/blog/2012/06/06/update-on-compromised-passwords/

Thinking About the Case

1. With the risk of litigation, loss of confidence and embarrassment, how do business organizations balance their public comments and transparency issues when attacks compromise their customers' privacy and information as well as their business operations?

2. Mary Wells Lawrence once said, "In this business, you can never wash the dinner dishes and say they are done. You have to keep doing them constantly." If you were a business executive or information technology manager, discuss how this statement relates to information technology risks, security, and disaster recovery.

3. Discuss any security situations that you have personally encountered and how they were handled by the business organization. Do you feel comfortable with how businesses are safekeeping your data and transaction activities?

References

Adams, J. (2012). How Superstorm Sandy Brought Disaster Recovery Home for Capital One, *American Banker*.

Anonymous. (2011). ID theft cases fall, but victims' costs rise. Retrieved April 23, 2013.

Anonymous. (2012a). Business Users of Macs Can Now Make Remote Deposits to Wells Fargo with Panini Scanners, *Business Wire*.

Anonymous. (2012b). Monthly Malware Statistics: April 2012. Retrieved April 24, 2013.

Anonymous. (2012c). Neustar Releases Survey Results on DDoS Attacks. (2012). *Wireless News*.

Anonymous. (2012d). The Revenue Drain of Downtime. Retrieved April 23, 2013, from http://www.netstandard.com/the-revenue-drain-of-downtime/

Anonymous. (2013a). Approved List of Digital Signature Certification Authorities. Retrieved April 22, 2013, from http://www.sos.ca.gov/digsig/

Anonymous. (2013b). New Data Suggests Cyber Attacks 'More Dangerous' Than International Terrorism. *Travel & Leisure Close-Up*.

Anonymous. (2013c). SurePassID Launches Secure Single Sign-On (Secure SSO) for Mobile at RSA Conference 2013, *PR Newswire*.

Bensinger, G. (2012). Corporate News: Netflix Blames Amazon For Overnight Blackout, *Wall Street Journal*, p. B.3.

Browdie, B. (2012). Citigroup Weathers Website Slowdown, *American Banker*.

Bryan-Low, C. (2011, Sep 02). Europe News: U.K. Charges Two More In Probe of Web Attacks, *Wall Street Journal*, pp. 4-4.

Chia, Terry. (2012, Aug 20). Confidentiality, Integrity, Availability: The three components of the CIA Triad. Retrieved August 5, 2013, from http://security.blogoverflow.com/2012/08/confidentiality-integrity-availability-the-three-components-of-the-cia-triad

Christman, A. (2013). Identity theft costs victims time, money, *McClatchy - Tribune Business News*.

Collins, J. C. (2012). Technology Q&A. *Journal of Accountancy*, 214(2), 76-79.

Darwell, B. (2012). Bot problem? Facebook estimates 8.7% of users are duplicate, miscategorized or spam accounts. Retrieved April 24, 2013, from http://www.insidefacebook.com/2012/08/01/bot-problem-facebook-estimates-8-7-of-users-are-duplicate-miscategorized-or-spam-accounts/

Dewdney, A. K. (1989). Computer Recreations: Of Worms, Viruses and Core War. *Scientific American*.

Finkle, J. (2012). Amazon.com cloudbursts at Christmas; Service outage pulls Netflix down across Americas, *National Post*.

Harris, C. (2011). IT Downtime Costs $26.5 Billion In Lost Revenue. Retrieved April 24, 2013, from http://www.informationweek.com/storage/disaster-recovery/it-downtime-costs-265-billion-in-lost-re/229625441

Linthicum, D. (2013). Calculating the true cost of cloud outages. Retrieved April 24, 2013, from http://www.infoworld.com/d/cloud-computing/calculating-the-true-cost-of-cloud-outages-212253

Nakashima, E., & Douglas, D. (2013). More companies admit to being hit by cyberattacks, *The Washington Post*, p. A.8.

Rapport, M. (2003). Many U.S. firms unprepared for business/IT outages, think firm finds. *Credit Union Times*, 14(13), 22.

Reckard, E. S. (2013). Online, mobile outage at BofA, *Los Angeles Times*, p. B.5.

Sarno, D. (2011, Mar 12). Twitter settles with FTC; The site agrees to tighten its security practices after hackers accessed users' data, *Los Angeles Times*, p. B.3.

Sherr, I. (2011, May 03). Hackers Breach Second Sony Service, *Wall Street Journal*, p. B.1.

Simpkins, J. (2011). Cyber Warfare Growing on a Global Scale – And We Have the Best Way to Profit. *Money Morning*. http://moneymorning.com/tag/cyber-terrorism-statistics/

Turner, K. (2012). Health Insurance Fraud Affects Everyone, *Standard - Speaker*.

Zetter, K. (2011). TSA Worker Gets 2 Years for Planting Logic Bomb in Screening System. Retrieved April 24, 2013, from http://www.wired.com/threatlevel/2011/01/tsa-worker-malware/

glossary

access controls—Hardware and software measures, such as user IDs and passwords, used to control access to information systems.

access point (AP)—An arrangement consisting of a device connected to the Internet on one end and to a router on the other end. All wireless devices link to the Internet through the router.

affiliate program—An arrangement by which a website promotes sales for another website through a link to the seller's site, and for which the affiliate is compensated. There are various schemes of compensation to affiliates.

agile methods—Software development methods that emphasize constant communication with clients (end users) and fast development of code, as well as modifications as soon as they are needed.

algorithm—A sequence of steps one takes to solve a problem. Often, these steps are expressed as mathematical formulas.

alliance—When organizations combine services to make them more attractive (and usually less expensive) than purchasing services separately. For example, in the travel industry, airlines collaborate with hotel chains and car-rental firms to offer travel and lodging packages.

antivirus software—Software designed to detect and intercept computer viruses.

applet—A small software application, usually written in Java or another programming language for the web.

application—A computer program that addresses a general or specific business or scientific need. General applications include electronic spreadsheets and word processors. Specific applications are written especially for a business unit to accommodate special activities.

application program interface (API)—Code in applications that helps link them to other applications. Using operating system APIs enables applications to utilize operating system features.

application service provider (ASP)—A firm that rents the use of software applications through an Internet link. The arrangement is known as Software as a Service (SaaS).

application software—Software developed to meet general or specific business needs.

application-specific software—A collective term for all computer programs that are designed specifically to address certain business problems, such as a program written to deal with a company's market research effort.

application systems support—Provision for software maintenance and user help on an information system.

arithmetic logic unit (ALU)—The electronic circuitry in the central processing unit of a computer responsible for arithmetic and logic operations.

artificial intelligence (AI)—The study and creation of computer programs that mimic human behavior. This discipline combines the interests of computer science, cognitive science, linguistics, and management information systems. The main subfields of AI are robotics, artificial vision, natural language processors, and expert systems.

assembly language—Second-generation programming languages that assemble several bytes into groups of characters that are human-readable to expedite programming tasks.

asymmetric (public key) encryption—Encryption technology in which a message is encrypted with one key and decrypted with another.

atomic transaction—A transaction whose entry is not complete until all entries into the appropriate files have been successfully completed. It is an important data entry control. (Atom=Indivisible)

audit trail—Names, dates, and other references in computer files that can help an auditor track down the person who used an IS for a transaction, legal or illegal.

authentication—The process of ensuring that the person who sends a message to or receives a message from another party is indeed that person.

autocategorization—Automatic sorting and indexing of information that is executed by specialized knowledge management software.

automatic taxonomy—A method in knowledge management to organize text and other nonstructured information in classes or categories.

B2B—Business-to-business, a term that refers to transactions between businesses, often through an Internet link.

B2C—Business-to-consumer, a term that refers to transactions between a business and its customers, often through an Internet link.

B2G—Business-to-government, a term that refers to transactions between a business and state or federal governments, often through an Internet link.

backbone—The network of copper lines, optical fibers, and radio satellites that supports the Internet.

backup—Periodic duplication of data in order to guard against loss.

backward compatibility—Compatibility of a device with another device that supports only an older standard. For example, USB 2.0 is backward-compatible with computers that support only USB 1.1 devices.

bandwidth—The capacity of the communications channel, practically its speed; the number of signal streams the channel can support, usually measured as the number of bits per second. A greater bandwidth also supports a greater bit rate, i.e., transmission speed.

banner—Advertisement that appears spread across the top or bottom of a webpage.

benchmarking—The measurement of time intervals and other important characteristics of hardware and software, usually when testing them before a decision to purchase or reject.

beta site—An organization that agrees to use a new application for a specific period and report errors and unsatisfactory features to the developer in return for free use and support.

beta version—A prerelease version of software to be tested by companies (called beta sites) that agree to use the application with actual data for several months.

Big Data—High volumes of data compiled from traditional business activities as well as newer nontraditional sources.

bill of materials (BOM)—A list showing an explosion of the materials that go into the production of an item. Used in planning the purchase of raw materials.

biometric—A unique, measurable characteristic or trait of a human being used for automatically authenticating a person's identity. Biometric technologies include digitized fingerprints, retinal pictures, and voice. Used with special hardware to uniquely identify a person who tries to access a facility or an IS, instead of a password.

bit—Binary digit; either a zero or a one. The smallest unit of information used in computing.

bits per second (bps)—The measurement of the capacity (or transmission rate) of a communications channel.

blackout/brownout—A period of power loss (blackout) or a significant fall in power (brownout). Power loss or irregularity may cause computers to stop working, or even damage them. Computers can be protected against blackouts and brownouts by using proper equipment, such as UPS (uninterruptible power supply) systems.

bleeding edge—The situation in which a business fails because it tries to be on the technological leading edge.

blog—A contraction of web log. A website where participants post their opinions on a topic or set of related topics; these postings are listed in chronological order.

Bluetooth—A personal wireless network protocol. It enables wireless communication between input devices and computers and among other devices within 10 meters.

bot—A small program installed by a hacker on a computer without the user's knowledge, designed to "hijack" the computer so the hacker can take advantage of the computer's resources and/or send spam to large numbers of people.

brainstorming—The process of a group collaboratively generating new ideas and creative solutions to problems.

brick-and-mortar—A popular term for companies that use physical structure for doing business directly with other businesses and consumers, such as stores. Often used to contrast with businesses that sell only online (pure play).

bridge—A device connecting two communications networks that use similar hardware.

broadband—High-speed digital communication, sometimes defined as at least 200 Kbps. T1, Cable modem, and DSL provide broadband.

Broadband over Power Lines (BPL)—A broadband service provided over electric power lines.

brownout—*See* blackout/brownout.

bus—The set of wires or soldered conductors in the computer through which the different components (such as the CPU and RAM) communicate. It also refers to a data communications topology whereby communicating devices are connected to a single, open-ended medium.

business analytics—Software that analyzes business data to help make business decisions, often at the strategic level. An alternative name for business intelligence.

business intelligence (BI)—Information gleaned from large amounts of data, usually a data warehouse or online databases; a BI system discovers not-yet-known patterns, trends, and other useful information that can help improve the organization's performance.

business recovery plan—Organizational plan that prepares for disruption in information systems, detailing what should be done and by whom, if critical information systems fail or become untrustworthy; also called business recovery plan and disaster recovery plan. Also known as business continuity plan.

byte—A standard group of eight bits.

C2C—Consumer-to-consumer business. The term usually refers to web-based transactions between two consumers via the servers of an organization, such as auctions and sales. eBay is an example of a C2C site.

case-based reasoning—A methodology of solving a new problem based on the solutions of similar problems, used in expert systems.

cash management system (CMS)—Information system that helps reduce the interest and fees that organizations have to pay when borrowing money and increases the yield that organizations can receive on unused funds.

central processing unit (CPU)—The circuitry of a computer microprocessor that fetches instructions and data from the primary memory and executes the instructions. The CPU is the most important electronic unit of the computer.

certificate authority (CA)—An organization that issues digital certificates, which authenticate the holder in electronic business transactions.

change management—A structured, disciplined approach that facilitates the adoption of new or modified systems by various groups and individuals within an organization.

character—The smallest piece of data in the data hierarchy.

chief information officer (CIO)—The highest-ranking IS officer in the organization, usually a vice president, who oversees the planning, development, and implementation of IS and serves as leader to all IS professionals in the organization.

chief security officer (CSO)—Also called chief information security officer (CISO), the highest-ranking officer in charge of planning and implementing information security measures in the organization, such as access codes and backup procedures.

chief technology officer (CTO)—A high-level corporate officer who is in charge of all information technology needs of the organization. Sometimes the CTO reports to the chief information officer, but in some companies this person practically serves as the CIO.

CIA triad—A concept which asserts that three basic elements are necessary for secure information systems: confidentiality, integrity, and availability (CIA).

ciphertext—A coded message designed to authenticate users and maintain secrecy.

clickstream software—Software that is a standard feature of web server software and is used to collect and analyze user activities on a website.

clickstream tracking—The use of software to record the activities of a person at websites. Whenever the person clicks a link, the activity is added to the record.

clock rate—The rate of repetitive machine cycles that a computer can perform; also called frequency. Measured in GHz.

closed system—A system that stands alone, with no connection to another system.

cloud computing—A model of computing in which local devices access applications and storage on remote servers, usually over the Internet.

cloud storage—The availability of network-accessible storage from an off-site computer or storage device.

clustering—A model of computing in which a "cluster" of smaller computers are linked via networks to use the computing power of multiple smaller computers, rather than one large supercomputer.

coaxial cable—A transmission medium consisting of thick copper wire insulated and shielded by a special sheath of meshed wires to prevent electromagnetic interference. Supports high-speed telecommunication.

co-location—The placement and maintenance of a web server with servers of other subscribers of the service provider. The servers are co-located in the same facility.

compact disc (CD)—Collective term for several types of lower-capacity storage optical discs, used for data storage and music or audio. Compare to digital video disc (DVD).

competitive advantage—A position in which one dominates a market; also called strategic advantage.

compiler—A program whose purpose is to translate code written in a high-level programming language into the equivalent code in machine language for execution by the computer.

composite key—In a data file, a combination of two fields that can serve as a unique key to locate specific records.

computer-aided design (CAD)—Special software used by engineers and designers that facilitates engineering and design work.

computer-aided manufacturing (CAM)—Automation of manufacturing activities by use of computers. Often, the information for the activity comes directly from connected computers that were used for engineering the parts or products to be manufactured.

content management system—Software that allows users to publish, edit, and update website content.

control unit—The circuitry in the CPU that fetches instructions and data from the primary memory, decodes the instructions, passes them to the ALU for execution, and stores the results in the primary memory.

controls—Constraints applied to a system to ensure proper use and security standards.

conversion—The process of abandoning an old information system and implementing a new one.

cookie—A small file that a website places on a visitor's hard disk so that the website can remember something about the visitor later, such as an ID number or username.

cost/benefit analysis—An evaluation of the costs incurred by an information system and the benefits gained by the system.

CPU clock—Circuitry in a computer's central processing unit (CPU) that synchronizes all tasks performed by the CPU.

create a new and unique product or service—A strategic move that can give an organization a competitive advantage.

create a standard—A strategic move that can give an organization a competitive advantage.

critical mass—In terms of strategic advantage, a body of clients that is large enough to attract many other clients.

crowdsourcing—A process for outsourcing a variety of tasks or problems to a distributed group of people, both online or offline.

CRT (cathode-ray tube)—A display (for a computer or television set) that uses an electronic gun to draw and paint on the screen by bombarding pixels on the internal side of the screen.

custom-designed (tailored) software—Software designed to meet the specific needs of a particular organization or department; also called tailored software.

customer relationship management (CRM) system—A set of applications designed to gather and analyze information about customers.

cut-over conversion (flash cut conversion)—A swift switch from an old information system to the new.

cyber terrorism—Terrorist attacks that target information systems or other online or technology infrastructure.

dashboard—A graphic presentation of organizational performance. Dashboards display in an easy-to-grasp visual manner metrics, trends, and other helpful information that is the result of processing of business intelligence applications.

data—Facts about people, other subjects, and events. May be manipulated and processed to produce information.

data dictionary—The part of the database that contains information about the different sets of records and fields, such as their source and who may change them.

data flow diagram (DFD)—A graphical method to communicate the data flow in a business unit. Usually serves as a blueprint for a new information system in the development process. The DFD uses four symbols for entity, process, data store, and data flow.

data integrity—Accuracy, timeliness, and relevance of data in a context.

data management module—In a decision support system, a database or data warehouse that allows a decision maker to conduct the intelligence phase of decision making.

data mart—A collection of archival data that is part of a data warehouse, usually focusing on one aspect of the organization such as sales of a family of products or daily revenues in a geographic region.

data mining—Using a special application that scours large databases for relationships among business events, such as items typically purchased together on a certain day of the week, or machinery failures that occur along with a specific use mode of the machine. Instead of the user querying the databases, the application dynamically looks for such relationships.

data modeling—The process of charting existing or planned data stores and flows of an organization or one of its units. It includes charting of entity relationship diagrams.

data processing—The operation of manipulating data to produce information.

data redundancy—The existence of the same data in more than one place in a computer system. Although some data redundancy is unavoidable, efforts should be made to minimize it.

data warehouse—A huge collection of historical data that can be processed to support management decision making.

data warehousing—Techniques to store very large amounts of historical data in databases, especially for business intelligence.

data word—The number of bits that a CPU retrieves from memory for processing in one machine cycle. When all other conditions are equal, a machine with a larger data word is faster.

database—A collection of shared, interrelated records, usually in more than one file. An approach to data management that facilitates data entry, update, and manipulation.

database administrator (DBA)—The individual in charge of building and maintaining organizational databases.

database approach—An approach to maintaining data that contains a mechanism for tagging, retrieving, and manipulating data.

database management system (DBMS)—A computer program that allows the user to construct a database, populate it with data, and manipulate the data.

debugging—The process of finding and correcting errors in software.

decision support system (DSS)—Information system that aids managers in making decisions based on built-in models. DSSs comprise three modules: data management, model management, and dialog management. DSSs may be an integral part of a larger application, such as an ERP system.

dedicated hosting—An arrangement in which a web hosting organization devotes an entire server to only the website of a single client organization, as opposed to having multiple clients' sites share one server.

denial of service (DoS)—The inability of legitimate visitors to log on to a website when too many malicious requests are launched by an attacker. Most DoS attacks are distributed (DDoS).

dialog module—The part of a decision-support system, or any other system, that allows the user to interact with the application. Also called interface.

dial-up connection—A connection to the Internet through a regular telephone and modem. Dial-up connections are slow, as opposed to broadband connections.

differentiation—A strategic initiative that can give an organization a competitive advantage by persuading consumers that its product or service is better than its competitors'.

digital certificate—Computer file that serves as the equivalent of an ID card.

digital signature—An encrypted digest of the text that is sent along with a message that authenticates the identity of the sender and guarantees that no one has altered the sent document.

digital subscriber line (DSL)—Technology that relieves individual subscribers of the need for the conversion of digital signals into analog signals between the telephone exchange and the subscriber jack. DSL lines are linked to the Internet on a permanent basis and support bit rates significantly greater than a normal telephone line between the subscriber's jack and the telephone exchange.

digital systems—Systems that communicate and process information in a form that follows the binary system of counting and binary methods of representing information, including sound and images.

digital video disc (DVD)—A collective term for several types of high-capacity storage optical discs, used for data storage and motion pictures. Also called digital versatile disc.

dimensional database—A database of tables, each of which contains aggregations and other manipulated information gleaned from the data to speed up the presentation by online processing applications. Also called multidimensional database.

direct access—The manner in which a record is retrieved from a storage device, without the need to seek it sequentially. The record's address is calculated from the value in its logical key field.

direct-attached storage (DAS)—Any data storage device that is directly connected to a computer as opposed to being connected via a communications network. When a disk is contained in the computer box or externally but directly linked to it, it is considered DAS.

disaster recovery plan—*See* business recovery plan.

DMZ—Demilitarized zone, a network of computers and other devices connected to the Internet where visitors are not allowed direct access to other resources connected to the DMZ. DMZs are used to serve visitors while minimizing risk of unauthorized access.

DNS (Domain Name System)—Hardware and software making up a server whose purpose is to resolve domain names (converting them back to IP numbers) and routing messages on the Internet.

domain name—The name assigned to an Internet server or to a part of a server that hosts a website.

dot-matrix printer—An older type of printer on which the printhead consists of a matrix of little pins; thus, each printed character is made up of tiny dots.

downstream—The movement of data bits from another computer to your computer via the Internet. Downstream speed of Internet connection services is usually greater than the upstream speed.

downtime—The unplanned period of time during which a system does not function.

drilling down—The process of finding the most relevant information for executive decision making within a database or data warehouse by moving from more general information to more specific details, such as from performance of a division to performance of a department within the division.

driver—The software that enables an operating system to control a device, such as an optical disc drive or joystick.

dynamic IP address—The IP address assigned to a computer that is connected to the Internet intermittently for the duration of the computer's connection.

dynamic webpage—A webpage whose contents change while the visitor watches it.

e-commerce—Business activity that is electronically executed between parties, such as between two businesses or between a business and a consumer.

economic order quantity (EOQ)—The optimal (cost-minimizing) quantity of a specific raw material that allows a business to minimize overstocking and save cost without risking understocking and missing production deadlines.

effectiveness—The measure of how well a job is performed.

efficiency—The ratio of output to input; the greater the ratio, the greater the efficiency.

electronic funds transfer (EFT)—The electronic transfer of cash from an account in one bank to an account in another bank.

electronic product code (EPC)—A product code embedded in a radio frequency identification (RFID) tag. Similar to the older UPC.

EMI (electromagnetic interference)—Unwanted disturbance in a radio receiver or electrical circuits caused by electromagnetic radiation from an external source. Fiber-optic cable is not susceptible to EMI.

employee knowledge network—Software that facilitates search of relevant knowledge within an organization. The software points an employee with need for certain information or expertise to coworkers who might have such information or expertise.

encapsulation—In object-oriented terminology, the combined storage of both the data and the procedures to manipulate the data.

encryption—The conversion of plaintext to an unreadable stream of characters, especially to prevent a party that intercepts telecommunicated messages from reading them. Special encryption software is used by the sending party to encrypt messages, and by the receiving party to decipher them.

enhance existing products or services—A strategic initiative that can give an organization a competitive advantage by adding to a product or service to increase its value to the consumer.

enterprise application—An application that fulfills a number of functions together, such as inventory planning, purchasing, payment, and billing.

enterprise resource planning (ERP) system—An information system that supports different activities for different departments, assisting executives with planning and running different interdependent functions.

entity—Any object about which an organization chooses to collect data.

entity relationship diagram (ERD)—One of several conventions for graphical rendition of the data elements involved in business processes and the logical relationships among the elements.

EPC (electronic product code)—The electronic equivalent of a universal product code (UPC), commonly embedded in an RFID (radio frequency identification) tag.

ergonomics—The science of designing and modifying machines to better suit people's health and comfort.

Ethernet—The design, introduced and named by Xerox, for a popular data communications protocol.

European Article Number (EAN)—A European standard of product code, similar to UPC but containing more information.

expert system (ES)—A computer program that mimics the decision process of a human expert in providing a solution to a problem. Current expert systems deal with problems and diagnostics in narrow domains. An ES consists of a knowledge base, an inference engine, and a dialog management module.

extranet—A network, part of which is the Internet, whose purpose is to facilitate communication and trade between an organization and its business partners.

fault tolerance—The ability of a system to continue to function despite a catastrophe or other usually disruptive events. Fault tolerance systems are usually redundant.

feasibility studies—A series of studies conducted to determine if a proposed information system can be built, and whether or not it will benefit the business; the series includes technical, economic, and operational feasibility studies.

Fiber to the Home (FTTH)—The connection of a home to the Internet through optical fiber technology. Often, other services, such as television and landline phone, are also provided through the same medium.

field—A data element in a record, describing one aspect of an entity or event. Referred to as attribute in relational databases.

file—In relational database terminology, a collection of related records.

File Transfer Protocol (FTP)—Software that allows the transfer of files over communications lines.

firewall—Hardware and software designed to control access by Internet surfers to an information system, and access to Internet sites by organizational users.

first mover—A business that is first in its industry to adopt a technology or method.

fixed wireless—A network of fixed transceivers to facilitate connection to the Internet. Requires line of sight between transceivers.

flash drive—A storage device containing flash memory. Flash drives are used in numerous electronic devices and often are designed to connect to a computer through a USB port.

flash memory—A memory chip that can be rewritten and can hold its content without electric power. Thumb drives, as well as ROM, are made of flash memory.

flat-panel monitor—A computer display device that has a slim profile, sharper images, and lower power consumption than older CRT monitors.

foreign key—In a relational database, a field in a table that is a primary key in another table. Foreign keys allow association of data between the two files.

fulfillment—Picking, packing, and shipping after a customer places an order online.

general-purpose application software—Programs that serve varied purposes, such as developing decision-making tools or creating documents; examples include spreadsheets and word processors.

geographic information system (GIS)—Information system that exhibits information visually on a computer monitor with local, regional, national, or international maps, so that the information can easily be related to locations or routes on the map. GISs are used, for example, in the planning of transportation and product distribution, or the examination of government resources distributed over an area.

Gigabit Ethernet—A network protocol often used in local area networks (LANs) supporting up to 1 Gbps.

global information system—Any information system that crosses national borders.

Global Trade Item Number (GTIN)—A number that uniquely identifies products and services. The GTIN is a global standard succeeding the EAN and UPC.

glocalization—The planning and designing of global websites so that they also cater to local needs and preferences.

graphical user interface (GUI)—A user interface that uses windows, icons, scroll bars, and other graphical images to help the user interact with the program.

group decision support system (GDSS)—Decision support system for a group of people rather than an individual. Often, a GDSS serves remote workers through the Internet, and provides mechanisms for bringing up ideas, discussing them, voting, and concluding a decision.

groupware—Any of several types of software that enable users of computers in remote locations to work together on the same project. The users can create and change documents and graphic designs on the same monitor.

hard disk—A stack of several rigid aluminum platters coated with easily magnetized substance to record data. Usually installed in the same box that holds the CPU and other computer components, but may be portable.

hardware—All physical components of a computer or computer system.

hijacking—In the context of networks, computers that are remotely taken advantage of by people who were not authorized to do so by the lawful owner. The computer is "hijacked" after a controlling application was surreptitiously installed on the computer's hard disk. Hijacked computers are exploited to participate in spamming or DDoS attacks.

honeypot—A duplicate database on a server connected to the Internet to trace an intruder. The server is dedicated specifically for detection of intrusions and is not productive. The honeypot is there to be attacked in lieu of a productive server. The traces can be used to improve security measures and possibly catch the intruder.

honeytoken—A bogus record in a database on a honeypot or productive server that is likely to draw an intruder's attention. If the intruder changes the record, the security officers know that the server has been attacked and can fix vulnerabilities.

host—A computer that contains files and other resources that can be accessed by "clients;" computers link to it via a network.

hot site—A location where a client organization hit by a disaster can continue its vital operations. The structure—often underground—is equipped with hardware and software to support the client's employees.

hotspot—An area in which a wireless device can connect to the Internet. The hotspot is created by installing an access point consisting of a device connected to the Internet on one end and to a router on the other end. All wireless devices link to the Internet through the router.

HTML5—The newest version of HTML/XML, which includes support for multimedia and mobile devices.

HTTPS—The secure version of HTTP.

hypermedia—A feature that enables a user to access information by clicking on selected text or graphics.

Hypertext Markup Language (HTML)—A programming language for webpages and web browsers.

Hypertext Transfer Protocol (HTTP)—Software that allows browsers to log on to websites.

Hypertext Transfer Protocol Secure (HTTPS)—*See* HTTPS.

identity theft—The criminal practice of obtaining enough personal information to pretend to be the victim, usually resulting in running up that person's credit cards or issuing new credit cards under that person's name.

IEEE 802.11—A family of standards for wireless communication. Several IEEE 802.11 standards have been approved by the Institute of Electrical and Electronics Engineers.

imaging—The transformation of text and graphical documents into digitized files. The document can be electronically retrieved and printed to reconstruct a copy of the original. Imaging has saved much space and expense in paper-intensive business areas.

impact printer—Printer that creates images on the page using mechanical impact. A dot-matrix printer is an impact printer.

implementation—In systems development, a phase that consists of two steps: conversion and training. Also called the delivery phase.

impression—In web advertising, the event of an ad displayed on a surfer's monitor.

inference engine—The part of an expert system that links facts and relationships in the knowledge base to reach a solution to a problem.

information—The product of processing data so that it can be used in a context by human beings.

information map—The description of data and information flow within an organization.

information system (IS)—A computer-based set of hardware, software, and telecommunications components, supported by people and procedures, to process data and turn it into useful information.

information systems auditor—A professional whose job it is to find erroneous or fraudulent entries in corporate information systems and investigate them.

information technology (IT)—Refers to all technologies that collectively facilitate construction and maintenance of information systems.

inheritance—In object-oriented terminology, the ability of a new (child) object to "inherit" some or all of the characteristcs of a previously developed (parent) object.

input—Raw data entered into a computer for processing.

input device—A tool, such as a keyboard or voice recognition system, used to enter data into an information system.

instant messaging (IM)—The capability for several online computer users to share messages in real time; also called chatting online.

intelligent agent—A sophisticated program that can be instructed to perform services for human beings, especially on the Internet.

internal memory—The memory circuitry inside the computer, communicating directly with the CPU. Consists of RAM and ROM.

Internet service provider (ISP)—An individual or organization that provides Internet connection, and sometimes other related services, to subscribers.

interpreter—A programming language translator that translates the source code, one statement at a time, and executes it. If the instruction is erroneous, the interpreter produces an appropriate error message.

intranet—A network using web browsing software that serves employees within an organization.

IP address—A unique number assigned to a server or another device that is connected to the Internet for identification purposes. Consists of 32 bits. The newer IPv6 protocol contains 128 bits, allowing many more unique IP addresses.

join table—In relational database manipulation, a table created by linking—that is, joining—data from multiple tables.

just-in-time (JIT)—The manufacturing strategy in which suppliers ship parts directly to assembly lines, saving the cost of warehousing raw materials, parts, and subassemblies.

key performance indicator (KPI)—A value used to measure performance in key areas of a business or organization; examples include occupancy ratios in hotels in hospitals, inventory turns in retail, or customer phone hold time in customer relations. KPIs are often shown in business analytic dashboard software.

keylogging—Automatically recording the keystrokes of a computer user. The logging is done by special software, usually surreptitiously with the intention of later using secret access codes.

knowledge base—The collection of facts and the relationships among them that mimic the decision-making process in an expert's mind and constitute a major component of an expert system.

knowledge management (KM)—The combination of activities involved in gathering, sharing, analyzing, and disseminating knowledge to improve an organization's performance.

knowledge workers—Employees whose main tasks involve collecting and organizing knowledge and information.

late mover—An organization that adopts a technology or method after competitors have adopted it.

liquid crystal display (LCD)—A flat-panel computer monitor in which a conductive-film-covered screen is filled with a liquid crystal whose molecules can align in different planes when charged with certain electrical voltage, which either blocks light or allows it to pass through the liquid. The combination of light and dark produces images of characters and pictures.

load balancing—The transfer of visitor inquiries from a busy server to a less busy server.

local area network (LAN)—A computer network confined to a building or a group of adjacent buildings, as opposed to a wide area network.

location-based services—Services that are enabled based on the location of a consumer combined with other data gathered from online and mobile apps, social media, and other sources. Location-based services offer the ability to target customers and gather more effective information about them.

lock in clients or suppliers—A strategic initiative that can give an organization a competitive advantage by forcing suppliers or buyers to use their products or modes of operation. Possessing bargaining power (the leverage to influence buyers and suppliers) is key to this approach.

logic bomb—A destructive computer program that is inactive until it is triggered by an event taking place in the computer, such as the deletion of a certain record from a file. When the event is at a particular time, the logic bomb is referred to as a time bomb.

Long-Term Evolution (LTE)—A standard method of wireless communications, specifically for high-speed data transmission for mobile phones. Also known as 4G LTE.

machine cycle—The steps that the CPU follows repeatedly: fetch an instruction, decode the instruction, execute the instruction, and store the result.

machine language—Binary programming language that is specific to a computer. A computer can execute a program only after the program's source code is translated to object code expressed in the computer's machine language.

magnetic disk—A disk or set of disks sharing a spindle, coated with an easily magnetized substance to record data in the form of tiny magnetic fields.

magnetic tape—Coated polyester tape used to store computer data; similar to tape recorder or video tape.

magnetic-ink character recognition (MICR)—A technology that allows a special electronic device to read data printed with magnetic ink. The data is later processed by a computer. MICR is widely used in banking. The bank code, account number, and the amount of a check are printed in magnetic ink on the bottom of checks.

mainframe computer—A computer larger than a midrange computer but smaller than a supercomputer.

management information system (MIS)—A computer-based information system used for planning, control, decision making, or problem solving.

manufacturing resource planning (MRP II)—The combination of MRP with other manufacturing-related activities to plan the entire manufacturing process, not just inventory.

many-to-many relationship—In databases, a relationship between two tables whereby every record in a table can be associated with several records in the other table.

mashup—An application created by integrating two or more existing applications, such as integrating a mapping application with a database of local charity associations.

massively open online course (MOOC)—An education delivery method that combines traditional course materials with interactive online forums for educators and students; a form of distance learning.

master production schedule (MPS)—The component of an MRP II system that specifies production capacity to meet customer demands and maintain inventories.

material requirements planning (MRP)—Inventory control that includes a calculation of future need.

m-commerce—*See* mobile commerce.

message digest—The first phase of the encryption process is to create a message digest from the file you wish to transmit, akin to a unique fingerprint of a file. Encryption software then encrypts the message digest to create a digital signature for that specific file.

metadata—Information about the data in a database, often called data dictionary.

metropolitan area network (MAN)—Network that links multiple LANs within a large city or metropolitan region and typically spans a distance of up to 50 kilometers/30 miles.

microprocessor—An electronic chip that contains the circuitry of either a CPU or a processor with a dedicated and limited purpose, for example, a communications processor.

microwaves—Short (high frequency) radio waves. Used in telecommunications to carry digital signals.

MIPS—Millions of instructions per second; an inaccurate measure of computer speed.

mirror server—An Internet server that holds the same software and data as another server, which may be located thousands of miles away.

mission-critical application—Application without which a business cannot conduct its operations.

mission statement—A paragraph that communicates the most important overarching goal of an organization for the next few years.

mobile applications developer—Person who develops software for smartphones and other mobile devices.

mobile commerce—Commerce conducted with the aid of mobile devices such as smartphones.

model—A representation of reality.

model management module—A collection of models that a decision-support system draws on to assist in decision making.

modem—Short for modulator/demodulator; a communications device that transforms digital signals to analog telephone signals, and vice versa, for data communications over voice telephone lines. The term is widely used for all devices that connect a computer to a wide area network, such as the Internet, even if the device does not modulate or demodulate.

motherboard—The primary circuit board in a computer, also called the system board.

mouse—An input device that controls an on-screen pointer to facilitate the point-and-click approach to executing different operations.

multicore processor—A processor that contains more than one central processing unit. Each core is equivalent to a CPU.

multidimensional database—*See* dimensional database.

multimedia software—Software that processes and displays various forms of information: text, sound, pictures, and video.

multiprocessing—The mode in which a computer uses more than one processing unit simultaneously to process data.

multitasking—The ability of a computer to run more than one program seemingly at the same time; it enables the notion of windows in which different programs are represented.

near-field communiations (NFC)—A standard communication protocol to create a radio connection between two devices within close proximity.

network—A combination of a communications device and a computer or several computers, or two or more computers, so that the various devices can send and receive text or audiovisual information to each other.

network administrator—The individual who is responsible for the acquisition, implementation, management, maintenance, and troubleshooting of computer networks throughout the organization.

network interface card (NIC)—Circuitry embedded or installed in a computer to support proper linking of the computer to a network.

network-attached storage (NAS)—An arrangement of storage devices linked to computers through a network.

neural network—An artificial intelligence computer program that emulates the way in which the human brain operates, especially its ability to learn.

node—A device connected to at least one other device on a network.

nonimpact printer—A printer that creates an image on a page without pressing any mechanism against the paper; includes laser, ink-jet, electrostatic, and electrothermal printers.

notebook computer—A computer as small as a book, yet with computing power similar to that of a desktop microcomputer.

object code—Program code in machine language, immediately processable by the computer.

object-oriented database model—A database model in which data is part of an object, that is processed using object-oriented programs.

object-oriented programming (OOP) programming language—A programming language that combines data and the procedures that process the data into a single unit called an "object," which can be invoked from different programs.

OC (optical carrier)—A family of several very high-speed technologies using optical fibers. Usually, the standard is marked as OC-3, OC-12, OC-48, etc.

offshoring—Outsourcing work to employees in other countries.

one-to-many relationship—In a database, a relationship between two tables such that each record in the one table can be associated with several records in the other table but each record in the other table can be associated with only one record in the first table.

online analytical processing (OLAP)—A type of application that operates on data stored in databases and data warehouses to produce summary tables with multiple combinations of dimensions. An OLAP server is connected to the database or data warehouse server at one end and to the user's computer at the other.

open source software—Software whose source code can be accessed by the general public.

open system—A system that interfaces and interacts with other systems.

operating system (OS)—System software that supports the running of applications developed to utilize its features and controls peripheral equipment.

optical disc—A disc on which data is recorded by treating the disc surface so it reflects light in different ways; includes CD and DVD.

optical tape—A storage device that uses the same principles as a compact disc.

organizational culture—An umbrella term referring to the general tone of a corporate environment.

output—The result of processing data by the computer; usually, information.

output device—A device, usually a monitor or printer, that delivers information from a computer to a person.

outsourcing—Buying the services of an information service firm that undertakes some or all of the organization's IS operations.

packaged software—General-purpose applications that come ready to install from a magnetic disk, CD, or file downloaded from a vendor's website.

parallel conversion—Using an old information system along with a new system for a predetermined period of time before relying only on the new one.

parallel processing—The capacity for several CPUs in one computer to process different data at the same time.

parameters—The categories that are considered when following a sequence of steps in problem solving.

peer-to-peer (P2P) file sharing—Software applications that enable two Internet users to send and receive to each other. The technology is highly objectionable to organizations that sell copyrighted materials because the software promotes violation of copyrights.

peer-to-peer LAN—A local area network (LAN) in which no central device controls communications.

personal area network (PAN)—A network of devices typically within a small radius that enables a user to use two or more devices wirelessly, such as a wireless keyboard and mouse.

personal computer—The collective name for several types of computers designed for individual computing: notebook computers, desktops, netbooks, and handheld computers.

personal digital assistant (PDA)—A type of handheld computer that was popular in the 1990s-2000s but has been superseded by smartphones and tablets. Many PDAs require the use of a special stylus to click displayed items and to enter handwritten information that is recognized by the computer.

phased conversion—Implementing a new information system one module at a time.

phishing—The criminal practice of luring Internet users to provide their personal information via email or the web. Phishing almost always results in fraud or identity theft.

pilot conversion—A trial conversion in which a new information system is introduced in one business unit before introducing it in others.

pixel—The smallest picture element addressable on a monitor, short for "picture element." In an LCD monitor, it is a triad of three transistors controlling the colors of red, green, and blue that can be switched on and off and kept on with varying amounts of electricity to produce various colors and hues.

plaintext—An original message, before encryption.

plug-and-play (PnP)—The ability of an operating system to recognize a new attachment and its function without a user's intervention.

podcast—To make a digital audio recording, usually of voice, and post the file on the web so that people can download and listen to it. People can subscribe to automatically download podcasts to their computers or devices.

port— (1) A socket on a computer to which external devices, such as printers, keyboards, and scanners, can be connected. (2) Software that enables direct communication of certain applications with the Internet.

primary key—In a database file, a field that holds values that are unique to each record. Only a primary key can be used to uniquely identify and retrieve a record.

process—Any manipulation of data, usually with the goal of producing information.

productivity—Efficiency, when the input is labor. The fewer labor hours needed to perform a job, the greater the productivity.

programmer/analyst—An entry-level position for IT professionals in computer programming. A programmer/analyst is partly involved in the analysis of business needs and ISs, but the greater part of the job involves setting up business applications.

programming—The process of writing software.

programming language—Set of syntax for abbreviated forms of instructions that special programs can translate into machine language so a computer can understand the instructions.

progressive elaboration—A process in systems development in which a vision of an initiative continually develops and influences the final product over time as more information is available.

project management—The set of activities that is performed to ensure the timely and successful completion of a project within the budget. Project management includes planning activities, hiring and managing personnel, budgeting, conducting meetings, and tracking technical and financial performance. Project management software applications facilitate these activities.

project portfolio management—A set of processes and methods used by project managers to determine which projects will meet the organization's operational and financial goals in relation to its strategic objectives as well as the needs of its customers.

proprietary software—Software owned by an individual or organizations. The owner can control licensing and usage terms of the software. Nonproprietary software is not owned by anyone and is free for use.

protocol—A standard set of rules that governs telecommunication between two communications devices or in a network.

prototyping—An approach to the development of information systems in which several analysis steps are skipped, to accelerate the development process. A "quick and dirty" model is developed and continually improved until the prospective users are satisfied. Prototyping has evolved into agile development methods.

proxy server—A computer that serves as an intermediary between two servers on the Internet, often for the purpose of security or filtering out certain information.

pure-play—A business operating with clients only via the web, as opposed to operating via stores or other physical facilities.

query—A request for information, usually addressed to a database.

radio frequency identification (RFID)—Technology that enables identification of an object (such as product, vehicle, or living creature) by receiving a radio signal from a tag attached to the object.

RAID (Redundant Array of Independent Disks)—A set of magnetic disk packs maintained for backup purposes. Sometimes RAID is used for storing large databases.

raise barriers to entrants—A strategic initiative that can give an organization a competitive advantage by making it difficult or impossible for other organizations to produce the product or service it provides.

RAM (random access memory)—The major part of a computer's internal memory. RAM is volatile; that is, software is held in it temporarily and disappears when the machine is unplugged or turned off, or it may disappear when operations are interrupted or new software is installed or activated. RAM is made of microchips containing transistors. Many computers have free sockets that allow the expansion of RAM.

rapid prototyping—Using software and special output devices to create prototypes to test design in three dimensions.

reach percentage—The percentage of web users who have visited a site in the past month, or the ratio of visitors to the total web population.

record—A set of standard field types. All the fields of a record contain data about a certain entity or event.

reduce costs—A strategic initiative that can give an organization a competitive advantage by lowering prices through having lower costs.

reengineering—The process by which an organization takes a fresh look at a business process and reorganizes it to attain efficiency. Almost always, reengineering includes the integration of a new or improved information system.

relational model—A general structure of a database in which records are organized in tables (relations) and the relationships among tables are maintained through foreign keys.

relational operation—An operation that creates a temporary table that is a subset of the original table or tables in a relational database.

repeater—A device that strengthens signals and then sends them on their next leg toward their next destination.

request for information (RFI)—A request to vendors for general, somewhat informal, information about their products.

request for proposal (RFP)—A document specifying all the system requirements and soliciting a proposal from vendors who might want to bid on a project or service.

resolution—The degree to which the image on a computer monitor is sharp. Higher resolution means a sharper image. Resolution depends on the number of pixels on the screen and the dot pitch.

return on investment (ROI)—A financial calculation of the difference between the stream of benefits and the stream of costs over the life of an information system; often used as a general term to indicate that an investment in an information system is recouped or smaller than the cost the system saves or the increase in revenue it brings about.

reverse auction (name-your-own-price auction)—An online auction in which participants post the price they want to pay for a good or service, and retailers compete to make the sale; also called a name-your-price auction.

RFI (radio frequency interference)—The unwanted reception of radio signals that occurs when using metal communication lines. Optical fibers are not susceptible to RFI.

ROM (read-only memory)—The minor part of a computer's internal memory. ROM is loaded by the manufacturer with software that cannot be changed. Usually, ROM holds very basic system software, but sometimes also applications. Like RAM, ROM consists of microchips containing transistors.

router—A network device, wired or wireless, that ensures proper routing of messages within a network such as a LAN and between each device on that network and another network, such as the Internet.

RSS—Really Simple Syndication, a type of application using XML for aggregating updates to blogs and news posted at websites.

SaaS (Software as a Service)—A software distribution method in which an application software provider (ASP) or vendor provides software over a network, often through the Internet. Payment is determined by the software made available, number of users, and the contract length of time.

scalability—The ability to adapt applications as business needs grow.

schema—The structure of a database, detailing the names and types of fields in each set of records, and the relationships among sets of records.

search advertising—Placing ads at search engine websites.

search engine optimization (SEO)—Tactics that allow a business to gain a high-ranking placement of their online entry in search engine results pages.

self-service—The customer's ability to determine the timing and services of their needs through an organization's website.

semistructured problem—An unstructured problem with which the decision maker may have had some experience. Requires expertise to resolve.

sensitivity analysis—Using a model to determine the extent to which a change in a factor affects an outcome. The analysis is done by repeating *if-then* calculations.

sequential storage—A file organization for sequential record entry and retrieval. The records are organized as a list that follows a logical order, such as ascending order of ID numbers, or descending order of part numbers. To retrieve a record, the application must start the search at the first record and retrieve every record, sequentially, until the desired record is encountered.

server—A computer connected to several less powerful computers that can utilize its databases and applications.

service-level agreement—A document that lists all the types of services expected of an outsourcing vendor as well as the metrics that will be used to measure the degree to which the vendor has met the level of promised services. Usually, the client makes the list.

shared hosting—An arrangement by which the websites of several clients are maintained by the hosting vendor on the same server.

smartphone—A cell phone that has a high-resolution color screen, is web and Internet-enabled, and runs mobile applications, or apps.

social engineering—Deceptive methods that hackers use to entice people to release confidential information such as access codes and passwords. Often, the crooks misrepresent themselves as technicians who need one's password for fixing a problem in a network.

software—Sets of instructions that control the operations of a computer.

software as a service (Saas)—A software distribution method in which an application software provider (ASP) or vendor provides software over a network, often through the Internet. Payment is determined by the software made available, number of users, and the contract length of time.

solid state disk (SSD)—Flash memory that serves as an internal or external storage medium as if it were a hard disk.

solid state storage—Computer storage that can be rewritten and retains its contents when electrical power is turned off; also known as flash memory.

source code—An application's code written in the original high-level programming language.

source data input device—A device that enables data entry directly from a document without need for human keying. Such devices include bar-code readers and optical character readers.

speech recognition—The process of translating human speech into computer-readable data and instructions.

spyware—A small application stored surreptitiously by a website on the hard disk of a visitor's computer. The application tracks activities of the user, including visits to websites, and transmits the information to the operator's server.

SSO (single sign-on)—Enabling employees to access several information systems by using a single password.

static IP address—An IP address permanently associated with a device.

storage—(1) The operation of storing data and information in an information system; (2) Any non-RAM memory, including internal and external hard disks, flash memory, and optical discs.

storage area network (SAN)—A device that enables multiple networked computers to save data on a group of disks located in a special area.

storage-as-a-service—Outsourcing corporate data storage to cloud storage vendors.

storage service provider (SSP)—A firm that rents storage space for software through an Internet link.

strategic advantage—A position in which one dominates a market; also called competitive advantage.

strategic information system (SIS)—Any information system that gives its owner a competitive advantage.

structured problem—A problem for whose solution there is a known set of steps to follow. Also called a programmable problem.

Structured Query Language (SQL)—The data definition and manipulation language of choice for many developers of relational database management systems.

stylus—A penlike marking device used to enter commands and data on a computer screen.

subsystem—A component of a larger system.

suite—A group of general software applications that are often used in the same environment. The strengths of the different applications can be used to build a single powerful document. Current suites are usually a combination of a spreadsheet, a word processor, presentation software, and a database management system.

supercomputer—The most powerful class of computers, used by large organizations, research institutions, and universities for complex scientific computations and the manipulation of very large databases.

supply chain—The activities performed from the purchase of raw material to the shipping of manufactured goods and collecting for their sale.

supply chain management (SCM) system—The coordination of purchasing, manufacturing, shipping, and billing operations, often supported by an enterprise resource planning system.

switch—A common networking device used as a central location to connect computers or devices to a local network.

switching costs—Expenses that are incurred when a customer stops buying a product or service from one business and starts buying it from another.

symmetric (secret or private key) encryption—Encryption technology in which both the sender and recipient of a message use the same key for encryption and decryption.

system—An array of components that work together to achieve a common goal or multiple goals.

system administrator—A computer professional who manages and maintains an organization's operating systems. Often referred to as "sys admin."

system requirements—The functions that an information system is expected to fulfill and the features through which it will perform its tasks.

system software—Software that executes routine tasks. System software includes operating systems, language translators, and communications software.

systems analysis—The early steps in the systems development process; to define the requirements of the proposed system and determine its feasibility.

systems analyst—An IT professional who analyzes business problems and recommends technological solutions.

systems design—The evaluation of alternative solutions to a business problem and the specification of hardware, software, and communications technology for the selection solution.

systems development life cycle (SDLC)—The oldest method of developing an information system, consisting of several phases of analysis and design, which must be followed sequentially.

systems integration—Interfacing several information systems.

T1 and T3 lines—Point-to-point dedicated digital circuits provided by telecommunications companies to provide high-speed communications for a fee.

table—A set of related records in a relational database.

tablet computer—A mobile computing device with a touch screen that uses a stylus or your fingers to execute commands; smaller than laptop computers but larger than smartphones.

targeted marketing—Promoting products and services to the people who are most likely to purchase them.

TCP/IP (Transmission Control Protocol/Internet Protocol)— A set of related protocols that can guarantee packets are delivered in the correct order and can handle differences in transmission and reception rates.

technology convergence—The combining of several technologies into a single device, such as mobile phone, digital camera, and web browser in a smartphone.

telecommunications—Communications over a long distance, as opposed to communication within a computer, or between adjacent hardware pieces.

throughput—A general measure of the rate of computer output or communications speed.

time to market—The time between generating an idea for a product and completing a prototype that can be mass-manufactured; also called engineering lead time.

top-level domain—The last part of a URL, a period and three letters that represent a major category into which URLs are divided, such as .com, .edu, and .gov.

total cost of ownership (TCO)—A financial estimate that allows business leaders to objectively evaluate the direct and indirect costs of a new organizational project.

touch screen—A computer screen that serves both as input and output device. The user touches the areas of a certain menu item to select options, and the screen senses the selection at the point of the touch.

trackback—A feature of some blog software that notifies bloggers when their posts have been mentioned elsewhere on the web.

trackball—A device similar to a mouse, used for clicking, locking, and dragging displayed information; in this case, the ball moves within the device rather than over a surface.

trackpad—A device used for clicking, logging, and dragging displayed information; the cursor is controlled by moving one's finger along a touch-sensitive pad.

traditional file approach—An older approach to maintaining data which has no mechanism for tagging, retrieving, and manipulating data, and which has been largely superseded by the database approach.

transaction—A business event. In an IS context, the record of a business event.

transaction processing system (TPS)—Any system that records transactions.

transmission rate—The speed at which data is communicated over a communications channel.

Transport Layer Security (TLS)—The successor of Secure Sockets Layer (SSL), the software in the web browser responsible for secure communication.

Trojan horse—A malicious piece of software hidden with a benign and legitimate software that one downloads or agrees to otherwise accept and install on one's computer. The Trojan horse then causes damage.

twisted pair cable—Traditional telephone wires, twisted in pairs to reduce electromagnetic interference.

Unicode—An international standard to enable the storage and display of characters of a large variety of languages—such as Asian, Arabic, and Hebrew—on computers.

Unified Modeling Language (UML)—An extensive standard for graphically representing elements of programming, specifically accommodating programming in object-oriented languages and web technologies.

Uniform Code Council (UCC)—An organization that promotes the use of uniform standards for bar codes.

Uniform Resource Locator (URL)—The address of a website. Always starts with *http://* or *https://* but does not have to contain *www*.

uninterruptible power supply (UPS)—A device that provides an alternative power supply as soon as a power network fails.

Universal Product Code (UPC)—A code usually expressed as a number and series of variable width bars that uniquely identifies the product by scanning.

universal serial bus (USB)—A ubiquitous socket that enables the connection of numerous devices to computers.

unstructured problem—A problem for whose solution there is no pretested set of steps, and with which the solver is not familiar—or is only slightly familiar—from previous experience.

upstream—The movement of data from your computer to another computer via a network, usually the Internet. Upstream speed through the services of Internet providers is typically lower than the downstream speed.

uptime—The percentage of time (so much time per year) that an information system is in full operation.

USB drive—Any storage device that connects to a computer through a USB socket, but especially flash drives.

user application development—Development of corporate applications by employees rather than IT professionals.

utilities—Programs that provide help in routine user operations.

value-added network (VAN)—A telecommunications network owned and managed by a vendor that charges clients periodic fees for network management services.

videoconferencing—A telecommunications system that allows people who are in different locations to meet via transmitted images and speech.

virtual memory—Storage space on a disk that is treated by the operating system as if it were part of the computer's RAM.

virtual private network (VPN)—Hardware and software installed to ensure that a network path that includes the Internet enables employees of the same organization or employees of business partners to communicate confidentially. The hardware and software create an impression that the entire communication path is private.

virtual private server—Part of a server that serves as an Internet server for a client of a web hosting company, while other clients share the same physical server.

virus—Destructive software that propagates and is activated by unwary users; a virus usually damages applications and data files or disrupts communications.

visual programming language—A programming language that provides icons, colors, and other visual elements from which the programmer can choose to speed up software development.

VoIP (Voice over Internet Protocol)—Technologies that enable voice communication by utilizing the Internet instead of the telephone network.

web hosting—The business of organizations that host, maintain, and often help design websites for clients.

webpage authoring tools—Software tools that make webpage composition easier and faster than writing code by providing icons and menus.

webmaster—The person who is in charge of constructing and maintaining the organization's website.

what-if analysis—An analysis that is conducted to test the degree to which one variable affects another; also called sensitivity analysis.

wide area network (WAN)—A network of computers and other communications devices that extends over a large area, possibly comprising national territories. Example: the Internet.

Wi-Fi—A name given to the IEEE 802.11 standards of wireless communication. Wi-Fi technologies are used in hotspots and in home and office networks.

wiki—A web application that enables users to add to and edit the content of webpages, or software that enables collaborative software used to create and revise websites.

WiMAX—The IEEE 802.16 standard for wireless networking with a range of up to 50 km (31 miles). (WiMAX stands for the organization that promotes that standard, Worldwide Interoperability for Microwave Access.)

wireless LAN (WLAN)—A local area network that uses electromagnetic waves (radio or infrared light) as the medium of communication. In recent years almost all WLANs have been established using Wi-Fi.

work order—A numbered (or otherwise uniquely coded) authorization to spend labor and other resources on the manufacturing of a product or rendering of a service. Usually, work orders are opened within a project number. The system of project number and work orders helps track costs and activities related to an assignment in an organization, typically one in the manufacturing sector.

workstation—A powerful microcomputer providing high-speed processing and high-resolution graphics. Used primarily for scientific and engineering assignments.

worm—A rogue program that spreads in a computer network. Unlike other computer viruses, worms do not need human intervention to spread.

XHTML—A standard that combines HTML standards and XML standards.

XML (Extensible Markup Language)—A programming language that tags data elements in order to indicate what the data means, especially in webpages.

yield management software—Software that helps maximize the capacity of airline seats and hotel rooms by analyzing which variables affect purchasing of such services and in what way.

subject INDEX

atomic transactions, **464**–465
AtTask, 407
attributes, 154, 228
auctions, 41–42, 264, 266–268,
    272–273
auditing decision support systems
    (DSSs), 331
auditing information systems, 402
audit trails, 93, **465**
authentication, **468**–474
autocategorization, **377**
auto industry
    building vehicles on websites, 57
    information systems (ISs), 73–74
    robots, 39
automated decision making, 339
Automated Staff Acquisition Platform
    (ASAP), 89
automatic taxonomy, **377**
automatic teller machines (ATMs),
    16, 121, 243
automation, 39, 52–53, 181–182
automobiles
    navigation systems, 123
    tweeting mechanical issues, 345
availability, 452
Avanquest WebEasy Professional, 151
AZERTY keyboards, 118

B

backbone, **196**
backups, **461**–462
    companies specializing in, 462
    databases, 227–228
    data warehouses, 240
    magnetic tapes, 127
    RAID (redundant array of
        independent disks), 461–**462**
    remote storage, 462
backward compatibility, **136**
Baidu, 310
balance sheet, 70
bandwidth, **189,** 304
banking industry
    apps for depositing checks, 123
    competitive advantage, 51
    data mining, 361
    mobile devices transactions, 6
    models, 331
    phishing and, 274–275
    source data input devices, 121
Bankway, 180
banners, **265,** 276
barcode scanners, 58, 64, 120,
    145, 146
barriers to entrants, **40, 64**

Basecamp, 159
BASIC, 152
BeAware, 441
benchmarking and software
    licensing, **435**
benefits management, 90–91
benefits selection, 338
Berkeley Software Distribution (BSD)
    UNIX, 171
beta sites, **402**
beta software, 54, **432**
Big Brother society, 22
Big Data, 84, 222, 241, 371
    data warehouses, **243**
    retail, 250–251
    social media, 243
big iron, 112
bill of materials (BOM), **76**
binary counting system, 6
biometrics, 53, **463**–464
    health care, 487
BI systems. *See* business intelligence
    (BI) systems
bit rate, 189
bits (binary digits), **111**
bits per second (bps), **189**
BitTorrent, 188
Blackberry devices, 475
Blackberry phones, 156, 276, 382
blackouts, **453**
bleeding edge, **58**
Blogger, 283
bloggers, 258
blogs, **258**–259
    freedom of speech, 22
    trackback, **259**
Blue Gene, 112
Blue Performance, 53
Bluetooth, 146, 191, **199**
Bluetooth mouse, 15
Blu-ray players, 418
BOM. *See* bill of materials (BOM)
bookselling industry decision support
    systems (DSSs), 335
bots, **460**
Boxee boxes, 418
bps. *See* bits per second (bps)
brainstorming, **73**
brand-name success, 44
brick-and-mortar businesses, 21, 65, **270**
bridges, **195**
"bring your own technology with
    you," 13
broadband, **189**
Broadband over Power Lines (BPL),
    192, 206

broadband services, 202–203
broadband telephony, 206–208
brownouts, **453**
Brussels Convention (1968), 311
brute force software, 457
BSD UNIX. *See* Berkeley Software
    Distribution (BSD) UNIX
buses, **117**
business alliances, 268–269
business analysis tools, 325
business analytics, **360**
Business Analytics Suite, 331
business applications, 342
business continuity plans, 477
    See also business recovery plans
businesses
    activities interdependence, 69
    analytics strategy, 241
    cloud computing, 241
    collecting data, 84
    globalization, **302**–303
    information map, **12**–13
    information systems (ISs), 13
    information use, 7
    multimedia, 161
    personal data, 92
    processing orders and payments, 5
    researching, 1–2
    shortening business cycle, 288
    storage media, 132–134
    strategic initiatives, 371
    unsolicited email, 276
business functions, 71
business intelligence applications,
    325, 361, 375
business intelligence (BI), 249, 368,
    382
    collecting, 369–371
    customer loyalty programs, 363
    dashboards, **371**–372
    data mining, 362
    mobile devices, 368
    top-of-the-line providers, 376
    zoos, 363
business intelligence (BI) systems, **18,**
    360, 395
business plan, 2–3
business process management (BPM)
    systems, 356
business process outsourcing, 425
business recovery plans, **476**–478
business-to-business (B2B), 56, 57,
    264
    advertising, 264–266
    electronic trade, 21
    exchanges and auctions, 266–268

online business alliances, 268–269

search engine optimization (SEO), **266**

trading, 264–269

web as global medium, 300

business-to-consumer (B2C), 57, **264,** 269–275, 277–279

auctions and reverse auctions, 272–273

content providers, 273

electronic bill presentment and payment (EBPP), 274

electronic trade, 21

e-tailing, 270–272

extra-organizational workforce, 277

mobile advertising, 272

mobile commerce, **277**–279

web as global medium, 300

business-to-government (B2G), **264**

buyers, locking in, **47**–48

buzzwords, 88

bytes, **111**

C

C#, 155

C++, 151, 155, 157

cable, 202–203

cable modem, 203

cable television, 189

CAD. *See* computer-aided design (CAD)

CADUCEUS, 343

call centers, outsourcing, 447

caller ID, 84, 457

CAM. *See* computer-aided manufacturing (CAM) systems

cameras, 14

CAN-SPAM act, 276

Carbonite, 258

card scanners, 487

careers

chief information officer (CIO), 25, **26**

chief information security officer (CISO), 25

chief security officer (CSO), **25**

chief technology officer (CTO), **26**

database administrators (DBAs), **24**

mobile applications developers, **25**

network administrator, 24–**25**

system administrators, **25**

systems analysts, **23**–24

webmasters, **25**

women, 24

CargoWiz, 79

Carnivore, 476

carpal tunnel syndrome, 132

car rental companies, 331

case-based expert systems (ESs), 343

case-based reasoning, **343**

CASE (computer-aided software engineering tools), 428

Cash Availability and Forecasting Environment (CASE), 355–356

cash flow forecasting system, 355–356

cash management systems (CMSs), **72**

CASM. *See* cost per available seat-mile (CASM)

Category 5 (Cat 5) cable, 190

Category 6 (Cat 6) cable, 190

cathode-ray tube (CRT) monitors, **124**

caveat emptor (buyer beware), 437–438

CDMA (Code Division Multiple Access) protocol, 201

CD-ROM (Compact Disc, Read Only Memory) CDs, 128

CD-R (recordable) CDs, 128

CD-RW (rewritable) CDs, 128

CDs. *See* compact discs (CDs)

cell phones, 186–187, 210

global positioning systems (GPS), 278

cellular networks, 146

censorship, 22

central processing units (CPUs), **110**

arithmetic logic unit (ALU), **115**

control unit, **115**

data word, **117**

machine cycle, **116**–117

microprocessors, **115**–116

multicore, 117

CEO. *See* chief executive officer (CEO)

CEO Desktop Deposit, 475

certificate authorities (CAs), **473**

certification, 409–411

CERT program (Carnegie Mellon), 411

CF (Compact Flash) flash memory card, 129

CGI, 285

change, 417

change management, **389**

characters, **223**–224

character sets, 304

chess, 341–342

chief executive officer (CEO), 25

chief information officer (CIO), 25, **26**

chief information security officer (CISO), 25

chief security officer (CSO), **25**

chief technology officer (CTO), **26**

China

censorship restrictions on Google, 310

market, 301

ChoiceView app, 447

Chrome, 55, 474

Chrysler Comprehensive Compensation (C3), 405

CIA triad (confidentiality, integrity, and availability), **452**

CIO. *See* chief information officer (CIO)

CIO Agenda Report (2012, Gartner), 36, 45

ciphertext, **468**

CISO. *See* chief information security officer (CISO)

Clarizen, 407

class diagrams, 399

classification, 360

click streams, 85

clickstream software, **369**–371

clickstream tracking, **263**

clients and certification, 410

clock rate, **116**–118

closed systems, **11**–12

cloud-based technologies *versus* outsourcing, 423

cloud computing, **13**

businesses, 241

group decision support systems (GDSS), 346

cloud storage, 110, **131,** 133–134

clustering, 360

clustering computers, **112**

CMSs. *See* cash management systems (CMSs)

coaxial cable, **190**

COBOL, 152, 153, 157

Cognos, 383

collaboration software, 163

collaborative logistics, 96

co-location service, **284**

commodities, 289

common metals detection, 345

communication and interactive technology, 261–262

communications software, 169

compact discs (CDs), **128,** 132

companies

backups specialization, 462

barriers to entrants, **40**

collaboration with retailers, 96
collection and analysis of consumer
    data specialization, 369–371
electronic copies of résumés, 88
failures on the web, 56–57
innovative technologies, 64–65
monopolistic power, 56
selling information, 239
strategic gap with competitors, 53
supply chain management (SCM)
    systems, 93
comparative advantage and
    manufacturing, 375
compensation, 90–91
competition and e-tailing, 271
competitive advantage, **37**
    achieving, 38–48
    alliances, **45**–47
    automation, 39
    barriers to entrants, **40**
    constant improvements and, 51
    differentiation, **44**
    enhancing products or services,
        44–45
    first movers, 73
    for-profit companies, 38
    industries, 48
    information systems (ISs), 51
    locking in suppliers or buyers,
        47–48
    minimizing lead time, 73
    as moving target, 51
    new and unique product creation,
        41–44
    online service, 39
    organizational change to gain, 50
    outsourcing, 430
    reducing costs, **39**
    robots, 39
    sales systems innovations, 12
    strategic information systems
        (SISs), 48
    switching costs, **41**
competitors
    imitating successful companies, 51
    strategic gap with, 53
compilers, **156**–157, 164, 169
complex simulation, 113
composite key, **230**
computer-aided design (CAD), **73,** 74,
    76, 113
computer-aided manufacturing
    (CAM) systems, **73,** 76, 113
Computer and Information Sciences
    undergraduate degrees
    (2010), 24

computers, 15
    access controls, **462**–464
    appropriate personal use of, 441
    buses, **117**
    central processing units (CPUs),
        115–117
    classifications, 111–115
    clock rate, **116**–117
    clustering, **112**
    components, 109–110
    credit decisions, 339
    expansion slots, 135
    health and, 132
    hijacking, **460**–461
    mainframe computers, **112**–113
    memory capacity, 117
    notebook computers, **113**
    personal computers (PCs), **113**
    personal digital assistants (PDAs),
        113–114
    power, 117–118
    processing and storing data, 111
    processing speed, 117–118
    servers, **113**
    smartphones, **114**–115
    supercomputers, **111**–112
    tablet computers, **114**
    technology convergence, **114**–115
    USB ports, 135
    workstations, **113**
computer security incident handler
    (CSIH) certification, 411
computer telephony integration
    (CTI), 84
computer-to-computer calls, 207
computer use policies, 441
computer vision syndrome (CVS),
    132
confidentiality, 452
Connect, 187
consumer privacy, 22, 92–93
consumer profiling, **271**
consumers
    e-commerce transactions law suits,
        311
    privacy, 452
consumer-to-consumer (C2C), **264,**
    272
content management systems, **286**
content providers, 273
controllers, 71
controls, **461**
    access, **462**–464
    application reliability, 461
    atomic transactions, **464**–465
    audit trails, **465**

backups, **461**–462
    data entry, 461
control unit, **115,** 116
converging technologies and
    networking, 210–211
conversion, **400**–402
cookies, 22, 239, **262**–263, 270, 271,
    288, 369, 447
coopetition, 272
copyrights, 309
Corendal Wiki, 260
cost accounting systems, 16, 71
cost/benefit analysis, **394**
cost per available seat-mile
    (CASM), 54
costs
    cloud storage, 134
    hardware, 136
    reducing, 39, 64
    savings, 390
    storage media, 134
countries
    civil rights, 309
    different standards, 310–311
    free speech, 313
    privacy, 312–313
    regulations and tariffs, 305–306
country-of-destination principle,
    311
country-of-origin principle, 311
Covisint website, 56–57, 268–269
C programming language, 152, 157
CPU clock, **116**
CPUs. *See* central processing units
    (CPUs)
Creative Suite, 151
credit-card processing, 286
credit cards, 122
    consumer privacy, 22
    e-commerce, 306
credit evaluation and expert systems
    (ESs), 344
credit score, 339
critical mass, **42**
CRM systems. *See* customer
    relationship management (CRM)
    systems
crowdsourcing, **277**
Crystal Clear, 403, 405
CS2/Dreamweaver, 162
CSI, 119
CSO. *See* chief security officer (CSO)
CTI. *See* computer telephony
    integration (CTI)
cultural differences, 308
custom-designed software, 423–424

data processing, **14**
data redundancy, **223,** 231
data storage devices, 13
data store, 397
data warehouses, **18,** 24, 58, 85, 128, **238,** 249, 359
  backups, 240
  Big Data, **243**
  customer loyalty programs, 362
  as data management module, 330
  data marts, **238**
  data mining, **360**–364
  extraction, transforming, and loading (ETL), 242
  linkages to identify purchases, 383
  mainframes, 240
  metadata, 242
  moving database data to, 238, 240–242
  online analytical processing (OLAP), **364**–369
  phases, 242
  retail, 250
data words, **117**–118
DB2, 231
DBAs. *See* database administrators (DBAs)
DBMSs. *See* database management systems (DBMSs)
DealerConnection, 56, 57
debit cards, 122, 306
debugging, **152,** 402
decimal counting system, 6
decision making, 326
  automating, 329, 339
  choice phase, 326
  collecting data, 6
  decision support systems (DSSs), **18**
  design phase, 326
  executive information systems (EISs), 336
  expert systems (ESs), **18**
  information, 7–8
  intelligence phase, 326, 330
  models, **326,** 331
  semi-structured problems, **327**–328
  structured problems, **327**–328
  tying data to physical location, 18–19
  unstructured problems, **327**–328
  "What if" questions, 18
decision support
  decision support systems (DSSs), 325–326
  expert systems (ESs), 325–326, **340**–445

geographic information systems (GIS), **347**–349
group decision support system (GDSS), **346**–347
decision support systems (DSSs), **18,** 325–326, **329**–338
  auditing, 331
  benefits selection, 338
  bookselling industry, 335
  data, 330
  databases, 330, 340
  data management module, **330**–331
  data warehouses, 330
  dialog module, **333**
  examples, 335–338
  financial services, 338
  food production, 335
  health care, 356
  intranets, 333
  model management module, **331**–333
  patients, 356
  sensitivity analysis, **335**
  stand-alone, 329
  tax planning, 336
  website planning and adjustment, 336–337
  yield management, **337**–338
de-commoditize, 289
dedicated hosting, **283**–284
DELETE SQL command, 233
delivery, 400
Delphi, 153
demodulation, 195
demographics, 364
denial of service (DoS) attacks, **459**–460, 488
Designer Pro, 159
desktop publishing, 159
destructive applications, 23
DEX handheld units, 217
DFDs. *See* data flow diagrams (DFDs)
diagnostic expert systems (ESs), 343
dialog module, **333**
dial-up connections, 195, 206
differentiation, **44**
digital cameras, 129
digital certificates, **473**–474
digital information, 6–7
digital signatures, **472**–473
digital subscriber line (DSL), **203**
digital systems, **6–7**
digital video discs (DVDs), 110, **128,** 132, 133
digital wallets, 307
dimensional databases, **365,** 368

direct access, **126**
direct access storage devices (DASDs), 126
direct-attached storage (DAS), **130,** 145
Direct Express Debit MasterCard, 73
disaster recovery planning, 452, 476
  See also business recovery plans
Discern Expert, 343–344
The Discipline of Market Leaders, 407
disk mirroring, 145
disk operating system (DOS), 55
displays, 14
distributed denial-of-service (DDoS) attacks, 459
DMZ (demilitarized zone), **467**
DNS (Domain Name System), **197**
documentation, 403
documents
  embedding links to websites, 160
  imaging, **122**–123
  indexing, 122
domain names, **255**
  extensions, 275
  resolution, 196
  top-level domain (TLD), **255**
Domain Name System. *See* DNS (Domain Name System)
domains, 340
DOS. *See* disk operating system (DOS)
dossier phenomenon, 92
dot-matrix printers, **126**
dots per inch (DPI), 125
Dove brand, 319
downstream, **201**
downtime, **453,** 480–481, 488
DPI. *See* dots per inch (DPI)
Dragon Naturally Speaking, 123
Dreamweaver, 151
drilling down, **365,** 383
drivers, **167**
Drupal, 170
DSL (digital subscriber line), 189, **203**
DSL modem, 203
DSSs. *See* decision support systems (DSSs)
DVDs. *See* digital video discs (DVDs)
Dvorak keyboards, 118
dynamically modified models, 331
dynamic IP addresses, **197**
Dynamic Systems Development Method (DSDM), 403
dynamic webpages, **285**

E

EBPP. *See* electronic bill presentment and payment (EBPP)
e-business, 37

File Transfer Protocol (FTP), **258**
finance
    cash management systems
      (CMSs), **72**
    information systems (ISs), 20,
      71–72
    investment analysis and service, 72
financial institutions and denial of
    service (DoS) attacks, 460
financial managers, 71
financial services, 85, 338
fingerprints, 463–464
FiOS (Fiber Optic Service), 204
Firefox, 55
firewalls, **466**–467
First Aid by American Red Cross, 150
first generation (1G) protocols, 201
first-generation programming
    languages, 151
first movers, **42**–44, 73
fixed variable models, 331
fixed wireless, **204**
Flash, 48
flash cut conversion, **401**
flash drives, **126**
flash memory, 110, **129**
flat-panel display monitors, **124**
floppy disks, 127–128
food manufacturers
    collaboration with paper manufac-
      turers, 96
    transit efficiency, 145–146
FoodPro, 335
food production decision support
    systems (DSSs), 335
FordDirect.com website, 57
forecasting, 360
foreign keys, 229, **230**
for-fee content, 273
for-profit companies competitive
    advantage, 38
FORTRAN, 152, 157
Fortune Magazine, 427
4G LTE. *See* Long-Term Evolution
    (LTE)
fourth-generation (4GLs) program-
    ming languages, 151–152
fourth generation (4G) protocols, 201
fraud and Internet, 274
freedom of speech, 22
frequently asked questions. *See* FAQs,
    39
fulfillment, **270**
functional business areas information
    systems (ISs), 19–21
furniture sales, 296

G

Galaxy Note II, 114
Gantt charts, 407
GB. *See* gigabytes (GB)
GDP. *See* gross domestic product
    (GDP)
General Public License (GPL), 171
general-purpose application software,
    158
GeoBase, 78
geographic information systems
    (GISs), **18**–19, **347**–349
geostationary (GEO) satellites,
    191–192
GHz. *See* gigahertz (GHz)
gigabytes (GB), 111
gigahertz (GHz), 116
Gigabit Ethernet, **197**
Gimp, 159
GISs. *See* geographic information
    systems (GISs)
global information systems, **300**
    applicable law, 313
    conflicting economic, scientific,
      and security issues, 308–309
    cultural differences, 308
    different standards, 310–311
    flexible websites and applications,
      304
    language differences, 304, 307
    legal barriers, 312–313
    localizing, 304
    multiple versions of websites, 304
    open source software, 309
    payment mechanisms differences,
      306–307
    political challenges, 309
    privacy laws, 312–313
    regulations and tariffs, 305–306
    technological challenges, 304–305
    time zones, 313–314
globalization, **302**–303, 375
global positioning systems (GPSs), 19,
    78, 119, 204
    cell phones, 278
    smartphones, 86
    3-D geographic software, 164
Global Trade Item Numbers (GTINs),
    311
Google Docs, 41, 160, 163
Google Drive, 160, 163
Google Earth, 19, 349
Google Maps, 19, 162, 164
Google Voice, 207
Google Wallet, 279, 307
GoToMeeting, 187

GoToMyPC, 454
"got-to-have-it" technology, 37
government databases cyber attacks,
    228
government-to-business, 264
government-to-consumer, 264
GPS. *See* global positioning system
    (GPS)
Gramm-Leach-Bliley Act (GLBA,
    1999), 452
graphical user interfaces (GUIs), **155,**
    166
    object database management
      systems (ODBMSs), 232
graphics programs, 159
grocery ordering services, 64–65
gross domestic product (GDP), 93
group decision support system
    (GDSS), **346**–347
groupware, **163**
GSM (Global System for Mobile)
    protocol, 201
GUIs. *See* graphical user interfaces
    (GUIs)

H

hackers, 24, 451
hacking, 455
    customer privacy protection, 488
    software defending against, 457
handheld devices, 14, 113, 124, 146
handheld scanners, 58
hard disks, 127–**128**
hardware, **109**
    backward compatibility, **136**
    blackouts, **453**
    bridges, **195**
    brownouts, **453**
    central processing units (CPUs),
      110
    compatibility, 136
    cost, 136
    drivers, **167**
    ergonomics, 136
    expansion slots, 135
    external ports, 135
    footprint, 136
    information systems (ISs), 13
    input devices, **110**
    internal memory, **110**
    leasing, 138
    modems, **195**
    motherboard, **110**
    natural disasters, 453
    network interface cards (NICs), **195**

noise, 136
output devices, **110,** 124–126
power, 135
power consumption, 136
purchasing, 111, 135–137
RAM (random access memory), **110**
repeaters, **195**
risks, 453–454
ROM (read-only memory), **110**
routers, **195**
scalability, 138
source data input devices, **120**–122
storage, **110,** 126–134
switches, **195**
technology convergence, **114**–115
updating, 138
vandalism, 454
Hawaii Five-O, 119
HBO app family, 418
HBO GO mobile platform, 418
HDTV. *See* high definition television (HDTV)
health care
    biometrics, 487
    decision support systems (DSSs), 356
    electronic records, 239–240
    networks and, 217–218
    positive patient identification (PPID) systems, 487
health care plans, 338
Health Guide patient monitoring and management system, 194
health information management (HIM), 344
Health Insurance Portability and Accountability Act (HIPAA, 1996), 240, 452
high definition television (HDTV), 125
hijacking, **460**–461
hits, 286
home lending operation, 295
honeypots, **457**
honeytokens, **457**
hospitality industry, 338
hosting service, 283–285
hosts, **196**
hotel industry customer relationship management (CRM), 105
hot sites, **478**–479
hotspots, **197**–198
How to Drive Your Competition Crazy (Kawasaki), 158
HR information systems. *See* human resources (HR) information systems

HRM. *See* human resource management (HRM)
HTML5, **257**
HTML. *See* Hypertext Markup Language (HTML)
HTTP. *See* Hypertext Transfer Protocol (HTTP)
HTTPS (HTTP Secure), **255, 471**
human resource (HR) information systems, 16
human resource (HR) information systems (ISs), 21
human resource management (HRM), 88–91
Hurricane by American Red Cross, 150
hypermedia, **160**–161
Hypertext Markup Language (HTML), **257**–258, 348
Hypertext Transfer Protocol (HTTP), **255**

I

IBM PCs, 55
iCloud, 131
ICQ, 261
identity theft, 22, 279, **455,** 488
IEEE 802.3, 197
IEEE 802.11, **197**–199, 218
IEEE 802.15, 199
IEEE 802.16, 199
IF-THEN rules, 340–341
Illustrator, 151, 159
imaging, **122**–123
impact analysis, 477
impact printers, **126**
implementation, **400**–402
impressions, **265**
InDesign, 151, 159
indexing documents, 122
industrial revolution, 22
industries and competitive advantage, 48
inference engine, **340**
information, **8**
    availability, 452
    businesses use of, 7
    confidentiality, 452
    context, 9–10
    cost of obtaining, 10
    versus data, 8–9
    decision making, 7–8
    disaster recovery planning, 452
    erroneous, 10
    generating, 9

identifying needed, 109
integrity, 452
managers and, 12–13
out-of-date, 10
partial, 10
problem solving, 7–8
producing, 12
relevant, 10
risks, 452
theft, 454–455
useful, 10
information map, **12**–13
information security
    economics, 479–481
    goals, 451–452
information systems auditor, **465**
information systems (ISs), **12**
    accounting, 20, 70–71
    antiquated, 54
    business intelligence (BI) systems, **18**
    careers, 23–26
    competitive advantage, 51
    computers, 15
    customer relationship management (CRM) systems, **17**–18, 82–87
    cyber terrorism, **456**
    data, 13
    data processing, **14**
    decision support systems (DSSs), **18**
    downtime, **453**
    employee involvement in, 423
    engineering, 73–74
    expert systems (ESs), **18**
    finance, 20, 71–72
    functional business areas, 19–21
    geographic information systems (GISs), **18**–19
    hardware, 13
    human resource (HR), 21
    human resource management (HRM), 88–91
    input, **14**
    inventory control subsystem, 11
    manufacturing, 77
    marketing, 20
    mobile phones, 20
    output, **14**
    people, 13
    planning, 387–391
    procedures, 13
    processing stages, 14–15
    purpose of, 7–8
    redundancy, 475–476, 480–481
    risks, 452–459
    securing, 451–452

software, 13
storage, **14**–15
strategic information systems
  (SISs), **37**
supply chain management (SCM)
  systems, **16**–17, **75**–81, 93–98
telecommunications, 13
transaction processing systems
  (TPSs), 16
information technology (IT), **13,**
  22–23
  describing role in mission
    statement, 388
  dynamic nature of, 8
  expediting transfer of knowledge,
    375
  importance of, 6
  job requirements, 8
  knowledge creation, 375
  knowledge workers and, 8
  offshoring, 425
  outsourcing, 425
  reengineering and, 50
  sources for new systems, 389
  strategic plan for implementing,
    389
  systems thinking, **13**
  targeted marketing, 85
  terrorism, 476
  turning knowledge into routine,
    automated processes, 375
information technology (IT) professionals certification, 410–411
information technology (IT) security
  workers, 474
information technology (IT) services
  and outsourcing, 425–428
inheritance, **231**
ink-jet printers, 125–126
innovative technologies, 64–65
input, **14**
input devices, 14–15, **110**
  imaging, **122**–123
  keyboards, 118
  mouse, **118**–119
  source data, **120**–122
  speech recognition, **123**–124
  touch screens, **119**
  trackballs, **119**
  trackpads, **119**
INSERT SQL command, 233
insider securities trading, 345
instant messaging (IM), **261**–262
InstantService, 262
insurance claims, 44–45
insurance companies, 48

antiquated software and hardware,
  48
  identifying profitable customer
    groups, 363
  neural nets, 342–343
integrity, 452
intellectual property, 40, 309
intelligent agents, **342**
intelligent transportation systems
  (ITS), 396
interaction diagrams, 399
interactive communication technology, 261–262
interactive voice recognition (IVR),
  123–124
internal memory, **110**
international commerce, 300–304
international information systems
  (ISs), 304
Internet, 21, 194
  auditing information systems, 402
  availability, 186
  backbone, **196**
  criminals, 274
  databases, 236–238
  enhancing existing products or
    services, 44–45
  fraud, 274
  government limits on, 309
  growth of, 13
  hosts, **196**
  large retailers, 362
  mobile phone access (China), 115
  networking services, 201–204, 206
  non-work related access, 441
  peer-to-peer (P2P) file sharing, 188
  phone calls, 44
  system linking, 77
  world-wide population using, 302
Internet Explorer (IE), 47, 55, 58, 474
Internet Protocol version 4 (IPv4),
  196
Internet Protocol version 6 (IPv6), 196
Internet Security Threat report, 23
Internet service providers (ISPs), 194,
  199, 476
  fixed wireless, 204
  Internet connections, 206–207
Internet telephony, 207
interpreters, **156**–157, 164, 169
interrupts, 116
intranets, 89, 195–196, **267**
  benefits database, 91
  decision support systems (DSSs),
    333
  knowledge sharing, 374–375

inventory, 93, 95–96
inventory control, 76–77
inventory control subsystem, 11
investigation, 393–394
investment analysis and service, 72
Invisible Keylogger Stealth, 454
iOS, 167
iPads, 114, 122, 123, 218, 310, 382,
  418, 475
iPhones, 32, 42–43, 122, 123, 151,
  156, 276, 310, 383, 418, 475
IP (Internet Protocol) addresses, 195,
  196–197
iPods, 260, 273, 418
iPod Touches, 64
IP telephony, 207
IrfanView, 159
iSCSI, 145
Isis, 188, 307
Isis Ready merchants, 188
ISPs. *See* Internet service providers
  (ISPs)
ISs. *See* information systems (ISs)
IT. *See* information technology (IT)
iterative programming, 403
iTunes, 48, 260, 388
IVR. *See* interactive voice recognition
  (IVR)

J

Jaguar supercomputer, 112
Java, 25, 151, 155, 157, 458
JavaScript, 155
Java servlets, 237, 285
jobs and information technology (IT)
  requirements, 8
join relational operation, 232
join tables, **229,** 232–233
Joomla!, 286
just-in-time (JIT) manufacturing, **77**
just-in-time (JIT) system, 208

K

keyboards, 14, 110, 118
keylogging, **454**
key performance indicators (KPIs),
  371–372
keystroke logging, 454
Kindle e-readers, 38, 65, 114, 389
Kindle Fire, 131, 370
Kindle Fire HD, 114
Kindle Owners Lending Library, 38
knowledge, 372–373, 375–376
knowledge management (KM)
  software, 375

knowledge management (KM)
systems, **372**
autocategorization, **377**
automatic taxonomy, **377**
capturing and sorting
organizational knowledge, 373
difficulty quantifying benefits, 395
employee knowledge networks,
373–**374,** 375
knowledge from the web, 375–376
knowledge workers, 8, **373**
konbini stores, 306
KPIs. *See* key performance indicators
(KPIs)

L

languages
character sets, 304
differences, 307
LANs. *See* local area networks (LANs)
laptops, 87, 113, 194
laser printers, 125–126
lasers, 190
late mover, **54**
latency, 129
LCD monitors. *See* liquid crystal
display (LCD) monitors
Lean Development (LD), 403
legacy systems, 54, 408–409
legal barriers and global information
systems, 312–313
legal jurisdictions on the web, 311
lending institutions, 339
libraries, 335
licensing applications, 431–435.
See also software licensing
life cycle, 392
light-emitting diode (LED), 190
LimeWire, 188
linear regression model, 332–333
Linear Tape-Open (LTO), 127
linking tables, 230
links, 161
Linux, 167–168, 170–171
Linux Mobile, 171
liquid crystal display (LCD) monitors,
124
Liquor Inventory System, 82
load balancing, **282**–283
local area networks (LANs), 15, 25,
193, 194
location-based services, **85**–86
locking in suppliers or buyers, 41,
47–48
logic bombs, **459**
Long-Term Evolution (LTE), **200**

Lotus 1-2-3, 41
Lotus Notes, 448
Lotus SmartSuite, 159
low earth orbit (LEO) satellites,
191–192
LTO. *See* Linear Tape-Open (LTO)

M

machine cycle, **116**–117
machine language, **151,** 156
Macintosh, 418
Mac OS, 48
Mac OS X, 156, 167, 168
magnetic disks, 110, 126, **127**–128,
133
magnetic-ink character recognition
(MICR), 121
magnetic tapes, 110, 126–**127,** 132,
133, 145
mainframe computers, **112**–113
data warehouses, 240
maintenance, 402–403
malicious code, 488
malware, 23
management information system
(MIS), **16**
Management Reporting Suite, 156
managers, 12–13
*Manifesto for Agile Software Develop-
ment,* 404
manufacturing, 75
comparative advantage, 375
departments as subsystems, 10
information systems (ISs), 76–77
just-in-time (JIT), **77**
monitoring and controlling, 78
relying on technology, 40
manufacturing resource planning
(MRP II), **77**
many-to-many relationship, **230**–231
MapPoint, 347
Mapquest, 162, 349
marketing, 20, 84–85
data mining, 360
market research, 83
Mars Climate Orbiter, 310
mashups, **161**–162, 349
massive open online courses
(MOOCs), **260**–261
master production schedule (MPS),
77
material requirements planning
(MRP), **76**–77, 104
MB. *See* megabytes (MB)
McAfee, 466
m-commerce, 277–279

MediaWiki, 260
medical devices, 46
Medical-grade Wireless Utility, 218
medical management and expert
systems (ESs), 343–344
megabits per second (Mbps), 191
megabytes (MB), 111
megahertz (MHz), 116
Melissa virus, 458
memory
allocation, 166–167
capacity, 117
RAM (random access memory), **110**
ROM (read-only memory), **110**
message digest, **472**
metadata, **234,** 242
methods, 154
metropolitan area networks (MANs),
193, 194
WiMAX (Worldwide Interoperability for Microwave Access), 199
MHz. *See* megahertz (MHz)
MICR. *See* magnetic-ink character
recognition (MICR)
microprocessors, **115**–116
Microsoft TechEd conference, 275
Microsoft Windows, 25, 48, 55, 459
Microwaves, **191**
military information, 308–309
millions of instructions per second.
See MIPS (millions of instructions
per second)
Mipis Software, 21
MIPS (millions of instructions per
second), **117**–118
mirror servers, **283**
MIS. *See* management information
system (MIS)
mission-critical applications, **477,**
480
mission statements, **388**
Mobile Advertising: Analysis and
Forecasts (2009), 272
mobile applications, 13, 156
mobile applications developers, **25**
mobile commerce, **277**–279
mobile communications, 201
mobile computing, 6, 13, 36, 109
mobile devices, 44
banking transactions, 6
business intelligence (BI), 368
malware, 23
mobile commerce, **277**–279
RFID readers, 278
spam, 276
mobile networks, 201

states Attorneys General, 55
static IP address, **197**
stock keeping units (SKUs), 181
stock transactions, 44
"Stop Online Piracy Act," 311
storage, **14**–15, **110**, 126–134, 145
   cloud storage, **131**
   data, 221–222
   direct access, **126**
   direct-attached storage (DAS), **130**
   magnetic disks, **127**–128
   magnetic tapes, **127**
   network-attached storage (NAS),
    130
   optical discs, **128**
   RAID (redundant array of independent disks), **130**
   scalability, **130**
   sequential storage, **126**
   solid-state storage, **129**
   storage area networks (SANs),
    130
storage area networks (SANs), **130**, 145
storage-as-a-service (SaaS), **131**
storage devices, 15
storage media, 132–134
storage service provider (SSP), **438**
stored data, 132–133
strategic advantage, **37**
   custom-design software, 424
   first movers, **42**–44
   late mover, **54**
strategic information systems (SISs),
   37, 40
   competitive advantage, 48
   creation, 48–50
   customers, 49
   economic justification, 49
   enhanced service, 53–54
   maintaining, 50–54
   massive automation, 52–53
   organizational change, 50
   organizational goal, 48
   organizational strategy, 49
   reengineering, **50**
   standard business practice, 51
   supporting nonstrategic activities,
    50
strategic moves, 36–37, 40
strategic planning, 37, 389
strategies, 36–37
   competitive advantage, 38–48
   as unfair business practices, 55–56
strong passwords, 455
structured problems, **327**–328

Structured Query Language (SQL), 25,
   152, **233**
stylus, **113**–114
subsystems, **10**–11
suites, **159**
supercomputers, 112–113
supermarket chains, 58
   data, 249–250
suppliers
   locking in, **47**–48
   reluctance to share information, 95
supply chain management (SCM),
   146
   information systems (ISs), **75**–81
   manufacturing resource planning
    (MRP II), **77**
   material requirements planning
    (MRP), **76**–77
   monitoring and control, 78
   radio frequency identification
    (RFID), **80**–81
   shipping, 78–79
supply chain management (SCM)
   systems, **16**–17, 19, 68, 75,
    280–282, 330
   after-the-sale-services, 95
   collaborative logistics, 96
   cycle time reductions, 94
   enterprise resource planning (ERP)
    systems, 93–94, **97**–98
   implementing, 93
   information systems (ISs), 93–98
   inventory, 94, 95–96
   production costs, 94
   relational databases, 229
   systems thinking, 16
   trust, 94–95
supply chains, 16, **75**, 94
   knowledge about, 71
   web, 280–282
Supply Chain Services, 288
support, 391, 402–403
Surface, 114
swap space, 167
switches, **195**
switching costs, **41**, 47
S.W.O.T. (Strengths, Weaknesses,
   Opportunities, and Threats), 299
Symantec Intelligence Report, 277
symmetric encryption, **469**
   Transport Layer Security (TLS), 471
sys admin. *See* system administrators
system administrators, **25**
system analysis, 393–394
system as a service (SaaS), 421
system requirements, 396

systems, **10**–12
systems analysts, **23**–24
systems design, **397**
   construction, 400
   data flow diagrams (DFDs), **397**–399
   system testing, 400
   Unified Modeling Language (UML),
    399
systems development
   agile methods, 391, **403**–406
   principles, 390
   progressive elaboration, **391**
   systems development life cycle
    (SDLC), **391**–403
systems development life cycle
   (SDLC), **391**
   economic feasibility study, 393,
    394–395
   feasibility studies, **394**–396
   implementation, **400**–402
   investigation, 393–394
   operational feasibility study, 393,
    396
   requirements definition, 393, 396
   support, 402–403
   systems design, **397**–400
   technical feasibility study, 393, 394
systems integration, **408**–409
system software, **150**, 164–169
systems thinking, 12–13, 16
system testing, 400

T

tables, **228**
   attributes, 228
   composing on the fly, 365
   composite key, **230**
   creation from existing tables, 232
   foreign keys, 229, **230**
   join, 232–233
   keys, 229–230
   linking, 230
   many-to-many relationship,
    230–231
   one-to-many relationship, **230**
   primary key, **230**
   relational database model, **228**
   relationships, 230–231, 235–236
   selecting columns from, 232
   temporary, 232
   tuples, 228
tablet computers, **114**
tablets, 13, 114, 418
   airlines industry, 53
   mobile advertising, 272

name & company INDEX

A

ABC, 185
Abercrombie & Fitch, 320
ABI Research, 456
Accenture, 170, 406–407, 426
Acenet, 284
Acquila, 170
Acxiom, 105, 271
Adidas, 257
Adobe, 48, 151, 159, 162, 187, 231, 458
ADP, Inc., 338
Adyen, 307
AES Corp., 305
Aetna, 84
Air Canada, 269
Air New Zealand, 269
Aite Group, 6
Amazon.com, 15, 17, 38, 40, 41, 42, 46, 51, 65, 85, 113, 131, 161, 233, 236, 237, 251, 264, 266, 270, 272, 273, 304, 356, 362, 364, 388–389, 448, 453, 460
Amazon Web Services (AWS), 241, 452–453
Amber Road, 305
Amerada Hess, 171
American Airlines, 51, 269
American Civil Liberties Union (ACLU), 476
American Express Co. (AmEx), 85, 187, 275, 344
American International Group (AIG), 362
American Productivity & Quality Center (APQC), 210
American Red Cross, 150
American Society of Composers, Authors and Publishers (ASCAP), 448
American Stock Exchange (AMEX), 345
AMR Corp, 51
AnnualCreditReport.com, 339
AOL, 44
Apache, 159

aplusnet, 283
Apple App Store, 150
Apple Computer, 40, 42–43, 48, 56, 114, 123, 131, 133, 151, 156, 158, 167, 272, 273, 382, 383, 475
ARC Advisory Group, 146
Ariba, 436
ASAP for Home Healthcare, 89
Ascentive LLC, 441
askart.com, 267
ASNA, 153
Aspect, 90
ASTD, 280
Astute Solutions, 319
AT&T, 146, 194, 196, 201, 204, 436
AT&T Bell Labs, 168
Aurora Information Systems, 335
Austrian Airlines, 269
Avanquest, 162
Avenue A, 239, 262

B

Backblaze, 462
Bank of America, 123, 361, 460
Bank of Montreal, 373
Barclays PLC, 274, 275
Barnes & Noble (B&N), 40, 281, 335
Baugh, Rob, 64
BayCare Health Systems, 487
BearingPoint, 169
Beckman Coulter, Inc., 95
Benioff, Mark, 435
Ben & Jerry's, 369
Best Buy, 121, 310
Bharti Airtel Ltd., 426
BIA/Kelsey, 279
Bing, 264
BMC Software, 47
BN.com, 40
Bonaparte, Napoleon, 40
Booz Allen Hamilton, 277
Bornemann Associates, 53
Boxfl, 207
BP PLC, 94
Brightcove, 418
British Airways, 198, 405

British Tesco, 208
Bureau of Justice Statistics, 279
Burlington Coat Factory, 171
Business Software Alliance (BSA), 173
Business Week, 50
Buy.com, 17, 46, 270

C

Cambria Suites, 267
Capgemini, 406, 426
Capital One Financial Corp., 67–68, 187
Carbonite, 462
CareTech Solutions, 427
Carle Foundation Hospital, 356
Carl's Furniture City, 296
CBS, 185
Cemex, 427
Center for Media and Communications Studies (CMCS), 312
Chanel, 44
Charles Schwab, 44
CheckPoints, 86
Chesterfield County, Virginia, 417
Chesterfield University, 417
Chevin, 156
Chevrolet, 57
Chevron Corp., 94
ChoiceBuys.com, 267
Choice Hotels International, 267
ChoicePoint, 271
Chronicle of Higher Education, 261
Cincinnati Zoo (CZ), 383
Cinergy, 206
Cisco Systems, 77, 187, 474
Citibank, 123, 172
Citigroup, 460
Citizens National Bank of Texas, 180–181
Citrix, 187
ClamWin, 458
Clarion, 267
ClawfootCollection.com, 284–285
ClickZ, 279
CMS Energy, 432